# The American Museum of Natural History Guide to Shells

THE AMERICAN MUSEUM OF NATURAL HISTORY

*Land, Freshwater, and*

# GUIDE TO SHELLS

*Marine, from Nova Scotia to Florida*

## By WILLIAM K. EMERSON
## and MORRIS K. JACOBSON

with the assistance of

HAROLD S. FEINBERG and WILLIAM E. OLD, JR.

 ALFRED A. KNOPF    NEW YORK    1976

THIS IS A BORZOI BOOK
PUBLISHED BY ALFRED A. KNOPF, INC.

Grateful acknowledgment is hereby made to the following
for permission to use the material indicated:

Dr. R. Tucker Abbott, for a schematic description of the
genus *Rissoina* used as a basis for the description in the
present work, and taken from his book *American Seashells*, 2nd ed. (Reinhold, N.Y.: Van Nostrand, 1974),
p. 76. Copyright © 1974 by R. Tucker Abbott.
The Charles T. Branford Company, Newton Centre,
Massachusetts, for material quoted from Julia Ellen Rogers,
*The Shell Book*, 1960 ed., pp. 191–2. Copyright © 1960
by the Charles T. Branford Company.
John B. Burch and the Wm. C. Brown Company, Dubuque,
Iowa, for a schematic description of the genus *Gastrocopta*
used as a basis for the description in the present work, and
taken from *How to Know the Eastern Land Snails*
(Dubuque, Iowa, 1962). Copyright © 1962 by John B. Burch.
Dover Publications, Inc., New York, N.Y., for line draw-
ings taken from Morris K. Jacobson and William K.
Emerson, *Shells from Cape Cod to Cape May, with
Special Reference to the New York City Area*, 1971 ed.,
pp. 121 and 123.

Library of Congress Cataloging in Publication Data
Emerson, William K.
The American Museum of Natural History guide to shells—
Nova Scotia to Florida.
Includes index.
1. Shells—Atlantic coast (United States)—Identification.
2. Shells—Nova Scotia—Identification.
I. Jacobson, Morris K., joint author. II. American Museum
of Natural History, New York. III. Title.
QL416.E43     1976     594′.04′7     74-21304

# CONTENTS

# ACKNOWLEDGMENTS

We gratefully acknowledge the assistance received from many colleagues in the preparation of this book. They include: Messrs. George L. Kennedy and Barry Roth, Drs. R. Tucker Abbott, Kenneth J. Boss, John B. Burch, Eugene V. Coan, Anthony D'Attilio, Richard S. Houbrick, Donald R. Moore, Joseph P. E. Morrison, Thomas E. Pulley, Joseph Rosewater, and Ruth D. Turner, who kindly lent specimens or provided information pertaining to their respective molluscan specialties.

The photography is the work of Messrs. Arthur Singer and James Coxe and Dr. David Berliner of the Department of Photography of the American Museum, excepting the photomicrography, which was generously contributed by Fr. Antonio M. Frias Martins of the Seminário-Colégio Do Santo Cristo, Azores, and Dr. Ernst Kirsteuer of the American Museum. Miss Frances Stiles redrafted most of the line drawings.

We are especially indebted to our colleagues, Messrs. Harold S. Feinberg and William E. Old, Jr., who gave unstintingly of their time and knowledge in furthering the completion of this task. Misses Lynne Judge and Joan Mey undertook the laborious job of typing the manuscript.

# The American Museum of Natural History Guide to Shells

# INTRODUCTION

This book describes, illustrates, and discusses the commoner shelled land, freshwater, and marine mollusks along the eastern coast of North America from Nova Scotia to Florida. The land shells are limited mostly to those found on the Atlantic coastal plain, the freshwater shells, similarly, are the species found in the rivers, lakes, streams, and ponds on that same coastal plain; and the marine shells include the more familiar intertidal species and those found in shallow water just below the low-tide line, as well as those cast up on shore by storms and waves. These are the shells the general collector is likely to find either alive *in situ* or in beach drift along the shore. Omitted are rare, uncommon, and deep-water species, or those found in isolated localities not easily reached.

These stipulations, of course, still leave an intimidatingly vast number of species eligible for inclusion here; and, given inevitable limitations of space, it was a difficult task throughout to decide which to take in and which to leave out. Conscientious as we have tried to be in carrying out this task—basing our selections upon both our personal collecting experiences and an extensive search of the literature—we doubt that we shall have succeeded in satisfying all collectors. Not a few will probably be surprised to find that species "common" in their experience are omitted, while "rare" ones have been included. The identities of the respectively "common" and "rare" animals, however, may well differ greatly from reader to reader. The fact is that we live in a region of richly varied topography, endowed with a wide range of habitats in which mollusks can flourish. As a result, what may be prevalent in one restricted area is rare or absent in another, even though both areas may appear to enjoy the same sort of ecological conditions. To take one example, *Ventridens cerinoideus* is one of the commonest land snails of the coastal plain of the Carolinas, yet is quite rare or even totally absent in many other localities. We hope, therefore, that the reader will be understanding of the problems we have encountered in this regard. Perhaps in later editions we will be able to rectify any omissions that turn out to be really glaring.

For the convenience of the collector, we have arranged the gastropods and bivalves by chapters according to their habitats: marine, freshwater, or terrestrial. Thus there are separate chapters devoted to the marine snails, the land snails, the freshwater snails and bivalves, and the marine bivalves. Zoologically speaking, this is not a satisfactory system, and it forces us to adopt some arbitrary decisions. For example, the salt marsh snails, family Melampidae, and others are actually air breathers, classified with the pulmonates, and thus really land snails. But their habitat in salt marshes prompts us to place them with the marine snails, since the collector will encounter them near the sea. Similarly, some marine snails are able to tolerate water of low salinity and almost completely fresh water, but practical considerations urge that they remain with the marine gastropods. Clench and Turner (1948) succinctly elucidate this treatment:

> In a strict sense, the terms marine, land, and freshwater refer only to habitat preferences and are only lightly superimposed upon the much broader and more exact systematic arrangement of our mollusks. Borderline families and genera and even species naturally overlap in the three major habitats so that their inclusion in any faunal study would be based upon their ecological preference rather than their systematic position.

The chitons, tooth shells, and cephalopods, all of which are inhabitants of the seas, are placed in a chapter entitled "Other Marine Mollusks."

# THE MOLLUSKS

The mollusks form one of the more important invertebrate groups in the animal kingdom. Second only to the insects in the number of living species, these animals are classified in the phylum Mollusca. Briefly, the mollusks are characterized by having a soft body (Lat. *mollis*, soft), which is commonly, though not always, protected by a limy exoskeleton, the shell. It is this shell, in all its myriads of forms, sizes, shapes, sculptures, and colors, that fascinated man long before the dawn of civilization and that today inspires biologists and amateurs alike to collect and study shells.

The living mollusks are divided into seven major groups, called "classes." The largest class, in terms of number of species, are the snails, or Gastropoda (Gr. *gaster poda*, stomach foot). As the snails comprise about three-quarters of all the living species of mollusks, they form the bulk of most shell collections. They are, moreover, the only molluscan class having members that have successfully left the primeval seas and invaded dry land. There are no land-dwelling clams or octopuses, nor are there any other terrestrial molluscan classes. All but the gastropods are restricted to aquatic environments; further, most of the other mollusks occur only in the seas, although many bivalves also inhabit bodies of fresh water.

The other six molluscan classes are, in the order of their importance as far as numbers are concerned: the clams, Bivalvia (two shells or valves), also called Pelecypoda (Gr. *pelekos poda,* hatchet foot). Next are the chitons, or pill-bug snails, the Polyplacophora (Gr. *polys placo pherin*, many-plate bearer), which have a shell made up of eight plates held together by a surrounding girdle; the octopuses and squids, Cephalopoda (Gr. *kephalos poda,* head foot) of which only three genera—two in our area—have shells of interest to the collector; the tusk shells, Scaphopoda (Gr. *skaphe poda,* boat foot) which resembles a miniature hollow elephant tusk; the Aplacophora (Gr. *a placo pherin*, no-plate bearers), an obscure group of wormlike creatures that have very little resemblance to shelled mollusks; and the Monoplacophora (Gr. *mono placo pherin*, one-plate bearer), a "living fossil" from vast ocean depths, looking like little limpets with vestiges of wormlike, segmented bodies. Of the seven classes listed, the collector for whom this book has been written will meet mainly the gastropods and bivalves in his or her peregrinations and collecting trips. Of the other five classes, less than a dozen species comprise the shallow-water and intertidal groups that might come to the collector's attention in this area.

It is appropriate here to discuss briefly the systematic hierarchy malacologists use to arrange the taxonomic categories within the phylum Mollusca. The major division of a *phylum* is the *class,* and the living mollusks are constituted in seven classes (see discussion above). Each class may be divided into *subclasses.* The next category is the *order,* which is sometimes divided into *suborders,* and these in turn may be divided into *infraorders.* Following in sequence are the categories *superfamily,* indicated orthographically by the ending *-acea; family,* with the ending *-idae; subfamily,* with the ending *-inae; genus;*

*subgenus; species;* and *subspecies.* By way of illustration, the "genealogy" of the Florida Chinese Alphabet Cone, *Conus spurius atlanticus* Clench, 1942, would be:

Phylum Mollusca

Class Gastropoda

Subclass Prosobranchia

Order Neogastropoda

Superfamily Conacea

Family Conidae

Subfamily Coninae

Genus *Conus* Linnaeus, 1758

Subgenus *Leptoconus* Swainson, 1840

Species *spurius* Gmelin, 1791

Subspecies *atlanticus* Clench, 1942

Only the generic, subgeneric, specific, and subspecific names are italicized. The names of the last two categories are always written in lower-case letters, whereas all the other categories are either capitalized or only the first letter is a capital, as in the case of generic names.

The author and the year that generic, subgeneric, specific, and subspecific names were described in the scientific literature are given for these categories. In most classifications, the authors and the dates are not cited for the higher categories.

---

# CONSERVATION AND THE COLLECTOR

This is an era of ecological awareness. The heedless exploitation of our natural surroundings so characteristic of former years is being steadily combatted both by education and by restrictive legislation. Of all the dangers facing the continued existence of many molluscan populations and even species themselves, the activities of the amateur shell collector are probably the least harmful. Industrial pollution and the destruction of natural habitats, together with natural disasters such as hurricanes and floods, cause infinitely more damage. The few specimens a shell enthusiast can collect do little to decrease the size of a population; moreover, he usually does not collect immature forms, and overlooks completely the larvae and the eggs, the promise of a future generation. It is true, nonetheless, that local populations, especially of larger and more spectacular shells, are seriously depleted at times by collecting activities—as has happened, for instance, in many places in the Florida Keys. Unless the collectors concerned learn to observe periods of restriction when no collecting is undertaken, and so enable the affected species to reestablish their numbers, such populations may well disappear entirely.

The collecting of live shells is already legally regulated on the West Coast, and such restrictions will probably be extended to other states as well. Where such laws are not yet on the books, the conscientious collector will want to observe prudent personal restrictions, being satisfied with the smallest number of live-collected specimens and disturbing as little as possible their natural habitats, such as coral heads, boulders, and rocks. Even worthier of merit is the collector who is satisfied with reasonably well-preserved beach specimens and prefers these to live-collected individuals of the same species. Most advanced is the student who collects only dead specimens and confines his live collecting to worthwhile ecological and natural history observations, and who records living specimens on film. When a live specimen is taken, it may be transferred to a tank or terrarium, its life history observed and recorded in a journal, and then returned to its natural habitat. Such practices may not materially aid in the preservation of molluscan populations. Rather, their value will lie in the awakening of a new attitude toward nature, recognizing the need to conserve all forms of life and to add to our knowledge of natural history.

There is another aspect of conservation that collectors can make it their duty to observe. Every curator has had the sad experience of being obliged to discard superb shell specimens he would have liked very much to keep for the museum collection. His available space is limited, and he must make room only for well-documented specimens. Now, what is a scientifically valuable specimen? It is one that is in reasonably well-preserved condition and is accompanied with a label bearing thorough and reliable data. But what constitutes such data? First, an accurate statement of the locality where it was collected, then a brief description of the actual conditions under which it was taken (whether in sand, on rocks, burrowing in mud, under leaves, etc.), next the date of collection and the name of the collector. Any specimen provided with such data will always be desirable to a museum; on the other hand, the most beautiful shell without such data is a piece of useless crockery. The collector should be aware that a shell collection without reliable data is worthless, a candidate sooner or later for disposal as trash. This is true of all shells, whether self-collected, obtained by exchange, or purchased from dealers.

# NAMES AND NOMENCLATURE

The matter of nonscientific names for shells is troublesome. With a handful of exceptions there are no truly "popular" or "common" names in conchology, such as we find for birds, mammals, reptiles, fish, and flowers. Some of the more spectacular shells and mollusks of commercial importance do enjoy names of widespread use. But with few exceptions, these names are not universally employed—for example, *Mya arenaria* in our area is known as the Soft-Shelled Clam or the Steamer Clam—or they may be employed in a confusing manner. Thus the same names may be used in various regions for different species of mollusks—or even for different kinds of animals —and the same species may go under various names in different parts of the country. Moreover, for the vast majority of the species, especially the smaller and less notable ones, names have never been applied that can be called either popular or common. The number of living molluscan species, conservatively estimated to be between 50,000 and 70,000, is too extensive for such a task. The majority of mollusks, therefore, are known only by their scientific names.

Nevertheless, in this book we have in most cases provided names that can be called neither common nor popular. They are rather merely English names, and they are not meant to replace the scientific names. They are a convenient handle to enable one reader to discuss a species with another reader without being troubled by unfamiliar, many-syllabled terms. They will ease the flow of the conversation. However, the average collector will in time, purposefully or not, learn to use the scientific names for most species, for these alone are afforded international recognition by scientists.

The difficulty of pronouncing and learning these Latinate "jaw breakers" has been much exaggerated. In our multiethnic population the names of many of our fellow citizens are every bit as difficult as such scientific terms, if not more so. There is little reason to be frightened off by this basically practical vocabulary.

To make mastery easier here, we have gone to great pains to provide the etymology and English meaning of the Latin or Greek names used in this book. Frequently these names prove to be descriptively quite apt and applicable to the shell in question. Then learning the name is easy. But just as frequently they seem to have nothing to do with the organisms they designate—like an undersized Mr. Long or a blonde Mrs. Black. However, apt or not, that name must prevail which conforms to the universally applied rules of the International Code of Zoological Nomenclature. Thus, though one large, handsome helmet shell is found in Florida and the West Indies, not in Madagascar, it is named *Cassis madagascariensis*, because that is the earliest nomenclaturally valid name introduced for this species, and it has priority over all other names that were subsequently applied to it. Numerous other, similar examples will appear in the course of this book.

A word should be said about the pronunciation of scientific names. In this matter there is no universal standard, and many different pronunciations are used. Each one is "correct." In English-speaking countries, two schools flourish: one assigns English values to the letters, the other uses what it takes to be the classical Latin pronunciation of ancient Rome. Most speakers employ a combination of the two. Recently Dr. R. Tucker Abbott of the Delaware Museum of Natural History produced a phonograph record with the pronunciation of many of the commoner marine shell names. Though without the authority of the International Code, this could prove to be a useful tool for the isolated collector. Other collectors will adopt the pronunciation they hear most frequently from their colleagues. Only one rule in this ruleless situation must be observed: no part of the word may be omitted; every letter and syllable should be pronounced.

Though the scientific names are the only feasible ones in the long run, they present an added difficulty: many of them are not stable; names are sometimes changed. This is particularly unfortunate because one of the purposes of the International Code of Zoological Nomenclature, which regulates the rules governing the names, is to achieve nomenclatural stability. But advancing biological knowledge or more thorough bibliographical research may result in nomenclatural refinement, and thus familiar names may be replaced by new or different ones. Fortunately, only a small number of such changes are required at one time, so that no collector need ever feel that he is being overwhelmed. For our part, we have tried to seek out and employ only the latest names in use, but inevitable and increasing progress is bound to overtake some of the nomenclature we have used.

When a great many species are contained in a single genus or when some of the species have minor characteristics in common, closely related groups of species may then be recognized within a genus, and such groups are called "subgenera." Since most of the genera discussed in this book contain only a few local species, we have not resorted to the use of subgeneric names, unless they are necessary to differentiate large groups, such as the tellins. They would add little to the reader's comprehension and merely present an added nomenclatural hazard to overcome. Moreover, these subgeneric names—enclosed in parentheses and placed between the generic and the specific trivial names—are used largely for taxonomic purposes, rarely for simple reference. Thus the name usually used in conversation among collectors and malacologists consists only of the generic and trivial parts, both together called the "species name." In the case of subspecies, the subspecific name follows that of the specific name, as in *Spisula solidissima raveneli*, which is commonly known as Ravenel's Surf Clam.

Each species name is followed by that of the author responsible for its introduction into the scientific literature. By knowing the author of a species, the interested reader can track down the original description. The author's name of a species, however, is not commonly used in conversation. Thus, for example, the complete citation for the Atlantic Surf Clam is *Spisula (Hemimactra) solidissima solidissima* (Dillwyn, 1817). But in conversation these clams are generally referred to simply as *Spisula solidissima*. Since the species was transferred to a genus other than the one into which Dillwyn, the author, had originally placed it—Dillwyn called it a *Mactra*—the author's name is placed in parentheses. We have not followed this practice in our book, for the presence or lack of parentheses associated with authors' names is often confusing to the beginning student. The date that follows the author's name—in this instance, 1817—is the year the species was described in the scientific literature. These dates are not generally given in popular handbooks, but they may be found in nomenclatural compilations and monographic studies.

Subspecies, or races, though difficult to define biologically, are much in use in modern taxonomy. They usually designate populations of a species that are distinguished from others of the same species by minor but consistent characteristics and that are restricted to an area separated from the typical or nominate subspecies. The subspecific name is added to the generic and specific names of the nominate subspecies. When subspecies are recognized, the nominate subspecies is designated by repeating the specific name. For example, the nominate subspecies of the bay scallop, *Argopecten irradians*, is cited as *Argopecten irradians irradians,* whereas southern populations are recognized as a subspecies: *Argopecten irradians concentricus.* However, for the sake of greater simplicity, we do not use the repetitive form of the nominate species and merely call the northern form *Argopecten irradians.*

Some biologists now question the utility and even the biological validity of the concept of subspecies. They think that many of the presently recognized subspecies are merely varying populations of single species that do not require subspecific names.

# DISTRIBUTION

The range of a species comprises the area between two geographical end points in which the species is known to occur. However, this does not indicate that such individuals are found everywhere in that area, but that discontinuous populations consisting locally of varying densities are distributed, usually in an irregular pattern, through the designated area. The distributional pattern is determined by the presence of compatible living conditions for each species, be it marine, freshwater, or terrestrial. Thus the search for a species must include not only the range of the species but also a knowledge of its ecological requirements; such information is given, briefly, wherever it is required in this book. Of course, dead shells may be scattered haphazardly by tides, currents, waves, and winds, but, in any case, a knowledge of the range of a species is frequently useful in aiding in the identification of specimens. In such instances, distributional data are given in the keys.

Ranges are sometimes limited by geographical features, both past and present; these serve as barriers to certain ecological conditions upon which some species depend for their existence. Cape Cod and Cape Hatteras are good examples of topographical barriers, and the ranges of many species find their limits here. Peninsular Florida, on the other hand, presents a more complex situation. In the geologic past, much of peninsular Florida was submerged beneath the sea. As a result, this region was much less of a land barrier to the distribution of marine organisms than it is at the present time. With the emergence of Florida, the ranges of many species became discontinuous, with populations being isolated to the north in the western Atlantic and to the west in the Gulf of Mexico. The species in question have not penetrated this land barrier, and they do not occur in the waters of southernmost Florida, but some appear on both sides of the peninsula. Further south, however, many species found in the Gulf of Mexico and the West Indies continue on to the northern coast of South America, to Brazil. We have not always noted this fact, since our chief interest is directed to the shells living further to the north.

---

# THE IDENTIFICATION KEYS

To aid in the identification or determination of species, keys have been provided for most groups. The keys use only the most easily observable characteristics, and they are applicable only to the genera and species discussed in this book, they cannot be used to identify species living beyond the geographical limits covered here. The tabular form employed in the keys serves to make their various steps more visible, and affords, at a glance, a better understanding of the characteristics that serve to separate related forms.

The method of employing the keys is simple, but needs, perhaps, a brief explanation. Major groups of species, such as families or genera, are first broken down into two larger divisions on the basis of two differing characteristics, each division indicated in the key by a single marginal dot. These two larger divisions are in turn broken down progressively into smaller and smaller dual alternatives as new characteristics are introduced, each new characteristic indicated by a successively increasing number of marginal dots. Finally a last set of alternatives is presented, and the remaining choice leaves only a single species, the name of the species requiring identification. The reader follows this path, gradually narrowing down the possibilities open to him by selecting one of a series of alternative choices until the name of the species in question has been determined.

As an example, let us take the Lightning Nerite, *Nerita fulgurans* (page 50). By referring to the illustrations and checking with the description of the introductory "guide species" of the nerites, the reader determines that his specimens belong to the genus *Nerita*. He then consults the key to the family Neritidae, here reproduced from page 49, to identify his specimens.

## KEY TO GENERA OF FAMILY NERITIDAE

&ast; Shell usually rough, heavy, large, more than 20 mm. (4/5 in.) in length
&ast;&ast; Color pattern of black and white only
&ast;&ast;&ast; Color pattern of alternating squarish black and white spots, operculum black     *Nerita tessellata*
&ast;&ast;&ast; Color pattern entirely black or with irregularly scattered patches or lines of white, operculum bluish gray to yellow     *N. fulgurans*
&ast;&ast; Color pattern includes black and red markings
&ast;&ast;&ast; Columellar area smooth, with blood-red stain     *N. peloronta*
&ast;&ast;&ast; Columellar area all white, roughened by deep axial ridges     *N. versicolor*
&ast; Shell smooth, glossy, thin, 18 mm. (3/4 in.) or less in length
&ast;&ast; Shell 16 to 18 mm. (2/3 to 3/4 in.) in length
&ast;&ast;&ast; Shell with bold pattern of large square, circular, or zigzag designs, color various     *Neritina virginea*
&ast;&ast;&ast; Shell with pattern of narrow, closely set zigzag lines, color generally greenish     *N. reclivata*
&ast;&ast; Shell under 10 mm. (2/5 in.) in length
&ast;&ast;&ast; Shell white with zebralike black stripes     *Puperita pupa*
&ast;&ast;&ast; Shell emerald green     *Smaragdia viridis*

After examining the key, the reader finds that the first division, which is indicated by the single marginal dot, reads:

&ast; Shell usually rough, heavy, large, more than 20 mm. in length
or
&ast; Shell smooth, glossy, thin, 18 mm. or less in length

Since the shell under examination is rough, heavy, and rather large, and not smooth, glossy, thin, or small, the reader sees that it belongs to the first of the two alternatives. This means that all alternatives under "Shell smooth," and so forth, are now eliminated from further consideration.

Now, the second alternative, indicated by two marginal dots, reads:

* * Color pattern of black and white only

or

* * Color pattern includes black and red markings

As the shell in question lacks red markings and shows only black and white, the first alternative is obviously correct—and all alternatives under the other division are eliminated. This leads to the third alternative, indicated by three marginal dots, which reads:

* * * Color pattern of alternating squarish black and white spots, operculum black

or

* * * Color pattern entirely black or with irregularly scattered patches or lines of white, operculum bluish gray to yellow

As the specimen in hand has a bluish or yellow operculum and shows no regularly alternating black and white dots, it clearly belongs to the second of the alternatives, and the species thus is *Nerita fulgurans.*

Some keys run to five or six alternatives, but the process of determination is the same as described above.

No two creatures of the same species are exactly alike. For this reason, the keys are best employed when more than one specimen is being examined. A single example may chance to be atypical, or be an immature specimen. Thus, if a single specimen does not fit into the key, a larger sample may be necessary in order to identify some species. And as some species are more variable than others, the descriptive text should be consulted to ascertain the range of natural variation in shell form, size, color, and color pattern. Finally, specimens should be compared with the appropriate illustrations in order to confirm determinations based on the keys and the descriptions found in the text.

When required for identification, the sizes of both adult and juvenile specimens of a species are indicated in the keys. The size attained by a species may vary greatly, depending on biological and environmental factors. Also, in some species the male shells differ from the female shells, which is called "sexual dimorphism" (Gr. two forms). The shell of the female in certain species of *Strombus,* for example, is larger than that of the male; in other groups, however, the males may attain a larger size than do the females. Frequently, too, an entire population found at any given time may represent one age group, such as yearlings; these individuals present only juvenile characteristics. In other samples, all age groups may be present, from tiny juveniles to large, fully mature individuals. Finally, in some instances the shells of a species living in protected intertidal habitats or offshore may have larger and more delicate shells than those of the same species inhabiting areas exposed to the action of the surf and to tidal bores. Thus the dimensions cited in the text must be taken only as the general size for adult specimens. At best, these measurements serve to convey to the reader the range in size commonly attained by each species. In the descriptive text, measurements are given for each species both in millimeters (mm.) and in inches (in.). One inch equals 25.37 millimeters. As one becomes familiar with the metric system, one finds that measurements expressed in millimeters are easier to visualize than dimensions cited as fractions of an inch—and this is especially true for tiny specimens. For example, a shell 4 mm. in height is approximately 1/6 in. and precisely 0.15748 in.

The illustrations of the shells are not to scale. Some are natural size, while others are enlarged or reduced in size. The size of each specimen is provided in the legend to the illustrations, the measurements being given in millimeters and denoting the largest dimension of the figured specimen—for instance, the diameter, height, and so forth.

# HOW TO USE THIS BOOK

Little more need be said about the procedures required to identify specimens. The easiest method is perhaps to examine a specimen carefully and make comparisons with pictures in the book. To distinguish two or more related species, the reader should next consult the appropriate identification keys and then read the descriptive text. A final check—not absolutely essential—might be the comparison of a doubtful specimen with other authoritatively named specimens in a museum exhibit or reference collection. Naturally, frequent consultation of the book, even when no name for a particular specimen is being sought, will enable the reader in time to assign without difficulty most of the shells to their proper families or genera. Such familiarity will permit the reader to distinguish, for example, an *Oliva* from a *Conus* or a *Cypraea*. When this elementary stage of knowledge is achieved, immediate reference can be made to the appropriate section of the book, and the identification of one's collection thus becomes a pleasurable pastime.

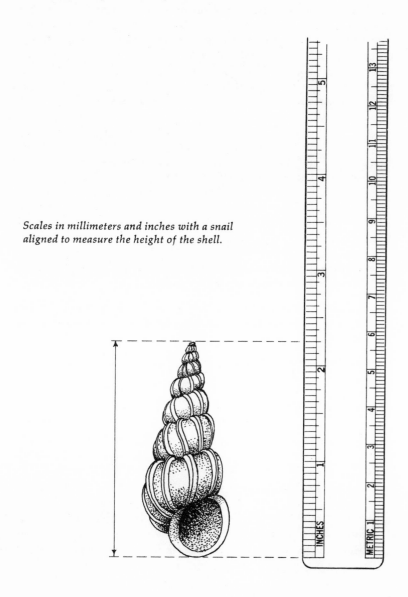

*Scales in millimeters and inches with a snail aligned to measure the height of the shell.*

# GLOSSARY

**Accessory plate.** A secondary limy structure formed by some bivalves to protect the soft anatomy.

**Adductor muscle.** One or two muscles in bivalves used to draw the valves together.

**Anisomyarian.** Bivalves with adductor muscles that are unequal in size.

**Aperture.** The principal opening of the body whorl in a gastropod shell.

**Apex.** The tip of the spire in gastropod shells.

**Apical.** At the apex or top.

**Apophysis** (*pl.* apophyses). A projecting peglike or fingerlike structure that supports a muscle in some bivalves.

**Aragonite.** A mineral composed, like calcite, of calcium carbonate, but differing from calcite in certain characters of crystallization, density, and cleavage.

**Axial.** Parallel to the axis of coiling in gastropods; applied to ribs, color bands, and so forth.

**Axis.** The center around which the whorls of a gastropod coil; a line of reference, or one about which parts are arranged symmetrically.

**Basal.** The bottom or lower part, the base.

**Beaded.** A form of sculpture resembling small beads.

**Beak.** The small tip of a bivalve shell, near the hinge.

**Bifurcated.** Divided into two branches or elements, especially in sculpture.

**Bivalve.** A clam or other representative of the class Bivalvia; a shell with two valves.

**Composite figure illustrating
the parts of a bivalve**

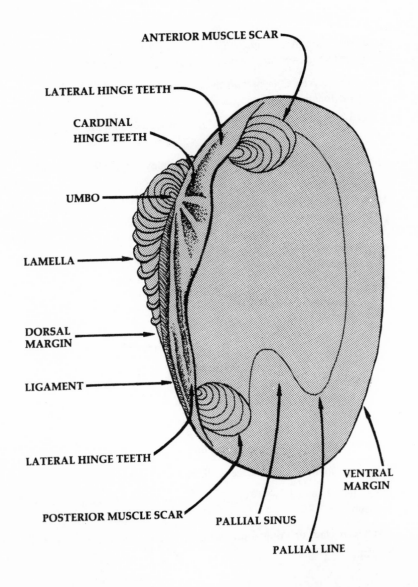

ANTERIOR MUSCLE SCAR

LATERAL HINGE TEETH

CARDINAL
HINGE TEETH

UMBO

LAMELLA

DORSAL
MARGIN

LIGAMENT

LATERAL HINGE TEETH

POSTERIOR MUSCLE SCAR

PALLIAL SINUS

PALLIAL LINE

VENTRAL
MARGIN

**Byssus.** The threads that certain bivalves secrete for attachment to solid objects.

**Calcareous.** Having the shell material composed of or containing calcium carbonate.

**Callum.** A sheet of shelly material in certain bivalves, covering a gap between the valves.

**Callus.** A shelly substance composing a thickened layer, as around the aperture in gastropods.

**Cancellate.** Having lines of sculpture intersecting at right angles.

**Cardinal teeth.** Those situated more or less in the central part of the hinge area in bivalves.

**Carina** (*pl.* carinae). A keel-like ridge.

**Cartilage pit.** A depression for the inner part of the ligament in bivalves.

**Chiton.** A horny, organic substance as in the ligament of bivalves, the operculum of some gastropods and Polyplacophora, etc.

**Chondrophore.** A large, spoon-shaped pit projecting from the hinge plate in some bivalves.

**Circumboreal.** Living in the region around the high latitudes of the northern hemisphere.

**Circumpolar.** Living in the waters surrounding or found in the vicinity of a terrestrial pole.

**Columella.** The axial pillar around which the whorls of the gastropod shell coil, commonly visible at the inner lip of the aperture.

**Commensalism.** The association of two or more individuals of different species in which one kind or more is benefited and the others are not harmed.

**Concave.** Hollowed out, excavated.

**Concentric.** Direction coinciding with that of growth lines, such as the curved ridges on a bivalve shell.

**Congener.** A term applied to species of the same genus.

**Conic.** Shaped like a cone.

**Conical.** Peaked, as in a cone.

**Convex.** Curved outward; bulging out.

**Cord.** Coarse, round sculpture on the surface of a shell.

**Corneous.** Having a chitinous or horny composition, such as in some gastropod opercula and the ligaments of bivalves.

**Costa** (*pl.* costae). Rounded ridge on the surface of a shell, larger than a cord.

**Crenulated.** Finely notched or delicately corrugated, as on the gastropod aperture or the ventral margin of the valves of bivalves.

**Decollate.** Truncated or cut off, for example in snail shells lacking the top several whorls of the spire.

**Decussate.** Having a latticed surface ornamentation of fine ribs, not necessarily crossing at right angles.

**Denticle.** A small projection resembling a tooth, situated around the margin of the gastropod aperture or on the exterior of bivalve shells.

**Denticulate.** With denticles.

**Detritus.** A product of disintegration or wearing away, especially of rocks and organic material.

**Dextral.** Right-handed; coiled in a right-hand spiral in a clockwise manner; said of snails having the aperture on the right side of the shell facing the observer when the apex is held upward; opposite of sinistral.

**Discoidal.** Round and flat like a disk; having the whorls of the gastropod shell coiled in one plane.

**Dorsal.** At or toward the hinge in bivalves; the back opposite the aperture in gastropods.

**Epifauna.** A term for the organisms that are attached or move on the surface of marine or freshwater bottom sediments.

**Fasciole.** A spiral band formed by the successive growth lines on the anterior or posterior canal in gastropods.

**Flexure.** A bending or angulation.

**Fusiform.** Spindle-shaped; an elongate form swelling in the central part, tapering at the extremities.

**Gastropod.** A snail, slug, nudibranch, or other representative of the class Gastropoda; *see* Univalve.

**Globose.** Rounded; subspherical.

**Glochidium** (*pl.* glochidia). A larval bivalve of freshwater mussels that is parasitic on fishes.

**Heterodont.** The hinge teeth of bivalves that are differentiated into cardinals and laterals.

**Heterostrophic.** Having apical whorls coiled in a direction apparently opposite to that of the succeeding whorls.

**Holarctic.** A term used to designate the combined biogeographic area of the Palearctic and Nearctic regions; an organism native to this area.

**Holostomatous.** In snail shells, having the apertural margin uninterrupted by siphonal canal, notch, or by other extension.

**Imbricated.** A shinglelike sculpture, arranged to lie regularly so as to overlap one another.

**Imperforate.** Not perforated or umbilicated; lacking an umbilicus.

**Incised.** Sculptured, with sharply depressed lines or grooves.

**Indo-Pacific.** The faunal province comprising the shallow waters of the Indian and tropical western Pacific Oceans; the organisms living in this province.

**Infauna.** A term for the organisms that live in marine or freshwater bottom sediments.

**Insertion teeth.** The parts of chiton plates that unite the valves to the girdle.

**Intromittent organ.** An external reproductive organ of males.

**Keel.** A prominent rib, or carina, usually marking a change of shape in the outline of the shell.

**Labial.** Pertaining to the lip of the shell.

**Lamella** (*pl.* lamellae). A thin plate or scale.

**Lappet.** A fold, small flap, lobe, or loose hanging portion.

**Composite figure illustrating
the parts of a gastropod (univalve)**

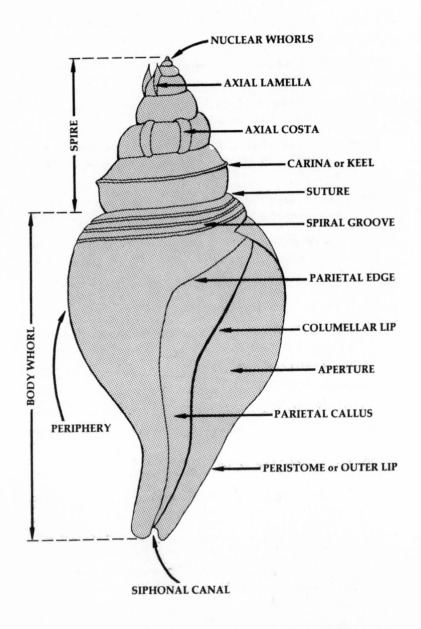

NUCLEAR WHORLS

AXIAL LAMELLA

AXIAL COSTA

CARINA or KEEL

SUTURE

SPIRE

SPIRAL GROOVE

PARIETAL EDGE

COLUMELLAR LIP

BODY WHORL

APERTURE

PARIETAL CALLUS

PERIPHERY

PERISTOME or OUTER LIP

SIPHONAL CANAL

**Lateral.** Pertaining to the side; at or near the hinge on either side of the cardinal area in bivalves; one of a series of radular teeth in gastropods.

**Lateral teeth.** Those situated on either side of the cardinal teeth in bivalves.

**Ligament.** Cartilage and elastic resilium dorsally connecting the shells of a bivalve.

**Lirate.** Having threadlike sculpture.

**Liration.** A line or pattern of threadlike sculpture.

**Lunule.** The heart-shaped area in front of the beaks in bivalves, one half being on each valve; a crescent-shaped marking or pattern.

**Maculate.** Splashed or spotted, blotched by color.

**Malleated.** Having the appearance of being hammered.

**Mantle.** The fleshy membrane that encloses the body of mollusks and secretes the shell and periostracum (*q.v.*)

**Mesoplax.** One of the accessory plates of some bivalves, especially pholads.

**Metaplax.** One of the accessory plates of some bivalves, especially pholads.

**Multispiral.** Consisting of many whorls, as in the opercula of trochids.

**Nacre.** Shell structure consisting of thin leaves of aragonite lying parallel to the inner surface of the shell and imparting a characteristic luster, commonly iridescent.

**Nacreous.** Consisting of, or having the character of nacre.

**Nearctic.** The biogeographic region including North America and nontropical Mexico; an organism native to this region.

**Neotropical.** The biogeographic region including tropical Mexico, Central America, South America, and the West Indies; an organism native to this region.

**Nodose.** Bearing tubercules or knobs.

**Nucleus.** The earliest formed part of the shell or operculum.

**Oblique.** To deviate from the perpendicular; slanting, as in the aperture of some gastropod shells.

**Obtuse.** Blunt or rounded at the extremity; not pointed.

**Ocellate.** Eyelike, spotted.

**Operculate.** Having an operculum.

**Operculum.** The horny or calcareous structure, formed by and attached to the foot, covering the apertural opening of some gastropod shells.

**Orbicular.** Circular, well rounded.

**Orifice.** A small opening into a cavity; a mouthlike opening.

**Ovate.** Egg shaped.

**Palatal.** Pertaining to the outer lip of the aperture of the gastropod shell.

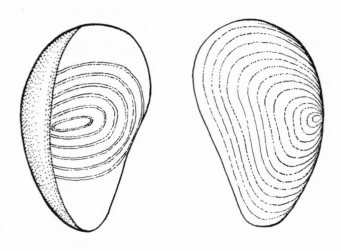

Operculum of *Latiaxis dalli* Emerson and D'Attilio, off southern Florida to Brazil. *Left,* underside; *right,* outside; greatly enlarged. Drawing by Anthony D'Attilio. (After Emerson and D'Attilio, 1963, p. 5)

**Palearctic.** The biogeographic region including Europe, Asia north of the Himalayas, and Africa north of the Sahara; an organism native to this region.

**Pallial.** Pertaining to the mantle.

**Pallial line.** The impression or scar on the inner surface of the bivalve shell marking the attachment of the mantle.

**Pallial sinus.** An indentation in the pallial line.

**Papilla.** Small nipplelike processes; minute nodes or bumps.

**Papillose.** Covered with pimplelike nodes.

**Parietal.** The inside wall of a coiled gastropod shell, within the aperture.

**Parietal shield.** A callus or glaze forming a thickening on the inner lip along the columellar border of the aperture of the gastropod shell.

**Paucispiral.** Having only a few whorls or turns.

**Pelagic.** Pertaining to open water, such as the seas.

**Penultimate.** Next to the last-formed; in gastropod shells, refers to whorl preceding the last or body whorl.

**Perforate.** A gastropod shell having a small opening at the base of the body whorl.

**Periostracum.** The skinlike, outermost covering of many shells.

**Periphery.** The edge or boundary of an area; the part of a shell or whorls farthest from the axis of coiling.

**Peristome.** The lip or margin of the aperture of a gastropod shell.

**Plait.** A plication; a fold on the columella or pillar of a gastropod shell.

**Porcelaneous.** Having a translucent, porcelainlike appearance.

**Predator.** An organism that captures or preys upon another organism for its food; a predaceous organism.

**Prodissoconch.** A shell secreted by the larva or embryo and preserved at the beak of some adult bivalves.

**Propodium** (*pl.* propodia). The anterior part of a snail's foot.

**Protandry.** Production first of sperm, and later in life, eggs by the same gonad.

**Protoconch.** The apical whorls of a shell; the embryonic shell of a gastropod.

**Punctate.** Describing pinprick-like sculptural depressions.

**Quadrate.** Rectangular in general outline.

**Rachiglossate radula.** One with two laterals and a single central tooth.

**Radula** (*pl.* radulae). The dental apparatus possessed by most of the Gastropoda and found in all other classes of mollusks, except the Bivalvia; composed of a ribbon to which are fixed chitinous teeth or plates.

**Reflected.** Turned backward or outward.

**Resilifer.** The socketlike structure that supports the internal ligament in certain bivalves.

**Resilium.** The internal ligament, in a resilifer, under compressed stress.

**Reticulated.** Describing sculpture characterized by distinct lines crossing each other like a network; cancellated.

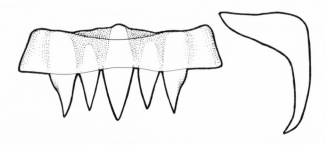

Radular dentition of *Calotrophon ostrearum* Conrad, from Peninsula Point, Florida. *Left*, central tooth; *right*, one lateral tooth; greatly enlarged. Drawing by Anthony D'Attilio. (After McLean and Emerson, 1970, p. 61)

**Riblets.** Small or rudimentary ribs.

**Rostrate.** Having a produced, beaklike end.

**Septum.** A decklike, shelly process; a shelly plate or partition.

**Shouldered.** The angulation of the whorl of gastropod shells, forming one edge of a sutural ridge or shelf.

**Sinistral.** Left-handed; coiled in a left-hand spiral, in a counter-clockwise manner; said of snails having the aperture on the left side of the shell facing the observer when the apex is held upward; opposite of dextral.

**Sinus.** An embayment or cavity in a shell, or a bend in the attachment scar of the mantle.

**Siphon.** A tubelike extension of the mantle by which water enters or leaves the mantle cavity.

**Siphonal fasciole.** Spiral growth lines marking the former position of the siphonal notch.

**Siphonal notch.** A narrow sinus terminating the siphonal canal.

**Spatulate.** Having the shape of a spatula; oblong with an attenuated base.

**Spinose.** Armed with sharp spines.

**Spire.** The visible parts of all the whorls of the gastropod shell except the last one, or body whorl.

**Stria** (*pl.* striae). A very fine line.

**Striate.** Describing fine sculpture consisting of microscopic grooves.

**Striation.** A form or pattern of striate sculpturing.

**Substrate.** An ecological term denoting the base on which an organism lives, for example, the sand, mud, and rocky bottom of aquatic environments.

**Sulcus.** A fissure, slit, or furrow.

**Suture.** The spiral line marking the junction between the whorls of a gastropod shell.

**Synonym.** In scientific nomenclature, one of two or more different names for the same taxonomic unit—for example, for the same species or the same genus.

**Taxodont.** Bivalves with numerous hinge teeth.

**Toxoglossate radula.** One with the radular teeth possessing an attached poison gland; the teeth usually harpoonlike.

**Transverse.** At right angles to the direction of the whorls; parallel to the columella or axis of the gastropod shell.

**Trematodes.** Parasitic flatworms, including the flukes.

**Trigonal.** Triangular or three-cornered in shape.

**Truncate.** Sharply or squarely cut off.

**Tubercle.** A small but prominent rounded elevation on the surface of a shell.

**Tunicate.** A marine chordate; commonly known as a sea squirt.

**Turbinate.** Having a broadly conical spire and a convex base, as in the shells of turbinid snails.

**Turreted.** Describing a tower-shaped shell with a long spire.

**Umbilicate.** Having an umbilicus.

**Umbilicus.** A small hollow, usually at the center of the base of the body whorl in a loosely spiral gastropod shell.

**Umbo** (*pl.* umbones). The earliest or upper part of the bivalve shell as viewed from the outside, opposite the hinge; *see* Beak.

**Univalve.** A snail or other representative of the class Gastropoda having a single shell.

**Varix** (*pl.* varices). Prominently raised ridges on the surface of the gastropod shell originally formed at the aperture.

**Ventral.** Toward that part of the bivalve shell opposite the hinge; away from the back.

# CHAPTER I

# MARINE SNAILS

Sea snails live in all kinds of marine habitats: on wave-washed rocks, in sand, on beaches exposed to the sea or in sheltered bays and lagoons, on man-made jetties and piles, and in saltwater marshes. Others live offshore down to the greatest depths of the ocean basins.

All seven classes of mollusks have representatives that live in the sea, but the gastropods and bivalves are the shells that the collector will most likely find along our shores. Under some conditions chitons are abundant, but tusk shells (scaphopods) are not commonly encountered by the novice. Aplacophorans and monoplacophorans are rarities taken mostly by dredging, the latter by oceanographic surveys working in extremely deep water. Of the cephalopods, only the Pearly Nautilus, an inhabitant of the South Seas, has an external shell. The internal, ram's-hornlike shells of *Spirula* and the unsightly internal pens of squids are occasionally found washed ashore in our area. And while the paperlike egg receptacles of the argonaut cephalopod are rarely taken from the Carolinas southward, a specimen found in good condition is a real treasure.

The shells of sea snails vary in size from minute forms little more than 1 mm. (1/25 in.) in size, to large, massive ones attaining 609 mm. (24 in.) in length and 456 mm. (18 in.) in width. They belong to the class Gastropoda and comprise about 75 percent of the living species of mollusks.

Most collectors are interested in marine gastropods or snails, and the larger part of each collection generally consists of these shells. The class Gastropoda includes three subclasses: Prosobranchia (gills forward; the auricle of the heart is situated anterior to the ventricle), Opisthobranchia (hind gills; the auricle of the heart is situated posterior to the ventricle), and Pulmonata (lung bearer; there is a functional lung in the mantle cavity). In some classifications Gastropoda is divided into two subclasses: the Streptoneura (twisted nerve; the main nerve track is twisted into the shape of a figure eight), and the Euthyneura (straight nerve; the nerve track has an oval shape). In this dual system of subclasses, the prosobranchs are in the Streptoneura and the opisthobranchs and pulmonates form the Euthyneura. We prefer to use the tripartite system, because the collector of land snails will find it more convenient to consult a separate chapter devoted to the terrestrial pulmonates. The characteristics of the three gastropod subclasses—Prosobranchia, Opisthobranchia, and Pulmonata—will be briefly discussed here.

The prosobranchs fall into three distinct divisions, or orders. These are the Archaeogastropoda (ancient gastropods), the Mesogastropoda (middle gastropods), and the Neogastropoda (new gastropods). On the basis of advanced anatomical similarities, some malacologists unite the mesogastropods and the neogastropods into a single order called Caenogastropoda (recent gastropods). The archaeogastropods, as the name implies, are considered to be the most primitive prosobranchs. They are all herbivorous, and thus have to live largely on hard bottoms on which grow the marine plants that nourish them. Fertilization, for the most part, takes place externally when ova from the female and sperm from the male are ejected into the water; in other cases, only the male performs thus, the ejected sperm being taken in by the female together with food and oxygen, and the ova fertilized internally. In only the single archaeogastropod superfamily Neritacea has the male developed an intromittent organ for copulation.

The archaeogastropod shell is frequently nacreous, and there are no species with highly turreted shapes. Since no archaeogastropod species has a siphon, the lip of the shell is entire, that is, unbroken by a siphonal canal or notch, a condition known as *holostomatous* (whole mouthed). The archaeogastropods include the slit shells (superfamily Pleurotomariacea), the keyhole limpets (superfamily Fissurellacea), the limpets (superfamily Patellacea), the top shells (superfamily Trochacea), and the nerites, or bleeding tooth shells (superfamily Neritacea). In addition, there are a large number of extinct fossil archaeogastropod superfamilies and families.

The second prosobranch order, Mesogastropoda, includes carnivores as well as herbivores. Fertilization is internal after copulation. Almost all the carnivorous mesogastropods have a siphon; hence the lip of the shell has a siphonal break, either a canal or a notch, a condition known as *siphonostomatous* (siphon mouthed). The carnivorous moon snails (superfamily Naticacea) are an outstanding exception. The most primitive herbivorous mesogastropods, as for example the periwinkles (superfamily Littorinacea), however, are holostomatous. The mesogastropods form a very large group, one that consists of twenty superfamilies, including several fossil groups. The most important are, besides the two mentioned above, the horn shells (superfamily Cerithiacea), the wentletraps (superfamily Epitoniacea), the conchs (superfamily Strombacea), the slipper shells (superfamily Calyptraeacea), the cowries (superfamily Cypraeacea), and the tun shells (superfamily Tonnacea). The mesogastropods also include some land and freshwater superfamilies.

The neogastropods are the most advanced of the prosobranchs. They are all carnivorous; thus all the shells, many of which are highly turreted, are siphonostomatous, some having amazingly long and well-decorated siphonal canals. Fertilization is internal. Neogastropods are frequently found on soft bottoms, in the sand and mud of which they can pursue their prey. There are no major extinct fossil groups. Included in this order are some of the most beautiful and desirable of all molluscan shells, such as the rock shells (superfamily Muricacea), the volutes (superfamily Volutacea), the cones (superfamily Conacea), the mitres (superfamily Mitracea), and the whelks (superfamily Buccinacea). The order Neogastropoda may be divided into two suborders: suborder Stenoglossa (narrow radula), and suborder Toxoglossa (arrow radula), which includes the cones and the mitres. The other neogastropod superfamilies are placed in Stenoglossa.

Although the representatives of the subclass Opisthobranchia are considered to be more advanced than the prosobranchs, since few of the species bear shells, they are thus of less interest to the shell collector. Where shells are present they tend to be quite small, and almost all have a "bubble" shape. Some opisthobranchs have internal shells, but most have no shells at all, like the beautiful but shell-less Nudibranchia (naked gills). These unshelled groups are not discussed in this book.

The subclass Pulmonata includes most of the terrestrial and many of the freshwater snails, and these air breathers are discussed in the chapters devoted to the land and freshwater gastropods. There are, however, a few pulmonates that live along the edge of the ocean and in saltwater marshes, where the collector of marine shells will encounter them. These are included in this chapter.

CLASS:

# GASTROPODA

*(stomach-footed)*

---

SUBCLASS:

## PROSOBRANCHIA

*(gills forward)*

= STREPTONEURA

*(twisted nerve)*

ORDER:

## ARCHAEOGASTROPODA

*(ancient stomach-footed)*

---

# FISSURELLACEA

## FISSURELLIDAE
*(keyhole limpets)*

These shells are cap shaped like the true limpets, but they differ from these (family Acmaeidae) (see pages 38–39) by the presence of a hole or slit, an orifice, at or near the center of the apex. In some deep-water species, the orifice at the apex is replaced by a notch at the margin of the shell. Immature Fissurellidae all have a marginal slit, but as the shell grows, the slit is increasingly surrounded by shelly material till it finally assumes its adult position. The keyhole limpets live on hard surfaces like coral, rocks, or other shells, and in life the thin mantle covers most of the outer surface. They are found mostly in warmer waters.

## KEY TO GENERA FISSURELLA, DIODORA, AND LUCAPINA

      \* Dorsal orifice circular or oval
      \* \* Internal callus truncate behind
   \* \* \* Orifice large, one-sixth of shell, white          *Lucapina sowerbii*
   \* \* \* Orifice one-seventh to one-ninth of shell,
        bluish black         *L. suffusa*
     \* \* Internal callus not truncate behind
   \* \* \* Orifice oval
\* \* \* \* Orifice small, one-twelfth of shell, internal
        callus light brown or reddish brown         *Fissurella angusta*
\* \* \* \* Orifice larger, one-sixth of shell, callus green
        with pinkish border         *F. rosea*
   \* \* \* Orifice circular, callus margined with dark
        reddish band         *F. barbadensis*
      \* Dorsal orifice not circular or oval
     \* \* Orifice triangular, shell white with         *Diodora dysoni*
        black rays
     \* \* Orifice keyhole shaped

* * * Surface sculpture very strong, with nodules
    and square pits where radial and concentric
    ribs intersect                                    *D. listeri*

* * * Surface sculpture weak, nodules and square
    pits absent                                       *D. cayenensis*

Genus *Fissurella* Lamarck

*Fissurella barbadensis* Gmelin
    Barbadan Keyhole Limpet

Pl. XVII, 1

ETYMOLOGY: Lat. *fissura*, notch, fissure.

SIZE: 25 to 40 mm. (1 to 1 3/5 in.) in length, 20 to 25 mm. (4/5 to 1 in.)
    in width.

DISTRIBUTION: Southeast Florida, Bermuda, and the Caribbean.

CHARACTERISTICS: Shell fairly heavy, conical, more or less elevated; apex
    pierced by an almost circular orifice that is bounded internally by a
    green callus margined with reddish brown sculpture of numerous
    irregular, radiating ribs. External color grayish white to pinkish buff,
    generally with purplish lines between the small ribs and with dark
    reddish brown or purple blotches between the larger ribs; interior with
    alternating bands of green and white.

This is the commonest of Floridian keyhole limpets, living on rocks in
reach of the waves. The shells are frequently covered with algal
growths and hence are not easy to detect. The shell is very variable
in shape and sculpture, but the species can be recognized by the
circular orifice, the green and white bands in the interior, and the red
margin around the callus of the orifice. Keyhole limpets are commonly
found living on hard surfaces such as rocks, coral, and the shells of
other mollusks.

The **Narrow Keyhole Limpet**, *Fissurella angusta* Gmelin (Lat.
*angustus*, narrow) (pl. XVII, 2), differs by having the front end
pointed, the orifice smaller (one-twelfth of the shell), and the internal
orifice callus light brown to reddish brown, without the reddish
margin. It is found from the Florida Keys to the Caribbean.

The **Rosy Keyhole Limpet**, *Fissurella rosea* Gmelin (pl. XVII, 3), is
smaller, 30 mm. (1 1/5 in.) in length, and more delicate. The orifice is
oval rather than round and comparatively large, one-sixth of the shell.

The internal orifice callus is green, with a pinkish border. The surface color consists of alternating straw-colored and pinkish rays; the interior is pale green and white. This is a common species in shell drift, and probably lives below the low-water line. It occurs from southeast Florida through the Caribbean to Brazil.

Genus *Diodora* Gray

*Diodora cayenensis* Lamarck
  Cayenne Keyhole Limpet

  Pl. XVII, 4

ETYMOLOGY: Diodora is an invented name without meaning; Cayenne is the capital of French Guiana.

SIZE: 25 to 40 mm. (1 to 1 3/5 in.) in length, 20 to 24 mm. (about 4/5 to 1 in.) in width.

DISTRIBUTION: Southern New Jersey to Florida, Bermuda, and the Caribbean to Brazil.

CHARACTERISTICS: Shell rather heavy, conical; base oval; apex with a keyhole-shaped orifice, one-sixth of shell, with an interior, truncated orifice callus set off by a deep pit behind. Color variable: whitish cream, pinkish to dark gray; interior white or bluish gray. Surface sculpture of numerous radial ribs crossed by concentric growth laminae.

This species varies considerably in height, shape, and color, and thus has been the unfortunate recipient of numerous synonyms. It can be recognized by the keyhole-shaped orifice and the relatively weak sculpture. It lives intertidally to deep water and is the commonest of the genus found. *Diodora alternata* Say is a later synonym.

**Lister's Keyhole Limpet,** *Diodora listeri* Orbigny (named for Martin Lister, an English naturalist of the seventeenth century) (pl. XVIII, 1), is of the same size as *D. cayenensis,* but differs chiefly in having much stronger axial ribs crossed by concentric lines, which form large scales or nodules and square interstitial pits where they intersect. This is a rarer species than *D. cayenensis,* with which it occurs in south Florida. It is more common in the West Indies.

**Dyson's Keyhole Limpet,** *Diodora dysoni* Reeve (Dyson was a collector in Central America) (pl. XVII, 5), is smaller, rarely reaching 20 mm. (4/5 in.) in length. In addition to its small size, the species is most easily recognized by its color pattern of bold black rays on a white background, and the triangular-shaped orifice. It is a moderately common species that is sometimes washed ashore. It ranges from south Florida through the West Indies to Brazil.

Genus *Lucapina* Sowerby

*Lucapina sowerbii* Sowerby
    Sowerby's Keyhole Limpet

    Pl. XVII, 6

ETYMOLOGY: Lucapina is an invented name without meaning; G. B. Sowerby was the name of three generations of English conchologists.

SIZE: 22 mm. (4/5 in.) in length, 12 mm. (1/2 in.) in width.

DISTRIBUTION: Southeast Florida to the Caribbean and Brazil.

CHARACTERISTICS: Shell small, thin, low conical; base oval; apex with large oval orifice, one-sixth of shell; internal callus narrow, truncate behind. Surface latticelike, white to buff with seven to nine irregularly placed broken or dotted rays of brown or flesh color; interior white, callus may be bounded by an olive green streak.

This species is not common, but can be taken under rocks at low tide. The soft parts are very large, and the mantle covers about one-third of the shell. The species is most readily recognized by the rather delicate shell and the relatively large oval orifice. It has been wrongly called *L. aspersa* Philippi.

The **Mauve Keyhole Limpet,** *Lucapina suffusa* Reeve (Lat. *suffusus,* overspread, tinged) (pl. XVII, 7), is larger, up to 36 mm. (1 1/2 in.) long, and has a latticelike surface. The color is mauve, fading to pink in worn specimens. The orifice is one-eighth of the shell and stained bluish black; the inside is grayish. The species is most readily recognized by the bluish black orifice and its large, conspicuous orange mantle when taken alive. It is found from south Florida through the West Indies to Brazil.

# PATELLACEA

# ACMAEIDAE

(*true limpets*)

These shells are conical or cap shaped, without spirals or an orifice at the top. Like the keyhole limpets, the true limpets live on hard substrates, feeding on seaweeds and other marine plants. They are generally found in temperate and warmer waters.

Genus *Acmaea* Eschscholtz

*Acmaea testudinalis* Müller
　　Tortoise-Shell Limpet

　　Pl. XVII, 8

ETYMOLOGY: Gr. *akmaios*, blooming, vigorous; Lat. *testudo*, tortoise.

SIZE: 25 to 40 mm. (1 to 1 3/5 in.) in length.

DISTRIBUTION: Arctic seas to Long Island Sound.

CHARACTERISTICS: Shell medium, cup shaped, oval in outline, rather thin. Exterior greenish or cream white with radiating dark brown, broken lines; interior glossy, central portion brownish, margin with alternating small brown and white areas.

This is one of the few true limpets on the East Coast; the genus is much more generously represented on the West Coast. It lives clinging to rocks near and under the intertidal lines. The specimens in the north are larger. A small form, which lives on eel grass and has parallel sides to its shell, has been named *A. alveus* Conrad (Lat. *alveus*, cavity) (pl. XVII, 9). Though formerly regarded as merely a habitat form of *A. testudinalis*—that is, a form influenced by its habitat on narrow blades of eel grass—recent anatomical studies indicate that it may be a distinct species. Limpets are generally found subtidally on hard objects, such as rocks, coral, and the shells of other mollusks.

The **Antillean Limpet,** *Acmaea antillarum* Sowerby (pl. XVII, 10), is more depressed and smaller. It has numerous spiral threads, and the surface is whitish, with few or many radial bands of brownish green. This is a rare shell in southern Florida, but common in the Caribbean.

The **White-ribbed Limpet,** *Acmaea leucopleura* Gmelin (Gr. *leukos, pleura,* white sided) (pl. XVII, 11), is only 15 mm. (3/5 in.) in diameter. It is thick, with fifteen to twenty large, rounded, white radial ribs on a white or brownish background. This, too, is largely a West Indian species occasionally found on the lower Florida Keys. The coarser ribbed form was formerly known as *A. jamaicensis* Gmelin.

SUPERFAMILY:

# TROCHACEA

---

FAMILY:

# TROCHIDAE
(*top and tegula shells*)

The shells in this family are usually low, broadly conical in shape, somewhat like an inverted top, and range from rather large to quite small. The shell material is nacreous, but this inner iridescent layer is generally covered by a limy outer layer that is variously, commonly colorfully ornamented. The circular operculum is thin and horny, unlike the heavy limy operculum of the related family Turbinidae (see pages 43–46). Top shells are herbivorous and generally inhabit hard substrates, where they find their food. Though most occur in warmer seas, some cold-water forms also exist.

---

## KEY TO GENERA MARGARITES, CALLIOSTOMA, AND TEGULA

* Operculum corneous, thin (family Trochidae)
** Shell quite small, less than 10 mm. (2/5 in.) in diameter

\*\*\* Shell smooth, glossy, yellow-olive — *Margarites helicinus*

\*\*\* Shell surface with spiral threads, color tan or rose — *M. groenlandicus*

\*\* Shell larger, 20 to 75 mm. (4/5 to 3 in.) in diameter

\*\*\* Shell high, with surface sculpture of beaded spiral cords

\*\*\*\* Shell with umbilicus

\*\*\*\*\* Umbilicus one-eighth to one-tenth of base

\*\*\*\*\*\* Shell 25 to 35 mm. (1 to 1 2/5 in.) in height, beads fine, chocolate brown bands between spiral cords — *Calliostoma javanicum*

\*\*\*\*\*\* Shell 15 to 18 mm. (3/5 to 3/4 in.) in height, beads coarse, brown intercordal bands lacking — *C. adelae*

\*\*\*\*\* Umbilicus one-eighteenth of base, peripheral cords smooth — *C. jujubinum*

\*\*\*\* Shell without umbilicus

\*\*\*\*\* Shell with acutely keeled periphery, strong sutural cords with reddish brown dots — *C. pulchrum*

\*\*\*\*\* Shell with rounded periphery, no spotted cords — *C. euglyptum*

\*\*\* Shell low, with surface sculpture other than beaded spiral cords

\*\*\*\* Area around callus white — *Tegula fasciata*

\*\*\*\* Area around callus green — *T. excavata*

---

Genus *Margarites* Gray

*Margarites helicinus* Phipps
Tiny Arctic Top Shell

Pl. XVIII, 2

ETYMOLOGY: Gr. *margarites*, pearl; and diminutive of *helix*, spiral.

SIZE: 7 mm. (about 1/4 in.) in width, 5 mm. (1/5 in.) in height.

DISTRIBUTION: Arctic seas to Cape Cod.

CHARACTERISTICS: Shell small, moderately depressed, shaped like an inverted top, smooth, thin, glossy, fragile. Color yellow olive, aperture pearly. Umbilicus small, deep; lip thin. Operculum horny, with many spirals.

This is one of the few *Margarites* species found near the shore in our area. Most species live in deep water, and are rarely found on beaches. *M. helicinus* is a very common species farther north at Gaspé, Quebec, and it has also been found in beach drift on beaches in Maine and Massachusetts.

The **Greenland Tiny Top Shell**, *Margarites groenlandicus* Gmelin (pl. XVIII, 3) is about the same size, 7 × 6.5 mm. (about 1/4 × 1/4 in.) but can be distinguished by its tan or rose color and its surface covered by closely set but rather weak spiral threads, whereas *M. helicinus* is smooth except for faint irregular growth lines. *M. groenlandicus* has been collected in the spring on dulse seaweed along the Cape Cod Canal; it ranges northward to the Arctic.

Genus *Calliostoma* Swainson

*Calliostoma jujubinum* Gmelin
Jujube Top Shell

Pl. XVII, 12

ETYMOLOGY: Gr. *kallos stoma*, beautiful mouth; a jujube is a Mediterranean fruit from which a brownish jam is made.

SIZE: 34 mm. (1 2/5 in.) in height, 21 mm. (4/5 in.) in width.

DISTRIBUTION: North Carolina to Texas and south to Colombia, the West Indies, and the Bahamas.

CHARACTERISTICS: Shell medium, solid, pyramid shaped; sides straight except for the rounded keels of earlier whorls. Color dark mahogany brown to yellowish brown, generally marked with irregular lighter blotches. Surface sculpture of minutely beaded spiral cords, the cords on the periphery being very fine and unbeaded. Aperture very oblique, basal. Umbilicus small, deep, bordered by beaded cords. Operculum horny, brown, multispiral; nucleus central.

This is the most abundant shallow-water species of the genus, and for most collectors probably the only one they will encounter without dredging. The fine-beaded surface sculpture, the brown color, the straight-sided pyramid shape, and the deep umbilicus make identification easy. The shells vary somewhat in outline and sculpture, but the few extra names given to such forms are not necessary. All the

Trochidae are top shells with horny opercula. They live on rocky or pebbly bottoms.

**Adele's Top Shell,** *Calliostoma adelae* Schwengel (named for Adele Koto, a diligent Floridian collector) (not illustrated) resembles *C. jujubinum* but is smaller, usually reaching only 15 mm. (3/5 in.) in height. In color it is golden tan to brown and the heavier spiral cords at the base of each whorl are white with brown markings. The beading on all the cords is coarser than in *C. jujubinum*, and there are six to eight spiral whorls on the base instead of the ten to fifteen found in *jujubinum*. In contrast to *C. javanicum*, it has no distinct color bands between the spiral cords. It was originally named in 1951 from specimens collected in Indian Key, Florida, but has since been found to be moderately common in shallow water in grass beds throughout southeastern Florida.

The **Javanese Top Shell,** *Calliostoma javanicum* Lamarck (pl. XVIII, 4) differs from *C. jujubinum* in having a wider umbilicus, a sharper angle at the periphery, and more regularly beaded spiral cords. It is 30 mm. (1 1/5 in.) in height, and in color it is mottled brownish red or tan with brownish markings. There are usually chocolate brown lines between the spiral cords. This species, which ranges from the lower Florida Keys to the West Indies, was formerly known as *C. zonamestum* A. Adams (Lat. *zona mixtus*, mixed zones) because of the chocolate lines, but Lamarck's name, based on mistaken locality data—the shell is not found in Java—is older.

There are several other beautiful species of *Calliostoma* in our region, but they are quite rare, deep-water species that are rarely found on the beaches. The interested reader should consult the monograph by Clench and Turner (1960).

The **Beautiful Top Shell,** *Calliostoma pulchrum* C. B. Adams (Lat. *pulcher*, beautiful) (pl. XVII, 13) is much smaller, 15 mm. (3/5 in.) in height, thin, and without an umbilicus. The color is ivory white or light yellowish brown, with small brownish red spots more or less evenly dispersed on beaded spiral cords. The strongest cords are just above the suture. This species ranges from North Carolina to Florida to the Caribbean, and is much rarer than *C. jujubinum*.

The **Sculptured Top Shell,** *Calliostoma euglyptum* A. Adams (Gr. *eu glyphein*, well sculptured) (pl. XVIII, 5) is about 25 mm. (1 in.) high and just as wide; it is pinkish brown in color, often mottled with white. The periphery is rounded, not keeled, and there is no umbilicus. The species ranges from North Carolina to Florida and Mexico. It is an uncommon species sometimes found in shallow water.

Genus *Tegula* Lesson

*Tegula fasciata* Born
Banded Tegula

Pl. XVIII, 6

ETYMOLOGY: Lat. *tegula*, roof tile; possibly *fascis*, bundle.

SIZE: 18 mm. (3/4 in.) in diameter, 12 mm. (1/2 in.) in height.

DISTRIBUTION: Southeast Florida and the West Indies.

CHARACTERISTICS: Shell turban shaped, low, smooth, solid. Yellowish to brown, mottled with red, brown, black, or white spots, often with a pale color band on the periphery; umbilicus and callus white. Aperture with two teeth on columella. Sculpture of fine spiral threads. Operculum circular, horny, with many spirals; nucleus central.

This is the commonest tegula top shell in our area. The individuals live on grass blades and under rocks at low tide, and are frequently found dead in beach drift. Like most Trochidae, the shell is iridescent under a thick, limy outer layer.

The **Excavated Tegula,** *Tegula excavata* Lamarck (pl. XVIII, 7) is slightly smaller, bluish gray in color, with a corrugated surface. The base is concave (excavated), and there is a blue-green or iridescent green area around the deep, round, narrow umbilicus. This is a common West Indian species that is sometimes found in Florida.

FAMILY:

# TURBINIDAE

(*turban and star shells*)

These shells are shaped like an inverted top, often quite heavy and bulky. An inner iridescent layer is covered by an outer limy layer variously sculptured and colored. The calcareous operculum is heavy, quite unlike the thin, horny operculum of the related family Trochidae (see pages 39–43). Like the latter, these snails are also herbivorous and cling to hard surfaces, generally in warmer and tropical seas. The well-known cat's eye is an operculum of a South Pacific species favored for its use in jewelry.

# KEY TO GENERA TURBO AND ASTRAEA

* Operculum calcareous, heavy (family
Turbinidae)
** Aperture very oblique, basal
*** Shell much wider than high, with triangular
peripheral spines             *Astraea phoebia*
*** Shell width and height more or less equal
**** Shell large, reaching 75 mm. (3 in.) with
hollow scutelike spines on base         *A. caelata*
**** Shell smaller, reaching 50 mm. (2 in.), basal
spines wanting
***** Shell grayish, surface with narrow, wavy
axial lines and with low, oblique peripheral
knobs         *A. americana*
***** Shell greenish, surface with heavy undulate
ridges swollen at base         *A. tuber*
** Aperture almost vertical, about one-half
of shell in height
*** Shell large, 75 mm. (3 in.), smooth, brownish, suture deep, channeled         *Turbo canaliculatus*
*** Shell small, 40 mm. (1 3/5 in.), brownish,
suture shallow, not channeled         *T. castanea*

---

Genus *Turbo* Linnaeus

*Turbo castanea* Gmelin
Chestnut Turban Shell

Pl. XVII, 14

ETYMOLOGY: Lat. *turbo*, whirlwind, whipping top; *castanea*, chestnut tree.

SIZE: 40 mm. (1 3/5 in.) high, 40 mm. (1 3/5 in.) wide.

DISTRIBUTION: North Carolina, Texas, and the West Indies.

CHARACTERISTICS: Shell medium, broadly conic; heavy, strong, rough. Color orange, buff, grayish, occasionally green, blotched with darker brown or white, flamelike spots. Aperture almost vertical, large, with outer lip directed downward. Umbilicus lacking. Operculum limy, heavy, white; convex on the outside, flat with a brownish layer on the inside.

This is a common turban shell living in grassy situations close to shore. The knobby surface sculpture and the wide, downward projecting lip make identification easy. The turban shells resemble the top shells, but differ by having a heavy, limy operculum. They live on coral rubble and rocky bottoms.

The **Channeled Turban,** *Turbo canaliculatus* Hermann (Lat. *canalis,* channel) (pl. V, 5) is larger, up to 75 mm. (3 in.) in height, and is a much rarer shell. It has a deep, channeled suture, and the surface sculpture consists of strong, smooth, spiral cords. The color is greenish yellow, usually mottled with white and brown. This species ranges from the lower Florida Keys to the West Indies. It was formerly called *Turbo spenglerianus* Gmelin (for L. Spengler, 1720–1807, an early Danish conchologist).

Genus *Astraea* Röding

*Astraea phoebia* Röding
   Long-Spined Star Shell

   Pls. V, 4; XVIII, 8

ETYMOLOGY: Gr. *astraios,* starry; Phoebus Apollo, the sun god.

SIZE: 65 mm. (2 3/5 in.) in width, 30 mm. (1 1/5 in.) in height.

DISTRIBUTION: Southeast Florida and the West Indies.

CHARACTERISTICS: Shell medium, low, strong, solid; base almost flat; periphery acutely keeled and ornamented with a series of strong, triangular spines. Color silvery white, iridescent. Either umbilicate or imperforate. Aperture very oblique, basal; operculum heavy, limy.

This pretty shell is found abundantly in shallow water on grassy bottoms. It is easily recognized by the silvery color, low outline, and strong triangular spines. Specimens with somewhat shorter spines have been erroneously identified as *Astraea brevispina* Lamarck, but that is a West Indian species not found in Florida, characterized by having an orange-red splotch around the umbilicus. Formerly known as *A. longispina* Lamarck (Lat. *longa spina,* long spine).

The **American Star Shell,** *Astraea americana* Gmelin (pl. XVIII, 9) is smaller, reaching only 40 mm. (1 3/5 in.) in height. Unlike *A. phoebia,* it is much higher than wide, and instead of having triangular spines, the surface is corrugated by rounded, wavy axial ridges that terminate in low, oblique peripheral knobs. The color is stony greenish or grayish white. *A. americana* lives in the same habitat as *A. phoebia,* but ranges further north to central Florida.

The **Green Star Shell,** *Astraea tuber* Linnaeus (Lat. *tuber,* bump, protuberance) (pl. V, 1) is about the same size as *A. americana,* but differs in having a green and white reticulated color scheme. There are several low, blunt axial ridges swollen at the base and shoulder, features that probably suggested the name to the great Swedish naturalist. The imperforate base is smooth. This is a common West Indian shell occasionally found in southeast Florida.

The **Engraved Star Shell,** *Astraea caelata* Gmelin (Lat. *caelare,* to engrave, carve) (pls. V, 3; XVIII, 10) grows to 75 mm. (3 in.) in height, 65 mm. (2 3/5 in.) in width. It resembles *A. tuber,* but is readily distinguished by the presence of several spiral rows of hollow, short, scalelike spines on the base of the whorls, the largest spines being on the last whorl. The color is greenish white, occasionally with a pale brown tinge, but most older shells, like many top and star shells in Florida, are encrusted with an amorphous layer of calcium that hides the color and fills in the hollow basal spines, making them look like rounded protuberances. The heavy white operculum is dull and the surface finely pebbled. This species ranges from off South Carolina to the West Indies, and is a common shell in moderately shallow offshore waters of the lower Keys. Occasionally specimens are found washed up on the beach.

FAMILY:

# PHASIANELLIDAE

*(pheasant shells)*

The shells of this family in our area are usually quite small, rather narrowly conic in shape; the outer limy layer covers an inner iridescent layer, which is often brightly colored. The calcareous operculum is small but heavy. The local pheasant shells live in shallow water on grassy bottoms; the family as a whole is confined to warmer seas.

## KEY TO GENUS TRICOLIA

* Shell with shouldered whorls, generally with very fine spiral grooves, or striae          *Tricolia bella*
* Shell with rounded whorls, spiral grooves lacking

\*\* Shell white, with varicolored spots and
   checkered appearance                                    *T. affinis*
\*\* Shell pale brown or reddish, with wavy lines    *T. affinis pterocladia*

---

Genus *Tricolia* Risso

*Tricolia bella* M. Smith
   Shouldered Pheasant Shell

   Pl. XVIII, 11

ETYMOLOGY: *Tricolia* possibly suggested by the three colors found in these
   shells: rose, brown, orange; and Lat. *bellus*, pretty.

SIZE: 5 mm. (1/5 in.) in height, 3 mm. (1/8 in.) in width.

DISTRIBUTION: Lake Worth to the Florida Keys and the Caribbean; Brazil.

CHARACTERISTICS: Shell very small, solid, conical, with red, pink, brown or
   orange-yellow spots or flame markings on a white base color. Surface
   with numerous very fine spiral cords rarely lacking. Upper margin of
   whorls shouldered by a shallow keel. Operculum heavy, limy, white,
   threaded near the margin.

This common species, *Tricolia bella,* can readily be recognized by the
shouldered, keeled whorls and the generally fine spiral lines. The
smooth form occurs and intergrades with the finely grooved form and
is most abundant from Miami to the lower Keys, but the shouldered
whorls can easily be seen in all specimens. This and the other local
species of pheasant shells, unlike many species found in warmer
waters in other parts of the world, are quite small, and some of the characteristics mentioned above can be seen only under magnification. The
animals live on *Thalassia* grasses in shallow water, but can also be
taken on limy gravel and beneath the holdfasts of sea fans. This species
was once called *Tricolia pulchella* C. B. Adams, but it was found that
this name had been used two years earlier for another species.

   The male and the female shells in *Tricolia* may differ considerably
in appearance, a condition zoologists call "sexual dimorphism" (Gr.
*di morphe*, two forms). In most cases, the male shell is noticeably
smaller than the female shell. But recently Dr. Robert Robertson of
the Academy of Natural Sciences of Philadelphia discovered that in
some *Tricolia* even the radular teeth of males and females are dissimilar, an unusual condition among most groups of snails. He as-
cribed this remarkable circumstance to the different feeding habits of

the two sexes. The female eats a kind of brown seaweed, while the male, usually perched on the female's back, especially during the mating season, gets its food by scraping the algae that grow on the surface of its mate's shell.

The **Checkered Pheasant Shell**, *Tricolia affinis* C. B. Adams (Lat. *affinis*, related to, kindred) (pl. XVIII, 12) is a little larger, reaching about 8 mm. (1/3 in.) in height. The shell is thin and has rounded whorls without a keel. The color pattern consists of irregularly arranged reddish, pink, orange, or brownish dots on a light orange-brown or pink background, giving a checkered appearance to the surface. Occasional specimens can also have whitish zigzag markings or blotches. There is a slitlike umbilicus. This is a common species ranging from the Florida Keys to the Caribbean. In the Keys it lives on turtle grass (*Thalassia testudineum*).

The **Algae Pheasant Shell**, *Tricolia affinis pterocladia* Robertson (Gr. *pteron cladon,* wing branch) (pl. XVIII, 13) differs by having a dull, pale brown (rarely reddish) ground color with a pattern of descending wavy lines instead of spots. It ranges from Fort Pierce to the Biscayne Bay area, and sporadically as far as Grassy Key. It is found alive only on the red algae, *Pterocladia*—hence its name—a plant growth found on rocks in shallow water. This subspecies has erroneously been called *Tricolia tessellata* Potiez and Michaud, a West Indian species that does not occur in Florida.

SUPERFAMILY:

# NERITACEA

FAMILY:

# NERITIDAE
(*nerites*)

The shells are moderately large to rather small, almost globular in shape, most of which consists of a large body whorl with a spire that barely rises above it. The operculum is shaped like a half moon, and is usually limy. In warmer seas, Neritidae cling in large numbers to wave-washed rocks. Some species of *Neritina* are found in brackish and even fresh water, and the closely related family Helicinidae (see pages 202–203) have adapted to live entirely on land.

## KEY TO FAMILY NERITIDAE

* Shell usually rough, heavy, large, more than 20 mm. (4/5 in.) in length
** Color pattern of black and white only
*** Color pattern of alternating squarish black and white spots, operculum black      *Nerita tessellata*
*** Color pattern entirely black or with irregularly scattered patches or lines of white, operculum bluish gray to yellow      *N. fulgurans*
** Color pattern includes black and red markings
*** Columellar area smooth, with blood-red stain      *N. peloronta*
*** Columellar area all white, roughened by deep axial ridges      *N. versicolor*
* Shell smooth, glossy, thin, 18 mm. (3/4 in.) and less in length
** Shell 16 to 18 mm. (2/3 to 3/4 in.) in length
*** Shell with bold pattern of large square, circular, or zigzag designs, color various      *Neritina virginea*
*** Shell with pattern of narrow, closely set zigzag lines, color generally greenish      *N. reclivata*
** Shell under 10 mm. (2/5 in.) in length
*** Shell white, with zebralike black stripes      *Puperita pupa*
*** Shell emerald green      *Smaragdia viridis*

Genus *Nerita* Linnaeus

*Nerita peloronta* Linnaeus
Bleeding Tooth

Pl. V, 2

ETYMOLOGY: Gr. *nerites*, sea snail, possibly from Nereus or Nereis, mythological sea creatures; Gr. *peloros odont*, huge tooth.

SIZE: 25 to 30 mm. (1 to 1 1/5 in.) in length, 20 to 25 mm. (4/5 to 1 in.) high.

DISTRIBUTION: Florida, the Caribbean, and Bermuda.

CHARACTERISTICS: Shell semiglobose, body whorl much larger than spire; thick, heavy, rough, generally coarsely sculptured with strong spiral cords. Color yellowish, with red and black zigzag markings. Inner lip smooth, with blood-red stain around two or three large white teeth. Operculum porcelainlike, orange brown.

The Bleeding Tooth is the most abundant nerite on rocks between the tide lines. Actually, no characteristic beyond its common name is needed for it to be recognized. In some populations the spiral cords are weak or lacking. The operculum has a peg on which it can swivel like a hinge.

The **Variegated Nerite,** *Nerita versicolor* Gmelin (Lat. *versicolor,* of changeable color) (pl. XVIII, 14) is smaller, reaching only 25 mm. (1 in.) in length. The shell is sculptured with strong spiral cords, ornamented with irregular black and red rectangular spots on a white background. The columellar margin of the inner lip, that is, the parietal area, is white and much roughened by strong spiral cords. This species has the same range and habitat as the Bleeding Tooth, but the two need never be confused.

The **Tessellated Nerite,** *Nerita tessellata* Gmelin (Lat. *tessella,* little cube) (pl. XVII, 15) is even smaller, barely reaching 20 mm. (4/5 in.) in length. The sculptured surface is ornamented with alternating squarish spots of black and white, red markings being altogether absent. In this it differs readily from *N. versicolor.* Moreover, the columellar margin is pebbled, and the operculum is finely pebbled and black. The range of this species is the same as that of the two species already discussed.

The **Lightning Nerite,** *Nerita fulgurans* Gmelin (Lat. *fulgur,* flash of lightning) (pl. XVIII, 15) reaches 25 mm. (1 in.) in length. It is usually black, with blurred, irregular white markings, differing in this from *N. tessellata,* whose markings are more or less regular. The operculum, moreover, is not black, but bluish gray to yellow. This species has the same range as the other nerites, but it prefers less saline habitats, and is found within the mouths of harbors where the water is somewhat freshened. Its name was probably inspired by its irregular, lightning-like white surface markings.

Genus *Neritina* Lamarck

*Neritina virginea* Linnaeus
  Virgin Nerite

  Pl. XVII, 16

ETYMOLOGY: Gr. diminutive of *Nerita*; Lat. *virgineus*, maidenly.

SIZE: 10 to 18 mm. (2/5 to 3/4 in.) in diameter, 6 to 12 mm. (1/4 to 1/2 in.) in height.

DISTRIBUTION: Florida to Texas, the Caribbean, and Bermuda.

CHARACTERISTICS: Shell small, globose, thin, glossy. Ground color olivaceous yellowish or brownish, with a pattern of crooked axial lines, circles, dots, mottlings, zebralike stripes, and bandings, often margined with black. Parietal area white or yellow, smooth. Operculum usually black.

This is a very abundant species on intertidal flats where the water is brackish. The color patterns are striking and astonishingly variable—as with human fingerprints, there are, among the literally billions of specimens, no two patterns alike. These patterns, however, are only surface thin and scrape off easily, leaving exposed a greenish gray surface. Linnaeus thought this species came from the Mediterranean; hence the name has nothing to do with the state of Virginia. But it is difficult to guess what Linnaeus saw in the shells of these prolific snails to make him think of virgins.

The **Olive Nerite,** *Neritina reclivata* Say (Lat. *reclinavi,* to lean backward) (pl. XVII, 17) resembles the Virgin Nerite in shape and size, but differs in being generally greenish or olive with a pattern of fine, close, angular black, brown, or lavender lines; the bold designs of *N. virginea* are wanting. This species ranges from Florida to Texas and the Caribbean, where it is found in brackish or even completely fresh water.

The **Zebra Nerite,** *Puperita pupa* Linnaeus (both names from Lat. *pupa,* puppet or doll) (pl. XVII, 18) is much smaller, rarely reaching 14 mm. (1/2 in.) in length, 10 mm. (2/5 in.) in height. This species, ranging from southeastern Florida to the Caribbean, is generally found in splash pools, though it has also been taken in shallow water at Torch Key. In some specimens, the zebralike markings become much wider, making the shell almost entirely black. The aperture is yellow rather than orange. Such shells may be *Puperita tristris* Orbigny, a species widespread in the Caribbean.

The **Emerald Nerite,** *Smaragdia viridis* Linnaeus (Gr. *smaragdos,* emerald; Lat. *viridis,* green) (pl. XVIII, 16) is much smaller, about 5 mm. (1/5 in.) in length, less than 3 mm. (1/8 in.) in height. It is proportionately lower than most nerites, and is most easily recognized by its green color, rarely with tiny white or purple markings. While a common Caribbean species, it is a very rare shell in Florida. *S. viridis* is also a Mediterranean species; sometimes the American form has been separated as the subspecies *S. viridis viridemaris* Maury (Lat. *viridis, mare,* green sea).

ORDER:

# MESOGASTROPODA
(*middle stomach-footed*)

# LITTORINACEA

## KEY TO GENERA OF FAMILIES LACUNIDAE AND LITTORINIDAE

* Columellar lip excavated with a smooth, crescent-shaped groove, shell thin, translucent (family Lacunidae) — *Lacuna vincta*

* Columellar lip not excavated, shell generally heavy, opaque (family Littorinidae)

** Shell without heavy surface sculpture

*** Shell large, generally 25 mm. (1 in.) or more in diameter

**** Shell somewhat thinner, whorls rounded; southern distribution — *Littorina angulifera*

**** Shell heavy and thick, suture shallow, whorls flat

***** Shell low conic, dark colored, smooth or with very shallow, fine irregular spiral lines; northern distribution — *L. littorea*

***** Shell high, narrow, light colored, spiral lines more pronounced; southern distribution — *L. irrorata*

*** Shell less than 25 mm. (1 in.)

**** Shell quite small, 8 to 11 mm. (about 1/3 to 1/2 in.)

***** Shell with no sign of umbilicus; northern distribution — *L. obtusata*

***** Shell with short umbilical slit; southern distribution — *L. mespillum*

**** Shell larger, 18 to 20 mm. (3/4 to 4/5 in.)

***** Suture very deep, whorls rounded; northern distribution — *L. saxatilis*

***** Suture shallow, whorls less rounded; southern distribution

****** Shell quite smooth, spiral lines
microscopic, numerous — *L. ziczac*

****** Shell somewhat rougher, grooves
deeper, widely spaced

******* Aperture large, one-half or more
of entire shell, flame markings
broken, zigzag — *L. lineolata*

******* Aperture small, less than one-half
of entire shell, flame markings
oblique, straight — *L. angustior*

** Shell with heavy nodular surface
sculpture

*** Nodules rounded, shell with
umbilical chink — *Tectarius muricatus*

*** Nodules pointed, shell without
umbilical chink

**** Operculum with few spirals,
columellar edge wide, dished — *Nodilittorina tuberculata*

**** Operculum with many spirals,
columellar edge narrower, not
dished — *Echininus nodulosus*

FAMILY:

# LACUNIDAE
(*chink shells*)

The shells are small, brownish, and most easily characterized by the presence of an excavated crescent-shaped groove on the columellar shelf. Immature shells are commonly found in the spring on the beaches of New York, where they cling to bits of seaweed and other floating objects.

Genus *Lacuna* Turton

*Lacuna vincta* Montagu
Common Chink Shell

Pl. XVII, 19

ETYMOLOGY: Lat. *lacuna*, pit; *vincere*, to vanquish.

SIZE: 13 mm. (about 1/2 in.) in height, 7 mm. (about 1/4 in.) in width, frequently smaller.

DISTRIBUTION: Labrador to New Jersey.

CHARACTERISTICS: Shell small, thin, high conic. Color light tan to brown, occasionally with a few darker bands. Columellar shelf with a smooth, crescent-shaped groove. Operculum brown, horny, with few spirals.

These shells are more common in the northern part of their range, where large specimens can be taken feeding on *Laminaria* seaweed. They are most easily identified, even when very young, by the excavated crescent groove on the columellar shelf.

FAMILY:

# LITTORINIDAE
(*periwinkles*)

Periwinkles are usually moderate in size, though some are quite small. They have sturdy shells, and some are sculptured with surface nodules and ridges. The operculum is dark and horny, and the outer lip is thin. There is never an umbilicus. Periwinkles live, clinging to rocks and grasses, in large numbers near the tide line, though some genera like *Tectarius* are rarely reached by the tide. The family is found worldwide and is eaten in Europe.

Genus *Littorina* Férussac

*Littorina littorea* Linnaeus
Common Periwinkle

Pl. XVII, 20

ETYMOLOGY: Both names from Lat. *littus, littoris*, seashore.

SIZE: Up to 42 mm. (1 3/4 in.) in height, 25 mm. (1 in.) in width.

DISTRIBUTION: Canada to Cape May, New Jersey.

CHARACTERISTICS: Shell low conical, heavy, lusterless; suture shallow, whorls flat. Color dull brown or ashy, occasionally with very narrow reddish or blackish lines. Lip heavy, sharply beveled. Operculum horny, brownish. Umbilicus lacking.

This snail, a favorite article of food in Europe, lived originally in Labrador, but has spread southward during the last hundred years down the East Coast to Cape May. It is a cold-water species, and it is unlikely that it will become established further south. In many places it has become the most abundant species living on rocks or other hard surfaces. In our northern populations and those in Europe, specimens attain a much larger size than those in our southern waters. The young shells are covered with strong revolving lines.

The **Marsh Periwinkle,** *Littorina irrorata* Say (Lat. *irrorare,* besprinkle) (pl. XVII, 21) is smaller, reaching only 25 mm. (1 in.) in height, and is relatively higher and less chunky. The color is grayish white, with blotches or streaks of dark purple or reddish brown. The surface is sculptured with regularly spaced, rather deep spiral grooves. This species ranges from Long Island, New York, to central Florida and Texas, but is generally found only as a fossil north of Chesapeake Bay.

The **Angulate Periwinkle,** *Littorina angulifera* Lamarck (Lat. *angulus fere,* angle bearing) (pl. XVII, 22) is about the size of the Common Periwinkle, but it is thinner in texture, more colorful, and has a deeper suture and more rounded whorls. It is sculptured with fine spiral grooves, and is whitish or orange to reddish brown with darker, wavy axial color bands. It ranges from southern Florida to the Caribbean, and is common on branches of mangrove trees.

The **Round Periwinkle,** *Littorina obtusata* Linnaeus (Lat. *obtusus,* blunt, dull) (pl. XIX, 1) is quite small, 12 mm. (1/2 in.) in height and 11 mm. (about 1/2 in.) in width, and is most easily recognized by its globular shape with a very small spire. It is heavy and smooth, and it varies in color from yellow to chestnut brown, occasionally with wide bands. The operculum is bright yellow or light brown. The species ranges from Labrador to Cape May, New Jersey, and lives under *Fucus* seaweed, where the rounded shell resembles the air bladders of the weed. It also occurs in northwestern Europe, where it grows considerably larger.

The **Narrow Periwinkle,** *Littorina angustior* Mörch (Lat. *angustus,* narrow) (pl. XIX, 2) is found together with the Lineolate Periwinkle and the Zigzag Periwinkle. It resembles the former in having deep, well-spaced spiral grooves, but it is smoother, the flame markings are oblique and straight rather than zigzag, and the aperture is smaller, always less than one-half of the entire shell. Formerly known as *L. lineata* Orbigny (Lat. *linea,* line), an unavailable name. This species is incorrectly cited by Abbott (1968) as *L. lineolata.*

The **Dwarf Periwinkle,** *Littorina mespillum* Mühlfeld (Lat. *mespi-lum,* medlar fruit—somewhat like a crab apple) (pl. XVIII, 17) is the smallest of the local periwinkles, rarely reaching 8 mm. (1/3 in.) in height. It has a globular shape and low spire like *L. obtusata,* but is easily separated by the presence of a narrow umbilical slit. There is a brown periostracum, under which the shell is light colored, smooth, and occasionally decorated with rows of small, round, blackish spots. Not a common shell, it is to be found in splash pools near the high-tide line. It ranges from the Florida Keys to the Caribbean.

The **Rough Periwinkle,** *Littorina saxatilis* Olivi (Lat. *saxatilis,* living among rocks) (pl. XIX, 3) reaches 18 mm. (3/4 in.) in height. It is thinner in texture than *L. obtusata,* and has a conic outline with a deep suture. The surface is marked with shallow, revolving lines, and the color is variable: yellowish, ashen, greenish or orange, frequently, especially with juveniles, prettily marked with wide spiral bands. The species ranges from the Arctic to New Jersey, and is a common species on wood pilings, wharves, and rocks.

The **Zigzag Periwinkle,** *Littorina ziczac* Gmelin (Gr. *zickzack,* origin uncertain) (pl. XIX, 4) reaches about 20 mm. (4/5 in.) in height, but is generally smaller. The shell is high conic in outline; smooth, with many microscopic incised lines; and prettily marked with many narrow, zigzag, oblique axial lines of brown or purplish brown. It ranges from southern Florida to the Caribbean, and is a very common species in crevices in rocky areas.

The **Lineolate Periwinkle,** *Littorina lineolata* Orbigny (Lat. *lineola,* diminutive of *linea,* line) (pl. XIX, 5) has the same range and habitat as *L. ziczac.* For a long time it was thought to be the male shell of the Zigzag Periwinkle, but is now recognized as a distinct species. The shell is smaller and darker, and the surface is roughened by more widely spaced and more prominent spiral striae or grooves. The aperture is relatively large, one-half or more of the entire shell. Abbott (1968) incorrectly identified this species as *Littorina floccosa* Mörch, 1876.

Genus *Tectarius* Valenciennes

*Tectarius muricatus* Linnaeus
   Beaded Periwinkle
   Pl. XIX, 6

ETYMOLOGY: Lat. *tectum,* roof; *muricatus,* spiny, same as in *murex.*

SIZE: 15 to 30 mm. (3/5 to 1 1/5 in.) in height, 15 to 17 mm. (3/5 to 3/4 in.) in width.

DISTRIBUTION: Southern Florida, the Caribbean, and Bermuda.

CHARACTERISTICS: Shell small, low conic, solid. Color ash-gray, with ten or eleven rows of rounded, white tubercles. Aperture tan or brown. Umbilicus a narrow slit. Operculum with few spirals, horny, dark brown.

This relative of *Littorina* lives far from the high-water mark and is well on its way to becoming a true land dweller. It is very abundant, living on rocks or bushes. Dr. Clench noted that the individuals living nearer the tide line tend to be larger because the flying spray enables them to engage in long periods of feeding.

The **True Prickly Winkle,** *Nodilittorina tuberculata* Menke (Lat. *nodus*, knot, and *littorina*—q.v., page 56—and Lat. *tuber*, bump, protuberance) (pl. XIX, 7) is 20 mm. (4/5 in.) in height, 14 mm. (about 3/5 in.) in width. The shell—small, low conic, and strong, brownish to leaden gray, sculptured with several rows of small sharp tubercles arranged axially under one another—resembles the False Prickly Winkle (see below) but differs as follows: it has a paucispiral operculum, whereas the False Prickly Winkle has one with many spirals; the columella is flattened and dished, not narrow, and the tubercles are lined up axially one under the other, not haphazardly. This common rock dweller near the high-tide line was formerly called *T. tuberculatus* Wood. It is found in southern Florida, the Caribbean, and Bermuda.

The **False Prickly Winkle,** *Echininus nodulosus* Pfeiffer (Lat. *echinus*, hedgehog; *nodus*, knot) (pl. XIX, 8) is 20 mm. (4/5 in.) in height, 15 mm. (3/5 in.) in width. The small shell is strong, low conic, and grayish brown, and is sculptured with two spiral, keellike rows of sharp nodules and two or three rows of small blunt nodules; the columella is not dished, and the operculum is multispiral. It lives together with the True Prickly Winkle, but can be distinguished by carefully comparing the specimens. (See under *Nodilittorina tuberculata*, above.) It ranges from southern Florida to the Caribbean.

# RISSOACEA

# RISSOIDAE

(*risso shells*)

These shells are small to tiny, from conic to depressed in shape, often strongly and regularly sculptured. The snails live at or near the tide line on all sorts of objects, and their empty shells are commonly found in beach drift. The family has been little studied, and the large number of described species are not easy to recognize.

## KEY TO GENUS RISSOINA

(*modified from Abbott, 1974*)

* Shell smooth, glossy white, without surface sculpture, 4 mm. (1/6 in.); range Carolinas to Florida, Texas, and the West Indies — *Rissoina browniana*, Pl. XVIII, 18
* Shell sculptured with riblets and/or spiral lines
** Axial ribs more prominent than spiral lines
*** With axial ribs only, spiral sculpture lacking
**** White or stained with yellow, 16 to 22 riblets, 5 to 6 mm. (1/5 to 1/4 in.); range south Florida and the West Indies — *R. bryerea*, Pl. XIX, 9
**** White, 11 to 14 riblets, 3 to 5 mm. (1/8 to 1/5 in.); range Carolinas to Florida, Texas, and the West Indies — *R. catesbyana*, Pl. XIX, 10
*** With both axial ribs and spiral lines
**** 4 to 5 mm. (1/6 to 1/5 in.); ribs strong, white to rusty; range southeast Florida to Texas, and the West Indies — *R. multicostata*, Pl. XVIII, 19
**** 6 to 7 mm. (about 1/4 in.); ribs weak, spirally striated between, white to yellowish; range Carolinas to the West Indies — *R. decussata*, Pl. XIX, 11
** Axial ribs not more prominent than spiral threads

\*\*\* Surface strongly cancellated, depressed
interspaces large and square, white, 5 to 7
mm. (about 1/5 to 1/4 in.); range southeast
Florida and the West Indies

*R. cancellata,*
Pl. XIX, 12

\*\*\* Surface not strongly cancellated, spiral
threads dominant, axial ribs faint, 5 to 10
mm. (1/5 to 2/5 in.); range southeastern
Florida and the West Indies

*R. striosa,*
Pl. XVIII, 20

---

Genus *Rissoina* Orbigny

*Rissoina catesbyana* Orbigny
Catesby's Risso Shell

Pl. XIX, 10

ETYMOLOGY: Dedicated to A. Risso (1777–1845), a European malacologist;
and possibly to Mark Catesby (1679–1749), traveler and naturalist.

SIZE: 3 to 5 mm. (1/8 to 1/5 in.) in height.

DISTRIBUTION: North Carolina to Florida, Texas, and the West Indies.

CHARACTERISTICS: Shell tiny, white, glossy; elongate-conical, with strong
rounded, slanting axial ribs. Outer lip thickened, inner lip narrow.

This family of tiny shells, many of which live on seaweed in shallow
bays and inlets, is of worldwide distribution, mostly in warmer seas.
The eight species or so found on the Atlantic coast differ from each
other in details of axial ribbing and grooving; some, however, are
smooth, e.g. *Rissoina browniana* Orbigny. The family has never been
satisfactorily monographed, and much confusion reigns regarding the
true names. The identification key, modified from Abbott, 1974, is
provisional. *Rissoina catesbyana* was formerly mistaken for *R. ches-
nelii* Michaud, a species apparently limited to Jamaica, West Indies.

The **Pointed Cingula,** *Cingula aculeus* Gould (possibly Lat. *cingulum,* a girdle; diminutive of *acus,* a spine) (pl. XIX, 13) is an almost
microscopic species, 3 mm. (1/8 in.) in length. It is light brown, conic,
with a deep suture and rounded whorls covered by regular microscopic, revolving lines with numerous short axial riblets under the
suture. It is not easy to find, but is said to be common in shallow water
from Nova Scotia to Maryland.

FAMILY:

# SKENEOPSIDAE

*(marine ram's horns)*

These shells are minute, the few whorls all on the same plane, giving them a planorbidiform, or flattened, appearance. The snails live in shallow water on seaweed, and under rocks and dead shells.

Genus *Skeneopsis* Iredale

*Skeneopsis planorbis* Fabricius
Tiny Marine Ram's Horn

Pl. XX, 1

ETYMOLOGY: Named for David Skene, a contemporary of Carolus Linnaeus (1707–1778); Lat. *planus orbis*, flat orb or circle.

SIZE: 1.5 to 2 mm. (about 1/12 in.) in diameter.

DISTRIBUTION: Greenland to Florida, but commoner to the north.

CHARACTERISTICS: Shell microscopic, thin, opaque, brownish, flat. Umbilicus large, aperture round, lip thin.

This is said to be a common shell, but its microscopic size makes it hard to detect. It lives on submerged rocks and seaweeds. Formerly placed in the genus *Skenea,* the shells resemble minute members of the freshwater family Planorbidae.

---

FAMILY:

# VITRINELLIDAE

*(minute glass snails)*

The Vitrinellidae are a large, complicated family with unusually tiny shells, less than 2 mm. (1/12 in.) in width, having the general outline of the Striate Glass Snail (see below). Almost all are flattened or very depressed, generally umbilicate, and have a thin, multispiral operculum. This family has been divided into many genera and subgenera, but though it formed the subject matter recently of a Ph.D. thesis, no truly monographic works have yet appeared. The best popular treatment, with excellent photographs of about twenty species, has been published by Jean Andrews in her book *Shells of the Texas Coast* (1972). Specimens of Vitrinellidae can be found in beach drift, if carefully searched for, or in sand in shallow water. Many species are thought to live commensally with marine worms, and Mrs. Andrews suggests that the tubes of these worms be examined for specimens that the worm used, together with grains of sand and bits of shell, to construct its tubular shelter.

# KEY TO FAMILY VITRINELLIDAE

      * Shell large, up to 10 mm. in diameter

      ** Shell up to 7 mm., thin, glassy, weakly sculptured     *Cochliolepis striata*

      ** Shell up to 10 mm., strong, keeled, with strong spiral ridges     *Cyclostremiscus beaui*

     * Shell quite small, 1 to 3 mm. in diameter

     ** Shape raised, trochiform     *Paraviturboides interruptus*

     ** Shell depressed to very depressed

    *** Umbilicus covered or closed

   **** Shell with three narrow peripheral keels, umbilical area with a raised ridge     *Cyclostremiscus suppressus*

   **** Shell very flat, no keels or ridges     *Teinostoma biscayense*

    *** Umbilicus open, uncovered

   **** Lip with pronounced sinus above     *Cyclostremella humilis*

   **** Lip entire, without sinus

  ***** Shell with 3 blunt peripheral keels     *Cyclostremiscus pentagonus*

  ***** Shell without keels

 ****** Sculpture of numerous fine zigzag markings     *Anticlimax pilsbryi*

 ****** Sculpture of growth lines only

******* Suture with an additional spiral cord     *Vitrinella helicoidea*

******* Suture simple, without additional cord     *Solariorbis blakei*

Genus *Cochliolepis* Dall

*Cochliolepis striata* Dall
Striate Glass Snail

Pl. XIX, 14

ETYMOLOGY: Lat. *cochlea*, snail shell, Gr. *lepis*, scale; Lat. *stria*, furrow, channel.

SIZE: 7 mm. (about 1/4 in.) in width, 1 mm. (1/25 in.) in height.

DISTRIBUTION: North Carolina to Texas and the Caribbean.

CHARACTERISTICS: Shell small, quite depressed; white, thin, glassy. Body whorl very large, marked with closely set, concentric spiral grooves. Lip thin, umbilicus small, constricted.

This is one of the largest species of the family in our area. Its flattened shape, large body whorl, and finely grooved surface will suffice to identify it. It lives in shallow coastal bays, commonly found living on or near marine worms.

Because of the amplitude and complexity of this family, we shall limit ourselves to brief comments on the commonest species in our area:

*Anticlimax pilsbryi* McGinty (opposite of *Climacia*, a name previously used for another species; H. A. Pilsbry, an American malacologist). 3 mm. (1/8 in.) in width. Southern Florida, Texas, Mexico. Umbilicate, sculptured with numerous fine, zigzag markings.

*Cyclostremella humilis* Bush (Gr. *kyklos strema*, circular aperture; -*stremella*, the diminutive form; Lat. *humilis*, humble). 2 mm. (1/12 in.) in width. North Carolina to Texas. Deeply umbilicate, sculptured with irregular growth lines only; suture deep, lip with sinus above, operculum paucispiral. This genus has recently been removed from the Vitrinellidae to its own family, Cyclostremellidae.

*Cyclostremiscus beaui* Fischer (Commander Beau was a French naval officer who died in 1859) (pl. XVIII, 21) is about 10 mm. (2/5 in.) in width, 4 mm. (1/6 in.) in height. The shell is flattened like a *Planorbis*, white, keeled above and below, and has several strong spiral ridges on the top. It is a rare shell, sometimes being found on the beaches at Cedar Keys, Sanibel, and Palm Beach, Florida, and ranges from North Carolina to the West Indies.

*Cyclostremiscus pentagonus* Gabb (Gr. *pente gonia*, five angle), (pl. XIX, 15). 2 mm. (1/12 in.) in width. Southeastern United States to Texas and the West Indies. With three blunt keels on the body whorl, umbilicus open, deep.

*Cyclostremiscus suppressus* Dall (Lat. *suppressus*, subdued, low). 2 mm. (1/12 in.) in width. West coast of Florida to Texas. With three narrow, sharp keels, umbilicus closed, but umbilical area surrounded by a raised ridge.

*Paraviturboides interruptus* C. B. Adams (Lat. *parvus turbo*, small turbo; Gr. *oides*, resembling) (pl. XIX, 16). 1 mm. (1/25 in.) in width. South Carolina to Texas, Panama, and the West Indies. Shape raised, trochiform, with eight to nine strong spiral ridges, umbilicus deep, narrow.

*Solariorbis blakei* Rehder (Lat. *sol orbis*, sun circle; Blake was the name of a ship). 1 mm. (1/25 in.) in width. Florida, Gulf states to Mexico. Smooth but irregular axial wrinkles along suture and around the deep, narrow umbilicus only.

*Teinostoma biscayense* Pilsbry and McGinty (Gr. *teino stoma*, stretched mouth; named for Biscayne Bay, Florida) (pl. XVIII, 22). 2 mm. (1/12 in.) in width. Southern and western Florida to Texas. Very flat, umbilicus completely filled by heavy callus.

*Vitrinella helicoidea* C. B. Adams (Lat. diminutive of *vitrum*, glass; Gr. *helix oides*, spiral like) (pl. XVIII, 23). 3 mm. (1/8 in.) in width. Southeastern United States to Texas and the West Indies. Suture with additional spiral cord, umbilicus narrow, deep.

SUPERFAMILY:

# ARCHITECTONICACEA

FAMILY:

# ARCHITECTONIDAE
(*sundial shells*)

These shells are rather solid, low, and circular in shape. The umbilicus is huge and surrounded by a beaded keel; this is the easiest way to recognize the family. In our area, the family is found only in warmer seas.

# KEY TO GENERA
# ARCHITECTONICA AND HELIACUS

* Shell large, up to 50 mm. (2 in.) in diameter     *Architectonica nobilis*
* Shell smaller, reaching 25 mm. (1 in.) or less in diameter
** Shell raised, height equal to diameter, color dark, up to 25 mm. (1 in.)     *Heliacus cylindricus*
** Shell depressed, diameter decidedly larger than height, color pale, up to 11 mm. (about 1/2 in.)     *Heliacus bisulcatus*

---

Genus *Architectonica* Röding

*Architectonica nobilis* Röding
Noble Sundial Shell

Pls. VI, 8; XVIII, 24

ETYMOLOGY: Lat. *architecton*, master builder; and *nobilis*, excellent, superior.

SIZE: 30 to 50 mm. (1 1/5 to 2 in.) in diameter, 25 mm. (1 in.) in height.

DISTRIBUTION: North Carolina to Florida, Texas, the West Indies, and the eastern Atlantic. Also from western Mexico to Peru.

CHARACTERISTICS: Shell medium to large, circular, depressed, widely conical, strong. Color cream, with reddish brown spots. Sculpture of four to five beaded spiral cords, basal sculpture stronger. Umbilicus large, deep, bordered by a heavily beaded spiral cord. Lip distorted by termination of cords, not expanded. Operculum thin, with few spirals, brown.

This striking and beautiful shell is moderately common in sand below the low-water line, and beach specimens are not rare. It was formerly called *Architectonica granulata* Lamarck, a later name.

Genus *Heliacus* Orbigny

*Heliacus cylindricus* Gmelin
Cylinder Sundial Shell

Pl. XIX, 17

ETYMOLOGY: Gr. *helix*, spiral, coil.

SIZE: 25 mm. (1 in.) in height and width.

DISTRIBUTION: Lower Florida Keys and the West Indies.

CHARACTERISTICS: Shell small, conic, elevated. Reddish brown to black, frequently with white spots on the periphery and above the suture. Sculptured with minutely beaded, closely set spiral cords. Umbilicus narrow, very deep; border scalloped.

This smaller sundial shell is said to be fairly common at low tide. The beaded surface, the crenulated but not expanded lip, and the bordered, deep umbilicus betray its relationship to *Architectonica*. It was formerly placed in the genus *Torinia* Gray.

The **Bifurrowed Sundial,** *Heliacus bisulcatus* Orbigny (Lat. *bis sulcare,* twice furrowed) (pl. XVIII, 25) is smaller, 8 to 13 mm. (1/3 to 1/2 in.) in diameter, and much more depressed. The color is gray to tan, and the surface is strongly sculptured with revolving beaded cords, the periphery having two rows of larger beads—whence its name. It lives intertidally on rocks and jetties along the southeastern coast of the United States, Texas, and in the West Indies.

SUPERFAMILY:
# TURRITELLACEA

FAMILY:
# TURRITELLIDAE
(*turret shells*)

These shells are elongate, very attenuated, and awl shaped, with many whorls sculptured with strong, closely set spiral ridges. A common family in the Pacific Ocean, only a few species occur in our area.

## KEY TO TURRITELLIDAE

\* Shell with light base color mottled with brown
   flame markings, whorls concave        *Turritella exoleta*

\* Shell with light base color, no other color
   markings, whorls flat or convex

\*\* Whorls flat, with numerous fainter spiral
    ridges                       *T. acropora*

\*\* Whorls convex, with 5 to 6 strong spiral ridges    *Tachyrhynchus erosus*

---

Genus *Tachyrhynchus* Mörch

*Tachyrhynchus erosus* Couthouy
   Eroded Turret Shell

   Pl. XX, 2

ETYMOLOGY: Gr. *tachys rhynchus*, quick snout or beak; Lat. *erosus*, corroded.

SIZE: 25 mm. (1 in.) in height, 7 mm. (about 1/4 in.) in width.

DISTRIBUTION: Nova Scotia to Cape Cod.

CHARACTERISTICS: Shell medium, elongate, cream to white. Surface sculpture
of five to six smooth, strong, spiral ridges on each whorl. Aperture
squarish, siphonal notch absent. Operculum round, multispiral,
corneous, brown.

The turret shells can be confused with the auger shells (family
Terebridae), but the sculpture is always spiral, never axial, and the
aperture, because of the missing siphonal canal, looks quite different.
The Eroded Turret is a rare shell on the beaches, but lives in fair
abundance in deeper offshore waters. The turret shells live burrowing
in sand and sandy mud, below the tide line.

   The **Boring Turret Shell,** *Turritella acropora* Dall (diminutive of
Lat. *turris*, tower; Gr. *acropora*, piercing, boring) (pl. XX, 3) is about
the same size, but differs immediately in that the latter whorls have
more numerous and weaker spiral lines. The shell is yellowish or
brownish in color, and is common just offshore from North Carolina
to Florida, Texas, and the West Indies.

   The **Geriatric Turret Shell,** *Turritella exoleta* Linnaeus (Lat. *exole-
tum*, full grown, mature) (pl. VI, 3) grows to 50 mm. (2 in.) in
height. The color is white to cream, ornamented with irregular axial
brownish flame markings. The whorls have a strong spiral ridge above

and below, and the space between is deeply concave. This rather pretty turret shell, which ranges from South Carolina, is found moderately commonly in southern Florida and the West Indies.

---

FAMILY:

# CAECIDAE

The shells are very small, tubular, the surface smooth, ringed, or more commonly longitudinally grooved. The embryonal shell is spiral-shaped, but as the snail matures this part is lost. The shells are frequently found in beach drift, mainly in warmer waters.

These tiny shells can be collected by straining sand in shallow water, and by closely examining sponges and eel grass, on which some live. Dead shells are sometimes common in beach drift. The mollusks begin life as minuscule, normally coiled snails but then grow in a single direction only; the original spiral whorls are lost and the opening is filled with a tiny septum, or caplike partition.

---

## KEY TO GENERA
## CAECUM AND MEIOCERAS

| | |
|---|---|
| * Shell tubular, swollen in the middle, septum rounded | *Meioceras nitidum* |
| * Shell cucumber-shaped, not swollen in the middle, septum pointed | |
| ** Shell with smooth surface, glossy, cream white | *Caecum carolinianum* |
| ** Shell with sculptured surface | |
| *** Sculpture predominantly of narrow axial rings | |
| **** Shell 3 mm. (1/8 in.), opaque white when alive, with apertural varix; North Carolina to Florida | *C. floridanum* |
| **** Shell 2 mm. (1/12 in.), translucent when alive, no varix; Cape Cod to North Carolina | *C. pulchellum* |
| *** Sculpture predominantly of longitudinal ribs | |
| **** Shell 4 to 5 mm. (1/6 to 1/5 in.), 24 ribs | |

crossed by numerous axial lines; Cape Cod
to North Carolina                    *C. cooperi*
**** Shell 3 mm. (1/8 in.), 14 ribs cut by axial
grooves; southern Florida and the Bahamas    *C. imbricatum*

---

Genus *Caecum* Fleming

*Caecum carolinianum* Dall
Carolina Caecum

Pl. XIX, 18

ETYMOLOGY: Lat. *caecum*, blind gut, from *caecus*, blind.

SIZE: 5 mm. (1/5 in.) in length, 1 mm. (1/25 in.) in width.

DISTRIBUTION: Cape Cod, Massachusetts, to southern Florida.

CHARACTERISTICS: Shell tiny, cucumber-shaped, glossy white, smooth except
for microscopic growth lines; one end closed by a pointed septum.
Aperture circular. Operculum thin, with many spirals.

The genus *Caecum* has a very wide distribution throughout the world,
and several species are found in our area, of which the following are
perhaps those most readily encountered.

The **Pretty Caecum,** *Caecum pulchellum* Stimpson (Lat. *pulcher,*
pretty) (pl. XX, 4) is only 2 mm. (1/12 in.) long. It is readily recognized by the sculpture, which consists of a series of narrow rings.
When alive, the shell is translucent. Cape Cod to North Carolina;
Texas.

The **Florida Caecum,** *Caecum floridanum* Stimpson (pl. XX, 5),
is 3 mm. (1/8 in.) long. It also is sculptured with narrow rings, but
the shell is larger and opaque in life. Moreover, to distinguish it even
more readily from *C. pulchellum,* the last one or two rings are
thickened into a heavy ridge at the aperture. North Carolina to
Florida.

**Cooper's Caecum,** *Caecum cooperi* S. Smith (William Cooper,
1798–1864, an American naturalist) (pl. XIX, 19), is rather large, 4 to
5 mm. (1/6 to 1/5 in.) in length. The surface sculpture consists of
about twenty-four rounded, longitudinal ribs, which are faintly crossed
by numerous fine lines. This is a species ranging from Maine to
northern Florida.

The **Rooftile Caecum,** *Caecum imbricatum* Carpenter (Lat. *imbricatus,* covered with tiles) (not illus.), also has longitudinal ribs on

its surface. But there are only about fourteen of these, and they are strongly cut by crossing grooves. This is a species found in southern Florida and the Bahamas.

The **Little Horn Caecum,** *Meioceras nitidum* Stimpson (Gr. *meion keras*, little horn, and Lat. *nitidus*, glossy) (pl. XIX, 20), is only 3 mm. (1/8 in.) long. It is readily distinguished from the true caecums by its shape, which is tubular with a swollen middle. The septum is rounded. The shell is glossy white or brownish, with irregular specks of opaque white. The early stages of the shell, which become detached long before the animal reaches maturity, resemble a tiny horn. Fairly commonly found on eel grass in southern Florida.

---

FAMILY:

# MODULIDAE

The family is composed of a few, small, top-shaped shells with grooved and knobby surfaces. There is a denticle below the columella. The snails are common in grassy areas in shallow parts of warmer seas.

Genus *Modulus* Gray

*Modulus modulus* Linnaeus
   Atlantic Modulus

   Pl. XIX, 21

ETYMOLOGY: Diminutive of Lat. *modus*, a measure.

SIZE: 10 to 16 mm. (2/5 to 2/3 in.) in height, 9 to 15 mm. (about 2/5 to 3/5 in.) in width.

DISTRIBUTION: Off North Carolina to southeast Florida, Texas, Bermuda, and the Caribbean.

CHARACTERISTICS: Shell small, low top-shaped. Strong, dull, grayish white, porcelainlike, occasionally flecked with purplish brown. Surface roughened and sculptured with a series of coarse spiral cords, the strongest being at the periphery. Outer lip thin, inner lip thick and with a prominent toothlike, purple-tinged narrow ridge. Umbilicus small. Operculum horny, with many spirals; thin, amber.

This is the commonest species of the single genus that comprises the family. The shell looks like a top shell (family Trochidae, see pages

39–43) but it is not iridescent, and the radula and soft parts show that it is close to the horn shells (family Cerithiidae) (see pages 75–80). The shells vary greatly and synonyms are many, but specific recognition is easy. It is prolific in shallow-water eel-grass flats, especially in sheltered bays.

FAMILIES:

# VERMICULARIIDAE, VERMETIDAE, AND SILIQUARIIDAE

*(worm shells)*

In the family Vermiculariidae, the early whorls of the shells are normally spirally coiled, but the later whorls are loosely coiled and form a long, wormlike, irregularly twisted tube. The surface is variously sculptured. In our area, they are found in temperate and warmer seas. Most authors include the vermiculariids in the family Turitellidae, which have similar, evenly and tightly coiled early whorls. They are placed here for the convenience of collectors.

In the family Vermetidae, the earliest whorls are minute, and few in number. Shortly after leaving the protection of the adult's shell, the juvenile vermetid attaches itself to some hard object. Thereafter, the newly formed whorls coil at right angles to the original whorls, to give a wormlike appearance. Tangled masses of these snails can be mistaken for worm tubes. The vermetids are widely distributed in shallow water, mostly in warmer seas.

The slit worm shells of the family Siliquariidae have long, irregularly coiled tubes with a series of minute holes arranged in a single, longitudinal row, or they have elongate slits on the middle of the whorl.

# KEY TO FAMILIES SILIQUARIIDAE, VERMICULARIIDAE, AND VERMETIDAE

* Shell with a row of slits in the middle of
  the whorl (family Siliquariidae)  • *Siliquaria squamata*
* Shell whorl solid, without slits
** Shells living individually, early whorls
  spirally coiled (family Vermiculariidae)

| | | |
|---|---|---|
| * * * | Early whorls dark | *Vermicularia spirata* |
| * * * | Early whorls white | *V. knorri* |
| * * | Shells living in twisted masses, early whorls weakly coiled (family Vermetidae) | |
| * * * | Shell long, wormlike, relatively fragile, sculpture weak, color gray to dull brown | *Petaloconchus nigricans* |
| * * * | Shells greatly twisted and coiled, often forming large masses | |
| * * * * | Shells heavy, light gray, surface longitudinally sculptured | *Spiroglyphus irregularis* |
| * * * * | Shells weaker, reddish brown to orange, surface roughened by growth lines | *Petaloconchus varians* |

---

Genus *Vermicularia* Lamarck

*Vermicularia spirata* Philippi
Common Worm Shell

Pl. VI, 2

ETYMOLOGY: Lat. *vermiculus*, like worm; *spiratus*, coiled

SIZE: Tube 5 mm. (1/5 in.) in diameter, coiled portion 12 to 25 mm. (1/2 to 1 in.).

DISTRIBUTION: Woods Hole, Massachusetts, to Florida and the Gulf Coast.

CHARACTERISTICS: Shell medium, early portion coiled, later portion wormlike, uncoiled. Shell thin, amber or yellowish brown, early whorls dark. Two to three longitudinal ridges that weaken on later portion. Operculum circular, thin.

The English malacologist J. E. Morton says of *Vermicularia* that "it is in fact little more than a turritellid [Turret Shell] which has taken a sessile posture embedded in a hard substratum and proceeded to uncoil its whorls." The shells live attached to coral, large shells, sponges, and calcareous algae. The degree of uncoiling varies with the nature of the object on which the shell rests; the harder the substrate, the sooner the shell begins to uncoil. The name *Vermicularia fargoi* Olsson was given to specimens with large coiled juvenile shells living in mud along the west coast of Florida and in Texas.

The **Florida Worm Shell,** *Vermicularia knorri* Deshayes (Knorr was a German malacologist) (pl. XX, 6), differs only in having the coiled portion white instead of dark. It lives in spongy masses, which may be washed up on shore, and ranges from North Carolina to Florida and the Gulf of Mexico.

The **Slit Worm Shell,** *Siliquaria squamata* Blainville (Lat. *siliqua,* pod; Lat. *squama,* fish scale) (pl. VI, 1), is 120 mm. (5 in.) in length and is characterized by having a long row of elongate slits in the middle of the whorl. The early whorls are not tightly coiled, and the later whorls are spiny. The species lives in southeast Florida and the West Indies, in deep water.

The **Variable Worm Shell,** *Petaloconchus varians* Orbigny (Gr. *petalos,* spread out, and *concha,* shell; *varius,* variegated) (pl. VI, 5), is 48 to 100 mm. (2 to 4 in.) in length, 4 mm. (1/6 in.) in diameter. The unevenly coiled, tubelike shells are usually intertwined and are fixed to hard surfaces. Sometimes they are numerous enough to form large reefs. There is hardly any regular coiling, even when the shells are still juvenile. The shells of this species are reddish brown outside, whitish inside, and the surface is ribbed longitudinally and generally roughened by growth wrinkles. The species is found in southern Florida and the West Indies. *Petaloconchus* is a genus in the family Vermetidae.

The **Dark Worm Shell,** *Petaloconchus nigricans* Dall (Lat. *nigricans,* blackish), is a more fragile growth form in which the sculpture is weaker and the color gray to purplish brown. It lives on the west coast of Florida.

The **Irregular Worm Shell,** *Spiroglyphus irregularis* Orbigny (Gr. *speira, glyphis,* coiled carving) (pl. VI, 4), has a heavier, more coiled shell than the preceding, and grows in confused, intricate, spaghetti-like masses. Shell with fine surface sculpture, and is light gray in color. It attaches to rocks and other shells, occupying the same range as the Variable Worm Shell.

Some true worms of the genus *Serpula* form tubes that superficially resemble worm shells. However, these tubes of genuine worms are chalky and lusterless, quite unlike the hard, porcelain-like molluscan worm shells. The latter, moreover, are commonly operculate, whereas no *Serpula* has an operculum.

SUPERFAMILY:

# CERITHIACEA

FAMILY:

# CERITHIIDAE
(*cerith horn shells*)

These shells are moderate sized to quite small, awl shaped, elongated, attenuated, usually strongly sculptured, the rounded aperture with a short, bent siphonal canal at the base and a flaring lip. These snails live in mud and grassy areas in warmer seas, but some forms occur in temperate waters.

## KEY TO GENUS CERITHIUM

* Shell reaching only 12 mm. (1/2 in.) in height — *C. lutosum* syn. *variabile*

* Shell reaching 25 to 35 mm. (1 to 1 2/5 in.)
** Shell stocky, width about one-half of height; largest nodules just below suture — *C. litteratum*
** Shell slender, width less than one-half of height
*** Siphonal canal long, twisted sharply to the left, surface sculpture of knobby axial ribs — *C. muscarum*
*** Siphonal canal short, straight, oblique, surface sculpture of spiral rows of beads or nodules
**** Spiral rows of beads separated by several rows of fine, granular cords; with several old varices in the form of short, white axial swellings — *C. atratum* syn. *floridanum*

**** Spiral rows of beads not separated by granular cords; old varices not prominent
***** Nodules of central rows sharp, large, shell outline uneven — *C. algicola*
***** Nodules of central rows barely larger than others, shell outline more even — *C. eburneum*

Genus *Cerithium* Bruguière

*Cerithium atratum* Born
　Florida Horn Shell

　Pl. XX, 7

ETYMOLOGY: Gr. *keration*, little horn; Lat. *atratus*, dressed in black.

SIZE: 30 to 35 mm. (1 1/5 to 1 2/5 in.) in height, 15 mm. (3/5 in.) in width.

DISTRIBUTION: North Carolina to southern Florida and Texas.

CHARACTERISTICS: Shell medium, rough, narrowly conic; spire high,
　turreted. Color white, with spirally grooved pattern of brownish
　dashes, each whorl with several rows of eighteen to twenty small
　beads separated by fine granular spiral threads, with several irregularly
　placed former varices in the form of white axial swellings. Aperture
　small, lip reflected, toothed within. Siphonal notch short, oblique.
　Operculum thin, horny, oval, with few spirals; nucleus basal.

The horn shells are common shallow-water inhabitants of tropical and
subtropical seas, and live in sand and sandy mud near the tide line
in warm seas. The shells of this genus are easily recognized. They are
high and narrow, with strongly sculptured surfaces, toothed outer lip,
and short siphonal canals. They bear some resemblance to a miniature
Alpine shepherd's horn. The species are less easy to separate, since
they vary greatly and individual specimens are often troublesome. The
present species was formerly known as *Cerithium floridanum* Mörch,
a later name.

　The **Lettered Horn Shell,** *Cerithium litteratum* Born (Lat. *literatus*,
marked with letters) (pl. XIX, 22), is 25 mm. (1 in.) in height but 13
mm. (about 1/2 in.) in width, and hence is most easily distinguished
from the other horn shells by its stocky shape. The color is whitish,
with many rows of black or reddish squares, the "lettered" part of the
name. The surface sculpture consists of numerous coarse, spiral lines
with most prominent nodules, nine to ten in number, appearing just
below the suture. Occasionally there are rows of smaller spines at the
periphery. The species ranges from southeast Florida to Bermuda and
the West Indies.

　The **Fly Horn Shell,** *Cerithium muscarum* Say (genitive plural of
Lat. *musca,* fly) (pl. XX, 8), is 25 mm. (1 in.) high and 10 mm. (2/5
in.) wide. The shell is gray and speckled, flylike, with brownish spots
arranged spirally. The siphonal canal is somewhat longer and sharply
twisted to the left. The sculpture consists of 9 to 11 knobby axial ribs
on each whorl. These knobby ribs, the "fly-specked" coloration, and

the longer siphonal canal are characteristic of the species, which ranges from southern Florida to the West Indies.

The **Ivory Horn Shell,** *Cerithium eburneum* Bruguière (Lat. *eburneus,* made of ivory) (pl. XX, 9), is 17 to 25 mm. (about 3/4 to 1 in.) high and moderately elongate; the color is white, cream, or brown, with reddish brown blotches; each whorl has four to seven spiral rows of from eighteen to twenty-two beads, the beads in the middle row being only slightly larger than the others. This species ranges from southeast Florida to the Bahamas and the Greater Antilles. It is very common in shallow water. The **Algae Horn Shell,** *Cerithium algicola* C. B. Adams (Lat. *alga cola,* seaweed dweller) (pl. XX, 10), also 25 mm. (1 in.) high, is colored like *C. eburneum,* but differs in having the nine to twelve beads of the middle row large and pointed, making the shell outline uneven. It ranges from southern Florida to the West Indies. According to Dr. Richard Houbrick, it is merely a form of *C. eburneum.* Many other forms of this variable species were named by Sowerby and other workers.

The **Dwarf Horn Shell,** *Cerithium lutosum* Menke (possibly Lat. *lutum,* mud, filth) (pl. XX, 11), is, as the English name indicates, much smaller than the other *Cerithium,* reaching only 12 mm. (1/2 in.) in height. It is stocky, usually dark blackish brown in color, and sculptured with three or four rows of even-sized beads. This shell, which was formerly called *C. variabile* C. B. Adams, is common under rocks in southern Florida, Texas, and the West Indies. It should not be confused with the False Horn Shell, *Batillaria minima,* which has a thin, untoothed outer lip and a circular operculum with many spiral lines.

# KEY TO FAMILIES CERITHIIDAE AND TRIPHORIDAE

    \* Shell sinistral (family Triphoridae, see
       p. 80)
  \*\* Shell chestnut brown, with dark band
     below the suture         *Triphora nigrocincta*
  \*\* Shell light colored, with reddish brown
     mottlings         *T. decorata*
    \* Shell dextral (family Cerithiidae)
  \*\* Shell ovate-conic, smooth except for tiny
     spiral grooves         *Litiopa melanostoma*
  \*\* Shell narrow, turreted

\* \* \* Surface sculpture of strong, screwlike
spiral ridges only           *Seila adamsi*

\* \* \* Surface sculpture beaded or latticelike

\* \* \* \* Siphonal notch weak or absent, sculpture
latticelike

\* \* \* \* \* Base rounded, suture well impressed;
distribution to Gulf of Saint Lawrence    *Diastoma alternatum*

\* \* \* \* \* Base squarish, suture weakly impressed;
distribution to Maryland         *D. varium*

\* \* \* \* Siphonal notch prominent, sculpture
beaded

\* \* \* \* \* Shell small, 5 mm. (1/5 in.) in height, base
convex               *Cerithiopsis greeni*

\* \* \* \* \* Shell large, 20 mm. (4/5 in.) in height,
base concave             *C. emersoni*

---

Genus *Diastoma*

*Diastoma alternatum* Say
     Alternate Miniature Horn Shell

     Pl. XX, 12

ETYMOLOGY: Gr. *dia*, *stoma*, through mouth; Lat. *alternus*, alternating.

SIZE: 5 to 6 mm. (1/5 to 1/4 in.) in height, 2 mm. (1/12 in.) in width.

DISTRIBUTION: Gulf of Saint Lawrence to Virginia.

CHARACTERISTICS: Shell tiny, narrow, high, turreted. Color gray to brown.
     Suture well impressed, whorls strongly rounded. Surface sculptured
     with a dense granular network of fine axial lines and spiral grooves.
     Siphonal notch barely perceptible.

This tiny shell is readily recognized by the even, granular surface
sculpture, the well-indented suture, and the practically absent siphonal
notch. It lives in vast numbers on eel grass in shallow water, and is
a frequent, brick red dead shell in beach drift. The immature shells
are triangular bits of dark brownish color, and were once thought to be
a different species under the name *Bittium nigrum* Totten. This and
the following species were formerly placed in the genus *Bittium*.

     The **Variegate Miniature Horn Shell,** *Diastoma varium* Pfeiffer
(Lat. *varius*, mottled, variegated) (pl. XX, 13), is slightly smaller,
reaching only 4 to 5 mm. (1/6 to 1/5 in.) in height. It differs from
*D. alternatum*, in addition to size, in having weaker sculpture, espe-

cially at the lower part of the body whorl. Moreover, its distribution is more southerly, from Maryland to Florida and Texas.

The **Sargassum Miniature Horn Shell,** *Litiopa melanostoma* Rang (Gr. *litos ope,* simple aperture; *melanos stoma,* black mouth) (pl. XIX, 23), is only 4 to 5 mm. (1/6 to 1/5 in.) high. It lives pelagically on sargassum weed, and looks like the small brown seeds of that plant. It should be sought for among stranded bundles of the weed. The shell is fragile, moderately elevated, the body whorl about twice as high as the spire. The surface is glossy and marked with numerous spiral lines. Just inside the aperture there is a strong ridge.

Genus *Cerithiopsis* Forbes and Hanley

*Cerithiopsis greeni* C. B. Adams
  Green's Miniature Horn Shell

  Pl. XIX, 24

ETYMOLOGY: Gr. *keration opsis,* having the appearance of a small horn;
  Jacob Green (1790–1841) was an American naturalist.

SIZE: 5 mm. (1/5 in.) in height.

DISTRIBUTION: Cape Cod to Florida.

CHARACTERISTICS: Shell minute, elongated, turreted, glossy, chocolate
  brown, suture moderately indented, surface with spiral rows of large
  beads; aperture with short siphonal canal, lip smooth.

This tiny shell can easily be distinguished from *Diastoma* of about the same size by the presence of the strong siphonal canal. The suture is less indented, the whorls less swollen, and the surface thickly sculptured with distinct beads. The species ranges from Cape Cod to Florida and the Caribbean. It lives in shallow water, often together with *Diastoma* and other minute shells.

The **Awl Miniature Horn Shell,** *Cerithiopsis emersoni* C. B. Adams (named for G. B. Emerson, 1797–1881, an American botanist) (pl. XX, 14), resembles *C. greeni* in shape and sculpture, but it is much larger, reaching 20 mm. (4/5 in.) in height. The whorls are flat and the base is concave. The species ranges from Massachusetts to Florida and the West Indies. Formerly called *C. subulata* Montagu (Lat. *subula,* awl), which is a different species according to Abbott (1974).

**Adams' Miniature Horn Shell,** *Seila adamsi* H. C. Lea (Gr. *seira,* cord; dedicated to Arthur Adams, an English conchologist) (pl. XX, 15), is about 11 mm. (about 1/2 in.) high. The entire surface is covered by sharp, evenly spaced spiral cords like the threads of a tiny wood screw. The base is concave. In life it is chocolate brown or light yellow-ish, but dead specimens fade to chalky white. It ranges from Massa-chusetts to Florida, Texas, and the West Indies.

---

FAMILY:

# TRIPHORIDAE

(*sinistral miniature horn shells*)

This family of tiny, slender, left-handed snails is ornamented with beaded spiral cords, usually three on a whorl. Aperture narrow and with a closed tubelike siphonal canal in fully mature individuals. Widely distributed, especially in warmer seas.

Genus *Triphora* Blainville

*Triphora nigrocincta* C. B. Adams
Sinistral Miniature Horn Shell

Pl. XIX, 25

ETYMOLOGY: Gr. *treis phora*, three bearing; Lat. *niger cinctus*, black girdle.

SIZE: 5 to 10 mm. (1/5 to 2/5 in.) in height.

DISTRIBUTION: Cape Cod to Florida and the West Indies.

CHARACTERISTICS: Shell tiny, narrow, sinistral, dark chestnut brown, a dark band below the poorly marked suture, surface sculpture of three rows of well formed beads on each whorl; lip thin, with a centrally located, vertical siphonal canal.

This shell looks very much like a member of the genus *Cerithiopsis* (see page 79) but is readily distinguished by having the aperture opening to the left rather than the right when the shell is held with the spire upward. Such left-handed shells are termed sinistral, from the Latin *sinister*, left. This is a shallow-water species, and can be found in fair numbers, sometimes clinging to submerged rocks and other hard objects. Some writers consider this to be a subspecies of *Triphora perversa* Linnaeus from Europe and hence call it *T. perversa nigrocincta*. The generic name probably refers to the three rows of beads on each whorl.

The **Mottled Sinistral Miniature Horn Shell**, *Triphora decorata*

C. B. Adams (pl. XX, 16), differs in being a little larger and in having a cream to gray color, with large, irregular mottlings of reddish brown. It is a rarer, southern species, ranging from southeast Florida to the West Indies.

FAMILY:

# POTAMIDIDAE

(*potam horn shells*)

The shells are elongated, attenuated, brownish, with many whorls, usually sculptured with rounded vertical riblets. The horn shells of the family Potamididae (Gr. *potamos*, river) are related to the horn shells of the family Cerithiidae, but differ in having an untoothed outer lip and a circular, multispiral operculum. Moreover, they are mainly brackish-water dwellers and intertidal mud lovers. They may occur in bewildering numbers.

## KEY TO GENERA
## CERITHIDEA AND BATILLARIA

| | |
|---|---|
| * Spiral sculpture as strong as axial sculpture | *Batillaria minima* |
| * Axial sculpture decidedly stronger than spiral sculpture | |
| ** Suture and base with spiral ridges | *Cerithidea scalariformis* |
| ** Sculpture of axial ribs only, spiral ridges absent | |
| *** Axial ribs smooth | |
| **** Axial ribs many, closely set, 25 to 30 on the next to last whorl | *C. costata* |
| **** Axial ribs few, more widely set, 15 to 20 on penultimate whorl; west coast of Florida only | *C. costata turrita* |
| *** Axial ribs beaded | *C. pliculosa* |

Genus *Cerithidea* Swainson

*Cerithidea costata* da Costa
  Ribbed Horn Shell

Pl. XX, 17

ETYMOLOGY: Gr. *keration*, little horn; Lat. *costa*, rib.

SIZE: 13 mm. (about 1/2 in.) in height, 5 mm. (1/5 in.) in width.

DISTRIBUTION: Florida and West Indies.

CHARACTERISTICS: Shell small, narrow, high turreted; suture deep, whorls very convex. Translucent, pale yellowish-brown. Sculpture of prominent axial ribs extending from suture to suture, 25 to 30 on the penultimate whorl. Aperture suboval, lip weakly turned back, untoothed. Operculum thin, brown, many spiraled; nucleus central.

A form or subspecies, *Cerithidea costata turrita* Stearns, which occurs in Tampa Bay and at Sanibel Island, differs mainly in having fewer and more widely spaced axial ribs on the penultimate whorl, fifteen to twenty instead of twenty-five to thirty.

Do not confuse with the **Plicate Horn Shell,** *Cerithidea pliculosa* Menke, which has vertical ribs, faintly beaded instead of smooth, and white axial swellings on the surface. It is found in Louisiana, Texas, and the West Indies.

The **Ladder Horn Shell,** *Cerithidea scalariformis* Say (Lat. *scala forma*, ladder-shaped) (pl. XX, 18), grows somewhat larger, reaching 30 mm. (1 1/5 in.) in height. It is russet brown in color, and has many conspicuous, dirty white spiral bands. The suture has a prominent spiral ridge, which becomes strong at the periphery. The axial ribs disappear at the base and are replaced by five or more spiral ridges. The outer lip is very thick, particularly above. It ranges from South Carolina to Florida and the West Indies.

The **False Horn Shell,** *Batillaria minima* Gmelin (possibly Lat. *batillum*, a small pan or chafing dish) (pl. XX, 19), is quite small, 11 to 18 mm. (about 1/2 to 3/4 in.) in height, 4 to 7 mm. (about 1/6 to 1/4 in.) in width. The shell is elongate, conelike, strong, rough; the color varies from completely black to almost white, often with broad or narrow, dark or light spiral bands. Some of these color varieties were given names, but since all the forms live together, such names can be disregarded. The sculpture is finely knobby, with coarse axial swellings and strong, uneven spiral threads. The aperture is narrow, toothless; the siphonal canal, short and oblique. This exceedingly abundant mud-dweller in brackish water should not be confused with

*Cerithium lutosum* (page 77). It is found in southern Florida and the Caribbean.

SUPERFAMILY:

# STROMBACEA

---

FAMILY:

# STROMBIDAE
(*conchs*)

The shells are small to large and massive; the body whorl takes up most of the shell. The lip is thickened and expanded, and is commonly winged above. The aperture is long and narrow, and the operculum is brown, horny, and claw shaped, and, while small, is strong. This is a large family of active snails living in warmer seas.

The family Strombidae constitutes one of the most prominent features of the Floridian molluscan fauna because of their large size and handsome, solid shells. The conchs are characterized by the presence of an indentation at the base of the outer lip through which the colorful, startlingly human-looking right eye can peep forth when the snail is in motion. This indentation is called the "stromboid notch." The operculum is not used, as in most operculate gastropods, as a protective door, but rather as an aid to locomotion. It serves as a propelling rod for the jumplike movement exhibited by these creatures, as well as, in time of need, a weapon of offense or defense.

---

## KEY TO GENUS STROMBUS

* Shell attaining more than 190 mm. (7 3/5 in.) in height, aperture pink      *Strombus gigas*
* Shell 180 mm. (7 1/5 in.) or less in height
** Shell whitish, heavy with greatly thickened outer lip, aperture cream white      *S. costatus*
** Shell lighter, outer lip less thickened, shell not white
*** Outer lip winged above      *S. raninus*

     * * * Outer lip not winged above

     * * * * Spines low, equal in size, frequently with zigzag
            color marking on columellar wall of aperture, top
            of lip sloping downward               *S. alatus*

     * * * * Spines long, strongest on penultimate whorl, color
            of parietal wall uniform, top of lip sloping upward    *S. pugilis*

---

Genus *Strombus* Linnaeus

*Strombus gigas* Linnaeus
    Queen Conch

    Pl. X, 2a & b

ETYMOLOGY: Gr. *strombos*, a kind of snail; Lat. *gigas*, giant.

SIZE: 190 to 300 mm. (7 3/5 to 12 in.) in height, and 160 to 210 mm. (6 2/5 to 8 2/5 in.) in width.

DISTRIBUTION: Southeast Florida, Bermuda, and the West Indies.

CHARACTERISTICS: Shell huge, massive, very heavy; outer lip strong, flaring. Color white to pinkish white, interior bright pink. Spire and upper part of body whorl with variously low, rounded spines, stromboid notch shallow, periostracum thick, horny, flaky. Operculum strong, brown, clawlike.

This is one of the largest gastropods in our area. Its appearance is so characteristic that the identity of the adult shell, at least, is never in question. The immature specimens, known as "rollers," look quite different; the outer lip is very fragile and commonly broken, and the entire surface of the body whorl is covered with numerous, rather wide and strong spiral cords. The soft parts are widely used as food in the West Indies, and overfishing has sharply reduced its numbers in the Florida Keys. To extract the animal easily, a hole is broken in one of the upper whorls, and few dead specimens can be found that have not been so damaged. The lovely bright pink color of the aperture tends to fade in the light. Occasionally a small pink pearl of slight monetary value is found in the mantle.

    The **Milk Conch,** *Strombus costatus* Gmelin (Lat. *costatus*, ribbed) (pl. VII, 4), is smaller, reaching only 100 to 175 mm. (4 to 7 in.) in height, and less massive. The shell is pale yellowish white under a heavy, flaking periostracum; the strong, moderately flaring outer lip and the aperture are creamy white. The surface of the body whorl is sculptured with rather thick spiral corrugations. This is a common shallow-water shell in the West Indies, and occasional specimens have been taken in southern Florida.

The **West Indian Fighting Conch,** *Strombus pugilis* Linnaeus (Lat. *pugil, pugilis,* boxer) (pl. VII, 3), is 52 to 100 mm. (2 to 4 in.) in height, 35 to 65 mm. (1 2/5 to 2 3/5 in.) in width. This species is rare in Florida, having been reported only from Lake Worth. It has a good-sized, strong, solid shell that is provided with spines near the suture, the longest spines being on the next to last whorl. The body whorl is smooth, salmon pink with a bluish-purple blotch at the base. The outer lip is weakly flaring and the top of the lip slopes upward. This is a lively shell, which probably got its name from its rapid, hopping movements rather than from any innate combative tendencies. Julia Rogers (1960) provides a vivid picture of the snail making for the water:

> It is an exciting experience to watch these conchs on a Florida beach contriving to get back to the water after being stranded by the tide. One rarely sees in Florida such an illustration of strenuousness. The extended hook [i.e., the operculum] is stuck into the wet sand, and over the shell rolls; the second stroke flings it into another direction. . . . Obstacles are avoided, corners are turned, wherever possible the conch makes a leap, and at last plunks joyfully into the water.

The **Florida Fighting Conch,** *Strombus alatus* Gmelin (Lat. *alatus,* winged) (pl. VII, 2), is the common fighting conch in Florida. It ranges from North Carolina to Florida, Texas, and Yucatán. It is especially abundant on Florida's west coast, and does not occur in the West Indies. The species differs in certain important respects from *S. pugilis:* the spines are shorter and of a uniform size, but they are often wanting on the body whorl; the shell is more slender and the spire relatively higher; the color ranges from mottled salmon or orange brown to dark brownish red, with zigzag patterns on the parietal wall, especially in younger individuals. The top of the outer lip, unlike in *S. pugilis,* slopes distinctly downward.

The **Hawk Wing Conch,** *Strombus raninus* Gmelin (Lat. *rana,* frog) (pl. VII, 1), is 40 to 110 mm. (1 3/5 to 4 1/2 in.) in height, 25 to 85 mm. (1 to 3 1/2 in.) in width. This shell is readily distinguished from the other *Strombus* species of similar size because the outer lip is distinctly winged and the tip almost reaches the same height as the apex. The color is brownish gray with chocolate brown or purplish mottling; the aperture is reddish. The sutural spines are low and blunt. This is a fairly common species living in shallow water among grasses, but heavy collecting in recent years has made live specimens scarce in accessible areas.

A midget form of this species from the southern part of Lake Worth, Florida, has been called the **Dwarf Hawk Wing,** *S. raninus nanus* Bales (Lat. *nanus,* dwarf). In size it ranges from 35 mm. (1 2/5 in.) to 67 mm. (2 1/2 in.) in height.

---

FAMILY:

# APORRHAIDAE

(*pelican's foot shells*)

The shells are moderate in size, strong, the spire high, and the outer lip is greatly expanded; in some species it is provided with long, pointed extensions.

Genus *Aporrhais* da Costa

*Aporrhais occidentalis* Beck
  American Pelican's Foot Shell

  Pl. XIX, 26

ETYMOLOGY: Gr. *aporrheo*, to flow away; Lat. *occidens*, the west.

SIZE: 50 to 65 mm. (2 to 2 3/5 in.) in height, 35 mm. (1 2/5 in.) in width.

DISTRIBUTION: Labrador to Massachusetts, in deeper water, to off North Carolina.

CHARACTERISTICS: Shell medium, strong, lusterless, chalky. Color ashen to yellowish. Outer lip greatly expanded, edge thickened. Surface sculpture of curved, rounded axial ribs and many minute spiral threads. Operculum corneous, brown, clawlike.

This northern species is rarely found on the beaches, but is commonly dredged by fishermen off the New England coast and is often discovered in the contents of fish stomachs. The winged lip makes it easy to identify, and also demonstrates its relationship to the true conchs, family Strombidae. A related species, *Aporrhais pespelicani* Linnaeus, is common in European waters.

# EPITONIACEA

# EPITONIIDAE
(*wentletrap shells*)

These shells are high, generally attenuated, usually chalky or pure white, rarely yellowish or brown, ornamented with variously strong axial ribs, or costae. The aperture is round, the lip strong and rounded, the operculum thin and horny. The English name comes from the German *Wendeltreppe,* spiral staircase. The wentletraps constitute an ancient worldwide family with many strange and beautiful forms, especially those living in deeper water. The beach collector to whom this book is mainly directed is not likely to find many of these, if any, but if interested, he should consult the monographs by Clench and Turner (1951, 1952) for the western Atlantic forms.

## KEY TO GENUS EPITONIUM

* Shell with spiral sculpture
** Spiral sculpture strong, costae few, well spaced
*** Shell reaching 36 mm. (1 1/2 in.), distinct basal ridge present            *Epitonium greenlandicum*
*** Shell reaching 14 mm. (about 3/5 in.), basal ridge absent            *E. championi*
** Spiral sculpture weak, costae many, closely spaced
*** Later whorls attached only by costae; range Massachusetts to Florida            *E. multistriatum*
*** Whorls attached throughout entire length; range confined to west coast of Florida            *E. multistriatum matthewsae*
* Shell without spiral sculpture
** Shell with some brown color, usually near suture

&#42;&#42;&#42; Shell large, up to 34 mm. (1 2/5 in.),
   costae bladelike, high, fragile, confined
   in U.S. to southern Florida       *E. lamellosum*

&#42;&#42;&#42; Shell reaching 20 mm. (4/5 in.),
   costae low, strong; range to
   Massachusetts       *E. rupicola*

 &#42;&#42; Shell all white, no brown color
   present

&#42;&#42;&#42; Costae discontinuous at suture, not
   lined up, shell slender       *E. tollini*

&#42;&#42;&#42; Costae lined up at suture, shell less
   slender

&#42;&#42;&#42;&#42; Costae with strong angle at shoulder
   of whorls       *E. angulatum*

&#42;&#42;&#42;&#42; Costae with weak or no angles at
   whorls       *E. humphreysii*

---

Genus *Epitonium* Röding

*Epitonium humphreysii* Kiener
   Humphrey's Wentletrap

   Pl. XX, 20

ETYMOLOGY: Gr. *epitonos*, stretched, strained, or *epitonion*, turncock, peg;
   G. Humphrey, ?1745–1830, was a shell dealer in England.

SIZE: 18 mm. (3/4 in.) in height, 7.5 mm. (1/3 in.) in width.

DISTRIBUTION: Cape Cod to Florida, except the lower Keys, and west to
   Texas.

CHARACTERISTICS: Shell medium, high, turreted, moderately strong. Color
   white. Sculpture of numerous white axial ribs, or costae, thin and
   bladelike on earlier whorls, rounded and thickened later on. Aperture
   circular, outer lip thick, inner lip narrower. Operculum thin, horny,
   dark brown, with few spirals (paucispiral).

This is one of the commoner, widely ranging wentletrap shells in our
area. The characteristic shape, the generally white color, and especially the usually strong costae make the genus easily recognizable.
Recognition of the various species is generally not so easy. Clench and
Turner write: ". . . few species are at all clear cut; they have a
tendency to merge into one another." The characteristics described in
this chapter can thus be taken only in a general sense; individual

specimens, especially juveniles, or when collected dead or beach worn, may present problems. The genus was formerly called *Scala* or *Scalaria*.

The **Angulate Wentletrap,** *Epitonium angulatum* Say (pl. XIX, 27), resembles Humphrey's Wentletrap in size, but differs in being generally somewhat wider, 9 mm. (about 2/5 in.) in width, and in having the costae expanded into an angle at the whorl shoulders. These angles are stronger on the early whorls than on the later ones, where they may even be absent on the body whorl. The costae of *E. humphreysii* are rounded rather than bladelike, but many specimens will be difficult to place with certainty. The species ranges from Long Island to Florida and Texas, but is not found in the lower Florida Keys.

**Tollin's Wentletrap,** *Epitonium tollini* Bartsch (Oscar Tollin sent specimens of this form to the United States National Museum) (pl. XX, 21), is 14 mm. (about 3/5 in.) in height and only 3 to 4.5 mm. (1/8 to 1/5 in.) in width; hence it is more slender than the other wentletraps. The costae are thin and bladelike. They differ by not being continuous at the suture but lining up irregularly with the costae on the whorls. The species is found on the west coast of Florida from Gasparilla Island to Marco, and has also been reported from Texas.

The **Lamellose Wentletrap,** *Epitonium lamellosum* Lamarck (pl. XX, 22), is the largest of the local shallow-water wentletraps, reaching a height of 32 mm. (about 1 1/4 in.) and a width of 15 mm. (3/5 in.). The costae are very thin and easily broken. Like most other epitoniids, the costae line up well at the sutures with those on the whorls above. The shell is white but has irregular brownish markings, especially at the suture. The species is rare, and ranges from Lake Worth, Florida, to Bermuda and the Caribbean. It is also found in Europe.

The **Banded Wentletrap,** *Epitonium rupicola* Kurtz (Lat. *rupes incola,* rock dweller) (pl. XIX, 28), also has brown markings, in the form of rather well-defined spiral bands at the suture. It is smaller than *E. lamellosum,* reaching only 20 mm. (4/5 in.) in height, and has lower and more rounded costae. It ranges from Massachusetts to Florida and Texas, and is common, especially in the north.

The **Many-ribbed Wentletrap,** *Epitonium multistriatum* Say (Lat. *multi stria,* many fine grooves) (pl. XX, 23), unlike the epitoniids discussed above, has faint but definite spiral lines in the areas between the costal ribs. The costae are low, very numerous, and quite closely set together, which is generally enough to identify the species. The aperture is oval rather than round, and the lip is only slightly thickened. It is 15 mm. (3/5 in.) in height and about 5 mm. (1/5 in.) in width, and ranges from Massachusetts to Florida and west to Texas.

**Matthews's Wentletrap,** *Epitonium multistriatum matthewsae* Clench & Turner (Charlotta Matthews was a collector on Sanibel Island) (pl. XX, 24), differs in being smaller (13 mm., or about 1/2 in., in height), and in having the whorls attached at a deep suture, whereas in *E. multistriatum multistriatum* the later whorls lie close together but are attached to one another only by the costae. This subspecies is known only from Fort Walton south to Marco on the west coast of Florida.

**Champion's Wentletrap,** *Epitonium championi* Clench & Turner (Dr. Merrill E. Champion, 1880–1963, was a prominent Harvard malacologist) (pl. XX, 25), has the spiral lines of *E. multistriatum* but differs immediately in having far fewer and much more widely spaced and stronger costae. The fine spiral grooves are stronger, and the aperture is oval, with the lip only slightly thickened. The species is 13 mm. (about 1/2 in.) high and ranges from Cape Cod to South Carolina.

The **Greenland Wentletrap,** *Epitonium greenlandicum* Perry (pl. XX, 26), is quite large, reaching 36 mm. (1 2/5 in.) in height and 13 mm. (about 1/2 in.) in width. In Alaska the same species grows to 61 mm. (2 2/5 in.). In addition to size, it differs from *E. championi* in having a pronounced thick spiral ridge, called the "basal ridge," toward the bottom of the body whorl. The spiral lines are quite coarse. The species is circumpolar, and in our area it ranges from Greenland to Montauk Point, Long Island. It is not common.

---

FAMILY:

# JANTHINIDAE

(*violet snails*)

The shells are low conic or globular, moderately large, rather frail, colored in various shades of violet and purple. The lip is thin, fragile, commonly with a centrally placed notch. These pelagic snails live attached upside down to a float of hardened mucus containing air bubbles, and are sometimes thrown on shore in large numbers, especially in the warmer areas. When disturbed, the animal can extrude a purplish fluid. They are predators on various kinds of jellyfish.

The violet snails may be washed ashore in vast quantities, most often in the south in Florida, but records show that the Gulf Stream has deposited isolated specimens as far north as Nantucket and Martha's Vineyard. Animals deprived of their mucus float sink to the bottom, where they perish.

## KEY TO GENUS JANTHINA

* Shell turbinate, like an inverted top in outline    *Janthina janthina*
* Shell more or less globose
** Outer lip deeply cleft by central notch or sinus    *J. umbilicata*
** Outer lip with shallow sinus or none
*** Base of outer lip prolonged in a rounded angle,
     color deep purple    *J. globosa*
*** Base of outer lip rounded, color pale    *J. pallida*

Genus *Janthina* Röding

*Janthina janthina* Linnaeus
    Common Violet Snail

    Pl. VI, 7

ETYMOLOGY: Gr. *ianthinos*, violet colored.

SIZE: Up to 40 mm. (1 3/5 in.) in height, 25 mm. (1 in.) in width.

DISTRIBUTION: Pelagic in most warmer waters, occasionally cast on shore by tides and storms.

CHARACTERISTICS: Shell medium, smooth, not glossy, fragile, turbinate; spire little elevated, periphery with rounded keel. Pale violet above, deep purple below. Aperture squarish, outer lip thin.

This species is the violet snail shell most often found, but frequently other species also occur, in smaller numbers. The size given is for those specimens found locally; in other parts of the world they grow a good deal larger. There is much confusion regarding the identity of these widely ranging pelagic snails, and they have been given many names (see Laursen, 1953).

    The **Dwarf Violet Snail,** *Janthina umbilicata* Orbigny (pl. XVIII, 26), is smaller, reaching only 19 mm. (4/5 in.) in diameter. The color is uniformly of one shade of violet, and the shell is somewhat glossy. The outline is globose, and the outer lip has a deep central notch or sinus dividing the lip into two rounded winglike structures. Perhaps this should be known by the earlier name *J. exigua* Lamarck.

The **Elongate Violet Snail,** *Janthina globosa* Swainson (Lat. *globosus*, globose) (pl. XVIII, 27), is larger than the previous species, attaining about 25 mm. (1 in.) in height, and is of a deep violet color throughout. The aperture is very large and terminates below in an angular projection. This species used to be called *J. prolongata* Blainville (Lat. *prolongata*, extended), but *J. globosa* Swainson (not *J. globosa* Blainville) antedates it by a few months.

The **Pale Violet Snail,** *Janthina pallida* Thompson (Lat. *pallidus,* pale) (pl. XXI, 1), differs from *J. globosa* Swainson in being more nearly globose and in having the outer lip terminating below in a smooth curve without a prolongation. The labial sinus is absent or very shallow, and the color is purplish white, with lavender along the lower margins of the lip. Called erroneously *J. globosa* Swainson by some workers.

SUPERFAMILY:

# HIPPONICACEA

FAMILY:

# HIPPONICIDAE
(*hoof shells*)

These shells are rather small, cap shaped, the apex curved backward. The embryonic shell is spirally coiled, but as growth proceeds the caplike shape is assumed. Most species rest on a shelly plate secreted by the foot. They attach to hard substrates such as rocks and other shells.

## KEY TO GENERA CHEILEA (FAMILY CALYPTRAEIDAE) AND HIPPONIX

* Shell with internal plate          *Cheilea equestris* (see p. 97)
* Shell without internal plate

** Shell stained with orange brown        *Hipponix subrufus*
** Shell white or gray                     *H. antiquatus*

---

Genus *Hipponix* DeFrance

*Hipponix antiquatus* Linnaeus
   White Hoof Shell

   Pl. XIX, 29

ETYMOLOGY: Gr. *hippos onyx*, Horse hoof; Lat. *antiquatus*, made old, obsolete.

SIZE: 15 mm. (3/5 in.) in diameter.

DISTRIBUTION: Southeastern Florida to the West Indies.

CHARACTERISTICS: Shell small, solid, cap shaped, with poorly developed uncoiled spire. Color white or gray. Surface usually with strong, irregular axial ribs crossed by fine striations. Periostracum weak, with short hairs.

This not very handsome cap-shaped shell, which faintly resembles a horse's hoof, is commonly found in beach drift. It lives on rocks and other shells just below the tide line. It is also found on the West Coast, from California to Peru.

The **Orange Hoof Shell,** *Hipponix subrufus* Lamarck (Lat. *subrufus*, almost reddish) (pl. XXII, 1), is similar, but differs chiefly in being stained with light orange brown instead of being white or gray. The surface sculpture is finely beaded, and the periostracum is fairly heavy. The species ranges from southeastern Florida to the West Indies and is less common than *H. antiquatus*.

# CALYPTRAEACEA

# CALYPTRAEIDAE
(*cup-and-saucer and slipper limpets*)

The shells are cap shaped like a limpet. On the inner surface there is a shelly structure or septum, which can take the form of either a shelf or a rounded cuplike extension. The Calyptraeidae are nearly worldwide in distribution, and range from shallow water to moderate depths, living on rocks or other shells. The shells of the family Capulidae are also so similar that they have been included in this discussion.

## KEY TO GENERA CALYPTRAEA, CRUCIBULUM, AND CREPIDULA

* Inner septum about one-half of aperture, free edge shorter than fused edge
* * Shell with outer surface much roughened by spiny ribs                                           *Crepidula aculeata*
* * Shell with outer surface smooth or slightly roughened by growth lines
* * * Apex fused to body whorl, free edge of septum sinuous
* * * * Shell variously arched, tan with strong brown markings, septum strong                         *C. fornicata*
* * * * Shell flat or concave, white, septum weak        *C. plana*
* * * Apex free, not fused to body whorl
* * * * Apex directed straight back, shell small, 12 mm. (1/2 in.)                                    *C. convexa*
* * * * Apex directed to right, shell large, 25 mm. (1 in.)                                           *C. maculosa*
* Inner septum cup shaped, considerably less than one-half of aperture, free edge larger than fused edges, or entirely free
* * Free edge of septum not fused to inner wall at any point, shell white                             *Crucibulum auricula*

** One edge of septum fused to body whorl,
   shell brownish

  *** Shell 6 mm. (1/4 in.), white, free edge of
    septum has thickened margin, open in front,
    twisted                                         *Calyptraea centralis*

  *** Shell 25 mm. (1 in.), wax yellow or brownish,
    free edge of septum has thin, evenly rounded
    margin                                      *Crucibulum striatum*

---

Genus *Calyptraea* Lamarck

*Calyptraea centralis* Conrad
    Lesser Cup-and-Saucer Limpet

    Pl. XXII, 2

ETYMOLOGY: Gr. *kalyptra,* a covering for the head

SIZE: 6 mm. (1/4 in.) in diameter, 2 mm. (1/12 in.) in height.

DISTRIBUTION: North Carolina to Florida and the West Indies.

CHARACTERISTICS: Shell very small, thin, cap shaped; base circular. Outer
    surface dull, roughened. Apex central, minutely coiled, glassy. Interior
    cup widely attached at one side, free edge open in front; margin
    thickened, slightly twisted.

This shell is quickly recognized by its small size, thin walls, and white
color. The interior cup is unique in the group of cup-and-saucer
limpets because of the thickened, twisted margin, which resembles the
columella of a typical gastropod shell. The species can be found in
shallow water attached to dead shells or stones. It was formerly called
*Calyptraea candeana* Orbigny (Lat. *candeo,* white).

    The **Striate Cup-and-Saucer Limpet,** *Crucibulum striatum* Say (Lat.
*crucibulum,* hanging lamp or earthen pot; Lat. *striatus,* with channels)
(pl. XXI, 2), reaches 25 mm. (1 in.) in diameter, 12 mm (1/2 in.) in
height. The moderately strong, medium-sized, cup-shaped, conical
shell has a twisted apex, and is dull wax yellow on the outside with
numerous wavy radiating lines. The interior is light brown and glossy.
The septum is white, and about one-third of its margin is attached to
the walls of the shell; the rest is free and evenly rounded. This species
lives in moderately deep water, but dead shells are occasionally
washed up on shore. Live specimens have been taken clinging to the
shell of the Sea Scallop, *Placopecten magellanicus.* The relatively

smooth outer surface, circular base, and characteristic septum make recognition of this species easy. It ranges from Nova Scotia to South Carolina.

The **Ear Cup-and-Saucer Limpet,** *Crucibulum auricula* Gmelin (Lat. *auricula,* ear) (pl. XXI, 3), is much smaller, and differs mainly in having the walls of the interior septum or cup entirely free. It is attached to the shell only at the base. The dull white surface is more strongly sculptured, and the edges of the shell are crenulated by the radiating ribs. This is an uncommon species in shallow water, and ranges from North Carolina and the Florida Keys to the West Indies.

Genus *Crepidula* Lamarck

*Crepidula fornicata* Linnaeus
Arched Slipper Limpet

Pl. XXII, 3

ETYMOLOGY: Lat. *crepidula,* small sandal; *fornix,* arch or vault.

SIZE: Shell reaching 45 mm. (1 3/5 in.) in length, 26 mm. (about 1 in.) in width.

DISTRIBUTION: Nova Scotia to Florida and Texas.

CHARACTERISTICS: Shell medium, strong, elongate cup shaped; apex turned to right and fused to body whorl. Smooth, height very variable. Color dull white or tan, variously marked with interrupted chestnut brown markings. Septum about one-half of aperture, white, relatively strong; outer margin sinuous.

This is one of the most abundant larger gastropods in bays along its range. It lives in shallow water fixed to stones, horseshoe crabs, dead shells, and to one another, in muddy areas forming "sticks" of clinging mollusks up to 8 inches long. Its abundance and clinging habits make it a pest in oyster beds, where the bivalves are suffocated under masses of slipper shells. On the other hand, dead slipper shells find a use as a convenient settling bed for young oyster spat. The animal is a protandric hermaphrodite—that is, the gonad of an individual first produces sperm and later in life bears ova. The species has been introduced into northern Europe, where, under the name of American Limpet, it is cursed as a serious nuisance. Contrary to popular belief, the startling Latin name of this species is derived from the noun *fornix,* meaning "arch," which aptly describes the shape of the shell.

The **Spotted Slipper Limpet,** *Crepidula maculosa* Conrad (Lat. *macula,* stain, blemish) (pl. XXII, 4), is smaller, 25 to 35 mm. (1 to 1 2/5 in.) in length, but very similar. However, the apex is free and turned to the right; the free end of the septum is concave rather than sinuous; and there is a prominent muscle scar on the right side in front of the septum. The brown color stains are generally arranged in lines that are broken up into spots. This species ranges from the west coast of Florida to Veracruz, Mexico. The young are difficult to distinguish from *C. fornicata,* with which this species was for a long time confused.

The **Convex Slipper Limpet,** *Crepidula convexa* Say (pl. XXI, 4), is smaller, 12 mm. (1/2 in.) in length, 8 mm. (1/3 in.) in width. The outer surface is faintly wrinkled, ash brown in color, usually with tiny stripes or dots of reddish brown. The interior is chestnut to bluish brown; the septum is deeply set, with a straight or shallowly concave free edge. The apex is free and extends straight back. This is a moderately common species in bays from Massachusetts to Florida, Mexico, and the West Indies.

The **White Slipper Limpet,** *Crepidula plana* Say (Lat. *planus,* level, flat) (pl. XXII, 5), reaches 30 mm. (1 1/5 in.) in length, 16 mm. (3/5 in.) in width. It is pure white, the surface occasionally roughened by irregular growth lines, and flat or concave in shape, since it usually inhabits the aperture of dead gastropods. It is a common shell on outer beaches. In bays it settles on rocks, bottles, oysters, scallops, or other *C. plana,* each habitat affecting the shape of the shell to some degree. The species ranges from Canada to Florida, the Gulf states, and the West Indies.

The **Spiny Slipper Shell,** *Crepidula aculeata* Gmelin (Lat. *acus,* needle) (pl. XXII, 6), is 20 to 30 mm. (4/5 to 1 1/5 in.) in length. The shell resembles other slipper limpets, but the outer brownish surface is sculptured with irregular, radiate, tuberculate, or spiny ribs. The species ranges from North Carolina to Florida and the West Indies, and is commonly found on the beach, where the spines are worn down but the raised ridges still betray its true identity.

The **False Cup-and-Saucer Limpet,** *Cheilea equestris* Linnaeus (Gr. *cheilos,* lip; and Lat. *equester,* pertaining to horsemen) (pl. XXII, 7), is larger, reaching 25 mm. (1 in.) in diameter. It is readily distinguished from *Hipponix* by the presence of a strong, horseshoe-shaped internal plate, which is sliced off and open in front. The surface is marked by closely set, narrow ridges, and the circular lip is crenulated. The species ranges from southeastern Florida to the West Indies, being more common in the latter area. It need not be confused with other members of the family Calyptraeidae because of the "sliced-away" internal plate, the surface ridges, and the crenulated lip margin.

FAMILY:

# CAPULIDAE

*(cap shells)*

The small shell is cap shaped, and only the small, pointed apex shows any signs of spirals. Unlike the Calyptraeidae, an internal septum, or plate, is wanting. The animals live fixed to rocks or scallop shells in shallow water of warmer regions. Dead shells are frequently found in beach drift.

Genus *Capulus* Montfort

*Capulus incurvatus* Gmelin
   Incurved Cap Shell

   Pl. XXII, 8

ETYMOLOGY: Lat. *capulus*, handle, sword hilt; *incurvus*, bent, bowed.

SIZE: 12 mm. (1/2 in.) in diameter.

DISTRIBUTION: North Carolina to Florida, and the West Indies.

CHARACTERISTICS: Shell small, white or cream colored, with a tiny, tightly coiled spire and with surface sculpture of rounded growth lines, crossed by numerous spiral cords.

The shells of this species differ from those of *Hipponix*, which also lack an internal shelf or deck, in being more fragile and in having finer sculpture. They inhabit rocks and stones in shallow water.

---

FAMILY:

# TRICHOTROPIDAE

*(hairy shells)*

The shells are small, thin, aperture large with flaring lip; sculpture of spiral keels, or carinae, periostracum thin, occasionally with sparse, hairlike extensions. This is a family of mostly cold-water snails. Some species are known to change sexes, a phenomenon known as "protandry" (at first an individual functions as a male, but later in life becomes a female).

Genus *Trichotropis* Broderip & Sowerby

*Trichotropis borealis* Broderip & Sowerby
Boreal Hairy Shell

Pl. XXII, 9

ETYMOLOGY: Gr. *trichos tropis,* hairy keel; *boreas,* north wind.

SIZE: 18 mm. (3/4 in.) in height, 13 mm. (about 1/2 in.) in width.

DISTRIBUTION: Labrador to Massachusetts Bay.

CHARACTERISTICS: Shell small, strong. Chalky white under a thick, yellowish
or brown periostracum with bristly cords. Body whorl large, with two
or three prominent spiral cords and frequently a few minor ones.
Suture deeply channeled, aperture broad, siphonal notch shallow.

This fairly common northern species occurs from below low water to
ninety fathoms. It is frequently found in fish stomachs. In spite of its
appearance, this family is placed in the same superfamily with the
slipper and cup-and-saucer limpets, and cap shells, families Calyptraeidae and Capulidae, respectively.

FAMILY:

# XENOPHORIDAE
(*carrier shells*)

The moderately large shell is shaped like a top shell, but the carrier
shells, especially those that inhabit shallow water, cement bits of rock,
coral, and the shells of other mollusks to their surface so that they
look like small heaps of ocean debris. Found in deep and shallow
water in warmer regions.

Genus *Xenophora* Fischer von Waldheim

*Xenophora conchyliophora* Born
Atlantic Carrier Shell

Pls. VI, 6; XXI, 5

ETYMOLOGY: Gr. *xenos phero,* strange bearer; *conchylion phero,*
shell-bearer.

SIZE: The true shell without the accretions is 60 mm. (2 2/5 in.) in diameter,
42 mm. (1 3/4 in.) in height.

DISTRIBUTION: North Carolina to Key West and the West Indies.

CHARACTERISTICS: Shell low conic, shaped like a flattened top, covered above with assortments of cemented stones, shells, or bits of coral; base flat, finely and evenly reticulated, the concentric ridges somewhat stronger than the axial. Operculum thin, with numerous concentric growth lines.

This slow-moving snail is well camouflaged to look like a heap of sea debris, but only slight experience is needed to penetrate the disguise. It is rather common in shallow water on sandy or pebbly bottoms.

SUPERFAMILY:

# NATICACEA

---

FAMILY:

# NATICIDAE
(*moon and ear snails*)

The shells range from tiny to quite large, and in shape are globular, low conic, or markedly flattened. The surface may be pleasingly colored. This is a very large family of carnivorous snails found in all seas. They have a huge foot, with which they plow through water-logged sand in search of molluscan prey.

The predacious moon snails fall easily into two groups, depending on the nature of the operculum: those with a shelly, or calcareous, operculum are placed in the subfamily Naticinae; and those with a corneous, or horny, operculum, in the subfamily Polinicinae. Recent studies have shown that the radular characteristics do not always conform to the duo-classification of the operculae, and hence tend to weaken the assignment of some species to their subfamilies. In general, however, these opercular differences hold up quite well. Representatives of both groups occur in our area. The moon snails live generally on bivalve flesh, which they reach by boring neat, countersunk holes in the shells; shells with such holes are common on most outer beaches. When the snail is active, the exposed soft parts are much larger than the shell, and the fleshy foot can be accommodated only by expulsion of large quantities of water, apparently the agent of the swollen condition. *Natica* moves rapidly through waterlogged sand in its hunt for prey, guided by a strong sense of smell. The eyes are much reduced or absent. The eggs are laid in rather large, pliable structures made of sand grains held together by solidified mucus. These are commonly called "sand collars."

## KEY TO FAMILY NATICIDAE

|  |  |
|---|---|
| * Shell very flat, earlike, aperture huge | |
| ** Shell white, very depressed | *Sinum perspectivum* |
| ** Shell strongly stained with brown, somewhat higher | *S. maculatum* |
| * Shell globose or depressed globose | |
| ** Shell with callus in umbilical region, which may cover all or much of umbilicus | |
| *** Operculum corneous | |
| **** Callus brown or purplish brown | *Polinices duplicatus* |
| **** Callus white | |
| ***** Shell milk white | *P. lacteus* |
| ***** Shell brown | *P. hepaticus* |
| *** Operculum shelly (porcelaneous) | |
| **** Shell up to 52 mm. (about 2 in.), operculum with deep concentric grooves | *Natica canrena* |
| **** Shell smaller, operculum smooth | |
| ***** Shell 25 mm. (1 in.), colorless, umbilicus usually completely covered | *N. clausa* |
| ***** Shell 6 to 8 mm. (1/4 to 1/3 in.), surface with brown markings, umbilicus partially open | *N. pusilla* |
| ** Shell with open umbilicus, operculum corneous | |
| *** Shell very large, 115 mm. (4 3/4 in.), bandless | *Lunatia heros* |
| *** Shell small, 25 mm. (1 in.), usually banded | *L. triseriata* |

Genus *Natica* Scopoli

*Natica canrena* Linnaeus
  Colorful Moon Snail

  Pl. IX, 3

ETYMOLOGY: Lat. *natica*, buttock, rump; *canrena*, from the Malayan word *Karang*, shell, shellfish.

SIZE: 52 mm. (about 2 in.) in diameter, 45 mm. (1 4/5 in.) in height.

DISTRIBUTION: North Carolina to Key West and the West Indies.

CHARACTERISTICS: Shell globose, smooth, glossy; body whorl large, aperture capacious, spire small. Color pale bluish white, with a variable pattern of wavy, fawn-colored lines and zigzag markings or spiral rows of dark brown spots. Umbilical region and callus white. Operculum ear shaped, calcareous, heavy, with about 10 deep concentric grooves on outer surface.

The **Miniature Moon Snail,** *Natica pusilla* Say (Lat. *pusillus,* very small) (pl. XXI, 6), is much smaller, 6 to 8 mm. (1/4 to 1/3 in.) in diameter. It is glossy white or pale brown, with faint brownish markings. The umbilicus is almost covered by the heavy buff-colored callus. The operculum is calcareous but smooth. This species ranges from Cape Cod to the Caribbean, and occasionally specimens are washed up on shore.

The **Northern Moon Snail,** *Natica clausa* Broderip and Sowerby (Lat. *clausa,* closed) (pl. XXI, 7), reaches about 25 mm. (1 in.) in diameter. It is rather colorless, and most easily recognized by the fact that the callus practically always covers the umbilicus. It ranges from the Arctic Ocean to North Carolina, but it lives intertidally only north of Massachusetts.

Genus *Polinices* Montfort

*Polinices duplicatus* Say
  Double Moon Snail or Shark Eye

  Pl. XXI, 8

ETYMOLOGY: Gr. Polynices (from *poly nice,* many victories) was the son of Oedipus; Lat. *duplicatus,* doubled.

SIZE: 58 mm. (2 1/3 in.) in diameter, 45 mm. (1 4/5 in.) in height.

DISTRIBUTION: Cape Cod to Florida and the Gulf States.

CHARACTERISTICS: Shell subglobose, low pyramidal to depressed oval, smooth, moderately glossy. Color tan or bluish gray. Umbilicus partially or almost entirely covered with a purplish brown or brown callus. Operculum ear shaped, horny, light brown.

The Shark Eye or Double Moon Snail is easily characterized by the heavy purplish brown callus that almost, but not completely, covers the umbilicus, a narrow, curved slit always remaining along the outer edge. The shell of males, especially among those found in the northern populations, is pyramidal in shape, and higher and heavier than the female shell. Southern specimens have a bluish gray and generally more depressed or oval shell than the buff-colored northern specimens. The Shark Eye, like all members of the family Naticidae, is predacious, drilling into the shell of the food mollusk and extracting the flesh by means of the radula housed in an extendible proboscis, or snout. The half-moon-shaped horny operculums are seasonally common objects on beaches. This snail is reported to swim by vigorously undulating its huge mantle.

The **Brown Moon Snail,** *Polinices hepaticus* Röding (Gr. *hepar,* the liver) (pl. XXII, 10), is a little smaller, reaching only 45 mm. (1 4/5 in.) in diameter. It is glossy and heavy, and elongate globose in shape. The color is purplish or orange brown, but the umbilical region and the callus are white. The upper portion of the deep umbilicus is covered by the callus. The species ranges from southeastern Florida to Texas and the Caribbean. It was formerly called *Polinices brunneus* Link, a later synonym.

The **Milky Moon Snail,** *Polinices lacteus* Guilding (Lat. *lacteus,* milky) (pl. XXII, 11), is generally similar to *P. hepaticus,* but it differs by being a little smaller, 40 mm. (1 3/5 in.), and entirely milk white in color. It ranges from North Carolina to Florida and the Caribbean.

Genus *Lunatia* Gray

*Lunatia heros* Say
    Hero Moon Snail

    Pl. XXI, 9

ETYMOLOGY: Lat. *luna,* moon; *heros,* demigod, hero.

SIZE: Up to 115 mm. (4 1/2 in.) in height, 90 mm. (3 1/2 in.) in diameter.

DISTRIBUTION: Gulf of Saint Lawrence to North Carolina.

CHARACTERISTICS: Shell large, globular, rather thin, inflated; body whorl
huge, spire small. Ashen brownish, moderately glossy, sometimes with
large bluish areas. Aperture with brownish stains, brilliantly polished.
Umbilicus deep, open. Operculum as in *Polinices* (page 102).

This is the largest moon snail in our area, and it is quite common
intertidally, especially in the north. The open umbilicus and the
globose shape serve to distinguish it easily from the Shark Eye
(*P. duplicatus*), with which it shares its range. The genus *Lunatia*,
formerly considered a subgenus of *Polinices*, includes those species
with a horny operculum and an open umbilicus. Like others in the
family, these, too, are drilling predators. They can often be dug up
alive on sandy beaches at low tide by opening the small hillocks they
throw up while plowing their way through waterlogged sand.

The **Spotted Moon Snail,** *Lunatia triseriata* Say (Lat. *tri series*,
three rows) (pl. XXII, 12), is very much smaller, reaching only 25 mm.
(1 in.) in diameter. There is a dull yellowish periostracum, and the
surface is usually ornamented with three wide spiral bands of brown
elongate spots, but frequently these bands are missing. There is no
umbilical callus, but the umbilicus may be partially hidden by an extension of the parietal lip. It occupies the same range as the Hero
Moon Snail.

Genus *Sinum* Röding

*Sinum perspectivum* Say
Common Baby Ear

Pl. XXI, 10

ETYMOLOGY: Lat. *sinum*, a large drinking vessel with swollen sides;
*perspicere*, to look through.

SIZE: 35 to 50 mm. (1 2/5 to 2 in.) in diameter, 8 mm. (1/3 in.) in height.

DISTRIBUTION: Virginia to Florida, the Gulf states, and the Caribbean.

CHARACTERISTICS: Shell moderate, very flat, thin. Aperture very large. Color
dull white. Periostracum thin, light brown. Surface with numerous fine
spiral lines above. Operculum absent.

The Baby Ear is well named because of its delicate, white texture.
The unique shape makes it impossible to mistake this genus. In life
the foot completely envelops the shell. The Baby Ear lives burrowing

in sand, where it finds its clam prey. Like some naticids, this species probably is a swimmer.

The **Spotted Baby Ear,** *Sinum maculatum* Say (Lat. *macula,* spot, satin) (pl. XXI, 11), is a little higher, 14 mm. (1/2 in.), and 40 mm. (1 3/5 in.) in diameter. The spiral sculpture is weaker, and the shell is brown or splotched with brown. This species has the same range as the Common Baby Ear.

SUPERFAMILY:

# TRIVIACEA

FAMILY:

# ERATOIDAE

(*miniature cowries*)

The shells are small and look like miniature cowries, but in spite of their outward appearance they are placed in a different superfamily from the Cypraeidae. The surface is not smooth and glossy, but is strongly ornamented with transverse, often bifurcating ridges. Eratoidae are confined to warmer seas, and dead shells are not uncommon in beach drift.

## KEY TO GENUS TRIVIA

* Shell tan, brownish, or pink in color, often with dark pink or brown spots
** Shell pink with weak and suffused brown spots    *Trivia suffusa*
** Shell tan or pink, with clearly delimited but irregular brown spots
*** Shell tan, with 3 pairs of brown spots, the central pair the largest    *T. pediculus*
*** Shell pink, with 2 to 4 small, dark reddish brown spots along the central dorsal line    *T. quadripunctata*
* Shell white, not spotted

&ast;&ast; Shell with distinct vertical dorsal groove separating the horizontal ribs above        *T. nix*
&ast;&ast; Shell without vertical dorsal groove, horizontal
ribs joined above        *T. candidula*

---

Genus *Trivia* Broderip

*Trivia pediculus* Linnaeus
    Coffee-bean or Louse Trivia

Pl. XXII, 13

ETYMOLOGY: Trivia is a surname of Diana, goddess of the hunt; *Lat.*
*pediculus*, louse.

SIZE: 15 mm. (3/5 in.) in length, 8 mm. (1/3 in.) in height.

DISTRIBUTION: Southern Florida and the West Indies.

CHARACTERISTICS: Shell quite small, oval, not glossy; surface roughened by
sixteen to nineteen strong horizontal ribs crossing the back and base
of the shell, broken by a deep, longitudinal dorsal furrow. Color tan to
brownish pink, with three pairs of large, irregular brown blotches on
the back, the central pair being the largest.

These small relatives of the cowries differ by having a strongly sculptured surface. They are usually common, and good, cleaned specimens
are frequently found in beach drift. They are known to feed on soft-
bodied tunicates.

The **Suffused Trivia,** *Trivia suffusa* Gray (pl. XXII, 14), is bright
pink, with a few faint, suffused brownish blotches and eighteen to
twenty-three (usually twenty) horizontal riblets, which are sometimes
beaded. The species ranges from southern Florida to the West Indies.

The **Four-spotted Trivia,** *Trivia quadripunctata* Gray (Lat. *quat-*
*tuor punctum*, four-dot) (pl. XXII, 15) is quite small, usually reaching
only 3 to 6 mm. (1/8 to 1/4 in.) in length. It is bright pink in color,
and has two to four very small, dark reddish brown spots on the
central dorsal line. There are nineteen to twenty-four horizontal ribs,
which are never beaded. In beach-worn specimens the brown spots
wear away and the pink color fades. This is a common species from
southeastern Florida to Yucatán and the West Indies.

The **Snowy Trivia,** *Trivia nix* Schilder (Lat. *nix*, snow) (pl. XXII,
16), reaches 9 mm. (2/5 in.) in length, and is characterized by having a
globular shape and a pure white color. It has about twenty-two to

twenty-six horizontal riblets, broken above by a strong dorsal furrow. It is a relatively uncommon shell, ranging from southeastern Florida to the West Indies.

The **Little White Trivia,** *Trivia candidula* Gaskoin (Lat. *candidulus,* shining white) (pl. XXII, 17), is also globose and white but smaller, reaching only 3 to 6 mm. (1/8 to 1/4 in.) in length. It lacks the strong dorsal furrow of *T. nix,* the horizontal riblets joining above. *T. candidula* ranges from North Carolina to Florida and Barbados.


SUPERFAMILY:

# CYPRAEACEA

---

FAMILY:

# CYPRAEIDAE
(*cowrie shells*)

The mature shell is small to large, extremely glossy, swollen and hump shaped, with a large, narrow basal aperture, both lips of which bear strong, evenly spaced teeth. This is a large family of very attractive shells confined to warmer seas.

The gleaming cowrie shells have always attracted mankind by the brilliance of their color and their smooth and pleasing shape. The shell was dedicated to Venus, the goddess of love as a fertility symbol, possibly because the long aperture bears a resemblance to the female organ. Several small species serve even today as currency in the South Seas. The immature shell differs strongly from the adult; it is shaped like a bubble shell, with a thin outer lip and a distinct but low spire. At this stage it is said to have a Bulla form. As the shell matures, the lips thicken, turn inward, and are armed with strong, regularly spaced, low teeth. The spire is gradually covered with gleaming shell matter till it becomes invisible. At intermediate stages, however, the spire is still visible, and this excites inexperienced collectors who think they have discovered a new species. Collectors are also occasionally fooled by finding a beach-worn specimen that has had its topmost shell layer eroded away, exposing a color not mentioned in the descriptions in books. The immature shell also differs in color, lacking the mature color pattern and frequently having a few wide, indistinct bands.

In life the shell is covered by two flaps of a usually highly ornamented fleshy mantle, which can be rapidly withdrawn when the
animal is disturbed. The cowries all live in warm water. The Italians
call them *porcellani*, or little pigs, possibly because of their elongated
plump shape. When Marco Polo returned from his trip to China,
bringing the brilliantly gleaming chinaware pottery back with him, his
countrymen exclaimed that it gleamed like the *porcellani*. This is the
origin, via the French, of our words "porcelain" and "porcelaneous."

## KEY TO GENUS CYPRAEA

* Shell large, up to 125 mm. (5 in.) in length

** Shell with sides inflated and with small, very
    numerous unocellated spots           *Cypraea cervus*

** Shell narrow, spots larger, less numerous, basal
    ones ocellated                       *C. zebra*

* Shell small, reaching only 38 mm. (1 1/2 in.) in
  length

** Shell rather depressed, base always entirely white   *C. spurca acicularis*

** Shell rather rounded horizontally, base white to
    ivory, with purplish spots between the teeth     *C. cinerea*

Genus *Cypraea* Linnaeus

*Cypraea zebra* Linnaeus
    Measled or Zebra Cowrie

    Pls. VIII, 1a & b; XXI, 12

ETYMOLOGY: Cypria is a surname of the goddess Venus.

SIZE: 50 to 100 mm. (2 to 4 in.) in length, 50 mm. (2 in.) in width.

DISTRIBUTION: Southeastern Florida to the West Indies.

CHARACTERISTICS: Shell medium to large, oblong, glossy, smooth surface.
    Color dark brown, with the back regularly speckled with white dots,
    those on the base with brown centers. Aperture long, narrow; lips
    strongly armed with regular teeth.

This species was formerly called *C. exanthema* Linnaeus (Lat. *exanthema*, measles), whence the popular name Measled Cowry, much
more appropriate to this spotted species than Zebra Cowry. Linnaeus

named *zebra* in 1758 and *exanthema* in 1767, not realizing that they were the same species, *zebra* being an immature form and *exanthema* an almost adult shell.

The cowries in Florida live in shallow water, and are often thrown up on the beach.

The **Deer Cowrie,** *Cypraea cervus* Linnaeus (Lat. *cervus*, buck or stag) (pl. VIII, 4a & b), is generally larger, up to 125 mm. (5 in.), rarely to 180 mm. (7 in.) in length. The shell is lighter in color and more inflated, and the spots are smaller and more numerous, none of them being ocellated or having a brown center like the basal spots in *C. zebra*. This species occurs in southern Florida, Cuba, and south to Yucatán. It is not the female of *C. zebra*, as some malacologists have speculated, but a distinct species.

The **Ashen Cowrie,** *Cypraea cinerea* Gmelin (Lat. *cinis, cineris,* ashes) (pl. VIII, 3; XXII, 18), is very much smaller, reaching only 18 to 38 mm. (3/4 to 1 1/2 in.) in length and 25 mm. (1 in.) in height. The back is whitish or light to orange brown, occasionally with brown or black dashes; the base is ivory white and the spaces between the teeth usually purplish. This species is frequently collected under stones in shallow water from southern Florida to the West Indies.

The **Yellow Cowrie,** *Cypraea spurca acicularis* Gmelin (Lat. *spurcus,* filthy, unclean; *acicula,* little pin) (pl. XXII, 19), is a little smaller, 11 to 28 mm. (about 1/2 to 1 1/8 in.) in length. It is readily separated from the Ashen Cowrie in that it is flatter and the base is pure white, without any color. The upper surface is covered with irregular flecks of orange or yellow brown, and the flattened margins are sometimes roughened like the edge of a pie crust. The shells live under rocks in shallow water from South Carolina and Florida to Yucatán and the West Indies, and are often found cast up on the beach. The belittling name given by Linnaeus to this pretty shell is quite undeserved. The "typical" or nominate subspecies, *C. spurca spurca* Linnaeus, lives in the Mediterranean.

---

FAMILY:

# OVULIDAE

(*cowrie allies*)

The shells are small to medium, commonly long and slender, glossy, with a slitlike aperture, notched at each end. Operculum lacking. The colorful and characteristic mantle may extend to cover the entire dorsal surface of the shell. Inhabitants of warmer seas, they feed on the polyps of soft coral.

## KEY TO GENERA
## SIMNIA AND CYPHOMA

\* Shell elongate ovate, divided near the center by a rounded transverse ridge, ends rounded
\* \* Transverse ridge strong, high
\* \* \* Shell cream orange to buff, lateral callus with a weak or absent transverse ridge      *Cyphoma gibbosum*
\* \* \* Shell white, with tints of lilac or pink, lateral callus with strong transverse ridge      *C. macgintyi*
\* \* Transverse ridge weak, color light buff      *C. signatum*
\* Shell long, slender, not divided near the center, ends pointed
\* \* Shell with short, twisted spiral fold at end of columella      *Simnia acicularis*
\* \* Shell without columellar fold      *S. uniplicata*

Genus *Simnia* Risso

*Simnia acicularis* Lamarck
Common Simnia

Pl. XX, 27

ETYMOLOGY: Gr. *Simnia* is one of the water sprites called Nereids; Lat. *acicula*, little pin.

SIZE: 12 mm. (1/2 in.) in length, 3 mm. (1/8 in.) in width.

DISTRIBUTION: North Carolina to the West Indies.

CHARACTERISTICS: Shell small, narrow, elongate-oval, glossy, strong. Lavender or yellow. Aperture long, narrow, lip without teeth. Columella flattened or dished, in adults bordered by a long whitish ridge; spire covered.

This handsome small ally of the true cowries lives on soft coral such as sea fans, taking on the color of its host. It is not a common species, and is best collected by vigorously shaking dried sea fans. The color is not very stable, and tends to fade rapidly unless well sheltered from light.

The **Single-toothed Simnia,** *Simnia uniplicata* Sowerby (Lat. *unus plicatus,* one-folded or -plicated) (pl. XX, 28), reaches 17 mm. (about 3/4 in.) in length. Its color is similar to *S. acicularis,* but the shell is somewhat wider and has a single strong, rounded ridge on the columella and a twisted spiral fold at the end. It ranges from Virginia to the West Indies, living in much the same habitat as the previous species.

Genus *Cyphoma* Röding

*Cyphoma gibbosum* Linnaeus
   Common Flamingo Tongue

   Pl. VIII, 2

ETYMOLOGY: Gr. *kyphoma,* hump; Lat. *gibbus,* hump.

SIZE: 28 mm. (1 1/8 in.) in length, 15 mm. (3/5 in.) in width.

DISTRIBUTION: North Carolina to the West Indies.

CHARACTERISTICS: Shell small, glossy, elongate oval with a single strong
   transverse ridge near the dorsal center; spire covered. Color cream
   orange to buff. Aperture narrow, long, lips toothless.

This is the commonest of the cyphomas in our area. Dead shells are often found in the beach drift, and live ones with gorgeous orange mantles richly sprinkled with irregular black rings can be seen crawling and feeding on sea fans in shallow water.

**McGinty's Flamingo Tongue,** *Cyphoma macgintyi* Pilsbry (Thomas L. McGinty is a well-known Floridian shell collector and student) (pl. XX, 29), is far less common. It is more elongate and narrower than *C. gibbosum,* and whitish in color, with tints of lilac or pink. There is a strong, rounded ridge running along one side, perpendicular to the strongly developed transverse ridge. This species has been reported only from the lower Florida Keys. Its mantle is decorated with numerous, generally rounded brown spots near the margins.

The **Fingerprint Flamingo Tongue,** *Cyphoma signatum* Pilsbry & McGinty (Lat. *signum,* sign, print) (pl. XX, 30), is similar, but the transverse dorsal ridge is much weaker and the front of the aperture wider than in the other two species. It is light buff in color. The mantle is ornamented with numerous crowded lines, like human fingerprints. It is by far the rarest of the flamingo tongues. The authors of this species originally wanted to name this *digitisignatus* because of the fingerprint markings on the mantle, but they eventually compromised.

SUPERFAMILY:

# TONNACEA

---

FAMILY:

# TONNIDAE
(*tun shells*)

These shells are medium to large and rather thin but not fragile. The body whorl is capacious, and the surface is strongly ridged spirally. This is a small family, found only in warmer seas.

The tun shells are easily characterized by their light, sturdy shells and strong spiral sculpture. They are found in shallow water on sandy bottoms, usually near reefs. These snails have expandable snouts, with which they engulf small prey. The newly hatched shells are tiny, smooth, golden brown, and flexible.

Genus *Tonna* Brünnich

*Tonna maculosa* Dillwyn
    Spotted Tun Shell

    Pls. IX, 5; XXII, 20

ETYMOLOGY: Lat. *tonna*, cask; *maculosus*, spotted, stained.

SIZE: 47 to 134 mm. (1 4/5 to 5 2/5 in.) in height, 32 to 96 mm. (1 1/4 to 3 4/5 in.) in width.

DISTRIBUTION: Southern Florida to the West Indies and Brazil.

CHARACTERISTICS: Shell medium to large, ovate globose, thin but strong, smooth. Color mottled with brown and white. Surface with strong spiral grooves. Aperture capacious, lip thin, operculum wanting.

This species is sometimes confused with *Tonna perdix* Linnaeus, a Pacific shell.

The **Giant Tun Shell,** *Tonna galea* Linnaeus (Lat. *galea*, helmet) (pl. X, 1), reaches 172 mm. (6 3/4 in.) in height and is more globose in shape. It is usually white to light coffee brown in color. The spiral sculpture is stronger and more widely spaced, and the lip has a thickened ridge below the margin. The columella is strongly twisted, and an umbilicus is present. This species has a very wide distribution from the Mediterranean and the west coast of Africa to the Indo-Pacific. In our area it ranges from North Carolina to Florida and Texas and south to Brazil. The smooth, golden-brown juveniles are common seasonally in beach drift.

FAMILY:

# FICIDAE
*(fig shells)*

A small family of medium-sized, elongate, thin, but strong shells. Aperture large, with long canal. Operculum lacking. Inhabitants of sandy bottoms in shallow to deep water of warmer seas.

Genus *Ficus* Röding

*Ficus communis* Röding
Common Fig Shell

Pl. IX, 4

ETYMOLOGY: Lat. *ficus*, fig; *communis*, common, ordinary.

SIZE: 60 to 100 mm. (2 1/2 to 4 in.) in height, 50 mm. (2 in.) in width.

DISTRIBUTION: North Carolina to the Caribbean.

CHARACTERISTICS: Shell large, pear-shaped, light but strong. Dull purplish or whitish brown in color, somewhat mottled. Surface sculpture reticulated with strong spiral ridges crossed by narrower and weaker axial lines.

The Common Fig Shell is a common beach shell, especially on Florida's west coast. It resembles the Pear Whelk (*Busycon spiratum*) in size and shape, but it is lighter and lacks the well-channeled suture. It was formerly called *Ficus papyratia* Say (Lat. paper). When the animal is extended, the foot is much larger than the shell, and the mantle forms wide lobes that cover much of the shell.

# CYMATIACEA

# CYMATIIDAE
(*triton shells*)

The shells are medium to quite large, with a prominent siphonal canal, and usually with apertural teeth. The shells of the triton family resemble some groups of rock shells (family Muricidae), and may be confused with them. Zoologically these families are quite distinct, and are placed in different orders of the prosobranchiate gastropods; the Cymatiidae are mesogastropods, whereas the Muricidae are neogastropods. A point to note in differentiating the two is that, though the rock shells have three or more varices on each whorl, the triton shells have no more than two. In addition, the hairy or rough periostracum found in many of the Cymatiidae is never seen on the Muricidae. The triton shells are found in warm and temperate seas.

## KEY TO GENERA CYMATIUM, CHARONIA, AND DISTORSIO

* Shell very large, 220 to 330 mm. (7 to 13 in.)
** Shell triangular, aperture more than twice as high as the spire — *Cymatium femorale*
** Shell conic, aperture less than spire in height — *Charonia variegata*
* Shell smaller, 45 to 138 mm. (1 4/5 to 5 1/2 in.) in height
** Shell with whorls and aperture distorted, white or tan, thin parietal shield present, surface latticed — *Distorsio clathrata*
** Whorls and aperture not distorted, shell varicolored, parietal shield absent
*** Siphonal canal narrow, long
**** Spire and body whorl globose — *Cymatium moritinctum*
**** Spire and body whorl conical — *C. vespaceum*

\* \* \* Siphonal canal wide, short
\* \* \* \* Outer lip with small paired, yellowish
    brown teeth                 *C. pileare*
\* \* \* \* Outer lip with large, unpaired white teeth    *C. nicobaricum*

---

Genus *Cymatium* Röding

*Cymatium femorale* Linnaeus
    Angular Triton Shell

    Pl. XI, 1

ETYMOLOGY: Gr. *kymation*, diminutive of *kyma*, wave; Lat. *femur*, thigh
    bone.

SIZE: Up to 220 mm. (8 in.) in height, 115 mm. (5 in.) in width.

DISTRIBUTION: Southeast Florida, Bermuda, and the Caribbean.

CHARACTERISTICS: Shell very large, strong, triangular, rough. Color golden
    to light reddish brown, varices with alternating bands of brown and
    white. Whorls shouldered, aperture longer than the somewhat extended
    spire. Shell usually with three to five heavily knobbed varices; surface
    with six to eight conspicuous spiral cords, the largest on the shoulder,
    weakly cancellated with numerous spiral and axial threads. Operculum
    rough, claw shaped, relatively small. Periostracum thin, rough, foliated,
    deciduous.

This beautiful triton shell is most easily recognized by its roughly
triangular shape and the wide, heavily corded shoulder of the body
whorl. The animals live a little beyond the low water on sandy bottoms.

The **Hairy Triton Shell,** *Cymatium pileare* Linnaeus (Lat. *pilus*,
hair) (pl. XXII, 21), is smaller, 138 mm. (5 1/2 in.) in height and 65 mm.
(2 3/5 in.) in width, and has a different fusiform, or spindle-shaped,
shell, with the oval aperture not as long as the spire. It is grayish to
golden brown in color, with alternating light and dark bands, especially on the varices. The surface is roughly sculptured with strong
spiral and weaker axial ridges, and the outer lip is decorated with
small, paired yellowish brown denticles. The whorls are not shouldered, and the extended spire is about equal to the body whorl in
length. The periostracum is thick, hairy, and brown. This species, like
several other triton shells, has a very wide distribution, occurring in
the Indo-Pacific region as well as in the Atlantic. The Atlantic form

has occasionally been designated as *C. martinianum* Orbigny, but recent studies show that it cannot be separated from the Pacific form. Some writers have tried to compromise by calling the Atlantic race *C. pileare martinianum*. *C. aquatile* Reeve is another synonym. In our area the species ranges from South Carolina to Texas and the Caribbean.

The **Dwarf Hairy Triton Shell,** *Cymatium vespaceum* Lamarck (possibly from Lat. *vespa*, wasp) (pl. XXII, 22), reaches only 45 mm. (1 4/5 in.) in height and 21 mm. (4/5 in.) in width. It is ovate in shape, with a longer and narrower siphonal canal, and the lip is much narrower. The roughly sculptured shell is yellowish brown, with patches of reddish brown on the varices. The periostracum is like that of *pileare*. This is a rarer species living in shallow to deeper water, and occurs in the Indo-Pacific as well as in our area, where it is found from southern Florida to the West Indies. It is the same as *C. gracile* Reeve, but not *C. gemmatum* Reeve, an Indo-Pacific species.

The **Doghead Triton Shell,** *Cymatium moritinctum* Reeve (possibly Lat. *marior tincta*, death color), was formerly confused with a different species, *C. cynocephalum* Lamarck (Gr. *kynos kephale*, dog's head) (pl. XXII, 23). It reaches only 45 mm. (1 4/5 in.) in height and 21 mm. (4/5 in.) in width, and is readily distinguished by having a globose spire with squarish shoulders and a long, narrow siphonal canal, so that it looks like a candied apple on a stick. The color is light tan to dark brown, with alternating dark and light bands on the varices. There are seven nodulose spiral cords and numerous fine spiral striae between. This species, which also occurs in the Indo-Pacific region, ranges from South Carolina to the Caribbean, but it is uncommon in our area. The eastern American populations were unnecessarily named *C. caribbaeum* Clench & Turner.

The **Golden-mouthed Triton Shell,** *Cymatium nicobaricum* Röding (named for the Nicobar Islands in the Bay of Bengal) was formerly called *C. chlorostomum* Lamarck (Gr. *chloros stoma*, green mouth) (pl. XXIV, 1). It reaches 85 mm. (3 2/5 in.) in height and 50 mm. (2 in.) in width, and is readily distinguished by its clumsy, rounded spire and quite small aperture, the outer lip of which is armed with a series of large, white teeth on the inside. The rough shell is light gray or reddish brown, with flecks of darker reddish brown on the five to nine coarse spiral threads. This species ranges from Florida to the Caribbean and also occurs, as its most recent name indicates, in the Indo-Pacific region.

Genus *Charonia* Gistel

*Charonia variegata* Lamarck
  Trumpet Triton Shell

  Pls. XI, 2a & b; XXII, 24

ETYMOLOGY: Charon, in Greek mythology, was the boatman who ferried the souls of the dead over the river Styx; Lat. *variegatus*, variegated.

SIZE: Up to 231 mm. (13 1/4 in.) in height, 168 mm. (6 1/2 in.) in width.

DISTRIBUTION: South Carolina to Florida and the West Indies. Also in Europe.

CHARACTERISTICS: Shell very large, rather heavy; spire high, attenuated; body whorl swollen, angularly shouldered. Color variegated, with buff, brown or purplish near the apex. Surface sculpture of strong spiral grooves. Outer lip with paired short white folds, the interspaces chocolate; the inner lip with numerous long white furrows. Operculum corneous, strong, elliptical.

This is one of the largest gastropods in our area. It is quite distinctive, and in adult and near-adult stages not easily confused with any other species. It does not grow as large as its Pacific relative, *Charonia tritonis* Linnaeus, and differs from it in other respects as well. This shell is used as a trumpet when the tip is broken off. *Charonia* is a predator on starfish, and those in the Pacific Ocean can even overcome and devour the harmful Crown of Thorns Starfish that has been destroying reef corals in many tropical areas in recent years.

Genus *Distorsio* Röding

*Distorsio clathrata* Lamarck
  Distorted Triton Shell

  Pl. XXII, 25

ETYMOLOGY: Lat. *distorsio*, distorting contortion; and *clathri*, trellis.

SIZE: 77 mm. (3 1/12 in.) in height, 43 mm. (1 3/4 in.) in diameter.

DISTRIBUTION: North Carolina to Texas, Mexico, and the West Indies.

CHARACTERISTICS: Shell large, solid, strongly sculptured. Color white diffused with yellowish or pinkish brown. Surface reticulated and strongly knobbed. Aperture surrounded by a large, thin, white parietal shield and grotesquely distorted by uneven teeth on both lips. Siphonal canal short, curved. Periostracum thin, brown. Operculum small, claw shaped.

This species lives in shallow to deeper water, and dead shells or recognizable fragments are often found on beaches. The lopsided whorls and the distorted aperture with the large, thin parietal shield make identification certain.

FAMILY:

# CASSIDAE

(*helmet shells*)

The shells are moderate to very large, often quite heavy and capacious. The aperture is toothed, and a glossy parietal shield is generally present. The family is usually found in warmer seas in shallow water.

## KEY TO FAMILY CASSIDAE

* Shell huge, reaching 230 to 280 mm. (9 to 11 in.)
** Shell cream colored, with 3 rows of tubercles
*** Tubercles large, not numerous, unequal    *Cassis madagascariensis*
*** Tubercles small, numerous, equal    *C. spinella*
** Color brownish cream, with dark brown, crescent-shaped markings    *C. tuberosa*
* Shell smaller, reaching only 91 mm. (3 1/2 in.) in height, frequently smaller
** Shell subcylindrical, quite small, 27 mm. (about 1 in.) high    *Morum oniscus*
** Shell oval, larger, up to 91 mm. (3 1/2 in.) high
*** Shell surface smooth, glossy    *Phalium cicatricosum*
*** Shell roughly sculptured
**** Sculpture of strong spiral grooves, reticulation weak; color creamy white, with brown blotches    *P. granulatum*
**** Sculpture strongly reticulated; color orange brown, with lighter and darker blotches    *Cypraecassis testiculus*

Genus *Cassis* Linnaeus

*Cassis madagascariensis* Lamarck
  Emperor Helmet Shell

  Pl. X, 7

ETYMOLOGY: Lat. *cassis*, helmet. Lamarck's specimens possessed erroneous locality data.

SIZE: Up to 216 mm. (8 2/3 in.) in height, 162 mm. (6 1/2 in.) in width.

DISTRIBUTION: North Carolina to southeastern Florida, the Bahamas, and the West Indies.

CHARACTERISTICS: Shell huge, heavy, cream colored, moderately glossy. Parietal shield very large, deep salmon color with a high gloss. Surface irregularly and coarsely latticed, and with three spiral rows of blunt spines, the topmost being the largest. Aperture narrow, stained with brown; outer lip with ten to twelve strong rounded white teeth, interspaces occasionally brown; inner lip with numerous unequal, horizontal wrinkles. Operculum short, semicircular, corneous.

The true helmet shells are characterized chiefly by their massive shape and huge parietal shield, which extends sharply beyond the periphery of the body whorl. The Emperor Helmet Shell is more typical of the Bahamas and the West Indies; however, it is known to occur uncommonly as far north as the Carolinas with the next discussed species. Both forms live in shallow and fairly deep water, and many are brought up by fishermen and divers for the tourist trade. The shell lends itself to the cutting of cameos, because the shell consists of dark, usually brownish layers sandwiched between white ones. Thus one can have either brown sculptured figures on a white background or white sculpture on a brown background.

**Clench's Helmet Shell,** *Cassis spinella* Clench (diminutive of Lat. *spina,* spine) (pl. X, 6), is larger than the Emperor Helmet Shell, reaching 280 mm. (11 in.) in height. It is chiefly characterized by having smaller, more regular, and more numerous surface tubercles. As *C. spinella* occupies the same range as *C. madagascariensis,* it may be in fact the female of that species. It is not unusual in some groups of marine snails to find sexual differences in the size of the shell, a condition known as "secondary sexual dimorphism"; in most such instances, the female shells are larger than the male.

The **King Helmet Shell,** *Cassis tuberosa* Linnaeus (Lat. *tuber,* protuberance, bump) (pl. X, 3), reaches 230 mm. (9 in.) in length and 175 mm. (7 in.) in height. The surface is finely reticulated and the brownish cream base color is mottled with dark brown, crescent-shaped markings. The triangular parietal shield is large, with a strong brown stain near the aperture. This species ranges from southeastern Florida to the West Indies. It is the commonest true helmet shell in its range.

Genus *Phalium* Link

*Phalium granulatum* Born
Scotch Bonnet

Pl. IX, 1

ETYMOLOGY: Gr. *phalios*, having patches of white; diminutive of Lat. *granum*, grain.

SIZE: Up to 91 mm. (3 1/2 in.) in height, 60 mm. (2 2/5 in.) in width.

DISTRIBUTION: North Carolina to Florida, the Gulf Coast, and the West Indies.

CHARACTERISTICS: Shell large, ovate, moderately strong. Cream to white overlaid with a series of uniformly arranged brown, squarish markings. Surface sculpture of numerous deeply incised grooves, latticed by faint axial ridges. Inner lip with a glazed area, lower portion extended shieldlike, papillose; outer lip thickened, coarsely and regularly crenulated.

This is a common shell in offshore waters, and specimens are frequently thrown up on shore. The shell, though easily recognizable, is highly variable, and several unnecessary subspecific names have been given to these variations. The Scotch Bonnet was recently declared the official state shell of North Carolina. This action has caused it to be overcollected for the souvenir market, much to the distress of the law's sponsors.

The **Smooth Scotch Bonnet,** *Phalium cicatricosum* Gmelin (Lat. *cicatricosus,* scarred) (pl. IX, 6; XXIII, 1), reaches only 60 mm. (2 2/5 in.) in height. It is readily distinguished from the true Scotch Bonnet by its generally smooth and shiny surface, which is occasionally finely malleated, or hammered, thus giving rise to its Latin name. The color is cream, lightly overlaid with faint buff markings. The species ranges from southeast Florida to the Caribbean and Bermuda. It is considered by Abbott (1968) to be a smooth form of the preceding species, and the dominant form in the West Indies and southward to Brazil. Small shells from Lake Worth, Florida, and the West Indies with a "crown" of nodules on the shoulder of the last whorl have been named *Phalium c. peristephes* Pilsbry & McGinty (Gr. *peristephes,* crowned).

The **Reticulated Helmet Shell,** *Cypraecassis testiculus* Linnaeus (Lat. Cypria, a surname of the goddess Venus, plus *cassis,* helmet; diminutive of Lat. *testis,* testicle) (pl. IX, 2), reaches 75 mm. (3 in.) in height, 48 mm. (2 in.) in width. This species is readily distinguished from the other helmet shells of equal size by the strongly reticulated, or latticed, surface and the oval shape, which possibly reminded Linnaeus of a human scrotum. The color is orange brown, with unevenly distributed white and purplish brown blotches. The parietal area is covered by an orange–cream colored glaze. The inner portion of the aperture has several rather strong wrinkles, the outer lip is thick and toothed. The shell is fairly common, but rarely occurs in large numbers in any single locality. It is found in southern Florida, Bermuda, and the West Indies.

Genus *Morum* Röding

*Morum oniscus* Linnaeus
   Atlantic Wood Louse

   Pl. XXIII, 2

ETYMOLOGY: Lat. *morum,* mulberry; *oniscus,* wood louse.

SIZE: Up to 27 mm. (about 1 in.) in height, 19 mm. (4/5 in.) in width.

DISTRIBUTION: Lower Florida Keys and the West Indies.

CHARACTERISTICS: Shell small, subcylindrical, strong, rough. Heavily speckled with brown on a whitish background. Sculptured with 3 spiral rows of blunt tubercles. Parietal wall glazed, minutely pebbled. Aperture narrow, outer lip thickened, weakly toothed. Periostracum thin, grayish.

This smallest of the helmet shells is fairly common in shallow water, and is frequently washed up on the shore. It looks quite unlike the other members of its family, and is not easily mistaken for any one of them.

FAMILY:

# BURSIDAE
*(frog shells)*

The shell is small or moderate in size, somewhat compressed laterally, with two peripheral varices. The aperture has two short siphonal canals, one above and one below. The family occurs mostly in warmer seas.

Genus *Bursa* Röding

*Bursa granularis* Röding
  Granular Frog Shell

  Pl. XXIII, 3

ETYMOLOGY: Lat. *bursa*, a purse.

SIZE: Up to 50 mm. (2 in.) in height, 28 mm. (1 1/8 in.) in width.

DISTRIBUTION: Southeast Florida and the West Indies.

CHARACTERISTICS: Shell medium in size, strong, ovate-conic; slightly flattened laterally, with strong peripheral varices. Color reddish brown, blotched with white. Aperture with two canals, one above and one below; lip thick, yellowish with white teeth. Surface sculpture of revolving lines, some beaded, and a row of knobs on the shoulder.

This is the only fairly common frog shell in our area. It is found in shallow water on or near reefs. The flattened shape, the peripheral varices, and the two apertural canals serve to identify it easily. The English name "frog shells" comes from earlier scientific designations of the genus: *Ranella* Lamarck (frog) and *Gyrineum* Link (tadpole). The name *B. cubaniana* Orbigny has been applied to the western Atlantic populations of this wide-ranging species, which is common in the Indo-Pacific region.

# ORDER:
## NEOGASTROPODA
*(new stomach-footed)*

SUPERFAMILY:

# MURICACEA

---

FAMILY:

# MURICIDAE
(*rock shells*)

These shells are generally heavy and solid, frequently with elaborate sculpture in the form of spines, ridges, scales, and knobs. The siphonal canal is often very long and armed with spines. There are usually 3 varices to a whorl, unlike the Cymatiidae (which are somewhat similar, though in the order Mesogastropoda), which have 2. Muricidae occur in all seas, but the largest number, and the most elegantly sculptured, are inhabitants of tropical and subtropical waters.

Rock shells are an extensive group of mostly tropical species whose beauty lies in their rich, often spiny surface sculpture rather than in their color. They are voracious predators who live on bivalves and other prosobranchs. Some species have a gland whose secretion, upon being exposed to the air, turns a lovely purple shade, the Tyrian purple so much favored by the ancient Greeks and Romans. The classification of the muricacean gastropods is presently undergoing extensive study by a number of workers, some of whom reduce the thaids to the rank of a subfamily (Thaidinae) within the family Muricidae.

---

## KEY TO FAMILY MURICIDAE

| | |
|---|---|
| \* Shell large, 75 to 115 mm. (3 to 4 3/5 in.) in height | |
| \*\* Shell rough but without spines | *Murex pomum* |
| \*\* Shell with open spines | |
| \*\*\* Spines short, strong, smooth, not foliated, shell whitish | *M. fulvescens* |
| \*\*\* Spines generally long, foliated or frilly at edges, shell frequently brownish or rusty | |
| \*\*\*\* Aperture large, ovate | *M. brevifrons* |
| \*\*\*\* Aperture small, rounded | |

\* \* \* \* \* Color dark, spines long; Florida but
       not the Keys                                    *M. florifer*
\* \* \* \* \* Color light, spines short; Florida
       Keys only                                       *M. dilectus*
       \* Shell small, 20 to 35 mm. (4/5 to
         1 2/5 in.) in height
      \* \* Shell relatively smooth, without
           spines or varices
     \* \* \* Shell surface relatively smooth or
            cancellated or latticed
    \* \* \* \* Shell surface strongly cancellated        *Urosalpinx tampaensis*
    \* \* \* \* Shell surface weakly or not at all
             cancellated, marked with strong,
             narrow spiral cords
   \* \* \* \* \* Aperture of shell rich mauve color       *Calotrophon ostrearum*
   \* \* \* \* \* Aperture of shell not mauve color
  \* \* \* \* \* \* Outer lip thin, distribution, Nova
              Scotia to east coast of Florida          *Urosalpinx cinerea*
  \* \* \* \* \* \* Outer lip thick, strongly toothed,
              distribution limited to west coast of
              Florida                                  *U. perrugata*
     \* \* \* Shell surface regularly beaded, color
            dark                                       *Morula nodulosa*
      \* \* Shell with spines and/or varices
     \* \* \* Shell with short spines only, arranged
            on axial ribs                              *Muricopsis oxytatus*
     \* \* \* Shell with varices
    \* \* \* \* Shell with 3 varices                       *Favartia cellulosa*
    \* \* \* \* Shell with only 2 peripheral varices
             at aperture
   \* \* \* \* \* Axial ribs rounded; distribution
             northern to east coast of Florida         *Eupleura caudata*
   \* \* \* \* \* Axial ribs sharp, often with spines at
             shoulder; distribution limited to
             west coast of Florida                     *E. sulcidentata*

Genus *Murex* Linnaeus

*Murex pomum* Gmelin
   Apple Murex

   Pls. XII, 3; XXIII, 4

ETYMOLOGY: Lat. *murex*, a fish armed with prickles and a long beak, a
   purple shell; and *pomum*, fruit, apple.

SIZE: 87 to 115 mm. (3 1/2 to 4 1/2 in.) in height, 53 to 68 mm. (2 to 2 1/2
   in.) in width.

DISTRIBUTION: North Carolina to the West Indies.

CHARACTERISTICS: Shell large, thick, rough, ovate, lusterless. Color
   brownish yellow to brown, many specimens with 3 dark brown,
   solid, or interrupted spiral bands. Siphonal canal short, broad,
   curved backwards. Operculum claw shaped, heavy, corneous.

This is the most familiar, larger rock shell in our area, living in shallow
water on sand and among sea grasses. Though quite variable, the shell
is readily recognized and not confused with other species. The juvenile
stages have a hairy periostracum. Individuals living in sheltered areas
have more delicate sculpture than those exposed to strong wave action.
Placed in the genus *Phyllonotus* Swainson (Gr. *phyllon,* leaf) or
*Chicoreus* Montfort (Gr. *kichorion,* endive or lettuce) by some
workers.

   The **Leafy** or **West Indian Murex,** *Murex brevifrons* Lamarck (Lat.
*brevis frons,* short leaf) (pls. XII, 7; XXI, 13), is quite large, 90 to 150
mm. (3 1/2 to 6 in.) in height, and 53 to 75 mm. (2 to 3 in.) in width.
The shell has three rounded varices armed with five thick, long, open
spines with foliated edges. The siphonal canal is broad and slightly
bent backwards, the space between the varices strongly lined spirally.
The color is variable, from cream or pinkish to rusty or purplish
brown, and the length of the spines is very variable. This is an uncommon shell in the Florida Keys, but quite abundant in the West Indies.
Some specialists place this and the following species in the genus
*Chicoreus.*

   The **Flowery** or **Lace Murex,** *Murex florifer* Reeve (Lat. *flos, floris,
ferro,* flower bearing) (pls. XII, 2; XXI, 14), is medium in size, 40 to 86
mm. (1 1/2 to 3 1/2 in.) in height, and 27 to 32 mm. (1 to 1 1/2 in.) in
width. It resembles *M. brevifrons,* but it is smaller and has a small,
round aperture rather than a large egg-shaped one, as in *M. brevifrons.*
In color it varies from cream to buff and light brown, the three varices
and spines often being chocolate brown. The spines are open and their
edges leafy. This species ranges from southern Florida to the Carib-

bean. Light-colored shells with short spines from the Florida Keys are known as *M. dilectus* A. Adams (Gr. *di lectus,* twice chosen). *M. dilectus* is more widely known by the later name *M. arenarius* Clench & Pérez Farfante (Lat. *arena,* sand), which is now considered a synonym. (Pl. XII, 1.)

The **Tawny** or **Giant Murex,** *Murex fulvescens* Sowerby (Lat. *fulvus,* yellowish or tawny) (pls. XII, 8; XXI, 15), is the largest *Murex* species in our area, reaching 180 mm. (7 in.) in height and 115 mm. (4 1/2 in.) in width. It is milky white to dirty gray, with numerous brown or brownish purple threads outside, and shiny white inside the aperture and the broad siphonal canal. There are six to ten varices armed with strong, short, unfoliated spines, the easiest way to distinguish this species from *M. florifer* and *M. brevifrons.* The species ranges from North Carolina around to Texas, where it is found during breeding seasons on reefs and oyster beds in shallow water. Placed in the genus *Hexaplex* Perry (Gr. *hex plex,* six plates) or *Muricanthus* Swainson (Lat. *murex* and Gr. *akantha,* spiny like a *Murex*) by some authors.

The **Pitted Murex,** *Favartia cellulosa* Conrad (Lat. *favus,* honey comb; *cellula,* small apartment or store room) (pl. XXIII, 5), is quite small, reaching only 20 to 25 mm. (1 in.) in height and 11 to 15 mm. (1/2 to 3/5 in.) in width. It is grayish white in color, with three rounded varices that only very rarely develop short spines. The surface is roughened by strong pitted spiral ridges, and the rather broad siphonal canal is sharply bent backwards, when it is not broken off. This is a common shallow-water species ranging from North Carolina to the Gulf of Mexico and the West Indies. It is especially common near oyster beds, which it occasionally raids.

The **Hexagonal Murex,** *Muricopsis oxytatus* M. Smith (Lat. *murex* and Gr. *opsis,* having the appearance of *murex;* Gr. *oxys,* sharp) (pl. XXIII, 6), is only 25 to 35 mm. (1 to 1 2/5 in.) in height. It is grayish white, narrowly spindle shaped or fusiform, and has seven usually spiny axial ridges. The siphonal canal is open and straight. This species, formerly known as *M. hexagonus* Lamarck, lives in shallow water from the Florida Keys to the West Indies.

The **Oyster Murex,** *Calotrophon ostrearum* Conrad (Gr. *kallos* beautiful and *trophon,* food; Lat. *ostra,* oyster) (pl. XXIII, 7), also reaches only 25 mm. (1 in.) in height. It has seven broad, rounded axial ridges crossed by numerous well-spaced spiral cords. The aperture is mauve colored and the siphonal canal bent backwards. In these two latter characteristics it differs from *Urosalpinx perrugata,* which it otherwise much resembles. Commonly associated with oyster beds, intertidally to 35 fathoms, from Biscayne Bay, and Key West to Tampa Bay.

The **Blackberry Drupe Murex,** *Morula nodulosa* C. B. Adams (Lat. *morum,* mulberry; Lat. *nodulus,* small knot) (pl. XXIV, 2), reaches 20 mm. (4/5 in.) in height, 10 mm. (2/5 in.) in width. The shell is small, broadly spindle shaped, and the surface is covered with rounded, regularly spaced blackish beads like the surface of a blackberry. The dark purple aperture has four or five whitish, well-developed denticles on the outer lip. This is a common species living under rocks in shallow water ranging from South Carolina to the West Indies. It was recently placed in the genus *Trachypollia* Woodring (Gr. *trachys polios,* rough gray).

Genus *Urosalpinx* Stimpson

*Urosalpinx cinerea* Say
  Atlantic Oyster Drill

  Pl. XXIV, 3

ETYMOLOGY: Gr. *oura salpinx,* tail trumpet; Lat. *cinis, cineris,* ashes.

SIZE: 25 mm. (1 in.) in height, 14 mm. (3/5 in.) in width.

DISTRIBUTION: Nova Scotia and Maine to eastern Florida.

CHARACTERISTICS: Shell small, spindle shaped or fusiform, strong. Color bluish ashy gray to white or orange, occasionally banded. Surface roughened by nine to twelve rounded axial ribs, ridges crossed by shallow, narrow spiral lines. Aperture brown with low, white teeth on thin outer lip; operculum corneous, amber colored.

This is the notorious Oyster Drill that is so destructive of young oysters. As the English name suggests, it drills quickly through the oyster shell and then devours the soft flesh inside. It is a distressingly abundant species in the intertidal zone to twenty-five feet. Exceptionally large specimens from the central eastern states have been named *follyensis* B. Baker after Folly Creek, Virginia, and white specimens from New York *aitkinae* Wheat, named for Helen J. Aitkin.

The **Tampa Oyster Drill,** *Urosalpinx tampaensis* Conrad (pl. XXIII, 8), is the same size. It differs in having a much thickened lip and a strongly cancelled surface formed by sharp axial and spiral crossing ridges. Its range is limited to the west coast of Florida, where it frequents oyster beds.

The **Gulf Oyster Drill,** *Urosalpinx perrugata* Conrad (Lat. *per-*

*rugatus*, completely wrinkled) (pl. XXIII, 9), differs from *U. cinerea* in having fewer and more widely spaced axial ridges, and fewer and stronger spiral cords, but the surface does not look cancellated. The aperture is rosy or yellow brown, and the outer lip considerably thickened. It also is limited to the west coast of Florida.

Genus *Eupleura* H. & A. Adams

*Eupleura caudata* Say
Thick-lipped Oyster Drill

Pl. XXIV, 4

ETYMOLOGY: Gr. *eu pleura*, well sided; Lat. *cauda*, tail.

SIZE: 25 mm. (1 in.) in height, 13 mm. (about 1/2 in.) in width.

DISTRIBUTION: South of Cape Cod to Florida.

CHARACTERISTICS: Shell small, strong, with broad peripheral varices on each side of the body whorl, which give a flattened appearance to the shell. Surface roughened by about 11 strong axial ribs crossed by numerous fine spiral lines. Outer lip very thick, strongly toothed. Siphonal canal long, almost closed. Operculum corneous, yellowish brown.

This species is also a predator, with much the same habitats as *Urosalpinx*. In the New York City area it is rarer intertidally than the Atlantic Oyster Drill, but quite common in 10 feet or so of water. Large specimens—**Etter's Oyster Drill,** *E. caudata*, form *etterae* B. Baker (pl. XXIII, 10)—constitute an ecological form.

The **Sharp-ribbed Oyster Drill,** *Eupleura sulcidentata* Dall (Lat. *sulcus dentatus*, furrow-toothed) (pl. XXIV, 5), differs from *E. caudata* by having fewer but sharper axial ridges, frequently armed with a sharp spine above. In color it is gray, brown, or pinkish, sometimes with a narrow spiral band. It is found only on the west coast of Florida.

FAMILY:

# THAIDIDAE
(*dogwinkles*)

These shells are usually small and heavy, with a low spire and a large body whorl. The surface is rough but not spiny, and if knobby, the knobs are low and rounded. This group of predatory snails is found living on rocky shores in many seas. Like Muricidae, they can secrete a purplish dye.

# KEY TO GENERA THAIS, NUCELLA, AND PURPURA

* Aperture more than twice as high as the spire · · · · · · · · · · · · · · · · · · *Purpura patula*
* Aperture little higher or equal to the spire
** Shell without shoulder nodules, highly variable; northern distribution · · · · · · · *Nucella lapillus*
** Shell with nodules on shoulder; southern distribution
*** Shell small, about 40 mm. (1 3/5 in.) in height
**** Nodules large, blunt, shell triangular, aperture lavender or rose · · · · · · · · *Thais deltoidea*
**** Nodules small, sharp, shell ovate-conic, aperture white, purple stain at lower corner · · · · · · · · · · · · · · · · · · · · *T. rustica*
*** Shell large, more than 70 mm. (2 4/5 in.) in height
**** Double row of shoulder nodules; range restricted to Gulf of Mexico · · · *T. haemastoma haysae*
**** Single row of shoulder nodules; range not restricted to Gulf of Mexico · · · · · · *T. h. floridana*

Genus *Thais* Röding

*Thais deltoidea* Lamarck
Deltoid Dogwinkle

Pl. XXIII, 11

ETYMOLOGY: Thais was the name of an Egyptian courtesan; Gr. *deltoidea*, deltalike.

SIZE: 41 mm. (1 2/3 in.) in height, 35 mm. (1 2/5 in.) in width.

DISTRIBUTION: Florida to the West Indies and Brazil.

CHARACTERISTICS: Shell small, triangular, heavy, solid. Color grayish white mottled with dull brown to black; parietal wall tinted lavender to rose. Sculpture of large, blunt nodules at the shoulder, occasionally a second row below, with fine spiral lines. Operculum semicircular, corneous, rough.

This moderately common dogwinkle lives on rocks, to which it clings with considerable force. Like most members of the family, which is considered by some malacologists to be a subfamily of Muricidae, it is highly variable, and the young look quite unlike the mature forms. The deltoid shape and the strong shoulder nodules, nevertheless, are usually seen in all variations.

The **Rustic Dogwinkle,** *Thais rustica* Lamarck (pl. XXIII, 12), is about the same size or a little smaller. It is less solid, and the shoulder nodules are smaller and less blunt. It has a white aperture with a small purple stain on the lower corner, and its shape is narrower and roughly ovate in shape. It has almost the same range as *T. deltoidea.*

The **Florida Dogwinkle,** *Thais haemastoma floridana* Conrad (Gr. *haema stoma*, blood mouth) (pl. XII, 5), is a much larger shell, reaching 75 mm. (3 in.) in height and 44 mm. (1 4/5 in.) in width. The shoulder nodules are present but are lower, and the shape is ovate-conic. Its most easily observed diagnostic character, aside from its large size, is the salmon color (not blood, as the name suggests) in the aperture. It is found from North Carolina to the West Indies and Central America.

**Hays' Dogwinkle,** *Thais haemastoma haysae* Clench (named for Markley L. Hays, a collector) (pl. XII, 6), is even larger, reaching 105 mm. (4 1/5 in.) in height and 50 mm. (2 in.) in width. It has a double row of strong shoulder nodules, a strong, rough shell, and an indented suture. However, not all specimens are easily placed, and some doubt has been expressed as to the validity of the name. A serious predator in oyster beds, it ranges from the west coast of Florida to Texas. *T. canaliculata* Gray may be an earlier name for this subspecies.

The **Northern Dogwinkle,** *Nucella lapillus* Linnaeus (possibly diminutive of Lat. *nux*, nut; Lat. *lapillus*, little stone (pl. XXIII, 13), was until recently in the genus *Thais*. It is 30 to 40 mm. (1 1/5 to 1 3/5 in.) in height and 18 to 22 mm. (3/4 to 4/5 in.) in width. The heavy shell is free of shoulder nodules, but the variations in color, shape, and surface sculpture are bewildering. Specimens intergrade from high, narrow shells with well-raised spires to short, dumpy shells with low spires; the color can be white, yellowish, orange or brown, occasionally banded; the surface is usually smooth but often strongly marked with spiral furrows; occasionally populations have a scaly surface, a form called *N. l. imbricatus* Lamarck. It is found from Labrador to the eastern end of Long Island, New York, and also in nothern Europe, where specimens grow much larger.

The **Wide-mouthed Dogwinkle,** *Purpura patula* Linnaeus (Lat. *purpura,* purple; *patulus,* standing open, wide) (pl. XII, 4), is 50 to 85 mm. (2 to 3 1/2 in.) high and 40 to 60 mm. (1 1/2 to 2 1/2 in.) wide. It is ovate-globose in shape, with a vast aperture and a small spire. The color is dull gray on the outside, with a salmon-pink columella; the outer lip is irregularly blotched with brown internally. The sculpture consists of six or seven spiral rows of low, sharp nodules and numerous incised spiral lines between. The pre-Columbian Indians obtained a purple stain by drawing a thread across the mouth of the animal. This probably suggested the generic name, though most dogwinkle species secrete a purplish dye. The present species ranges from Florida to the West Indies. A very similar shell on the west coast of America with a white line on the upper edge of the inner lip is recognized as a subspecies, *P. patula pansa* Gould.

FAMILY:

# CORALLIOPHILIDAE

(*coral shells*)

Coral snails, closely related to the Muricidae and Thaididae, have small, mostly solid, whitish or light colored shells, commonly ornamented with spines, or rarely smooth. The horny operculum is similar to that of the genus *Thais.* The small family, also known as Magilidae, occurs in tropical and subtropical waters living on coral and rocky bottoms. Some are parasites of corals; a radula is lacking. Species of the genus *Magilus* (etymology unknown), which inhabit the Indo-Pacific region, live inbedded in coral heads, with only a tube extending from the aperture exposed on the growing surface of the coral.

Genus *Coralliophila* H. & A. Adams

*Coralliophila abbreviata* Lamarck
Abbreviated Coral Shell

Pl. XXIII, 14

ETYMOLOGY: Gr. *korallion philos*, coral loving.

SIZE: 19 to 38 mm. (about 4/5 to 1 1/2 in.) in height, 26 mm. (1 in.) in width.

DISTRIBUTION: Off South Carolina and southeastern Florida to the West Indies and Brazil.

CHARACTERISTICS: Shell medium, solid, broadly ovate-conic, often misshapen; shoulders rounded. Surface sculpture of numerous narrow but strong, raised spiral cords. Color grayish white. Aperture often tinted yellow or orange.

This heavy, chunky shell with the strongly sculptured surface is common in shallow water at the base of the corals and sea fans on which it feeds.

SUPERFAMILY:

# BUCCINACEA

FAMILY:

# BUCCINIDAE
(*whelks*)

These shells vary from small to quite large, ovate-conic to spindle shaped, with a short basal notch at the aperture. The sculpture ranges from fine- to well-ribbed forms, but the shells have no spines. This is a very large family, with genera and species ranging from frigid to tropical seas. Like most neogastropods, these snails are generally predators and scavengers.

## KEY TO FAMILY BUCCINIDAE

* Shell large, usually more than 75 mm. (3 in.) in height
** Shell smooth, or with shallow spiral lirations

    \*\*\* Shell thin, large, 150 mm. (6 in.) in height,
        spiral lirations weak                   *Colus stimpsoni*

    \*\*\* Shell strong, smaller, 75 mm. (3 in.) in
        height, spiral lirations strong

  \*\*\*\* Shell narrow, suture shallow, body whorl
        narrow, spiral bands weak; living       *C. islandicus*

  \*\*\*\* Shell squat, suture deep, body whorl much
        swollen, spiral bands strong; extinct     *C. stonei*

      \*\* Shell surface heavily sculptured

    \*\*\* Shell sculpture of 7 to 10 wide, heavy
        brown spiral ridges               *Neptunea decemcostata*

    \*\*\* Shell sculpture of 8 to 19 wide, low axial
        undulations and occasionally spiral cords   *Buccinum undatum*

      \* Shell small, not exceeding 35 mm. (1 2/5
        in.) in height

      \*\* Shell surface smooth or with shallow
        spiral lirations

    \*\*\* Shell not exceeding 20 mm. (4/5 in.),
        chalky, with heavy, black periostracum   *Colus pygmaeus*

    \*\*\* Shell up to 35 mm. (1 2/5 in.), glossy,
        purplish brown, with bands of chevron-
        shaped spots, periostracum thin       *Pisania pusio*

      \*\* Shell with strong surface sculpture

    \*\*\* Sculpture consisting of spiral rows of
        larger or smaller rounded knobs      *Engina turbinella*

    \*\*\* Sculpture other than rounded knobs

  \*\*\*\* Surface strongly cancellate       *Cantharus cancellaria*

  \*\*\*\* Sculpture chiefly of wide spiral ridges, not
      cancellate                      *C. tinctus*

---

Genus *Buccinum* Linnaeus

*Buccinum undatum* Linnaeus
   Wavy Whelk

   Pl. XXIII, 15

ETYMOLOGY: Lat. *buccina* or *bucina*, trumpet; *undatus*, wavy.

SIZE: 50 to 100 mm. (2 to 4 in.) in height, 50 mm. (2 in.) in width.

DISTRIBUTION: Arctic seas to New Jersey.

CHARACTERISTICS: Shell large, high conic, solid. Chalky gray to yellowish.
   Each whorl usually has eight to nineteen low, wide axial undulations

not extending to its base, occasionally with narrow spiral cords.
Operculum oval, concentric, chitinous.

This is a common shell of moderately deep water in the north; more
southerly, it is found as a rather worn beach specimen, often showing
signs of having been occupied by a hermit crab. Its size, shape, and
wavy surface sculpture make it easy to recognize. Though it is a
known scavenger, it is a common article of food in England. The egg
masses, which are sometimes washed up on the beach, are grayish
white and composed of many small, transparent, tough membranous
sacs each filled with unborn shells. Sailors used to call these masses
"sea wash-balls," and used them in place of soapy washcloths.

Genus *Colus* Röding

*Colus islandicus* Gmelin
 Iceland Whelk

 Pl. XV, 1

ETYMOLOGY: Lat. *colus*, distaff.

SIZE: 75 mm. (3 in.) in height, 35 mm. (1 2/5 in.) in width.

DISTRIBUTION: Arctic to Labrador; dead shells washed up as far south as
 New York.

CHARACTERISTICS: Shell medium, narrowly spindle shaped, strong, chalky.
 Surface has regularly spaced, moderately deep revolving lines.
 Periostracum velvety, horn colored.

This northern species, which is also found in northern Europe, is occasionally found as dead, broken, wave-worn shells as far south as the
beaches of New York. The rough encrustations usually covering all
or most of the shells are the remains of *Hydractinia*, a corallike
animal that lives commensally with hermit crabs. Hence the shells
we find here are strays, brought down by currents and brought
inshore by hermit crabs.

 **Stimpson's Whelk,** *Colus stimpsoni* Mörch (William Stimpson
was a prominent New England malacologist of the nineteenth century) (pl. XV, 2), is much larger, reaching 130 mm. (5 in.) in height.
It is a more fragile shell, and the spiral lines are closely set and
weaker. It occurs from Labrador to North Carolina, but south of
Maine it is found only in deep water or as a stray on the beach.

 **Stone's Whelk,** *Colus stonei* Pilsbry (Witmer Stone was a collec-

tor) (pl. XXIII, 16), is an extinct species occurring as a fossil in
Pleistocene deposits along the coasts of New York and New Jersey.
Specimens are occasionally found washed up on the beaches as far
south as Cape Hatteras, and the species has been collected in fossil
beds on Gardiner's Island in Long Island Sound, and on southern
Nova Scotia. The shell differs from the other species of *Colus* by having a shorter, dumpier shape, a deep suture and swollen body whorl,
and a surface covered with prominent spiral cords. Some authors
place it in the genus *Atractodon* Charlesworth.

The **Pygmy Whelk,** *Colus pygmaeus* Gould (pl. XXIV, 6), looks
like its larger congeners, but it is less than 1 inch in height. This alone
is sufficient to identify it. It is chalk white, with incised spiral lines,
and is as fragile as Stimpson's Whelk. It ranges from the Gulf of
Saint Lawrence to deep water off North Carolina, and is an uncommon live shell in shallow water in northern New England and
Canada. Lucky collectors can sometimes catch a codfish or a halibut
with its stomach bulging with nicely cleaned, though offensively
smelling, specimens.

Genus *Neptunea* Röding

*Neptunea decemcostata* Say
    Ten-ridged Whelk

    Pl. XXI, 16

ETYMOLOGY: Lat. *Neptunus*, god of the sea; *decem costa*, ten rib.

SIZE: 100 mm. (4 in.) in height, 60 mm. (2 1/2 in.) in width.

DISTRIBUTION: Nova Scotia to off North Carolina.

CHARACTERISTICS: Shell large, strong, widely spindle shaped. Grayish white
    or pale or reddish yellow. Surface has 7 to 10 strong, raised, reddish
    brown spiral cords.

This shell, which lobstermen often take up in their pots, is readily
recognized by its strong spiral ridges. Occasional specimens occur on
northern beaches down to Cape Cod. It has been reported as much
esteemed as an article of food, but local fishermen do not eat it. The
Ten-ridged Whelk may be a subspecies of the Northwest Whelk,
*N. lyrata* Gmelin (Gr. *lyra*, lute), a common species from the Arctic
Ocean to the waters off California.

Genus *Cantharus* Röding

*Cantharus tinctus* Conrad
 Gaudy Lesser Whelk

 Pl. XXIV, 7

ETYMOLOGY: Gr. *kantharos*, a tankard or drinking pot used by Bacchus and his followers; Lat. *tingere*, to dye, tinge.

SIZE: 15 to 25 mm. (3/5 to 1 in.) in height, 15 mm. (3/5 in.) in width.

DISTRIBUTION: North Carolina to Florida, Texas, and the West Indies.

CHARACTERISTICS: Shell small, solid, rough, spindle shaped. Color variously purplish, yellowish brown, or blue gray with lighter or whitish splotches, or entirely white. Surface sculpture of low, weak axial ribs crossed by numerous spiral cords forming weak beads at the junctures. Aperture wide, ovate; outer lip thickened, strongly toothed inside, inner lip weakly plaited.

This fairly common shell in shallow water is readily distinguished from *Engina turbinella* by the wider, less constricted aperture, the weaker surface sculpture, and the more ovate shape. It is found alive on grassy bottoms around submerged pilings and jetties and on oyster bars.

The **Cross-barred Lesser Whelk,** *Cantharus cancellaria* Conrad (Lat. *cancelli,* lattice) (pl. XXIV, 8), is much like *C. tinctus,* but differs in being narrower, with a higher spire; it is also less heavy. The surface sculpture consists of sharp spiral threads and narrow axial ribs, which result in a beaded and latticelike structure. It is moderately common in shallow water from the west coast of Florida to Texas and Yucatán, but is rarer off the southeastern shore, from Florida to North Carolina.

The **Spotted Lesser Whelk,** *Engina turbinella* Kiener (Eng. engine; Lat. *turbinella,* little whirlwind) (pl. XXIII, 17), is 11 mm. (about 1/2 in.) in height, 6 mm. (1/4 in.) in width. The small shell is ovate spindle shaped, dark purple or blackish brown, with about ten low, rounded white knobs on the periphery of each whorl; there are also some spiral rows of smaller knobs at the base. The aperture is narrow, and has six to eight whitish teeth on the outer lip. This easily recognized species is fairly common under rocks at low tide. It ranges from the lower Florida Keys to the West Indies.

The **Pisan Lesser Whelk,** *Pisania pusio* Linnaeus (named either for the natives of Pisa, Italy, or for an Admiral Pisani; Lat. *pusio,* little boy) (pl. XXIII, 18), is 25 to 45 mm. (1 to 1 4/5 in.) in height, about

20 mm. (4/5 in.) in width. This small, strong shell is narrowly elongate-ovate in shape. The shiny, smooth surface is purplish brown, with spiral bands of irregular dark and light spots, which are often chevron or arrow shaped. The outer lip is toothed within; the aperture has a short siphonal canal below and a small, rounded sinus above. This species is commonly found on coral reefs near shore; it is taken occasionally in Florida, but it is more common in some places in the West Indies.

FAMILY:

# COLUMBELLIDAE

(*dove shells*)

Dove shells are small, spindle shaped, slender or chunky, smooth to weakly sculptured, moderately shiny, commonly quite colorful. This is a large family of mainly warm-water species, though some are found in temperate seas. Owing to their small size and attractive coloration, they are very popular with necklace makers.

## KEY TO FAMILY COLUMBELLIDAE

* Shell generally smooth, little surface sculpture
** Shell small, less than 8 mm. (1/3 in.) in height, slender — *Mitrella lunata*
** Shell larger, more than 10 mm. (2/5 in.) in height
*** Aperture shorter than the spire, apex generally lost — *Nitidella ocellata*
*** Aperture longer than the spire, apex commonly intact
**** Aperture narrow, sinuous, outer lip considerably thickened in center, toothed within — *Columbella rusticoides*
**** Aperture not sinuous, outer lip not thickened in center — *Nitidella nitida*
* Shell generally rough or with strong axial ribs or ridges

✱ ✱ Shell less than 8 mm. (1/3 in.) in height,
    strongly decussate                      *Anachis obesa*
 ✱ ✱ Shell more than 10 mm. (2/5 in.) in height
✱ ✱ ✱ Shell squat, with deep, evenly spaced
    spiral striae, axial ridges wanting,
    aperture narrow, sinuous         *Columbella mercatoria*
 ✱ ✱ ✱ Shell slender, with axial ridges and
    variously strong spiral striae, aperture
    short, wide, straight
✱ ✱ ✱ ✱ Spiral striae crossing axial ridges,
    subsutural striae strongest       *Anachis translirata*
✱ ✱ ✱ ✱ Spiral striae not crossing axial ridges,
    subsutural striae not strongest     *A. avara*

---

Genus *Columbella* Lamarck

*Columbella mercatoria* Linnaeus
   Common Dove Shell

   Pl. XXIII, 19

ETYMOLOGY: Diminutive of Lat. *columba*, dove; *mercator*, merchant.

SIZE: 17 mm. (about 3/4 in.) in height, 11 mm. (about 1/2 in.) in width.

DISTRIBUTION: Southeastern Florida to West Indies.

CHARACTERISTICS: Shell small, oval, solid, squat. Color variable: yellow,
   pink, or orange background with white and brown interrupted spiral
   bars, often only spotted; surface has numerous deep, well-spaced spiral
   striae. Lip thickened in center with about 12 white teeth, interspaces
   white.

This is an abundant shallow-water species that is, however, not found
on Florida's west coast. Its squat shape and heavy outer lip armed
with white teeth and its bright color make it easily recognizable.
Linnaeus selected the name because the shell often appeared in trade
as necklaces and other ornaments. The generic name *Pyrene* (Pyrene
was the name of a Greek nymph) has been erroneously applied instead of *Columbella*.

   The **Rustic-like Dove Shell,** *Columbella rusticoides* Heilprin (Lat.
*rusticus,* rural) (pl. XXIII, 20), is more slender, with a higher spire, a
more subdued color, and a smoother surface. The outer lip is nar-

rower and the teeth are weaker, their interspaces brownish instead of white. The species ranges from the west coast of Florida to the Florida Keys. It has also been reported near Havana. The name was given by Heilprin because the shell resembles a European shell called *Columbella rustica*.

Genus *Anachis* H. & A. Adams

*Anachis avara* Say
  Greedy Dove Shell

  Pl. XXIV, 9

ETYMOLOGY: Pliny called the diamond *anachis*, but the more usual word in Latin is *antis*; Lat. *avarus*, greedy.

SIZE: 15 mm. (3/5 in.) in height, 6 mm. (1/4 in.) in width.

DISTRIBUTION: Massachusetts to Florida and west to Texas.

CHARACTERISTICS: Shell elevated, high conical, whorls flattened. Sculpture of variable number of raised axial ribs (seven to twenty-one) and numerous spiral cords on the interspaces, but not crossing the raised ribs. Color straw yellow to chestnut brown, usually with conspicuous white, round or elliptical mottlings. Aperture elliptical; outer lip slightly thickened, with four to twelve small teeth. Operculum small, corneous, elliptical.

This graceful dove shell is found in eel grass and on hard bottoms just below mean low water, but specimens are often found washed up on shore. A recent study shows that the southern populations vary from the northern populations in several respects, but not consistently enough to be separated as distinct subspecies. The Texas form has, nevertheless, been called *A. avara semiplicata* Stearns (Lat. *semi plicatus*, half folded). It is glossier than the northern *A. avara*, and less strongly sculptured. The same study concluded that the subspecies *A. avara similis* Ravenel, which appears in older shell books, is unidentifiable. A smaller form, 8 mm. (1/3 in.) in height, without any spiral lirations or striae on the upper whorls, has been called *Anachis floridana* Rehder. It has been reported from near Cape Canaveral, Waveland, and Tampa Bay in southern Florida.

The **Well-ribbed Dove Shell,** *Anachis translirata* Ravenel (Lat. *lira*, ridge between two furrows, and *trans*, across) (pl. XXIV, 10), is larger, 18 mm. (3/4 in.) in height, and proportionately wider. The surface sculpture is stronger, the spiral striae being more noticeable and crossing *over* the axial ridges. This feature, however, is seen only in completely fresh and unworn shells. Identification is made more certain by the presence of a single stria, just below the suture, that is wider and stronger than all the other striae. This stria is absent in *A. avara*. *A. translirata* has a dull surface, and while it resembles *A. avara* in color, it lacks the conspicuous white mottling. The species ranges from Massachusetts to Florida, and is frequently found occupying the same habitat as *A. avara*.

The **Fat Dove Shell,** *Anachis obesa* C. B. Adams (Lat. *obesus*, stout, plump) (pl. XXI, 17), is most easily recognized by its smaller size, reaching only 6 mm. (1/4 in.) in height. The color is whitish with brown bands or entirely reddish brown. The surface is strongly reticulate, but the color bands do not cross the axial ribs. This is a common shallow-water species ranging from Virginia to Florida. It also occurs in the Gulf states and the West Indies.

The **Lunar Dove Shell,** *Mitrella lunata* Say (diminutive of Lat. *mitra*, mitre, and *luna*, moon) (pl. XXIII, 21), is about the same size as the Fat Dove Shell, 5 mm. (1/5 in.) in height, but narrower, and smooth and glossy. The color is variable: often it is reddish brown or fawn, with two or three series of crescent-shaped whitish spots, but brown or whitish unspotted shells, or with variously shaped whitish and brownish markings, also occur. This species ranges from Massachusetts to Florida, Texas, and the West Indies. Specimens can often be taken clinging to seaweed thrown on shore.

Genus *Nitidella* Swainson

*Nitidella nitida* Lamarck
    Glossy Dove Shell

    Pl. XXIII, 22

ETYMOLOGY: Lat. *nitidus*, shining, glistening.

SIZE: 15 mm. (3/5 in.) in height, 7 mm. (about 1/4 in.) in width.

DISTRIBUTION: Southeastern Florida and the West Indies.

CHARACTERISTICS: Shell small, long egg shaped, strong, smooth, glistening. Aperture long, three-fourths of the entire shell. Color whitish, marbled with brown. Operculum small, corneous.

This is a very common shell living under rocks, detritus, and seaweed at low tide.

The **Spotted Dove Shell,** *Nitidella ocellata* Gmelin (diminutive of Lat. *oculus*, eye) (pl. XXIV, 11), is about the same size, but the length

of the aperture is less than one-half the shell. The color is dark
blackish or reddish brown, with many small white dots, the ones
below the suture being the largest. The apex is frequently missing in
mature shells. The species is found from Palm Beach to the Florida
Keys and the West Indies.

FAMILY:

# MELONGENIDAE

(*crown conchs and busycon whelks*)

These snails—with shells mostly large, conic, spindle- or pear-
shaped—are active predators and scavengers. The busycons consume
large numbers of bivalves, opening the clams by placing the lip of
their shell between the clam's valves. Once the valves of the clam are
forced open, the snail inserts its proboscis and consumes the soft
body of the bivalve by rasping away the tissue with its radula. The
proboscis of a 3-inch *Melongena* may be extended as much as 6 inches
to reach the snail's prey. The few species of the family are found in
tropical and temperate waters; the busycons are restricted to the
western Atlantic, and the genus *Melongena* is limited to the New
World. The large, fleshy foot of the busycons (called *scungili*) is
considered to be a delicacy in Italian cuisine.

## KEY TO GENERA
## MELONGENA AND BUSYCON

| | |
|---|---|
| * Shell generally with 1 to 3 rows of sharp, large spines | *Melongena corona* |
| * Shell elongate pear shaped, without spiral rows of large spines | |
| * * Shell with larger or smaller rounded knobs on shoulder of body whorl only | |
| * * * Shell with swollen, rounded ridge around middle of body whorl, sinistral; distribution Gulf of Mexico to Yucatán | *Busycon kieneri* |
| * * * Shell without middle swollen ridge | |
| * * * * Shell almost always sinistral, very large; distribution South Carolina to Yucatán | *B. perversum* |

**\*\*\*\*** Shell almost always dextral, smaller;
 distribution Cape Cod to Florida                    *B. carica*
  **\*\*** Shell with smooth shoulder on body whorl
   when mature
 **\*\*\*** Shell well shouldered, with a wide, deep
  sutural channel; distribution Cape Cod to
  northeastern Florida                              *B. canaliculatum*
 **\*\*\*** Shell with weakly sloping shoulders, sutural
  channel narrow, shallow; distribution north to
  North Carolina only                               *B. spiratum*

---

Genus *Melongena* Schumacher

*Melongena corona* Gmelin
 Crown Conch

 Pl. XV, 6 and 8

ETYMOLOGY: Gr. *melon genos*, a kind of apple; Lat. *corona*, crown.

SIZE: 98 to 205 mm. (4 to 8 in.) in height, 70 to 127 mm. (3 to 5 in.) in width.

DISTRIBUTION: Florida, Alabama, and Yucatán.

CHARACTERISTICS: Shell medium to large, generally thick and solid. Color
 ivory, with variable spiral bands of light brown to dark reddish brown.
 Surface sculpture of one to three spiral rows of usually large, sharp
 spines on the shoulder and various places on the body whorl. Outer lip
 thin, operculum clawlike.

This predatory species is exceedingly variable in shape, size, color,
and nature and number of rows of spines. Clench and Turner (1956)
showed that the young issue from the egg as small but fully formed
snails unable to swim. Hence they tend to stay in one place, and
populations develop with more or less fixed characteristics, different
even from closely neighboring populations. Several of these forms
have been given subspecific names, but their taxonomic value has
been questioned.

Genus *Busycon* Röding

*Busycon carica* Gmelin
 Knobbed Whelk

 Pl. XIII, 3

ETYMOLOGY: Gr. *bousycon*, a large, coarse fig; and Lat. *carica*, a dried fig from Caria, a province in Asia Minor.

SIZE: 150 mm. (6 in.) in height, 75 mm. (3 in.) in width.

DISTRIBUTION: Cape Cod to central eastern Florida.

CHARACTERISTICS: Shell large, dextral, solid, pear shaped. Color yellowish gray, with brownish purple axial streaks in juveniles; interior orange yellow or brick red. Surface smooth, with about nine low tubercles on the shoulder of the body whorl. Operculum strong, brown, corneous.

This species is one of the larger gastropods on the northern part of our coast. It lives in shallow water, generally in bays, but dead shells are frequently thrown up on the beaches by storms. The eggs are enclosed in flattened, membranous capsules the size of a half-dollar piece, attached at one end to a tough, cordlike structure. Though the shell is almost always dextral, sinistral specimens have been reported. Specimens from North Carolina southward are much heavier, and have a prominent ridge crossing the siphonal canal; the name *B. eliceans* Montfort has been applied unnecessarily to this form.

The **Perverse** or **Lightning Whelk,** *Busycon perversum* Linnaeus (Lat. *perversus*, turned to the wrong side) (pl. XIII, 2), attains 450 mm. (16 in.) in height, and is most easily distinguished by being almost always sinistral. The color is grayish or white, and in immature forms pretty, longitudinal, violet brown stripes appear. This shell in recent years was called *B. contrarium* Conrad, which actually is a small, extinct, spineless species. It was also named *B. sinistrum* Hollister. The range of this species, our largest whelk, is from New Jersey to Campeche, Mexico.

**Kiener's Whelk,** *Busycon kieneri* Philippi (named for Louis Charles Kiener, an early French malacologist) (pl. XIII, 1), is also sinistral, but differs by having a very heavy, polished shell with a rounded swollen ridge around the middle of the body whorl. It rarely exceeds 250 mm. (10 in.) in height, and ranges from off western Florida to Yucatán. *B. gibbosum* Conrad is a synonym. Dr. Thomas E. Pulley considers this to be a variant of the Perverse Whelk, for he reports that intergrades between the two forms occur frequently.

The **Pear Whelk,** *Busycon spiratum* Lamarck (Lat. *spira*, coiled) (pl. XV, 5), grows to 125 mm. (5 in.) in height and 75 mm. (3 in.) in width. It has smooth, sloping shoulders, with a moderately deep, narrowly channeled suture. The surface has fine spiral sculpture, and the color is creamy, with irregular brown axial lines. It ranges from

North Carolina to Florida and the Gulf states. This shell is much stronger than the fig shells (genus *Ficus*) (see page 113), which it somewhat resembles in shape. The species was formerly called *B. pyrum* Dillwyn, which is a later name. Additionally, several growth forms of this species have been named. Shells with smoothly rounded whorls were called *B. pyruloides* Say; those with a keel on the shoulder, *B. plagosus* Conrad; and narrow, high-spired forms, *B. texanum* and *B. galvestonense* Hollister.

The **Channeled Whelk,** *Busycon canaliculatum* Say (Lat. *canalis,* channel) (pl. XIV, 1), grows to 200 mm. (8 in.) in height and 125 mm. (5 in.) in width. It is most easily recognized by the deep, widely channeled suture and the heavy, velvety periostracum. The shell is thin, yellow or fawn colored; the outer lip is thin and the whorls strongly shouldered, the shoulders being prettily beaded in very young specimens. The species lives in shallow water in bays, and ranges from Cape Cod to Saint Augustine, Florida.

---

FAMILY:

# NASSARIIDAE
(*basket shells*)

These shells are small, conic, and either smooth or well sculptured. The nuclear whorls are finely grooved. Many forms have a parietal shield. The snails are carnivores, although some live on diatoms and consume other plant life in the absence of carrion. This is a world-wide group, often occurring locally in vast numbers.

---

## KEY TO GENERA NASSARIUS AND ILYANASSA

* Shell with enameled parietal shield      *Nassarius vibex*
* Shell without parietal shield
** Suture deep, whorls shouldered above      *N. trivittatus*
** Suture shallow, whorls not shouldered
*** Spire longer than body whorl      *N. acutus*
*** Spire and body whorl approximately equal

**** Shell light colored, surface sculpture strong;
    range mainly southern                        *N. albus*

**** Shell dark colored, surface sculpture weak;
    range mainly northern                    *Ilyanassa obsoleta*

---

Genus *Nassarius* Dumeril

*Nassarius vibex* Say
   Bruised Basket Shell

   Pl. XXIII, 23

ETYMOLOGY: Lat. *nassa*, a wicker basket for catching fish; *vibex*, bruise.

SIZE: 16 mm. (2/3 in.) in height, 9 mm. (about 2/5 in.) in width.

DISTRIBUTION: Cape Cod to Florida and the West Indies.

CHARACTERISTICS: Shell small, widely conic, chunky, strong. Grayish brown
   or ashen, with brown or purplish brown splotches. Surface roughened
   by about a dozen heavily beaded or tuberculated axial ridges. Aperture
   enameled, with the enamel extending over part of the adjacent body
   whorl as a parietal shield. Operculum narrow, corneous.

This small basket shell is commoner in the south than in the north,
where it occurs in shallow water in a few restricted localities. It is
most easily recognized by its dark color, dumpy shape, and the enamel
wash extending over the parietal area.

   The **Narrow Basket Shell,** *Nassarius acutus* Say (Lat. *acutus,*
sharp) (pl. XXIII, 24), is approximately the same size, but it is a
narrower shell, with the spire longer than the body whorl. The
enameled parietal shield is wanting, and the color is lighter: cream-
white to yellowish, occasionally with a narrow brown band connecting the tubercles on the axial ridges. The species ranges from North
Carolina to Florida and Texas.

   The **White Basket Shell,** *Nassarius albus* Say (Lat. *albus,* white)
(pl. XXIII, 25), is also a chunky shell, 8 to 15 mm. (1/3 to 3/5 in.) in
height, white or pale yellow generally spotted with brown. It lacks
the parietal shield of *N. vibex,* and the body whorl and spire are
about the same size. It is a common shell, and ranges from North
Carolina to Florida and the West Indies. In older books it is called
*N. ambiguus* Pulteney, but that name was used earlier for a different

species. *N. consensus* Ravenel is today considered to be merely a variation of *N. albus.*

The **Three-lined Basket Shell,** *Nassarius trivittatus* Say (Lat. *tri vitta,* three-banded) (pl. XXIII, 26), is about 18 mm. (3/4 in.) high, rather light shelled, and greenish or yellowish white, occasionally with light brown bands. The surface is regularly latticed, and the suture is deep and the whorls shelved above. This latter characteristic alone is enough to identify it. The outer lip is thin, and the corneous operculum has one edge shallowly serrated. It is a northern species, and ranges from Nova Scotia to Georgia.

The **Mud Basket Shell,** *Ilyanassa obsoleta* Say (Gr. *ilys* and Lat. *nassa,* muddy fishing basket; Lat. *obsoleta,* worn out, decayed) (pl. XXV, 1), can reach 25 mm. (1 in.) in height, but is usually smaller. It is dark reddish brown, but thickly encrusted with mud and algae. The shell has a weak lattice surface sculpture, and a bluish white band can frequently be seen in the aperture. The corneous operculum has smooth edges. This is an overabundant species living on mud flats from the Gulf of Saint Lawrence to northern Florida, and has been introduced on the west coast. The shells are usually heavily eroded. Julia Gardner, the eminent American paleontologist, believes the name was inspired by the weak surface sculpture, but Thomas Say probably had the eroded condition of the shells in mind when he decided to call the species worn out or decayed. Until recently *Ilyanassa* was considered only as a subgenus of *Nassarius,* but studies of feeding habits and radular morphology convinced most malacologists that the name has generic value.

---

FAMILY:

# FASCIOLARIIDAE

*(tulip shells and horse conch)*

These shells are large, strong, thick, and spindle shaped, with an elevated spire. There are generally two to four shallow folds (plicae) on the columella. This family boasts the largest gastropod on the East Coast, a species that is also one of the largest living snails. They occur in warmer seas in shallow waters, and are active predators on clams and gastropods.

---

# KEY TO GENERA FASCIOLARIA, PLEUROPLOCA, AND LEUCOZONIA

| | |
|---|---|
| * Shell small, usually less than 50 mm. (2 in.) in height | |
| * * Shell, including shoulder nodules, brown, usually with a narrow white basal ridge terminating in a low palatal spine | *Leucozonia nassa* |
| * * Shell brown to blackish, shoulder nodules and smaller basal tubercles white | *L. ocellata* |
| * Shell large to very large, 100 to 600 mm. (4 to 24 in.) in height | |
| * * Shell huge, 600 mm. (24 in.) in height, strongly sculptured with rounded axial ridges and spiral cords | *Pleuroploca gigantea* |
| * * Shell 100 to 150 mm. (4 to 6 in.) in height, little surface sculpture | |
| * * * Shell ornamented with narrow, spaced brown bands, with a prominent ridge at upper angle of aperture | *Fasciolaria hunteria* |
| * * * Shell mottled, suffused with brown color, color bands indefinite, apertural lamella lacking | *F. tulipa* |

---

Genus *Fasciolaria* Lamarck

*Fasciolaria tulipa* Linnaeus
   True Tulip Shell

   Pl. XIV, 5

ETYMOLOGY: Lat. *fasciola*, small band or bandage; and *tulipa*, a flower.

SIZE: Up to 150 mm. (6 in.) in height, 80 mm. (3 in.) in width.

DISTRIBUTION: North Carolina to Florida and the West Indies.

CHARACTERISTICS: Shell large, strong, spindle shaped, smooth except for two or three narrow spiral grooves below the suture where the surface is wrinkled. Color variable, light orange or red with interrupted, indefinite, blotched bands of brown and buff. Columella has two oblique shallow folds below.

This beautiful shallow-water species is quite common in the southern part of its range. Its large, graceful, spindle-shaped shell and handsome but subdued coloring always arouse admiration. Giant specimens reach 250 mm. (10 in.) in height, and in the lower Keys a beautiful orange-red variety is frequently found.

The **Banded Tulip Shell,** *Fasciolaria hunteria* Perry (Captain John Hunter was an early governor of New South Wales, Australia) (pl. XIV, 4), is smaller, reaching about 100 mm. (4 in.) in height. It has the same graceful shape as *F. tulipa,* but the shell is entirely smooth and the mottled buff ground color is decorated with straight, well-defined, narrow brown spiral bands. At the upper angle of the aperture a white parietal ridge is formed. This species shares the same northern range as *F. tulipa.* It was formerly known as *F. distans* Lamarck, and some authors consider it to be a subspecies of *F. lilium* Fischer, a similar species with several named forms living in the Gulf of Mexico and southward to Yucatán.

Genus *Pleuroploca* P. Fischer

*Pleuroploca gigantea* Kiener
Florida Horse Conch

Pls. X, 4, and XIV, 3

ETYMOLOGY: Gr. *pleuron,* rib or side, and *ploke,* anything plaited; Lat. *gigantea,* gigantic.

SIZE: Up to 600 mm. (2 ft.) in height, 150 mm. (6 in.) in width.

DISTRIBUTION: North Carolina to Florida, Texas, and Mexico.

CHARACTERISTICS: Shell huge, spindle shaped, very strong and heavy. Color grayish white to pale salmon under a rough, brown strong flaky periostracum; aperture orange. Surface sculpture of heavy, wide, rounded axial ridges crossed by numerous strong spiral cords. Columella with three strong diagonal folds. Operculum oval, corneous, brown.

This is the largest gastropod in our area and one of the largest in the world, only a single Indo-Pacific species exceeding it in size. The young have a bright orange shell, and the predaceous animal at all stages is a brilliant red. Large specimens live well in saltwater tanks, and are frequently exhibited in public aquariums.

Genus *Leucozonia* Gray

*Leucozonia nassa* Gmelin
Common Lesser Tulip Shell

Pl. XXV, 2

ETYMOLOGY: Gr. *leukos zone*, white belt or girdle; Lat. *nassa*, a wicker basket for catching fish.

SIZE: 35 to 50 mm. (1 2/5 to 2 in.) in height, 25 mm. (1 in.) in width.

DISTRIBUTION: Florida to the West Indies.

CHARACTERISTICS: Shell small, squat, spindle shaped, solid. Light to dark brown, moderately glossy, usually with a narrow white band at the base that commonly terminates in a small spine at the outer lip. Surface sculpture of about nine wide, blunt shoulder nodules and numerous faint spiral striae. Columella white, with three or four weak folds.

This small member of the tulip shells has the spindle-shaped shell and the few shallow columellar folds characteristic of the family. The bright red extruded animal forms a pleasing contrast with the rich brown color of the shell. The species is moderately common in shallow water, but does not occur in Texas. It was formerly called *Leucozonia cingulifera* Lamarck (Lat. *cingulum fero*, belt-bearing).

The **White-spotted Lesser Tulip Shell,** *Leucozonia ocellata* Gmelin (diminutive of Lat. *oculus*, eye) (pl. XXV, 3), is a little smaller, reaching only 25 mm. (1 in.) in height, but it has the same type of squat, spindle-shaped, heavy shell. The color is brown to blackish, but the large, rounded shoulder nodules are white, as are the three to four spiral rows of smooth tubercles below. This species has the same range and habitat as *L. nassa.*

SUPERFAMILY:

# VOLUTACEA

FAMILY:

# VOLUTIDAE

(*volutes*)

This is a family of beautiful shells highly prized by collectors. The wide aperture is notched in front and the columella commonly bears several folds. The apex may originate in a large bulbous whorl. These carnivorous snails are largely tropical in distribution, but cold-water forms are also known, some from very deep water.

Genus *Scaphella* Swainson

*Scaphella junonia* Lamarck
Juno's Volute

Pl. XIV, 2

ETYMOLOGY: Diminutive of Gr. *skaphe,* a bowl or dug-out boat; Juno was the queen of the gods in Roman mythology.

SIZE: 115 mm. (4 3/5 in.) in height, 47 mm. (almost 2 in.) in width.

DISTRIBUTION: North Carolina to Florida.

CHARACTERISTICS: Shell large, smooth, solid, moderately glossy, broadly spindle-shaped. Color cream, decorated with spiral rows of small reddish brown dots. Aperture long, narrow. Columella has four folds. Operculum, small, corneous.

The volutes are a largely tropical family of very attractive and desirable shells. They can be recognized by their broadly spindle shape and by the usual presence of two or more strong oblique folds on the columella. The few species found on the East Coast all live in deep water, and are mostly obtained by scuba diving or dredging. The Juno Volute is the only one that is occasionally driven ashore by strong winds and waves, especially on Florida's west coast. The monographs by Clench (1946) and Weaver and duPont (1970) should be consulted for a discussion of the other Floridian volutes.

---

FAMILY:

# OLIVIDAE
(*olive shells*)

Olive shells are small to moderate in size, the body whorl enlarged and concealing all the other whorls except at the apex. The columella bears several narrow wrinkles or folds. The shell surface is smooth, shiny, and often colorful. These snails burrow into sandy bottoms in shallow, warmer waters, where they prey on other sand dwellers.

Genus *Oliva* Bruguière

*Oliva sayana* Ravenel
Lettered Olive

Pl. XV, 3; XXV, 4

ETYMOLOGY: Lat. *oliva*, olive; Thomas Say (1787–1834) is called the father of American conchology.

SIZE: 50 to 60 mm. in height (2 to 2 1/2 in.), 25 mm. (1 in.) in width.

DISTRIBUTION: North Carolina to Florida and the Gulf States.

CHARACTERISTICS: Shell medium, elongate oval or olive shaped; spire very low; smooth, glossy, strong. Color grayish tan, closely ornamented with numerous purplish and chocolate brown zigzag markings. Aperture narrow, columella with numerous sharp folds; operculum and periostracum lacking.

This is the commonest eastern American representative of a widely ranging tropical and subtropical family. These predaceous and nocturnal animals live in sand. The shell is protected by propodia, two mantlelike flaps. The color of the present species varies in intensity, some specimens being quite pale or even all white, others with strong color bands. A golden variety named *citrina* by Johnson is particularly striking.

The **Netted Olive,** *Oliva reticularis* Lamarck (Lat. *reticulum*, diminutive of *rete*, net) (pl. XXV, 5), is smaller, reaching only 40 mm. (1 3/5 in.) in height. The color pattern of the shells is roughly similar to that of *O. sayana*, but decidedly paler. Dr. Abbott points out that *O. reticularis* furthermore differs from *O. sayana* by having a much shallower canal at the suture, the apical whorls slightly convex rather than concave, and the sides more swollen. It is a rare species off South Carolina to southern Florida, but common in the West Indies.

## KEY TO GENERA OLIVELLA AND JASPIDELLA

* Shell 5 to 6 mm. (1/5 to 1/4 in.) in height, generally dark mahogany in color      *Olivella pusilla*
* Shell larger, 11 to 30 mm. (about 1/2 to 1 1/5 in.), color varied but not mahogany
** Shell with unglazed parietal wall      *Jaspidella jaspidea*
** Shell with glazed parietal wall
*** Shell entirely white, often with bluish tinge, apex occasionally orange or purplish      *Olivella floralia*
*** Shell whitish with some sort of color pattern

\* \* \* \* Shell with wide, bluish gray spiral bands,
     parietal callus well developed      *O. mutica*

\* \* \* \* Color pattern of brown shadings, fasciole
     white, callus lacking      *O. nivea*

---

Genus *Olivella* Swainson

*Olivella mutica* Say
    Variable Dwarf Olive

    Pl. XXV, 6

ETYMOLOGY: Diminutive of Lat. *oliva*, olive; *mutilus*, mutilated, or *mutare*, to change.

SIZE: 10 mm. (2/5 in.) in height, 6 mm. (1/4 in.) in width.

DISTRIBUTION: Cape Hatteras to Florida and the Bahamas.

CHARACTERISTICS: Shell small, elongate oval, spire well raised, glossy, strong. Color variable, gray to light brown or yellowish, with wide, bluish gray spiral bands. Upper parietal wall has a well-developed callus. Operculum thin, corneous.

This is one of the commonest of the dwarf olive shells in our area. The animals are predators living in water-logged sand in shallow depths. The dwarf olives differ from the true olives, in addition to their smaller size, by having higher spires and by possessing an operculum.

The **Snowy Dwarf Olive,** *Olivella nivea* Gmelin (Lat. *niveus,* pertaining to snow) (pl. XXV, 7), reaches 25 mm. (1 in.) in height. The shell is white with shadings of brown, commonly with two bands of darker purplish brown; the fasciole—the wide, raised spiral ridge—at the base of the shell is all white. The species ranges from Miami to the Florida Keys, where it used to be much more plentiful. It also occurs in the West Indies.

The **Tiny Dwarf Olive,** *Olivella pusilla* Marrat (Lat. *pusillus,* very little) (pl. XXV, 8), is only 5 to 6 mm. (1/5 to 1/4 in.) in height, and quite narrow. The color varies in tones of rich mahogany brown, but some individuals are gray or even white. This is the commonest dwarf olive in Florida, living in shallow water in bays, especially on the west coast.

The **Rice** or **Flowery Dwarf Olive,** *Olivella floralia* Duclos (Lat.

*floralis,* belonging to Flora, goddess of flowers) (pl. XXV, 9), reaches 15 mm. (3/5 in.) in height. It is more slender than *O. mutica* or *O. nivea,* and the apex is quite sharp. The shell is all white, often with a bluish tinge, and the apex is sometimes orange or purplish. This common shallow-water species ranges from North Carolina to the West Indies.

The **Jasper Dwarf Olive,** *Jaspidella jaspidea* Gmelin (Lat. *iaspis,* jasper, a precious stone) (pl. XXV, 10), reaches 18 mm. (about 4/5 in.) in height. It is usually white or brown, often finely flecked with brown lines; the fasciole, or basal ridge, has irregular brown spots or bars. It is distinguished from all the other dwarf olives by the fact that it is the only one that has an unglazed, dull parietal wall; in all other species the parietal wall is richly glazed. It is this fact, plus some peculiarities in the radular teeth, that induced Dr. Olsson to erect the genus *Jaspidella* for it in 1956. It ranges from the east coast of Florida to the West Indies.

---

FAMILY:

# VASIDAE

(*vase shells*)

These are heavy and ponderous shells, sculpture consisting of spiral ridges crossed by vertical ribs to produce sharp nodes at the shoulders; the inner lip has strong spiral cords. The periostracum may be thick or scaly, the operculum horny. This is a small group confined to shallower waters in warmer seas.

Genus *Turbinella* Lamarck

*Turbinella angulata* Lightfoot
    West Indian Chank Shell

    Pl. X, 5

ETYMOLOGY: Diminutive of Lat. *turbo,* spinning top; *angulatus,* angular.

SIZE: 180 to 360 mm. (7 to 14 in.) in height, 95 to 152 mm. (4 to 6 in.) in width.

DISTRIBUTION: Key West, Florida, to the Bahamas and the Caribbean.

CHARACTERISTICS: Shell huge, heavy, solid, broadly spindle shaped. Color creamy white under a thick, light brown periostracum. Aperture yellowish, pink, or orange; in adults, has a richly colored, porcelainlike parietal shield. Columella with 3 narrow horizontal folds. Sculpture of six to eight prominent blunt tubercles on the top of each whorl and rather weak spiral lines, which are absent on the center of the body whorl. Operculum corneous, hard, dark brown.

This huge and heavy shell, readily recognized by the large, rounded tubercles on the shoulders of the whorls, is a common species in shallow water in the Bahamas, and several have been taken in Key West and the Dry Tortugas. However, chances are that the souvenir specimens on sale in Miami probably came from the Bahamas. The immature forms lack the brilliantly colored parietal shield, and the spiral lines generally cover the entire shell. The earlier generic name, *Xancus* Röding, 1798 (Sanskrit, *sankha*, shell), was set aside by a special opinion of the International Commission on Zoological Nomenclature in favor of the later name, *Turbinella* Lamarck, 1799, for the convenience of anthropologists and businessmen who deal in the Indian Sacred Chank Shell, *Turbinella pyrum* Linnaeus, which is revered in the Hindu religion. Some authors place the chank shells in their own family, Turbinellidae, which was formerly called Xancidae.

Genus *Vasum* Röding

*Vasum muricatum* Born
Caribbean Vase Shell

Pls. XV, 9; XXV, 11

ETYMOLOGY: Lat. *vasum*, vase; *muricatus*, from *murex*, a sharp, pointed stone, or purple shell.

SIZE: 60 to 125 mm. (2 1/2 to 5 in.) in height, 62 to 80 mm. (2 1/2 to 3 1/2 in.) in width.

DISTRIBUTION: Southern Florida to the West Indies and Central America.

CHARACTERISTICS: Shell medium, solid, vase shaped, heavy, rough. Color white under a strong, very thick, dark periostracum. Surface sculpture of fine axial threads and rough, strong spiral cords, with one or two spiral rows of large blunt spines at the shoulder and two to five rows at the base; aperture narrow, white with a purplish tinge. Several folds in the center of the columella. Operculum corneous, thick, claw-shaped.

This is a not-uncommon shallow-water shell that prefers sheltered waters for its habitat. The rough, heavy, solid vase-shaped shell is not easily confused with any other species. There is some variation in the size and number of shoulder spines.

FAMILY:

# MARGINELLIDAE

*(margin or rim shells)*

This is a family of mostly small, highly polished, porcelainlike (porcelaneous) shells living in sand in shallow water, mostly in warmer seas. The body whorl usually covers most of the shell, and the outer lip is generally thickened by a rounded margin; hence the name "margin shells." The colorful animals have a wide, lacelike mantle that envelops the shell when it crawls. They are active carnivores.

## KEY TO FAMILY MARGINELLIDAE

    * Shell very small, 2 to 4 mm. (1/12 to 1/6 in.) in height

    ** Shell white to cream with orange bands, spire 1/2 height of body whorl     *Dentimargo aureocincta*

    ** Shell white, unbanded, spire less than one-half of body whorl

    *** Shell globular, aperture as long as shell, apex submerged     *Granulina ovuliformis*

    *** Shell pear shaped, spire low but distinct, aperture shorter than shell     *Granula lavalleeana*

    * Shell larger, 6 to 19 mm. (1/4 to about 4/5 in.)

    ** Spire high, one-half height of body whorl, color tan     *Dentimargo eburneola*

    ** Spire low or submerged

    *** Shell narrow, almost cylindrical

    **** Shell thin, translucent, outer lip concave in center, found only on west coast of Florida     *Volvarina veliei*

    **** Shell strong, opaque

    ***** Shell whitish tan, with 3 bright orange bands     *V. avena*

    ***** Shell white, with 3 indistinct straw-colored areas at suture, center, and base     *V. avenacea*

    *** Shell pear shaped or rounded conic, spire low, blunt

* * * * Shell with spire submerged, surface
colorful, marked with color bands and
undulate axial lines — *Persicula catenata*

* * * * Shell white with bluish or pinkish
tinge, never with color bands or
surface spots — *Prunum bellum*

* * * * Shell with blunt, low spire, outer lip
with strongly raised margin, shell
usually with 3 faint color bands

* * * * * Shell base-color golden or brownish
orange, not spotted, color bands
sometimes absent — *P. apicinum*

* * * * * Shell color pale tan or ivory, surface
spotted or flecked

* * * * * * Shell narrow; range South Carolina,
New Jersey — *P. roscidum*

* * * * * * Shell broad; range from southeastern
Florida to the Caribbean — *P. guttatum*

---

Genus *Dentimargo* Cossmann

*Dentimargo aureocincta* Stearns
Golden-lined Margin Shell

Pl. XXV, 12

ETYMOLOGY: Lat. *dentis margo*, tooth edge, rim; Lat. *aurum cingulum*, gold belt.

SIZE: 4 mm. (1/6 in.) in height, 1.75 mm. (1/12 in.) in width.

DISTRIBUTION: North Carolina to the Caribbean.

CHARACTERISTICS: Shell very small, glossy, rounded conic or pear shaped; spire well raised, about one-half the height of the body whorl. Color white to cream, with two narrow pale orange bands. Columella with four oblique folds, outer lip weakly toothed, operculum wanting.

Shells of this common species may be taken intertidally to depths of more than 500 feet. These margin shells were formerly placed in the genus *Marginella* Lamarck, but living representatives of this genus do not occur in the New World, according to Barry Roth and Eugene V. Coan.

The **Tan Margin Shell,** *Dentimargo eburneola* Conrad (Lat. *eburneous*, pertaining to ivory) (pl. XXV, 13), is larger, reaching 9 mm. in height. It has the high spire of the genus *Dentimargo,* and is easily recognized by its yellow tan to yellowish shell, without bands or spots. It ranges from North Carolina to the Caribbean. Until recently it was called *Marginella denticulata* Conrad.

Genus *Prunum* Herrmannsen

*Prunum apicinum* Menke
   Plum Margin Shell

   Pl. XXIV, 12

ETYMOLOGY: Lat. *prunum,* plum; *apex,* point.

SIZE: 11 mm. (about 1/2 in.), in height, 7 mm. (about 1/4 in.) in width.

DISTRIBUTION: North Carolina to the Gulf states and the West Indies.

CHARACTERISTICS: Shell small, very glossy, strong, roundly conic; spire distinct but very slightly raised. Outer lip with strong, thickened margin, the upper termination partly covering the spire. Color golden to brownish orange, commonly with three broad, faint, darker color bands. Outer lip untoothed, and with two or three brown spots.

This is by far the commonest margin shell in our area, living in shallow grassy areas. In Florida an occasional gray specimen is found. The members of the genus *Prunum* have a low, blunt spire, and the nuclear whorls may be dark colored.

The **White-spotted Margin Shell,** *Prunum guttatum* Dillwyn (Lat. *guttae,* specks) (pl. XXV, 14), is much larger, reaching 22 mm. (about 4/5 in.) in height. The color is pale tan, with three faint violet bands on the body whorl, and the entire surface is irregularly spotted with white flecks. The thickened, heavily margined outer lip bears two to three dark spots. This is a common species living in shallow water in coral and sand, and ranging from southeastern Florida to the Caribbean.

The **Dewy Margin Shell,** *Prunum roscidum* Redfield (Lat. *roscidus,* dewy) (pl. XXV, 15), is only 6 mm. (1/4 in.) high, and resembles *P. apicinum* except that it is noticeably narrower. It is ivory white to pinkish gray in color, with three very faint darker bands; the surface is spotted with faint, irregularly formed whitish spots. This rather uncommon species is occasionally found as far north as Cape May, New Jersey, and ranges southward to South Carolina.

The **Handsome Margin Shell,** *Prunum bellum* Conrad (Lat. *bellus,* handsome, beautiful) (pl. XXIV, 13), reaches only 6 mm. (1/4 in.) in height. It is a glossy white shell, often with a bluish or rosy tint.

The untoothed outer lip is rather thick. This species ranges from North Carolina to Key West, and is common in moderately deep water.

The **Chained Margin Shell,** *Persicula catenata* Montagu (diminutive of Lat. *persicus,* pear; Lat. *catenatus,* chained) (pl. XXV, 16), is 6 mm. (1/4 in.) in height. It is a beautiful shell, readily recognized by the tan surface ornamented with strongly undulate reddish brown axial lines and three dark spiral bands, separated by bands of elongate white spots that are set off by narrow, dark, V-shaped markings. The spire is sunken below the upper margin of the body whorl. It ranges from southeast Florida to the West Indies, although it is not commonly found.

The **Tiny Margin,** or **Snow Flake, Shell,** *Granula lavalleeana* Orbigny (diminutive of Lat. *granum,* seed, grain; F. Lavallée, a collector, was vice-consul in Trinidad) (pl. XXI, 18), is one of the smallest margin shells in our area, reaching only 3 mm. (1/8 in.) in height. It has the ovate shape of *P. apicinum,* but is completely white. The present species was formerly called *Persicula minuta* Pfeiffer.

Genus *Volvarina* Hinds

*Volvarina avena* Kiener
Oat-grained Margin Shell

Pl. XXIV, 14

ETYMOLOGY: Lat. *volvere,* to roll; *avena,* oat.

SIZE: 6 to 12 mm. (1/4 to 1/2 in.) in height, 4 mm. (1/6 in.) in width.

DISTRIBUTION: North Carolina to the West Indies.

CHARACTERISTICS: Shell small, long, narrow, glossy; spire rounded, moderately raised. Color whitish tan, with three well marked orange bands.

This species is readily recognized by the long, narrow, often cylindrical shape, different from the usual ovate shape of other margin shell species, and the distinct orange bands. It is one of the commonest margin shells in our area. This and the following two species were formerly placed in the genus *Hyalina* Schumacher.

The **Little Oat Margin Shell,** *Volvarina avenacea* Deshayes (Lat. *avenaceus,* resembling oats) (pl. XXV, 17), is usually smaller than *V. avena,* and readily distinguished by its pure, opaque white color with a very faint, indistinct area of straw color below the suture, at the middle of the body whorl, and near the base. It has the long, narrow outline of its genus. This is a common shallow-water shell, ranging from North Carolina to the West Indies. *V. succinea* Conrad is a synonymic form in which most of the shell is amber colored.

**Velie's Margin Shell,** *Volvarina veliei* Pilsbry (named for Dr. J. W. Velie, who first collected the species) (pl. XXIV, 15), is 12 mm. (1/2 in.) high. It is uncommonly thin in texture for a margin shell, which are usually quite strong. It is yellowish to whitish in color, the outer lip thick and concave at the center. It is commonly found on mud flats living inside the valves of dead pen shells, genus *Atrina,* on the west coast of Florida. Specimens have been dredged off South Carolina.

The **Teardrop Margin Shell,** *Granulina ovuliformis* Orbigny (diminutive of Lat. *granum,* seed, grain; Lat. *ovuli formis,* egg shaped) (pl. XXV, 18), is a tiny shell only 3 mm. (1/8 in.) in height. It is globular in shape, glossy, and white. The aperture reaches beyond the hidden apex and is as long as the entire shell. The marginellid columellar folds are minute. This tiny margin shell is common in shallow water, and is often found in beach drift from North Carolina to the West Indies. It is not easily confused with *Granula lavalleeana,* although they are the same size and color.

SUPERFAMILY:

# MITRACEA

FAMILY:

# MITRIDAE
(*miter shells*)

Miter shells are generally spindle shaped, with a high spire; those in our area are quite small. The largest, most colorful, and most desirable forms live in the Indo-Pacific region. Most miters have a series of plicae, or folds, on the columella, the uppermost being the largest. The animals are carnivores living in sand, under rocks, and on coral reefs.

# KEY TO GENERA
# MITRA, VEXILLUM, AND THALA

\* Shell reaching 24 to 30 mm. (about 1 to 1 1/5 in.) in height

\*\* Shell orange to brownish orange, axial ribs strongly beaded                                    *Mitra nodulosa*

\*\* Shell yellow or fawn colored, surface sculpture of weak spiral lines only                        *M. barbadensis*

  \* Shell reaching only 6 to 12 mm. (1/4 to 1/2 in.) in height

\*\* Shell very small, narrow, 6 mm. (1/4 in.) in height, dark brown, surface sculptured with lines crossing at right angles                             *Thala foveata*

\*\* Shell reaching 12 mm. (1/2 in.) in height, sculptured with low, widely spaced axial ribs, a white band on body whorl                            *Vexillum albocincta*

---

Genus *Mitra* Lamarck

*Mitra nodulosa* Gmelin
    Beaded Miter Shell

    Pl. XXIV, 16

ETYMOLOGY: Gr. *mitra*, turban; diminutive of Lat. *nodosus*, full of knots.

SIZE: 25 mm. (1 in.) in height, 11 mm. (about 1/2 in.) in width.

DISTRIBUTION: North Carolina to the West Indies.

CHARACTERISTICS: Shell small, narrowly ovate, spire high, solid, glossy; sculptured with strong beaded axial ribs. Color orange to brownish orange. Columella with 3 strong white folds, the uppermost the largest.

This small representative of a large and very beautiful warm-water family is a very common shell, frequently found washed up on shore. It lives in shallow water under rocks. Like many species of the family Volutidae, Mitridae also have oblique folds on the columella, but in the latter case the uppermost is usually the largest.

The **Barbados Miter,** *Mitra barbadensis* Gmelin (pl. XXIV, 17), reaches 30 mm. (1 1/5 in.) in height, and is quite similar to the Beaded Miter in shape. It differs in having a much smoother surface, sculptured only with very weak spiral threads. The suture is shallow and the sides almost flat. In color it is yellow brown to fawn, with occasional whitish flecks. This is a common beach and shallow-water shell, ranging from southeastern Florida to the West Indies.

The **Dwarf Florida Miter,** *Thala foveata* Sowerby (Lat. *fovea,* hole) (pl. XXV, 19), is much smaller, reaching only 6 mm. (1/4 in.) in height. It is dark brown in color, and the surface is strongly and regularly marked with nodulose spiral and axial ridges. It is found in southeastern Florida, and is not uncommon under stones in shallow water. Formerly placed in the genus *Mitra.* Dall's *Mitra floridana* is a synonym.

The **White-banded Miter,** *Vexillum albocincta* C. B. Adams (Lat. *albus cincta,* white girdle) (pl. XXV, 20), is only 12 mm. (1/2 in.) high. It is broadly spindle shaped, and weakly sculptured with low, widely separated axial ribs. The color is chocolate brown, with a narrow white band above the center of the body whorl. The four columella folds are brown, the uppermost being the largest. It ranges from southeastern Florida to the West Indies. Until recently it was called *Mitra sulcata* Gmelin, an unavailable name.

---

FAMILY:

# CANCELLARIIDAE

(*nutmeg, or cross-barred shells*)

These shells are moderate to small in size, the outer surface strongly cross-ribbed or latticed (cancellated), the columella commonly with strong folds, the outer lip ridged within. An operculum is lacking. The radular teeth are poorly developed, or the radula may be wanting. These snails live in shallow to deep water, generally in warmer seas, but some genera occur in cooler climes. Many bizarre forms are highly prized by collectors.

Genus *Cancellaria* Lamarck

*Cancellaria reticulata* Linnaeus
    Common Nutmeg

    Pl. XXV, 21

ETYMOLOGY: Lat. *cancelli,* a grating made like a lattice; diminutive of Lat. *rete,* net.

SIZE: 26 to 55 mm. (about 1 to 2 1/5 in.) in height, 32 mm. (about 1 1/4 in.) in width.

DISTRIBUTION: North Carolina to Florida and Texas.

CHARACTERISTICS: Shell medium, ovate conic, strong, surface strongly cross-ribbed or reticulate. Columella with two or three strong folds, the central or uppermost being the largest. Outer lip with evenly spaced, narrow ridges within. Color cream, irregularly banded with reddish brown markings, often in wide bands.

This is a very common Florida beach shell, living everywhere in shallow water. The rough surface, generally reddish brown color, and strong columellar folds make it easy to recognize. Occasionally completely white individuals are found. A much smoother form from the Florida Keys has been named *C. reticulata adelae* Pilsbry. This form is not common.

The **Delicate Nutmeg,** *Trigonostoma tenerum* Philippi (Gr. *trigonos stoma,* triangular mouth; Lat. *tener,* delicate, tender) (pl. XXV, 22), reaches 19 mm. (about 4/5 in.) in height and a little less in width. It is thin but fairly strong, and the surface bears the characteristic cross-ribbed surface. The aperture is roughly triangular in shape, extended in an acute angle below, and with the lips above somewhat flaring; the umbilicus is large and funnel shaped. In color the shell is a light reddish brown. This is an uncommon species found in sand and mud along the southwest coast of Florida.

SUPERFAMILY:

# CONACEA

FAMILY:

# CONIDAE
(*cone shells*)

Cone shells vary from small to very large, the body whorl constituting most of the shell, with the spire varying from nearly flat to highly elevated. The aperture is long and narrow, and the operculum, when present, is small, incapable of closing the aperture. The beguiling shape and frequently rich coloration make this one of the most highly valued family of shells for collectors. The poison from these predaceous snails can be toxic to man, and human deaths have resulted from the sting of some South Sea species.

## KEY TO GENUS CONUS

* Shell with strongly raised pyramidal spire, whorls usually stepped

** Shell large, reaching 48 mm. (about 2 in.), the surface of the upper half quite smooth, faint spiral lines on the lower half ............ *Conus floridanus*

** Shell small, reaching only 25 mm. (about 1 in.) in height

*** Shell narrow, sides straight, strong spiral grooves on lower half, color light ............ *C. jaspideus stearnsii*

*** Shell stout, sides rounded, spiral grooves covering entire surface, color bright ............ *C. jaspideus*

* Shell with low spire, raised slightly centrally

** Shell with knobby tubercles on whorl shoulders, color usually chocolate brown ............ *C. regius*

** Shell with whorl shoulders smooth

*** Shell whitish, with various brown markings ............ *C. spurius atlanticus*

*** Shell color solid orange or lemon yellow, occasionally with a single narrow white band ............ *C. daucus*

Genus *Conus* Linnaeus

*Conus spurius atlanticus* Clench
Florida Chinese Alphabet Cone

Pls. XV, 7; XXV, 23

ETYMOLOGY: Lat. *conus*, cone; *spurius*, illegitimate child.

SIZE: 65 to 80 mm. (2 3/5 to 3 1/4 in.) in height, 38 to 47 mm. (1 1/2 to 1 4/5 in.) in width.

DISTRIBUTION: Florida.

CHARACTERISTICS: Shell large, cone shaped, solid, smooth, moderately glossy under a thin periostracum; sides straight. Color whitish, ornamented with variously shaped and arranged orange spots. Spire concave, elevated centrally.

This is one of the commonest and most readily recognized cone shells in our area. It is frequently found washed up on the beaches and alive under boulders in shallow water. Though all cones possess some sort of poison apparatus, it is only the venom of the fish-eating species that has proved to be highly toxic and deadly to man; the Floridian cones are not known to be poisonous to human beings, living largely on worms, mollusks, and other invertebrates, though some may be fish eaters. In any case, it is wise to handle all living cones with care.

The typical subspecies, *C. spurius spurius* Gmelin, with fewer, larger, and darker spots, is found in the Caribbean.

The **Carrot Cone,** *Conus daucus* Hwass (Lat. *daucus,* carrot) (pl. XXV, 24), is smaller, reaching only 50 mm. (2 in.) in height. It looks very much like the Chinese Alphabet Cone in outline, but differs in being colored solid brownish orange to lemon yellow, occasionally with a light band across the middle. This is a rarer species, but specimens can occasionally be found on the beach. It lives in Florida and the West Indies.

The **Crown Cone,** *Conus regius* Gmelin (Lat. *regius,* kingly, royal) (pls. XV, 4; XXV, 26), is 50 to 75 mm. (2 to 3 in.) in height, 30 to 40 mm. (1 1/5 to 1 3/5 in.) in width. It differs largely by having the shoulders of the whorls armed with large, knobby tubercles of varying size. Its color pattern is exceedingly variable, and a great number of names were needlessly given these forms. As Dr. Clench (1942) remarks, "In a large series, these [color pattern] variations are almost completely linked together by intermediates, which show a homogeneity that would not be suspected if only a few isolated specimens were studied." The color is generally deep chocolate brown, occasionally brownish red and variously ornamented with cream-colored bands, blotches, and spots. The species is found in southern Florida and the West Indies. It is a reef dweller, and live specimens are not easily come by, but dead shells are sometimes taken on the beaches.

The **Florida Cone,** *Conus floridanus* Gabb (pl. XXV, 25), reaches 48 mm. (about 2 in.) in height and 24 mm. (about 1 in.) in width. It differs sharply from the previous cones in having the spire pyramid shaped and strongly raised, and the whorls stepped, with straight, perpendicular sides. The color pattern consists of two more or less solid bands of brown or yellowish brown on a whitish background. The spire also has dashes of color. The species can be found from North Carolina to Florida, where it is moderately common.

The **Jasper Cone,** *Conus jaspideus* Gmelin (Lat. *iaspis,* jasper) (pl. XXV, 27), is about the same size as the subspecies (see below) *C. jaspideus stearnsii*—23 mm. (about 1 in.) in height and 12 mm. (about 1/2 in.) in width—and resembles it closely. It differs by being fatter, with rounded rather than straight sides, and it is usually marked with wide, deep spiral grooves over the entire body whorl; in *C. j. stearnsii* these grooves are usually found only on the lower half. The colors of the Jasper Cone Shell are brighter and the mottlings reddish brown and larger. The "typical," or nominate, subspecies occurs in southern Florida, the West Indies, and Mexico.

**Stearns' Cone,** *Conus jaspideus stearnsii* Conrad (Robert Edward Carter Stearns was an active nineteenth-century malacologist) (pl. XXV, 28), resembles *C. floridanus* in having a raised, pyramid-like spire with strongly shouldered whorls, but is less than half its size, reaching at most 20 mm. (4/5 in.) in height and 9 mm. (about 2/5 in.) in width. In color it is a dirty white, overlaid with irregular areas of light to dark brown blotches. It ranges from North Carolina to Florida.

---

FAMILY:

# TEREBRIDAE

(*auger shells*)

Auger shells are long, narrow, attenuated; the surface sculpture is generally axially arranged, not spirally as in the Turritellidae, which have the same general shape. The operculum is narrow, and the aperture is provided with a short, twisted siphonal notch or canal. These snails live in sand and mud in warmer seas, where they prey on small invertebrates. Some forms possess a poison apparatus much like the Conidae, but their bite is not known to be dangerous to humans. In some classifications the terebras are grouped together with the Conidae and the Turridae, in the order Toxoglossa (arrow-tongue).

---

## KEY TO GENERA TEREBRA AND HASTULA

* Axial ribs extending from top to bottom of whorls
(genus *Terebra*)

    ✶✶ Shell outline uniformly awl-shaped, sides
        tapering regularly, surface rough
    ✶✶✶ Whorls concave                              *Terebra concava*
    ✶✶✶ Whorls flat or convex
  ✶✶✶✶ Subsutural band wide, consisting of strong beads    *T. dislocata*
  ✶✶✶✶ Subsutural band narrow, beads weak           *T. protexta*
      ✶✶ Shell outline not tapering gradually to the
          summit, surface smooth, glossy            *T. hastata*
       ✶ Axial ribs confined to top of whorl, not reaching
         across to bottom (genus *Hastula*)
      ✶✶ Shell up to 40 mm. (1 3/5 in.) in height, lighter in
         color, surface with myriads of closely set
         microscopic pimples                   *Hastula cinerea*
      ✶✶ Shell up to 25 mm. (1 in.) in height, color darker,
         surface punctae widely separated; species
         confined to shores of Gulf of Mexico        *H. salleana*

---

### Genus *Terebra*

*Terebra dislocata* Say
   Common Auger Shell

   Pl. XXIV, 18

ETYMOLOGY: Lat. *terebra*, borer, auger; *dislocatus*, disarranged.

SIZE: 50 mm. (2 in.) in height, 12 mm. (1/2 in.) in width.

DISTRIBUTION: Virginia to Florida, Texas, and the West Indies.

CHARACTERISTICS: Shell medium, slender, rough, multiwhorled, high,
   narrowly conical. Color gray, or pinkish or orangish white. Surface
   sculpture of about twenty-five short, strong axial ribs on each whorl,
   separated from other whorls by a beaded spiral band below the suture;
   spiral cords weak. Aperture small; outer lip thin, leading to a short,
   curved siphonal notch. Operculum corneous, thin, yellowish brown.

Shells of this common species are found intertidally and in shallow
water on muddy sand. These snails are carnivores, living on marine
worms and other small invertebrates.

    The **Fine-ribbed Auger Shell,** *Terebra protexta* Conrad (Lat. *pro
textus*, in front of the weaving) (pl. XXIV, 19), reaches only 20 to 25
mm. (4/5 to 1 in.) in height. It is dull white or brownish in color. The
axial ribs are more widely spaced than in *T. dislocata*, and are crossed
by seven to nine strong spiral cords on each whorl. The subsutural

band is less pronounced, and the beads much weaker. This species ranges from North Carolina to Florida and Texas; it lives in somewhat deeper water than the Common Auger Shell.

The **Concave Auger Shell,** *Terebra concava* Say (pl. XXIV, 20), is recognized chiefly by the distinctly concave-sided whorls, causing the roughly beaded subsutural lines to project beyond the rest of the surface. In addition, there are about twenty very small beads arranged in a spiral row and some very weakly incised spiral lines in the middle of each whorl. The shell, which is about 25 mm. (1 in.) in length, is yellowish gray and moderately glossy. It ranges from North Carolina to Florida in shallow water.

The **Shiny Auger Shell,** *Terebra hastata* Gmelin (Lat. *hastatus*, armed with a spear) (pl. XXIV, 21), differs from the other auger shells by having a "fatter" outline, with the upper whorls of the spire tapering more rapidly than the lower whorls. The shell reaches 40 mm. (1 3/5 in.) in height; it is glossy and bright yellow or light brown, with a white band below the suture. The species ranges from southeastern Florida, where it is rather rare, to the West Indies.

Genus *Hastula*

*Hastula cinerea* Born
   Gray Atlantic Auger Shell

   Pl. XXIV, 22

ETYMOLOGY: Diminutive of Lat. *hasta*, spear; *cinis, cineris*, ashes.

SIZE: Up to 50 mm. (2 in.) in height, 10 mm. (2/5 in.) in width.

DISTRIBUTION: Southeastern Florida and the West Indies.

CHARACTERISTICS: Shell medium, slender, glossy, high turreted; apex sharp. Color cream or bluish brown, occasionally dark spotted near the suture. Surface sculpture of numerous small riblets at the top of each whorl, not extending to the bottom, and with very fine rows of closely set microscopic punctae.

The shells of the genus *Hastula* differ from true *Terebra* in having the axial ridges arranged only along the top of the whorls. This is a slight morphological difference, but more fundamental differences are found in the anatomy, radula, and life history of both groups. It is only recently that *Hastula* was afforded generic recognition; it was formerly considered to be a subgenus. Both genera live together in shallow water.

**Sallé's Auger Shell,** *Hastula salleana* Deshayes (A. Sallé was a prominent traveler and collector) (pl. XXIV, 23), is smaller than *H. cinerea,* reaching only 25 mm. (1 in.) in height; it is somewhat darker in color. The tiny punctae on the surface are far less numerous and much more widely separated. It has been recorded only from the west coast of Florida to Texas and the coast of Mexico, thus being confined to the shores of the Gulf of Mexico.

FAMILY:

# TURRIDAE

(*turret shells*)

The turret shells constitute by far the largest single family of gastropods. About 250 genera and subgenera are presently recognized, and there are estimated to be about 1,500 living species; at least as many extinct fossils are known, and many new species are being described yearly. Recently the description of 50 new forms off the West Coast of North America appeared in print, showing how, in even comparatively well-explored areas, many unknown forms still exist.

The correct determination or identification of most turrid species is a frustrating experience for amateur and professional alike. The generic and particularly the specific differences are not easily detected, especially if large series of shells are being examined. Unfortunately, there is no reliable monograph of the East Coast species available, and the authors of the most generalized shell books do not always agree on the names of the shells they discuss.

Luckily, though the determination of genus and species is difficult and complicated for most forms of turrids, it is comparatively easy, at least, to recognize what shells belong to the turret shell family. They are characterized by the presence of a notch, which varies in size and prominence, near the upper end of the outer lip, and it may extend to the suture itself. This is called the "turrid notch," for it is most conspicuous in turrid shells. A similar notch occurs in some cone and auger shells, but is not as prominent. When these snails crawl, the upper end of the aperture is held toward the back of the animal. Therefore, the turrid notch is also called the "posterior," or "anal," notch. The shells vary in form, but are mostly spindle shaped, slender, and long, and have high, sharp spires. In size they range from less than 6 mm. (1/4 in.) to some that attain more than 125 mm. (5 in.) in length.

These snails are included in the same superfamily, Conacea, as the poison-bearing cone and auger shells, and many genera of turret shells do possess similar poison sacs and dartlike radular teeth, the sort of radula termed "toxoglossate." Other genera, however, have a radula with many teeth, similar to the volutes and rock shells, the so-called rachiglossate radula. Most turrids inhabit deep water, and are not easily found on the beaches. They are worldwide in distribution.

In this book we will have to limit ourselves to the few commoner shallow-water species, a scanty sampling of the exceeding richness of the group.

## KEY TO FAMILY TURRIDAE

\* Shell large, more than 10 mm. (2/5 in.) in height
\*\* Shell with row of light-colored spiral nodules
\*\*\* Nodules split by spiral lines, shell grayish brown *Monilispira leucocyma*
\*\*\* Nodules not split, shell blackish brown *M. albinodata*
\*\* Shell without prominent nodules
\*\*\* Shell quite smooth, with undulate axial ridges only *Cerodrillia thea*
\*\*\* Shell surface roughened by lightly beaded axial ribs and spiral lirations *Crassispira ostrearum*
\* Shell small, less than 10 mm. (2/5 in.) in height
\*\* Shell thin, translucent, relatively smooth; range North Carolina to Florida and the Tortugas *Kurtziella limonitella*
\*\* Shell thicker, opaque; range Massachusetts to Florida
\*\*\* Shell waxy yellow, relatively smooth, acutely shouldered axial ridges *Mangelia cerina*
\*\*\* Shell darker brown, surface strongly cancellated, ridges not shouldered *M. plicosa*

Genus *Crassispira* Swainson

*Crassispira ostrearum* Stearns
    Oyster Turret Shell

    Pl. XXIV, 24

ETYMOLOGY: Lat. *crassus spira*, fat coil or twist; *ostrea*, oyster.

SIZE: 15 to 19 mm. (about 3/5 to 4/5 in.) in height, 6 mm. (1/4 in.) in width.

DISTRIBUTION: North Carolina to southern Florida.

CHARACTERISTICS: Shell small, strong, slender, long; spire higher than aperture. Color light to dark brown. Surface sculpture of about twenty strong axial ribs, lightly beaded by numerous closely set spiral striations, a single smooth spiral cord below the suture. Turrid notch not deep, U shaped.

This is among the larger of the common turret shells in our area. It lives in shallow water, where it clings to the undersides of boulders and rocks.

The **Tea-colored Turret Shell,** *Cerodrillia thea* Dall (Gr. *keros*, wax, and Eng. drill; late Lat. *thea*, tea) (pl. XXV, 29), is about 15 mm. (3/5 in.) high, with a high, slender spire about twice as high as the aperture. It is much smoother than the Oyster Turret, the surface having a number of wide, smooth, wavelike axial ridges with some fine spiral threads at the base. The turrid notch is wide and rounded, and in color it is like steeped tea. This fairly common species lives on sand bars in protected waters only along the west coast of Florida.

The **White-beaded Turret Shell,** *Monilispira leucocyma* Dall (Lat. *monile spira*, necklace coil or twist; Gr. *leukos kyma*, white wool) (pl. XXIV, 25), is 14 mm. (about 3/5 in.) in height, 5 mm. (1/5 in.) in width. The small, slender shell has a high spire; the color is grayish chocolate brown ornamented with low, cream-colored nodules split by rather deep spiral grooves. The rest of the shell and base has strong spiral cords. This common species is found on sand bars from southern Florida to Texas and in the West Indies. It is readily recognized by its slender shape and the split, light-colored nodules arranged in a spiral line.

The **White-banded Turret,** *Monilispira albinodata* Reeve (Lat. *albus nodus*, white knot) (pl. XXV, 30), is about 10 mm. (2/5 in.) high. It is dumpier in shape than most turrets, with the usual spindle shape deformed by the very short base. In color it is brown to orange, and it is ornamented with a spiral row of prominent white or pale yellowish beads that are roundish, not split as in *M. leucocyma*. In addition, there are some narrow white spiral bands on the body whorl. In appearance this looks a little like a horn shell (genus *Cerithium*) but the family sign, the turrid notch, discloses its true identity. This species can be found in shallow water from southern Florida to the West Indies. The species name *albinodata* Reeve appears to apply to a different west American species (see Keen, 1971, p. 734); if this is the case, this well-known western Atlantic shell would require another name.

Genus *Mangelia* Risso

*Mangelia cerina* Kurtz & Stimpson
Waxy Turret Shell

Pl. XXV, 31

ETYMOLOGY: The generic term is without meaning; Gr. *keros*, wax.

SIZE: 6 to 10 mm. (1/4 to 2/5 in.) in height, 3 mm. (1/8 in.) in width.

DISTRIBUTION: Massachusetts to Florida.

CHARACTERISTICS: Shell usually tiny, narrow, spindle shaped. Color waxy yellow. Spire equal to body whorl in height; turrid notch distinct, not in contact with suture. Surface has a number of heavy, acutely shouldered, wavelike axial ridges and a smooth, wide area below the suture; the base has fine spiral lines.

This is a very common shallow-water species found in bays and protected waters. It is not easily confused with other species. The name was sometimes written *Mangilia* in the supposition that Risso named it for G. Mangili, an eighteenth century naturalist. But Risso wrote *Mangelia*, in French *mangélie*, and there is no indication that he had Mangili or anything else in mind when he coined the word.

The **Plicate Turret Shell**, *Mangelia plicosa* C. B. Adams (Lat. *plicare*, to fold) (pl. XXV, 32), is 6 to 8 mm. (1/4 to 1/3 in.) in height. In color it is gray or reddish brown, with about twelve heavy axial ridges thickly cancellated by almost equally strong spiral cords. The whorls are weakly shouldered and the suture shallow. This species is readily collected in shallow protected waters, on grass or mud bottoms. It ranges from Cape Cod to Florida and Texas.

The **Lemon-colored Turret Shell**, *Kurtziella limonitella* Dall (J. D. Kurtz was an American conchologist; Span. *limon*, lemon) (pl. XXVI, 1), reaches 10 mm. (2/5 in.) in height. The shell is thin, lemon yellow, translucent, and the whorls have strong, rounded axial ridges and numerous very fine, evenly spaced spiral threads. The species lives on mud flats, ranging from North Carolina to the Tortugas.

# SUBCLASS:

# OPISTHOBRANCHIA

(*gills behind*)

# = EUTHYNEURA

(*straight nerves*)

As we saw in the introduction to this chapter, the subclass Opisthobranchia (Gr. *opisthon branchion*, hind gill), though forming an important and probably more advanced group than the Prosobranchia, is of lesser interest to the shell collector because, of the numerous forms constituting this subclass, only a few have shells, and these are, with some important exceptions, generally of the "bubble" type, that is, the shell looks like a bubble: its inflated body whorl covers all the other whorls and the spire is frequently sunk below the summit. In many cases the shell is tiny, compared with the size of the soft parts, and the animal cannot withdraw into it; and in some forms the shell is vestigial, remaining as nothing more than an internal plate. In one of the larger groups of Opisthobranchia, the Nudibranchia, a tiny shell is found in the embryonic stage but is lost long before the snail matures.

# ORDER:
# ENTOMOTAENIATA
*(notched band)*

---

# PYRAMIDELLACEA

---

FAMILY:
# PYRAMIDELLIDAE
*(pyramid shells)*

The numerous members of the family Pyramidellidae (diminutive of Lat. *pyramis*, pyramid), although belonging to the subclass Opistho-branchia, look quite unlike the bubble shells. The pyramid shells resemble prosobranchs with high, spired shells, such as the ceriths. They are usually quite small and slender, with many whorls. Until recently the pyramids were indeed classed with the prosobranchs, but a study of the anatomy and embryology by two British scientists, Vera Fretter and Alastair Graham, revealed that these snails are opisthobranchs. The small pyramid shells are parasites dwelling on other gastropods and bivalves, and live by sucking the juices from them, very much like fleas and mosquitos living on the blood of vertebrates. The operculum is horny, and a radula is lacking.

The family Pyramidellidae is a very difficult group to understand, and unfortunately no modern monographic work is available for our fauna. Besides the genus *Pyramidella* Lamarck (diminutive of Lat. *pyramis*, pyramid), the commonest genera in the family are *Odostomia* Fleming (Gr. *odos stoma*, tooth mouth) and *Turbonilla* Risso (diminutive of Lat. *turbo*, spinning top). Most of the species are tiny and require detailed descriptions; identification, therefore, is not easy. Space limitations require us thus to restrict our discussion to descriptions of the genera and listings of the commoner shallow-water species, with the addition of brief remarks that serve to characterize each species.

# KEY TO GENERA PYRAMIDELLA, TURBONILLA, AND ODOSTOMIA

* Shell with few whorls, 6 to 7; single tooth in
  aperture                                    *Odostomia* Fleming
* Shell multiwhorled, 10 whorls or more
** Shell with strong spiral folds on columella,
   surface generally smooth                   *Pyramidella* Lamarck
** Aperture without folds, surface with axial ribs   *Turbonilla* Risso

Genus *Pyramidella* Lamarck

CHARACTERISTICS: Shell multiwhorled, narrow, spire sharply pointed, columella with strong spiral folds.

*P. dolobrata* Lamarck. Up to 30 mm. (1 1/5 in.) (pl. XXVI, 2). Florida Keys to the Caribbean. Shell large for family, narrowly pyramidal in shape. Color yellowish white, with three or four narrow brownish spiral stripes. Columella with two or three strong folds; operculum with a lateral notch to accommodate the columellar folds. This is by far the largest pyramid shell in our area, most of the others being about 5 to 13 mm. (about 1/5 to 1/2 in.) in height.

*P. crenulata* Holmes. 14 mm. (about 3/5 in.). South Carolina to western Florida. Suture crenulated.

Genus *Turbonilla* Risso

CHARACTERISTICS: Shell generally small to tiny, long, very narrow, multiwhorled; nuclear whorls horizontal to the axis of shell, therefore heterostrophic; later whorls with strong axial ribs. Color generally pale, aperture without folds or denticles.

*T. interrupta* Totten. 6 mm. (1/4 in.) (pl. XXVI, 3). Canada to the West Indies. Shell pale yellow, with numerous straight axial ribs wider than the interspaces.

*T. reticulata* C. B. Adams. 3 mm. (1/8 in.). North Carolina to West Indies. Shell tiny, axial threads very fine.

*T. conradi* Bush. 9 mm. (about 2/5 in.). Tampa Bay to Tarpon Bay, Florida. Shell grayish, spaces between ribs wider than the slightly rounded ribs.

*T. dalli* Bush. 8 mm. (1/3 in.). Cape Hatteras to Palm Beach and Sarasota, Florida. Shell stout, bluish white, transparent, ribs oblique, strong.

*T. hemphilli* Bush. 9 mm. (about 2/5 in.). Sarasota to Sanibel, Florida. Like *T. dalli* but more slender, apex more pointed.

*T. belotheca* Dall. 11 mm. (about 1/2 in.). Palm Beach to the West Indies. Shell white, shining, ribs oblique, broad.

*T. elegantula* Verrill. 6 mm. (1/4 in.). Woods Hole, Massachusetts. Wax yellow, axial ribs broad and low, interspaces as wide as ribs, with prominent spiral cords. *T. winkleyi*, *T. vinae*, and *T. mighelsi*, all named by Bartsch, appear to be forms of this variable species.

Genus *Odostomia* Fleming

CHARACTERISTICS: Shell very small, generally white, with few whorls, narrowly ovate-conic in shape, aperture with columellar fold, surface variously sculptured, but not with axial ribs.

*O. impressa* Say. 5 mm. (1/5 in.) (pl. XXVI, 4). Massachusetts Bay to Gulf of Mexico. Whorls with 4 deep, closely spaced spiral grooves.

*O. seminuda* C. B. Adams. 4 mm. (1/6 in.) (pl. XXVI, 5). Canada to Gulf of Mexico. Spire and upper half of body whorl with strong squarish reticulations, lower body whorl and base with strong spiral grooves only. Lives parasitically on *Crepidula*.

*O. trifida* Totten. 4 mm. (1/6 in.) (pl. XXVI, 6). Canada to New Jersey. Whorls with 3 narrow, widely spaced spiral grooves. Lives parasitically on *Mya* (Soft-shelled Clam).

*O. bisuturalis* Say. 5 mm. (1/5 in.). Canada to Delaware Bay. Sutural line double.

*O. modesta* Stimpson. 3 mm. (1/8 in.). Woods Hole, Massachusetts. Shell quite broad, shining yellowish white, surface quite smooth.

*O. fusca* C. B. Adams. 6 mm. (1/4 in.) (pl. XXVI, 7). Canada to Florida. Shell light brown, semitransparent, outline rather swollen. This and the next species may be placed in the genus *Sayella* Dall, a group of fragile, pupiform shells with convex whorls.

*O. producta* C. B. Adams. 5 mm. (1/5 in.). Massachusetts Bay to New Jersey. Shell light yellowish brown, translucent, smooth, quite narrow.

# ORDER:

# CEPHALASPIDEA

(*head shield*)

Formerly

# TECTIBRANCHIATA

(*shell-covered gills*)

Among the opisthobranchs, which are mostly hermaphroditic, and considered to be more highly advanced than the prosobranchs, it is mainly the members of the order Cephalaspidea and the superfamily Pyramidellacea of the order Entomotaeniata (see page 174) that bear external shells typical of marine snails. The others, by far the larger number, have no shells at all, tiny shells that are lost very early in their lives, or weak, platelike internal shells. We omit all these—the nudibranchs, sea hares, and their kin—as this book is devoted to shells.

The cephalaspidean shells can readily be distinguished, with few exceptions, from the prosobranch shells, since they are bubble shaped, the body whorl being very large and usually ovate and mostly covering the other whorls. The spire is frequently sunk into an apical pit below the top of the huge body whorl. The outer lip is thin, and the aperture long and narrow but wider at the base. In a few cases the animal is not able to retract its entire body into the shell, but in many other species, especially members of the true bubbles (family Bullidae), the shell is strong and affords the animal good protection. Most cephalaspideans do not have an operculum.

## KEY TO ORDER CEPHALASPIDEA

* Shell with body whorl about one-half the height of the shell, spire distinctly raised, operculum present  *Rictaxis (Acteon)*

    * Shell with huge body whorl generally enclosing all the other whorls, spire frequently sunken, operculum absent
      ** Shell large, usually more than 10 mm. (2/5 in.) in height
    *** Shell strong, colorful, mottled, solid, animal completely retractable into shell        *Bulla*
    *** Shell delicate, fragile, animal retractable into shell
  **** Shell opaque with colorful periostracum
 ***** Shell large, 30 mm. (1 1/5 in.), decorated with narrow spiral color bands        *Hydatina*
 ***** Shell small, 12 mm. (1/2 in.), decorated with a network of reddish lines        *Micromelo*
  **** Shell translucent or transparent, white or faintly tinged with amber or yellow, animal not completely retractable into shell
 ***** Shell relatively narrow, striated only at both ends, center smooth        *Atys*
 ***** Shell globose or broadly cylindrical, finely sculptured over entire surface        *Haminoea*
      ** Shell small, usually less than 7 mm. (about 1/4 in.) in height
    *** Spire usually sunk below top of body whorl        *Cylichna*
    *** Spire not sunk below top of body whorl or slightly raised        *Retusa (Acteocina)*

---

SUPERFAMILY:

# BULLACEA

---

FAMILY:

# BULLIDAE
(*true bubble shells*)

The shells are medium to large, rather strong, rounded-ovate or broadly cylindrical; flaring aperture as large as the entire shell and enveloping the other whorls; spire sunken, frequently lower than the top of the aperture; surface smooth, or the last whorl may be finely striated spirally. Chiefly inhabitants of warm seas, these snails live on sandy or muddy bottoms where they feed on other mollusks.

Genus *Bulla* Linnaeus

*Bulla umbilicata* Röding
Common True Bubble Shell

Pl. XXVI, 8

ETYMOLOGY: Lat. *bulla*, a bubble, and *umbilicatus*, umbilical.

SIZE: 25 mm. (1 in.) in height, 15 mm. (3/8 in.) in width.

DISTRIBUTION: North Carolina to the West Indies.

CHARACTERISTICS: Shell solid, strong, widely cyclindrical or moderately swollen in shape, the body whorl enveloping the entire shell and the aperture reaching higher than the sunken spire; surface of body whorl with fine spiral striations; color whitish, strongly mottled with brown flecks and blotches, occasional specimens banded.

This is a very abundant species, found on mud flats near the low tide line, where it lives by swallowing other mollusks whole and crushing their shells by means of internal stomach plates. *B. occidentalis* A. Adams is a synonym. Some authorities consider this to be the same species as the following one, which has priority by six years, and they call both forms *B. striata* Bruguière.

The **Striate Bubble,** *Bulla striata* Bruguière (Lat. *stria,* a shallow canal) (pl. XXVI, 9), is larger, up to 35 mm. (1 2/5 in.) in height, and similar in shape. But it is heavier and somewhat compressed above; it is most easily recognized by the usual presence of quite strong spiral grooves near the base of the body whorl and in the pit of the sunken spire. The color is brighter than in *Bulla umbilicata* and the columella has a white callus, frequently stained with brown. It ranges from the west coast of Florida to Texas and the West Indies.

FAMILY:

# ATYIDAE
(*paper bubble shells*)

The shells of this family are small, generally thin and fragile, ovate but more slender and less "bubbly" in shape than the true bubble shells; body whorl huge, sculptured with fine spiral lines above and below, smooth centrally; white or pale yellowish in color; aperture lunate, widened below, inner lip frequently reaching above the sunken spire. These snails live in muddy and sandy bottoms and some may be found in brackish waters; most occur in warmer seas.

Genus *Atys* Montfort

*Atys caribaea* Montfort
    Caribbean Paper Bubble

    Pl. XXVI, 10

ETYMOLOGY: *Atys* is a name in Gr. mythology, belonging to, among others, the son of Hercules; Montfort's spelling of "Caribbean" must be preserved under the rules of nomenclature.

SIZE: 8 to 11 mm. (about 1/3 to 1/2 in.) in height, 4 mm. (1/6 in.) in width.

DISTRIBUTION: Southeastern Florida to the West Indies.

CHARACTERISTICS: Shell thin, milk white, translucent, narrowly ovate, aperture extending beyond the spire; center smooth, fine spiral striations above and below.

This small species lives in shallow water and specimens in fairly large numbers can be found in beach drift after a storm, especially during the breeding season.

**Sanderson's Paper Bubble,** *Atys sandersoni* Dall (Sanderson Smith was a prominent malacologist of the 19th century) (pl. XXVI, 11), is approximately the same size as the Caribbean Paper Bubble, but it is thicker, the sides are flatter, and the spiral lines finer and more numerous. It ranges from North Carolina to the West Indies, and is fairly numerous in shallow to deeper water.

---

## KEY TO GENUS HAMINOEA

* Outer lip of shell begins on the left side of the apical depression at the sunken spire, color greenish yellow, surface with many straight, incised spiral lines; southern distributional range          *Haminoea elegans*
* Outer lip begins on the right side of apical depression at the sunken spire
** Shell very swollen, globose, greenish yellow, spiral lines very fine          *H. antillarum*

\*\* Shell narrower and more cylindrical
\*\*\* Shell bluish or yellowish white, spiral grooves
    straight; range Cape Cod to North Carolina     *H. solitaria*
\*\*\* Shell white, spiral grooves wrinkled; range
    Florida to Texas and the West Indies     *H. succinea*

---

Genus *Haminoea* Turton & Kingston

*Haminoea solitaria* Say
  Solitary Paper Bubble

  Pl. XXVI, 12

ETYMOLOGY: Gr. *hama noeo*, seen together.

SIZE: 6 mm. (1/4 in.) in height, 3 mm. (1/8 in.) in diameter.

DISTRIBUTION: Gulf of Saint Lawrence to Florida.

CHARACTERISTICS: Shell exceedingly thin and fragile. Yellowish or bluish in
    color in life, opaque white when dead. Only moderately inflated, the
    sides almost cylindrical. Entire surface marked with faint spiral lines.

This is the only fairly large bubble shell in the northern part of our
area. Occasional giant forms reaching 18 mm. (3/4 in.) can be found
near New York City. This gigantic form has been named *Haminoea
insculpta* Totten. The name of the genus probably comes from the
fact that the animal cannot retract its soft parts into the shell, so that
soft parts and shell are "seen together." The shells are all very fragile,
and occasionally have a bluish or amber tinge. The shell, of course,
can be seen only when the soft parts have been removed. In life the
mollusks are unsightly blobs of grayish flesh living on muddy bottoms
in shallow water.

    The **Antillean Paper Bubble,** *Haminoea antillarum* Orbigny (pl.
XXI, 19), reaches 17 mm. (about 3/4 in.). It is globose and quite swollen
in shape. The shell is thin but strong, the color is greenish yellow, and
the surface is covered with microscopic wavy striae. It ranges from
western Florida and the Gulf states to the West Indies.

    The **Amber Paper Bubble,** *Haminoea succinea* Conrad (Lat. *suc-
cinum*, amber) (pl. XXVI, 13), is similar to the Antillean Paper Bubble,
but the sides are distinctly flattish and the shell is not swollen. The
entire surface is sculptured with minute, wrinkled axial lines, and the
color is translucent white. This species ranges from Florida to Texas
and the West Indies.

The **Elegant Paper Bubble,** *Haminoea elegans* Gray (Lat. *elegans,* elegant) (pl. XXVI, 14), reaches almost 20 mm. (4/5 in.) in height. It is brownish or greenish yellow in color, and the surface has many fine, straight spiral grooves. Unlike the other members of the genus, the outer lip of this species rises on the left side of the apical pit in which the spire is sunken. To see this, the shell should be held with the apex facing the viewer and the outer lip to the right.

---

FAMILY:

# RETUSIDAE
*(barrel bubble shells)*

These minute to small cylindrical shells have a bluntly rounded or truncated spire, giving the chunky appearance of a barrel. The apex is commonly raised. Whorls are slightly to deeply channeled by the suture. A single fold occurs on the inner lip. Widely distributed in warm and cold waters.

Genus *Retusa* Brown

*Retusa canaliculata* Say
   Channeled Barrel Shell

   Pl. XXVI, 15

ETYMOLOGY: Lat. *retusus,* blunted, and *canalis,* channel.

SIZE: 5 mm. (1/5 in.) in height.

DISTRIBUTION: Nova Scotia to Florida, Texas, and the West Indies.

CHARACTERISTICS: Shell white, smooth, solid, and cylindrical, with straight sides. The suture channeled; inner lip with a thick, curved lamella.

The tiny shell is distinguished from other bubbles of similar size by its apex, which is not sunken but slightly raised. This is a common shell in beach drift, and is easily sifted in shallow water, especially from sand obtained in estuaries. Its characteristic habitat is in bays of variable low to intermediate salinity. Formerly placed in the genus *Acteocina.*

**Candé's Barrel Bubble,** *Retusa candei* Orbigny (Ferdinand de Candé was a French naval officer and shell collector) (pl. XXIV, 26), is similar in size and appearance, but differs in being widest in the middle of the shell rather than the shell being cylindrical with straight sides. The protoconch projects strongly from the spire instead of only a little, as in *R. canaliculata*. The protoconch of both species is not on the same axis as the shell, but horizontal to it. This condition is known as "heterostrophic" (Gr. *hetero strophe*, different turning), a feature found in the pyramid shells (see pages 174–176). Unlike the Channeled Barrel Bubble, Candé's Bubble is an ocean dweller in shallow water of normal salinity.

SUPERFAMILY:

# PHILINACEA

FAMILY:

# SCAPHANDRIDAE
(*chalice bubble shells*)

The only genus of this large family in our region resembles the Retusidae (Superfamily Bullacea) in size and color, but the shells are not truncated or flattened above and the spire is always sunken. In shape they can be either ovate or cylindrical. These widely distributed snails burrow into soft bottoms, where they prey on other mollusks.

# KEY TO GENUS CYLICHNA

* Shell inflated, sides rounded *Cylichna oryza*
* Shell cylindrical, sides parallel
* * Shell with two distinct lamellae or teeth at the base of the columella; range North Carolina to Texas and the West Indies *C. bidentata*
* * Shell without columellar nodules or teeth; range Arctic seas to Massachusetts *C. alba*

Genus *Cylichna* Lovén

*Cylichna oryza* Totten
Rice Bubble Shell

Pl. XXIV, 27

ETYMOLOGY: Gr. *kylichne*, chalice, cup; and Lat. *oryza*, rice.

SIZE: 5 mm. (1/5 in.) in height.

DISTRIBUTION: Cape Cod, Massachusetts, to Charleston, South Carolina.

CHARACTERISTICS: Shell tiny, white, ovate, the sides swollen, spire well
sunken; sculptured with fine spiral lines above and below, the center
being smooth.

This species is readily recognized by its roundish shape; specimens are
found together with *Retusa canaliculata* in the beach drift. It apparently prefers the same type of habitat.

The **White Chalice Bubble,** *Cylichna alba* Brown (Lat. *albus*, white)
(not illus.), differs from *C. oryza* by having its sides not swollen
but almost parallel and the shape cylindrical. The entire surface has
minute spiral lines. This is a northern species ranging from the Arctic
seas to Massachusetts. It is frequently found in the stomachs of fish
taken off the coast of New England and often appears in beach drift.

The **Two-toothed Chalice Bubble,** *Cylichna bidentata* Orbigny
(Lat. *bi dens*, twice tooth) (pl. XXVI, 16), is quite small, reaching only
3 mm. (1/8 in.) in height. It is narrow like *C. alba,* but differs in that
the base of the columella has a spiral fold and a low nodule, giving
the impression that it has two teeth. Spiral lines are found on
both ends of the shell. It ranges from North Carolina to Florida and
Texas, and the West Indies, where it lives in shallow to deep water
and is often taken in beach drift.

.　.　.

# ACTEONACEA

# ACTEONIDAE
(*baby bubble shells*)

A family of small, cylindrical bubble shells having a short, raised spire and a long, narrow aperture. A single plait is present in the inner lip. Widely distributed worldwide.

Genus *Rictaxis* Dall

*Rictaxis punctostriatus* C. B. Adams
  Pitted Baby Bubble

  Pl. XXVI, 17

ETYMOLOGY: Lat. *rictus*, mouth wide open, and *axis; puncto striatus*, dotted striated.

SIZE: 3 to 6 mm. (1/8 to 1/4 in.) in height, 1.5 to 2 mm. (about 1/12 in.) in width.

DISTRIBUTION: Cape Cod to Florida and the West Indies.

CHARACTERISTICS: Shell quite small, strong, narrowly ovate. White or with rustlike stain. Spire well raised; aperture about one-half the height of the shell. Lower half of body whorl has numerous spiral rows of fine pits. Operculum thin, horny.

This is a primitive opisthobranch still preserving such prosobranch characters as separate sexes and an operculum. It is a very common species in shallow water. Until recently it was placed in the genus *Acteon* Montfort (Gr. *actaeos*, coast dweller) but it was found to have a very un-*Acteon*-like radula. Large—7 to 10 mm. (about 1/4 to 2/5 in.)—and very much thicker shells are called *Rictaxis candens* Rehder (Lat. *candens*, white). They range from Florida to Cuba.

FAMILY:

# HYDATINIDAE

*(lined bubble shells)*

These globose shells are thin, fragile, mostly large and inflated; periostracum thin but tough and well developed. The soft parts of these warm water snails are large and often colorful, and the foot extends well beyond the shell.

Genus *Hydatina* Schumacher

*Hydatina vesicaria* Lightfoot
  Bladder Bubble Shell

  Pl. XXVI, 18

ETYMOLOGY: Gr. *hydatis*, a watery vesicle or blister; Lat. *vesica*, bladder.

SIZE: 30 mm. (1 1/5 in.) in height and width.

DISTRIBUTION: Southern Florida to the West Indies.

CHARACTERISTICS: Shell globelike, very thin; surface polished, ornamented with many narrow, closely set, wavy brown spiral lines. Aperture is capacious and the spire is sunken. Periostracum tough, yellowish gray.

These fragile shells are found on sandy bottoms in shallow water during the summer, when the snails breed. Formerly mistaken for *H. physis* Linnaeus, an Indo-Pacific species.

The **Miniature Melon Shell,** *Micromelo undatus* Bruguière (Gr. *micros, melo,* small melon, and Lat. *unda,* wave or billow) (pl. XXVI, 19), is similar in shape and texture, but is smaller, reaching only 12 mm. (1/2 in.) in height and width. It is easily recognized by its creamy or white shell covered with a network of reddish, often wavy lines. This pretty little bubble, which ranges from the lower Florida Keys to the West Indies, is not commonly found at low tide.

SUBCLASS:

# PULMONATA

*(lunged)*

ORDER:

# BASOMMATOPHORA

*(carrying eyes basally)*

The members of the order Basommatophora (Gr. *basis,* base; *omma,* eye; and *pherein,* bearing, hence sessile-eyed) are primitive pulmonates or air-breathing mollusks that have not been able to break completely the bonds that link them to their primeval ocean home. They are rarely found far from water; even the more advanced ones, which moved inland, live either in fresh water or not very far from it. The other order of pulmonates, the Stylommatophora (Gr. *stylos,* pillar or column, hence stalk-eyed) have been so successful in moving to the land that they have colonized even mountaintops and deserts.

SUPERFAMILY:
# MELAMPACEA

---

FAMILY:
# MELAMPIDAE
(*marsh snails*)

These shells are small to tiny, usually smooth, ovate to rounded conic, with the aperture variously armed with teeth or denticles. They spend most of the time out of water secreted under leaves and boards in saltwater marshes. The family was formerly called Ellobiidae.

---

## KEY TO FAMILY
## MELAMPIDAE (= ELLOBIIDAE)

| | |
|---|---|
| \* Shell tiny, 3 to 4 mm. (1/8 to 1/6 in.) in height | |
| \*\* Shell spirally sculptured | |
| \*\*\* Shell globulose, thick, sculpture heavy | *Pedipes mirabilis* |
| \*\*\* Shell ovate, spire conic, thin, sculpture weak | *Laemodonta cubensis* |
| \*\* Shell conic, without spiral sculpture | *Marinula succinea* |
| \* Shell larger, 8 to 18 mm. (1/3 to 3/4 in.) in height | |
| \*\* Shell conic, widest above the midpoint | genera *Melampus, Pira* |
| \*\* Shell not widest above the midpoint | |
| \*\*\* Shell cylindrical olive shaped, 18 mm. (3/4 in.) in height | *Ellobium auricula* |
| \*\*\* Shell ovate, spindle shaped | |
| \*\*\*\* Aperture with one or more parietal teeth and 4 to 10 palatal ridges | genus *Detracia* |
| \*\*\*\* Aperture with parietal teeth but no palatal ridges | |
| \*\*\*\*\* Outer lip thin | *Ovatella myosotis* |
| \*\*\*\*\* Outer lip thickened | *Tralia ovula* |

Genus *Ellobium* Röding

*Ellobium auricula* Bruguière
Pellucid Marsh Snail

Pl. XXIV, 28

ETYMOLOGY: Gr. *ellobion*, earring; Lat. *auricula*, ear.

SIZE: 18 mm. (3/4 in.) in height, 9 mm. (about 2/5 in.) in width.

DISTRIBUTION: Cedar Keys south to Florida Keys, the West Indies.

CHARACTERISTICS: Shell bubble or cylindrical olive shaped, smooth, translucent, grayish, dull. Body whorl much larger than the spire. Aperture narrow, widest below with a single rounded denticle on the columella near the base; lip simple, thin.

These shells are found dead in fair numbers on the Florida Keys, but living specimens seem to be rare. In 1899, near Miami, some snails were discovered imbedded in soft, rotten mangrove branches lying in mud. More recently, in 1958, Dr. Morrison of the U.S. National Museum found some live specimens under thick wet mangrove leaf mold, near Flamingo, and in 1960 a fairly large colony was located, again near a mangrove swamp, on Key Largo. The species was formerly called *Auriculastra pellucens* Menke, a later name.

Genus *Pedipes* Bruguière

*Pedipes mirabilis* Mühlfeld
Stepping Marsh Snail

Pl. XXI, 20

ETYMOLOGY: Lat. *pes, ped,* foot; *mirabilis,* admirable

SIZE: 3 to 5 mm. (1/8 to 1/5 in.) in length.

DISTRIBUTION: Southern Florida and the Keys, westward to Port Aransas, Texas, and the West Indies.

CHARACTERISTICS: Shell quite small, globose or elongate globose, very solid, usually strongly sculptured spirally. Color light to rather dark reddish brown. Three well-developed white teeth on the inner (parietal) margin of the aperture, the uppermost the largest; outer (palatal) margin usually with a single, centrally placed denticle. Lip simple, much thickened within.

This tiny shell is variable in shape and size, and in immature stages it has a different apertural dentition. For this reason it has been given many unnecessary names, which are now regarded as synonyms. It occurs in ephemeral colonies that perish when conditions become unfavorable, but new ones are readily established. It prefers a hard substrate, clinging to stones, pebbles, and dead shells. The name *Pedipes* was originally given by Adanson, a pre-Linnaean author, in an attempt to Latinize the French word *piéton* (pedestrian), because of the snail's loping method of walking, caused by the division of the foot into an anterior and posterior portion, each one moving separately.

The **Cuban Marsh Snail,** *Laemodonta cubensis* Pfeiffer (Gr. *laimos*, throat, and *odont*, tooth) (pl. XXVI, 20), is of the same size as *Pedipes* but differs in being rather thin, the color of light straw, and with a higher spire and finer spiral sculpture, and in having three parietal and two palatal teeth. It ranges from the Florida Keys to the Bahamas and the West Indies.

The **Amber Marsh Snail,** *Marinula succinea* Pfeiffer (diminutive of Lat. *marinus*, marine; *succinum*, amber) (pl. XXVI, 21), is slightly larger, 4 mm. (1/6 in.) high, conic and more pointed, smooth, with three parietal teeth, the two upper ones much larger than the lowest. The outer lip is toothless and very thin. This species is also found in Florida, the Bahamas, and the West Indies.

Although, as can be seen, these three snails all occupy more or less the same habitats, the latter two are more difficult to find than *Pedipes*.

Genus *Detracia* Gray

*Detracia bullaoides* Montagu
  Bubble-shaped Marsh Snail

  Pl. XXVI, 22

ETYMOLOGY: Formed from the proper name De Tracy; Lat. *bullaoides*, bubblelike.

SIZE: 11 mm. (about 1/2 in.) in height, 5 mm. (1/5 in.) wide.

DISTRIBUTION: Southern Florida, Cedar Keys to Florida Keys, the West Indies.

CHARACTERISTICS: Shell small, ovate, spindle shaped, heavy, thick, shining. Dark brownish, occasionally with white revolving bands. Aperture narrow, widest below, a single heavy lamella on the columellar margin; outer lip thin with six to eight narrow horizontal ridges.

The Bubble-shaped Marsh Snail is readily distinguished from other marsh snails of approximately the same size by their more elongate, almost spindle-shaped outline. They are found under logs and other drift at the high-tide line, or under rocks not far from the beach.

The **Floridian Marsh Snail,** *Detracia floridana* Pfeiffer (pl. XXVI, 23), 8 mm. (1/3 in.) in height and 5 mm. (1/5 in.) in width, is wider and lighter in color than *D. bullaoides*, usually with several darker bands. It is further distinguished from *D. bullaoides* by the presence of two rather than one parietal (columellar) ridges in the aperture, the lower one always being the heavier one. The outer or palatal wall has about ten almost equal white horizontal ridges. This species is common in less saline marshes, where *Melampus bidentatus* does not live. In 1950 Dr. J. P. E. Morrison found such a concentration of the Floridian Marsh Snail in the Pocomoke River estuary in Virginia that he estimated there were more individuals of the *Detracia* in one square mile than there were human beings in the entire world. It will be interesting to see if such high population densities can be maintained despite the deleterious activities of mankind. This species has been found in Delaware and Chesapeake Bays, eastern and western Florida, and along the Gulf coast to Louisiana.

**Clark's Marsh Snail,** *Detracia clarki* Morrison (named for Austin H. Clark, late curator of echinoderms at the National Museum) (pl. XXVI, 24), 13 mm. (about 1/2 in.) in height, 7 mm. (about 1/4 in.) in width, is roughly similar in shape to *Melampus*, but differs in having a heavier columellar ridge that is dished or has the outer margin curved upward like a railing as it enters the aperture. It also attains a larger size than *M. bidentatus*. It has been reported from several localities along the Florida Keys as well as in Virginia Key in Biscayne Bay.

## KEY TO GENERA MELAMPUS AND PIRA

*(after Morrison, 1958)*

| | |
|---|---|
| * Shell without incised spiral sculpture | *Melampus coffeus* |
| * Shell with incised spiral sculpture | |
| ** Sculpture of incised spiral lines on body whorl above the shoulder | *M. bidentatus* |
| ** Sculpture of a single central row of periostracal hairs or pit scars on each whorl of spire | *Pira monilis* |

Genus *Melampus* Montfort

*Melampus bidentatus* Say
　　Common Marsh Snail

　　Pl. XXVI, 25

ETYMOLOGY: Gr. *melas*, black, and *pous*, *pod*, foot; Lat. *bidentatus*, two-toothed.

SIZE: Up to 10 mm. (2/5 in.) in height, 6 mm. (1/4 in.) in width.

DISTRIBUTION: Canada and New England to Florida and west to Texas.

CHARACTERISTICS: Shell small, rather thin, ovate-conic, widest above; spire short, body whorl 3/4 to 5/6 of entire shell. Color horn or brownish, sometimes with narrow revolving lines; smooth, shining but often eroded. Body whorl above shoulder with incised spiral lines. Aperture long, widest below, lip thin; inner lip white, enameled, with two toothlike folds; outer lip usually has one to four short horizontal ridges.

These small snails occur in huge numbers in tidal salt marshes, where they live on sedges and in wet places under washed-up debris. The brown color bands are more frequently found on young specimens. *Melampus lineatus* Say is a synonym.

The **Coffee-bean Marsh Snail,** *Melampus coffeus* Linnaeus (pl. XXVI, 26), is larger, 18 mm. high (3/4 in.) and heavier, the surface is fawn colored usually with one to three narrow, cream-colored bands, and it lacks the incised lines on the body whorl. It lives in large numbers on mudflats or marsh grasses and low shrubs in southern Florida and on the Keys.

The **Pear Marsh Snail,** *Pira monilis* Bruguière (Lat. *pirum*, pear; *monile*, necklace) (pl. XXVI, 27), is 15 mm. (3/5 in.) high and differs from *Melampus* by having, on each spiral whorl, a single central row of periostracal hairs, which become a row of pit scars when the hairs fall out. Moreover, the second parietal denticle is set far inside the shell aperture, whereas in the other two species it is near the outside. This shell has been mistakenly called *Melampus flavus* Gmelin, an Indo-Pacific species. It ranges from southern Florida through the West Indies to South America.

The **Mouse-eared Marsh Snail,** *Ovatella myosotis* Draparnaud (diminutive of Lat. *ovatus*, oval; Gr. *myosotis*, mouse ear) (pl. XXVI, 28), is 8 mm. (1/3 in.) in height, 3 mm. (1/8 in.) in width. The small, elongate-ovate shell is translucent, thin, smooth, and shining, in color light horn or brown, often tinted with violet. The spire is high, the body whorl somewhat higher than the spire. The narrow aperture has three white teeth on the inner lip, the lowest one formed by the inward turning of the lip. The outer lip is thin. In immature stages there is a row of tiny hairs along the suture. This species is found in crevices of wood or rock just at the tide line. It can be recognized by its narrow shape, shiny, generally dark color, and the three apertural teeth. It is more slender than *Melampus* and smaller and narrower than *Detracia*. It is a common inhabitant of jetties. It was formerly placed in the genera *Phytia* and *Alexia*.

The **Egg-shaped Marsh Snail,** *Tralia ovula* Bruguière (Tralia might be a proper name; Lat. *ovula*, a little egg) (pl. XXVI, 29), is 13 mm. (about 1/2 in.) high, 7 mm. (about 1/4 in.) wide. This species can be recognized by its rather large size, dark, almost black, shiny color, and most of all by the thickened outer lip with its single revolving internal ridge. The range is from Miami to the West Indies, but the shell has not often been collected. A synonym is *T. pusilla* Gmelin.

SUPERFAMILY:

# SIPHONARIACEA

---

FAMILY:

# SIPHONARIIDAE
(*false limpets*)

These shells closely resemble typical limpets (family Acmaeidae), but differ in the presence of a small but distinct siphonal groove that projects beyond the margin of the shell. The surface is generally strongly ridged and the interior highly polished. This family of air-breathing snails live attached to rocks near the high-tide line in warmer waters. These limpets can be distinguished by the presence of the lateral siphonal groove and the lateral location of the muscle-scar gap. In true limpets (families Acmaeidae and Patellidae) there is no siphonal groove, and the gap is placed anteriorly. They are popularly called "false limpets" because, though they do not have gills, they breathe atmospheric air. Dr. Abbott points out that, because of this mode of respiration, they are more closely related to the common garden snails than to the gill-bearing limpets they so closely resemble.

Genus *Siphonaria* Sowerby

*Siphonaria alternata* Say
  Say's False Limpet

  Pl. XXI, 21

ETYMOLOGY: Gr. *siphon*, and Lat. *alternatum*.

SIZE: 15 to 20 mm. (3/5 to 4/5 in.) long, 15 mm. (3/5 in.) wide.

DISTRIBUTION: Southeastern Florida (and Sarasota) to the Keys.

CHARACTERISTICS: Shell limpetlike, strong. Gray to cream. Surface
  roughened by about twenty to twenty-five small, radiating white ribs
  with smaller riblets between. Interior glossy tan, occasionally with
  dark brown spots or stripes. A small but distinct siphonal groove on
  the right side projects slightly beyond the outer margin. Muscle scar
  horseshoe shaped, gap located at side near groove.


The **Striped False Limpet,** *Siphonaria pectinata* Linnaeus (Lat.
*pecten*, comb) (pl. XXVI, 30), differs in having a relatively smooth
shell decorated with numerous narrow, forking brown lines. This
species has a wide distribution from the Mediterranean, the Azores
and Cape Verde Islands, and the west coast of Africa to the West
Indies. The Georgian, Floridian, and West Indian form differs slightly
in having forked or bifurcated lines, whereas elsewhere the lines are
single. This species was also called *Siphonaria lineolata* Orbigny and
*S. naufragum* Stearns. The latter name, meaning "shipwreck," was
proposed by Stearns because he found specimens living on driftwood.

# CHAPTER II

# LAND
# SNAILS

With few exceptions, most notably the tree snails, *Liguus* and *Orthalicus* in Florida, the land snails of the region discussed in this book represent a small, uncolorful, and inconspicuous element of the fauna. The shells of most of the indigenous species are predominantly somber brown or horn colored, and few species have striking sculptural features. The specific and generic characteristics are frequently obscure, and call for close and careful observation, especially since so many of the species are small to tiny in size.

To these native constituents of our terrestrial snail fauna, there has been added a prominent and possibly growing foreign element. These introduced species are more aggressive and vigorous than the native snails, and constitute the only group that is occasionally destructive to agriculture. The foreign snails are often more colorful and larger. They betray their alien origin by clustering around the sites where they first arrived, and they may spread to other urban areas. They are rarely found in the wooded American heartland.

Only brief mention can be made of the biology of the terrestrial pulmonates. The harsher conditions of life on land, as compared to life in the sea, are reflected, in part, by the fact that by far the greater number of land snails are hermaphrodites, enabling each individual to be a potential bearer of young. This major evolutionary achievement of the terrestrial gastropods has helped make the pulmonates one of the most successful land dwellers. The few nonhermaphroditic land snails of our region are confined to Florida and the neighboring states, and have limited ranges. They are characterized by being operculates.

Most land mollusks are herbivores. The native ones prefer to eat decaying vegetation in which small fungi and mycelium threads are found. The introduced species, however, mostly consume living vegetation. Some eat cultivated garden and farm products, thus constituting a nuisance, if not a hazard, to gardeners and farmers. Much study has been devoted to the control of these pests. In addition, there are a few predaceous species, such as the genera *Euglandina* and

*Haplotrema,* which feed on various kinds of worms as well as on other mollusks. Some slugs, unshelled pulmonates not treated in this book, are known to be omnivorous, feeding upon both plants and animals. Slugs can be serious pests in greenhouses and gardens.

All the pulmonate land snails discussed in this chapter belong to the order Stylommatophora (Gr. *stylos omma pherein,* pillar eye bearer), which are characterized by having their eyes borne at the tip of pillars, the snail's "horns" of popular speech. The pillar on which each eye rests is invaginable, that is, it can be drawn in like the finger of a glove pulled back from the inside tip. The order Basommatophora (Gr. *baso omma pherein,* base eye bearer) carry their eyes at the base of retractable, but not invaginable, tentacles. These snails, which also are air breathers, inhabit freshwater and salt marshes.

Finally, a word might be said about collecting land snails. Little equipment is necessary: a tool, like a hand rake or any convenient substitute, to stir up the ground surface, any and all sorts of convenient containers, small and large, to hold the catch, and most importantly, a notebook and pencil to record ecological and distributional data. Fruitful areas for snail collecting are moist, shaded spots in forest ravines. Limestone cliffs shaded by heavy foliage are ideal habitats. Flat, forested areas are richest at the margins rather than in the thicker parts, and coniferous forests, though not barren, tend to yield little. Other good spots are deserted forest garbage dumps. There many snails are found clinging to the undersides of corrugated boards and other light, moisture-conserving cover.

When to search? Ideally, in the morning after rainy nights, or on any spring or summer night with a strong flashlight or lantern. At such times snails become active and freely leave their hiding places.

Land snail collecting is not unattended by a certain unpleasantness or even danger. We call brief attention to such things to avoid as thistles, poison ivy and poison oak, ticks, chiggers, scorpions, mosquitos, and above all, poisonous snakes.

We have already pointed out that land shells are not as richly colored, variously formed, or highly sculptured as the shells of most marine prosobranch snails. On the other hand, the internal anatomy, especially the sexual apparatus, is highly diversified in land snails. Unfortunately, these complicated internal features are not reflected in the morphology of the shells, and thus many land genera, which differ markedly from one another in their internal anatomical characters, have very similar-looking shells.

For this reason, we have included in some discussions the species of more than one genus or, occasionally, even two or more families, especially when only a few species are involved. However, when a genus includes a relatively large number of species, or when the shells are sufficiently distinct, we have discussed these in separate sections. The reader will thus be able to identify species by the use of the shell alone and by comparison with the shells of other species without having to delve into differences of the radulae and reproductive anatomy.

# KEY TO LAND SHELL GENERA AND/OR FAMILIES

| | |
|---|---|
| * Shell with operculum | |
| * * Shell width equal to or greater than height | *Helicina* |
| | *Lucidella* |
| * * Shell width considerably less than height | *Chondropoma* |
| | *Truncatella* |
| * Shell without operculum | |
| * * Shell height greater than width | |
| * * * Lip sharp, simple, lip teeth wanting | |
| * * * * Shell shape ovate-conic | Bulimulidae |
| | *Achatina* |
| | Succineidae |
| | *Cochlicella* |
| * * * * Shell shape turreted, white or light colored | Subulinidae |
| * * * * Shell shape oblong, color brownish or pinkish | *Euglandina* |
| | *Cionella* |
| * * * Lip thickened and/or expanded, lip teeth often present | Urocoptidae |
| | *Gulella* |
| | *Cerion* |
| | Pupillidae |
| * * Shell height equal to or less than width | |
| * * * Lip sharp, simple, lip teeth wanting | Endodontidae |
| | Zonitidae |
| | *Haplotrema* |
| | Sagdidae |
| | Camaenidae |
| | Helminthoglyptidae |
| | *Hygromia* |
| | *Helicella* |

* * * Lip thickened and/or expanded, lip teeth
    often present

       *Vallonia*
       Polygyridae
       Helicidae
       *Strobilops*

CLASS:

# GASTROPODA

SUBCLASS:

## PROSOBRANCHIA

*(gills placed before the heart)*

ORDER:

## ARCHAEOGASTROPODA

*(early or primitive prosobranchs)*

# HELICINACEA

# HELICINIDAE
(*helicinid snails*)

These shells are small, low conic or depressed, smooth; the aperture is a half moon in shape, the operculum is horny or limy. The presence of an operculum distinguishes the members of this and the following family, Pomatiasidae (page 204), from all other local land shells. The Helicinidae are chiefly a tropical and subtropical family, with the richest development in the West Indies and Southeast Asia. Absent from Europe, Africa, and northern Asia, they are represented in the midwestern United States by a single, rapidly disappearing species. Though they are air breathers, they differ radically from the pulmonates, and are directly descended from the archaeogastropod prosobranch family Neritidae. This serves to explain the presence of an operculum, an organ present in only a very few aberrant Pulmonata. In the struggle to maintain themselves as air-breathing land dwellers, the helicinids are at a disadvantage when compared to the terrestrial pulmonates, since in the helicinids the sexes are separate and only the females can give birth to young. In the case of the hermaphroditic pulmonates, however, each adult is potentially capable of producing offspring.

Genus *Helicina* Lamarck

*Helicina orbiculata* Say
  Common Florida Helicina

  Pl. XXVII, 1

ETYMOLOGY: Diminutive of Gr. *helix*, spiral; Lat. *orbiculatus*, circular.

SIZE: 6 to 8 mm. (1/4 to 1/3 in.) in diameter, 5 to 7 mm. (about 1/5 to 1/4 in.) in height.

DISTRIBUTION: Islands off Georgia to Florida and westward to Oklahoma.

CHARACTERISTICS: Shell small, globose-conic, solid, not glossy. White to buff, sometimes pink, often with brownish bands. Umbilicus lacking.

Lip slightly expanded, somewhat thickened. Operculum ear shaped, corneous.

The Helicinidae form an important part of the molluscan land fauna of tropical America, especially the Greater Antilles. They may be found in large numbers on low bushes and grasses.

**Clapp's Helicina,** *Helicina clappi* Pilsbry (named for William F. Clapp, a prominent malacologist of the early twentieth century) (pl. XXVII, 2), is less globose and lower than *H. orbiculata*, and the body whorl is more angular at the periphery. The color is occasionally livelier, being pale citrine, white with two red bands, or uniformly red. The species is confined to southern Florida and the Keys.

Genus *Lucidella* Swainson

*Lucidella tantilla* Pilsbry
  Tiny Lucidella

  Pl. XXVIII, 1

ETYMOLOGY: Diminutive of Lat. *lucidus*, shining; Lat. *tantillus*, so little.

SIZE: 3 mm. (1/8 in.) in diameter, 2 mm. (1/12 in.) in height.

DISTRIBUTION: Southern Florida and the Keys.

CHARACTERISTICS: Shell minute, much depressed, glossy. Faintly yellowish. Surface has regular, fine, clear-cut axial striae. Umbilical area covered with a papillose callus; lip rounded, thickened.

This shell is easily distinguished from other flattened lilliputians by the presence of the heavy callus covering the umbilical area. Other features are visible under slight magnification. This species, as Pilsbry writes, "is probably a hurricane-borne waif from Cuba." It can be found where land shells usually congregate, under damp leaves and in moist, shady areas.

# ORDER:
# MESOGASTROPODA
(*middle prosobranchs*)

---

FAMILY:
# POMATIASIDAE
(*land periwinkles*)

These shells are small, narrowly conic or cylindrical, surface minutely but strongly sculptured with axial lines; operculum horny, ornamented with a thin and variously sculptured outer layer of calcium; lip thickened, often double. The early whorls are usually lost as the shell matures. The members of this family, like those of the Helicinidae, are not pulmonates, but are land prosobranchs related to the mesogastropod family of marine periwinkles (Littorinidae). The Pomatiasidae are well developed in the Antilles, especially in Cuba, Jamaica, and Hispaniola, where scores of endemic species occur. Related groups are found in South and Central America, Europe, North Africa, and Asia. Some writers afford special recognition for the New World species by placing them in the family Chondropomidae.

Genus *Chondropoma* Pfeiffer

*Chondropoma dentatum* Say
Dentate Land Periwinkle

Pl. XXIX, 1

ETYMOLOGY: Gr. *chondros*, grain; *poma*, operculum.

SIZE: 10 to 12 mm. (2/5 to 1/2 in.) in height, 6 to 7 mm. (about 1/4 in.) in diameter.

DISTRIBUTION: Miami and south to Key West, Florida.

CHARACTERISTICS: Shell small, oblong-conic, truncated, with about four whorls remaining; dull. Surface closely decussated; suture with unevenly spaced, tiny, toothlike serrations. Light tan, sometimes with faint spiral bands or spots. Umbilicus narrow, lip white, little expanded. Operculum oval, corneous, with thin, limy outer layer.

These land periwinkles are commonly found on the undersides of limestone blocks, but they move about freely on the surface of the rocks after rains. *C. dentatum* is closely related to a Cuban species from Matanzas.

The **Bahamian Land Periwinkle,** *Opisthosiphon bahamensis* Pfeiffer (Gr. *opisthon siphon*, rear siphon) (pl. XXVIII, 2), is about 9 mm. (about 2/5 in.) in height. It looks very much like *C. dentatum,* but differs chiefly in having a wide, double lip and a tiny, erect, hollow tube at the upper angle of the aperture that enables the animal to breathe when the operculum is in place. The generic name refers to this tiny breathing tube. This species, a native Bahamian, was known in our area only in Key West, Florida, but has not been recorded recently.

FAMILY:

# TRUNCATELLIDAE

(*looping snails*)

These shells are small, cylindrical; their immature whorls, which are much narrower, are discarded as the shell matures. The lip is often doubled, and the operculum is horny. This is a widely distributed family living under protective material like detached seaweed, boards, and rocks above high tide. Local populations of looping snails may consist of numerous individuals. The popular name is based upon the animal's way of walking; locomotion is accomplished by looping along like measuring or inch worms, using first the snout and then the foot.

# KEY TO GENUS TRUNCATELLA

* Shell with simple lip               *Truncatella pulchella*
* Shell with lip doubled by presence of a thick,
   prominent rib behind inner lip
** Shell with 8 to 11 coarse, well-shaped axial ribs
     on last whorl                           *T. scalaris*
** Shell with 22 to 28 closely set axial ribs on last
     whorl, or with ribs lacking and replaced by
     scallops under the suture              *T. bilabiata*

---

Genus *Truncatella* Risso

*Truncatella bilabiata* Pfeiffer
   Double-lipped Looping Snail

   Pl. XXVII, 3

ETYMOLOGY: Diminutive of Lat. *truncus*, deprived of some parts; Lat. *bi labium*, two lipped.

SIZE: 4 to 5 mm. (1/6 to 1/5 in.) in length (truncated specimens), 2 mm. (1/12 in.) wide.

DISTRIBUTION: Southern half of Florida.

CHARACTERISTICS: Shell small, almost cylindrical. Light tan or pinkish tan to whitish gray. Three and one-half to four whorls after truncation, rather solid. Sculpture of fine, closely set ribs, twenty-two to twenty-eight on the last whorl. Umbilicus lacking; lip appears to be doubled by the presence of a thick prominent rib behind the inner lip.

In this species and in *T. pulchella* (see below), specimens may be found without any axial ribs; the ribs are replaced by narrow, fine scalloping just below the suture, the surface otherwise being smooth and glossy. The earlier truncated whorls are small, turreted, and not cylindrical.

The **Trellis Looping Snail,** *Truncatella scalaris* Michaud (Lat. *scala*, ladder) (pl. XXIX, 2), is similar, but the axial ribs are coarser and more widely spaced, there being eight to eleven on the last whorl. The shell is buff to dark reddish brown, and the lip is similar to that of the previous species. *T. scalaris* is rather rare in southern Florida, where it occurs in several isolated populations. This species was formerly known as *T. clathrus* Lowe (Lat. *clathri,* trellis) but *scalaris* has two years' priority.

The **Pretty Looping Snail,** *Truncatella pulchella* Pfeiffer (diminutive of Lat. *pulcher,* pretty) (pl. XXVII, 4), differs from the other two species in having a simple lip without the added outer ridge. It is yellow or light amber in color. Both ribbed, as in *T. bilabiata,* and rib-less forms with narrow sutural scalloping occur here also. It is the most widely spread locally of the looping snails, ranging from North Carolina to Florida and westward to Texas, as well as to the West Indies.

## SUBCLASS:

# PULMONATA

*(lung breathers)*

## ORDER:

# BASOMMATOPHORA

*(eyes at base of tentacles)*

## SUPERFAMILY:

# MELAMPACEA

## FAMILY:

# CARYCHIIDAE

*(swamp snails)*

These shells are minute, white, often translucent; aperture narrow, with internal ridges. Lip usually expanded, often thick. This widely distributed family lives on land near bodies of fresh water. Pilsbry, after reviewing related fossil genera and living ones in other parts of the world, concluded that they generally represented "dead ends" of evolution. One genus in southeastern Europe consists entirely of blind cave dwellers. Pilsbry writes: "The experiment of sessile-eyed land pulmonates seems to have been rather unsuccessful in the long run." Apparently because of their reliance upon water, they could not compete with the stalk-eyed snails, the Stylommatophora.

Genus *Carychium*

*Carychium exiguum* Say
    White Swamp Snail

    Pl. XXIX, 3

ETYMOLOGY: Gr. *karichion*, horn; Lat. *exiguus*, little.

SIZE: 2 mm. (1/12 in.) in height, 1 mm. (1/25 in.) in diameter.

DISTRIBUTION: Canada and Maine to North Carolina and westward to Colorado.

CHARACTERISTICS: Shell minute, turreted, narrow, smooth, with faint growth striae. Whitish horn color, translucent. Umbilicus slitlike, aperture with two parietal lamellae; lip expanded, thickened.

This basommatophoran (sessile-eyed) land snail is found inland but never far from water. It is thus more closely related to the freshwater pulmonates. Slender specimens, named *Carychium exile* H. C. Lea, are now considered to be variants of this species.

The **Mexican Swamp Snail,** *Carychium mexicanum* Pilsbry (pl. XXIX, 4), differs by its smaller size, only 1–1.5 mm., and chiefly by its greatly thickened lip. It occurs throughout Florida, and has been found in South Carolina and Texas. Formerly known as *C. floridanum* Clapp, a later name.

# ORDER:

# STYLOMMATOPHORA

## SUBORDER:

# ORTHURETHRA
*(straight, unflexed ureter)*

## SUPERFAMILY:

# CIONELLACEA

## FAMILY:

# CIONELLIDAE
*(apple-seed snails)*

A small family of tiny, glossy, translucent, horn-colored shells with a sharp, simple lip. Individuals often occur in huge numbers, even in urban lots and parks.

Genus *Cionella* Jeffreys

*Cionella lubrica* Müller
   Apple-seed Snail

   Pl. XXVII, 5

ETYMOLOGY: Diminutive of Gr. *kion*, pillar; Lat. *lubricus*, slippery.

SIZE: 6 mm. (1/4 in.) in height, 3 mm. (1/8 in.) in diameter.

DISTRIBUTION: Canada and United States, except some southern states.

CHARACTERISTICS: Shell quite small, cylindrical but gradually tapering upward. Yellowish, corneous, smooth and glossy, weakly transparent. Umbilicus lacking, lip simple.

This is a Palaearctic (northern Old World) genus, with only the single species in North America. The apple-seed snails live in leaf mold, under bits of wood and stone, and in stone crevices, and can be found in urban lots as well as in woodlands. Occasionally huge swarms of shells can be found, congregating possibly, as Pilsbry speculates, for mating. Pilsbry also calls them "enviably weatherwise," because they are said to become active six to eight hours before rain.

---

FAMILY:

# VALLONIIDAE

These snails form a small family. The shells are minute, flattened, slightly raised, or ovate-conic; surface commonly sculptured with raised ribs; aperture round, lip generally well developed, rarely sharp or simple; umbilicus usually prominent. Specimens are common in city gardens and flower pots.

Genus *Vallonia* Risso

*Vallonia pulchella* Müller
Handsome Vallonia

Pl. XXVIII, 3

ETYMOLOGY: Vallonia is said to have been the classical goddess of valleys; Lat. *pulchellus*, diminutive of *pulcher*, beautiful.

SIZE: 2 mm. (1/12 in.) in diameter, 1 mm. (1/25 in.) in height.

DISTRIBUTION: In North America east of the Rocky Mountains, from Nova Scotia to Kentucky. Introduced into Texas and California.

CHARACTERISTICS: Shell tiny, depressed. Glassy white or pale, corneous, semitransparent. The three to three and one-half whorls are

microscopically striate. Lip opaque and well reflected about the
circular aperture. Umbilicus large, about one-quarter of diameter.

This pleasing little shell has a wide distribution in the northern
hemisphere, as do the other two species of *Vallonia* described below.
It is at times very common, and can be taken under moist boards,
stones, bricks, shrubbery, or flower pots, even in city lots and gardens.
A board left in a sheltered spot in contact with the soil and kept
persistently moist will in time attract a colony of *Vallonia*.

The **Ribbed Vallonia,** *Vallonia costata* Müller (Lat. *costa*, rib)
(pl. XXVIII, 4), differs from *V. pulchella* mainly in the presence of
raised, widely spaced oblique axial ribs. They are readily visible under
light magnification.

The **Off-center Vallonia,** *Vallonia excentrica* Sterki (pl. XXVIII, 5),
differs from the other two species "by the more oblong contour of the
shell and umbilicus, the last whorl widening more towards the
aperture . . . and by the smaller and lower spire" (Pilsbry). Some
scholars express doubt about the validity of this form as a species.

The **Tiny Star Shell,** *Planogyra asteriscus* Morse (Lat. *planus*, flat,
Gr. *gyros*, whorl; Gr. *aster*, star) (pl. XXVII, 6), is a minute speck of a
shell, less than 2 mm. in diameter and less than 1 mm. in height. This
mite can be distinguished from its larger relative, *Vallonia*, by its
brown instead of whitish color; its level, flattened spire; and its thin,
unreflected instead of expanded lip. The periostracum is ornamented
with thin, high, irregularly spaced, axial ribs on the body whorl. This
species ranges from Canada to New York and westward to Michigan,
living only in very wet, boggy places and swampy thickets, where it
inhabits the deeper layers of fallen leaves. It is not an easy snail to
find.

The **Tiny Harp Snail,** *Zoogenetes harpa* Say ("The name *Zoogenetes* signifies that reproduction is by living young instead of eggs"
[Pilsbry]) (pl. XXVIII, 6), is 3 mm. (1/8 in.) in height, 3 mm. (1/8 in.)
in diameter. This member of the family Valloniidae is readily recognized by its raised, ovate-conic shell, as the dimensions show. The
thin, translucent shell is olive green and rather glossy. The last two
of the four whorls are sculptured with low, widely spaced, oblique
axial ribs, and the lip is thin and not reflected. This is another northern
species ranging from Canada to New York and westward to Oklahoma, living generally in mountainous country. It is a hardy snail,
hibernating on leaves just below the surface, not deeply buried. It

also occurs in the northern regions of Europe and Asia. The writers once collected a series on the Gaspé Peninsula in Quebec by leaving a piece of corrugated cardboard on the ground near their cabin. Every morning a few specimens were found under the board.

SUPERFAMILY:

# PUPILLACEA

FAMILY:

# PUPILLIDAE
(*pupa snails*)

This is a very large family of minute, ovate, cylindrical or pupa-shaped shells, worldwide in distribution. The color is brownish or white, the lip is expanded, and the aperture is commonly armed with teeth. For the most part these snails live in leaf mold, where they cling to tiny branches or twigs. Some, like *Vertigo ovata,* live on the shores of forest ponds and streams. Specimens of *Vertigo* have been collected alive even on sunny winter days when the temperature hovered below freezing. Another rich source of dead but well-preserved pupillid specimens is in dry river drift.

These tiny creatures can best be collected when bags of promising forest debris are taken home, dried out, and then carefully sifted and examined under a magnifying glass. Frequently the apertures of the shells are obstructed by dried mucus or dirt, thus hindering the examination for the presence of apertural denticles. Cleaning this obstruction is a delicate job, done with infinite patience and the finest of insect pins. An easier job is to submerge the shells in a fluid, which is then subjected to supersonic vibrations in a machine such as dentists use to clean dentures. To facilitate description, the various apertural denticles have been given technical names, which are clarified in the accompanying labeled illustration. As in all cases, the keys and descriptions refer to mature specimens only; the immature forms lack important diagnostic characteristics or have these insufficiently developed.

Shell collectors customarily avoid tiny shells, but in our rather unexciting land snail fauna, these lilliputians form a most interesting and structurally pleasing element. It would be a mistake to disregard them.

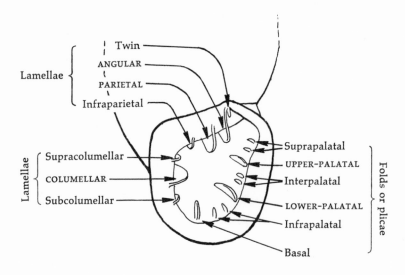

*Terminology of pupillid teeth, the five primary lamellae and folds indicated by capitals. Diagrammatic (after Pilsbry, 1948, p. 869).*

## KEY TO FAMILY PUPILLIDAE

   \* Shell without conspicuous apertural denticles
     and lamellae
  \*\* Shell with 3 1/2 whorls, low conic
\*\*\* Shell with distinct spiral striae           *Pupisoma dioscoricola*
\*\*\* Shell without spiral striae               *P. minus*
  \*\* Shell with 5 1/2 to 6 1/2 whorls, high
\*\*\* Shell with thin lip                 *Columella edentula*
\*\*\* Shell with more or less wide, reflected lip
\*\*\*\* Shell quite cylindrical, occasionally with 1
      to 3 tiny denticles               *Pupilla muscorum*

**** Shell with gradually tapering sides,
     normally with an inconspicuous denticle    *Pupoides albilabris*
  * Shell with conspicuous apertural denticles
    and lamellae
  ** Shell with outer lip indented in middle,
    brownish    Genus *Vertigo*
  ** Shell with outer lip rounded, tannish brown
    to white    Genus *Gastrocopta*

---

Genus *Pupilla* Leach

*Pupilla muscorum* Linnaeus
  The Moss Pupa Snail

  Pl. XXIX, 5

ETYMOLOGY: Diminutive of Lat. *pupa*; *muscus*, moss.

SIZE: 3 to 4 mm. (1/8 to 1/6 in.) in height, 1 mm. (1/25 in.) in diameter.

DISTRIBUTION: Canada and Maine to New Jersey and westward to Oregon
  and New Mexico.

CHARACTERISTICS: Shell tiny, quite cylindrical. Brownish, white behind lip,
  moderately solid. Umbilicus slitlike; lip narrowly reflected.

This small shell differs from *Columella* and *Pupoides* by its much
more cylindrical shape, the sides being quite parallel except at the
three topmost whorls. The aperture occasionally has one to three tiny
teeth. The species is also found in Europe and North Africa.

    The **Toothless Pupa Snail,** *Columella edentula* Draparnaud (dimin-
utive of Lat. *columna,* column; *edentatus,* rendered toothless) (pl.
XXIX, 6), is a tiny snail only 2 mm. (1/12 in.) in height, 1 mm. (1/25
in.) in diameter. It can be recognized by its tiny size, five to six whorls,
and the thin, smooth, brownish shell with narrow umbilicus and
sharp, thin lip. It ranges from Canada to Virginia and westward to
Oregon.

    The **White-lipped Pupa Snail,** *Pupoides albilabris* C. B. Adams
(Gr. *pupoides,* pupa-like; Lat. *albus labris,* white lip) (pl. XXVII, 7),
measures 5 mm. (1/5 in.) in height, 2 mm. (1/12 in.) in diameter. The
shell is roughly cylindrical but gently tapering above. The aperture,
which commonly has a minute denticle, is surrounded by a wide, white
reflected lip. The dark cinnamon-colored shell is usually coated with

dirt when alive. This species ranges from Maine to Florida and westward to Arizona. The related *Pupoides modicus* Gould (Lat. *modicus*, intermediate, moderate) (pl. XXIX, 7), is found on some islands off Georgia and from Cedar Key to Key West in Florida, as well as in the Bahamas. It differs by being smaller, only 4 mm. (1/6 in.) in height, narrower, and by having a more strongly striated surface.

The **Low Pupa Snail**, *Pupisoma minus* Pilsbry (Gr. *soma*, body; Lat. *minus*, smaller) (pl. XXVIII, 7), measures no more than 1.35 mm. (about 1/25 in.) in height, 1.25 mm. (about 1/25 in.) in diameter. This species differs from the other pupillids in having a low shell, the height only slightly exceeding the diameter, as the measurements show. Moreover there are only three and one-half whorls, the last one more than twice the size of the entire spire. This unpupillid shape may have induced Stoliczka, the author of the name *Pupisoma*, to indicate that, though the shell is not pupilla-like, the soft anatomy or the body (*soma*) is pupilloid. The shell is cinnamon colored, smooth but not glossy, and the lip is thin and sharp, widened near, but not covering, the umbilicus. This speck of a mollusk ranges from South Carolina to Florida.

The closely related **Yam Pupa Snail**, *Pupisoma dioscoricola* C. B. Adams (Dioscoracea is the botanical name for the yam family) (not illustrated), differs mainly in having the surface sculptured with distinct spiral striae. The widened portion of the thin lip in this species covers the umbilicus. This shell, only slightly larger than *P. minus*, is found from South Carolina to Florida and westward to Alabama and Texas. It also occurs in the West Indies and South America.

---

# KEY TO GENUS GASTROCOPTA

*(adapted from Burch, 1962)*

   \* Teeth on parietal wall well developed
  \*\* Palatal folds situated on callus ridge,
       aperture almost entirely filled by large
       teeth
 \*\*\* Shell larger than 3 mm. (1/8 in.), white,
       6 1/2 to 7 1/2 whorls, aperture squarish          *Gastrocopta armifera*
 \*\*\* Shell smaller than 3 mm., white or bluish
       white, 5 1/2 whorls, aperture triangular          *G. contracta*
  \*\* Palatal folds not situated on callus ridge,
       teeth not filling aperture
 \*\*\* Lip heavily callused within

\* \* \* \* Palatal fold strongly bifid, cinnamon to
  light brown ................................................ *G. procera*
\* \* \* \* Palatal fold weakly or not at all bifid, pale
  brown or white ............................................ *G. rupicola*
  \* \* \* Lip not callused within, shell slender, pale
    brown to white ................................ *G. pellucida hordeacella*
    \* Teeth on parietal wall not well developed
    \* \* Aperture without palatal fold, white,
      translucent ............................................ *G. corticaria*
    \* \* Aperture with palatal fold
    \* \* \* Shell ovate-conic, spire almost oval,
      corneous, white or gray ........................ *G. tappaniana*
    \* \* \* Shell elongate, spire tapering, white or
      corneous .............................................. *G. pentodon*

---

Genus *Gastrocopta* Wollaston
  Pupa Snails

ETYMOLOGY: Gr. *gastros*, stomach or belly, and *koptein*, to cut.

SIZE: 2 to 4 mm. (1/12 to 1/6 in.) in height.

DISTRIBUTION: North America except the Pacific slope.

CHARACTERISTICS: Shell very small, cylindrical or conic. Color light brown
  to white. Outer lip well rounded, umbilicate. Aperture with varying
  number of denticles.

The *Gastrocopta* are one of the two groups of local pupillids that are
provided with apertural denticles. They differ from *Vertigo*, the other
toothed pupillids, because the outer lip is rounded and does not bear a
central indentation. In color the *Gastrocopta* tend to be paler. The
local species of *Gastrocopta* fall conveniently into two groups, those
with well-developed parietal teeth and those with weak ones. These
two larger groups are then progressively divided, as can be seen by
consulting the keys. These tiny shells are collectively called pupa
snails.

*Gastrocopta armifera* Say (Lat. arm bearer) (pl. XXIX, 8) is rather
large, 3 to 4.8 mm. (about 1/8 to 1/5 in.) in height. The shell is
characterized by its oblong shape, large size, waxy appearance, and
large teeth, almost filling the squarish aperture. The palatal fold is
situated on a callus ridge. In life the shell is usually coated with a layer
of dirt. This is the commonest species in our area, Canada to Florida.

*Gastrocopta contracta* Say (Lat. draw together) (pl. XXVII, 8) is smaller, 2.5 mm. (about 1/8 in.) in height. The shell is more globose, white or bluish white, and the aperture is triangular in outline. The teeth are even more strongly developed in this species than in *G. armifera*. Canada to Florida.

*Gastrocopta procera* Gould (Lat. high, tall) (pl. XXIX, 9) is also small, not exceeding 3 mm. (1/8 in.) in height. The palatal fold is split into two teeth and not situated on a callus ridge, as it is in the two former species. The teeth, though large, do not seem to fill the aperture. The cylindrical shell is cinnamon brown, and the lip heavily callused within. Maryland to South Carolina.

*Gastrocopta rupicola* Say (Lat. rock dweller) (pl. XXVII, 9) is about 2.5 mm. (about 1/8 in.) in height. It is similar to *G. procera*, but lighter in color and less cylindrical in shape. The palatal fold is weakly or not at all bifid. It lives on limestone rocks and in ruins of old limestone buildings. South Carolina to Florida, especially the Keys.

*Gastrocopta pellucida hordeacella* Pilsbry (Lat. transparent; barley) (pl. XXIX, 10) reaches 2.3 mm. (about 1/12 in.) in height. The shell is extremely slender, and the lip, unlike *G. procera* and *G. rupicola*, is not callused within. Pale brown to white. New Jersey to Florida. The nominate form *G. pellucida* is West Indian.

*G. corticaria* Say (Lat. cortex or tree bark) (pl. XXIX, 11) has the teeth weakly developed on the parietal wall, and there is no palatal fold. The shell is 2.5 mm. (about 1/8 in.) in height, translucent white. It is best recognized by its greatly reduced teeth, smaller than in any other *Gastrocopta* species. It often crawls on trees a foot or two above the ground. Canada to Florida.

*G. pentodon* Say (Gr. five teeth) (pl. XXIX, 12) is only 1.5 mm. (about 1/12 in.) in height. The bluish white, waxy shell, with a single parietal tooth, is conic in shape, and the lip teeth are arranged on a white callus rim. There is a palatal fold. Canada to Florida.

*G. tappaniana* C. B. Adams (pl. XXIX, 13) reaches 2 mm. (1/12 in.) in height. It, too, has weak parietal teeth and a palatal fold. It is more ovate than *G. pentodon*, and prefers to live in low, moist situations, whereas the latter prefers dryer surroundings. Canada to Florida.

## KEY TO GENUS VERTIGO

* Lower palatal fold unusually long, almost reaching opposite side, shell brown or cinnamon        *Vertigo milium*
* Lower palatal fold short or not unusually long

\*\* Shell cylindrical
\*\*\* Aperture with 4 small teeth, almost equal in length,
    dark olive brown to chestnut brown        *V. modesta*
\*\*\* Aperture with 5 teeth, unequal in length, lower
    palatal tooth longest; shell amber to light cinnamon  *V. bollesiana*
 \*\* Shell tapering, 8 to 9 strong teeth in small aperture,
    shell auburn to chestnut brown        *V. morsei*
 \*\* Shell ovate
\*\*\* Aperture with 6 to 9 well-developed teeth almost
    filling aperture, shell auburn or dark brown    *V. ovata*
\*\*\* Aperture with 5 poorly developed teeth, shell auburn  *V. ventricosa*

---

Genus *Vertigo* Müller
   Brown Pupa Snails

ETYMOLOGY: Lat. *vertere*, to turn.

SIZE: 1.8 mm. (about 1/12 in.) to 3 mm. (1/8 in.) in height.

DISTRIBUTION: Generally in entire northern North America, a few species
   reaching South Carolina and Florida.

CHARACTERISTICS: Shell oval, cylindrical oblong or ovate, glossy. Some
   shade or tint of brown. Narrowly umbilicate, outer lip with a sharp
   indentation. Aperture variously ornamented with denticles or lamellae.

The species of *Vertigo* differ from *Gastrocopta* in the presence of a
sharp indentation in the middle of the outer lip. Otherwise the shells
are very much alike, except that the color of *Vertigo* tends to be
darker brown.

    *Vertigo ovata* (New Lat. *ovatus,* egg shaped) (pl. XXVIII, 8) is
about 2.5 mm. (about 1/8 in.) in height. The shell is ovate, glossy,
brown, and smooth. The teeth are well developed. It prefers very
moist situations on the margins of woodland ponds and streams. It
is the commonest and most widely spread *Vertigo* species in our area.
Canada to Florida.

    *Vertigo ventricosa* Morse (Lat. *venter,* belly) (pl. XXIX, 14) reaches
2 mm. (1/12 in.) in height. It is similar to *V. ovata,* but constantly
smaller, and with weaker and fewer apertural teeth. It is a localized
northern species found only from Canada to New York.

    *Vertigo morsei* Sterki (named for E. S. Morse, 1838–1925, a
zoologist) (not illus.) has a tapering rather than cylindrical shell.
It reaches 3 mm. (1/8 in.) in height and resembles *V. ovata,* but has

six narrower whorls rather than five wider ones. Chestnut brown to auburn. Found only in New Jersey and New York.

*Vertigo modesta* Say (Lat. *modestus,* modest) (pl. XXIX, 15) reaches about 2.5 mm. (about 1/8 in.) in height. It is readily recognizable because it has only 4 equal teeth arranged like a cross. Dark olive-brown to chestnut. Canada to Connecticut.

*Vertigo bollesiana* Morse (named for a Mr. Bolles) (pl. XXIX, 16) is only 1.5 mm. (about 1/16 in.) in height. It resembles *V. modesta,* but is smaller and has 5 small and unequal teeth, the lower palatal one being the largest. Amber to light brown. Canada to New York, in hardwood forests.

*Vertigo milium* Gould (Lat. *millet*) (pl. XXIX, 17) is 1.8 mm. (about 1/12 in.) in height. It differs from all the other species of *Vertigo* in our area by having an unusually long palatal fold that crosses the aperture and almost reaches the opposite side. The oval shell is pale cinnamon in color. Canada to Florida.

---

FAMILY:

# STROBILOPSIDAE

(*labyrinth snails*)

The shells are tiny, mostly low conic or dome shaped, rarely depressed. The brownish surface is characteristically sculptured with closely set but well-developed axial ribs, and the aperture has several variously developed, long internal ridges, or lamellae. The snails live in decaying logs in moderately humid forests, especially in North America west of the Rockies, but are found also in South America, Japan, China, and the Philippines, and as a fossil in Europe.

The identification of the shells depends to some degree upon the number, location, and size of the folds located internally on the base of the last whorl. To examine these, it is necessary to remove the upper whorls and spire of the shell, leaving the basal part of the whorls exposed.

---

## KEY TO GENUS STROBILOPS

* Shell depressed, umbilicus large, one-half to
  one-third of diameter, axial sculpture weak          *Strobilops hubbardi*

    \* Shell elevated, dome shaped, umbilicus small,
one-sixth to one-twelfth of diameter, axial
sculpture strong

    \*\* Shell with periphery of last whorl angular,
palatal fold lacking, shell less elevated           *S. aenea*

    \*\* Shell with periphery of last whorl rounded,
palatal fold present, shell more elevated

    \*\*\* Shell larger, 2.75 mm. (about 1/8 in.) or more
in diameter, basal folds nearly equal         *S. affinis*

    \*\*\* Shell smaller, 2.5 mm. (about 1/10 in.) or less
in diameter, basal folds unequal

\*\*\*\* Axial ribs weakly developed on base, closely
set, interspaces little wider than ribs      *S. labyrinthica*

\*\*\*\* Axial ribs strongly developed on base, widely
set, interspaces twice the width of the ribs     *S. texasiana*

---

Genus *Strobilops* Pilsbry

*Strobilops labyrinthica* Say
    Labyrinth Snail

    Pl. XXVIII, 9

ETYMOLOGY: Gr. *strobilos ops*, having the appearance of a pine cone; Lat.
*labyrinthus*, a labyrinth.

SIZE: 2.3 mm. (about 1/10 in.) in diameter, 1.8 mm. (about 1/12 in.) in
height.

DISTRIBUTION: Canada and Maine to Georgia and westward to Kansas and
Arkansas.

CHARACTERISTICS: Shell dome shaped, periphery rounded, moderately strong,
sculptured with prominent axial ribs, the ribs a little narrower than
their interspaces, growing weaker on the base. Color chestnut brown.
Internal basal folds strongly unequal. Umbilicus narrow, about
one-eleventh of diameter. Lip thickened, aperture showing the
termination of one or more upper internal parietal lamellae.

These tiny shells, which much resemble old-fashioned beehives, are
found on decaying and dead leaves in moderately humid forests. Like
all tiny shells, they are best collected by taking home promising leaf
mold, drying it, and examining it for snails with the aid of a magnifying glass.

    The **Texas Labyrinth Snail,** *Strobilops texasiana* Pilsbry & Ferriss (pl. XXVIII, 10), is similar to *S. labyrinthica*, but the axial ribs are widely spaced and continue strongly on the base. Moreover, *S. texasiana* has a more southerly distribution, from Virginia to Florida and westward to Texas.

The **Allied Labyrinth Snail,** *Strobilops affinis* Pilsbry (Lat. *affinis*, allied to) (pl. XXVIII, 11), differs by being larger—2.75 mm. (about 1/8 in.) in diameter, 2.5 mm. (about 1/10 in.) in height—and rather thin and glossy. Otherwise it resembles *S. labyrinthica* in the closely set axial ribs weakening on the base. The species ranges from Canada to New Jersey and westward to Minnesota.

The **Bronze Labyrinth Snail,** *Strobilops aenea* Pilsbry (Lat. *aeneus*, made of copper or bronze) (pl. XXVIII, 12), differs from the other species of labyrinth snails by having an angular, almost keeled periphery. The shell, 2.4 to 2.8 mm. (about 1/6 to 1/8 in.) in diameter, is low domed, dark brown with a red golden sheen, and the inner palatal fold is lacking. It ranges from Canada to Florida.

**Hubbard's Labyrinth Snail,** *Strobilops hubbardi* A. D. Brown (named for Eber Ward Hubbard, a New York physician and malacologist) (pl. XXIX, 18), differs readily by being depressed rather than dome shaped. It is 2.6 mm. (about 1/10 in.) in diameter, 1.2 mm. (about 1/25 in.) in height. The axial sculpture is weak and the umbilicus is large, about one-fourth of the base. Like other labyrinth snails, it possesses the typical parietal lamellae and basal folds, the "labyrinth" part of the creatures. It differs so much from the others in the genus that in 1927 Pilsbry proposed a subgeneric name for it, appropriately *Discostrobilops*.

# SUBORDER:

# MESURETHRA

*(ureter reduced to a lateral opening of the kidney)*

## SUPERFAMILY:

## CLAUSILIACEA

### FAMILY:

### CERIONIDAE

*(peanut snails)*

These shells are moderate in size, and cylindrical, with a low, rapidly tapering spire; generally light colored, aperture with a single basal tooth, lip narrowly reflected. This is a family found only in the Neotropics, and is especially well developed in Cuba—where it probably originated—and the Bahamas. A few species occur elsewhere in the West Indies, but the family is strangely absent from Jamaica. These snails live close to salt water.

Genus *Cerion* Röding

*Cerion incanum* Binney
Florida Peanut Snail

Pl. XXIX, 19

ETYMOLOGY: Gr. *kerion*, honeycomb; Lat. *incanus*, quite gray.

SIZE: 20 to 35 mm. (about 4/5 to 1 2/5 in.) long, 8 to 13 mm. (1/3 to 1/2 in.) wide.

DISTRIBUTION: Southern Florida and the Florida Keys.

CHARACTERISTICS: Shell moderately large, solid, cylindrical, with rapidly tapering upper spire. White, occasionally with a bluish tint, or gray. Surface nearly smooth, but with some low axial ribs on last whorl. Aperture white or light brown, small tooth on parietal (upper) margin. Lip white, narrowly reflected; umbilicus slitlike.

This is a common species on the Keys, found clinging to bushes, tree trunks, or even blades of grass, always within a few hundred feet of the ocean. Though the shell is variable, this single species is the only one on the U.S. mainland. The family is highly developed in Cuba, and is found commonly in the Bahamas. There is also a single living species on Curaçao. In the 1920s a scientist unwisely undertook to plant colonies of many Cuban and Bahamian *Cerion* species on several of the Keys. Most did not flourish, but such foreign specimens can still occasionally be found. In at least one case interbreeding did take place. Pilsbry was right when he wrote: "It is hoped that the interesting snail faunas of other keys will be left undisturbed."

# HETERURETHRA

*(ureter directed laterally to the intestine and then anteriorly to the orifice)*

## SUCCINEACEA

## SUCCINEIDAE

*(amber snails)*

These shells are small, thin, and fragile; horn colored, and translucent or flesh colored and opaque; body whorl huge, spire small to tiny, lip thin, simple. This is a family of primitive pulmonates with a worldwide distribution. Found everywhere in suitable places, but some species prefer very moist conditions.

Genus *Succinea* Draparnaud

*Succinea ovalis* Say
Oval Amber Snail

Pl. XXVII, 11

ETYMOLOGY: Lat. *succinum*, amber, and *ovalis*, oval.

SIZE: Up to 27 mm. (about 1 in.) in height, 11 mm. (about 1/2 in.) in width.

DISTRIBUTION: Canada and Maine to North Carolina, westward to Nebraska.

CHARACTERISTICS: Shell large for genus, ovate, greenish yellow, fragile, thin, glossy transparent, body whorl and aperture huge, spire about one-third of shell length.

This is probably the commonest species of the genus in our area. It is usually found clinging to grasses and low bushes at the edge of forests, especially after rains.

The **Golden Amber Snail,** *Succinea aurea* Lea (Lat. *aureus,* golden) (pl. XXVIII, 13), is also a small shell, but in the proportion of spire to length it resembles *S. ovalis.* Canada to South Carolina and westward to Indiana.

The **Worm Amber Snail,** *Catinella vermata* Say (Lat. *vermis,* worm or grub) (pl. XXVII, 10), is smaller, 8 to 11 mm. (about 1/3 to 1/2 in.), and the spire is proportionately larger, being about one-half the length of the shell. It was formerly called *Succinea avara* Say. Canada and Maine to Florida and westward to New Mexico.

The shells of the next two species have the shape and appearance of the other amber snails, but the shell is opaque, dull, flesh or ocher tinted or gray, and rather strong. They have been put into the subgenus *Calcisuccinea* Pilsbry, or calcified amber snails.

The **Florida Amber Snail,** *Succinea luteola floridana* Pilsbry (Lat. *luteus,* muddy or yellowish) (pl. XXVIII, 14), generally has a long, narrow shell, and the spire is large, about one-half the length of the shell. The **Field Amber Snail,** *Succinea campestris* Say (Lat. *campester,* pertaining to a field) (pl. XXIX, 20), is short, wide, and oval, the spire being only about one-fourth of the length. South Carolina to Florida.

SUBORDER:

# SIGMURETHRA
*(ureter reflexed S-like)*

INFRAORDER:

# HOLOPODOPES
*(kidney transversely placed)*

SUPERFAMILY:

## ACHATINACEA

FAMILY:

## ACHATINIDAE

This is a family of generally very large snails found originally only in Africa, south of the Sahara, and perhaps in some of the surrounding islands, including Zanzibar and Madagascar. The shell is strong, ovate-conic, colored usually with browns and occasionally pink; the lip is simple, not expanded.

Genus *Achatina* Lamarck

*Achatina fulica* Bowdich
    Giant African Snail

    Pl. XXVIII, 15

ETYMOLOGY: Gr. *achates*, agate; Lat. *fulica*, coot or water-hen.

SIZE: Reaching 100 mm. (4 in.) and more in height, 65 mm. (2 3/5 in.) in
    diameter.

DISTRIBUTION: Africa, introduced into many warmer regions of the world.

CHARACTERISTICS: Shell huge, glossy, quite strong. Brown with lighter,
    irregular axial stripes. Umbilicus lacking; lip simple.


This species is a serious and extremely unsanitary agricultural pest
that escaped the vigilance of U.S. customs officials and has appeared
recently in large numbers in North Miami, Florida. The importation
resulted when a child brought home from Hawaii three pet snails and
released them in his yard. In a short time the neighborhood was over-
run with the pests. At one time it was thought that the invasion had
been controlled and the Miami colony isolated, but new outbreaks
far from the scene of the original infestation subsequently were reported. Those who live in the southern states may have to resign
themselves to the continuing presence of this snail. Unrelenting war
will have to be waged to control the species, and extermination may
now be impossible.

There is another hazard connected with the presence of *Achatina*.
At one stage of its life, the Giant African Snail looks superficially like
some of our native tree snails of the genus *Orthalicus*. Careless and
overenthusiastic attempts at eradication of *Achatina* may result in the
extermination of these beneficial snails, so that the innocent may
suffer with the guilty.

---

FAMILY:

# SUBULINIDAE
(*awl snails*)


These shells are often quite small to tiny and shaped like rice grains,
but several larger forms exist. The color is usually white, but some
species are yellow and glassy, others larger and brownish. Many

generic characteristics are based largely on the soft anatomy. Some tropical species have been accidentally introduced with plants grown in hothouses in the northeastern United States; here they are sometimes a nuisance because they may eat the petals of orchids and other flowers.

## KEY TO FAMILIES
## SUBULINIDAE AND STREPTAXIDAE

| | |
|---|---|
| * Shell cylindrical, aperture with 4 teeth | *Gulella bicolor* |
| * Shell tapering, aperture without teeth | |
| ** Shell large, 27 mm. (about 1 in.), stout, sharply decollate | *Rumina decollata* |
| ** Shells smaller, slender, not decollate | |
| *** Shell 17 to 20 mm. (about 4/5 in.) in height, translucent, smooth, base of columella truncate | *Subulina octona* |
| *** Shell 7 to 10 mm. (about 1/4 to 2/5 in.) in height, opaque, base of columella not truncate | |
| ***** Shell sculpture of evenly spaced arcuate lines, whorls high, shell reaching 10 mm. (2/5 in.) | *Lamellaxis gracilis* |
| ***** Shell sculpture uneven, whorls low, shell reaching only 7 mm. (about 1/4 in.) in height | *L. micrus* |

Genus *Rumina* Risso

*Rumina decollata* Linnaeus
    Decollated Awl Snail

    Pl. XXVII, 12

ETYMOLOGY: Probably Lat. *rumen*, throat; *decollatus*, decapitated.

SIZE: 22 to 30 mm. (about 4/5 to 1 1/5 in.) long in truncated state, 10 mm. (2/5 in.) in maximum width.

DISTRIBUTION: North Carolina to Florida and westward to Texas.

CHARACTERISTICS: Shell moderately large, tapering cylindrical, apex truncated, thin, opaque, moderately glossy. Whitish or flesh tinted. Surface striate, somewhat malleated (hammered). Umbilicus slitlike; lip thin.

This shell is easily recognized by its relatively large size, and decollate or truncated condition. The young stage is much narrower, the apex blunt. It is an introduction from the Mediterranean region, and it has become very common in urban gardens and lots. It has also been found in hothouses in the northeastern states. The animal is omnivorous, and besides eating vegetable matter, readily attacks and eats other snails. William G. Binney, a prominent American malacologist of the nineteenth century, kept a few in his home in Charleston to help him clean out the shells of other snails for his collection. Some conchologists use ants for the same purpose.

The **Miniature Awl Snail,** *Subulina octona* Bruguière (Lat. *subula,* an awl, and *octa* (?), eight) reaches 17 mm. (about 3/4 in.) in height. The shell is long and slender, tapering to a blunted apex; it is thin, translucent, polished, light yellowish in color. The short columella is truncated below, and the aperture is without teeth. There is no umbilicus. This exceedingly abundant snail in gardens, patios, and lots in southern Florida and the Keys lives under leaves, bits of wood, and in garden trash. Frequently small white, hard-shelled little eggs can be seen in the last few whorls through the semitransparent wall of the shell. This is a West Indian species which commerce has introduced into most warm countries of the world. The Miniature Awl Snail serves as one of the hosts in the life cycle of a trematode worm that causes serious malfunction of the liver in cats (pl. XXVII, 13).

The **Graceful Awl Snail,** *Lamellaxis gracilis* Hutton (Lat. *lamella, axis,* axle plate; *gracilis,* graceful) (pl. XXVII, 14), is a much smaller shell, about 10 mm. (2/5 in.) long, pale gray and translucent with a smooth surface. It inhabits the southeastern states.

The **Tiny Awl Snail,** *Lamellaxis micrus* Orbigny (Gr. *micron,* very small) (pl. XXVII, 15), is similar to *L. gracilis,* but the surface is ornamented with widely spaced axial ribs and it has a wider, bullet-shaped spire and a smaller aperture. Introduced into Florida. Occasionally other introduced subulinids also turn up, especially in hothouses even in the northern states.

# STREPTAXACEA

# STREPTAXIDAE

This is a predaceous family widely distributed in the Old World tropics, including India, China, and southeast Asia, and introduced into the Neotropics. A single species has become established in the southeastern United States.

Genus *Gulella* Pfeiffer

*Gulella bicolor* Hutton
    Bicolored Awl Snail

    Pl. XXIX, 21

ETYMOLOGY: Diminutive of Lat. *gula*, a throat.

SIZE: 7 mm. (1/4 in.) in height.

DISTRIBUTION: Introduced in scattered localities in South Carolina, Florida, Mississippi, Louisiana, and Texas.

CHARACTERISTICS: Shell small, 7 mm. (1/4 in.) in height, white or glossy, narrow, cylindrical, translucent, aperture armed with 4 small teeth. In life the reddish tinge of the soft parts can be seen through the translucent shell.

Once firmly established, this carnivorous snail may successfully displace some of our native snails.

SUPERFAMILY:

# RHYTIDACEA

FAMILY:

# HAPLOTREMATIDAE

This small family of predatory mollusks, with shells characterized by a flattened shape, huge umbilicus, and thin lip with a flattened or depressed area on the upper margin, is limited to North America, with several interesting species in the West Coast states.

Genus *Haplotrema* Ancey

*Haplotrema concavum* Say
Disk Cannibal Snail

Pl. XXIX, 22

ETYMOLOGY: Gr. *haplos trema*, simple orifice; Lat. *concavus*, hollowed.

SIZE: 11 to 18 mm. (about 1/2 to 3/4 in.) in diameter, 5 to 8 mm. (1/5 to 1/3 in.) in height.

DISTRIBUTION: Canada and Maine and south to western Florida, westward to Arkansas.

CHARACTERISTICS: Shell moderately large, depressed, strong. Moderately glossy, yellowish. Umbilicus broadly open; lip thin, slightly flattened or depressed at upper margin.

This shell is easily identified by its large size, huge umbilicus, and the small depressed area in the upper lip margin. It is a predator, feeding on other mollusks and rainworms. The animal is long and slender, and is thus able to plunge fiercely into the aperture of a retracted food snail, where it consumes its victim to the last morsel in the topmost whorl. There is reason to believe that *Haplotrema* will dine cannibalistically on immature individuals of its own species. It is found in moist, shaded situations where other snails live.

# BULIMULACEA

# BULIMULIDAE
(*tree snails*)

A family with many species having large to small shells characterized by an ovate-conic or spindle-shaped shell. A few low-spired, depressed forms are found in South America, where other beautiful forms also occur. The lip is varied, sometimes thin and simple, but often strongly reflected and expanded. Many are monocolored, but numerous other forms with bright and lively colors also occur. The nuclear whorls are well sculptured, and these sculptural differences serve to separate several of the many genera into which the family has been divided. Members are limited to tropical and temperate regions.

There are numerous genera in South America where the family has had its greatest development, and it is also represented in Australia, Melanesia, and New Zealand. North America has only a few peripheral species, mainly in Florida, Texas, and Mexico. The Floridian bulimulids are largely arboreal or live in bushes.

## KEY TO GENERA DRYMAEUS, ORTHALICUS, AND LIGUUS

* Shell relatively small, up to 32 mm. (about 1 1/4 in.) long, narrow
** Shell fragile, translucent, colored areas spirally arranged
*** Shell up to 32 mm. (about 1 1/4 in.), colored areas in spiral rows of interrupted bands — *Drymaeus dormani*
*** Shell up to 23 mm. (about 1 in.), colored areas in uninterrupted spiral bands — *D. dominicus*
** Shell thicker, opaque, colored areas axially arranged — *D. multilineatus*
* Shell large, up to 70 mm. (about 3 in.), broad
** Shell usually light and thin, not glossy

&#42;&#42;&#42; Colored areas spirally arranged        *Orthalicus floridensis*
&#42;&#42;&#42; Colored areas axially arranged         *O. reses*
 &#42;&#42; Shell usually heavier, glossy, highly colorful    *Liguus fasciatus*

Genus *Drymaeus* Albers

*Drymaeus dormani* W. G. Binney
     Dorman's Tree Snail

     Pl. II, 3

ETYMOLOGY: Gr. *drymaios*, forest living.

SIZE: 32 mm. (about 1 1/4 in.) in length, 16 mm. (2/3 in.) in diameter.

DISTRIBUTION: Central and northern Florida.

CHARACTERISTICS: Shell small, elongate-conic, thin, fragile, transparent,
     smooth. Light waxen color, with three to five interrupted spiral rows of
     reddish brown patches. Umbilicus very narrow; lip thin, simple or
     slightly reflected.

The genus *Drymaeus* differs from other bulimulid genera in having a
regular, gridlike sculpture on the protoconch. This can readily be seen
under slight magnification. Dorman's Tree Snail is characterized by its
relatively small, extremely fragile, translucent wax-colored shell,
generally marked by reddish brown, squarish patches arranged in
spiral rows. Individuals with unbanded shells sometimes occur.

The **Dominican Tree Snail,** *Drymaeus dominicus* Reeve (probably
based on the West Indian island Dominica) (pl. XXVII, 16), is similar
but smaller, 20 to 23 mm. (about 4/5 to 1 in.) long, pale buff, and
usually marked by three to five uninterrupted reddish brown bands,
although sometimes these bands are lacking. Southern and eastern
Florida.

The **Lined Tree Snail,** *Drymaeus multilineatus* Say (Lat. *multi
lineatus,* many lined) (pl. II, 1), has a similar shape, but it is
stronger, opaque, not glossy, and of an ivory yellow color, with many
uneven axial stripes. It inhabits southern Florida and lives in trees
and bushes, frequently in large numbers. It is also found in Central
America.

FAMILY:

# ORTHALICIDAE

(*tree snails*)

These shells are moderately large, egg shaped or narrowly pyramidal, smooth but rarely glossy, usually ornamented with brownish or purplish brown bands and streaks. This family of tree snails is confined to the warmer areas of the Americas.

Genus *Orthalicus* Beck

*Orthalicus floridensis* Pilsbry
Common Florida Tree Snail

Pls. II, 5; XXVIII, 16

ETYMOLOGY: Gr. *orthos*, upright, *alichos*, similar.

SIZE: 55 to 70 mm. (about 2 to 2 3/4 in.) high, 30 to 40 mm. (1 1/5 to 1 3/5 in.) wide.

DISTRIBUTION: Southernmost Florida and the Keys.

CHARACTERISTICS: Shell large, not glossy, moderately thin. White to creamish buff, marked with spiral chestnut brown stripes, occasionally some with irregularly spaced, oblique axial stripes as well. Umbilicus lacking; lip simple, dark brown.

This shell is readily recognized by its large size, light color, and mainly by the spiral color bands. It is found on tree trunks and branches, never living very far from the sea. The occasional bands are the places where the lip was formed in the snail's earlier stages of growth.

The **Lazy Florida Tree Snail,** *Orthalicus reses* Say (from Lat. *reses*, sluggish, inert) (pl. XXVIII, 17), is similar, but differs in having irregular color bands arranged mainly in an axial (upright) direction. A form with darker, bolder bands and a black spot on the apex has been called subspecies *O. reses nesodryas* Pilsbry (Gr. *nesos dryas*, island nymph). It has been found only on the Florida Keys. Thomas Say evidently saw *O. reses* for the first time in the dry season, when it is cemented stoutly to the tree trunk on which it lives. Nothing more "sluggish and inert" can then be imagined.

The **Banded Florida Tree Snail,** or "Lig" Snail, *Liguus fasciatus* Müller (Lat. *ligo*, bind up; *fascia*, band) (pls. IV, 1–18, XXVIII, 18), is similar to *Orthalicus* in shape, but the shell is usually much stronger, glossier, and far more showily decorated. However, some thin and undecorated white shell populations also occur. The rich color variations have led to the formation of a *Liguus* cult of collectors, whose aim it is to collect every one of the numerous named subspecies, varieties, and forms. From the point of view of systematics, however, there is little reason to doubt that only a single, richly varied species is involved. The genus had its origin in Cuba, and the ancestors of the Floridian shells unquestionably came from there, transported to southern Florida and the Keys by frequent hurricanes, clinging tenaciously to storm-driven tree trunks. The presence of isolated populations on keys and water-surrounded hammocks in the Everglades have produced localized colonies with characteristic color patterns because of restricted gene flow. These forms, when brought together, interbreed readily, and thus the numerous named "forms and varieties" are not taxonomically valid. Anyone interested in arranging a *Liguus* collection in a "systematic" manner should consult Pilsbry (1946).

Like many other creatures, *Liguus* is suffering dreadfully as the result of human activity, and many populations, especially around Miami, have already been eliminated. This is particularly regrettable because, in addition to being the most beautiful pulmonate in America —perhaps in the world—the animal is useful economically, as an eater of fungi that are harmful to trees.

---

FAMILY:

# UROCOPTIDAE

(*rock snails*)

The shells are elongate, quite narrow, often needlelike, with many whorls and a rounded, untoothed aperture. The early juvenile whorls in many species are discarded as the shell matures. The family Urocoptidae (from Gr. *ouros copt*, tail cut off) is limited to the tropics of the New World, and is richly developed in the West Indies, especially in Cuba and Jamaica. Representatives of the family also occur in the southwestern United States and Mexico. Some of the Mexican forms attain the size and shape of small cigars.

Genus *Cochlodinella* Pilsbry & Vanatta

*Cochlodinella poeyana* Orbigny
Poey's Truncate Rock Snail

Pl. XXIX, 23

ETYMOLOGY: Diminutive of Gr. *cochlos*, snail; named for Felipe Poey, famous Cuban naturalist.

SIZE: 10 to 14 mm. (about 2/5 to 3/5 in.) in length, 3 mm. (1/8 in.) wide.

DISTRIBUTION: Miami area and the Florida Keys.

CHARACTERISTICS: Shell small, tapering cylindrical, apex truncated. Grayish white or pale brown, moderately fragile, lusterless. Sculpture of fine, closely set oblique axial striae. Aperture ovate; lip reflected, often free of body whorl.

The immature shell and the adult, truncated shell of *C. poeyana* look quite different; the former has a narrow, rapidly tapering shell and a rounded, bulbous protoconch. The shells are usually collected clinging to the undersides of rocks and slabs of stone. This species is also found in Cuba, and the Florida colonies were obviously introduced from that island by hurricanes, as were several other Cuban land and tree snails.

The **Pontiff Rock Snail,** *Microceramus pontificus* Gould (Gr. *micros keramus*, small earthen ware) (pl. XXIX, 24), is 8 to 12 mm. (1/3 to 1/2 in.) in height, 3 to 4 mm. (1/8 to 1/6 in.) in diameter. This relative of *Cochlodinella* is wider, lower, and dumpier in shape, and above all it does not discard its apex as it matures. It has a lusterless, rough, rather strong shell, whitish with a cream or brownish tinge, and marked with irregular, coarse, oblique axial ribs terminating in white papillae at the suture. The aperture is round and the lip narrowly expanded. Found in southern Florida. Like other urocoptids, the genus *Microceramus* is also richly developed in Cuba.

The **Floridian Rock Snail,** *Microceramus floridanus* Pilsbry (pl. XXVII, 17), differs only in being smaller, 5 to 7 mm. high (about 1/5 to 1/4 in.), and less attenuated at the apex, with finer ribbings and lower and less regularly spaced white sutural papillae. This species is less common than *M. pontificus*, occurring in a few localities within the range of the latter.

# AULACOPODA

*(foot with marginal furrow)*

SUPERFAMILY:

# ENDODONTACEA

FAMILY:

# ENDODONTIDAE

*(disk snails)*

The Endodontidae (from Gr. *endon*, within, and *odous*, tooth) are rather primitive pulmonates with a worldwide distribution. The shells are generally small to tiny, but giants occur in the genus *Anguispira*. Since most American endodontids do not form a thickened lip and do not develop teeth or other apertural structures as they mature, it is difficult, aside from size, to tell when a specimen is fully grown.

In our region the Endodontidae are characterized by having depressed, brownish shells with a strong surface sculpture of axial ribs and riblets, a large umbilicus, and a thin lip with a round, untoothed aperture. The animals are gregarious, and frequently live in large colonies. In the coastal states disk snails occur in leaf mold and forest debris, but they may inhabit urban areas as well.

# KEY TO FAMILY ENDODONTIDAE

&ast; Shell large, 15 to 30 mm. (about 3/5 to
1 1/5 in.) in diameter

&ast;&ast; Shell generally dull

&ast;&ast;&ast; Axial ribs closely set, weak basally · · · · *Anguispira alternata*

&ast;&ast;&ast; Axial ribs more widely set, strong
basally · · · · · · · · · · · · · · · · · · · · · · · · · · · · *A. alternata crassa*

&ast;&ast; Shell bright, glossy · · · · · · · · · · · · · · · · · *A. fergusoni*

&ast; Shell small, 5 to 9 mm. (about 1/5 to
2/5 in.) in diameter

&ast;&ast; Umbilicus huge, one-half of base · · · · · *Discus patulus*

&ast;&ast; Umbilicus smaller, less than one-third
of diameter

&ast;&ast;&ast; Shell ornamented with flame markings · · *D. rotundatus*

&ast;&ast;&ast; Shell uniformly brownish

&ast;&ast;&ast;&ast; Shell with rounded periphery · · · · · · · · · *D. cronkhitei*

&ast;&ast;&ast;&ast; Shell with angular periphery · · · · · · · · · *D. cronkhitei catskillensis*

&ast; Shell tiny, 1.1 to 3 mm. (about 1/25 to
1/8 in.) in diameter

&ast;&ast; Shell darker, generally brownish, 1 to
1.5 mm. (about 1/25 to 1/12 in.) · · · · · *Punctum minutissimum*

&ast;&ast; Shell paler, yellowish or corneous

&ast;&ast;&ast; Shell yellowish with greenish tinge,
parallel lines distinct · · · · · · · · · · · · · · · *Helicodiscus parallelus*

&ast;&ast;&ast; Shell corneous, parallel lines barely
discernible · · · · · · · · · · · · · · · · · · · · · · · · · *H. singleyanus*

---

Genus *Anguispira* Morse

*Anguispira alternata* Say
Striped Forest Snail

Pl. II, 10

ETYMOLOGY: Gr. *anguis spira*, snake coil; Lat. *alternata*, alternating.

SIZE: 15 to 30 mm. (3/5 to 1 1/5 in.) in diameter, 9 to 17.5 mm. (about 2/5 to 3/4 in.) in height.

DISTRIBUTION: From Canada to Georgia and west to South Dakota and Kansas.

CHARACTERISTICS: Shell generally depressed, sometimes low conic, thin but opaque, usually with strong rounded axial ribs. Umbilicus large, one-fifth to one-fourth of diameter. Color pale yellow or horn, copiously blotched with irregular flame markings above and often a belt of spots below the periphery. Lip thin, not expanded; aperture without lamellae or teeth.

This shell can readily be recognized by the large size, large umbilicus, generally strong sculpture and characteristic color, which varies but is always recognizable. Colonies of albino specimens can sometimes be found. The animal of *A. alternata* is distinctive because the soft parts are rather brightly colored, and it produces an orange slime trail. The name *Anguispira* was given to the genus owing to the resemblance of the color of *A. alternata,* the type species, to a snakeskin.

This widely distributed species breaks down into many forms, some of which have been given specific or subspecific names. Most of these, however, are not found in the region we are treating. A form that is smaller than *A. alternata,* with a smooth, shining surface, weaker striation, and brighter color, has been called *A. fergusoni* Bland—**Ferguson's Forest Snail** (pl. II, 11) is common in eastern New York and extends to South Carolina. The subspecies *Anguispira alternata crassa* Walker (Lat. *crassus,* gross), the **Heavy Forest Snail** (pl. XXIX, 25), is heavy, and has strong ribs extending from spire to base. It ranges from Virginia to Florida.

The **Common Disk Snail,** *Discus cronkhitei* Newcomb (Gr. *diskos,* disk; and named for a Mr. Cronkhite) (pl. XXVIII, 19), like most species of the genus *Discus,* is a small shell, 5 to 7 mm. (about 1/4 in.) in diameter, and about 3 mm. (1/8 in.) in height. It is a flat, dull, brown shell, strongly sculptured with fine axial ribs; the umbilicus is large, about one-third of the diameter, and the lip is thin. There are six to eight ribs per mm. This is a common species living in fields and at the edges of forest areas, and it is also found in urban areas. It ranges from Canada and Maine to Maryland, and westward to the West Coast. The subspecies *Discus cronkhitei catskillensis* Pilsbry differs only in having an obtuse keel at the periphery of the last whorl. It is found from Canada to Pennsylvania and west to Minnesota. It is the commoner form in New York and New Jersey. (Pl. XXIX, 26.)

The **Open Disk Snail,** *Discus patulus* Deshayes (Lat. *patulus,* standing open) (pl. XXIX, 27), reaches 8 to 9 mm. (about 1/3 to 2/5 in.) in size. It is most readily recognized by its huge umbilicus, forming about one-half of the entire base. This feature makes the shell look convex. The ribs are coarser and more widely separated, with only three to four ribs per mm. This species ranges from Canada to western Florida and westward to Iowa and Arkansas. In the coastal states it is found in the hilly western sections, under loose bark and in soft, rotten wood.

The **Rotund Disk Snail,** *Discus rotundatus* Müller (Lat. *rotundus,* wheel-shaped, spherical) (pl. XXIX, 28), is 6 to 7 mm. (about 1/4 in.) in diameter. The slightly raised shell has narrow whorls, and the brownish color is ornamented with reddish flame markings or blotches. Thus it looks like a miniature version of *Anguispira alternata* (page 239). This is a species accidentally introduced from Europe, and it occurs in isolated colonies in New York City, Boston, New Jersey, and undoubtedly in other urban and suburban areas.

The **Parallel Disk Snail,** *Helicodiscus parallelus* Say (Gr. *helix diskos,* spiral disk) (pl. XXIX, 29), is only 3 mm. (1/8 in.) in diameter and 1 mm. (1/25 in.) in height. The tiny shell is pale yellow with a greenish tinge; the entire surface is clearly marked with several equidistant spiral striations. There are a few small conical teeth inside the aperture. The species ranges from Canada and Maine to Virginia and westward to Oklahoma. Pilsbry writes that it "is a timid creature, hard to observe, as it takes alarm when approached with a lens, though apparently blind. It lives on decaying wood in shady or humid places, on damp leaves. It is generally distributed, and may usually be found in leaf siftings and in drift debris on streams."

**Singley's Disk Snail,** *Helicodiscus singleyanus* Pilsbry (pl. XXVIII, 20), is even smaller, about 2.5 mm. (about 1/8 in.) in diameter. It is thin, corneous, and translucent, with only faint signs of parallel lines on the top. It ranges from New Jersey to Florida and westward to New Mexico.

The **Minute Disk Snail,** *Punctum minutissimum* Lea (Lat. *punctum,* point or dot; *minutissimus,* very minute) (pl. XXVIII, 21), is only about 1.5 mm. (about 1/12 in.) in diameter. This tiniest of shells is horn colored, translucent, shining; the fine axial cords are crossed by microscopic spiral striae. This speck of a shell can be found in leaf siftings from Canada and Maine to Florida and westward to the West Coast.

The **Glassy Disk Snail,** *Punctum vitreum* H. B. Baker (Lat. *vitreus,* glassy) (not illustrated) is no larger, but differs in being lighter in color and almost transparent; the axial ribs are much more widely spaced. Baker writes that "under the binocular [microscope], *P. minutissimum* looks as if it were molded out of bronze, but *P. vitreum* appears as if it were cut from yellowish crystal." *P. vitreum* ranges from New Jersey to Virginia; it is not commonly encountered.

# KEY TO GENERA OF ZONITIDAE, VITRINIDAE, AND EUCONULIDAE

\* Shell with huge body whorl, tiny spire, aperture larger than rest of shell when viewed from the side — *Vitrina* (Vitrinidae)

\* Shell with body whorl not more than double the penult whorl, and aperture not larger than rest of shell when viewed from the side

\*\* Shell sculpture elaborate, strong axial ribs and strong spiral sculpture underneath — *Striatura*

\*\* Shell smooth or with weak sculpture

\*\*\* Shell diameter almost equal to height — *Euconulus* (Euconulidae)

\*\*\* Shell diameter decidedly greater than height

\*\*\*\* Shell with denticles in aperture

\*\*\*\*\* Shell tiny, 3 mm. (1/8 in.) — *Paravitrea*

\*\*\*\*\* Shell large to quite large, 7 to 15 mm. (about 1/4 to 3/5 in.) — *Ventridens*

\*\*\*\* Shell without apertural denticles

\*\*\*\*\* Shell white, opalescent — *Hawaiia*

\*\*\*\*\* Shell not white

\*\*\*\*\*\* Whorls rapidly increasing in width, body whorl at least twice the width of penultimate

\*\*\*\*\*\*\* Shell with widely spaced axial grooves in addition to growth lines — *Retinella*

\*\*\*\*\*\*\* Shell with axial growth lines only

\*\*\*\*\*\*\*\* Shell much depressed, very glossy, light colored; urban and suburban dwellers — *Oxychilus*

\*\*\*\*\*\*\*\* Shell rather high, dark colored, moderately glossy; inhabits woods and meadows — *Mesomphix*

\*\*\*\*\*\* Whorls slowly increasing in width, body whorl only slightly wider than penultimate

\*\*\*\*\*\*\* Shell with axial growth lines only — *Zonitoides*

* * * * * * * Shell with well-marked spiral
sculpture                                      *Guppya* (Euconulidae)

SUPERFAMILY:

# ZONITACEA

FAMILY:

# ZONITIDAE
(*zonite snails*)

These shells are minute to moderate in size, depressed, generally very fragile, smooth and shiny, commonly translucent or transparent, with a thin, nonreflected lip, and an umbilicus that varies in size. Most groups lack apertural teeth. This family is worldwide in distribution, and many unique forms are found on the islands of the South Pacific.

## KEY TO GENUS RETINELLA

* Axial grooves few, widely spaced
** Shell with spiral striae beaded                    *Retinella burringtoni*
** Shell with spiral striae unbeaded
*** Shell smaller, 3.5 to 4 mm. (about 1/6 in.),
white with greenish tinge                             *R. binneyana*
*** Shell larger, 4.5 to 5.2 mm. (about 1/5 in.),
amber with greenish tinge                             *R. electrina*
* Axial grooves many, closely spaced
** Shell with tiny, almost invisible umbilicus        *R. indentata*
** Shell with distinct umbilicus, one-seventh of
diameter                                              *R. rhoadsi*

Genus *Retinella*

*Retinella electrina* Gould
  Amber Retinella

  Pl. XXVII, 18

ETYMOLOGY: Lat. *retineo*, hold back, restrain; *electrum*, amber.

SIZE: 4 to 5 mm. (1/6 to 1/5 in.) in diameter, 2.5 mm. (1/8 in.) in height.

DISTRIBUTION: Canada and Maine to Virginia and westward to Washington State.

CHARACTERISTICS: Shell depressed, thin, fragile, almost transparent, clear. Amber with greenish tinge. Sculpture of faint growth lines interspersed with rather widely spaced, strong radial grooves, spiral sculpture microscopic. Last whorl decidedly wider than the others. Umbilicus deep and wide, one-fourth of diameter; lip thin.

*Retinella* is a genus of generally small shells in which the soft anatomy and details of the radula are of prime importance in systematics. Hence the recognition of species by the shell alone is not always easy. The genus itself is usually recognizable by the low, glassy, light-colored shell, and especially by the presence of the more or less widely separated, deep axial grooves interspersed among the axial growth lines.

**Binney's Retinella,** *Retinella binneyana* Morse (named for the nineteenth-century American malacologist W. G. Binney) (pl. XXVII, 19), is similar to the *R. electrina*, but about one-third smaller. In addition, it has a whitish color with a greenish tinge. In the coastal states it ranges from Canada to New Jersey, but it is more common to the north than *R. electrina*.

The **Indented Retinella,** *Retinella indentata* Say (pl. XXVIII, 22), has a tiny umbilicus that is, moreover, hidden under a minute expansion of the basal lip. To the naked eye it is quite invisible, and Thomas Say, who described the species in 1825, wrote "umbilicus none." The radial grooves are more closely set than in either of the two species already described. It ranges from Canada and Maine to Virginia and westward to Kansas. The Amber and the Indentated Retinellas are by far the commonest species within their range, and are most easily distinguished by the presence or absence of the umbilicus.

**Rhoads' Retinella,** *Retinella rhoadsi* Pilsbry (named for Samuel N. Rhoads, a well-known mammalogist who was also interested in mollusks) (pl. XXXII, 1), is similar to *R. indentata*, but the umbilicus is larger and more visible, and it shows the penultimate whorl within. It is found from Canada to North Carolina.

**Baker's Retinella,** *Retinella burringtoni* Pilsbry (named for Horace Burrington Baker, a leading malacologist of this century) (pl. XXXII, 2), small—less than 4 mm. (1/6 in.) in diameter—and differs from the others in having the fine, distinct spiral striae weakly but distinctly beaded. It ranges from Connecticut to Virginia.

In addition to these more common species, there are several others with rather restricted ranges, not likely to come to the attention of the ordinary collector. Pilsbry (1946) should be consulted for these.

Recently some of the previously subgeneric names of *Retinella* have been raised to generic status, so that *Retinella electrina*, for instance, is sometimes called *Perpolita electrina*, and *Retinella indentata* is *Glyphyalinia indentata*.

# KEY TO GENERA MESOMPHIX AND OXYCHILUS

|   |   |
|---|---|
| * Shell much depressed, very glossy, light colored; urban and suburban species | |
| ** Shell small, 6 mm. (1/4 in.) in diameter, exudes garlicky odor in life | *Oxychilus alliarius* |
| ** Shell larger, garlic odor absent | |
| *** Shell large, reaching 16 mm. (2/3 in.) in diameter, umbilicus large, color brownish above, very pale below | *O. draparnaldi* |
| *** Shell smaller, 10 mm. (2/5 in.) in diameter, umbilicus narrow, whitish splotch about umbilicus | *O. cellarius* |
| * Shell moderately depressed or conic, dark color, moderately glossy; wood and meadow species | |
| ** Umbilicus large, one-fifth of diameter | *Mesomphix cupreus* |
| ** Umbilicus very small, one-twelfth of diameter | |
| *** Embryonic shell and spire nearly smooth | *M. inornatus* |
| *** Embryonic shell and spire strongly striate | *M. vulgatus* |

# COLOR PLATES

*The legends that follow identify the corresponding figures in the immediately succeeding insert of color plates. The page number in each legend refers to the place in the text where the given shell is discussed.*

PLATE II / Land and Freshwater Snails

*All shells shown approx. ⅔ natural size*

1.  Lined Tree Snail, *Drymaeus multilineatus*, p. 234.
2.  Chinese Mystery Snail, *Viviparus malleatus*, p. 289.
3.  Dorman's Tree Snail, *Drymaeus dormani*, p. 234.
4.  Profound Forest Snail, *Allogona profunda*, p. 270.
5.  Common Florida Tree Snail, *Orthalicus floridensis*, p. 235.
6.  English Garden Snail, *Cepaea nemoralis*, p. 279.
7.  Common Garden Snail, *Cepaea hortensis*, p. 280.
8.  Georgian Mystery Snail, *Viviparus georgianus*, p. 289; 8a, northern form, 8b, wide-banded Florida form, 8c, non-banded Florida form.
9.  Variegated Bush Snail, *Hemitrochus varians*, p. 280.
10. Striped Forest Snail, *Anguispira alternata*, p. 239.
11. Ferguson's Forest Snail, *Anguispira fergusoni*, p. 240.
12. Elongate Cannibal Snail, *Euglandina rosea*, p. 276.
13. Wheeled Apple Snail, *Marisa cornuarietis*, p. 292.
14. Stagnant Pond Snail, *Lymnaea stagnalis*, p. 306.

Plate IV

Banded Florida Tree Snail, *Liguus fasciatus* Müller, p. 236.

*All shells shown approx. ⅔ natural size*

Depicted are 18 of the 52 or more named color forms found in Florida:

1. *testudineus* Pilsbry
2. *ornatus* Simpson
3. *aurantius* Clench
4. *barbouri* Clench
5. *delicatus* Simpson
6. *lignumvitae* Pilsbry
7. *pictus* Reeve
8. *castaneus* Simpson
9. *castaneozonatus* Pilsbry
10. *versicolor* Simpson
11. *marmoratus* Pilsbry
12. *vonpaulsoni* Young
13. *subcrenatus* Pilsbry
14. *fuscoflamellus* Frampton
15. *livingstoni* Simpson
16. *eburneus* Simpson
17. *floridanus* Clench
18. *splendidus* Frampton

PLATE VII / Marine Snails

*All shells shown approx. ½ natural size*

1. Hawk Wing Conch, *Strombus raninus*, p. 85.
2. Florida Fighting Conch, *Strombus alatus*, p. 85.
3. West Indian Fighting Conch, *Strombus pugilis*, p. 85.
4. Milk Conch, *Strombus costatus*, p. 84.

---

PLATE VIII / Marine Snails

*All shells shown approx. ⅔ natural size*

1. Measled Cowrie, *Cypraea zebra*, p. 108;
   1a, mature color pattern, 1b, immature color pattern.
2. Common Flamingo Tongue, *Cyphoma gibbosum*, p. 111.
3. Ashen Cowrie, *Cypraea cinerea*, p. 109.
4. Deer Cowrie, *Cypraea cervus*, p. 109;
   4a, mature color pattern, 4b, immature color pattern.

PLATE IX / Marine Snails

*All shells shown approx. ⅔ natural size*

1. Scotch Bonnet, *Phalium granulatum*, p. 120.
2. Reticulated Helmet Shell, *Cypraecassis testiculus*, p. 121.
3. Colorful Moon Snail, *Natica canrena*, p. 102.
4. Common Fig Shell, *Ficus communis*, p. 113.
5. Spotted Tun Shell, *Tonna maculosa*, p. 112.
6. Smooth Scotch Bonnet, *Phalium cicatricosum*, p. 120.

PLATE XII  /  Marine Snails

*All shells shown approx. ⅔ natural size*

1. Lace Murex, *Murex dilectus*, p. 126.
2. Flowery Murex, *Murex florifer*, p. 126.
3. Apple Murex, *Murex pomum*, p. 126.
4. Wide-mouthed Dogwinkle, *Purpura patula*, p. 132.
5. Florida Dogwinkle, *Thais haemastoma floridana*, p. 131.
6. Hays' Dogwinkle, *Thais haemastoma haysae*, p. 131.
7. Leafy Murex, *Murex brevifrons*, p. 126.
8. Tawny Murex, *Murex fulvescens* (immature specimen), p. 127.

---

PLATE I

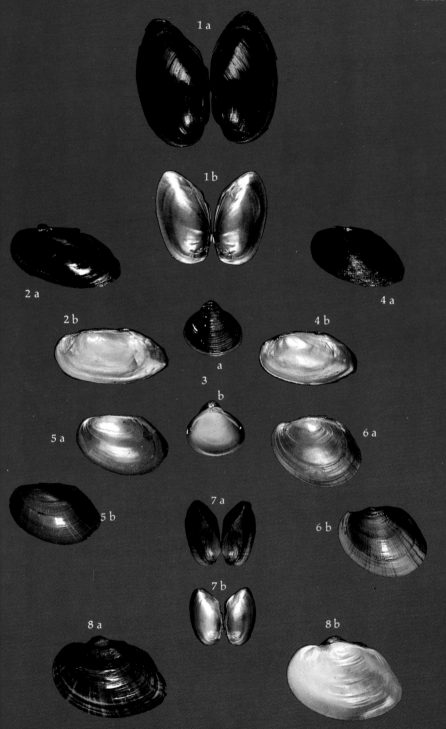

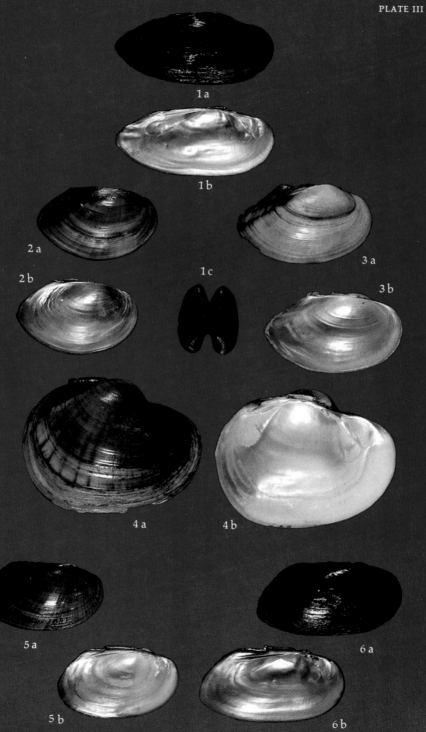

PLATE III

1 a

1 b

2 a

3 a

1 c

2 b

3 b

4 a

4 b

5 a

6 a

5 b

6 b

PLATE V

PLATE V

PLATE VII

PLATE VI

PLATE IX

PLATE X

PLATE XI

PLATE X

PLATE XIII

PLATE X

PLATE XV

PLATE XV

# BLACK-AND-WHITE
# PLATES

*The page number in each legend refers to the place in the text where the given shell is discussed.*

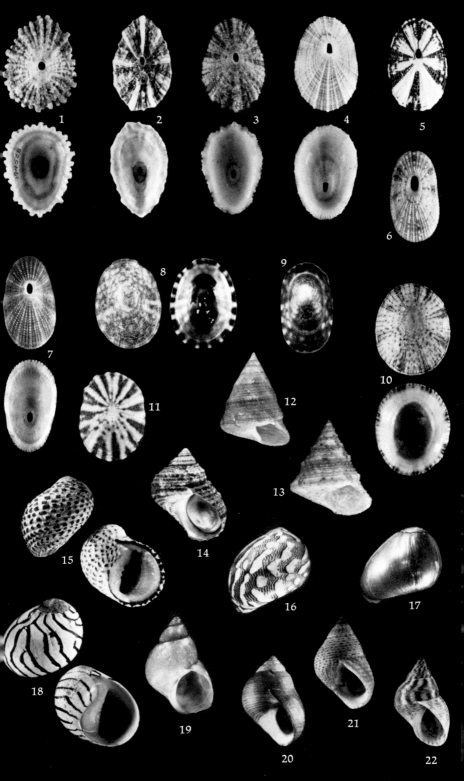

PLATE XVIII / Marine Snails

1. Lister's Keyhole Limpet, *Diodora listeri*, 39 mm., p. 36.
2. Tiny Arctic Top Shell, *Margarites helicinus*, 8 mm., p. 40.
3. Greenland Tiny Top Shell, *Margarites groenlandicus*, 10 mm., p. 41.
4. Javanese Top Shell, *Calliostoma javanicum*, 26 mm., p. 42.
5. Sculptured Top Shell, *Calliostoma euglyptum*, 18 mm., p. 42.
6. Banded Tegula, *Tegula fasciata*, 16 mm., p. 43.
7. Excavated Tegula, *Tegula excavata*, 18 mm., p. 43.
8. Long-spined Star Shell, *Astraea phoebia*, 43 mm., p. 45.
9. American Star Shell, *Astraea americana*, 30 mm., p. 45.
10. Engraved Star Shell, *Astraea caelata*, 53 mm., p. 46.
11. Shouldered Pheasant Shell, *Tricolia bella*, 5 mm., p. 47.
12. Checkered Pheasant Shell, *Tricolia affinis*, 7 mm., p. 48.
13. Algae Pheasant Shell, *Tricolia affinis pterocladia*, 7 mm., p. 48.
14. Variegated Nerite, *Nerita versicolor*, 24 mm., p. 50.
15. Lightning Nerite, Nerita fulgurans, 33 mm., p. 50.
16. Emerald Nerite, *Smaragdia viridis*, 7 mm., p. 52.
17. Dwarf Periwinkle, *Littorina mespillum*, 10 mm., p. 58.
18. Brown's Risso Shell, *Rissoina browniana*, 4 mm., p. 60.
19. Many-ribbed Risso Shell, *Rissoina multicostata*, 4 mm., p. 60.
20. Striose Risso Shell, *Rissoina striosa*, 10 mm., p. 61.
21. Beau's Glass Snail, *Cyclostremiscus beaui*, 10 mm., p. 64.
22. Biscayne Glass Snail, *Teinostoma biscayense*, 2 mm., p. 65.
23. Helix Glass Snail, *Vitrinella helicoidea*, 4 mm., p. 65.
24. Noble Sundial Shell, *Architectonica nobilis*, 43 mm., p. 66.
25. Bifurrowed Sundial Shell, *Heliacus bisulcatus*, 6 mm., p. 67.
26. Dwarf Violet Snail, *Janthina umbilicata*, 12 mm., p. 91.
27. Elongate Violet Snail, *Janthina globosa*, 26 mm., p. 92.

Plate XIX / Marine Snails

1. Round Periwinkle, *Littorina obtusata*, 9 mm., p. 57.
2. Narrow Periwinkle, *Littorina angustior*, 12 mm., p. 57.
3. Rough Periwinkle, *Littorina saxatilis*, 12 mm., p. 58.
4. Zigzag Periwinkle, *Littorina ziczac*, 17 mm., p. 58.
5. Lineolate Periwinkle, *Littorina lineolata*, 15 mm., p. 58.
6. Beaded Periwinkle, *Tectarius muricatus*, 18 mm., p. 58.
7. True Prickly Winkle, *Nodilittorina tuberculata*, 17 mm., p. 59.
8. False Prickly Winkle, *Echininus nodulosus*, 14 mm., p. 59.
9. Bryer's Risso Shell, *Rissoina bryerea*, 9 mm., p. 60.
10. Catesby's Risso Shell, *Rissoina catesbyana*, 3 mm., pp. 60, 61.
11. Decussated Risso Shell, *Rissoina decussata*, 8 mm., p. 60.
12. Cancellated Risso Shell, *Rissoina cancellata*, 6 mm., p. 61.
13. Pointed Cingula, *Cingula aculeus*, 3 mm., p. 61.
14. Striate Glass Snail, *Cochliolepis striata*, 9 mm., p. 64.
15. Pentagon Glass Snail, *Cyclostremiscus pentagonus*, 2 mm., p. 64.
16. Interrupted Glass Snail, *Parviturboides interruptus*, 1 mm., p. 65.
17. Cylinder Sundial Shell, *Heliacus cylindricus*, 11 mm., p. 66.
18. Carolina Caecum, *Caecum carolinianum*, 5 mm., p. 70.
19. Cooper's Caecum, *Caecum cooperi*, 4 mm., p. 70.
20. Little Horn Caecum, *Meioceras nitidum*, 2.5 mm., p. 71.
21. Atlantic Modulus, *Modulus modulus*, 13 mm., p. 71.
22. Lettered Horn Shell, *Cerithium litteratum*, 32 mm., p. 76.
23. Sargassum Miniature Horn Shell, *Litiopa melanostoma*, 5 mm., p. 79.
24. Green's Miniature Horn Shell, *Cerithiopsis greeni*, 5 mm., p. 79.
25. Sinistral Miniature Horn Shell, *Triphora nigrocincta*, 4 mm., p. 80.
26. American Pelican's Foot, *Aporrhais occidentalis*, 49 mm., p. 86.
27. Angulate Wentletrap, *Epitonium angulatum*, 16 mm., p. 89.
28. Banded Wentletrap, *Epitonium rupicola*, 16 mm., p. 89.
29. White Hoof Shell, *Hipponix antiquatus*, 18 mm., p. 93.

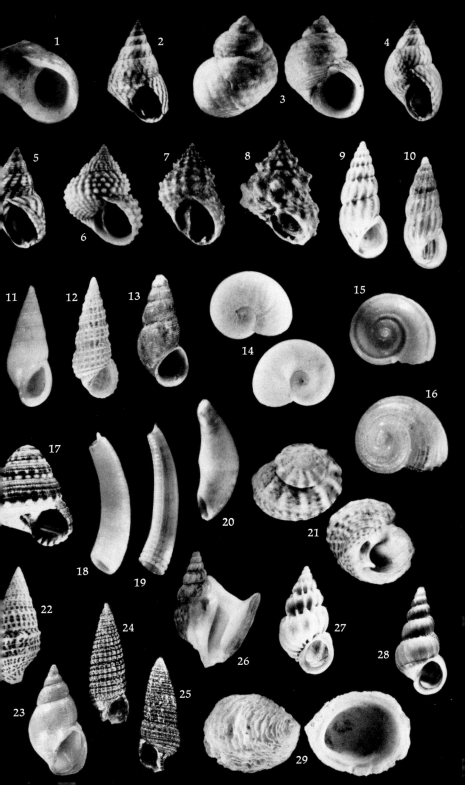

PLATE XX / Marine Snails

1. Tiny Marine Ram's Horn, *Skeneopsis planorbis*, 2 mm., p. 62. (after Hubendick and Waren, 1971)
2. Eroded Turret Shell, *Tachyrhrynchus erosus*, 18 mm., p. 68.
3. Boring Turret Shell, *Turritella acropora*, 29 mm., p. 68.
4. Pretty Caecum, *Caecum pulchellum*, 2.5 mm., p. 70.
5. Florida Caecum, *Caecum floridanum*, 4 mm., p. 70.
6. Florida Worm Shell, *Vermicularia knorri*, 42 mm., p. 73.
7. Florida Horn Shell, *Cerithium atratum*, 32 mm., p. 76.
8. Fly Horn Shell, *Cerithium muscarum*, 25 mm., p. 76.
9. Ivory Horn Shell, *Cerithium eburneum*, 24 mm., p. 77.
10. Algae Horn Shell, *Cerithium algicola*, 21 mm., p. 77.
11. Dwarf Horn Shell, *Cerithium lutosum*, 12 mm., p. 77.
12. Alternate Miniature Horn Shell, *Diastoma alternatum*, 8 mm., p. 78.
13. Variegate Miniature Horn Shell, *Diastoma varium*, 4 mm., p. 78.
14. Awl Miniature Horn Shell, *Cerithiopsis emersoni*, 13 mm., p. 79.
15. Adam's Miniature Horn Shell, *Seila adamsi*, 11 mm., p. 79.
16. Mottled Sinistral Miniature Horn Shell, *Triphora decorata*, 10 mm., p. 80.
17. Ribbed Horn Shell, *Cerithidea costata*, 10 mm., p. 82.
18. Ladder Horn Shell, *Cerithidea scalariformis*, 24 mm., p. 82.
19. False Horn Shell, *Batillaria minima*, 16 mm., p. 82.
20. Humphrey's Wentletrap, *Epitonium humphreysii*, 19 mm., p. 88.
21. Tollin's Wentletrap, *Epitonium tollini*, 7 mm., p. 89.
22. Lamellose Wentletrap, *Epitonium lamellosum*, 25 mm., p. 89.
23. Many-ribbed Wentletrap, *Epitonium multistriatum*, 13 mm., p. 89.
24. Matthews's Wentletrap, *Epitonium multistriatum matthewsae*, 8 mm., p. 90.
25. Champion's Wentletrap, *Epitonium championi*, 10 mm., p. 90.
26. Greenland Wentletrap, *Epitonium greenlandicum*, 37 mm., p. 90.
27. Common Simnia, *Simnia acicularis*, 19 mm., p. 110.
28. Single-toothed Simnia, *Simnia uniplicata*, 21 mm., p. 111.
29. McGinty's Flamingo Tongue, *Cyphoma macgintyi*, p. 111.
    a) Specimen with covering mantle intact, 33 mm.; b) apertural view of specimen without mantle, 30 mm.
30. Fingerprint Flamingo Tongue, *Cyphoma signatum*, 33 mm., p. 111.

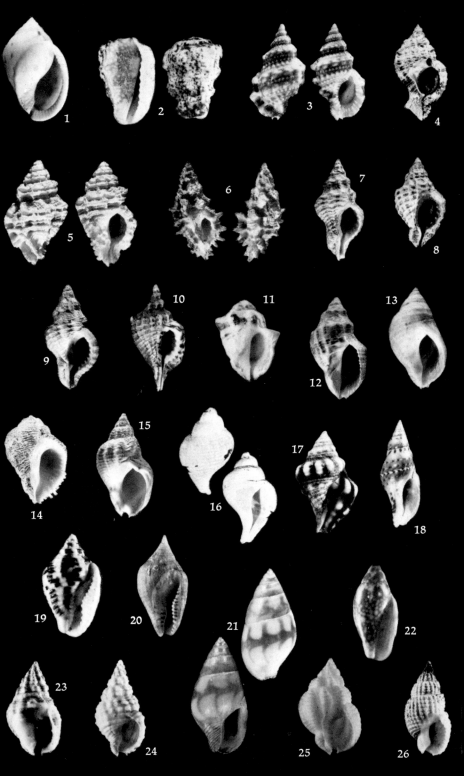

Plate XXIV / Marine Snails

1. Golden-mouthed Triton Shell, *Cymatium nicobaricum*, 67 mm., p. 116.
2. Blackberry Drupe Murex, *Morula nodulosa*, 19 mm., p. 128.
3. Atlantic Oyster Drill, *Urosalpinx cinerea*, 27 mm., p. 128.
4. Thick-lipped Oyster Drill, *Eupleura caudata*, 25 mm., p. 129.
5. Sharp-ribbed Oyster Drill, *Eupleura sulcidentata*, 20 mm., p. 129.
6. Pygmy Whelk, *Colus pygmaeus*, 19 mm., p. 136.
7. Gaudy Lesser Whelk, *Cantharus tinctus*, 24 mm., p. 137.
8. Cross-barred Lesser Whelk, *Cantharus cancellaria*, 31 mm., p. 137.
9. Greedy Dove Shell, *Anachis avara*, 18 mm., p. 140.
10. Well-ribbed Dove Shell, *Anachis translirata*, 11 mm., p. 140.
11. Spotted Dove Shell, *Nitidella ocellata*, 12 mm., p. 141.
12. Plum Margin Shell, *Prunum apicinum*, 12 mm., p. 158.
13. Handsome Margin Shell, *Prunum bellum*, 6 mm., p. 158.
14. Oat-grained Margin Shell, *Volvarina avena*, 13 mm., p. 159.
15. Velie's Margin Shell, *Volvarina veliei*, 7 mm., p. 160.
16. Beaded Miter Shell, *Mitra nodulosa*, 31 mm., p. 161.
17. Barbados Miter, *Mitra barbadensis*, 37 mm., p. 161.
18. Common Auger Shell, *Terebra dislocata*, 45 mm., p. 167.
19. Fine-ribbed Auger Shell, *Terebra protexta*, 19 mm., p. 167.
20. Concave Auger Shell, *Terebra concava*, 18 mm., p. 168.
21. Shiny Auger Shell, *Terebra hastata*, 27 mm., p. 168.
22. Gray Atlantic Auger Shell, *Hastula cinerea*, 33 mm., p. 168.
23. Sallé's Auger Shell, *Hastula salleana*, 24 mm., p. 169.
24. Oyster Turret Shell, *Crassispira ostrearum*, 18 mm., p. 171.
25. White-beaded Turret Shell, *Monilispira leucocyma*, 10 mm., p. 171.
26. Candé's Barrel Bubble, *Retusa candei*, 4 mm., p. 182.
27. Rice Bubble Shell, *Cylichna oryza*, 5 mm., p. 184.
28. Pellucid Marsh Snail, *Ellobium auricula*, 18 mm., p. 189.

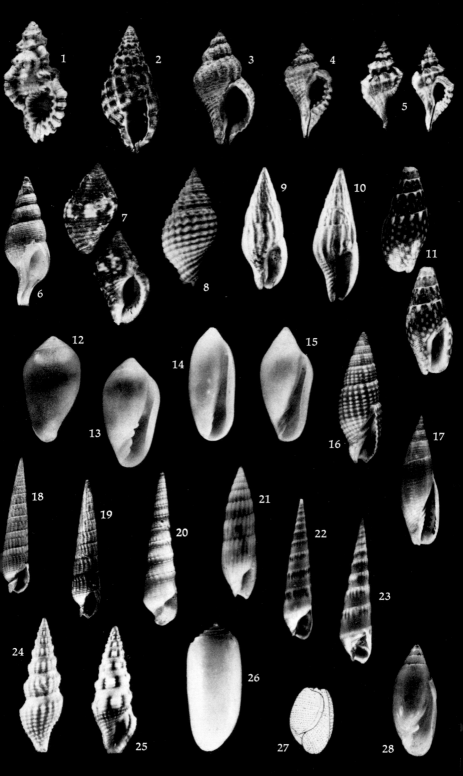

PLATE XXV / Marine Snails

1. Mud Basket Shell, *Ilyanassa obsoleta*, 24 mm., p. 147.
2. Common Lesser Tulip Shell, *Leucozonia nassa*, 58 mm., p. 149.
3. White-spotted Lesser Tulip Shell, *Leucozonia ocellata*, 22 mm., p. 150.
4. Lettered Olive, *Oliva sayana*, 67 mm., p. 151.
5. Netted Olive, *Oliva reticularis*, 49 mm., p. 152
6. Variable Dwarf Olive, *Olivella mutica*, 10 mm., p. 153.
7. Snowy Dwarf Olive, *Olivella nivea*, 18 mm., p. 153.
8. Tiny Dwarf Olive, *Olivella pusilla*, 7 mm., p. 153.
9. Rice Dwarf Olive, *Olivella floralia*, 12 mm., p. 153.
10. Jasper Dwarf Olive, *Jaspidella jaspidea*, 17 mm., p. 154.
11. Caribbean Vase Shell, *Vasum muricatum*, 89 mm., p. 155.
12. Golden-lined Margin Shell, *Dentimargo aureocincta*, 5 mm., p. 157.
13. Tan Margin Shell, *Dentimargo eburneola*, 5 mm., p. 157.
14. White-spotted Margin Shell, *Prunum guttatum* 20 mm., p. 158.
15. Dewy Margin Shell, *Prunum roscidum*, 12 mm., p. 158.
16. Chained Margin Shell, *Persicula catenata*, 7 mm., p. 159.
17. Little Oat Margin Shell, *Volvarina avenacea*, 9 mm., p. 159.
18. Teardrop Margin Shell, *Granulina ovuliformis*, 3 mm., p. 160.
19. Dwarf Florida Miter, *Thala foveata*, 6 mm., p. 162.
20. White-banded Miter, *Vexillum albocincta*, 10 mm., p. 162.
21. Common Nutmeg, *Cancellaria reticulata*, 40 mm., p. 162.
22. Delicate Nutmeg, *Trigonostoma tenerum*, 27 mm., p. 163.
23. Florida Chinese Alphabet Cone, *Conus spurius atlanticus*, 64 mm., p. 164.
24. Carrot Cone, *Conus daucus*, 42 mm., p. 165.
25. Florida Cone, *Conus floridanus*, 50 mm., p. 165.
26. Crown Cone, *Conus regius*, 60 mm., p. 165.
27. Jasper Cone, *Conus jaspideus*, 19 mm., p. 166.
28. Stearns' Cone, *Conus jaspideus stearnsii*, 20 mm., p. 166.
29. Tea-colored Turret Shell, *Cerodrillia thea* 16 mm., p. 171.
30. White-banded Turret Shell, *Monilispira albinodata*, 11 mm., p. 171.
31. Waxy Turret Shell, *Mangelia cerina*, 7 mm., p. 172.
32. Plicate Turret Shell, *Mangelia plicosa*, 6 mm., p. 172.

PLATE XXVI / Marine Snails

1. Lemon-colored Turret Shell, *Kurtziella limonitella*, 6 mm., 172.
2. Giant Pyramid Snail, *Pyramidella dolobrata*, 29 mm., p. 175.
3. Interrupted Turbonille, *Turbonilla interrupta*, 10 mm., p. 175.
4. Impressed Odostome, *Odostomia impressa*, 5 mm., p. 176.
5. Half-smooth Odostome, *Odostomia seminuda*, 4 mm., p. 176.
6. Three-toothed Odostome, *Odostomia trifida*, 3 mm., p. 176.
7. Brown Odostome, *Odostomia fusca*, 4 mm., p. 176.
8. Common True Bubble Shell, *Bulla umbilicata*, 16 mm., p. 179.
9. Striate Bubble, *Bulla striata*, 22 mm., p. 179.
10. Caribbean Paper Bubble, *Atys caribaea*, 6 mm., p. 180.
11. Sanderson's Paper Bubble, *Atys sandersoni*, 7 mm., p. 180.
12. Solitary Paper Bubble, *Haminoea solitaria*, 20 mm., p. 181.
13. Amber Paper Bubble, *Haminoea succincta*, 10 mm., p. 181.
14. Elegant Paper Bubble, *Haminoea elegans*, 12 mm., p. 182.
15. Channeled Barrel Shell, *Retusa canaliculata*, 6 mm., p. 182.
16. Two-toothed Chalice Bubble, *Cylichna bidentata*, 3 mm., p. 184.
17. Pitted Baby Bubble, *Rictaxis punctostriatus*, 4 mm., p. 185.
18. Bladder Bubble Shell, *Hydatina vesicaria*, 42 mm., p. 186.
19. Miniature Melon Shell, *Micromelo undatus*, 12 mm., p. 186.
20. Cuban Marsh Snail, *Laemodonta cubensis*, 3 mm., p. 190.
21. Amber Marsh Snail, *Marinula succinea*, 4 mm., p. 190.
22. Bubble-shaped Marsh Snail, *Detracia bullaoides*, 9 mm., p. 190.
23. Floridian Marsh Snail, *Detracia floridana*, 6 mm., p. 191.
24. Clark's Marsh Snail, *Detracia clarki*, 13 mm., p. 191.
25. Common Marsh Snail, *Melampus bidentatus*, 10 mm., p. 192.
26. Coffee-bean Marsh Snail, *Melampus coffeus*, 18 mm., p. 192.
27. Pear Marsh Snail, *Pira monilis*, 11 mm., p. 192.
28. Mouse-eared Marsh Snail, *Ovatella myosotis*, 6 mm., p. 192.
29. Egg-shaped Marsh Snail, *Tralia ovula*, 11 mm., p. 193.
30. Striped False Limpet, *Siphonaria pectinata*, 21 mm., p. 194.
    a) Interior view; b) exterior view.

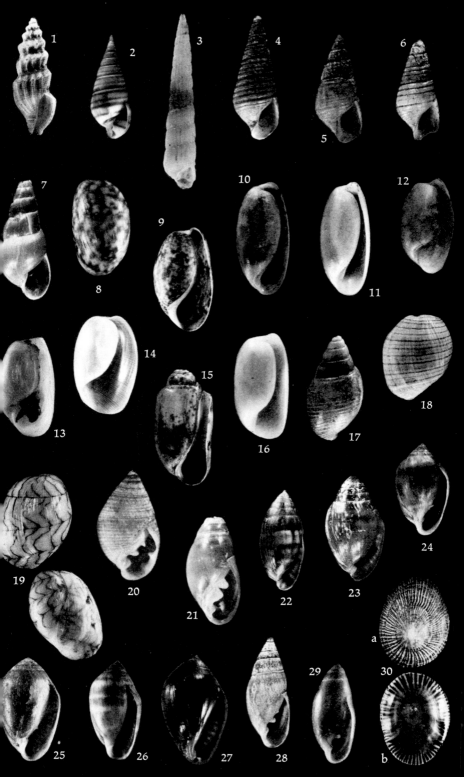

PLATE XXVII / Land Shells

1. Common Florida Helicina, *Helicina orbiculata*, 7 mm., p. 202.
2. Clapp's Helicina, *Helicina clappi*, 6.5 mm., p. 203.
3. Double-lipped Looping Snail, *Truncatella bilabiata*, 5 mm., p. 206.
4. Pretty Looping Snail, *Truncatella pulchella*, 6.5 mm., p. 207.
5. Apple-seed Snail, *Cionella lubrica*, 5.5 mm., p. 210.
6. Tiny Star Shell, *Planogyra asteriscus*, 2 mm., p. 212.
7. White-lipped Pupa Snail, *Pupoides albilabris*, 4.5 mm., p. 215.
8. Contracted Pupa Snail, *Gastrocopta contracta*, 2.3 mm., p. 218.
9. Rock-dwelling Pupa Snail, *Gastrocopta rupicola*, 2.2 mm., p. 218.
10. Worm Amber Snail, *Catinella vermata*, 10 mm., p. 225.
11. Oval Amber Snail, *Succinea ovalis*, 21 mm., p. 226.
12. Decollated Awl Snail, *Rumina decollata*, 31.5 mm., p. 229.
13. Miniature Awl Snail, *Subulina octona*, 14 mm., p. 230.
14. Graceful Awl Snail, *Lamellaxis gracilis*, 11 mm., p. 230.
15. Tiny Awl Snail, *Lamellaxis micrus*, 5.5 mm., p. 230
16. Dominican Tree Snail, *Drymaeus dominicus*, 14 mm., p. 234.
17. Floridian Rock Snail, *Microceramus floridanus*, 8.5 mm., p. 237.
18. Amber Retinella, *Retinella electrina*, 4.5 mm., p. 244.
19. Binney's Retinella, *Retinella binneyana*, 3.5 mm., p. 244.
20. Copper Great Zonite, *Mesomphix cupreus*, 25 mm., p. 247.
21. Many-toothed Zonite Snail, *Paravitrea multidentata*, 3 mm., p. 248.
22. White Zonite Snail, *Hawaiia minuscula*, 2.3 mm., p. 249.
23. Lesser Zonite Snail, *Striatura exigua* (after Pilsbry, 1946), 2.2 mm., p. 252.
24. Millet Zonite Snail, *Striatura milium* (after Pilsbry, 1946), 1.5 mm., p. 253.

PLATE XXVIII / Land Shells

1. Tiny Lucidella, *Lucidella tantilla*, 2.5 mm., p. 203.
2. Bahamian Land Periwinkle, *Opisthosiphon bahamensis*, 2.5 mm., p. 205.
3. Handsome Vallonia, *Vallonia pulchella*, 2.5 mm., p. 211.
4. Ribbed Vallonia, *Vallonia costata*, 2.2 mm., p. 212.
5. Off-center Vallonia, *Vallonia excentrica*, 2.2 mm., p. 212.
6. Tiny Harp Snail, *Zoogenetes harpa*, 3 mm., p. 212.
7. Low Pupa Snail, *Pupisoma minus*, 1.5 mm., p. 216.
8. Ovate Brown Pupa Snail, *Vertigo ovata*, 2.5 mm., p. 219.
9. Labyrinth Snail, *Strobilops labyrinthica*, 2.3 mm., p. 221.
10. Texas Labyrinth Snail, *Strobilops texasiana*, 2.2 mm., p. 221.
11. Allied Labyrinth Snail, *Strobilops affinis*, 2.8 mm., p. 222.
12. Bronze Labyrinth Snail, *Strobilops aenea*, 2.5 mm., p. 222.
13. Golden Amber Snail, *Succinea aurea*, 9 mm., p. 226.
14. Florida Amber Snail, *Succinea luteola floridana*, 13.5 mm., p. 226.
15. Giant African Snail, *Achatina fulica*, 115 mm., p. 228.
16. Common Florida Tree Snail, *Orthalicus floridensis*, 62 mm., p. 235.
17. Lazy Florida Tree Snail, *Orthalicus reses*, 42.5 mm., p. 235.
18. Banded Florida Tree Snail, *Liguus fasciatus*, 43.5 mm., p. 236.
19. Common Disk Snail, *Discus cronkhitei*, 5.5 mm., p. 240.
20. Singley's Disk Snail, *Helicodiscus singleyanus* (lip broken), 2.4 mm., p. 241.
21. Minute Disk Snail, *Punctum minutissimum*, 1.3 mm., p. 241.
22. Indented Retinella, *Retinella indentata*, 4.5 mm., p. 244.

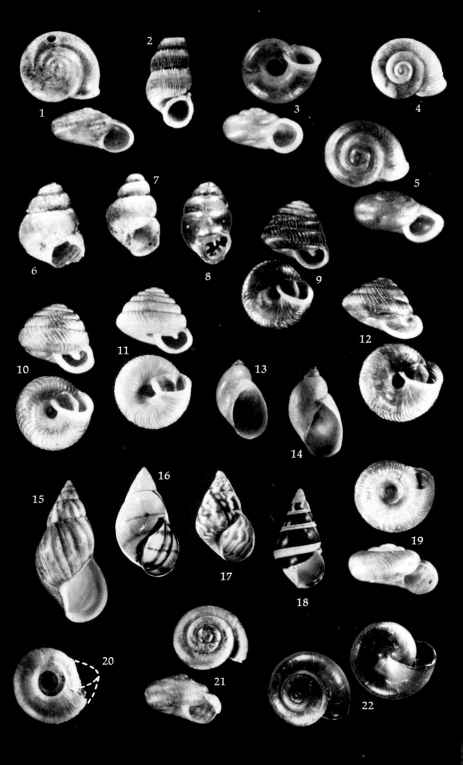

PLATE XXIX / Land Shells

1. Dentate Land Periwinkle, *Chondropoma dentatum,* 10 mm., p. 204.
2. Trellis Looping Snail, *Truncatella scalaris,* 4 mm., p. 206.
3. White Swamp Snail, *Carychium exiguum,* 2 mm., p. 209.
4. Mexican Swamp Snail, *Carychium mexicanum,* 1.4 mm., p. 209.
5. Moss Pupa Snail, *Pupilla muscorum,* 3.5 mm., p. 215.
6. Toothless Pupa Snail, *Columella edentula,* 2.2 mm., p. 215.
7. Medium Pupa Snail, *Pupoides modicus,* 4 mm., p. 216.
8. Armed Pupa Snail, *Gastrocopta armifera,* 4.1 mm., p. 217.
9. Tall Pupa Snail, *Gastrocopta procera,* 2.2 mm., p. 218.
10. Transparent Pupa Snail, *Gastrocopta pellucida hordeacella,* 2.2 mm., p. 218.
11. Tree Pupa Snail, *Gastrocopta corticaria,* 2.5 mm., p. 218.
12. Five-toothed Pupa Snail, *Gastrocopta pentodon,* 1.6 mm., p. 218.
13. Weak-toothed Pupa Snail, *Gastrocopta tappaniana,* 1.8 mm., p. 218.
14. Belly Brown Pupa Snail, *Vertigo ventricosa,* 1.8 mm., p. 219.
15. Modest Brown Pupa Snail, *Vertigo modesta,* 2.5 mm., p. 220.
16. Bolles' Brown Pupa Snail, *Vertigo bollesiana,* 1.5 mm., p. 220.
17. Millet Brown Pupa Snail, *Vertigo milium,* 1.5 mm., p. 220.
18. Hubbard's Labyrinth Snail, *Strobilops hubbardi,* 2.5 mm., p. 222.
19. Florida Peanut Snail, *Cerion incanum,* 25.5 mm., p. 223.
20. Field Amber Snail, *Succinea campestris,* 14 mm., p. 226.
21. Bicolored Awl Snail, *Gulella bicolor,* 5.5 mm., p. 231.
22. Disk Cannibal Snail, *Haplotrema concavum,* 19.5 mm., p. 232.
23. Poey's Truncate Rock Snail, *Cochlodinella poeyana,* 14 mm., p. 237.
24. Pontiff Rock Snail, *Microceramus pontificus,* 10.5 mm., p. 237.
25. Heavy Forest Snail, *Anguispira alternata crassa,* 16 mm., p. 240.
26. Catskill Disk Snail, *Discus cronkhitei catskillensis,* 4.5 mm., p. 240.
27. Open Disk Snail, *Discus patulus,* 8.5 mm., p. 240.
28. Rotund Disk Snail, *Discus rotundatus,* 5.5 mm., p. 241.
29. Parallel Disk Snail, *Helicodiscus parallelus,* 3 mm., p. 241.
30. Garlic Cellar Snail, *Oxychilus alliarius,* 5 mm., p. 248.

PLATE XXX / Land Shells

1.  Common Cellar Snail, *Oxychilus cellarius*, 9.5 mm., p. 247.
2.  Draparnaud's Cellar Snail, *Oxychilus draparnaldi*, 13.4 mm., p. 248.
3.  Depressed Belly-tooth Snail, *Ventridens suppressus*, 6.2 mm., p. 250.
4.  False Belly-tooth Snail, *Ventridens ligera*, 12.5 mm., p. 250.
5.  Tawny Beehive Snail, *Euconulus fulvus*, 3 mm., p. 254.
6.  Auricular Polygyra, *Polygyra auriculata*, p. 260.
    a) 14.5 mm; b) 17 mm.
7.  Uvular Polygyra, *Polygyra uvulifera*, 13.5 mm., p. 260.
8.  Two-horned Uvular Polygyra, *Polygyra uvulifera bicornuta*, 15 mm., p. 260.
9.  Florida Pill Snail, *Stenotrema florida*, 13 mm., p. 263.
10. Fraternal Pill Snail, *Stenotrema fraternum*, 9.5 mm., p. 263.
11. Spiny Pill Snail, *Stenotrema spinosum*, 13.5 mm., p. 268.
12. Profound Forest Snail, *Allogona profunda*, 28 mm., p. 270.
13. Hopeton Forest Snail, *Triodopsis hopetonensis*, 9 mm., p. 272.
14. Tricky Forest Snail, *Triodopsis fallax*, 12 mm., p. 273.
15. Lunar Wallet Snail, *Lacteoluna selenina*, 4.5 mm., p. 277.
16. Speckled Garden Snail, *Helix aspersa*, 26 mm., p. 278.
17. Milk Escargot, *Otala lactea*, 34 mm., p. 279.
18. Cuban Caracole Snail, *Zachrysia provisoria*, 26 mm., p. 280.
19. Furrowed Little Helix, *Hygromia striolata*, 10 mm., p. 282.

PLATE XXXI / Land Shells

*All shells shown approx. ⅔ natural size*

1a,b,c.  White-lipped Forest Snail, *Triodopsis albolabris*, p. 268.
2a,b,c.  Giant Forest Snail, *Mesodon normalis*, p. 269.
3a,b,c.  Common White-lipped Forest Snail, *Mesodon thyroidus*, p. 269.
4a,b,c.  Say's Forest Snail, *Mesodon sayanus*, p. 269.
5a,b,c.  Ripe Forest Snail, *Mesodon zaletus*, p. 270.
6a,b,c.  Raised Forest Snail, *Mesodon elevatus*, p. 270.
7a,b,c.  Engraved Forest Snail, *Mesodon perigraptus*, p. 271.
8a,b,c.  Chilhowee Forest Snail, *Mesodon chilhoweensis*, p. 269.
9a,b,c.  Tooth-bearing Forest Snail, *Triodopsis dentifera*, p. 271.
10a,b,c.  Three-toothed Forest Snail, *Triodopsis tridentata*, p. 271.
11a,b,c.  Juxtaposed Forest Snail, *Triodopsis juxtidens*, p. 273.
12a,b,c.  Fraudulent Forest Snail, *Triodopsis fraudulenta vulgata*, p. 274.

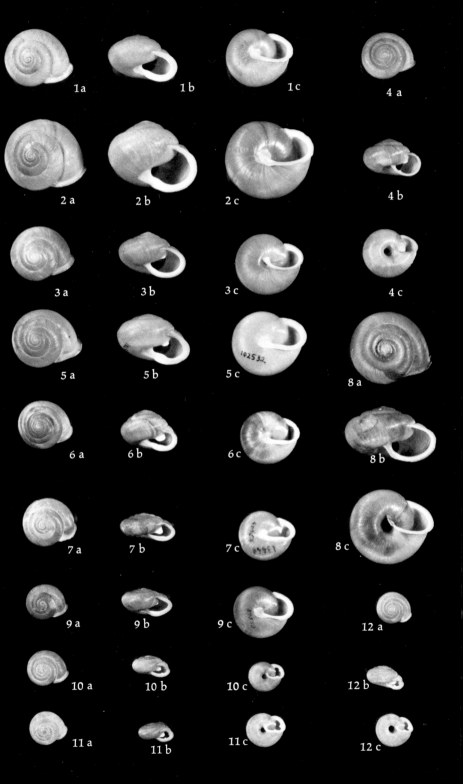

1a     1b     1c     4a

2a     2b     2c     4b

3a     3b     3c     4c

5a     5b     5c     8a

6a     6b     6c     8b

7a     7b     7c     8c

9a     9b     9c     12a

10a     10b     10c     12b

11a     11b     11c     12c

PLATE XXXII / Land Shells

1. Rhoads' Retinella, *Retinella rhoadsi* (broken lip), 2.5 mm., p. 244.
2. Baker's Retinella, *Retinella burringtoni*, 3.5 mm., p. 245.
3. Plain Great Zonite, *Mesomphix inornatus*, 14 mm., p. 247.
4. Common Great Zonite, *Mesomphix vulgatus*, 28 mm., p. 247.
5. Woven Belly-tooth Snail, *Ventridens intertextus*, 14 mm., p. 251.
6. Waxen Belly-tooth Snail, *Ventridens cerinoideus*, 6 mm., p. 251.
7. Tree Zonite Snail, *Zonitoides arboreus*, 5 mm., p. 251.
8. Shining Zonite Snail, *Zonitoides nitidus*, 6.5 mm., p. 252.
9. Clear Glass Snail, Vitrina limpida, 5.5 mm., p. 253.
10. Wild Beehive Snail, *Euconulus chersinus*, 2.5 mm., p. 255.
11. Sterki's Beehive Snail, *Guppya sterkii*, 1.2 mm., p. 255.
12. Guppy's Beehive Snail, *Guppya gundlachi*, 2.5 mm., p. 256.
13. Ceres Polygyra, *Polygyra cereolus*, 13 mm., p. 258.
    a) Apertural view, showing internal lamella; b) dorsal view.
14. Blisterlike Polygyra, *Polygyra pustuloides*, 5.5 mm., p. 261.
15. Hairy Pill Snail, *Stenotrema hirsutum*, 7 mm., p. 263.
16. Compressed Forest Snail, *Mesodon appressus*, 15.5 mm., p. 271.
17. Rugel's Forest Snail, *Mesodon rugeli*, 13 mm., p. 273.

Plate XXXIV / Freshwater Shells

1. Chinese Mystery Snail, *Viviparus malleatus*, 48 mm., p. 289.
2. Japanese Mystery Snail, *Viviparus japonicus*, 55 mm., p. 290.
3. Lesser Mystery Snail, *Campeloma decisum*, 25 mm., p. 290.
4. Southern Lesser Mystery Snail, *Campeloma geniculum*, 24.5 mm., p. 290.
5. Lesser Ram's Horn, *Gyraulus parvus*, 4 mm., p. 313.
6. Hairy Ram's Horn, *Gyraulus hirsutus*, 6 mm., p. 313.
7. Deflected Ram's Horn, *Gyraulus deflectus*, 5.5 mm., p. 313.
8. Dilated Ram's Horn, *Micromenetus dilatatus*, 2 mm., p. 313.
9. Hudson Ram's Horn, *Promenetus hudsonicus*, 2.5 mm., p. 313.
10. Jenks's Ram's Horn, *Planorbula jenksii*, 6.5 mm., p. 314.
11. Wavy Freshwater Mussel, *Strophitus undulatus*, 66 mm., p. 323.
12. Caried Lamp Mussel, *Lampsilis cariosa*, 116 mm., p. 324.
13. Lance Filter Clam, *Elliptio lanceolata*, 61 mm., p. 327.
14. Shepard's Filter Clam, *Elliptio shepardiana*, 122 mm., p. 327.
15. Rhomboid Fingernail Clam, *Sphaerium rhomboideum*, 11 mm., p. 329.
16. Striated Fingernail Clam, *Sphaerium striatinum*, 9 mm., p. 330.
17. Pregnant Fingernail Clam, *Sphaerium partumeium*, 10 mm., p. 330.
18. Doubtful Fingernail Clam, *Pisidium dubium*, 8 mm., p. 331.

PLATE XXXV / Freshwater Shells

1. Keeled Mystery Snail, *Lioplax subcarinata*, 22.5 mm., p. 291.
2. Pilsbry's Mystery Snail, *Lioplax pilsbryi*, 24 mm., p. 291.
3. Florida Apple Snail, Pomacea paludosa, 47 mm., p. 292.
4. Three-keeled Valve Snail, *Valvata tricarinata*, 5 mm., p. 294.
5. Two-keeled Valve Snail, *Valvata bicarinata*, 6.2 mm., p. 294.
6. True Valve Snail, *Valvata sincera*, 3.5 mm., p. 294.
7. Salt Hydrobia, *Hydrobia salsa*, 3 mm., p. 296.
8. Miry Hydrobia, *Amnicola limosa*, 4.5 mm., p. 297.
9. Natural Hydrobia, *Amnicola integra*, 4.5 mm., p. 297.
10. Pupalike Hydrobia, *Lyogyrus pupoides*, 2.5 mm., p. 298.
11. Faucet Snail, *Bithynia tentaculata*, 10 mm., p. 298.
12. Tuberculate Thiara Snail, *Melanoides tuberculata*, 26 mm., p. 300.
13. Chain River Horn Snail, *Goniobasis catenaria*, 16 mm., p. 302.
14. Parallel Freshwater Limpet, *Ferrissia parallela*, 4.8 mm., p. 308.
    a) Dorsal view; b) lateral view.
15. Brook Freshwater Limpet, *Ferrissia rivularis*, 5 mm., p. 308.
    a) Dorsal view; b) lateral view.
16. Off-center Freshwater Limpet, *Hebetancylus excentricus*, 6 mm., p. 309.
    a) Dorsal view; b) lateral view.
17. Dury's Ram's Horn, *Helisoma duryi*, 22.5 mm., p. 312.
18. Confused River Mussel, *Anodonta implicata*, 93 mm., p. 322.
19. Heavy-toothed Filter Clam, *Elliptio crassidens*, 90 mm., p. 327.
20. Pearl Mussel, *Margaritifera margaritifera*, 109 mm., p. 328.
21. Furrowed Fingernail Clam, *Sphaerium similis*, 21 mm., p. 330.

Plate XXXVI / Freshwater Shells

1. Totten's Hydrobia, *Hydrobia totteni*, 4.2 mm., p. 296.
2. Fat Hydrobia, *Gillia altilis*, 7.5 mm., p. 297.
3. Wetherby's Hydrobia, *Notogillia wetherbyi*, 6.5 mm., p. 297.
4. False Schisto Snail, *Pomatiopsis lapidaria*, 6 mm., p. 297.
5. Thiara Snail, *Tarebia granifera*, 23 mm., p. 299.
6. Virginian River Horn Snail, *Goniobasis virginica*, 22.5 mm., p. 301.
7. Livid River Horn Snail, *Goniobasis livescens*, 15 mm., p. 301.
8. Floridian River Horn Snail, *Goniobasis floridensis*, 22.4 mm., p. 301.
9. Swamp Pond Snail, *Lymnaea palustris*, 19 mm., p. 305.
10. Succinea-like Pond Snail, *Lymnaea columella*, 18 mm., p. 306.
11. Explorer Pond Snail, *Lymnaea catascopium*, 19 mm., p. 306.
12. Humble Pond Snail, *Lymnaea humilis*, 10 mm., p. 306.
13. Cuban Pond Snail, *Lymnaea cubensis*, 8.5 mm., p. 306.
14. Ear-shaped Pond Snail, *Lymnaea auricularia*, 27 mm., p. 307.
15. Dark Freshwater Limpet, *Laevapex fuscus*, 4.5 mm., p. 309.
16. Keeled Ram's Horn, *Helisoma anceps*, 11 mm., p. 312.
17. Bell-mouthed Ram's Horn, *Helisoma campanulatum*, 12 mm., p. 312.
18. Staircase Ram's Horn, *Helisoma scalare*, 12.5 mm., p. 312.
19. Three-whorled Ram's Horn, *Helisoma trivolvis*, 17 mm., p. 311.
20. Common Tadpole Snail, *Physa heterostropha*, 15 mm., p. 314.
21. Polished Tadpole Snail, *Aplexa hypnorum*, 15 mm., p. 315.
22. Dusky Caruncle Mussel, *Toxolasma pullum*, 38 mm., p. 324.
23. Lesser Caruncle Mussel, *Toxolasma parvum*, 25 mm., p. 324.
24. Inverted Mussel, *Alasmidonta heterodon*, 47 mm., p. 325.

Plate XXXVIII / Marine Bivalves

1. Blood Ark, *Anadara ovalis*, 46 mm., p. 350.
2. Chemnitz's Ark, *Anadara chemnitzi*, 27 mm., p. 350.
3. Brazil Ark, *Anadara brasiliana*, 50 mm., p. 350.
4. Adams' Miniature Ark, *Arcopsis adamsi*, 16 mm., p. 349.
5. Comb Bittersweet, *Glycymeris pectinata*, 25 mm., p. 352.
6. Wavy Bittersweet, *Glycymeris undata*, 42 mm., p. 352.
7. Decussate Bittersweet, *Glycymeris decussata*, 40 mm., p. 352.
8. American Bittersweet, *Glycymeris americana*, 63 mm., p. 352.
9. Lateral Mussel, *Musculus lateralis*, 10 mm., p. 358.
10. Chestnut Mussel, *Lioberus castaneus*, 24 mm., p. 358.
11. Cinnamon Chestnut Mussel, *Botula fusca*, 12 mm., p. 359.
12. Kitten's Paw, *Plicatula gibbosa*, 24 mm., p. 370.
13. Common Jingle Shell, *Anomia simplex*, 37 mm., p. 373.
14. Prickly Jingle Shell, *Anomia squamula*, 16 mm., p. 373.
15. Rough Jingle Shell, *Pododesmus rudis*, 41 mm., p. 373.
16. Delicate File Shell, *Lima scabra tenera*, 50 mm., p. 375.
17. Pellucid File Shell, *Lima pellucida*, 22 mm., p. 375.

PLATE XXXIX / Marine Bivalves

1. Scorched Mussel, *Brachidontes exustus*, 18 mm., p. 357.
2. Hooked Mussel, *Ischadium recurvum*, 39 mm., p. 357.
3. Paper Mussel, *Amygdalum papyrium*, 23 mm., p. 358.
4. Black Mussel, *Musculus niger*, 56 mm., p. 358.
5. Discord Mussel, *Musculus discors*, 34 mm., p. 358.
6. Mahogany Date Mussel, *Lithophaga bisulcata*, 51 mm., p. 359.
7. Antillean Date Mussel, *Lithophaga antillarum*, 71 mm., p. 359.
8. Black Date Mussel, *Lithophaga nigra*, 60 mm., p. 359.
9. Scissor Date Mussel, *Lithophaga aristata*, 49 mm., p. 360.
10. Amber Pen Shell, *Pinna carnea*, 220 mm., p. 361.
11. Rigid Pen Shell, *Atrina rigida*, 230 mm., p. 362.
12. Naked Pen Shell, *Atrina seminuda*, 180 mm., p. 362.
13. Sawtooth Pen Shell, *Atrina serrata*, 240 mm., p. 362.
14. Winged Pearl Oyster, *Pteria colymbus*, 46 mm., p. 364.
15. Lister's Tree Oyster, *Isognomon radiatus*, 35 mm., p. 366.
16. Ravenel's Scallop, *Pecten raveneli*, 41 mm., p. 368.
17. Thorny Scallop, *Chlamys sentis*, 41 mm., p. 368.
18. Ornate Scallop, *Chlamys ornata*, 33 mm., p. 368.
19. Calico Scallop, *Argopecten gibbus*, 33 mm., p. 369.
20. Bay Scallop, *Argopecten irradians*, 70 mm., p. 369.
21. Spiny File Shell, *Lima lima*, 35 mm., p. 374.
22. Rough File Shell, *Lima scabra*, 69 mm., p. 375.
23. Horse Oyster, *Ostrea equestris*, 46 mm., p. 377.
24. Leafy Oyster, *Ostrea frons*, 44 mm., p. 377.

PLATE XL / Marine Bivalves

1. Sponge Oyster, *Ostrea permollis*, 30 mm., p. 377.
2. Pennsylvania Lucina, *Lucina pensylvanica*, 43 mm., p. 380.
3. Miniature Lucina, *Lucina amianta*, 6 mm., p. 381.
4. Many-lined Lucina, *Lucina multilineata*, 5 mm., p. 381.
5. Florida Lucina, *Lucina floridana*, 27 mm., p. 381.
6. Comb Lucina, *Lucina pectinata*, 10 mm., p. 381.
7. Basket Lucina, *Lucina nassula*, 10 mm., p. 382.
8. Buttercup Lucina, *Anodontia alba*, 76 mm., p. 382.
9. Dwarf Tiger Lucina, *Codakia orbiculata*, 11 mm., p. 383.
10. Cross-hatched Lucina, *Divaricella quadrisulcata*, 18 mm., p. 383.
11. Dentate Lucina, *Divaricella dentata*, 26 mm., p. 384.
12. Corrugated Jewel Box, *Chama congregata*, 25 mm., p. 385.
13. False Jewel Box, *Pseudochama radians*, 51 mm., p. 385.
14. Spiny Jewel Box, *Arcinella cornuta*, 37 mm., p. 386.
15. Flat Lepton, *Mysella planulata*, 6 mm., p. 387.
16. Northern Cardita, *Cyclocardia borealis*, 21 mm., p. 388.
17. Chestnut Astarte, *Astarte castanea*, 31 mm., p. 389.

PLATE XLI / Marine Bivalves

1. Eastern Oyster, *Crassostrea virginica*, 73 mm., p. 377.
2. Philippi's Lucina, *Anodontia philippiana*, 67 mm., p. 382.
3. Tiger Lucina, *Codakia orbicularis*, 55 mm., p. 383.
4. Leafy Jewel Box, *Chama macerophylla*, 37 mm., p. 385.
5. West Indian Jewel Box, *Arcinella arcinella*, 57 mm., p. 386.
6. Florida Cardita, *Carditamera floridana*, 35 mm., p. 388.
7. Wavy Astarte, *Astarte undata*, 32 mm., p. 390.
8. Boreal Astarte, *Astarte borealis*, 35 mm., p. 390.
9. Giant Atlantic Cockle, *Dinocardium robustum*, 107 mm., p. 393.
10. Van Hyning's Cockle, *Dinocardium robustum vanhyningi*, 115 mm., p. 393.
11. Prickly Cockle, *Trachycardium egmontianum*, 75 mm., p. 393.
12. Yellow Cockle, *Trachycardium muricatum*, 39 mm., p. 393.
13. Ravenel's Egg Cockle, *Laevicardium pictum*, 9 mm., p. 394.
14. Dwarf Northern Cockle, *Cerastoderma pinnulatum*, 11 mm., p. 395.
15. Atlantic Surf Clam, *Spisula solidissima*, 130 mm., p. 397.
16. Ravenel's Surf Clam, *Spisula solidissima raveneli*, 75 mm., p. 397.
17. Channeled Surf Clam, *Raeta plicatella*, 60 mm., p. 398.
18. Wedge Rangia, *Rangia cuneata*, 49 mm., p. 398.
19. Lesser Razor Clam, *Ensis minor*, 64 mm., p. 401.
20. Scaly Razor Clam, *Siliqua squama*, 69 mm., p. 401.
21. Alternate Tellin, *Tellina alternata*, 56 mm., p. 404.

PLATE XLIII   /   Marine Bivalves

1. Rose Petal Tellin, *Tellina lineata*, 45 mm., p. 405.
2. Faust Tellin, *Tellina fausta*, 98 mm., p. 405.
3. Agile Tellin, *Tellina agilis*, 16 mm., p. 406.
4. Delicate Tellin, *Tellina tenella*, 9 mm., p. 407.
5. DeKay's Tellin, *Tellina versicolor*, 10 mm., p. 409.
6. Sybarite Tellin, *Tellina sybaritica*, 6 mm., p. 409.
7. Tampa Tellin, *Tellina tampaensis*, 20 mm., p. 409.
8. Wedge Tellin, *Tellina candeana*, 11 mm., p. 411.
9. Rainbow Tellin, *Tellina iris*, 12 mm., p. 411.
10. Remarkable Scraper, *Strigilla mirabilis*, 13 mm., p. 411.
11. Pea Scraper, *Strigilla pisiformis*, 9 mm., p. 412.
12. Baltic Macoma, *Macoma balthica*, 30 mm., p. 413.
13. Chalky Macoma, *Macoma calcarea*, 26 mm., p. 413.
14. Coquina Clam, *Donax variabilis*, 25 mm., p. 415.
15. Fossor Coquina Clam, *Donax variabilis fossor*, 100 mm., p. 415.
16. Giant False Donax, *Iphigenia brasiliana*, 56 mm., p. 416.
17. Blood-stained Sand Clam, *Sanguinolaria sanguinolenta*, 33 mm., p. 417.
18. Divided Sand Clam, *Tagelus divisus*, 27 mm., p. 418.

Plate XLIV / Marine Bivalves

1. Concentric Nut Clam, *Nuculana concentrica*, 8 mm., p. 342.
2. Atlantic Pearl Oyster, *Pinctada imbricata*, 80 mm., p. 364.
3. Winged Tree Oyster, *Isognomon alatus*, 68 mm., p. 365.
4. Bicolored Tree Oyster, *Isognomon bicolor*, 51 mm., p. 366.
5. Zigzig Scallop, *Pecten ziczac*, 56 mm., p. 367.
6. Imbricated Scallop, *Chlamys imbricata*, 49 mm., p. 369.
7. Iceland Scallop, *Chlamys islandica*, 53 mm., p. 369.
8. Southern Bay Scallop, *Argopecten irradians concentricus*, 72 mm.. p. 369.
9. Mossy Scallop, *Aequipecten muscosus*, 31 mm., p. 369.
10. Elevated Aligena, *Aligena elevata*, 7 mm., p. 387.
11. Fragile Surf Clam, *Mactra fragilis*, 90 mm., p. 396.
12. Stimpson's Surf Clam, *Spisula polynyma*, 89 mm., p. 398.
13. Arctic Wedge Clam, *Mesodesma arctatum*, 34 mm., p. 398.
14. Common Razor Clam, *Ensis directus*, 150 mm., p. 401.
15. Fragile Razor Clam, *Siliqua costata*, 45 mm., p. 401.
16. Great Tellin, *Tellina magna*, 94 mm., p. 404.
17. Lister's Tellin, *Tellina listeri*, 68 mm., p. 404.
18. Smooth Tellin, *Tellina laevigata*, 75 mm., p. 405.
19. Vulgar Sand Clam, *Tagelus plebeius*, 95 mm., p. 418.
20. Cancellate Semele, *Semele bellastriata*, 12 mm., p. 420.
21. Gaper Soft-shelled Clam, *Mya truncata*, 64 mm., p. 438.
22. True Angel Wing, *Cyrtopleura costata*, 162 mm., p. 444.
23. Common Piddock, *Zirfaea crispata*, 68 mm., p. 445.
24. Gould's Shipworm, *Bankia gouldi*, 6 mm. (after Clench and Turner, 1946), p. 447.
    a) Outer surface of pallet (greatly enlarged); b) inner surface of pallet; c) external view of shell; d) internal view of shell.

Plate XLV / Marine Bivalves

1. Common Abra, *Abra aequalis*, 9 mm., p. 421.
2. Conrad's False Mussel, *Mytilopsis leucophaeata*, 18 mm., p. 425.
3. Hard-shelled Clam, *Mercenaria mercenaria*, 90 mm., p. 428.
4. Southern Quahog, *Mercenaria campechiensis*, 105 mm., p. 429.
5. White Pygmy Venus, *Chione pygmaea*, 10 mm., p. 430.
6. Conrad's Lattice Venus, *Transennella conradina*, 9 mm., p. 431.
7. Spotted Venus, *Macrocallista maculata*, 55 mm., p. 434.
8. Disk Venus, *Dosinia discus*, 69 mm., p. 435.
9. Soft-shelled Clam, *Mya arenaria*, 84 mm., p. 438.
10. Contracted Box Clam, *Corbula contracta*, 10 mm., p. 439.
11. Dietz's Box Clam, *Corbula dietziana*, 12 mm., p. 440.
12. Caribbean Box Shell, *Corbula caribaea*, 7 mm., p. 440.
13. Spengler's Burrowing Gaper Clam, *Spengleria rostrata*, 29 mm., p. 441.
14. False Angel Wing, *Barnea truncata*, 49 mm., p. 444.
15. Campeche Angel Wing, *Pholas campechiensis*, 76 mm., p. 444.
16. Common Shipworm, *Teredo navalis*, 6 mm., p. 446.
    a) Exterior view of shell; b) block of wood infested with burrows of shipworms; c) shipworm removed from burrow, showing external soft parts, shell (far right), and pallets (far left).
17. Three-lined Pandora, *Pandora trilineata*, 26 mm., p. 449.
18. Northern Glass Clam, *Lyonsia hyalina*, 17 mm., p. 450.

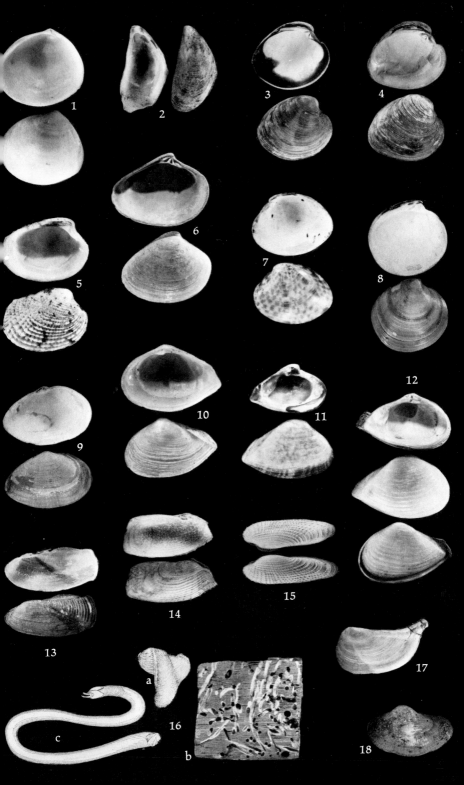

PLATE XLVI / Marine Bivalves

1.  Cross-barred Venus, *Chione cancellata*, 29 mm., p. 430.
2.  Purple Venus, *Chione intapurpurea*, 32 mm., p. 430.
3.  Gray Pygmy Venus, *Chione grus*, 11 mm., p. 430.
4.  Pointed Venus, *Anomalocardia auberiana*, 18 mm., p. 432.
5.  Gem Venus Clam, *Gemma gemma*, 4 mm., p. 432.
6.  Brown Gem Clam, *Parastarte triquetra*, 3 mm., p. 432.
7.  Codfish Venus, *Pitar morrhuanus*, 35 mm., p. 433.
8.  Lightning Venus, *Pitar fulminatus*, 37 mm., p. 433.
9.  Gould's Wax Venus, *Gouldia cerina*, 7 mm., p. 433.
10. Elegant Venus, *Dosinia elegans*, 70 mm., p. 434.
11. False Angel Wing, *Petricola pholadiformis*, 54 mm., p. 435.
12. Southern False Angel Wing, *Petricola lapicida*, 20 mm., p. 436.
13. Jonas's Rock Borer, *Rupellaria typica*, 21 mm., p. 436.
14. Smith's Piddock, *Diplothyra smithii*, 7 mm., p. 446.
15. Gould's Pandora, *Pandora gouldiana*, 26 mm., p. 449.
16. Lea's Spoon Clam, *Periploma leanum*, 30 mm., p. 451.
17. Unequal Spoon Clam, *Periploma margaritaceum*, 26 mm., p. 452.

PLATE XLVII / Other Marine Mollusks

1. Stimpson's Tusk Shell, *Dentalium entale stimpsoni*, 29 mm., p. 456.
2. Ivory Tusk Shell, *Dentalium eboreum*, 35 mm., p. 457.
3. Texas Tusk Shell, *Dentalium texasianum*, 28 mm., p. 457.
4. Carolina Tooth Shell, *Cadulus carolinensis*, 9 mm., p. 457.
5. Four-cusped Tooth Shell, *Cadulus quadridentatus*, 10 mm., p. 458.
6. Ram's Horn Shell, *Spirula spirula*, 21 mm., p. 459.
7. Paper Nautilus, *Argonauta argo*, 79 mm., p. 459.
8. Brown Paper Nautilus, *Argonauta hians*, 34 mm., p. 459.
9. Gray Chiton, *Chaetopleura apiculata*, 12 mm., p. 463.
10. Red Northern Chiton, *Ischnochiton ruber*, 16 mm., p. 464.
11. Florida Slender Chiton, *Stenoplax floridana*, 39 mm., p. 464.
12. Pitted Chiton, *Stenoplax papillosus*, 8 mm., p. 464.
13. Fuzzy Chiton, *Acanthopleura granulata*, 66 mm., p. 465.

Genus *Mesomphix* Rafinesque

*Mesomphix inornatus* Say
  Plain Great Zonite

Pl. XXXII, 3

ETYMOLOGY: Gr. *mesos omphalos,* middle umbilicus; Lat. *inornatus,* not decorated.

SIZE: 8 mm. (1/3 in.) high, 20 mm. (4/5 in.) wide.

DISTRIBUTION: Quebec and the coastal states from Maine to Virginia and westward to Indiana.

CHARACTERISTICS: Shell large for the family, low, yellowish or olive-tan, opaque, lip thin, umbilicus very narrow, protoconch and spire rather smooth.

The shells of the genus *Mesomphix* are higher and larger than most other zonitids. There are about a dozen species in the United States, but only three of these can be commonly found in our area. They live under moist leaf mulch and fallen trees.

The **Common Great Zonite,** *Mesomphix vulgatus* H. B. Baker (from Lat. *vulgatus,* common) (pl. XXXII, 4), is like *M. inornatus,* but it is larger 18 mm. (3/4 in.) high and 27 mm. (about 1 in.) wide, and heavier. It is somewhat darker in color, with darker and lighter streaks. The protoconch and spire are marked with strong axial striations. It ranges from Maryland to Florida and westward to Arkansas.

The **Copper Great Zonite,** *Mesomphix cupreus* Rafinesque (Lat. *cuprum,* copper) (pl. XXVII, 20), is as large as *M. vulgatus* but somewhat higher and with a decidedly wider umbilicus. It is darker in color, brownish olive to yellow, and is quite smooth; the aperture is bluish white and is also smooth. Its range extends from Vermont to South Carolina and westward to Illinois and Missouri.

The **Common Cellar Snail,** *Oxychilus cellarius* Müller (Gr. *oxeos cheilos,* sharp lip) (pl. XXX, 1), is somewhat larger, reaching about 10 mm. (2/5 in.) in diameter. It is imperfectly transparent, with a faint yellowish or amber tint above and whitish about the umbilicus. Thus it is larger and smoother than *O. alliarius,* and has no garlic odor.

The cellar snails, genus *Oxychilus* Fitzinger, are flatter, shinier, and paler in color than the *Mesomphix.* Since they are all immigrants from Europe, they tend to flourish in urban or suburban areas, never far from human habitation, rather than in isolated woods and fields as the native snails do. They are found in city lots, under debris and stones, and in dank cellars or other undisturbed moist situations.

The **Garlic Cellar Snail,** *Oxychilus alliarius* Miller (Lat. *allium,* garlic) (pl. XXIX, 30), is the smallest of the three species discussed, reaching only 6 mm. (1/4 in.) in diameter. When collected alive and handled roughly, it gives off a distinct scent of garlic. It is amber or light horn color above and whitish about the umbilicus, and is somewhat more striate and less smooth than the other two species. It has been found in several northern cities.

**Draparnaud's Cellar Snail,** *Oxychilus draparnaldi* Beck (named for the French malacologist J. Draparnaud) (pl. XXX, 2), is the largest of the three, reaching more than 16 mm. (2/3 in.) in diameter. The umbilicus is proportionately larger than in the other two species, and the color is pale brown above, much paler beneath. Shells less than 10 mm. (2/5 in.) in diameter are very difficult to distinguish from *O. cellarius*.

Genus *Paravitrea* Pilsbry

*Paravitrea multidentata* Binney
   Many-toothed Zonite Snail

   Pl. XXVII, 21

ETYMOLOGY: Gr. *para,* near, Lat. *vitreus,* glassy; *Vitrea* is a zonite genus of the Old World.

SIZE: 2.5 to 3 mm. (about 1/8 in.) in diameter, 1 mm. (1/25 in.) in height.

DISTRIBUTION: Canada and Maine to North Carolina.

CHARACTERISTICS: Shell small, spire low, very thin, pellucid, shining. Horn colored. Whorls narrow, slowly widening. Umbilicus very narrow; lip thin. Two or more rows of very minute white teeth radiating from the umbilicus can be seen through the base of the shell.

This "gemlike" snail, as Pilsbry calls it, is readily recognized by the almost flat spire, narrow whorls, and rows of tiny internal teeth, one row of which can be seen without a microscope in the aperture. When the animal is alive, the transparent shell has a roseate tinge.

There are several other species of *Paravitrea* living in the mountains on the western border of the coastal states. Pilsbry (1946) should be consulted for the discussion of these forms.

Genus *Hawaiia* Gude

*Hawaiia minuscula* Binney
White Zonite Shell

Pl. XXVII, 22

ETYMOLOGY: Lat. *minusculus*, minuscule.

SIZE: 2.5 mm. (about 1/8 in.) in diameter, 1.2 mm. (about 1/25 in.) in height.

DISTRIBUTION: From Canada to Florida and westward to the mountain states to Alaska.

CHARACTERISTICS: Shell minute, depressed, thin, silky, smooth. Pale gray, somewhat opalescent. Umbilicus large, about one-third of diameter; lip thin.

The small, shiny, whitish or gray shell with its large umbilicus can be taken for a bleached dead shell of some other zonitid until it is realized that weathered shells never have a gloss. The species is also found in the West Indies.

The proposal of the generic name *Hawaiia* for this species was due to an error. G. K. Gude applied the name to a mainland species that had been accidentally introduced to the Hawaiian Islands, not knowing the natural province of this snail. As Pilsbry dourly put it later: "The singularly inappropriate generic name . . . was owing to the circumstances that its author had only a hazy idea of the shell he was naming and knew nothing whatever about its long history in scientific literature." When it was found desirable to remove these whitish snails from the genus *Vitrea* where they had earlier been put, it was found that, appropriate or not, Gude's name was the earliest for the group and under the rules of priority it had to take precedence.

---

# KEY TO GENUS VENTRIDENS

\* Shell with apertural structures at mature and/or immature growth stage

\*\* Shell with minute umbilicus — *Ventridens cerinoideus*

\*\* Shell with distinct umbilicus, one-eighth of diameter

\*\*\* Shell with basal lamella only — *V. suppressus*

\*\*\* Shell with basal lamella and additional tooth opposite columella on outer wall — *V. suppressus virginicus*

&ast; Shell with no internal or apertural
structures at all growth stages
&ast;&ast; Shell glossy, upper surface of body whorl
with axial striae only                *V. ligera*
&ast;&ast; Shell lusterless, upper surface of body
whorl with axial striae and spiral lines    *V. intertextus*

---

Genus *Ventridens* W. G. Binney

*Ventridens suppressus* Say
Depressed Belly-tooth Snail

Pl. XXX, 3

ETYMOLOGY: Latin *venter dens*, belly tooth; *suppressus*, subdued, depressed.

SIZE: 5.5 to 7 mm. (about 1/4 in.) in diameter, 3.5 to 4 mm. (about 1/6 in.) in height.

DISTRIBUTION: From Canada and Maine to North Carolina and westward to Michigan.

CHARACTERISTICS: Shell small, depressed, glossy. Pale horn color, opaque whitish near the aperture, semitransparent. Umbilicus narrow, one-eighth of diameter; lip thin but with a prominent, entering basal tooth just within the aperture.

This small belly-tooth snail is characterized by the prominent basal tooth and the small but distinct umbilicus. In the immature shell there are two to five teeth in the aperture, but the adult animal presents only one.

The subspecies *V. suppressus virginicus* Vanatta, the **Virginian Belly-toothed Snail** (not illustrated), is similar, but in the adult stage there is, in addition to the basal tooth near the columella, another short, obtuse lamella opposite, inside the outer wall. It has been found in Virginia, Delaware, western New York, and westward to Michigan.

The **False Belly-tooth Snail,** *Ventridens ligera* Say (possibly from Gr. *elachus*, that which weighs little—hence the Spanish *ligero*, light— but Pilsbry writes that the etymology is uncertain) (pl. XXX, 4), reaches 11 to 15 mm. (about 1/2 to 3/5 in.) in diameter and 9 to 12 mm. (about 2/5 to 1/2 in.) in height. This most widely spread of the local *Ventridens* is easily recognized by its yellowish, raised glossy shell, with varnished base and a white opaque spot on the base near the aperture. The sculpture consists only of axial wrinkles, which weaken on the base. In spite of its generic name, it is the only *Ventridens* in our area that lacks internal teeth at all stages of its growth. It ranges from New York to Virginia and westward to Arkansas and Oklahoma, and lives in fields at the margin of forests.

The **Woven Belly-tooth Snail,** *Ventridens intertextus* Binney (Lat. *intertextus,* interwoven) (pl. XXXII, 5), is similar, but readily distinguished by its lusterless surface and the presence of distinct spiral lines on the upper surface of the body whorl, in addition to the axial growth lines. In *V. ligera* the spiral lines, if present, are very faint, and appear on the base only. The umbilicus is sometimes completely closed. It can be found from Canada and New York to Florida, but it is less common than *V. ligera* on the coastal plain.

The **Waxen Belly-tooth Snail,** *Ventridens cerinoideus* Anthony (Lat. *cerinus,* wax colored) (pl. XXXII, 6), differs chiefly in having a minute umbilicus, partly hidden by an extension of the lower lip. In the juvenile stage there are two entering lamellae on the base, but in maturity these are reduced to two low denticles just inside the aperture. The species is common on the coastal plain, but it has a more southern distribution than *V. suppressus.* It ranges from Virginia to Florida, and is very common in the eastern part of the Carolinas.

Genus *Zonitoides* Lehmann

*Zonitoides arboreus* Say
    Tree Zonite Snail

    Pl. XXXII, 7

ETYMOLOGY: Gr. *zonites oidea,* zonitelike.

SIZE: 5 to 6 mm. (1/5 to 1/4 in.) in diameter, 2.5 to 3 mm. (about 1/8 in.) in height.

DISTRIBUTION: Throughout the United States except Nevada, and in Canada.

CHARACTERISTICS: Shell low, translucent, moderately glossy. Olive buff. Weakly sculptured with growth lines, the base smoother. Umbilicus large, one-fourth of diameter; lip thin.

This is the most widely spread and one of the commonest land snails of the region. It is found in city parks and lots, as well as in woodlands, and almost everywhere where conditions are favorable. It is a hothouse pest because it nibbles the edges of ornamental flowers, and in the South it is accused of damaging the sugar cane by eating the root hairs of the plants. Though a native of America, it has been spread widely by commerce, and has recently been reported even from far-off Kenya.

The **Shining Zonite Snail,** *Zonitoides nitidus* Müller (Lat. *nitidus,* shining or glittering) (pl. XXXII, 8), is similar, but the shell is larger, 6 to 7 mm. (about 1/4 in.) in diameter, higher, and much more glossy, and the umbilicus is smaller. It lives in very wet situations at the very edge of ponds and streams, whereas *Z. arboreus* prefers dryer situations farther removed from bodies of water.

The two species of *Zonitoides* are not easy to separate unless live-taken specimens are compared. In addition to the differentiation indicated above, *Z. nitidus* with the soft parts inside is almost black, whereas *Z. arboreus* is light brown.

---

# KEY TO GENUS STRIATURA

* Shell with large umbilicus, about one-third of diameter, well sculptured
** Shell with axial ribs widely spaced, oblique, well raised, 2.5 mm. (about 1/10 in.) in diameter, greenish     *Striatura exigua*
** Shell with axial ribs closely set, barely raised, 1.5 mm. (about 1/16 in.) in diameter, pale yellow to grayish     *S. milium*
* Shell with small umbilicus, one-fifth of diameter, sculpture weak, steel gray, 3 mm. (1/8 in.) in diameter     *S. ferrea*

---

Genus *Striatura* Morse

*Striatura exigua* Stimpson
    Lesser Zonite

    Pl. XXVII, 23

ETYMOLOGY: Possibly from Lat. *striatus,* furnished with channels, and *exiguus,* very small.

SIZE: 2.5 mm. (about 1/10 in.) wide, 1 mm. (1/25 in.) high.

DISTRIBUTION: Canada and Maine to Cape May, New Jersey, and westward to Michigan.

CHARACTERISTICS: Shell very small, corneous green, widely umbilicate, surface sculpture of widely spaced, oblique, raised axial riblets and fine spiral striae.

This tiny shell lives in low, wet ground under leaves. Under even slight magnification it is a very handsomely ornamented object, much more so than other small zonites. The genus can be recognized by the small shells with few whorls, pale color, and generally elaborate surface sculpture. It is commoner in the northern part of its range.

The **Millet Zonite Snail,** *Striatura milium* Morse (from Lat. *milium,* millet seed) (pl. XXVII, 24), also has a wide umbilicus, but the shell is yellowish corneous or gray and very much smaller, being only 1.5 mm. (about 1/16 in.) in diameter. The axial ribs are not so oblique, are very closely set, and barely raised above the spiral sculpture. It ranges from Canada and Maine to New Jersey and westward to Michigan.

The **Ferrous Zonite Snail,** *Striatura ferrea* Morse (Lat. *ferreus,* pertaining to iron) (pl. XXXIII, 1), is larger, reaching 3 mm. (1/8 in.) in diameter. The shell is steel gray, not shining, and has a very narrow umbilicus, and the sculpture is much weaker. Superficially it resembles *Retinella indentata* (page 244), but, as Morse wrote, "The dead color alone is sufficient to distinguish it." It ranges from Canada to Maine to North Carolina.

FAMILY:

# VITRINIDAE
(*glass snails*)

The shells of this family have a large, expanded body whorl and an insignificant spire. They are very fragile and thin. These aberrant zonite snails were only recently afforded the rank of a family.

Genus *Vitrina* Draparnaud

*Vitrina limpida* Gould
    Clear Glass Snail

    Pl. XXXII, 9

ETYMOLOGY: From Lat. *vitrum* and *limpidus,* transparent glass.

SIZE: 6 mm. (1/4 in.) in diameter, 5 mm. (1/5 in.) in height.

DISTRIBUTION: Canada and Maine to New York and westward to northern Michigan.

CHARACTERISTICS: Shell discoid, thin, fragile, transparent, shining. Colorless or pale green. Sculpture very faint. Whorls two and one-half to three, the last large and much expanded. Umbilicus lacking; lip thin, fragile.

Because of the huge body whorl and the fragile glassy texture, this shell cannot be mistaken for any other zonite. It is characteristic of the northern forests where, according to Pilsbry, it is most easily collected alive in autumn after the first frost. Its life span is apparently only one year.

SUPERFAMILY:

# ARIOPHANTACEA

FAMILY:

# EUCONULIDAE
(*beehive snails*)

This is a small family of thin shells living throughout the Holarctic region, often in mountainous areas. The shells may be domed, but low conic to flattened forms also occur. They are amber or brownish to brownish green in color, sometimes glassy, and they generally have weak surface sculpture.

Genus *Euconulus* Reinhart

*Euconulus fulvus* Müller
Tawny Beehive

Pl. XXX, 5

ETYMOLOGY: Gr. *eu* and *conulus*, real little cone; and Lat. *fulvus*, tawny.

SIZE: 2.4 mm. (1 1/12 in.) high, 3.1 mm. (1/8 in.) wide.

DISTRIBUTION: In northern regions throughout the world; in coastal states from Canada to Virginia.

CHARACTERISTICS: Shell very small, broadly conic, minutely umbilicate, thin, fragile, glossy; pale brown, marked with faint spiral and axial lines.

The shells of this genus look like tiny old-fashioned beehives. They live among damp leaves in well-shaded places, and can best be collected by leaf sifting. The shells are also common in drift debris of creeks and rivers. Their broadly conic, beehive-like shells readily distinguish them from other zonites. The genus was first called *Conulus* (little cone), but this name had been used for a different genus previously. Hence the *eu* (Gr. real) was added to distinguish it.

The **Wild Beehive,** *Euconulus chersinus* Say (Gr. *chersinos*, of a wild place) (pl. XXXII, 10), is similar, but the shell is yellowish white in color, less glossy, and more finely sculptured. In addition, the spire is more elevated—the height is greater than the width—it has more numerous and narrower whorls and a narrower aperture. It ranges from New Jersey to Florida and westward to Illinois and Louisiana.

Genus *Guppya* Mörch

*Guppya sterkii* Dall
Sterki's Beehive Snail

Pl. XXXII, 11

ETYMOLOGY: Named for R. J. L. Guppy of Trinidad, a student of West Indian geology and conchology; and Victor Sterki, a Swiss-American malacologist who specialized in minute mollusks.

SIZE: 1.3 mm. (about 1/20 in.) in diameter, .75 mm. (about 1/32 in.) in height.

DISTRIBUTION: Ontario to Florida and westward to Ohio and Louisiana.

CHARACTERISTICS: Shell minute, depressed. Yellowish, translucent. Sculptured with minute, moderately spaced spiral striae and weak growth wrinkles. Base flat. Umbilicus lacking, periphery rounded, lip thin.

This is one of the tiniest of American land snails, and can be collected only by examining leaf siftings under a magnifying glass. It is most readily recognized by the imperforate, flattened base and especially by the incised spiral lines. *Guppya* is generally a genus of the warmer climates, and *G. sterkii* is unique in inhabiting the colder areas of the United States, as well as Canada.

**Guppy's Beehive Snail,** *Guppya gundlachi* Pfeiffer (named for Juan Gundlach, a devoted German-born student of the natural history of Cuba) (pl. XXXII, 12), is larger, 3 mm. (1/8 in.) in diameter, and has a small umbilicus. The spirally incised lines are readily discernible. This is a subtropical species, found in Florida and Texas on the American mainland.

The **Miami Beehive Snail,** *Guppya miamiensis* Pilsbry (not illustrated), has been found only in southern Florida and on some of the Florida Keys. It resembles *G. gundlachi* in having an umbilicus, but it is smaller and lacks the incised spiral lines.

# INFRAORDER:

# HOLOPODA

*(foot without marginal furrow)*


# SUPERFAMILY:

## POLYGYRACEA


# FAMILY:

## POLYGYRIDAE

*(polygyra land snails)*

These shells are small to moderate in size, depressed-conic to disklike-flattened in shape, generally brownish or light buff in color with an expanded lip and a semilunar to triangular aperture, generally armed with many teeth. This family is limited to North America, with a single West Indian genus and a few insular species in other genera. The flattened shells of the genus *Polygyra* are most richly developed in Florida and elsewhere in the South; the higher shells of *Mesodon* and *Triodopsis* are more common in the North, where most species live east of the Mississippi River. These shells are probably the most conspicuous molluscan elements in the deciduous forests of the Northeast.

# KEY TO THE GENUS POLYGYRA

   \* Aperture with parietal tooth only

   \* \* Shell with internal lamella; southern
distribution                         *Polygyra cereolus*

   \* \* Shell without internal lamella; northern
distribution                         *P. septemvolva*

   \* Aperture with parietal and 2 lip teeth,
frequently highly convoluted

   \* \* Shell surface with periostracal hairs

  \* \* \* Shell 6 to 7 mm. (about 1/4 in.) wide, hairs
closely set                         *P. avara*

  \* \* \* Shell 4 to 5 mm. (1/6 to 1/5 in.), hairs sparsely
set

 \* \* \* \* Shell very small, 4 mm. (1/6 in.) in diameter,
umbilicus partly covered by extension of inner
lip                         *P. pustula*

 \* \* \* \* Shell larger, 5.5 mm. (about 1/4 in.) in diameter,
umbilicus entirely free              *P. pustuloides*

   \* \* Shell without periostracal hairs

  \* \* \* Basal tooth at umbilical termination turning
inward at right angle                *P. postelliana*

  \* \* \* Basal tooth at umbilical side terminating in a
straight wall

 \* \* \* \* Basal lip near umbilicus flattened to surface of
last whorl                     *P. uvulifera*

 \* \* \* \* Basal lip near umbilicus raised and thickened    *P. auriculata*

---

Genus *Polygyra* Say
   Polygyra Land Snails

   Pl. XXXII, 13

*Polygyra cereolus* Mühlfeld
   Ceres Polygyra

ETYMOLOGY: Gr. *poly gyra*, many whorled; possibly from Ceres, the goddess
of agriculture.

SIZE: 7 to 18 mm. (about 1/4 to 3/4 in.) in diameter, about 4 mm. (1/6 in.)
in height.

DISTRIBUTION: Southern Florida, from Citrus and Seminole counties to the
Florida Keys.

CHARACTERISTICS: Disklike, with many narrow whorls (five and one-half to more than nine); moderately shining, thin. Faintly yellowish to horn brown. Surface strongly marked with axial ridges, which disappear at the base. Periphery roundly keeled or more or less angular. Peristome narrow, rounded, reflected, with a single low tubercle on the parietal lip. A thin, narrow ridge or lamella occurs on the inner wall inside the last half of the body whorl.

This is the common species of the more southern sections of Florida. It is the most frequently encountered land snail in Miami and the Florida Keys, occurring everywhere, under rubbish, garden debris, or stones. The flat, many-whorled shape and the aperture with the single tooth make it easy to recognize. Often there is an astonishing difference in size in the mature individuals in a single small colony; this is unusual in land snails. A small population of the Ceres Polygyra under a rock can contain individuals with such differences in size as are indicated in the dimensions given above. The significance of this is not understood. The smaller shells have been called *P. carpenteriana* Bland, but this name is best disregarded. According to Pilsbry, this species is restricted to calcareous soil, whereas the following one (*P. septemvolva*) prefers more acid conditions. The subspecific name *P. cereolus floridana* Hemphill was given to some colonies of shells with raised, slightly domed spires. Such specimens are found in isolated areas in Lee and Monroe Counties.

The **Seven-whorled Polygyra,** *Polygyra septemvolva* Say (Lat. *septem volva,* seven whorl) (pl. XXXIII, 2), reaches 7 to 15 mm. (about 1/4 to 3/5 in.) in diameter, 3 to 4 mm. (1/8 to 1/6 in.) in height. It is very similar in appearance to the Ceres Polygyra, and differs morphologically only in lacking the internal ridge or lamella on the last whorl. The side of the body whorl must be broken open near the aperture to see if the lamella is present—for *cereolus*—or absent—for *septemvolva*. The two species can also be distinguished by their ranges, that of *septemvolva* being more to the north from Georgia, and from Duval to Dade counties in Florida, and that of *cereolus* to the south and in the Keys. There is an overlap of the two species in Dade County. Recently some doubt has been thrown upon the significance of the internal lamella, but for the present it seems to be the best and easiest method of distinguishing the two species, with some reservations.

The name given by Thomas Say is not well chosen, since mature specimens with five to almost ten whorls are found under the same rock. The poorly defined subspecies *P. septemvolva volvoxis* Pfeiffer (Lat. *volvoxis*, rolled) occurs in Georgia, South Carolina, and some areas of northern Florida. It is said to be smaller than "typical" *septemvolva*, and to have fewer whorls.

The **Auricular Polygyra,** *Polygyra auriculata* Say (Lat. *auricula*, small ear) (pl. XXX, 6), reaches 17 mm. (about 3/4 in.) in diameter and 8 mm. (1/3 in.) in height. This species is easily distinguished from *P. septemvolva*, with which it is frequently found together, by its higher shape, wider and fewer whorls, and above all by the highly restricted aperture, the obstructions startlingly resembling the convolutions of a tiny human ear. It is more difficult to distinguish from the following species, *P. uvulifera*, as we explain below. For the moment it helps to know that *auriculata* has a more northern range, from northern Florida to Tampa on the west coast, whereas *uvulifera* ranges to the south, below Tampa.

The **Uvular Polygyra,** *Polygyra uvulifera* Shuttleworth (Lat. *uvula fero*, small grape or uvula bearing) (pl. XXX, 7), also reaches 18 mm. (3/4 in.) in diameter and 8 mm. (1/3 in.) in height. It can be distinguished from *auricula* only by careful examination. The difference lies in the nature of the basal lip: in *P. uvulifera* the area is strongly depressed to the surface of the last whorl, whereas in *auricula* the basal lip near the umbilicus is raised and thickened. The typical form is quite smooth, but it is restricted to the area around Tampa (Clearwater Island, Longboat Key, Pass-a-Grille, Gasparilla Island, etc.). In most of their range, the shells have the surface marked by strong axial or vertical striations. This widely spread striated form is called *P. uvulifera striata* Pilsbry. A colony of shells around Pompano in Broward County has been named *P. uvulifera margueritae* Pilsbry. They have a higher body whorl, 10 mm. (2/5 in.), the spire is raised, and the surface sculpture is stronger. Another form from Seminole, Orlando, and Orange counties is called *P. uvulifera bicornuta* Pilsbry (pl. XXX, 8), because the parietal margin of the lip extends into two low structures like horns. The name *uvulifera* is based upon the uvula-like structure of the highly convoluted lip.

**Postell's Polygyra,** *Polygyra postelliana* Bland (James Postell was a collector) (pl. XXXIII, 3), is only 10 mm. (2/5 in.) in diameter and 5 mm. (1/5 in.) in height. This shell superficially resembles the previous two species, but it differs in being smaller and in the nature of the basal apertural tooth. In the former two species, the basal tooth terminates in a straight wall at the umbilical side of the aperture, but in *P. postelliana* at this point, it turns inward at a right angle and then recurves further. This feature is visible in the aperture, but it can best be seen by removing part of the outer wall near the aperture. Postell's Polygyra occurs in isolated spots in northern Florida and in the coastal regions of the Carolinas and Georgia, and thus is found more to the north than the other two species with a convoluted aperture. The shell is usually sculptured with variously strong axial ribs.

The **Greedy Polygyra,** *Polygyra avara* Say (Lat. *avarus,* greedy) (pl. XXXIII, 4), is small, reaching only 7 mm. (about 1/4 in.) in diameter, 4 mm. (1/6 in.) in height. It is dark cinnamon in color, and the relatively smooth surface is covered in life with short, closely spaced hairs. The ear-shaped aperture is pale brown, the lip is thin, and there are two teeth on the outer lip and a rather strong fold on the parietal edge. In life the shell may be more or less covered with dirt held in place by the hairs. The hairs drop off quickly in dead shells, but they leave fine pits on the surface where they were affixed. The range of this species is limited to the northeastern and central portions of Florida, but it is said to occur also in Polk County and the Miami area. Thomas Say may have called this shell *avara* because, like a miser, it is hidden from the collector by its tiny shell and its hairy, dirt-covered surface.

The **Blister Polygyra,** *Polygyra pustula* Férussac (Lat. *pustula,* small blister) (pl. XXXIII, 5), is very small, not exceeding 4 mm. (1/6 in.) in diameter and 2 to 3 mm. (1/12 to 1/8 in.) in height. It is easily distinguished from *avara* by its smaller size, about one-half that of *avara.* Moreover, the surface hairs are sparser, and the umbilicus is half hidden by the columellar margin of the outer lip. Around the umbilicus there is a spiral groove that is absent in *avara.* It ranges from South Carolina to Miami, Florida, but being so small and living in isolated colonies, it is not easily detected, and is especially rare around Miami. The name *pustula* must refer to its small size and rounded shape.

The **Blisterlike Polygyra,** *Polygyra pustuloides* Bland (pl. XXXII, 14), is somewhat larger, reaching 5.5 mm. (about 1/4 in.) in diameter; and the umbilicus is larger and completely uncovered and the deep basal groove of *P. pustula* is lacking. It is lighter in color, and differs from *avara* by being smaller, and having much sparser surface hairs and a larger and rounder umbilicus. It ranges from South Carolina to Georgia, but in Florida it is found only in Tallahassee County, in the "panhandle."

# KEY TO GENUS STENOTREMA

| | |
|---|---|
| * Shell with carinate periphery | |
| ** Periostracum with long hairlike processes, basal tooth not raised centrally | Stenotrema barbigerum |
| ** Periostracum without long hairlike processes, basal tooth sharply raised centrally | S. spinosum |
| * Shell with rounded periphery | |
| ** Shell with open or partly covered umbilicus | S. leai |
| ** Shell without umbilicus, or with umbilicus slitlike | |
| *** Base of shell excavated in umbilical region | S. fraternum |
| *** Base rounded | |
| **** Shell small, about 6 mm. (1/4 in.); northern range | S. hirsutum |
| **** Shell larger, about 10 mm. (2/5 in.) | |
| ***** Southern range except Florida | S. stenotrema |
| ***** Range limited to Florida | S. florida |

Genus *Stenotrema* Rafinesque

*Stenotrema stenotrema* Pfeiffer
Southern Pill Snail

Pl. XXXIII, 6

ETYMOLOGY: Gr. *steno trema,* narrow aperture.

SIZE: 8 to 13 mm. (1/3 to 1/2 in.) in diameter, 5 to 9 mm. (about 1/5 to 2/5 in.) in height.

DISTRIBUTION: Virginia to Georgia and west to Oklahoma and Arkansas.

CHARACTERISTICS: Shell with rounded periphery. Periostracum usually with short papillalike hairs. Basal tooth gently curved, widest toward the center but not rising to the level of the basal lip. Labial notch well marked and located toward the center.

The shells of *Stenotrema* are generally rounded, and hence have been given the common name of "pill shells." They are easily recognized by their rounded shape, frequently hirsute surface, and especially by the long white or faint pinkish tooth that strongly restricts the aperture. Moreover, the aperture is located on the base of the shell rather than on the side, as in most ground snails; that is, the aperture is basal rather than lateral. The genus is restricted to North America, and has a wide range in the eastern half of the United States.

This species is widely spread throughout the western parts of the southern coastal states, but is not found in Florida. It is the commonest *Stenotrema* species in its range, occurring especially in the hilly and mountainous western sections. It resembles the Hairy Pill Snail (*S. hirsutum*) (see below), but the aperture is decidedly narrower, the parietal tooth higher, and the basal lip wider. In addition it has a generally more southern range.

The name *S. florida* Pilsbry (pl. XXX, 9) is given to a larger species restricted to the western Panhandle of Florida. It is olive tan in color, the basal tooth is not so high, and its outer end hooks rather abruptly inward. The basal notch is extremely small or missing. It is the only member of its genus known to occur in Florida, where it is endemic.

The **Hairy Pill Snail,** *Stenotrema hirsutum* Say (Lat. *hirsutus,* shaggy or hairy) (pl. XXXII, 15), reaches 9 mm. (about 2/5 in.) in diameter and 6 mm. (1/4 in.) in height, but smaller specimens are more common, 6 × 4 mm. (1/4 × 1/6 in.), especially in the northern part of its range. The round, pill-like shape and the rather strong, hairy periostracum make it easily recognizable. It is the commonest *Stenotrema* in the woodlands of the Northeast, but it is rarer in the more southern part, where its range slightly overlaps that of *S. stenotrema*. It ranges from Canada and Maine to Georgia and westward to Kansas.

**Lea's Pill Snail,** *Stenotrema leai* Binney (Isaac Lea was a prominent nineteenth-century American malacologist) (pl. XXXIII, 7), reaches about 9 mm. (about 2/5 in.) in diameter and 5.5 mm. (about 1/4 in.) in height. The shell is more depressed, there are no surface hairs, the notch is barely perceptible, the base is excavated, and there is a large umbilicus, sometimes partly covered by the columellar edge of the basal lip. It lives in damp places near water, and ranges from Canada and Maine to Virginia and westward to South Dakota and Texas.

The **Fraternal Pill Snail,** *Stenotrema fraternum* Say (Lat. *frater,* brother) (pl. XXX, 10), reaches 10 mm. (2/5 in.) in diameter, 7 mm. (about 1/4 in.) in height. It resembles *S. leai*, but differs in that the umbilicus is reduced to a slit, and the whorls are wider. *S. fraternum* ranges from New Hampshire to Georgia and westward to Minnesota and Oklahoma, but occupies drier habitats than *S. leai*.

The **Spiny Pill Snail,** *Stenotrema spinosum* Lea (Lat. *spinosus,* spiny) (pl. XXX, 11), reaches 15 mm. (3/5 in.) in diameter, 6.5 mm. (about 1/4 in.) in height. It is lens shaped, and has a low spire and an acutely keeled periphery. This last feature is sufficient to separate it from the other pill snails discussed so far. In addition, the basal tooth is very high in the center. It ranges from Virginia to Georgia and westward to Alabama and Tennessee, and is most commonly found in hilly country under rocks and forest debris. Its Latin name demonstrates that there need be no good reason for its selection, unless one cares to regard the acute keel as a spiny structure.

The **Bearded Pill Snail,** *Stenotrema barbigerum* Redfield (Lat. *barbiger,* having a beard) (pl. XXXIII, 8), reaches 10 mm. (2/5 in.) in diameter, 5 mm. (1/5 in.) in height. It has the sharp peripheral keel of *S. spinosum,* but differs in possessing a strong periostracum, with radial ridges that extend into long hairs at the suture and the periphery. It differs also in having the basal tooth not much raised in the center. The labial notch is shallow. Like *S. spinosum, S. barbigerum* is found in the mountainous areas, but it ranges only from the Carolinas to Georgia and westward to Alabama and Tennessee.

Genus *Praticolella* Martens

*Praticolella griseola* Pfeiffer
Grizzled Meadow Snail

Pl. XXXIII, 9

ETYMOLOGY: Probably Lat. *pratum,* meadow; med. Lat. *griseus,* white mottled with black or brown.

SIZE: 11 to 13 mm. (about 1/2 in.) in diameter, 8 to 9 mm. (about 1/3 to 2/5 in.) in height.

DISTRIBUTION: Florida and Texas.

CHARACTERISTICS: Shell small, depressed globose, glossy, opaque, rather strong. Gray, encircled with brown bands of varying width. Umbilicus hidden, lip narrowly reflected, thickened within.

This small shell is common especially in southern Florida, probably introduced from the Rio Grande valley. It has been introduced into Cuba, and can be expected to increase its range steadily, like many other tropical tramps.

The **Insignificant Meadow Snail,** *Praticolella jejuna* Say (Lat. *jejunus,* insignificant) (pl. XXXIII, 10), is smaller, 6 to 8 mm. (1/4 to 1/3 in.) in diameter and 4 to 5 mm. (1/6 to 1/5 in.) in height, cinnamon buff in color, and without spiral bands. It is readily identified by the lip, thickened within but reflected only at the base, and by the presence of a cinnamon or white streak behind the lip. The umbilicus is minute. The species is widely distributed in Florida.

## KEY TO THE SPECIES OF GENERA MESODON, TRIODOPSIS, ALLOGONA

* Lip tooth small or wanting
** Parietal tooth usually absent
*** Umbilicus covered
**** Shell globose, height/diameter ratio average about 77 percent
***** Thinner, lighter colored; denizen of mountain areas  *Mesodon normalis*
***** Thicker, darker colored; denizen of coastal plain  *Triodopsis albolabris major*
**** Shell moderately depressed, height/ diameter ratio average 67 percent  *T. albolabris*
*** Umbilicus open
**** Lip tooth absent, shell large, up to 40 mm. (1 3/5 in.); confined to region of the Great Smokies  *Mesodon chilhoweensis*
**** Lip tooth present, shell smaller, 25 to 30 mm. (1 to 1 1/5 in.), distribution wide
***** Shell unbanded, lip tooth narrow, acute  *M. sayanus*
***** Shell usually banded, lip tooth wide, rounded  *Allogona profunda*
** Parietal tooth usually present
*** Shell relatively high, height/ diameter ratio about 70 to 80 percent
**** Shell with umbilicus open, partly hidden  *Mesodon thyroidus*
**** Shell with umbilicus covered
***** Parietal tooth weak, baso-columnar portion of lip thickened  *M. zaletus*
***** Parietal tooth strong, basal lip not thickened  *M. elevatus*

**\* \* \*** Shell relatively depressed, height/
diameter ratio about 45 to 50
percent

**\* \* \* \*** Axial ridges smooth           *M. appressus*

**\* \* \* \*** Axial ridges cut by minute spiral
lines

**\* \* \* \* \*** Axial ridges without additional
wrinkles           *M. perigraptus*

**\* \* \* \* \*** Axial ridges with additional
microscopic wrinkles       *Triodopsis dentifera*

**\*** Two lip teeth usually present

**\* \*** Basal lip tooth converted into a
bladelike lamella and set off by a
notch where it joins outer arc of
lip

**\* \* \*** Surface with short, stiff hairs      *T. denotata*

**\* \* \*** Surface without hairs

**\* \* \* \*** Periphery with sharp keel      *T. obstricta*

**\* \* \* \*** Periphery rounded          *T. fosteri*

**\* \*** Basal lip without bladelike lamella

**\* \* \*** Outer lip tooth not recessed

**\* \* \* \*** Outer end of parietal tooth directed
to a point below lip tooth

**\* \* \* \* \*** Umbilicus open, periostracum
smooth; in northeastern states    *T. tridentata*

**\* \* \* \* \*** Umbilicus closed, periostracum
with fuzz; North Carolina to
Florida           *Mesodon inflectus*

**\* \* \* \*** Outer end of parietal tooth directed
to a point at or above outer lip
tooth

**\* \* \* \* \*** Lip with callus ridge from basal
tooth toward umbilicus       *Triodopsis hopetonensis*

**\* \* \* \* \*** No callus ridge on basal lip     *T. juxtidens*

**\* \* \*** Outer lip tooth receding or bent
inward

**\* \* \* \*** Umbilicus completely covered    *Mesodon rugeli*

**\* \* \* \*** Umbilicus open

**\* \* \* \* \*** Umbilicus wide, showing first
whorl           *Triodopsis fraudulenta*

**\* \* \* \* \*** Umbilicus narrow

**\* \* \* \* \* \*** Whorls 6 to 6 1/2; range South
Carolina and Alabama       *T. vannostrandi*

\* \* \* \* \* \* Whorls 5 to 5 1/2, more loosely
coiled; range Pennsylvania to
Georgia       *T. fallax*

---

# GENERA MESODON, TRIODOPSIS, AND ALLOGONA

Genera *Mesodon* Rafinesque, *Triodopsis* Rafinesque, *Allogona* Pilsbry

ETYMOLOGY: Gr. *meso odon*, middle tooth; Gr. *tri odous ops*, three tooth near; Gr. *allos goné*, different genitalia.

SIZE: 14 mm. (about 3/5 in.) to more than 40 mm. (1 3/5 in.) in diameter.

DISTRIBUTION: Generally the eastern portion of North America.

CHARACTERISTICS: Shell varied, medium to quite large. With or without an umbilicus. Globose with a cone-shaped spire to quite depressed. Aperture with white, expanded lip with one or two lip teeth, commonly wanting, parietal tooth or ridge present or absent. Color some shade of brownish horn or yellow buff, frequently with a faint olive tinge.

The three genera are confined to within the borders of the United States and Canada; mostly they occupy the eastern half of the continent. They are common in woodlands, living under forest debris, fallen tree trunks, or on sheltered portions of rocky cliffs. Some species are also found in lots or in parks within the boundaries of large cities. Size differences of specimens are due largely to availability locally of suitable habitats, and do not reflect differences between species. Those living in most favorable habitats tend to attain maximum size. Nevertheless, in some cases, names have been given to ecological morphs (forms).

It is important to bear in mind that usually all forms are umbilicate in the immature state; hence it is only when specimens are mature that the presence or absence of a covered umbilicus can be determined and this character used to identify specimens.

We treat all three genera together since the generic distinction rests largely on the nature of the sexual apparatus. Briefly, the penis of *Triodopsis* is provided with a penis sheath, a feature absent in *Mesodon*. In the case of *Allogona* the penis has a stimulator (*Reizkörper* in German), which is absent in all other members of the family Polygyridae. The shells of all three, however, are so similar that it is impossible to distinguish the genera on shell features alone. The identification key will show how we intermingle the shells of the three genera involved.

All the species we discuss in this section share with most other North American native land shells a dull, unexciting horn color and a relatively simple shape; a notable exception is the banded *Allogona*. Both features serve to camouflage the organisms on the dun-colored forest floor on which they live. The desire to collect these specimens has to be acquired and carefully nurtured, but even brief experience will quickly turn an indifferent attitude into one of consuming interest.

*Triodopsis albolabris* Say
 White-lipped Forest Snail

Pl. XXXI, 1

ETYMOLOGY: Lat. *albus labrum*, white lip.

SIZE: 20 to 35 mm. (4/5 to 1 2/5 in.) in diameter, 11 to 23 mm. (about 1/2 to 1 in.) in height.

DISTRIBUTION: From Canada and Maine southward to the Georgia coast and westward to the states bordering on the Mississippi River.

CHARACTERISTICS: Shell depressed, globose, lusterless. Axial ridges microscopically wrinkled; occasionally with a single parietal tooth. Umbilical edge of the white, expanded lip extended to cover the umbilicus completely.

This is a very common species, which shares much of its range with *Mesodon thyroidus* (see page 269). The two species resemble each other superficially, but can be readily distinguished by the closed umbilicus in *Triodopsis albolabris* and the open umbilicus in *M. thyroidus*. In addition, *M. thyroidus* usually has a parietal tooth, while *T. albolabris* usually does not.

The name *T. albolabris major* or *T. major* Binney has been given to very large shells, up to 43 mm. (1 3/4 in.) in diameter, which are larger, higher, and more globose in outline than typical *T. albolabris*. Colonies of *T. a. major* occur in the coastal areas of North Carolina, South Carolina, Georgia, and northern Florida. Sometimes specimens of *major* are difficult to separate from large typical *T. albolabris* or from *Mesodon normalis* (see below).

The **Giant Forest Snail,** *Mesodon normalis* Pilsbry (Lat. *norma,* the rule, a pattern) (pl. XXXI, 2), is decidedly larger, reaching 37 mm. (1 1/2 in.) in width, 28 mm. (1 1/8 in.) in height. The umbilicus is closed, the color is olive to light tan, and there is usually a yellow spot in back of the lip. Its range is in the mountains of North Carolina, South Carolina, and Georgia and westward to Alabama and Tennessee. This species resembles *T. albolabris,* especially subspecies *major,* rather closely, but when specimens of each are examined simultaneously the distinction becomes clear. *M. normalis* is much more globose and somewhat differently colored. Moreover, it is confined to the interior mountains whereas *T. albolabris* is found in the low areas of the mountains and *T. a. major* is found on the coastal plain. Until recently this species was considered to be a subspecies of *Mesodon andrewsae,* and was known as *M. andrewsae normalis.*

The **Chilhowee Forest Snail,** *Mesodon chilhoweensis* Lewis (named for Chilhowee Mountain in Tennessee) (pl. XXXI, 8), reaches 40 mm. (1 3/5 in.) in diameter and 24 mm. (about 1 in.) in height. It is a magnificent snail, usually referred to as the "queen of the Mesodons." The color is like that of the other ground snails, and it is most readily recognized by its large size and large, deep umbilicus. It is confined to Tennessee and to the mountains in the extreme western corner of North Carolina. This actually places it somewhat out of the territory covered by this book, but it is hard to omit what is perhaps the most spectacular ground snail in the eastern United States. Specimens are not uncommon under leaves and forest debris in mountain forests, and can also be taken under cliff and rock overhangs.

**Say's Forest Snail,** *Mesodon sayanus* Pilsbry (named for Thomas Say, the father of American conchology) (pl. XXXI, 4), looks like a smaller edition of *M. chilhoweensis.* It reaches 25 mm. (1 in.) in diameter, 15 mm. (3/5 in.) in height, and is glossy and pale yellow in color; the umbilicus is open. The lip is quite narrow, and there is always a small, acute tooth on the basal margin near the columella, and usually another on the parietal wall. This snail is found from Canada to North Carolina and westward to Michigan, living among leaves on woodland hillsides as well as in stone fences and under logs in pastures.

The **Common White-lipped Forest Snail,** *Mesodon thyroidus* Say (Gr. *thyrea,* shield) (pl. XXXI, 3), varies in size from 17 to 28 mm. (about 3/4 to 1 1/8 in.) in diameter and 11 to 18 mm. (about 1/2 to 3/4 in.) in height. It resembles the true White-lipped Forest Snail, *Triodopsis albolabris,* but differs in having the lower lip concealing but not filling the umbilicus. In addition there is almost always a small parietal tooth present. This is probably the most widely distributed and commonest larger-shelled pulmonate in the eastern United States. It ranges from Canada and Maine to the Florida Panhandle and westward to Oklahoma and Texas. The name *M. bucculenta* Gould was given to small shells with a very narrow or covered umbilicus, but it is of doubtful taxonomic value.

The **Profound Forest Snail,** *Allogona profunda* Say (Lat. *profundus,* deep, profound) (pls. II, 4; XXX, 12), reaches 34 mm. (1 2/5 in.) in diameter, 18 mm. (3/4 in.) in height. This species, with its depressed shell, is easily identified by a cinnamon-colored band, a large, deep (profound) umbilicus, and the fact that the ends of the lip are turned toward one another. (In most congeners the lower end is flattened out at the columella.) The color band is sometimes absent, and occasional specimens have additional bands on the base. The species ranges from New York to North Carolina and westward to Nebraska. The "different genitalia" in the generic name *allo goné* refers to the fact that the male organ has a stimulator on it, something lacking in related genera.

The **Ripe Forest Snail,** *Mesodon zaletus* Binney (probably in error for Lat. *exoletus,* full grown, overmature) (pl. XXXI, 5), is 31 mm. (about 1 1/5 in.) in diameter, up to 25 mm. (1 in.) in height. It closely resembles *Triodopsis albolabris,* but differs in being somewhat higher and less wide, the last whorl being narrower when viewed from above, the aperture less broad and not so oblique. However, an easier distinction can be seen immediately in the microscopic sculpture. In *T. albolabris* the axial lines are wrinkled and the shell is quite dull, whereas in *M. zaletus* the lines are not wrinkled and the shell has a glossier appearance. Moreover the parietal tooth is usually present in *M. zaletus* and usually absent in *T. albolabris,* and the basal lip near the umbilicus is thickened. The species ranges from Canada to North Carolina and westward to Wisconsin and Oklahoma. It is not found on the coast, but inhabits the hills and uplands. The shell was first taken to be a gerontic or overaged form of *T. albolabris.* When it was judged to be a different species, the name *exoletus* was given to it, but the name *zaletus* has priority.

The **Raised Forest Snail,** *Mesodon elevatus* Say (Lat. *elevatus,* raised) (pl. XXXI, 6), reaches 28 mm. (1 1/8 in.) in diameter, 20 mm. (4/5 in.) in height. It is very distinct because of its relatively high spire, solid texture, compact whorls, and large, strong parietal tooth or ridge. It differs from *M. zaletus,* with which it shares its upland habitat, in being higher, having a stronger parietal tooth, and in the lack of thickness in the basal edge of the lip near the umbilicus. Occasionally colonies with a medial color band are found. These have been called *M. elevatus tennesseensis* Lea, but the name is unnecessary. It is found from New York to South Carolina and westward to Arkansas.

The **Compressed Forest Snail,** *Mesodon appressus* Say (Lat. *appressus,* pressed, contracted) (pl. XXXII, 16), has a very depressed shell, 19 mm. (about 4/5 in.) in diameter, 9 mm. (about 2/5 in.) in height. The shell is brownish horn in color, and has a closed umbilicus. It is similar to the shell of the next species below, the Engraved Forest Snail, *M. perigraptus,* but differs in the nature of the microscopic surface sculpture. In *appressus* the axial ridges are smooth or slightly papillose, in *perigraptus* they are crossed by narrow, incised, more or less regularly spaced spiral lines. Slight magnification is sufficient to show this. Moreover, *appressus* is smaller, darker in color, and has a longer parietal tooth with a rounded outline. The species ranges from Virginia and North Carolina westward to Indiana. It is more common in its midwestern locale, and is a common species in city lots in Cincinnati.

The **Engraved Forest Snail,** *Mesodon perigraptus* Pilsbry (Gr. *peri graptus,* around engraved) (pl. XXXI, 7), measuring 23 mm. (about 1 in.) in diameter and 12 mm. (about 1/2 in.) in height, resembles *M. appressus,* but it is larger and higher, has a more rounded periphery, a lighter color, a smaller parietal tooth truncate at the tip, and a surface sculpture marked by spiral incised lines as well as rounded axial ribs. It is confined to the uplands from North Carolina to western Florida, and reaches westward to Arkansas. For many years it was held to be a form of *M. appressus,* until Pilsbry, in 1893, detected the spiral lines.

The **Tooth-bearing Forest Snail,** *Triodopsis dentifera* Binney (Lat. *dens fero,* tooth bearing) (pl. XXXI, 9), is a depressed shell, 28 mm. (1 1/8 in.) in diameter, 16 mm. (about 3/5 in.) in height. It somewhat resembles *T. albolabris,* with which it shares much of its range from Canada and Maine to North Carolina, but it can be readily distinguished by the smaller, thinner, and more depressed shell and by the presence of a parietal tooth. It is a far less common species. The axial ridges are cut by spiral lines and wrinkles. It has a dull surface, as compared to the glossy surface of *M. perigraptus.* The species lives in broken or mountainous country.

The **Three-toothed Forest Snail,** *Triodopsis tridentata* Say (Lat. *tri dentatus,* three toothed) (pl. XXXI, 10), reaches 20 mm. (4/5 in.) in diameter, 11 mm. (about 1/2 in.) in height. The shell is umbilicate, the umbilicus being one-seventh of the base, pale to dark buff, slightly glossy, and the periphery is rounded. There are three teeth in the lip, the outer and basal lip teeth not recessed or entering, and the parietal tooth directed toward a point below the outer lip tooth. This shell and the other species to follow are all depressed, and have one or more lip teeth. It is important to examine these teeth carefully in order to distinguish the different species. In the next four species the outer lip tooth is on the same plane as the lip, that is, it is not recessed and does not enter the aperture. The four succeeding species have this tooth either recessed or entering the aperture, or both. The Three-toothed Forest Snail ranges from Canada and Maine to Georgia and westward to Mississippi and Iowa, and is the commonest of these toothed, depressed ground snails; indeed, it can be collected in large numbers. The forms in the south are larger. Several subspecies have been described, but none of these are found in the coastal states. A form called *T. tridentata edentilabris* Pilsbry, which lacks labial teeth, is now recognized as being abnormal or immature.

The **Bent Forest Snail,** *Mesodon inflectus* Say (Lat. *inflectus,* bent) (pl. XXXIII, 11), is 14 mm. (about 3/5 in.) in diameter, 8 mm. (1/3 in.) in height, and it resembles *T. tridentata.* It differs in having the umbilicus closed and a periostracum with low, fuzzlike processes. The two lip teeth and the curved parietal tooth resemble those of *T. tridentata.* It ranges from North Carolina to western Florida and westward to Louisiana and Oklahoma, and it is absent from the northeastern states, where *T. tridentata* is so common. The shell is also quite similar to *M. rugeli* (see below), but lacks a recessed outer tooth.

The **Hopeton Forest Snail,** *Triodopsis hopetonensis* Shuttleworth (Hopeton was the name of an old plantation on the Altamaha River whose proprietor was interested in shells) (pl. XXX, 13), is 13 mm. (about 1/2 in.) in diameter, 6 mm. (1/4 in.) in height. The shell looks like a smaller *T. tridentata,* but the umbilicus is smaller (only one-sixth of the base), and the parietal tooth is directed to a point above the outer lip tooth. In *T. tridentata* the parietal tooth is directed to a point below the outer lip tooth. In addition, there is a callus ridge reaching from the basal tooth toward the umbilicus. This is a coastal plain species from Virginia to Florida and Alabama, often living near bodies of salt or brackish water. It is a common urban snail in many coastal cities.

A race of *T. hopetonensis* with a very narrow umbilicus (one-ninth of the base) and somewhat reduced lip teeth has been called subspecies *T. h. chincoteagensis* Pilsbry. It is found on Chincoteague Island, Virginia. Another race, from New Bern and Wilmington, North

Carolina, has a normal umbilicus, but the teeth are extremely reduced. It is called *T. h. obsoleta* Pilsbry.

A recent study by J. Vagvolgyi (1968) concluded that *T. hopetonensis*, as well as *T. vannostrandi* (see below), are mere hybrid forms of *T. fallax* (see below), and do not deserve taxonomic recognition. However, not all students accept these findings.

**Van Nostrand's Forest Snail,** *Triodopsis vannostrandi* Bland (named for Henry D. Van Nostrand) (pl. XXXIII, 12), is 14 mm. (about 3/5 in.) in diameter, 9 mm. (about 2/5 in.) in height. This species closely resembles *T. hopetonensis,* but differs in having a higher spire, a higher periphery, and in being more coarsely sculptured, as well as having the outer lip tooth bent inward. It lacks the internal callus tubercle of *T. fallax* (see below). The subspecies *T. v. goniosoma* Pilsbry (Gr. *gonios soma,* angular body), from northern Florida, has a weak but distinct keel at the periphery.

The **Tricky Forest Snail,** *Triodopsis fallax* Say (Lat. *fallax,* deceitful, tricky) (pl. XXX, 14), is 13 mm. (about 1/2 in.) in diameter, 8 mm. (1/3 in.) in height. This species can be most certainly determined by the presence of a unique internal ridge or tubercle on the columellar axis; the side of the shell just behind the aperture has to be broken open to see this. Otherwise, *fallax* is lower than *T. vannostrandi* and smaller than *T. fraudulenta* (see below), from which it further differs by its smaller umbilicus and dished aperture.

Vagvolgyi's study gave *T. fallax* a much wider application than it has had hitherto, since he included both *T. fraudulenta* and *T. vannostrandi,* but not *T. fraudulenta vulgata* (see below), in this species complex. More investigations will be needed to settle this question.

The **Juxtaposed Forest Snail,** *Triodopsis juxtidens* Pilsbry (Lat. *juxta dens,* near tooth) (pl. XXXI, 11), is 19 mm. (about 4/5 in.) in diameter and 10 mm. (2/5 in.) in height. This shell resembles *T. tridentata,* but it differs by having the two lip teeth set quite closely together and the parietal tooth directed to a point above the outer lip tooth. It is larger than *T. hopetonensis,* and differs by the absence of the basal lip ridge. This is a common snail ranging from Vermont to Georgia, and is particularly abundant in the hilly parts of New Jersey and along the Delaware River southward.

**Rugel's Forest Snail,** *Mesodon rugeli* Shuttleworth (named for Ferdinand Rugel, 1806–1879, a collector of plants and shells) (pl. XXXII, 17), is 18 mm. (3/4 in.) in diameter, 9 mm. (about 2/5 in.) in height. This shell resembles *M. inflectus,* but the outer lip tooth, which is not recessed in *M. inflectus,* is strongly recessed and bent inward in *M. rugeli.* There is also a fuzzy, bristly, often dirt-covered periostracum that is not seen in other, similar shells. This bristly periostracum peels off in weathered specimens, but the dirt in living specimens cannot easily be removed without damaging the bristles. The umbilicus is covered. The species ranges from Virginia to Georgia and westward to Kentucky and Alabama in the hilly interior. It, like *M. inflectus,* does not occur in the plains.

The **Fraudulent Forest Snail,** *Triodopsis fraudulenta vulgata* Pilsbry (Lat. *fraudulenta vulgata,* common cheat, since "it posed for many years as *T. fallax,*" Pilsbry) (pl. XXXI, 12), is 19 mm. (about 4/5 in.) in diameter, 10 mm. (2/5 in.) in height. The shell is buff to sea-foam yellow, and the umbilicus is very large, showing the first whorl inside. It resembles *T. tridentata* and *T. juxtidens,* but differs from both in that the outer lip tooth is much wider than the basal tooth. From *T. tridentata* it further differs in that the outer tooth is bent inward; from *T. juxtidens,* in that the aperture is strongly dished.

The subspecies *T. fraudulenta fraudulenta* has a much more constricted aperture, since the parietal tooth is higher than in *T. f. vulgata.* The former is restricted to an area in the high mountain regions of Virginia and West Virginia, whereas *T. f. vulgata* is a common inhabitant of the foothills. On the basis of computerized statistics, Vagvolgyi believes that the populations of *T. f. vulgata* were closer to *neglecta* Pilsbry from the Ozarks than to *fraudulenta.*

**Foster's Forest Snail,** *Triodopsis fosteri* F. C. Baker (T. Dale Foster, 1897–1936, was a Midwestern malacologist) (pl. XXXIII, 13), is 22 mm. (about 4/5 in.) in diameter, 11 mm. (about 1/2 in.) in height, with coarse but not papillose sculpture and a filled umbilicus. It resembles *Mesodon appressus* (see page 271), with which it was confused for a long time, but differs in the presence of a bladelike lamella on its basal lip and in lacking the microscopic surface papillae that can be seen in *M. appressus.* Moreover, the parietal tooth in *T. fosteri* is stronger, and the rounded periphery is widest at the center of the body whorl, not above it as in *M. appressus.*

This shell is a native of the west from Alabama to Iowa, but in 1865 it was introduced into Burlington, New Jersey, and more recently into a garden in New York City, where it has adapted with amazing success. Fortunately it eats only minute fungi in rotting leaves, and hence in no way constitutes a menace or even a nuisance.

The **Marked Forest Snail,** *Triodopsis denotata* Férussac (Lat. *notatus,* well marked) (pl. XXXIII, 14), is 26 mm. (about 1 in.) in diameter, 13 mm. (about 1/2 in.) in height. The umbilicus is filled, there is a rounded keel above the periphery, and the surface has a periostracum with closely set papillae bearing small, triangular scales and short, stiff, closely set hairs. These characteristics are sufficient to set off the species from any other in the range. In addition, this species as well as the following one, *T. obstricta*, and the preceding one, *T. fosteri*, also have a long, bladelike lamella along the basal lip instead of the more usual lip tubercle or tooth. The Marked Forest Snail ranges from Canada and Vermont to Georgia and westward to Illinois and Arkansas, in low, hilly country.

The **Constricted Forest Snail,** *Triodopsis obstricta* Say (Lat. *obstrictus*, tied, bound) (pl. XXXIII, 15), is about the same size, 27 mm. × 14 mm. (1 1/8 × 3/5 in.), but the periostracum is not hirsute, and the periphery is armed with a strong, sharp keel. The keel, however, varies in strength in different populations, and a complete series of intergrades from strongly keeled forms to rounded, keelless forms can be assembled. Intergrades have been called *T. carolinensis* Lea. *T. obstricta* ranges from South Carolina and Georgia westward to Louisiana and Arkansas, and thus has a more southerly distribution than *T. denotata*. However, there is a large area of overlap in the center.

SUPERFAMILY:

# OLEACINACEA

---

FAMILY:

# OLEACINIDAE

(*cannibal snails*)

This is a large family of predaceous snails with shells that are mostly elongate but that differ considerably in size and ornamentation. The members of the genus *Euglandina* generally have relatively large, elongate-ovate to spindle-shaped (fusiform) shells. They are found on the American mainland from Brazil to Texas, Florida, and South Carolina. Other genera of the family flourish in the West Indies and in the Mediterranean region.

Genus *Euglandina* Fischer & Crosse

*Euglandina rosea* Férussac
　　Elongate Cannibal Snail

　　Pl. II, 12

ETYMOLOGY: Gr. *eu*, real, and Lat. diminutive of *glans*, gland; Lat. *rosa*, rose.

SIZE: 50 to 75 mm. (2 to 3 in.) in length, 21 to 27 mm. (about 4/5 to 1 in.) in width.

DISTRIBUTION: North Carolina to Key West.

CHARACTERISTICS: Shell quite large, oblong with tapering apex, opaque, strong. Pink or buff pink above, ocher buff below. Surface glossy, sculptured with irregular longitudinal striae. Aperture pink, columella truncate below; lip simple.

This species varies greatly in size, shape, color, and sculpture, and several confusing subspecific names have been given to it. But it is well to remember that only a single, variable species is involved. This snail is a rapacious predator, feeding chiefly on other ground snails. Pilsbry describes its manner of attack: "Gliding rapidly toward [the food snail], when within striking distance the *Euglandina* lunged swiftly, seizing the snail by the back. The almost instantaneous withdrawal of the victim did not loosen the hold of the *Euglandina*, which quit the repast only after the greater part had been devoured." In addition to the normal two sets of tentacles, the Elongate Cannibal Snail also has two lateral, sickle-shaped lappets, which lend it a fierce appearance, like a long-mustachioed Cossack.

　　The **Graceful Cannibal Snail,** *Varicella gracillima floridana* Pilsbry (diminutive of Lat. *varix;* Lat. *gracillima*, most graceful) (not illus.) is much smaller and far more slender, measuring only 7.5 mm. (1/3 in.) in height, 1.6 mm. (1/16 in.) in width. It is readily distinguished from the subulinids by its more slender and graceful shape and especially by the handsome, widely set, axial ribs, of which about 25 appear on the last whorl. There are also closely set, microscopic parallel striae in the spaces between the ribs. Typical *gracillima* come from Cuba and differ by having fewer ribs and striae. The Graceful Cannibal Snail is the only local member of a widely spread West Indian genus which is particularly well represented in Jamaica. The Floridian population occurs from Miami to Key West, and these snails are found in leaf mold and under stones.

SUPERFAMILY:

# POLYGYRACEA

---

FAMILY:

# SAGDIDAE
(*wallet snails*)

This is a rather small family confined to the Neotropics, that is, the tropical and subtropical areas of the New World. The shells vary in size from minute to quite large, and from depressed to high dome shaped; the lip is thin and not reflected or expanded. The genus *Sagda* Beck (possibly from Gr. *sagido,* wallet), which includes the largest members of the family, is found only in Jamaica, where they form one of the most prominent elements of the land snail fauna.

Genus *Lacteoluna* Pilsbry

*Lacteoluna selenina* Gould
    Lunar Wallet Snail

    Pl. XXX, 15

ETYMOLOGY: Lat. *lac lactis*, milk, and *luna*, moon; Gr. *selene*, moon.

SIZE: 5 mm. (1/5 in.) in diameter, 3 mm. (1/8 in.) in height.

DISTRIBUTION: Southern Florida and the West Indies.

CHARACTERISTICS: Shell small, spire depressed, thin, fragile; silky but not polished. Milky bluish-white. Umbilicus small; lip thin.

This fragile shell is common on calcareous soils and under stones, leaves, and rubbish in the Florida Keys. It is native to the West Indies.

The **Plaited Wallet Snail,** *Thysanophora plagioptycha* Shuttleworth (Gr. *thysanos phero,* tail bearing; *pleko,* plaited, entwined) (pl. XXXIII, 16), is smaller than *Lacteoluna selenina,* about 3 mm. (1/8 in.) in diameter and conic in shape, being almost as wide as it is high. It is pale brown, semitransparent, somewhat glossy. In life the surface is covered by very oblique narrow ribs composed of periostracal material, not shell. It is a common species in southern Florida.

# HELICACEA

# HELICIDAE, HELICELLIDAE, CAMAENIDAE, AND HELMINTHOGLYPTIDAE

The shells in the families Helicidae and Helicellidae are small to rather large, those of the latter as the name suggests, usually being the smaller; in form they are generally depressed, but some are high spired. The Helicellidae are always umbilicate; the surface is weakly sculptured, and the colors are generally subdued.

These families are found in Europe, North Africa, Asia Minor, and the Atlantic islands. The local species were introduced through the agency of man, with one possible exception. The sexual anatomy of these hermaphrodites includes a dart sac on the vagina, which secretes tiny shelly love darts (*Liebespfeile* in German), used as stimulators prior to sexual intercourse. The name *Helix* was used by Linnaeus for a heterogeneous group of shells, including marine and freshwater as well as land snails. He placed in the genus *Helix* shells in which the aperture was constricted internally to a half-moon shape by the bottom of the penultimate whorl. Thus, the number of shells originally assigned by early naturalists to the genus *Helix* was tremendous.

The shells of the Helicacean families Camaenidae and Helminthoglyptidae (see below, pages 280–1) are so similar to the helicids that they have been included in this discussion. The familial differences are largely determined by the soft anatomy.

# HELICIDAE

Genus *Helix* Linnaeus

*Helix aspersa* Müller
Speckled Garden Snail
Pl. XXX, 16

ETYMOLOGY: Gr. *helix*, spiral; Lat. *aspersus*, speckled.

SIZE: 32 to 38 mm. (1 1/4 to 1 1/2 in.) in diameter, 29 mm. to 33 mm.
(1 1/6 to 1 1/8 in.) in height.

DISTRIBUTION: Charleston, South Carolina, and other southern cities.

CHARACTERISTICS: Shell obliquely globose, rather thin, spire moderately
raised. Surface wrinkled or otherwise roughened. Color yellow, with
interrupted spiral bands of chestnut brown. Umbilicus generally
lacking; lip white, reflected.

This species, originally from the Mediterranean area, was imported
into the United States, where it escaped, and in many areas is a
grievous garden pest. It can best be controlled by switching its role
and regarding it not as a nuisance to be exterminated, but as a table
delicacy to be nurtured. The rough, wrinkled surface and the variously
patterned yellow and dark brown markings make this species easy to
recognize. It is also found in southern and western Europe and in
many warmer areas in the world.

The **Milk Escargot,** *Otala lactea* Müller (Gr. *ous ostis,* ear; Lat. *lac
lactis,* milk) (pl. XXX, 17), reaches 28 to 36 mm. (1 1/8 to 1 1/2 in.)
in diameter. It is much more depressed than *H. aspersa,* and the shell
is smoother, almost glossy, and stronger. It is best recognized by the
shiny, dark brown, almost black aperture and lip. The rest of the
shell is creamy white, variously mottled and/or banded with brown
shadings. This immigrant from the Mediterranean region has established flourishing colonies at Pass-a-Grille and other areas in Florida.
It will probably spread even more. It is also reported on some islands
near Savannah, Georgia.

Genus *Cepaea* Held

*Cepaea nemoralis* Linnaeus
English Garden Snail

Pl. II, 6

ETYMOLOGY: Gr. *kepaios,* garden; Lat. *nemoralis,* inhabiting woods.

SIZE: 17 to 20 mm. (3/4 to 4/5 in.) in diameter, 13 to 18 mm. (about 1/2 to
3/4 in.) in height.

DISTRIBUTION: Widely introduced into the northern and central coastal
states from northern Europe.

CHARACTERISTICS: Shell small, depressed-globular, glossy. Yellow or rufous with one to five dark brown bands, often bandless. Umbilicus lacking; lip narrowly reflected, brown.

Large colonies of these handsome snails flourish in widely separated areas from Massachusetts to Virginia, usually near or in urban areas. There is a wide range of variation, especially in the number and nature of the spiral bands.

The **Common Garden Snail,** *Cepaea hortensis* Müller (Lat. *hortensis*, living in gardens) (pl. II, 7), is similar, differing mainly in having a white lip instead of a dark brown one. There is much evidence that this species is not only native to America, but is certainly pre-Columbian. It has been found on several offshore islands from Quebec and Prince Edward Island to Massachusetts. It has also been reported from some urban areas.

FAMILY:

# CAMAENIDAE

The **Cuban Caracole Snail,** *Zacrysia provisoria* Pfeiffer (probably from Chryseis, daughter of the priest Chryses in *The Iliad*; Lat. *provisor*, provider) (pl. XXX, 18), is small, 25 to 29 mm. (1 to 1 1/6 in.) in diameter, yellow to horn colored, somewhat glossy, sculptured with regular, rather coarse, closely set axial striae; the lip is thickened within and there is no umbilicus. This is an immigrant from Cuba, where the genus has several spectacular representatives. It is easily found in many spots in Miami. The Cuban Caracole is a member of the family Camaenidae, one of the most widely spread land-snail families in the world, but this introduced species is the only representative in the eastern United States.

FAMILY:

# HELMINTHOGLYPTIDAE

The **Variegated Bush Snail,** *Hemitrochus varians* Menke (from Gr. *hemi*, half, and Lat. *trochus*, dim, and Lat. *varius*, variegated) (pl. II, 9), is another immigrant from the Bahamas. It is small, about

16 mm. (3/4 in.) in diameter and height, conical, solid, smooth and glossy, and the spire is elevated. The species is highly variable in color, sometimes being unicolored, white or rose tinted, but often marked by spiral bands or spots or streaks of brown. The apex can be pink, purplish, or white. This snail is found on Virginia and Biscayne Keys, and is strung on necklaces sold to tourists in the Bahamas. It also is not a true helicid, but belongs to the family Helminthoglyptidae (Gr. *helmins*, worm; *glyptos*, sculptured). The shell, however, looks like a true helicid.

FAMILY:

# HELICELLIDAE

Genus *Helicella* Férussac

*Helicella elegans* Gmelin
  Elegant Little Helix

  Pl. XXXIII, 17

ETYMOLOGY: Diminutive of Gr. *helix*, spiral; Lat. *elegans*, elegant.

SIZE: 6 mm. (1/4 in.) in height, 9 mm. (about 2/5 in.) in width.

DISTRIBUTION: Introduced into Charleston, New Orleans, and other cities in the south from the Mediterranean area.

CHARACTERISTICS: Shell small, conic, solid; keeled at suture and periphery. Cream to light buff, with a few olive buff dots and streaks. Umbilicus small; lip thin.

This introduced species is common in Saint Peter's Churchyard in Charleston. Another species similarly introduced is the **Wrinkled Little Helix,** *Helicella caperata* Montagu (Lat. *capero,* to be wrinkled) (pl. XXXIII, 18), about 8 to 12 mm. (1/3 to 1/2 in.) in diameter, depressed, surface dull, opaque white with reddish brown spiral bands; it has been taken in Norfolk and Chincoteague, Virginia.

The **Fat Little Helix,** *Cochlicella ventrosa* Férussac (diminutive of Gr. *cochlos,* snail shell, Lat. *venter,* belly) (pl. XXXIII, 19), is elevated 9 to 12 mm. (2/5 to 1/2 in.) high, white with reddish brown axial bands.

The **Hairy Little Helix,** *Hygromia hispida* Linnaeus (Gr. *hygros,* wet; Lat. *hispidus,* shaggy, hairy) (pl. XXXIII, 20), is depressed, small,

7 to 9 mm. (1/4 to 2/5 in.) in diameter, pale cinnamon brown, and covered with short hairs; umbilicate, lip thin. This is a Palearctic species introduced into Canada, Maine, and Massachusetts.

The **Furrowed Little Helix,** *Hygromia striolata* C. Pfeiffer (Lat. *stria,* furrow) (pl. XXX, 19), is similar but larger, 10 to 11 mm. (2/5 to 1/2 in.) in diameter, somewhat darker in color, and is hirsute only in its early stages. It is very common in Quebec, where Pilsbry believes it was imported in colonial times. A colony has been reported from Naushon Island, Massachusetts.

Other species of foreign land snails can be found on sale in Italian markets in New York, Boston, and elsewhere. Some of them may in time escape and become part of the local fauna. For a brief description of these market snails, see Jacobson and Emerson (1971, pp. 106–110).

# CHAPTER III

---

# FRESHWATER SHELLS

Some species of gastropods and bivalves live in fresh water. The gastropods fall readily into two large groups—those with an operculum and those without. The latter are considered to be more highly developed. In almost all the operculates, the sexes are separate, the valve snails (family Valvatidae) being the only exception, and they all breathe by means of gills. The inoperculate forms are all hermaphroditic, and breathe by means of a modified "lung," though occasionally some, under certain conditions, tend to develop a sort of supplementary gill. They differ from the land pulmonates in bearing their eyes at the base of short, retractable, but not invaginable tentacles (hence they are called Basommatophora, "base eye bearers"). Because they breathe air, the pulmonates are less affected by water pollution than the water-breathing operculates, and they are usually the last mollusks to survive in bodies of water approaching maximum devitalization.

The freshwater bivalves of our area also constitute two major groups: the larger, heavier, darker naiads or freshwater mussels (families Unionidae and Margaritiferidae) and the smaller, thinner fingernail clams (family Sphaeriidae). The former are unique in having to pass through a parasitic juvenile stage in the gills, skin, or fins of fishes before metamorphosing into adults. In the case of the fingernail clams, many brood their young, which are retained in the parent until they attain the miniature form of the adult. At this stage, they are released to continue their growth and development.

Many of our freshwater mollusks are visually unattractive, for they lack the striking colors and the startling shapes and sculpture of their marine relatives. There are notable exceptions, however, such as the handsome banded *Marisa cornuarietis* and the striped freshwater mussels, with their pastel-colored, iridescent nacreous interiors. The majority, although less attractive, frequently, however, work a sort of quiet magic on the devoted student, amateur as well as professional, who rank high among the most indefatigable and enthusiastic of collectors.

Freshwater mollusks offer certain advantages to the collector, as they can be enormously abundant in favored places. They can be collected with little equipment, under the most adverse conditions, in all seasons, and at any time of the day. The collector may be rewarded by picking up and carefully examining submerged twigs, bits of wood, stones, and other objects. A simple kitchen sieve securely tied to a stick makes an efficient dredge in sandy and muddy bottoms. It is not productive to go to greater depths of lakes, because such places may be anaerobic, and therefore barren. Some of the local naiads live with the shell half buried, and others are covered by the bottom sediments, commonly in the lee of rocks and boulders. They can be seen in clear water, where their presence is betrayed by the two siphonal openings projecting out from the sand, and the collector soon becomes expert in detecting them. In murky waters, feeling around with hand or bare foot can yield a good catch. Usually many dead but well-preserved specimens can be found on the shores and beaches of lakes and rivers. Muskrats, who particularly relish mussel meat, leave nicely cleaned shells near their burrows, and these await the collector. Finally, it may be added that any body of fresh water, from large lakes and rivers to small brooks and streams and temporary forest ponds and meadow swales may contain some form of molluscan life. Among the exceptions are the waters strongly affected by industrial pollution and those in vacation areas which are excessively treated with copper sulfate or other chemicals to inhibit the growth of aquatic plant life. Other exceptions are highly acid waters, such as those with large amounts of decaying oak and other hardwood leaves, which are also inimical to molluscan life. This is why stagnant swamp waters are not the best places to hunt for snails.

## KEY TO THE
## FRESHWATER GASTROPODS
### (*adapted from Harman and Berg, 1971*)

| | |
|---|---|
| * Shells limpetlike | Ancylidae |
| * Shells whorled | |
| ** Whorls on one plane | |
| *** Shells banded | *Marisa* |
| *** Shells unbanded | Planorbidae |
| ** Whorls on more than one plane | |
| *** Shell sinistral | Physidae |
| *** Shell dextral | |

&ast;&ast;&ast;&ast; Shell not operculate Lymnaeidae
&ast;&ast;&ast;&ast; Shell with operculum
&ast;&ast;&ast;&ast;&ast; Spire slightly elevated, shell small,
 5 mm. (1/5 in.) in diameter Valvatidae
&ast;&ast;&ast;&ast;&ast; Spire moderately to extremely elevated
&ast;&ast;&ast;&ast;&ast;&ast; Whorls flattened Pleuroceridae, Thiaridae
&ast;&ast;&ast;&ast;&ast;&ast; Whorls inflated
&ast;&ast;&ast;&ast;&ast;&ast;&ast; Adults 15 mm. (3/5 in.) or greater in
 height, often considerably more Viviparidae, *Pomacea*
&ast;&ast;&ast;&ast;&ast;&ast;&ast; Adults less than 15 mm. (3/5 in.) in
 height, often considerably less Hydrobiidae

CLASS:

# GASTROPODA

*(stomach-footed)*

---

SUBCLASS:

## PROSOBRANCHIA

*(gills placed before the heart)*

ORDER:

## MESOGASTROPODA

*(middle gastropods, usually operculate)*

SUPERFAMILY:

# VIVIPARACEA

---

FAMILY:

# VIVIPARIDAE

(*mystery snails*)

The shells of this family are small to moderately large, ovate or broadly triangular, with a thin, unreflected lip, a dark, glossy periostracum, and a strong, horny operculum. The surface is usually smooth, but some tropical forms bear keels and transverse ridges. They may be very numerous in lakes, streams, and rivers.

---

## KEY TO GENERA VIVIPARA, CAMPELOMA, AND LIOPLAX

| | |
|---|---|
| * Shell widely ovate-conic, height/diameter ratio about 75 percent, thin shelled | |
| ** Shell reaching 40 mm. (1 3/5 in.), light colored, almost always banded | *Viviparus georgianus* |
| ** Shell darker, reaching 65 mm. (2 3/5 in.), unbanded | |
| *** Shell with 1 to 4 spiral rows of tiny pits | *V. malleatus* |
| *** Shell with incised lines, narrower | *V. japonicus* |
| * Shell narrowly ovate-conic, height/width ratio about 60 percent | |
| ** Early whorls with a medial keel or carina | |
| *** Shell dark, almost blackish green, umbilicus lacking; range western Florida | *Lioplax pilsbryi* |
| *** Shell pale brownish to olivaceous green, with small umbilicus; range New York to North Carolina | *L. subcarinata* |
| ** Whorls rounded, without keel or carina, tip usually eroded | |
| *** Shell with strongly shouldered whorls; range North Carolina to western Florida | *Campeloma geniculum* |
| *** Shell whorls not shouldered | |

**** Shell usually with bluish tinge in aperture;
      range Canada to South Carolina         *C. decisum*

**** Shell smaller, with reddish brown tinge in
      aperture; north central Florida only       *C. floridense*

---

Genus *Viviparus* Montfort

*Viviparus georgianus* Lea
    Georgian Mystery Snail

    Pl. II, 8a–c

ETYMOLOGY: Lat. *vivipara*, live bearing.

SIZE: 38 mm. (1 1/2 in.) in height and 28 mm. (1 1/8 in.) in width.

DISTRIBUTION: Quebec to central Florida and westward to the Mississippi
    Valley.

CHARACTERISTICS: Shell medium to large, subglobose, moderately strong,
    shiny. Light olive green, usually with three to four brownish bands,
    but sometimes unbanded. Lip entire, with a thin black line along the
    margin. Operculum horny, reddish amber, growth lines concentric.

This large snail, abundant in many lakes, ponds, and rivers, used to be
confined to the southern states, but as Dr. Clench of Harvard writes,
it has, since the middle of the nineteenth century, spread to many
northern states as well. In 1916 it appeared in the Boston Public
Gardens, and in the 1950s it was first noticed in Central Park in New
York City and has since spread rapidly on Long Island. Wherever it
appears it soon establishes itself as a prolific species, but the shells
are often fearfully eroded by acidy waters. Specimens from Quebec,
in the extreme north of the range, and in Florida, from the southern
limits, are pronouncedly smaller than those from the region about the
Great Lakes. Several of the extreme forms were given superfluous
subspecific names. The species used to be called *Viviparus contectoides*
Binney (Lat. *contego*, cover or hide).

    The **Chinese Mystery Snail,** *Viviparus malleatus* Reeve (from Lat.
*malleus,* hammer) (pls. II, 2; XXXIV, 1), differs by being larger, 65 mm.
(2 3/5 in.) high, more globose, and in lacking color bands. There
are one to four spiral rows of tiny scar pits, the situations of lost
periostracal hairs. This species is a native of the Far East, and was
first noticed in San Francisco in 1892, where it was being offered for

sale in a Chinese food market. In 1914 it was reported in Boston, and soon thereafter in Philadelphia. By the time it was first noticed in New York, in the 1940s, it had already established itself so firmly that today there is hardly a lake or pond near the great metropolis that does not have a large colony. It causes no ecological upset, but serves as food for muskrats as well as for gourmets. It is sometimes placed in the genus *Cipangopaludina* Hannibal (Cipango was an island described by Marco Polo, possibly Japan; Lat. *palus, paludis,* a swamp).

The **Japanese Mystery Snail,** *Viviparus japonicus* Martens (pl. XXXIV, 2), is similar, but the shell is narrower, higher, and less globose. It also lacks the rows of scar pits, which in this species are replaced by a few incised spiral lines. *V. japonicus* has frequently been confused in the literature with the Chinese Mystery Snail. It is not as successful an intruder as the latter, and in our area it has been reported only in the Concord River in Massachusetts.

Genus *Campeloma* Rafinesque

*Campeloma decisum* Say
  Common Lesser Mystery Snail

Pl. XXXIV, 3

ETYMOLOGY: Possibly Lat. *campe,* a crooked turn; *decisus,* cut off.

SIZE: 25 mm. (1 in.) in height, 15 mm. (3/5 in.) in width.

DISTRIBUTION: Nova Scotia and Maine to South Carolina.

CHARACTERISTICS: Shell small to medium, high conic-ovate, smooth, moderately glossy, heavy. Olive green, with a few dark lines marking the location of former lips. Growth lines coarse. Lip entire, thin. Operculum dark horn, concentric.

The shell is usually heavily eroded, a feature that probably suggested its name to Thomas Say. It lives in lakes and streams, usually burrowing in the soft mud, where it can be taken by straining or simply delving in the muck. It is an omnivorous beast that can be baited with dead organisms or fecal material. The olive green color, the rather elevated shape, and the eroded shell make this species easy to recognize.

The **Southern Lesser Mystery Snail,** *Campeloma geniculum* Conrad (Lat. *geniculum,* little knee) (pl. XXXIV, 4), is larger, 43 mm. × 35 mm. (1 3/4 × 1 2/5 in.), and heavier, with strongly shouldered whorls. It is a southern species, ranging from North Carolina to western Florida (but not in the peninsula) and westward to Alabama. The heavy, shouldered shell and its southern distribution make it easy to identify. This shell also erodes very readily.

The **Floridian Lesser Mystery Snail,** *Campeloma floridense* Call (not illustrated), is smaller, thinner, and has a reddish brown instead of bluish white coloration in the aperture. It is limited to central Florida, in the upper reaches of the Saint John River system.

Genus *Lioplax* Troschel

*Lioplax subcarinata* Say
  Keeled Mystery Snail

  Pl. XXXV, 1

ETYMOLOGY: Gr. *leios plax*, smooth plate; Lat. *sub*, almost, *carinatus*, keeled.

SIZE: 21 mm. (about 4/5 in.) in height, 13 mm. (about 1/2 in.) in width.

DISTRIBUTION: New York to North Carolina.

CHARACTERISTICS: Shell medium, thin, early whorls carinate. Pale brownish to olivaceous green. Sculpture of very fine, often beaded spiral lines crossed by thin growth lines. Umbilicus small; lip thin, entire.

This species is readily separated from *Campeloma decisum* by the keeled upper whorls. Clench and Turner (1955) report that there are gaps in the known range of this species, the largest one being between southernmost Virginia and Lake Waccamaw in North Carolina. Perhaps more collecting in this region will change the picture.

**Pilsbry's Mystery Snail,** *Lioplax pilsbryi* Walker (pl. XXXV, 2), differs by being darker, almost blackish green in color, larger, 28 mm. × 20 mm. (about 1 1/8 × 4/5 in.), and lacking an umbilicus. It has a limited distribution, in western Florida in the Chipola River, and in neighboring Alabama.

FAMILY:

# AMPULLARIIDAE (PILIDAE)
(*apple snails*)

These shells are usually globose, apple shaped, but some flattened forms (genus *Marisa*) are also known. The surface is smooth, greenish brown or buff, commonly with bands, and there is a horny or sometimes shelly operculum. The family is found throughout the world, in tropical and subtropical regions. The African genus *Lanistes* Montfort has sinistral shells; all others are dextral.

Genus *Pomacea* Perry

*Pomacea paludosa* Say
Florida Apple Snail

Pl. XXXV, 3

ETYMOLOGY: Lat. *pomum*, apple; *palus*, swamp.

SIZE: 63 mm. (2 1/2 in.) in height, 57 mm. (2 1/4 in.) in width.

DISTRIBUTION: Southern Georgia and peninsular Florida.

CHARACTERISTICS: Shell globose, smooth, moderately strong. Pale olive or brown, with greenish or brownish spiral lines. Spire small, low; body whorl huge. Lip simple but strong. Operculum corneous.

This is a very abundant species, common in slow-flowing or stagnant water. Unlike most water-dwelling operculate snails, *Pomacea* is able to breathe both water and air, the snail winding part of its mantle into a tube and extending it above the water surface. It lays small, hard-shelled white eggs, fixed in large numbers to wood and sedges just above the water line. Two species of birds, the limpkin (*Aramus guarauna pictus*) and the everglade kite (*Rostrhamus sociabilis plumbeus*) feed on the Florida Apple Snail, the latter exclusively so; it has a beak adapted to get under the operculum and extract the soft parts. *P. paludosa* was formerly placed in the genus *Ampullaria*.

The **Miami Apple Snail,** *Pomacea miamiensis* Pilsbry (not illustrated), differs by having a much heavier shell and a thicker lip. It is smaller, 43 mm. (1 3/4 in.) in height, and does not show the spiral bands. It was described in 1899 from a creek flowing from the Everglades near Miami, but is probably extinct now in this area. It may merely be an ecological form of *P. paludosa* influenced by its surroundings.

The **Wheeled Apple Snail,** *Marisa cornuarietis* Linnaeus (Lat. *mas, maris*, husband; *cornu arietis*, ram's horn) (pl. II, 13), looks very much like a large ram's horn or wheel snail (genus *Helisoma*), with all the whorls on one plane and the two sides excavated. However, unlike the true planorbids, it has a small, amber operculum. It reaches about 60 mm. (2 2/5 in.) in diameter and 18 mm. (3/4 in.) in height.

It is yellowish, and usually prettily banded. This originally South American species has invaded many regions in the Neotropics, but has only recently appeared in Florida, where it is flourishing. It has been welcomed because it is a voracious feeder on the beautiful but troublesome water hyacinth. The hope is that it will serve as a natural control of this floating weed, which is choking Florida's streams and rivers.

SUPERFAMILY:
# VALVATACEA

FAMILY:
# VALVATIDAE
(*valve snails*)

These shells are small to tiny, thin, depressed to disklike; operculum corneous, nucleus central. This family of generally hermaphroditic snails is found only in the colder and temperate regions of the northern hemisphere. There is only a single living genus *Valvata*. The nymph of a caddis fly in North America forms a *Valvata*-like shelter of cemented sand grains. Such a nymph was erroneously classified as a snail by a prominent conchologist, and named *Valvata granosa*.

## KEY TO GENUS VALVATA

* Shell low, spire not raised above upper
keel or margin of body whorl     *Valvata bicarinata*
* Shell higher, spire distinctly raised
** Shell with 1 to 3 keels     *V. tricarinata*
** Shell without keels
*** Aperture completely rounded     *V. sincera*
*** Aperture rounded but flattened above     *"simplex"* (keelless form of *V. tricarinata*)

Genus *Valvata* Müller

*Valvata tricarinata* Say
   Three-keeled Valve Snail

   Pl. XXXV, 4

ETYMOLOGY: Lat. *valva*, valve, and Gr. *tri*, three, Lat. *carinatus*, keeled.

SIZE: 3 to 5 mm. (1/8 to 1/5 in.) in diameter, 2.3 to 3 mm. (1/10 to 1/8 in.) in height.

DISTRIBUTION: Canada and northeastern United States to Virginia.

CHARACTERISTICS: Shell small, thin, translucent. Light tan or greenish, with flattened whorls, armed with one to three keels, sometimes lacking. Umbilicus deep. Aperture rounded; lip thin. Operculum multispiral.

The valve snails differ from other operculates in being hermaphroditic, a difference important enough to give this single genus its own family and superfamily. In addition, it has a single feathery gill that can be retracted when the snail retires behind its operculum. It lives in fine silt in lakes and rivers, where it can easily be strained out. The shell is variable in the nature and number of keels, and a few unnecessary subspecific names have been attached to them. It has been shown that some specimens may start out as one of the named "subspecies," and as they grow, by suppressing some or developing new keels, end up as another.

The **Two-keeled Valve Snail,** *Valcata bicarinata* Lea (pl. XXXV, 5), differs from the occasional two-keeled *tricarinata* as follows: it is larger and lower, and the upper surface of the whorls slope downward from the carina to the suture, a characteristic not found in *V. tricarinata*. Moreover, the spire is so low that it does not reach above the level of the upper carina of the body whorl, and the umbilicus is wider and shallower. This is a common valve shell of the coastal plains, and is found in scattered colonies as far south as Georgia.

The **True Valve Snail,** *Valvata sincera* Say. Lat. *sincerus,* real, natural, genuine) (pl. XXXV, 6), has no keels, and the aperture is completely, "sincerely," rounded. Because of this it can be distinguished from the no-keeled form of *V. tricarinata*, in which the upper part of the aperture is flattened. The no-keeled form of *V. tricarinata* has been known as subspecies *V. simplex* Gould, but the name can be disregarded, since such keelless forms appear in the same colonies as typical *tricarinata* and those with one or two keels. *Valvata sincera* has a more northerly distribution, not occurring south of New York.

# RISSOACEA

# HYDROBIIDAE

(*hydrobia and faucet snails*)

This is a family of small to tiny shells living mostly in bodies of fresh water, but they may be found in brackish water. Some unique forms occur in the ancient lakes of the Balkans, while others inhabit caves and are blind. The shells vary in shape and ornamentation.

The Hydrobiidae have recently been the subject of intensive study, and many new species and genera from Georgia and Florida have been described, especially by Dr. Fred G. Thompson of the University of Florida. Many of these species are known only from their restricted type-localities, and frequently systematic differences rest upon details of the minute anatomy. The inclusion of these species in this book is hence inadvisable.

## KEY TO FAMILY HYDROBIIDAE

* Shell larger, up to 12 mm. (1/2 in.) in
  height                                    *Bithynia tentaculata*
* Shell smaller, 4 to 8 mm. (1/6 to 1/3 in.)
  in height
* * Shell with last whorl not attached near
  aperture to penultimate whorl. 2.5 mm.
  (1/8 in.) high                            *Lyogyrus pupoides*
* * Shell with last whorl attached near
  aperture to penultimate whorl
* * * Shell with large body whorl, small spire,
  8 mm. (1/4 in.) high, 6 mm. (1/12 in.)
  wide
* * * * Body whorl globose, shoulder rounded
  or weakly angled; range New York to
  South Carolina                           *Gillia altilis*
* * * * Shoulder of body whorl strongly angled;
  range southern Florida                    *Notogillia wetherbyi*

      ✱ ✱ ✱ Shell with body whorl not unusually
           large

     ✱ ✱ ✱ ✱ Shell elevated, narrow, about 3 times
          higher than wide, 6 mm. (1/4 in.) high,
          2 mm. (1/12 in.) wide         *Pomatiopsis lapidaria*

     ✱ ✱ ✱ ✱ Shell more depressed, about 2 times
          higher than wide, frequently less

    ✱ ✱ ✱ ✱ ✱ Shell with umbilicus

  ✱ ✱ ✱ ✱ ✱ ✱ Protoconch raised above following
          whorls                   *Amnicola integra*

  ✱ ✱ ✱ ✱ ✱ ✱ Protoconch not raised above following
          whorls                   *A. limosa*

    ✱ ✱ ✱ ✱ ✱ Shell without umbilicus

  ✱ ✱ ✱ ✱ ✱ ✱ Aperture proportionately small, one-third
          of shell height           *Hydrobia totteni*

  ✱ ✱ ✱ ✱ ✱ ✱ Aperture proportionately larger,
          one-half of shell height      *H. salsa*

---

Genus *Hydrobia* Hartmann

*Hydrobia totteni* Morrison
    Totten's Hydrobia

    Pl. XXXVI, 1

ETYMOLOGY: Gr. *hydor*, water; named for General Joseph G. Totten
    (1788–1864), military engineer and scientist.

SIZE: 3.5 mm. to 4 mm. (1/8 to 1/6 in.) in height, 1.5 mm. (1/12 in.) wide.

DISTRIBUTION: Labrador to Florida.

CHARACTERISTICS: Shell tiny, ovate-conic, apex blunt, smooth. Yellow
    brown, translucent. Whorls inflated. Aperture oval, about one-third of
    entire shell; lip thin. Umbilicus wanting. Operculum paucispiral,
    corneous.

This common inhabitant of brackish marshes is found abundantly on
ulva seaweed. Dr. Gould had his troubles with this unspectacular,
tiny species and wrote: "This shell is so plain as to present no striking mark of distinction and it is consequently not easy to describe."
It was formerly called *Hydrobia minuta* Totten.

    The **Salt Hydrobia,** *Hydrobia salsa* Pilsbry (Lat. *salsus*, salted)
(pl. XXXV, 7), is smaller, about 3 mm. (1/8 in.) high, brownish gray

or a little greenish; the whorls are less inflated, and the aperture is about one-half the height of the shell. This species lives together with Totten's Hydrobia, but it ranges only from Massachusetts to New Jersey.

The **Miry Hydrobia,** *Amnicola limosa* Say. Lat. *amnis cola,* dweller in a rapid stream; *limosus,* slimy, miry) (pl. XXXV, 8), is a tiny shell, 4.5 mm. (1/5 in.) in height, 3 mm. (1/8 in.) in diameter. It is broadly conic, with a dull, bronze green or burnished color; the much inflated body whorl constitutes more than half the shell. The apex is flattened, the lip is thin, and the umbilicus is narrow and deep. Every author dealing with this species records its abundance in all sorts of bodies of fresh water. One even wrote of it as being as abundant as sand. It lives in sand or mud, and on many kinds of water plants. It can be recognized by its small size and large body whorl. It ranges from Labrador to Florida and westward to Utah.

The **Natural Hydrobia,** *Amnicola integra* Say (Lat. *integrum,* unchanged, real) (pl. XXXV, 9), is similar, but can readily be distinguished by having the protoconch raised above the following whorls instead of being on the same plane. It occupies the same habitats as the Miry Hydrobia but is less common, and moreover is restricted to a northern range, from New York to New Jersey and westward to Utah. It barely touches the area under discussion in this book.

The **Fat Hydrobia,** *Gillia altilis* Lea (Theodore Gill, 1837–1914, was a physician and naturalist; Lat. *altilis,* nourished, fattened) (pl. XXXVI, 2), is 8 mm. (1/3 in.) in height, 6 mm. (1/4 in.) in width. This species is most easily recognized by its rather large, almost globose, light brown shell, with its short spire and large body whorl slightly angled above. It is an abundant species, ranging from New York to South Carolina.

**Wetherby's Hydrobia,** *Notogillia wetherbyi* Dall (A. G. Wetherby, 1833–1902, was an active naturalist) (pl. XXXVI, 3), differs in having strongly angled shoulders, a thickened lip, and a dark olivaceous color. It is found only in the ponds and streams of northern Florida.

The **False Schisto Snail,** *Pomatiopsis lapidaria* Say (Gr. *poma opsis,* lid appearing; Lat. *lapis,* stone) (pl. XXXVI, 4), is 6 mm. (1/4 in.) in height, 2.5 mm. (1/8 in.) in diameter. This amphibious species is readily recognized by the narrow, conically elevated dark brown shell, the thin but reflected lip, the narrow umbilicus, and the rather high body whorl, about twice the height of the penultimate whorl. This species is anatomically close to the genus *Oncomelania,* the vector in the Far East of the dreadful fluke snail disease, schistosomiasis. But the role of *Pomatiopsis* in the life cycle of human parasitism in North

America has not been demonstrated. Its range is from New York south to Georgia, and west to Iowa.

The **Pupalike Hydrobia,** *Lyogyrus pupoides* Gould (Gr. *lyos gyra,* loosely whorled; *pupoides,* resembling a pupa) (pl. XXXV, 10), is only 2.5 mm. (1/8 in.) in height and less than 1 mm. (1/25 in.) in diameter. This tiny species is best recognized by the last part of the body whorl, which is free of contact with the penultimate whorl, whence its generic name. The shell itself is narrowly elongate-ovate, and while chestnut brown in color, is usually covered by a blackish encrustation. It ranges from Maine to Connecticut, and lives in ponds and streams on submerged sticks and stones.

The **Faucet Snail,** *Bithynia tentaculata* Linnaeus (Bithynia was a Roman province in Asia Minor; Lat. *tentare,* to handle, feel) (pl. XXXV, 11), reaches 8 to 12 mm. (1/3 to 1/2 in.) in height, 5 to 7 mm. (1/5 to 1/4 in.) in diameter. This species is best recognized by its relatively large conic shell, whose heavy, concentrically sculptured operculum, does not pull back into the aperture. It is greenish or light horn color under a thin, dark dirt layer, and the lip is thin; there is no umbilicus. The shell is an immigrant from northeastern Europe, and was introduced, probably as ballast, in the Great Lakes. It was first noticed in 1871, and is now found over much of the northeastern section of the United States, but not in northern New England. Its common name comes from the fact that its presence was first noted by large numbers of people when it entered the water systems of some cities on the Great Lakes and issued forth from drinking faucets. Screens now prevent this.

Recently it was shown that *Bithynia* also has a deleterious effect upon some native species of freshwater gastropods. In upstate New York the river horn snails (family Pleuroceridae) can survive in moderately polluted water. But when they share such a habitat with the introduced Faucet Snail, they quickly succumb to the stronger competition and vanish locally. Incidentally, it was also noted that in clear, unpolluted water both types of snails do coexist.

# CERITHIACEA

# THIARIDAE

(*thiara snails*)

These medium, high-spired, but occasionally low or globose shells are smooth or strongly sculptured, the apertures are faintly or strongly angled below, and the operculums are horny. This is a large family, richly developed in warmer regions but with some temperate representatives. In some countries these snails are eagerly sought as food. Some authors include the North American Pleuroceridae (see page 300) as a subfamily of the Thiaridae.

Genus *Tarebia* H. & A. Adams

*Tarebia granifera* Lamarck
Thiara Snail

Pl. XXXVI, 5

ETYMOLOGY: *Tarebia* seems to be an invented word without special meaning; Lat. *granum fero*, grain bearing.

SIZE: 36 mm. (1 1/2 in.) in height, 11 mm. (about 1/2 in.) in width.

DISTRIBUTION: Lithia Spring near Tampa and other springs and streams in Florida.

CHARACTERISTICS: Shell medium, moderately strong, narrow elevated-conic; spire acute, whorls flattened and faintly shouldered. Yellowish buff or light reddish brown, shiny. Lower part of body whorl with several strong spiral ridges, rest of shell covered by even, rounded pustules arranged in spiral rows. Aperture sharply angled above and below. Lip entire, thin.

This is a Far Eastern species that was accidentally introduced into this country on water plants. An interested dealer in Tampa marketed them under the name "Philippine Horn of Plenty," and escaped specimens flourished. Specimens in Lithia Spring literally carpet the floor, but die if the water falls below 70 degrees. The snail in Asia is the vector of a vicious lung parasite, but it can enter the human body only if crabs, infected by the snail, are eaten raw. So far only the snail is with us; as yet no one has found any signs of the lung fluke itself. Nor is it certain that any local crustacean can serve as intermediate host.

The **Tuberculate Thiara Snail,** *Melanoides tuberculata* Müller (pl. XXXV, 12), is similar to *Tarebia granifera,* but longer, narrower, and darker in color. The surface sculpture is weaker, and the lower part of the aperture is more rounded. It is found in several scattered localities in southern Florida and Texas, and probably in other neighboring states. In the San Antonio (Texas) zoo it is the bearer of a fluke parasite that attacks the eyes of water birds.

FAMILY:

# PLEUROCERIDAE

(*river horn snails*)

These shells are small, usually narrowly conic and strong, smooth but often highly sculptured, the sculpture being very variable. This confusing family is confined to North America, and most forms occur in the lime-rich streams and rivers of the southeastern states.

## KEY TO GENUS GONIOBASIS

* Shell smooth or relatively weakly striate
** Shell wider, larger, base angled at outer lip, 30
  × 12 mm. (1 1/5 × 1/2 in.), varicolored, dull     *Goniobasis virginica*
** Shell lower, 23 mm. (about 1 in.), wider, lip angle
  weak; range chiefly in interior basin     *G. livescens*
* Shell with strongly knobbed surface
** Shell sculpture strong, whorls with heavy basal
  keel; range southern Georgia and northern
  Florida     *G. floridensis*
** Shell sculpture weaker, whorls without basal
  keel; range North Carolina to Georgia     *G. catenaria*

Genus *Goniobasis* Rafinesque

*Goniobasis virginica* Gmelin
   Virginian River Horn Snail

Pl. XXXVI, 6

ETYMOLOGY: Gr. *gonia*, corner, angle; *basis*, base.

SIZE: 31 mm. (1 1/4 in.) in height, 12 mm. (1/2 in.) in width.

DISTRIBUTION: Lower Connecticut River to Virginia.

CHARACTERISTICS: Shell medium, high conic, strong; whorls moderately
   rounded, smooth but often with many strong spiral ridges. Color
   various: yellow, yellow green, fawn, or chestnut, frequently with two
   dark chestnut bands showing also in the aperture. Lip entire, sharply
   angled, and almost canaliculate below. Operculum paucispiral,
   chitinous, fragile.

This is a widely spread member of a group that has been richly
developed in the mountain streams and rivers of Alabama, Kentucky,
Tennessee, and throughout the entire mountainous region of the
Southeast. The shells live generally in rushing water and shoals,
clinging strongly to submerged rocks. The damming activities of the
TVA, which submerged such rapids and shoals, played havoc with
vast populations, and probably entire species of these creatures.
Progress for mankind does not come cheap. The Virginian River Horn
Snail, however, has adapted to slow-flowing waters, and is not un-
common in our area. The shell, though variable, is readily recognized
by its relatively large size, high conic shape, and angled base of the
outer lip. It is the freshwater relative of the marine horn snails, family
Cerithiidae (see pages 75–80).

   The **Livid River Horn Snail,** *Goniobasis livescens* Menke (Lat.
*livesco,* become livid) (pl. XXXVI, 7), differs by being lower, 23 mm.
(about 1 in.) in height, and not so slender. The shell is almost always
smooth. The livid color is seen best in dead shells. This is a species of
the Great Lakes and the Ohio Valley, and reaches our area only in
northern and central New York along the Erie Canal.

   The **Floridian River Horn Snail,** *Goniobasis floridensis* Reeve
(pl. XXXVI, 8), is about the same size, but differs sharply in being
dark chocolate brown, almost black in color, and especially in the
heavy, rough surface sculpture, which consists of strong axial ribs,
nodulose at the points where they are crossed by heavy spiral ridges,
the peripheral ridge being the strongest. In addition, the suture is
placed below a heavy keel at the base of the whorls. This species is

confined to a strip of land reaching from northern and central Florida to the neighboring areas of Georgia and Alabama. It lives in large freshwater springs and spring-fed streams and rivers, but it is also at home in still waters. It is variable in sculpture, and was formerly confused with the following species.

The **Chain River Horn Snail,** *Goniobasis catenaria* Say (Lat. *catena*, chain) (pl. XXXV, 13), differs in having weaker and more regular surface sculpture. It lacks the heavy, keellike ridge. It occurs from North Carolina to Georgia in the same habitats as *G. floridensis*.

CLASS:

# PULMONATA

*(lung breathers)*

---

ORDER:

## BASOMMATOPHORA

*(eyes at base of tentacles)*

---

# LYMNAEACEA

# LYMNAEIDAE
(*pond snails*)

The shells of this family of air-breathing (pulmonate) snails are dextral (opening to the right when held spire up), small to medium in size, generally rather thin and fragile, horn colored, and with a thin lip. There is never an operculum. The family is worldwide in distribution; forms have been found in high mountain lakes and even in some hot springs.

There is much confusion regarding the nomenclature and taxonomy of these snails. The shell is highly variable and strongly affected by the environment. Hence it is not a very reliable guide, in general, for determination of species. Recent anatomical, cytological, and antigenic studies indicate that there are far fewer species and genera than is commonly supposed. This is, however, truer of the worldwide species than the relatively few found in our area, where the shell alone, as will be seen, generally suffices. Nevertheless, one recent scholar (Walter, 1969) suggested that several of these species are actually nothing more than various forms of *Lymnaea catascopium* Say. The lymnaeids are important economically because in several cases they are vectors of serious animal diseases. In the Great Lakes area *Lymnaea* and *Physa* are vectors for the trematode that causes "swimmer's itch." In general, we follow Hubendick (1951) in assuming that there is only one genus *Lymnaea*, with several subgenera. We also follow his simplified taxonomy.

## KEY TO GENUS LYMNAEA

* Shell about 40 mm. (1 3/5 in.) in height, often larger, body whorl large, spire narrow, acute   *Lymnaea stagnalis*
* Shell less than 40 mm. (1 3/5 in.) in height, often greatly so
** Spire considerably smaller than body whorl

∗ ∗ ∗ Body whorl vast, earlike, upper margin of lip
almost horizontal                                    *L. auricularia*

∗ ∗ ∗ Body whorl *Succinea*-like, upper margin of lip
very oblique                                         *L. columella*

∗ ∗ Spire and body whorl about equal in height

∗ ∗ ∗ Shell 14 mm. (about 3/5 in.) or more in height

∗ ∗ ∗ ∗ Shell thickened, wide (height/width ratio less
than 2:1), seldom malleated; found in large
lakes                                               *L. catascopium*

∗ ∗ ∗ ∗ Shell thin, narrow (height/width ratio more
than 2:1), often malleated; found in shallow,
stagnant water                                      *L. palustris*

∗ ∗ ∗ Shell 13 mm. (about 1/2 in.) or less in height

∗ ∗ ∗ ∗ Shell glossy, columella not twisted; Floridian   *L. cubensis*

∗ ∗ ∗ ∗ Shell dull, columella twisted; northern
distribution                                        *L. humilis*

---

Genus *Lymnaea* Lamarck

*Lymnaea palustris* Müller
Swamp Pond Snail

Pl. XXXVI, 9

ETYMOLOGY: Gr. *limnaios*, pertaining to marshes; Lat. *palus*, swamp.

SIZE: 20 mm. (4/5 in.) in height, 10 mm. (2/5 in.) in diameter; in our area
frequently smaller.

DISTRIBUTION: Canada and Maine to Virginia and throughout northern
North America.

CHARACTERISTICS: Shell small to medium, elevated, ovate with acutely conic
spire; thin, dull, smooth but often malleated. Color some shade of
brown. Columella sharply twisted. Umbilicus generally covered by
extension of columellar margin of lip, which is thin and fragile.

This common pond snail lives in shallow, slow-flowing or stagnant
water and varies greatly in size and shape. The forms from the West
are generally larger, reaching as much as 35 mm. (1 2/5 in.) in height.
Naturally, many useless names have been given to these forms.
Frank C. Baker, a leading authority on the group in America, stated
that the malleated or "hammered" forms develop in very stagnant
water.

The **Succinea-like Pond Snail,** *Lymnaea columella* Say (diminutive of Lat. *columna,* column) (pl. XXXVI, 10), is commonly smaller in size, but differs markedly in having a much larger body whorl and aperture in relation to the spire. This feature alone is sufficient to identify it. It looks so much like an amber snail (genus *Succinea*) (see pages 225–6) that a subgenus called *Pseudosuccinea* F. C. Baker was erected for it. It ranges from Canada to Florida and westward to Kansas and Texas.

The **Explorer Pond Snail,** *Lymnaea catascopium* Say (Gr. *katasko-pos,* reconnoitering ship) (pl. XXXVI, 11), is hard to distinguish from the Swamp Pond Snail, *L. palustris.* However, it is heavier, lighter in color, 14 to 20 mm. (about 3/5 to 4/5 in.) in height, the spire is less elevated, and it is rarely malleated. Moreover, the surface sculpture consists of extremely coarse spiral striae supporting raised periostracal hairs. It ranges southward as far as Maryland and westward to Iowa, living in larger lakes and rivers.

The **Humble Pond Snail,** *Lymnaea humilis* Say (Lat. *humilis,* lowly) (pl. XXXVI, 12), looks like *palustris,* but it is consistently and noticeably smaller, rarely growing much beyond 10 mm. (2/5 in.) in height. It is also generally narrower. In contrast to *palustris,* which prefers to stay in water, *humilis* can frequently be found, in huge numbers, on silty banks completely out of water. It has even been collected in seepage areas on the steep slopes of ravines. This seems to indicate that it is well on its way to becoming a land snail like the sessile-eyed (basommatophoran) *Carychium,* the Swamp Snail. It ranges as far south as South Carolina and westward to the Pacific coast. *L. humilis* has recently been placed in the genus *Fossaria* (Lat. *fossa,* a ditch).

The **Cuban Pond Snail,** *Lymnaea cubensis* Pfeiffer (pl. XXXVI, 13), is a small shell, 7 to 10 mm. (about 1/4 to 2/5 in.) high, ovate or roundly ovate in shape, with a low spire and a glossy surface. The columella, unlike most lymnaeids, is not twisted. It is a subtropical species found in several areas throughout Florida. The Cuban Pond Snail is the only lymnaeid, aside from *L. columella,* with its characteristic huge aperture, found in Florida. This should make identification easier.

The **Stagnant Pond Snail,** *Lymnaea stagnalis* Linnaeus (Lat. *stag-num,* pool or swamp) (pl. II, 14), is an inland species found generally around the Great Lakes and thus in upstate New York. It is mentioned here because it is the largest of American *Lymnaea,* reaching 58 mm. (more than 2 in.) in height. It is quite a striking object, with its large, ovate body whorl, capacious aperture, and short, very acute spire. It is a fragile shell, and the lip breaks easily. We once collected a large series in the Niagara River not far above the Falls. It also occurs in Europe, and for a time the American form was considered to be a different subspecies, *L. s. jugularis* Say (probably Lat. *jugulum,* throat).

The **Ear-shaped Pond Snail,** *Lymnaea auricularia* Linnaeus (Lat. *auricula,* ear) (pl. XXXVI, 14), is a large, irregularly rounded shell, 28 mm. (1 1/8 in.) high and 21 mm. (about 4/5 in.) wide, with a fragile, extremely inflated ear-shaped body whorl, a huge aperture, and a very small spire. It is a European species that occurs sporadically in our country, and is sometimes successful even in polluted pools. Fixed colonies have been reported from upper New York State and elsewhere in the general region, but it has more often appeared in ephemeral populations in city parks and ponds. This species was recently placed in the genus *Radix* (Lat. *radix,* root).

SUPERFAMILY:

# ANCYLACEA

FAMILY:

# FERRISSIIDAE (ANCYLIDAE)
(*freshwater limpets*)

The shells in this family are small to tiny, limpetlike, fragile, and horn colored; the apex is behind the center, often pushed slightly to the right. This is a worldwide group found clinging to such submerged objects as water weeds, shells, stones, and bits of wood. In some forms, a small septum like that of *Crepidula* (see page 96) is formed on the inner surface as the shell matures. The freshwater limpets are related to the air breathers like the basommatophoran pulmonates Physidae, Lymnaeidae, and Planorbidae (see pages 314, 304, and 309).

# KEY TO GENERA HEBETANCYLUS, LAEVAPEX, FERRISSIA

* Shell depressed, apex posterior and strongly shifted to the right; range Georgia and Florida — *Hebetancylus excentricus*

* Shell more elevated, apex situated slightly posterior, not shifted to right

** Shell with fine radial striations on the apex, none on newer portions of shell — *Laevapex fuscus*

** Shell with smooth apex, newer portions of shell with radial striations

*** Shell with elongate base, sides almost parallel — *Ferrissia parallela*

*** Shell with oval base, sides rounded — *F. rivularis*

---

Genus *Ferrissia* Walker

*Ferrissia parallela* Haldeman
Parallel Freshwater Limpet

Pl. XXXV, 14

ETYMOLOGY: Named for James H. Ferriss (1849–1926), a skillful collector.

SIZE: 4 to 5.5 mm. (1/6 to 1/4 in.) in length, 2 to 2.5 mm. (1/12 to 1/8 in.) in width.

DISTRIBUTION: Canada and New England to South Carolina.

CHARACTERISTICS: Shell quite small, limpet shaped without a whorled spire; rather elevated, very thin, pellucid. Horn colored, occasionally with a greenish tinge. Base elliptical, sides almost parallel. Apex smooth, later portions of shell radially striate.

These small freshwater limpets may be found on plants, sedges, floating wood, stones, pebbles, debris, and on dead mussel shells. Their small size and dingy color, usually hidden by a thin layer of muck, make them very difficult to find.

The **Brook Freshwater Limpet,** *Ferrissia rivularis* Say (Lat. *rivus,* small stream or brook) (pl. XXXV, 15), is higher than *Hebetancylus excentricus* (see below), and the apex is nearly central on the posterior half. This species has a more northerly distribution, being absent from the southeastern states.

The **Dark Freshwater Limpet,** *Laevapex fuscus* C. B. Adams (Lat. *levis,* smooth, and *apex; fuscus,* swarthy) (pl. XXXVI, 15), differs from the other limpets in having the apex striate and the newer portions of the shell smooth. The color of the apical region is dark brown, while the outer edges are light brown or buff. This species ranges to Florida, where a larger, heavier form of the same species was unnecessarily named *Ferrissia peninsulae,* by Pilsbry.

The **Off-center Freshwater Limpet,** *Hebetancylus excentricus* Morelet (Lat. *hebes, hebetis,* blunt, and *ancile,* curved; Lat. *ex.,* from and *centrum,* point) (pl. XXXV, 16), is small, 5 mm. (1/5 in.) long, 3 mm. (1/8 in.) wide. It can most easily be recognized by the apex, which is placed very near the posterior end and clearly shifted toward the right side. It is found in large numbers along the Tamiami Trail and elsewhere in Florida, and has also been found on the coastal islands off Georgia. It is an immigrant from Cuba and the West Indies.

---

FAMILY:

# PLANORBIDAE

The Planorbidae, or ram's horn snails (Lat. *planus orbis,* flat orb or circle), are easily recognized by their planiform shape with all their whorls on one plane. Originally these snails must have had a properly raised spire, but the spire became telescoped to the level of the body whorl, like an old-fashioned collapsible drinking cup, the shell thus assuming its familiar flattened shape. That this was so can be seen by comparing both sides of the shell, let us say, of a specimen of the genus *Helisoma,* or the true ram's horns. It will then be observed that one side represents the telescoped spire, with about three flattened or slightly rounded whorls and a shallow suture. The other side will show a few rounded whorls leading to a deep umbilicus.

If now the shell is put with the telescoped-spire side up, the aperture will fall to the left, thus demonstrating that this is indeed a sinistral shell, as are all species of the genus *Helisoma.* In some genera (*Gyraulus, Planorbula, Promenetus,* and *Micromenetus*), however, the shell seems to be dextral, that is, if the telescoped-spire side is up, then the aperture falls to the right. But this is not so. The truth is that in these cases the spire was pushed down, not only to the level of the body whorl, but beyond it, so that it came out of the other end, the umbilicus, so to speak. The result is a pseudodextral shell that has also been called ultrasinistral. The soft parts of the animals in these pseudodextral shells preserve, nevertheless, their original sinistral arrangement.

Sometimes, in early spring, the reader might come across a number of individuals forming a chain of ram's horns, each in close contact with the others. This is a mating chain of copulating individuals formed because, like all Basommatophora (sessile-eyed pulmonates), each animal has separate male and female sexual orifices (the more advanced snails, or Stylommatophora, the stalk-eyed pulmonates, have only one). Thus a single animal can simultaneously serve as male for one animal and female for another, and so on. The result is that a mating chain of copulating creatures is formed.

---

# KEY TO FAMILY PLANORBIDAE

*(adapted from Harman and Berg, 1971)*

\* Shell 10 mm. (2/5 in.) or greater in
   diameter, body whorl inflated, high     genus *Helisoma*
\* Shell less than 10 mm. (2/5 in.) in
   diameter, body whorl depressed or
   carinate
\*\* Shell with 4 to 6 internal denticles,
   diameter 6.5 mm. (about 1/4 in.),
   height 2.5 mm. (about 1/8 in.)     *Planorbula jenksii*
\*\* Shell without internal denticles
\*\*\* Shell extremely flattened, body whorl
   with median carina, diameter 3 mm.
   (1/8 in.), height 1 mm. (1/25 in.)     *Promenetus hudsonicus*
\*\*\* Shell not extremely flattened,
   discoidal
\*\*\*\* Shell with carina at summit, diameter
   1.6 mm. (1/12 in.), height 0.7 mm.
   (about 1/25 in.)     *Micromenetus dilatatus*
\*\*\*\* Shell 2 mm. (1/12 in.) or more in
   diameter
\*\*\*\*\* Shell more or less centrally carinate,
   aperture strongly deflected at outer
   lip, diameter 8 mm. (1/3 in.), height
   2.3 mm. (1/8 in.)     *Gyraulus deflectus*
\*\*\*\*\* Shell without carina

****** Shell with periostracal hairs,
diameter 7 mm. (about 1/4 in.),
height 2.5 mm. (about 1/8 in.)      *G. hirsutus*

****** Shell without periostracal hairs,
diameter 5 mm. (1/5 in.), height 1.5
mm. (about 1/12 in.)      *G. parvus*

---

Genus *Helisoma* Swainson

*Helisoma trivolvis* Say
     Three-whorled Ram's Horn

     Pl. XXXVI, 19

ETYMOLOGY: Gr. *helix soma*, twisted body; Lat. *tri volvo*, for three-whorled.

SIZE: From 14 mm. (about 3/5 in.) in diameter and 7 mm. (about 1/4 in.) in
height, to 27 mm. (about 1 in.) in diameter and 14 mm. (about 3/5 in.)
in height.

DISTRIBUTION: Alaska, Canada, Maine, and eastern United States to
Maryland.

CHARACTERISTICS: Shell medium to large, coiled in one plane, sinistral, dull
to shiny. Pale yellow, light horn, or chestnut in color. Surface with
coarse growth lines, body whorl rounded, high. Spire compressed to a
flat-bottomed, cup-shaped depression, the opposite side with slightly
rounded whorls. Deep, open umbilicus. Lip thin, expanded, thickened
within.

This is a very common species, found everywhere in gently flowing
or standing bodies of water. The animals cling to hard surfaces like
submerged branches or rocks, but sometimes they can be taken
crawling across the soft bottom. In a very immature stage, the shell
looks like a flat-topped pond snail (genus *Physa*) (see pages 314–15).
Occasionally specimens are found with one or more strong, narrow
humps on the body whorl. These merely represent former lips of the
growing animal. Like most freshwater shells, this species is highly
variable, and many needless subspecific names have been applied to it.

     The **Magnificent Ram's Horn,** *Helisoma magnificum* Pilsbry (not
illustrated) appears to be only an oversized form of *H. trivolvis*, 37 ×
25 mm. (1 1/2 × 1 in.). It achieved this size because it found itself in
a very favorable environment (see *Nautilus*, vol. 42, p. 116). This form

is reported only from Greenfield Pond, an impounded lake near Wilmington, North Carolina.

The **Keeled Ram's Horn,** *Helisoma anceps* Menke (Lat. *anceps,* two headed) (pl. XXXVI, 16), differs by being generally smaller, 11 to 15 mm. (about 1/2 to 3/5 in.) in diameter, with a strong keel on the body whorl that reaches to the aperture and strongly distorts it. It can, however, be most easily recognized by the fact that it is considerably more excavated on both sides, spire and base, the spire forming a deep pit, like an inverted cone. This species is one of the few *Helisoma* that have an ultrasinistral shell as explained on pages 309–10. It is found in the same type of habitat as *H. trivolvis,* but we have rarely found both species living together.

The **Bell-mouthed Ram's Horn,** *Helisoma campanulatum* Say (late Lat. *campana,* a bell) (pl. XXXVI, 17), differs chiefly in that the aperture in mature individuals is expanded into a structure looking like the mouth of a bell. The juvenile forms, lacking the bell mouth, differ from other *Helisoma* species by their rounded, narrow, noticeably contracted whorls with a very deep suture. This is an inland species generally found away from the coastal plain. Having a more northerly distribution than the other ram's horns described in this book, it ranges from interior New Jersey and New York to Vermont and westward to Michigan.

**Dury's Ram's Horn,** *Helisoma duryi* Wetherby (pl. XXXV, 17), is limited to Florida. It is a very confusing species, of which Pilsbry writes, "These mollusks do not seem to know what is expected of a 'normal' snail." This comment was brought about by the extreme variability of the species. The only fixed characteristics seem to be "the great height of the last whorl, the very shallow spire, the few rapidly increasing whorls of the base and the high gloss" (Pilsbry). The most peculiar charactèristic appears in a small number of the specimens. This is a high extension of the flat-topped spire, which rises well above the body whorl and makes the shell look like a Babylonian ziggurat. The typical planorbiform shape is thus effectively destroyed. Even single populations can have flattened individuals as well as ziggurat-shaped ones of various heights.

The **Staircase Ram's Horn,** *Helisoma scalare* Jay (Lat. *scala,* staircase) (pl. XXXVI, 18), is also limited to Florida. It preserves the ziggurat form even when adult. As Pilsbry noted, it differs from *H. duryi* specimens of this shape by having "the lower border of the peristome (lip) more advanced." It is also common as a Pliocene fossil.

Genus *Gyraulus* Charpentier

*Gyraulus parvus* Say
  Lesser Ram's Horn

  Pl. XXXIV, 5

ETYMOLOGY: Diminutive of Gr. *gyros*, spiral; Lat. *parvus*, in small degree.

SIZE: 4 to 5 mm. (1/6 to 1/5 in.) in diameter, 1 to 1.5 mm. (about 1/25 to 1/12 in.) in height, frequently smaller.

DISTRIBUTION: North America, east of the Rocky Mountains and south to South Carolina.

CHARACTERISTICS: Shell quite small, very flat, disklike, thin, lustrous. Color reddish or grayish brown. Periphery rounded, last whorl enlarging rapidly. Lip thin, entire.

This small planorbid, with its nondescript coloration, is an abundant snail in nearly every pond or slowly flowing brook, where it can be collected easily from the underside of floating wood, lily pads, and leaves.

The **Hairy Ram's Horn,** *Gyraulus hirsutus* Gould (Lat. *hirsutus*, rough, shaggy) (pl. XXXIV, 6), is somewhat bigger, up to 7 mm. (about 1/4 in.) in diameter. It can be recognized by its dull surface covered by several revolving lines of periostracal hairs. The range is roughly the same as *parvus*, but the species is less common.

The **Deflected Ram's Horn,** *Gyraulus deflectus* Say (pl. XXXIV, 7), reaches 8 mm. (1/3 in.) in diameter. It can be most easily recognized by the keeled rather than rounded margin, by the fact that the body whorl increases less rapidly, and especially by the aperture, which is sharply deflected downward. Distributed from New England to Maryland.

The **Dilated Ram's Horn,** *Micromenetus dilatatus* Gould (Gr. *micros*, small, and *Menoetes*, one of the companions of Aeneas) (pl. XXXIV, 8), is tiny, less than 2 mm. (1/12 in.) in diameter. It differs from the Lesser Ram's Horn, *Gyraulus parvus*, in having a keel at the summit of the body whorl, the lower part well rounded. It consists of three rapidly increasing whorls. An inhabitant of quiet pools and ponds throughout the eastern United States.

The **Hudson Ram's Horn,** *Promenetus hudsonicus* Pilsbry (pl. XXXIV, 9), is a bit bigger, 3 mm. (1/8 in.) in diameter, and differs in being lens shaped, with a keel at the middle of the body whorl. It is grayish amber in color, reddish brown when taken alive. So far it seems to have been taken only in lower New York State and neighboring New

Jersey and Connecticut, where it is common in ponds and small streams.

**Jenks's Ram's Horn,** *Planorbula jenksii* H. C. Carpenter (Lat. *planus orbis,* flat orb; named for the late E. H. Jenks of Rhode Island, an enthusiastic conchologist of his day) (pl. XXXIV, 10), is readily distinguished from all the other Ram's Horns by the presence of four to six white teeth inside the aperture. These teeth can clearly be seen through the thin, bronze-colored shell. The shell has a fine glossy bronze color and a smoothly rounded, unkeeled body whorl. This species is limited to New England and New York, where it is commonly found in ephemeral woodland ponds and brooks. Occasionally many of these shells are seen scattered on the forest floor, but these are the remains of populations that had lived in ponds that subsequently dried up, resulting in the mass mortality of these aquatic snails. The presence of fingernail clams (family Sphaeriidae) in similar sites led to erroneous reports of land-dwelling bivalves.

FAMILY:

# PHYSIDAE

*(pond snails)*

This family, together with the Lymnaeidae, Planorbidae, and Ferrissidae, are the only pulmonate freshwater shell families in our area. The shells are thin, fragile, small, and shiny, with a huge body whorl and small spire. The lip is thin. The aperture always opens to the left; hence the shell is sinistral, in contrast to the related dextral Lymnaeidae. This family is worldwide in distribution.

Genus *Physa* Draparnaud

*Physa heterostropha* Say
  Common Tadpole Snail

  Pl. XXXVI, 20

ETYMOLOGY: Gr. *physa,* bellows; *hetero,* other, and *strophe,* twist (referring to the sinistral rather than dextral shell).

SIZE: Varying from 8 mm. (1/3 in.) in height and 6 mm. (1/4 in.) in width, to 22 mm. (about 4/5 in.) in height and 12 mm. (1/2 in.) in width, depending on location.

DISTRIBUTION: Eastern and central North America, from the Arctic to the Gulf of Mexico.

CHARACTERISTICS: Shell small to medium, sinistral, ovate, shining but not polished. Color amber to bronze brown. Body whorl much larger than spire; spire variously raised. Lip simple, thin, fragile.

This species is most easily recognized by its sinistral shell (aperture to the left when the shell is held spire up), and by its ovate shape with the large body whorl. It is a common shell in all kinds of bodies of fresh water, and frequently it is the only species found in small, even polluted, streams and ponds. The shells vary greatly in outline, some being rounded, others ovate; in the proportion of the size of the body whorl to the spire, some spires being very small, others raised; in possessing sloping or shouldered whorls; in the shape and size of the aperture; and in the absence or presence of microsculpture. All these characteristics intergrade perfectly. Nevertheless, they have led to a great deal of naming, most of it apparently superfluous. Judging by the shell alone, there is only a single, polymorphic species of *Physa* in eastern North America, *heterostropha* Say. There is some evidence to show that certain forms may have anatomical differences that might be used to separate them into different species, but this has not yet been satisfactorily demonstrated, and the shells of these animals, at any rate, do not differ sufficiently for the collector to recognize more than one species.

In one case, shells with a large body whorl and strongly shouldered were called *Physa ancillaria* Say (Lat. *ancillaris*, a servant), but this is now known to be a river form, which, because it relies more on its gills for breathing, has to develop a larger capacity to hold fresh water. In our opinion, the reader is safe in calling all the pond snails in our area *Physa heterostropha* Say and disregarding such names as *P. sayii* Tappan, *P. integra* Haldeman, *P. elliptica* Lea, *P. gyrina* Say and others, all of which were based largely on variable shell features.

The **Polished Tadpole Shell**, *Aplexa hypnorum* Linnaeus (Lat. *a plexus*, not braided; possibly from Hypnos, the Greek god of sleep) (pl. XXXVI, 21), reaches 15 mm. (3/5 in.) in height, 6 mm. (1/4 in.) in width. This close relative of *Physa* also has a sinistral shell, but it differs in being more slender and graceful, with a sharply conic, well-elevated spire. This is one of our most handsome freshwater pulmonates because of its brilliant polish, graceful outline, and bright yellow or deep bronze color. It can be strained from such ephemeral bodies of water as temporary swales or ponds, as well as from small streams, roadside ditches, and larger lakes and rivers.

Dr. Augustus A. Gould, the great American malacologist of the nineteenth century, wrote engagingly of the tadpole snails as follows:

It is quite interesting to keep a number of them in a vessel of water and to observe their motions and habits. The manner in which they open their mouths and display their lingual organ, the manner in which they rise to the surface and open the air cavity, into which its structure permits no water to enter, and above all, the beautiful and unaccountable manner in which it glides along, will never fail to excite astonishment.

CLASS:

# BIVALVIA (PELECYPODA; LAMELLIBRANCHIA)

SUBCLASS:

## PALAEOHETERODONTA

ORDER:

## UNIONOIDA (SCHIZODONTA)

# UNIONACEA

---

# UNIONIDAE

(*freshwater mussels*)

The freshwater mussels are known as "filter clams" or "button clams," but they are more commonly called "naiads" or "naiades" (Gr. *naias*, river nymph). Although they are worldwide in distribution, the richest development has taken place in North America, where the most numerous and beautiful species occur. Most of the spectacular species, however, are found only in the interior basin* of the United States and in the mountainous areas of the Southeast. The naiads in our area are sober-looking creatures, with little except the brilliant internal nacre of various colors to excite the ordinary collector. The wide distribution of the group is due partly to a peculiar characteristic of the reproductive process. The eggs do not hatch directly into young mussels, but into larval forms called "glochidia" (Gr. *glochis*, arrow, so called because of their shape). These must attach themselves to the skin, gills, or fins of fish where, as "blackheads," they undergo a period of parasitic existence. Here the internal anatomy is metamorphosed almost as much as insect anatomy in the pupa stage. The young naiad then drops to the bottom and develops to maturity. In the meantime, the tiny naiads have been removed far from their place of birth by the host fish.

The naiads are plastic organisms that respond readily to the environmental conditions present in the great variety of microhabitats available to them. Moreover, most mussels, when they have more or less achieved maturity, tend to remain in a single spot, some species being even unable to dig in again once they have been dislodged from the substrate. Hence the shells of a single species, exposed all their lives to the effects of a restricted ecological niche, can vary tremendously in shell characters from locality to locality. Shells of the same species living in hard bottoms are shorter and rounder

---

* The interior basin referred to here, and elsewhere in the remarks on distribution, comprises the area drained by the Mississippi and Ohio rivers. It is separated from the coastal plain by the Appalachian Mountains.

than those found in mud or soft sand. Lake dwellers tend to have different outlines from river dwellers, and those found in small streams are less swollen than river shells, and so on. Earlier malacologists were not aware of the significance of these differences, and named, unnecessarily, many different forms of a single species. The result is that the naiads are probably the most overnamed group of mollusks. One European mussel, *Anodonta cygneus,* has received more than five hundred names, and some others have been given more than one hundred. Nowhere has this caused more confusion than in the United States, where more species occur than in any other region in the world. Even today, American naiadologists are painfully working their way out of this morass of Latin and Greek neologisms.

The variability of shell morphology frequently makes identification of some species a difficult task. The descriptions given below cannot apply to all variants comprising a species. Rather, they define typical examples of a species in which some individuals may vary significantly. Fortunately, certain shell features are more useful diagnostic characters than others: the periostracum, for example, the umbonal sculpture (which, however, is usually destroyed in mature shells), and especially the hinge teeth.

For many years the valves of naiads were utilized extensively in the manufacture of pearl buttons. With the advent of plastics, however, synthetic materials have largely replaced shells as a source for buttons. At the present time great quantities of American naiad shells are exported to Japan for use in the cultured pearl industry. Tiny beads are cut from the shells to be used as the base, or seed, on which nacreous layers are formed by the soft parts of marine pearl oysters, which may produce commercially valuable pearls in two to five years.

The hinge teeth of all bivalves, marine as well as freshwater, comprise two basic kinds. The short teeth immediately under the beak, or umbo, of the shell are termed the "cardinal teeth," and the long, ridgelike teeth to the side or sides of the cardinal teeth are called "lateral teeth." In the naiads, however, they are called "pseudocardinals" and "pseudolaterals," respectively, because zoologists believe that in an evolutionary sense they have had a different origin than those of the other bivalves. Nevertheless, for the sake of brevity, we have used the shorter terms, cardinals and laterals, for the naiads.

# KEY TO FAMILIES
# UNIONIDAE AND MARGARITIFERIDAE

* Shell without or with much reduced hinge teeth
** Umbones barely raised, hinge margin almost straight
*** Upper and lower margins almost parallel, rays broad   *Anodonta imbecilis*
*** Lower margin convex, rays narrow   *A. couperiana*
** Umbones raised, hinge margin convex
*** Hinge plate relatively heavy   *Strophitus undulatus*
*** Hinge plate very narrow, linelike
**** Shell thin, often with bands or rays, nacre bluish white   *Anodonta cataracta*
**** Shell thicker, especially at lower anterior end, bandless and rayless, nacre generally copper or salmon colored   *A. implicata*
* Shell with well-developed hinge teeth
** Shell with cardinal teeth only, laterals absent or vestigial
*** Shell arched in maturity, always unrayed   *Margaritifera margaritifera*
*** Shell not arched, usually with rays   *Alasmidonta undulata*
** Shell with both cardinal and lateral teeth
*** Sexual dimorphism practically absent
**** Shell usually heavier to very heavy   *Elliptio crassidens*
**** Shell thinner
***** Length less than twice the height
****** Shell compressed, rhomboid, periostracum rough, dull; distribution also northern   *E. complanata*
****** Shell inflated, elongate, pointed, periostracum not dull; southern distribution
******* Shell 80 to 100 mm. (3 1/5 to 4 in.) in length, yellow or chestnut, rather thin   *E. icterina*
******* Shell reaching only 70 mm. (2 4/5 in.), dark brown, rather thick; range Florida only   *E. buckleyi*

\* \* \* \* \* Length more than twice the height      *E. lanceolata*

\* \* \* \* \* Length more than three times the
height      *E. shepardiana*

   \* \* \* Sexual dimorphism usually well
marked

  \* \* \* \* Shell reaching no more than 40 mm.
(1 3/5 in.) in length

\* \* \* \* \* Shell with 2 laterals in right valve,
1 lateral in left valve      *Alasmidonta heterodon*

\* \* \* \* \* Shell with 2 laterals in left valve,
1 lateral in right valve

\* \* \* \* \* \* Growth lines heavy, periostracum
satiny      *Toxolasma pullum*

\* \* \* \* \* \* Growth lines fine, periostracum shiny    *T. parvum*

  \* \* \* \* Shell reaching 60 to 100 mm. (2 2/5
to 4 in.) in length

\* \* \* \* \* Shell opaque, periostracum dull, rays
wanting      *Lampsilis ochracea*

\* \* \* \* \* Shell translucent, strongly rayed

\* \* \* \* \* \* Periostracum rough over entire
surface      *Villosa villosa*

\* \* \* \* \* \* Periostracum smooth, roughened on
posterior slope only      *V. vibex*

  \* \* \* \* Shell reaching 112 to 160 mm. (4 1/2
to 6 2/5 in.) in length

\* \* \* \* \* Length more than twice the height      *Ligumia nasuta*

\* \* \* \* \* Length less than twice the height

\* \* \* \* \* \* Sexual dimorphism not prominent,
periostracum yellow, not shiny, wide
rays over entire surface      *Lampsilis radiata*

\* \* \* \* \* \* Sexual dimorphism pronounced,
periostracum shiny, bright wax or
yellow

\* \* \* \* \* \* \* Shell very inflated, rays over entire
surface; interior basin species found
on coastal plain only in Potomac
River system      *L. ovata*

\* \* \* \* \* \* \* Shell less inflated, without rays or
rays confined to posterior slope      *L. cariosa*

Genus *Anodonta* Lamarck

*Anodonta cataracta* Lamarck
  Fragile Freshwater Mussel

  Pl. III, 3a & b

ETYMOLOGY: Gr. *an odontos*, without teeth; *kataraktos*, cataract.

SIZE: Up to 165 mm. (6 1/2 in.) in length, 86 mm. (3 1/2 in.) high.

DISTRIBUTION: Canada and Maine to Georgia and westward to Michigan.

CHARACTERISTICS: Shell large, elongate, inflated, thin, smooth, shiny. Straw
  yellow or lighter or darker green, occasionally with bands and rays.
  Hinge teeth lacking; hinge plate very narrow, linelike. Nacre bluish
  white, iridescent.


This is a common species in rivers, creeks, ponds, and lakes, where
it lives in soft mud and sand. It is quite fragile, and has a tendency,
when placed on display in a cabinet, to crack and come apart. The
species is most easily recognized by its inflated, fragile shell and
complete lack of hinge teeth. The genera *Anodonta* and *Strophitus*
of the family Unionidae belong in the subfamily Anodontinae, in
which both male and female shells are alike.

The **Confused River Mussel,** *Anodonta implicata* Say (Lat. *impli-
catus*, perplexed, confused) (pl. XXXV, 18), is similar enough to cause
confusion. It is somewhat smaller, 123 mm. (about 5 in.) long, 69
mm. (about 2 4/5 in.) high, and the color is darker, either yellowish
or brownish, and rays are always absent. The nacre is generally pale
copper or salmon color, instead of being bluish white. And finally
there is a pronounced thickening of the shell at the lower anterior
(rounded) end, a feature most prominent in mature shells. This species ranges from the Potomac River northward to Canada. It is
especially abundant in the region of Cape Cod, Massachusetts,
where it reaches its biggest size.

The **Feeble Freshwater Mussel,** *Anodonta imbecilis* Say. (Lat. *im-
becillus*, weak, feeble) (pl. I, 5a & b), attains 90 mm. (3 3/5 in.) in
length, 42 mm. (1 3/5 in.) in height, and is readily distinguished from
other *Anodonta* by its beaks, or umbones, which are entirely unele-
vated, the upper margin forming almost a straight line. The base is
also rather straight, and is nearly parallel to the upper, or hinge,
margin. The shell is quite fragile, and the periostracum is green and
shiny. This species has a wide distribution in the interior basin beyond the Appalachians to the Gulf of Mexico, and on the coast it extends from Maryland to Florida. It is a common species in the Erie
Canal.

**Couper's Freshwater Mussel,** *Anodonta couperiana* Lea (pl. III, 2a & b), is up to 110 mm. (4 2/5 in.) long and 67 mm. (about 2 3/5 in.) high, and differs from *A. imbecilis* by having green rays and a curved lower, or ventral, margin. It ranges from Georgia to Florida, and is especially abundant in central Florida.

The **Wavy Freshwater Mussel,** *Strophitus undulatus* Say (Lat. *strophium,* twisted cord; *undulatus,* wavy) (pl. XXXIV, 11), reaches 90 mm. (3 1/2 in.) in length, 55 mm. (2 1/2 in.) in height. It, too, is a hingeless mussel, but it differs from *Anodonta* in being less inflated, somewhat stronger, and in having a much thicker hinge plate, which even occasionally shows little stumps of vestigial hinge teeth. In color it is brownish yellow to black, rarely with narrow rays. It ranges from the Saint Lawrence River to South Carolina and the interior basin. It has also been called *S. rugosus* Swainson and *S. edentulus* Say.

Genus *Lampsilis* Rafinesque

*Lampsilis radiata* Gmelin
   Rayed Lamp Mussel

   Pl. III, 5a & b

ETYMOLOGY: Probably Gr. *lampas,* torch; Lat. *radiatus,* emit rays.

SIZE: Reaches 138 mm. (5 1/2 in.) in length, 86 mm. (3 1/3 in.) in height.

DISTRIBUTION: Saint Lawrence River system to North Carolina and
   westward to the Great Lakes.

CHARACTERISTICS: Shell medium to large, somewhat inflated. Generally
   yellowish or brownish green, with dark greenish or blackish rays.
   Periostracum somewhat roughened, not shiny. Lateral teeth well
   developed, cardinals weak.

This is one of the commoner species of *Lampsilis* in our area. The genus *Lampsilis,* together with the genera *Toxolasma, Alasmidonta, Ligumia,* and *Villosa,* discussed below, belong in the subfamily Lampsilinae, in which the female shell differs markedly from the male shell, a condition known as "secondary sexual dimorphism." The present species, however, is an exception, for the shells of both sexes are almost alike.

The **Ocher Lamp Mussel,** *Lampsilis ochracea* Say (Gr. *ochros,* pale yellow) (pl. I, 6a & b), is smaller, reaching only 73 mm. (about 3 in.) in length, and 44 mm. (1 3/4 in.) in height. The shell is thinner, and the hinge teeth are delicate. The periostracum is brownish and dull, and narrow, usually obscure rays cover the entire surface. The female differs by being distinctly higher and less rounded at the posterior end, that is, the end farther from the umbones. Along the coastal plain, this species ranges from Nova Scotia to Georgia.

The **Caried Lamp Mussel,** *Lampsilis cariosa* Say (Lat. *cariosus,* full of caries, rotten) (pl. XXXIV, 12), reaches 130 mm. (5 1/4 in.) in length, 85 mm. (3 1/2 in.) in height. It can be recognized by the bright wax or shiny, straw yellow periostracum and the usual absence of rays; if any are present, they are confined to the shorter or posterior portion. The species ranges from Nova Scotia to Georgia. The female shell differs strongly from the male by being more inflated and having the posterior portion much higher and the rear margin less rounded, almost straight.

The **Ovate Lamp Mussel,** *Lampsilis ovata* Say (pl. III, 4a & b), is a species of the interior basin that was introduced sometime in the 1890s to the Potomac River drainage, the only area where it can be found on the coastal plain. It resembles *L. cariosa,* but it differs in being larger, reaching 160 mm. (almost 6 1/2 in.) in length and 108 mm. (about 4 1/2 in.) in height. It is more inflated and has a prominent posterior ridge, which in the former species is almost nonexistent. Moreover, *L. ovata* is generally rayed over the entire surface.

The **Dusky Caruncle Mussel,** *Toxolasma pullum* Conrad (Gr. *toxon,* bow—formerly genus *Carunculina,* Lat. *caruncula,* piece of flesh; *pullus,* dusky) (pl. XXXVI, 22), is only 32 mm. (1 1/4 in.) in length and 19 mm. (3/4 in.) in height. This species can be recognized by its small size; dark brownish, olive, or blackish color; frequently satiny finish; and heavy concentric growth lines. The female shell is proportionately higher and less rounded, sometimes truncate behind. The former generic name refers to a fleshy projection (a real "caruncle") on the mantle edge whose function seems to be to lure fish in the neighborhood and impregnate them with ejected glochidia. This is a common species along the muddy margins of lakes. It ranges only from North Carolina to Georgia.

The **Lesser Caruncle Mussel,** *Toxolasma parvum* Barnes (Lat. *parvus,* small, little) (pl. XXXVI, 23), is a species more characteristic of the interior basin, but it reaches our area in western Florida and Georgia and in central New York. It differs from *C. pullum* in lacking the heavy growth lines and in having a smoother periostracum. In addition, the posterior ridge in *C. pullum* is higher, and there is a second less prominent ridge above it. In *C. parvum* the posterior ridge is poorly defined. It reaches 40 mm. (about 1 3/5 in.) in length and 23 mm. (1 in.) in height. *Toxolasma paula* Lea is a synonym.

The **Inverted Mussel,** *Alasmidonta heterodon* Lea (possibly Gr. *allos,* stranger; *hetero odont,* other tooth) (pl. XXXVI, 24), reaches 52 mm. (2 1/8 in.) in length and 26 mm. (1 in.) in height. The shells of this species are best recognized by their relatively small size, and especially by the fact that the right valve has two lateral teeth and the left valve only one, the opposite of the conditions in all other associated naiads. The color is olive brown to blackish brown, occasionally with rays. The female shell is rhomboid, swollen, and truncate behind; the male shell is oval. This species is rather rare, and its distribution from New Brunswick, Canada, to North Carolina is erratic and discontinuous. It seems to have died out in many polluted streams in the Northeast, but it is widely distributed in the Connecticut River system.

Although the **Undulate Mussel,** *Alasmidonta undulata* Say (Lat. *undulatus,* wavy, undulate) (pl. I, 8a & b), is in the same genus as *A. heterodon,* the shell is quite different. (As a matter of fact, the two species are placed in different subgenera, the former in the subgenus *Alasmidonta* and the latter in the subgenus *Prolasmidonta.*) It is usually larger, reaching 80 mm. (about 3 1/2 in.) in length, and the dentition is quite distinct. The cardinal teeth are stumpy, and there is a barely visible lateral tooth in the left valve and none at all on the right valve. In this way it differs from other naiads. The "undulate" part of the shell consists of wavy ridges that extend some distance on the ridge. The periostracum is greenish or reddish or yellowish brown, with rays over the entire surface. It ranges from the Saint Lawrence to North Carolina. It is a common species in the northern Atlantic slope, and is often locally abundant. Other *Alasmidonta* species with restricted ranges are treated by Johnson (1971). These are *A. triangulata* Lea, *A. arcula* Lea, and *A. varicosa* Lamarck.

The **Nose Mussel,** *Ligumia nasuta* Say (*ligumia* appears to be an invented word without meaning; Lat. *nasutus,* large-nosed) (pl. III, 1a, b, c), reaches 112 mm. (4 1/2 in.) in length and 44 mm. (1 3/4 in.) in height. These shells are most easily recognized by the shiny periostracum, the heavy, elongate shell with pointed, lancelike posterior, and the small cardinal teeth. The color is greenish yellow, olive, or brownish, often with narrow rays. The nacre is bluish white or salmon. The lower margin of the male shell tapers uniformly to a posterior point, but the female shell has an extra rounded projection below. The species differs from the other lancelike naiad, *Elliptio lanceolata* (see page 327), by its weaker hinge teeth, rayed periostracum, and sexual dimorphism. Moreover, its distribution, from the Saint Lawrence River, Canada, to the James River, Virginia, is more northern than *E. lanceolata.*

The **Bruised Mussel,** *Villosa vibex* Conrad (Lat. *villosus,* shaggy; *vibex,* bruise) (pl. I, 7a & b), reaches 100 mm. (4 in.) in length and 47 mm. (2 in.) in height. This species is mainly characterized by its thin, translucent shell with rather broad rays. The shell is elliptical, inflated; the smooth periostracum has a roughened posterior slope. The color is light reddish brown to almost black, with numerous broad rays. The hinge plate is very narrow and the hinge teeth delicate. The female shell is broadly rounded posteriorly, and the male shell has a bluntly truncate posterior. It ranges from North Carolina to Florida and westward to Mississippi. The generic name formerly was *Micromya,* but that name had been given earlier to a genus of insects.

The **Shaggy Mussel,** *Villosa villosa* Wright (Lat. *villosus,* shaggy, hairy) (pl. I, 4a & b), is smaller, reaching only 65 mm. (2 1/2 in.) in length. It differs from the Bruised Mussel by possessing a peculiar type of roughened periostracum which gives a satiny luster to the entire surface. The rays can be seen only by transmitted light. It is rarer than *V. vibex,* and ranges only from Florida to southern Georgia. In addition to these species of *Villosa,* Johnson (1971) also discusses *V. delumbis* Conrad and *V. constricta* Conrad.

Genus *Elliptio* Rafinesque

*Elliptio complanata* Lightfoot
 Flattened Filter Clam

 Pl. III, 6a & b

ETYMOLOGY: Probably Gr. *elleiptikos,* elliptical; Lat. *complanatus,* flattened.

SIZE: 115 mm. (4 3/5 in.) in length, 50 mm. (2 in.) in height.

DISTRIBUTION: Atlantic coastal plain, from the Gulf of Saint Lawrence to Georgia.

CHARACTERISTICS: Shell medium to large, almost elliptical or rhomboid, rather thick, compressed; periostracum rough. Yellowish brown to black, sometimes with green rays. Hinge teeth strong, well developed.

This is a bewilderingly variable shell that has been given more than one hundred names. Nevertheless, it is not hard to recognize. Its compressed, not inflated shape, the more or less rhomboid or elliptical outline, the rough, dark periostracum, and the well-developed hinge teeth serve to identify it. It is the most widely distributed and abundant freshwater mussel in the Atlantic slope region. Frequently, in many areas it is the only species found. It lives in lakes, ponds, rivers, and small streams, in all sorts of substrates. Fish hobbyists place it in their tanks to filter organic impurities from the water. The warmer water species of *Elliptio,* especially those from the lakes and ponds of Florida, however, adjust better to life in tropical fish aquaria. The genus *Elliptio* is in the subfamily Pleurobeminae, in which male and female shells are practically identical.

The **Heavy-toothed Filter Clam,** *Elliptio crassidens* Lamarck (Lat. *crassus dens,* solid tooth) (pl. XXXV, 19), differs mainly in that its shell is much thicker and heavier. Also, the outline is less elliptical, tending to be somewhat circular. The species is common in the Ohio-Mississippi and Alabama-Coosa River drainages, but in our area is confined to southern Georgia and Florida.

The **Jaundiced Filter Clam,** *Elliptio icterina* Conrad (Lat. *icter-icus,* jaundiced) (pl. I, 2a & b), is smaller than *E. complanata,* reaching only 80 to 100 mm. (3 1/5 to 4 in.) in length, somewhat thinner, more inflated, and elongate in outline, with the posterior margin ending in a point. The periostracum is smooth and shiny, and bright yellow or chestnut specimens are occasionally seen. The species is quite variable, and has received about fifty different names. It ranges from North Carolina to Florida and is very abundant, sometimes being the only naiad in its habitat. It was formerly called *Elliptio strigosa* Lea (Lat. *strigosus,* lank, lean).

The **Lance Filter Clam,** *Elliptio lanceolata* Lea (Lat. *lanceola,* little lance) (pl. XXXIV, 13), is most easily recognized by the fact that it is more than twice as long as it is high, 75 × 28 mm. (3 × 1 1/8 in.), and the dorsal and ventral margins are roughly parallel. It is found from Pennsylvania to western Florida.

**Shepard's Filter Clam,** *Elliptio shepardiana* Lea (pl. XXXIV, 14), is even longer and narrower than *E. lanceolata,* being more than 3 times as long as it is high, 127 × 29 mm. (about 5 × 1 1/5 in.). Its narrow, knifelike outline makes it unmistakable. Unfortunately, this striking shell is restricted to the Altamaha River drainage of Georgia, where it is not at all common.

**Buckley's Filter Clam,** *Elliptio buckleyi* Lea (pl. I, 1a & b), is a common species in the lakes, ponds, streams, and rivers of central and southern Florida. The shell is small, generally about 70 mm. (2 4/5 in.) in length, usually well inflated, strong, and with a brilliantly polished, brown periostracum, often weakly rayed in immature forms. The internal nacre is bluish or reddish, never white. As the animal ages, it loses the surface gloss and the shell turns darker and rougher.

There are several other species of filter clams (genus *Elliptio*) in the southern part of the Atlantic Slope, as follows: *E. dariensis* Lea, *E. fraterna* Lea, *E. waccamawensis* Lea, *E. hopetonensis* Lea, and *E. arctata* Conrad. They are not easily characterized, and they have a restricted distribution. The reader is referred to Johnson (1971).

FAMILY:

# MARGARITIFERIDAE

(*pearl mussels*)

The shells of this family are very like those of the Unionidae (see page 318). They are generally arched, or broadly arc shaped, especially along the lower, or ventral, margin, and the hinge teeth are poorly developed. There are two weak cardinal teeth in the left valve and one in the right. The laterals are short, weak, or may be lacking. It is largely major differences in gill structure that separate the pearl mussels, despite their uniolike shell, from the Unionidae.

Genus *Margaritifera* Schumacher

*Margaritifera margaritifera* Linnaeus
Pearl Mussel

Pl. XXXV, 20

ETYMOLOGY: Lat. *margarita fero*, pearl bearing.

SIZE: Up to 150 mm. (6 in.) in length, 65 mm. (2 3/5 in.) in height.

DISTRIBUTION: Circumboreal; in coastal North America from Labrador to Pennsylvania.

CHARACTERISTICS: Shell medium to large, elongate, not inflated, smooth, moderately thick; base arcuate in mature individuals. Color blackish. Hinge has two moderately strong cardinal teeth in the left valve, one in the right; lateral teeth entirely absent. Nacre whitish or suffused with pink or purple.

This species ranges from eastern North America, across northern Europe and Siberia to the Pacific coast. It is absent from the Rocky Mountains. It used to be fished extensively for the valuable pearls contained by some individuals. The shell is most easily recognized by the arcuate shape of mature individuals, the smooth, blackish periostracum, and the complete absence of lateral teeth. The animals mature slowly, and some are thought to reach an age of one hundred.

SUPERFAMILY:

# CORBICULACEA

FAMILY:

# SPHAERIIDAE (PISIDIIDAE)
(*fingernail clams*)

These shells are small to minute, and generally thin and translucent, but heavier, opaque forms also exist. The hinge area is narrow and the teeth are small and weak. The family is worldwide in distribution, and specimens abound in suitable locations.

## KEY TO GENERA SPHAERIUM AND PISIDIUM

* Shell with beak almost central or skewed toward anterior end, valves equilateral — genus *Sphaerium*
** Shell large, more than 13 mm. (about 1/2 in.) in length, strong, brown, glossy
*** Shell rhomboid in outline — *S. rhomboideum*
*** Shell oval in outline, ends rounded
**** Shell large, 20 mm. (4/5 in.) or more, striae strong, regular — *S. simile*
**** Shell smaller, about 13 mm. (about 1/2 in.) striae strong, irregular — *S. striatinum*
** Shell small, 10 mm. (2/5 in.) or less in length, fragile — *S. partumeium*
* Shell with beak skewed to posterior end, inequilateral — genus *Pisidium*

Genus *Sphaerium* Scopoli

*Sphaerium rhomboideum* Say
Rhomboid Fingernail Clam

Pl. XXXIV, 15

ETYMOLOGY: Gr. *sphairikos*, globular.

SIZE: 13 mm. (about 1/2 in.) in length, 10.5 mm. (about 1/2 in.) in height.

DISTRIBUTION: Canada and Maine to New York and westward to Montana.

CHARACTERISTICS: Shell moderately large, somewhat truncate at both ends, lending it a rhomboid appearance; inflated, thin, glossy. Color brown. Striae fine and regular.

This is a northern species that is easily recognized by the good-sized shell, the fine, regular striae, and especially the distinctly rhomboid shape. The young are even more strongly rhomboid than the mature forms. These clams live on muddy bottoms with weed and algae, where they can easily be recovered by a kitchen strainer tied to a stick.

The **Furrowed Fingernail Clam,** *Sphaerium simile* Say (Lat. *simile*, furrow) (pl. XXXV, 21), is larger, reaching 20 mm. (4/5 in.) in length. It can easily be recognized by its oval shape with rounded ends, and the strong, evenly spaced, regular striae, much stronger than in *S. rhomboideum*, with which it need never be confused, though both share much of the same range. *S. simile,* however, can be found further south, to Virginia.

The **Striated Fingernail Clam,** *Sphaerium striatinum* Lamarck (Lat. *striatus,* furrowed) (pl. XXXIV, 16), differs from *S. sulcatum* in being smaller, usually about 13 mm. (about 1/2 in.) in length, lighter in color, and in having much coarser and more irregular striae. The species lives in streams, ponds, and lakes with sandy bottoms. Reverend Herrington, a student of the Sphaeriidae, calls this the commonest species of the family in our area. It is found in much of Canada and most of the United States.

The **Pregnant Fingernail Clam,** *Sphaerium partumeium* Say (Lat. *parturio,* be pregnant) (pl. XXXIV, 17), is quite small, seldom exceeding 10 mm. (2/5 in.) in length. The shell is thin and fragile, often translucent or transparent, glossy, pale yellowish horn color, and with very fine striae. It ranges from Canada to Florida and westward to California. The southern specimens are somewhat thicker and larger. The name given by Temple Prime reflects the fact that this species, as well as many other fingernail clams, give birth to live young, retaining the unborn clams within their shell. Some writers thought these tiny, immature forms were a different species.

The fingernail clams, like most freshwater mollusks, are strongly affected by their environment and hence vary in shape, size, color, sculpture, etc. Many of these variations were given names by scholars unaware of the influence of ecological factors on morphology. Fortunately, Reverend Herrington's studies have brought much order out of this chaos. Nevertheless, the valid species are not always easy to distinguish and the interested reader is referred to Herrington's monograph (1962), which contains details of the rarer and more difficult species. Among these are the following: *Sphaerium fabale* Prime, *S. lacustre* Prime, *S. occidentale* Prime, *S. securis* Prime, and *S. transversum* Say.

Genus *Pisidium* Pfeiffer

*Pisidium dubium* Say
  Doubtful Fingernail Clam

  Pl. XXXIV, 18

ETYMOLOGY: Pisidia was the name of a country in Asia Minor in classical times; Lat. *dubius*, uncertain, doubtful.

SIZE: Up to 9 mm. (about 2/5 in.) in length, 8 mm. (1/3 in.) in height.

DISTRIBUTION: Canada and Maine to Florida and westward to Michigan.

CHARACTERISTICS: Shell very large for genus, oblique, inflated, inequilateral. Beak skewed toward posterior end. Walls thin, surface dark and shining, striae generally faint.

This is by far the largest species of the genus and can generally be recognized by this fact alone. Most of the other *Pisidium* are 2 to 4 mm. (1/12 to 1/6 in.) in length when mature. The fact that they are so small in size and that their shape is variable makes determination of species particularly difficult. This is done on the basis of the very small hinge teeth. Reverend Herrington's monograph (1962) and the identification manual of J. B. Burch (1972) are helpful. The genus itself is readily recognized by the small, askew shell and usually minute size. They live in all sorts of bodies of fresh water, in sand or mud. According to Reverend Herrington, the following additional species occur in our area: *Pisidium adamsi* Prime, *P. aequilaterale* Prime, *P. casertanum* Poli, *P. compressum* Prime, *P. fallax* Prime, *P. ferrugineum* Prime, *P. nitidum* Jenyns, *P. obtusale* Pfeiffer, and *P. variabile* Prime, but it is only the real devotee who will undertake to name up a collection.

# CHAPTER IV

# MARINE
# BIVALVES

The easiest way to collect clams and other kinds of bivalves is to pick up specimens washed up on the beaches. These are commonly found as single valves, one of a pair that formed the shell of the living bivalve. These disarticulated valves are transported shoreward by waves and currents, and are finally deposited in the beach drift. But in life the two valves are united, guided into place by an interlocking series of hinge teeth and pressed firmly together usually by two, less commonly by one, adductor muscle. Many species of bivalves burrow actively in the sand and mud of the sea bottom. These inhabitants are members of the infauna, for they live in the sandy or muddy surface layers. Some bivalves live upon or are associated with rocks, stones, corals, other shells, pilings, seaweed, and even on the roots of trees. These bivalves are representatives of the epifauna, for they live on, over, or in hard objects. Other epifaunal inhabitants attach to hard substrates by byssal threads, like blue mussels (family Mytilidae), or by cement, like the oysters (family Ostreidae). Scallops (family Pectinidae), which have evolved a rapid mode of locomotion, flit through the water by jet propulsion, and are "free-living" epifaunal constituents. Still others, also living infaunally, can burrow into wood, peat, coral, or rock, such as the shipworms (family Teredinidae) and the piddocks (family Pholadidae). For the casual collector, most forms, whether representatives of the infauna or epifauna, can usually be found, somewhat the worse for wear, it is true, washed up on the beaches. Any serious attempt at collecting live specimens requires sieves, tined pitchforks, chisel and hammer, and other gear.

The classification of the Bivalvia has been the subject of much dispute. Several widely differing systems have been proposed, each based upon different criteria, such as gill structure or hinge morphology, but these have not proved to be entirely reliable guides. In this book we have adopted, with some modifications, the system proposed in 1965 by Dr. Norman D. Newell of The American Museum of

Natural History, which is also used in the authoritative *Treatise on Invertebrate Paleontology*. This classification, which places much emphasis upon extinct fossil forms, is based largely upon shell characteristics, especially the nature of the hinge teeth.

As we examine the hinge teeth of bivalves we notice that they fall into several groups. One group has numerous more or less equally sized hinge teeth arranged in a row like a comb; this arrangement is called "taxodont" (Gr. *taxis*, arrangement, and *odous, odont*, tooth). But not all shells with taxodont teeth are thought to belong to a single group. They are placed into smaller groups, called "subclasses." In the subclass Palaeotaxodonta (ancient taxodonta) are those shells which have the row of teeth bent into an angle at or near the center; at the apex of the angle is a deep to shallow chondrophore pit. In this group are found the families Nuculidae and Nuculanidae of the order Nuculoida. The ark shells (family Arcidae), on the other hand, have the row of teeth in an unbroken straight or slightly curved line. The ark shells are placed in the order Arcoida of the subclass Pteriomorphia (Gr. *pteron morphe*, wing form).

In the subclass Pteriomorphia are also placed groups that retain only a vestige of their former taxodont dentition. These are sea mussels (superfamily Mytilacea), pearl oysters (superfamily Pteriacea), scallops (superfamily Pectinacea), and oysters (superfamily Ostreacea).

The subclass Cryptodonta (hidden teeth) consists of a small number of related bivalves that have lost all indications of their taxodont dentition. Among others, the awning clams (superfamily Solemyacea), are included here.

The largest group of Bivalvia are the ones that have a more or less full set of hinge teeth consisting of two radically different kinds of short, strong teeth directly under the umbo, or beak, called "cardinal teeth," and the long, lamellalike teeth located to one or both sides of the cardinal teeth called "lateral teeth." Groups that have this sort of tooth arrangement, often much modified, are in the subclass Heterodonta (other or differing teeth). In this huge subclass, which is broken down into several orders, are placed more species and genera than in all the other bivalve subclasses combined. In the order Veneroida of the subclass Heterodonta are found such interesting and beautiful bivalves as the lucina clams (superfamily Lucinacea), the chamas (superfamily Chamacea), the heart clams (superfamily Cardiacea), the trough shells (superfamily Mactracea), the razor or jackknife clams (superfamily Solenacea), the tellins (superfamily Tellinacea), and the most beautiful of all, the Venus clams (superfamily Veneracea). In addition, there are several other smaller and less interesting groups.

In the suborder Myina of the order Myoida, subclass Heterodonta, are found the soft clams (superfamily Myacea), the gapers (superfamily Gastrochaenacea), and the Arctic clams (superfamily Hiatellacea). In the suborder Pholadina of the order Myoida we find the piddocks (superfamily Pholadacea) and the shipworms (superfamily Pholadacea). It must be admitted that the hinge teeth arrangement of the last-named orders and suborders are so highly modified that it is hard to recognize them as belonging to the Heterodonta.

The peculiarly flattened pandora shells (superfamily Pandoracea) are in the bivalve subclass Anomalodesmata (Gr. *anomalos*, uneven, irregular, and *desmos*, band or ligament), which also includes many extinct groups and rare, deep-water representatives.

In the course of our discussion of the bivalves, we will frequently refer to the left and right valves of the clam and the anterior (front) or posterior (back) of the valves. Since it is difficult to distinguish the front end of a clam from the back end, we offer the following instructions as guides.

The mollusk should be held so that the umbones point upward and the edges of the valves face the observer. If now the shell is turned so that the ligament located near the beaks faces the observer, then the part toward the observer is the posterior, the part away from him the anterior part of the shell. The ligament is a strong, brown, cartilaginous bit of matter whose function it is to act as a spring and separate the valves, thus serving as the counterbalance to the adductor muscles, which operate to keep the valves closed. The ligament is usually external, and can easily be seen as a brownish body of varying size. In some bivalve groups, however, it is internal, lying in a narrow pit inside the valve, near the umbo.

If only one valve, deprived of the ligament, is available, the following indications may be used to determine the anterior and posterior sides. Inside the valve, a faintly impressed line will be seen running more or less concentrically with the basal margin and some distance from it. This impression is called the "pallial line" (Lat. *pallium*, mantle). It marks the point at which in life the mantle, the delicate membrane surrounding the viscera of the mollusk, was attached. In most clam shells this pallial line bears a more or less deep indentation at one end. This indentation, termed the "pallial sinus" (Lat. *sinus*, bay) invariably marks the posterior portion of the valve. It represents the line of attachment of the siphons, which in life provide the organism with food and oxygen and serve to expel body wastes. Thus, in summary, both the pallial sinus and the ligament normally mark the posterior of the valves. Once the anterior and posterior portions are determined, it is a simple matter to distinguish the left valve from the right.

In contrast to the members of the other six classes of living mollusks, the bivalves lack the dental apparatus called a "radula." Instead of rasping their food, bivalves, which do not have a head, trap tiny particles of organic matter, especially plants or algae, in strands of mucus, or filter planktonic microorganisms through their gills.

## KEY TO THE BIVALVE GENERA WITH COMB-TEETH (TAXODONT, PRIONODESMATIC) DENTAL SERIES

* Dental series continuous, not broken by chondrophore
** Hinge plate long, generally straight or very slightly arched, shell trapezoidal or ovate, frequently strongly sculptured radially
*** Shell with ventral byssal gape
**** Posterior end winged, shell moderately strong      *Arca*
**** Posterior end rounded, shell thin      *Barbatia*
*** Shell without byssal gape      *Arcopsis, Anadara, Noetia*
** Hinge plate short, strongly arched, shell circular, usually lightly sculptured      *Glycymeris*
* Dental series broken in two by a subcentrally located chondrophore
** Shell short, small, not glossy      *Nucula*
** Shell elongate, larger, periostracum glossy
*** Shell relatively strong, ligament lodged in an elongated dorsal pit, sculpture generally concentric, strong      *Nuculana*
*** Shell very fragile, ligament not in dorsal pit, no concentric sculpture      *Yoldia*

CLASS:
# BIVALVIA

---

SUBCLASS:
## PALAEOTAXODONTA
*(with comblike teeth)*

ORDER:
## NUCULOIDA

---

# KEY TO FAMILIES
## NUCULIDAE AND NUCULANIDAE

* Shell triangular, length and height about equal, strong, small, less than 7 mm. (about 1/4 in.) — *Nucula proxima*
* Shell elongate, longer than high, usually delicate, large, 10 to 60 mm. (2/5 to 2 2/5 in.)
** Shell moderately strong, 10 to 20 mm. (2/5 to 4/5 in.) in length, chondrophore pit narrow, surface marked by concentric lines or ridges
*** Concentric markings covering entire surface, strong — *Nuculana acuta*
*** Concentric markings on ventral portion of shell only, weak — *N. concentrica*
** Shell quite delicate, 25 to 60 mm. (1 to 2 2/5 in.) in length, glossy, smooth, chondrophore broadly triangular
*** Posterior extension long, color vivid green, basal margin evenly rounded — *Yoldia limatula*
*** Posterior extension short, color pale green, basal margin abruptly turned upward near posterior end — *Y. sapotilla*

---

SUPERFAMILY:

# NUCULACEA

---

FAMILY:

# NUCULIDAE
(*nut clams*)

These shells are small, obliquely triangular, smooth but not shiny. The periostracum is dull olive and the interior is pearly. The margins are finely toothed, and the hinge teeth are numerous. Found in all seas in deep to shallow water, but mostly in cooler regions.

Genus *Nucula* Lamarck

*Nucula proxima* Say
Common Nut Clam
Pl. XXXVII, 1

ETYMOLOGY: Diminutive of Lat. *nux*, nut; *proximus*, allied to.

SIZE: 6.5 mm. (about 1/4 in.) in length, 6.5 mm. (about 1/4 in.) in height.

DISTRIBUTION: Nova Scotia to Texas.

CHARACTERISTICS: Shell quite small, thick, solid, obliquely triangular, smooth but not lustrous. Periostracum light olive, interior pearly. Ventral margin finely crenulated. Hinge teeth numerous, chevron shaped, separated subcentrally by a chondrophore pit.

This is the species of nut clam most often found in our area, especially to the north. The oblique shape, the pearly interior, and the characteristic small, chevron-shaped teeth serve to identify it readily. The species lives in shallow water, where it is readily dredged, but dead valves, usually singly, are not uncommon on bay beaches. Other species of *Nucula* live in deeper water, and can be procured only by dredging or in the stomachs of bottom-feeding fish. Among such species are *N. delphinodonta* Mighels (dolphin toothed), which is only 3 mm. (1/8 in.) in length and has fewer hinge teeth and an uncrenulated lower margin; and *N. tenuis* Montagu (delicate, fine), like *N. proxima* but more delicate, the interior white but not pearly and rounded rather than triangular.

SUPERFAMILY:

# NUCULANACEA

FAMILY:

# NUCULANIDAE
(*elongate nut clams*)

These shells are elongate, rather fragile, and the posterior end is extended. The periostracum is gleaming, greenish or yellow. Hinge teeth are numerous with a subcentrally placed chondrophoral pit; the margin is smooth. This widely distributed family used to be grouped with the Nuculidae.

Genus *Nuculana* Link

*Nuculana acuta* Conrad
   Pointed Nut Clam

   Pl. XXXVII, 2

ETYMOLOGY: Diminutive of Lat. *nucula*, little nut; *acutus*, pointed.

SIZE: 10 mm. (2/5 in.) in length, 5 mm. (1/5 in.) in height.

DISTRIBUTION: Cape Cod to the West Indies.

CHARACTERISTICS: Shell small, elongate, moderately strong; posterior edge
   with a sharp, elongated point. Hinge teeth small, numerous on both
   sides of chondrophore. Color white under a thin yellowish periostracum.
   Surface sculptured with numerous rather strong, concentric grooves.
   Ligament at bottom of long umbonal trench.

This small elongate nut clam lives burrowing in mud just below the
low-tide line, but single valves are not uncommonly found on the
beach, especially in the north. It is readily recognized by the elongate shape and the strongly grooved surface.

The **Concentric Nut Clam,** *Nuculana concentrica* Say (pl. XLIV,
1), is similar, but reaches 18 mm. (3/4 in.) in length. It is easily
differentiated from *N. acuta* because the surface near the umbones
and just below is smooth, and the concentric grooves on the rest of
the shell are much finer. The pale yellowish shell is semiglossy. This
species ranges from northwest Florida to Texas, and though living
below the low-tide line, individual valves are not uncommonly
found in beach drift in certain areas.

The **File Nut Clam,** *Yoldia limatula* Say (named for Alfonse
d'Aguirre y Gadea, Count of Yoldi of Denmark, a famous collector;
Lat. *limatus*, filed down) (pl. XXXVII, 3), is 25 to 60 mm. (1 to 2 2/5
in.) in length, 25 mm. (1 in.) in height. The medium-sized thin,
elongate, fragile shell, with its varnished light green periostracum
and posterior end drawn out to an obtuse point, is a fairly common
species living near the shores of bays and inlets, on mud bottoms.
The interior is bluish white, and the hinge teeth are arranged on
both sides of a broadly triangular cartilage pit, which is larger than
the narrow pit found in the shells of the genus *Nuculana*. The range
is from Canada to Cape May, New Jersey, and the species also occurs
in northern Alaska.

The **Short Nut Clam,** *Yoldia sapotilla* Gould (Span. *sapotilla*, a
plumlike fruit whose seed resembles this bivalve) (pl. XXXVII, 4), is
smaller, reaching only 35 mm. (1 2/5 in.) in length, and paler in

color. The posterior extension or rostrum is much shorter, and the basal margin turns abruptly upward as it nears the posterior extension, whereas in Y. *limatula* the margin is evenly rounded. This species ranges from the Arctic seas to North Carolina, but it is quite rare, being found occasionally on beaches after a hard blow. It has also been discovered in fish stomachs.

SUBCLASS:

# CRYPTODONTA

*(hidden teeth)*

ORDER:

# SOLEMYOIDA

SUPERFAMILY:

## SOLEMYACEA

FAMILY:

## SOLEMYIDAE

*(awning clams)*

The shells in this family are oblong, with ends rounded, somewhat swollen; the periostracum is strong, extending in awninglike fringes beyond the margin of the shell. They live, in burrows, in shallow water with muddy bottoms.

# KEY TO GENUS SOLEMYA

* Shell large, reaching 75 mm. (3 in.), heavy, interior
  grayish blue; range Nova Scotia to Connecticut        *Solemya borealis*
* Shell smaller, fragile, interior purplish white
** Shell 15 to 25 mm. (3/5 to 1 in.) in length, cartilage
  pit bordered by two ridges; range Nova Scotia to
  Florida                                                *S. velum*
** Shell 6 mm. (1/4 in.) in length, cartilage pit bordered
  by a single ridge; range west coast of Florida to
  West Indies                                            *S. occidentalis*

---

Genus *Solemya* Lamarck

*Solemya velum* Say
  Common Awning Clam

  Pl. XXXVII, 5

ETYMOLOGY: Lat. *solen mya*, tube or sheath sea-mussel; *velum*, veil.

SIZE: 15 to 25 mm. (3/5 to 1 in.) in length, 10 mm. (2/5 in.) in height.

DISTRIBUTION: Nova Scotia to Florida.

CHARACTERISTICS: Shell small, very fragile, oblong. Periostracum polished,
  light brown, split by lines radiating from umbo, projects awninglike
  beyond shell margin. Interior purplish white, hinge teeth obsolete.

These small bivalves with very primitive anatomy are unmistakable,
resembling no other bivalve species. They live in bays on mud bottoms, but can also flit through the water like scallop shells. Fragments are sometimes found on shore.

The **Northern Awning Clam,** *Solemya borealis* Totten (Lat. *boreas,*
north wind) (not illus.), is larger, reaching 75 mm. (3 in.) in length.
It is more compressed, heavier, and grayish blue instead of purplish
white internally, and the upper margin is straighter. This species is
moderately common offshore, and has been taken on several beaches
in Massachusetts. It ranges from Nova Scotia to Connecticut.

The **West Indian Awning Clam,** *Solemya occidentalis* Deshayes
(Lat. *occidens,* the west) (not illus.), is very much smaller, reaching only 6 mm. (1/4 in.) in length. It also differs from *S. velum* in
having only a single ridge bordering the cartilage pit, whereas the
former has two. This is a southern species, ranging from the west
coast of Florida to the West Indies.

SUBCLASS:

# PTERIOMORPHIA

*(winged-shaped)*

ORDER:

# ARCOIDA

*(serrate teeth)*

SUPERFAMILY:

## ARCACEA

FAMILY:

## ARCIDAE

*(ark shells)*

SUBFAMILY:

## ARCINAE

*(ark shells with byssal gape)*

These shells are small to quite large, commonly with rather strong sculpture, radially ridged or latticelike. The hinge teeth are typically taxodont (teeth small, numerous, arranged in an unbroken line). Because of the comb or sawlike teeth, the Arcidae, Nuculidae, and Nuculanidae were at one time referred to as "prionodesmaceans" (Gr. *prion desmos,* saw ligament) and were placed in the order Prionodesmacea. The Arcidae are worldwide in distribution, living in shallow to moderately deep water.

Genus *Arca* Linnaeus

*Arca zebra* Swainson
 Turkey Wing

 Pl. XXXVII, 6

ETYMOLOGY: Lat. *arca,* chest, box; *zebra,* from the Amharic.

SIZE: 90 mm. (3 3/5 in.) in length, 40 mm. (1 3/5 in.) in height.

DISTRIBUTION: North Carolina to Texas and the Lesser Antilles.

CHARACTERISTICS: Shell medium to large, strong, rough, with large byssal opening below; posterior margin winged. Color tan, with reddish brown, zebralike markings. Sculpture of low radiating ribs. Hinge with numerous subequal teeth, weakest centrally. Periostracum brown, matted.

This species lives fixed by a strong byssus on rocks, shells, or mangrove roots. It is readily recognized by its color, with the zebralike markings. Dead valves are common on many beaches. It was formerly called *Arca occidentalis* Philippi, a name proposed later.

The **Mossy Ark,** *Arca imbricata* Bruguière (Lat. *imbricatus,* covered with tiles) (pl. XXXVII, 7), is smaller, 50 × 20 mm. (2 × 4/5 in.), and resembles the Turkey Wing in shape. It differs in its much finer surface sculpture, which consists of fine, beaded radiating ribs, and in its lack of zebralike markings. Its color is dull brown. It lives from North Carolina to Texas and the West Indies, and was formerly called *Arca umbonata* Lamarck, a later name.

# KEY TO GENERA BARBATIA AND ARCOPSIS

* Shell small, reaching 10 mm. in length      *Arcopsis adamsi*
* Shell larger, 25 mm. or more
** Shell reddish brown in color      *Barbatia cancellaria*
** Shell generally white, under yellowish or brown periostracum

| | |
|---|---|
| * * * Shell very swollen, thin, ribs fine | *B. tenera* |
| * * * Shell flattened, sculpture strong | |
| * * * * Ribs well beaded, shell large, up to 60 mm. (2 2/5 in.) in length | *B. candida* |
| * * * * Surface reticulated, shell small, up to 20 mm. (4/5 in.) in length | *B. domingensis* |

Genus *Barbatia* Gray

*Barbatia candida* Helbling
   White Bearded Ark

   Pl. XXXVII, 8

ETYMOLOGY: Lat. *barbatus*, bearded; *candidus*, white.

SIZE: 60 mm. (2 2/5 in.) in length, 25 mm. (1 in.) in width.

DISTRIBUTION: North Carolina to Texas and the Caribbean.

CHARACTERISTICS: Shell medium, thin, obliquely trapezoidal, posterior
   margin rounded. Color white. Sculptured with low, coarse, slightly
   beaded radiating ribs. Byssal notch small.

This is a fairly common species, living like other members of the subfamily fixed by a byssus to a strong holdfast. It has fewer hinge
teeth, and is thinner than most ark shells. Its shape varies irregularly,
affected by its immediate environment, but its white color, thin
texture, and coarse, beaded ribs are characteristic.

The **Red Brown Ark,** *Barbatia cancellaria* Lamarck (Lat. *cancelli,*
lattice) (pl. XXXVII, 9), reaches 50 mm. (2 in.) in length and 28 mm.
(1 1/8 in.) in height. The shells are compressed and colored red
brown throughout. The surface is sculptured with finely beaded ribs
and irregular growth lines. This species ranges from southern
Florida to Texas and the West Indies.

The **Dominican Ark,** *Barbatia domingensis* Lamarck (after the
Dominican Republic) is quite small, 12 to 18 mm. (1/2 to 3/4 in.) in
length. It is readily recognized by the heavily reticulated white to
cream surface. It lives from North Carolina to Texas and the West
Indies, in holes and crevices of jetties and under rocks in shallow
water.

The **Thin Ark,** *Barbatia tenera* C. B. Adams (Lat. *tenerus,* thin,
tender) (pl. XXXVII, 10), is 35 mm. (1 2/5 in.) in length and 24 mm.
(about 1 in.) in height. The shells are thin but quite swollen, and

are sculptured with many rather wide beaded ribs. The color is white, with a thin brown periostracum, and the species ranges from southern Florida to Texas and the Caribbean. In 1939 a form of this species was named *Arca* (*Barbatia*) *balesi* by Pilsbry & McLean in honor of Dr. Blenn R. Bales (1876–1946), an enthusiastic Florida collector. Though this name is now considered a synonym, the bivalve is still called Doc Bales' Ark by collectors, and is so cited in popular books.

**Adams' Miniature Ark,** *Arcopsis adamsi* Dall (Lat. *arca*, box, and Gr. *opsis*, having the appearance of; Charles B. Adams, 1814–1853, was a diligent New England conchologist) (pl. XXXVIII, 4), is quite small, 12 mm. (about 1/2 in.) in length, 7 mm. (about 1/4 in.) in height. It is white, inflated, and almost rectangular in shape, and has a strongly cancellated surface. The ligament holding the valves together is very short, limited to a strong triangular area between the umbones. This species lives from North Carolina to Brazil, usually fixed to hard objects by a white byssus.

---

SUBFAMILY:

# ANADARINAE
(*ark shells without a byssal gape*)

---

## KEY TO GENERA ANADARA AND NOETIA

| | |
|---|---|
| * Shell with ribs divided centrally by a groove | |
| * * Groove deep, length of shell decidedly greater than height | *Anadara floridana* |
| * * Groove faint, length only slightly greater than height | *Noetia ponderosa* |
| * Ribs entire, without central groove | |
| * * Shell shape rectangular, length greater than height | *Anadara transversa* |
| * * Shell length and height approximately equal | |
| * * * Shell shape oval | *A. ovalis* |
| * * * Shell shape trigonal | |
| * * * * Left valve overlapping right valve at base | *A. brasiliana* |
| * * * * Left valve not overlapping right valve | *A. chemnitzi* |

Genus *Anadara* Gray

*Anadara transversa* Say
  Transverse Ark

  Pl. XXXVII, 11

ETYMOLOGY: Name invented by Gray, no meaning. The derivation from the supposed Gr. *ana dara* is without foundation.

SIZE: 30 mm. (1 1/5 in.) in length, 21 mm. (about 4/5 in.) in height.

DISTRIBUTION: Cape Cod to Florida and Texas.

CHARACTERISTICS: Shell medium, obliquely trapezoidal, strong. Color white, with grayish brown periostracum. Radial sculpture strong. Left valve slightly overlaps the right.

The shells of the subfamily Anadarinae lack the byssal gape characteristic of the subfamily Arcinae. The Transverse Ark is a common species, especially in the northern part of its range, where it lives in mud just below the low-water line. Dead valves are frequently found on the beach.

The **Blood Ark,** *Anadara ovalis* Bruguière (Lat. *ovum,* egg) (pl. XXXVIII, 1), reaches 30 to 60 mm. (1 1/5 to 2 2/5 in.) in length. It differs from *A. transversa* chiefly in its rounder, more oval shape. Its blood is red instead of a watery blue, as in most bivalves. The valves are said to be chalky in the north but porcelaneous in the south. The species lives from Cape Cod to the Gulf states and the West Indies. It was formerly called *Arca pexata* Say and *Arca campechiensis* Gmelin, which is a different species.

**Chemnitz's Ark,** *Anadara chemnitzi* Philippi (Johann Chemnitz, 1730–1800, was a famous German iconographer-conchologist) (pl. XXXVIII, 2), is most easily recognized by being as high as it is long, 30 × 30 mm. (1 1/5 × 1 1/5 in.). It is trigonal in shape, the umbones are high and inflated, and the anterior ribs are heavily beaded. This species ranges from Florida to Texas and the West Indies.

The **Brazil Ark,** *Anadara brasiliana* Lamarck (pl. XXXVIII, 3), is very similar, but it is larger, reaching 40 mm. (1 3/5 in.) in length, and has lower umbones, and the left valve strongly overlaps the right. It is found from North Carolina to Texas and the West Indies. It was formerly called *Anadara incongrua* Say because of the strongly overlapping left valve, which gives an incongruous look to the shell.

The **Cut-ribbed Ark,** *Anadara floridana* Conrad (pl. XXXVII, 12), is a large species, reaching 125 mm. (5 in.) in length and 52 mm. (2 in.) in height. It is readily identified because each of its faintly beaded, wide, squarish ribs has a shallow furrow running down the center. For this reason it was formerly called *A. secticostata* Reeve (Lat. *secare costa,* cut rib). The species lives in deep water, but is not infrequently found washed onto beaches after strong storms. It ranges from North Carolina to Texas and the Greater Antilles.

The **Ponderous Ark,** *Noetia ponderosa* Say (named for Noe, Noah; Lat. *ponderosus,* heavy) is about 60 mm. (2 1/2 in.) in length and 42 mm. (1 3/4 in.) in height. The shell is trigonal in shape and very heavy, with a ponderous hingeline. The beaks are widely separated, and the squarish axial ribs have a faint central groove. The periostracum is velvety, black, and heavy. This species ranges from Virginia to Key West and Texas and lives in deeper water. Dead valves, joined together by the strong hinge are frequently found on beaches, especially after a strong blow. Fossil-like single valves occur as far north as Massachusetts. These northern populations were evidently exterminated by the cooling of the waters during the Pleistocene. *Noetia* and *Arcopsis,* together with similar arcidlike genera, are sometimes placed in the family Noetiidae. (Pl. XXXVII, 13.)

SUPERFAMILY:

# LIMOPSACEA

FAMILY:

# GLYCYMERIDIDAE
(*bittersweet shells*)

These shells are orbicular in outline, and the taxodont teeth are arranged in an arched line. The sculpture is weaker than in the Arcidae. This group is found in warmer waters.

## KEY TO GENUS GLYCYMERIS

* Shell with heavy, fanlike sculpture      *Glycymeris pectinata*
* Shell with weak sculpture of radiating striae
** Umbones facing posteriorly, ligamental area
    mostly anterior      *G. decussata*

    \* \* Beaks facing each other directly, ligamental
        area central

\* \* \* Shell smaller, 50 mm. (2 in.), inflated, creamy
       with brownish markings           *G. undata*

\* \* \* Shell large, 125 mm. (5 in.), compressed, tan
       with a few somewhat darker areas    *G. americana*

---

Genus *Glycymeris* da Costa

*Glycymeris pectinata* Gmelin
    Comb Bittersweet

    Pl. XXXVIII, 5

ETYMOLOGY: Gr. *glykys meris*, sweet part or morsel; Lat. *pecten*, comb.

SIZE: 33 mm. (1 1/3 in.) in length, 31 mm. (1 1/4 in.) in height.

DISTRIBUTION: North Carolina to Florida and the West Indies.

CHARACTERISTICS: Shell small, compressed, heavy, orbicular in outline;
    umbo central. Color dirty white, with irregular yellowish brown
    cross-markings. Surface sculpture of about twenty rounded, fanlike
    radial ribs. Hinge area reduced, strongly curved. Periostracum thin,
    brownish.

This is a moderately common shallow-water species living in sand.
On shore dead shells rapidly lose their bright color, but the species
can still be recognized by the heavy ribs.

    The **Wavy Bittersweet,** *Glycymeris undata* Linnaeus (Lat. *unda,*
wave) (pl. XXXVIII, 6), is about 50 mm. (2 in.) in size. It differs from
the Comb Bittersweet by having a smoothish shell, only weakly
marked by radiating and concentric striae. The color is creamy white,
thickly marked with brown blotches. It is found from North Carolina to Florida and the West Indies. Formerly called *Glycymeris
lineata* Reeve, a later name.

    The **Decussate Bittersweet,** *Glycymeris decussata* Linnaeus (Lat.
*decussare,* to cross like an X) (pl. XXXVIII, 7), is about 50 mm. (2
in.) in size. The surface is relatively smoothly sculptured, like *G. undata,* though the radial striae are somewhat deeper. The difference
between the two lies chiefly in the umbones and ligamental area: in
*G. undata* the umbones face each other directly and the ligamental
area is central; in *G. decussata* the umbones are turned to one side,
the back of the shell, with most of the ligamental area placed

frontally. The species is found from southeastern Florida to the West Indies.

The **American Bittersweet,** *Glycymeris americana* DeFrance (pl. XXXVIII, 8), is a rare shell, single valves seldom occurring on the beach. It is much larger than its congeners, reaching 125 mm. (5 in.) in size. It is very compressed and the surface is smoothish, with weak radial striae. The color is dull tan with darker mottlings. It is found in deeper water, from North Carolina to Florida and the Caribbean.

ORDER:

# MYTILOIDA

SUPERFAMILY:

## MYTILACEA
(*sea mussels*)

FAMILY:

## MYTILIDAE

The rather weak shells of this family are usually fan shaped, with the beak at the narrower, anterior end. Hinge teeth are absent or reduced to a few nodules near the tip. There is usually a threadlike byssus, by which the animal can anchor itself to hard substrates. Some species can bore into rock and corals. In many countries, sea mussels serve as important articles of food.

### KEY TO GENERA OF FAMILY MYTILIDAE

* Shell more or less fan shaped, posterior margin wider than anterior
** Shell with byssus; not a driller in stone
*** Shell with umbones at extreme tip          *Mytilus*
*** Shell with umbones behind extension of anterior margin (except *Ischadium recurvum*)

* * * * Shell smooth, teeth near ligament absent
* * * * * Shell large, 85 to 150 mm. (3 2/5 to 6 in.), generally strong     *Modiolus, Geukensia*
* * * * * Shell small, generally delicate     *Amygdalum, Lioberus & Botula*

   * * * * Shell sculptured with radiating ribs and with toothlike crenulations near ligament     *Brachidontes, Ischadium*

     * * Shell without byssus, cylindrical; borer in rock or coral     *Lithophaga*

      * Shell irregularly ovate, posterior margin little wider than anterior, center smooth, both ends with radial ribs     *Musculus*

---

Genus *Mytilus* Linnaeus

*Mytilus edulis* Linnaeus
Blue Mussel

Pl. XXXVII, 14

ETYMOLOGY: Lat. *mytilus*, sea mussel; *edere*, to eat.

SIZE: 75 mm. (3 in.) in length, 25 mm. (1 in.) in height.

DISTRIBUTION: Arctic seas to South Carolina, as well as Alaska to California and Europe.

CHARACTERISTICS: Shell medium to large, elongate triangular, moderately strong, smooth, umbones terminal, pointed. Color violet blue, occasionally light brown, with or without bluish rays. Four small teeth near umbo. Periostracum bluish black, shiny, strong.

It is hardly necessary to say much about this very common and useful bivalve. Everybody knows it either as a persistent inhabitant in bays and ocean inlets, where it lives in bewildering numbers, strongly matted together on hard surfaces, or as a delectable article of diet especially sought after in Europe. The animals anchor themselves with strong brownish byssal threads, and in the case of the Blue Mussel, these byssal threads can be cast off and new ones produced so that the animal is able to engage in a certain amount of laborious movement.

The shells of the order Mytiloida all have lost one of the two adductor muscles usually found in bivalves, or if there still are two, one is greatly reduced to a mere slender strand. This condition came about because the umbo had moved to one end of the shells, so that the valves opened lengthwise rather than sideways. Thus the function of one of the muscles was much increased and the need for the other much reduced. Bivalves with this condition have been called Anisomyaria (Gr. *anisos mya*, unequal sea-mussel), a name that is still found in some classifications of the Bivalvia.

Genus *Modiolus* Lamarck

*Modiolus modiolus* Linnaeus
   Horse Mussel

   Pl. XXXVII, 15

ETYMOLOGY: Diminutive of Lat. *modus*, a dry measure.

SIZE: 100 to 150 mm. (4 to 6 in.) in length, 75 mm. (3 in.) in width.

DISTRIBUTION: Arctic Ocean to North Carolina.

CHARACTERISTICS: Shell large, narrowly pear shaped, heavy, coarse. Pale lilac white under a heavy, shiny, brownish periostracum, which is shaggy below. The rounded anterior end of the shell extends beyond the umbones.

The Horse Mussel is a shell from offshore waters, where it solidly anchors itself with its byssus to hard underwater objects. But strong storms often hurl these holdfasts onto the beach, so that *M. modiolus* is not an uncommon beach shell, especially in New England. For a short time the species was placed in the genus *Volsella* Scopoli, 1777, a much earlier but overlooked name; however, the International Commission on Zoological Nomenclature—the "Supreme Court" of nomenclature—voted to conserve the better-known though later name, *Modiolus* Lamarck, 1799.

The **Tulip Mussel**, *Modiolus americanus* Leach (pl. XXXVII, 16), is smaller, 85 mm. (3 2/5 in.) in length, 40 mm. (1 3/5 in.) in height. It is similar to *M. modiolus*, but is thinner shelled and yellowish brown in color, with a purplish or reddish stain in the interior near the umbo; there are light-colored rays. This is a southern species, ranging from North Carolina to Florida, Texas, and the Caribbean. In earlier books it is called *Modiolus tulipa* Lamarck, whence its common English name.

The **Ribbed Mussel**, *Geukensia demissa* Dillwyn (Lat. *demissus*, brought down, humble) (pl. XXXVII, 17), is 75 to 100 mm. (3 to 4 in.) in length. It is easily distinguished from the previous two species because its surface is ornamented with numerous, crowded radial ridges. These ridges divide, or bifurcate, as they approach the lower margin. The periostracum is thin, varnished, and yellow green or brown in color. This species lives in salt marshes, the lower half buried in muddy or peaty bottoms, with only the wide posterior edge showing above the bottom. It ranges from Canada to North Carolina. *G. plicatula* Lamarck is a synonym.

In the south, from Florida to Texas and Yucatán, specimens of *Geukensia demissa* have radial ridges that are beaded rather than smooth. Shells with this type of surface sculpture are recognized as a subspecies, *G. demissa granosissima* Sowerby (Lat. *granosus*, grainy). Also, at one time *G. demissa* was called *Brachidontes demissus*. But the genus *Brachidontes* Swainson is distinguished by the presence of toothlike crenulations just behind the ligament. As the Ribbed Mussel does not have these crenulations, it was placed in the genus *Modiolus*. Recent anatomical studies, however, suggest that this species is referable to the genus *Geukensia* Poel.

The **Lemon Mussel,** *Brachidontes modiolus* Linnaeus (Gr. *braches dontes*, short tooth; Lat. *modus*, a dry measure) (pl. XXXVII, 18), is much smaller, only 46 mm. (1 4/5 in.) in length and 17 mm. (about 3/4 in.) in height. It is a long and slender shell, bluish gray under a bright yellow periostracum; the wider, posterior surface is ribbed, the narrower, anterior one smooth. There are four tiny teeth near the umbo. This species ranges from southern Florida to the West Indies. It lives in deeper water, but single valves are occasionally found on the beach. Formerly known as *B. citrinus* Röding (Lat. *citrus*, citrus tree), a synonym.

The **Scorched Mussel,** *Brachidontes exustus* Linnaeus (Lat. *exurere*, to scorch, burn up) (pl. XXXIX, 1), is only 37 mm. (1 1/2 in.) in length and 20 mm. (4/5 in.) in height. It resembles *B. modiolus*, but it is wider, brownish rather than yellowish, and has only two tiny teeth near the umbo. It is a common species ranging from North Carolina to Florida, Texas, and the West Indies.

The **Hooked Mussel,** *Ischadium recurvum* Rafinesque (Gr. *ischadion*, dried fig; Lat. *recurvus*, bent, crooked) (pl. XXXIX, 2), reaches 50 mm. (2 in.) in length, 25 mm. (1 in.) in width. The narrower end is extended into a strong, moderately hooked umbo, and there is no extension of the shell reaching beyond the umbones as in the species of *Brachidontes* and *Modiolus*. The color is purplish gray, and the surface is strongly sculptured with bifurcated radial ridges. This species, formerly placed in the genus *Brachidontes*, ranges from North Carolina to Florida, Texas, and the West Indies. At times living specimens have been introduced as far north as Cape Cod, but these individuals perish during the winter.

The **Paper Mussel**, *Amygdalum papyrium* Conrad (Lat. *amygdalum*, almond; *papyrus*, paper) (pl. XXXIX, 3), is 34 mm. (1 2/5 in.) in length and 12 mm. (1/2 in.) in height. It has the shape of *Brachidontes*, but it is very compressed and fragile. The surface is smooth, with only fine growth lines showing; the color is grayish green or yellowish brown, with an iridescent interior. This is a common shell in bays, where it lives half buried in the mud at the roots of marsh marine grasses. It ranges from Maryland to Florida.

Genus *Musculus* Röding

*Musculus niger* Gray
   Black Mussel

   Pl. XXXIX, 4

ETYMOLOGY: Lat. *musculus*, muscle; *niger*, black.

SIZE: 50 to 75 mm. (2 to 3 in.) in length, 35 mm. (1 2/5 in.) in width.

DISTRIBUTION: Arctic seas to North Carolina; also in Alaska and Washington State.

CHARACTERISTICS: Shell medium, irregularly oval, fairly strong. Color dark brown. Umbones placed far from the margin. Surface has a narrow, smooth, triangular central area bordered on both sides by areas with finely marked radial striae. Periostracum moderately strong, shiny.

This close relative of *Mytilus* differs decidedly in the shape of the shell and the peculiar surface sculpturing. It is a fairly common species in offshore waters, but specimens are also found on shore, especially in the more northern part of its range. There are several other *Musculus* species known from our area, but they are rarely found on beaches. These are *Musculus discors* Linnaeus (Arctic seas to Long Island, New York), *Musculus lateralis* Say (North Carolina to Florida, Texas, and the West Indies). See pl. XXXIX, 5 and pl. XXXVIII, 9 for comparison.

The **Chestnut Mussel**, *Lioberus castaneus* Say (Gr. *leios*, smooth, and Lat. *berus*, water snake; *castanea*, chestnut tree) (pl. XXXVIII, 10), is only 28 mm. (1 1/8 in.) in length and 15 mm. (3/5 in.) in height. It is quite swollen, thin, and glossy, with a strong chestnut brown periostracum and an interior of iridescent bluish white. It is a moderately common species found from Florida and Texas to the West Indies.

The **Cinnamon Chestnut Mussel,** *Botula fusca* Gmelin (Lat. *botulus,* sausage; *fuscus,* swarthy) (pl. XXXVIII, 10), is only 20 mm. (4/5 in.) in length and 9 mm. (about 2/5 in.) in height. It is elongate, grayish in color, and best recognized by a series of strongly impressed, arched growth lines indicative of the places where normal growth of the shell was interrupted, like the rings in a tree. Not a common species, it ranges from the Florida Keys to the West Indies.

Genus *Lithophaga* Röding

*Lithophaga bisulcata* Orbigny
Mahogany Date Mussel

Pl. XXXIX, 6

ETYMOLOGY: Gr. *lithos phagen,* stone eater; Lat. *bisulcus,* cloven.

SIZE: 51 mm. (about 2 in.) in length, 17 mm. (about 3/4 in.) in height, including the calcareous deposit.

DISTRIBUTION: Florida and Texas to Brazil.

CHARACTERISTICS: Shell moderate, elongate, almost cylindrical, pointed at posterior end (opposite the umbones), each valve divided by a narrow, oblique furrow. Color mahogany brown, thickly encrusted with a heavy calcareous layer that extrudes beyond the posterior margin of the shell.

This is the commonest of the date mussels, so called because of their shape and color. They bore in rocks, coral, and even in other shells, such as *Strombus, Spondylus,* and so forth. They can be freed only by careful use of hammer and chisel. Anyone ambitious enough to undertake this arduous type of collecting should read the paper by Dr. Bales (1940) in *The Nautilus,* who seems to have had more experience in this type of collecting than anybody we know.

The **Antillean Date Mussel,** *Lithophaga antillarum* Orbigny (pl. XXXIX, 7), reaches 110 mm. (4 2/5 in.) in length, 25 mm. (1 in.) in height. It differs by being light yellowish brown in color, and in its surface ornamentation of numerous fine, radiating striae, whereas *L. bisulcata* is quite smooth. Moreover, the shell is not encrusted with the calcareous formation of *L. bisulcata.* This West Indian species was collected by Doc Bales in the Florida Keys; it ranges from Florida to the Caribbean, and is less common than the former.

The **Black Date Mussel,** *Lithophaga nigra* Orbigny (pl. XXXIX, 8), reaches 65 mm. (2 3/5 in.) in length and 20 mm. (4/5 in.) in height. It is readily distinguished by its blackish brown, indeed almost black color, and by its highly iridescent interior. It is free also of the calcareous incrustation. It is found from the Florida Keys to the West Indies.

The **Scissor Date Mussel,** *Lithophaga aristata* Dillwyn (Lat. *arista,* ear of corn) (pl. XXXIX, 9), reaches 44 mm. (1 4/5 in.) in length and 14 mm. (about 3/5 in.) in height. It bears a strong calcareous incrustation like *L. bisulcata,* but the deposit extends beyond the posterior end, where the triangular-shaped extensions twist and cross each other like the beak of a scissorbill bird. This species is found in the Florida Keys, and ranges to Texas and the Caribbean. It is almost cosmopolitan in distribution in warmer seas.

SUPERFAMILY:

# PINNACEA

FAMILY:

# PINNIDAE
(*pen shells*)

These shells—large, wedge-shaped, fragile and translucent, with surface smooth or variously sculptured—are common shells in shallow water in warmer seas. They attach by a byssus at the umbo to a hard object deep in the sand. The projecting valves, which are sharp edged and are often overgrown with algae, present a hazard to bare feet of unwary collectors. Probably for this reason they are sometimes called "razor clams." The true razor clams, however, belong to the family Solenidae (see page 399).

## KEY TO GENERA PINNA AND ATRINA

* Shell with interior divided by a shallow, centrally
  placed longitudinal sulcus or groove      *Pinna carnea*
* Shell without interior sulcus
** Anterior muscle scar large, touching the upper margin
  of the internal nacreous layer      *Atrina rigida*

** Anterior muscle scar small, not touching margin
of nacreous layer
*** Shell relatively strong, dark purplish or black, spines
when present large, hollow                                  *A. seminuda*
*** Shell thin, light tan or pale brownish green, surface of
numerous axial ribs with small, not hollow spines          *A. serrata*

---

Genus *Pinna* Linnaeus

*Pinna carnea* Gmelin
    Amber Pen Shell

    Pl. XXXIX, 10

ETYMOLOGY: Lat. *pinna* (or *penna*), feather, wing; *caro, carnis*, flesh.

SIZE: 270 mm. (11 in.) in length, 122 mm. (5 in.) in height.

DISTRIBUTION: Lake Worth, Florida, to the Caribbean.

CHARACTERISTICS: Shell large, thin, very fragile, translucent, wedge shaped.
    Color varying from light tan to pink or salmon. Surface sculptured
    with radiating ribs, less commonly with a few thornlike spines. Interior
    marked by a centrally placed, shallow longitudinal furrow or sulcus.

This is a rather rare shell in Florida, where it lives, like other pen
shells, with the terminal pointed umbo buried in the sand. Only the
upper part of the shell protrudes above the bottom. The shell is kept
in place by a strong byssus attached to buried rocks or other hard
objects. The byssus of some Mediterranean species has been spun
into fibers, woven into a fabric called "cloth of gold," and made
into beautiful silklike scarves and shawls. The large posterior adductor muscle and all the flesh are eaten as a delicacy in many countries. Turner and Rosewater (1958) have an interesting account of
the economic importance of this bivalve, which in the United States
is entirely overlooked. The fragile shell tends to split as it dries up,
and this, together with its large size and not very attractive appearance keeps it from being favored in shell collections.

The shells of the genus *Pinna* are recognized by the presence of
the internal furrow or sulcus; the genus *Atrina* Gray lacks this feature. In the past *Pinna carnea* was confused with *Pinna rudis*
Linnaeus, a European species which is rarely found in the West
Indies. The etymology of the name *Atrina* is debatable, some writers
deriving it from the Latin *atrium*, opening, others from *ater*, black.
Neither derivation is very convincing, and chances are that Gray

merely made up a euphonious artificial word without meaning, as he did in many other instances.

The **Rigid Pen Shell,** *Atrina rigida* Lightfoot (Lat. *ater* (?), black colored) (pl. XXXIX, 11), reaches 286 mm. (11 1/4 in.) in length and 180 mm. (about 7 in.) in height. It lacks the internal furrow of *Pinna*, and is purplish brown to nearly black in color. The surface sculpture varies from smooth to spiny. This species ranges from North Carolina to the West Indies; it is very abundant, and large numbers of dead shells frequently litter the beaches after a hard blow.

The **Naked Pen Shell,** *Atrina seminuda* Lamarck (pl. XXXIX, 12), is a little smaller, reaching 243 mm. (about 9 3/4 in.) in length. Externally this species resembles the Rigid Pen Shell, and to detect the difference, the interior of the valves must be examined. It will be seen immediately that the internal surface of both species is divided into two areas, an upper (actually posterior) crystalline layer and a lower (actually anterior) pearly layer. In *A. rigida* the large posterior muscle scar touches the upper margin of the pearly layer, and in older specimens, even protrudes strongly beyond it into the crystalline area. In *A. seminuda* the smaller muscle scar lies well below and separated from the upper margin of the pearly area. In other respects the shells are similar, varying in thickness and color, and in whether, depending upon the selective effect of the environment, the surface is smooth or spiny. In addition, if the soft parts can be examined, it will be seen that *A. rigida* has a bright, golden orange mantle, much more vivid than the pale yellow mantle of *A. seminuda*. The Naked Pen Shell ranges from North Carolina to Texas and the Caribbean, but is strangely absent from the Florida Keys.

The **Sawtooth Pen Shell,** *Atrina serrata* Sowerby (Lat. *serra,* saw) (pl. XXXIX, 13), is also quite large, reaching 295 mm. (11 1/2 in.) in length. It is readily distinguished from the other pen shells by its thinner shell and much more numerous, narrower, crowded ribs armed with very small solid thorns or spines. The color varies from greenish to brown. Like *A. seminuda*, the small, circular muscle scar is set well below the margin of the nacreous layer. *A. serrata* ranges from North Carolina to Texas and the West Indies.

ORDER:

# PTERIOIDA

(*winged shells*)

SUPERFAMILY:

## PTERIACEA

FAMILY:

## PTERIIDAE

(*pearl oysters*)

The shell is highly iridescent, or pearly, with the exterior covered by a strong, generally roughened periostracum. The hinge margin is straight, and may extend posteriorly as a winglike projection. The pearl oysters are attached to hard objects by a strong byssus, which passes through a hole under the wing of the right valve. In the tropical Pacific Ocean, related species are extensively fished for their commercially valuable pearls.

## KEY TO GENERA PTERIA AND PINCTADA

* Edges of hinge margin exceedingly unequal,
  posterior edge with large winglike extension    *Pteria colymbus*
* Edges of hinge margin more or less equal        *Pinctada imbricata*

Genus *Pteria* Scopoli

*Pteria colymbus* Röding
 Winged Pearl Oyster

Pls. XVI, 1a & b; XXXIX, 14

ETYMOLOGY: Gr. *pteron*, wing; *kolymbus*, diver.

SIZE: 89 mm. (3 1/2 in.) in length, 59 mm. (2 1/4 in.) in height.

DISTRIBUTION: Southern Florida to Texas and the Caribbean.

CHARACTERISTICS: Shell medium, moderately strong, oval; hinge margin straight with posterior edge drawn out in a sharp winglike extension. Left valve inflated, right valve flattened. Color dark brown, with incomplete lighter-colored radial lines. Interior pearly; periostracum matted, shaggy.

This common pearl oyster lives attached to gorgonian sea whips and sea fans. When storms dislodge the holdfasts, gorgonia and pearl oysters are swept ashore together. The unmistakable identifying characteristic of this species is the sharp, winglike extension at the hinge margin. The pearls found in this and the *Pinctada* pearl oysters are beautiful, but too rare and too small, at least in Florida, to be of commercial value.

The **Atlantic Pearl Oyster,** *Pinctada imbricata* Röding (possibly from Lat. *pincta*, pint; Lat. *imbricatus*, overlapping) (pl. XLIV, 2), is 75 mm. (3 in.) in length, 72 mm. (slightly under 3 in.) in height. It has the same pearly interior as *Pteria*, but the ears on both ends of the straight hinge margin are small and about equal in size. The color is variable—tan, reddish brown, or green—and commonly beautifully mottled with yellow or varying shades of light brown. The surface is generally sculptured with rough ridges or lamellae, which curl up and overlap; in very young specimens these lamellae are spiny. This pearl oyster, formerly known as *P. radiata* Leach, ranges from southern Florida and Texas to the West Indies, but it is rarer than *Pteria colymbus*. The derivation of the generic name from the Spanish *pintada* ("painted," not "dotted") is fanciful.

FAMILY:

# ISOGNOMONIDAE
(*tree oysters*)

The greatly compressed shell of this family is best characterized by the peculiar hinge with short, rectangular grooves and by the pearly interior layer, which does not reach to the margin of the valves. The shape of the shell varies greatly. The family is found worldwide in warm seas.

## KEY TO GENUS ISOGNOMON

* Shell large, 80 mm. (3 1/5 in.), fan shaped, 8 to 12
  hinge grooves                                *Isognomon alatus*
* Shell small, 25 mm. (1 in.), elongate or spatulate,
  4 to 8 grooves
** Shell internally without a ridge; elongate, grooves
  small, squarish                              *I. radiatus*
** Shell internally with low, curved ridge along pallial
  line, spatula shaped, grooves rectangular        *I. bicolor*

Genus *Isognomon* Lightfoot

*Isognomon alatus* Gmelin
    Winged Tree Oyster

    Pl. XLIV, 3

ETYMOLOGY: Gr. *isos gnomon*, equal carpenter's square; Lat. *alatus*, winged.

SIZE: 80 mm. (3 1/5 in.) in height and length.

DISTRIBUTION: Southern Florida, Texas, and the Caribbean.

CHARACTERISTICS: Shell medium to large, very flat, fan shaped. Color gray or purplish with pearly interior. Surface has roughened growth lines. Hinge has eight to twenty-one rectangular grooves filled with brown resilium.

This is a common oyster clinging to the roots of mangrove trees and on rocks in quiet bay waters. Competition for space may result in some distortions of the shape during growth, but the exceedingly flat valves and the presence of the rectangular grooves at the hinge margin serve to identify the species. Formerly placed in the genus *Pedalion* Dillwyn (Gr. rudder).

The **Bicolored Tree Oyster,** *Isognomon bicolor* C. B. Adams (pl. XLIV, 4), is smaller, 28 mm. (1 1/8 in.) in length and 18 mm. (3/4 in.) in height. It is yellow with purple blotches, and very irregular in shape. There are only four to eight resilium sockets, and the surface is heavily and irregularly sculptured. Internally there is a low, curved ridge along the pallial line that separates the shell into two differently colored sections. This species ranges from the Florida Keys to Texas and the Caribbean.

**Lister's Tree Oyster,** *Isognomon radiatus* Anton (Lat. *radiatus,* with rays), is 60 mm. (2 2/5 in.) in length and 25 mm. (1 in.) in height. It is elongate and very variable in shape, depending upon the situation in which it lives. The four to eight resilium sockets are very small and squarish rather than oblong in shape, and are widely spaced. The color of the shell is yellowish or light violet brown, frequently with a few irregular radial stripes. It ranges from southern Florida to the West Indies, where it is occasionally found at low tide on rocks. It was formerly called *I. listeri* Hanley, a later name (pl. XXXIX, 15).

SUPERFAMILY:

# PECTINACEA

FAMILY:

# PECTINIDAE
(*scallop shells*)

The pectens, or scallop shells, are fanlike, commonly brilliantly colored, and are favorites among shell collectors. Their use in art, as religious objects, in heraldry, and as the trademark of an international petroleum company have made them one of the best-known shells to the layman, and the toothsome white, fleshy muscle has been relished by generations of gourmets. They have been called the "butterflies of the sea" because of the fluttering swimming movement attained by opening and closing the valves and ejecting water from the mantle in a form of jet propulsion. Some permanently cement one valve to a hard object in the adult stage. Others become attached to rocks and other firm substrates by a byssus.

# KEY TO GENERA
# OF FAMILY PECTINIDAE

| | |
|---|---|
| * Lower valve much deeper than upper | *Pecten* |
| * Lower valve and upper valve more or less equal in depth | |
| * * Hinge ears strongly unequal in size | *Chlamys* |
| * * Hinge ears about equal in size | |
| * * * Shell large, 200 mm. (8 in.), relatively fragile, lightly sculptured | *Placopecten* |
| * * * Shell frequently smaller, 35 to 75 mm. (1 2/5 to 3 in.), rarely 145 mm. (5 4/5 in.), surface sculpture very strong | |
| * * * * Shell sculpture of about 20 radiating ridges | *Argopecten; Aequipecten* |
| * * * * Shell sculpture dominated by a few heavy ridges ornamented with large hollow nodules or blisters | *Nodipecten* |

Genus *Pecten* Müller

*Pecten ziczac* Linnaeus
  Zigzag Scallop

  Pl. XLIV, 5

ETYMOLOGY: Lat. *pecten*, comb; origin of *ziczac* unknown.

SIZE: 100 mm. (4 in.) in length, 90 mm. (3 3/5 in.) in height.

DISTRIBUTION: North Carolina to Florida and the West Indies.

CHARACTERISTICS: Shell medium to large, fan shaped. Ears at hinge about equal in size. Lower valve deeply cupped. Color light tan to brownish red, sculptured with about 20 strong, whitish, radiating ribs. Upper valve almost flat, reddish or purple with lighter zigzag markings. Radiating ribs flattened.

This is a fairly common species of scallop shell, but beach shells are rarely found with both valves still intact. Nevertheless, even single valves are readily recognized. The scallops live in lively schools of flitting individuals, since they are one of the few bivalves that can swim by opening and closing their valves rapidly, changing directions by closing off part of the mantle and thus directing a jet of water opposite to the desired trajectory, somewhat like a jet plane or space rocket. At one time all scallop shells were called *Pecten,* but now some fifty generic names are available, six of which may be used for the species discussed here. These genera are now generally accepted, although some of them may not be justified on biological grounds.

The scallops are best known to the public as tasteful morsels of whitish flesh in shore dinners. These bits are the single large adductor muscle of this anisomyarian bivalve, whose shells are widely known as the trademark of the Shell Oil Company. The scallop shell also figured in religious, artistic, and heraldic fields. In 1957 Shell Oil published a useful book dealing with the scallop in all its many manifestations, with a large portion devoted to culinary matters.

**Ravenel's Scallop,** *Pecten raveneli* Dall (Edmund Ravenel, 1797–1871, was a prominent naturalist and collector) (pl. XXXIX, 16), is similar to *P. ziczac* but somewhat smaller, about 50 mm. (2 in.) in size. It differs by having more ribs on the lower valve, twenty-five instead of twenty, as in the Zigzag Scallop. In addition, the strong ribs of *P. raveneli* are whitish in color, whereas in *P. ziczac* the ribs are weaker and colored like the rest of the valve. Ravenel's Scallop is a far less common species, ranging from North Carolina to Florida, Texas, and the West Indies.

The **Thorny Scallop,** *Chlamys sentis* Reeve (Gr. and Lat. *chlamys,* a light outer garment; Lat. *sentis,* thorn) (pl. XXXIX, 17), reaches 25 to 35 mm. (1 to 1 2/5 in.) in size, and the valves are almost equally dished. The two hinge ears are very different in size, one being considerably smaller than the other. The species of the genus *Chlamys* Röding can be recognized by this feature alone. There are about fifty ribs, all armed with tiny, thornlike scales. The color is variable and brilliant, red, orange red, brownish purple, white, or mottled specimens occurring together. This species can be found from North Carolina to the West Indies.

Various close relatives of *C. sentis* live in the same area, though in much less abundant numbers. Among these: the **Ornate Scallop,** *Chlamys ornata* Lamarck (pl. XXXIX, 18), whose sculpture consists of eighteen groups of three closely packed riblets each; the **Imbricated Scallop,** *Chlamys imbricata* Gmelin, with only eight to ten ribs, covered by large, cuplike scales (pl. XLIV, 6); and **Mildred's Scallop,** *Chlamys mildredae* Bayer (named for the collector M. Royce), with thirty ribs, every third or fourth one being larger.

The **Iceland Scallop,** *Chlamys islandica* Müller (pl. XLIV, 7), reaches 100 mm. (4 in.) in length. The larger ear is about twice the size of the smaller, and the color, usually dirty gray or cream, is occasionally nicely tinged with peach, yellow, or purple. This species ranges from the Arctic Seas to Massachusetts, and though very common offshore, is not usually found on beaches.

The **Calico Scallop,** *Argopecten gibbus* Linnaeus (*Argo,* the name of the ship Jason sailed in, and *pecten,* comb; *gibbus,* hunched) (pl. XXXIX, 19), is about 30 mm. (1 1/5 in.) in size. The hinge ears are about equal—which distinguishes the genus *Argopecten* Monterosato —and the rather swollen valves differ slightly in depth. There are about twenty strong, squarish ribs. The lower valve is whitish, the upper lavender, reddish, or white, colorfully mottled with purple or red. It ranges from North Carolina to Florida, the Gulf of Mexico, and the West Indies. It is at present the object of intensive fishing activity.

The **Bay Scallop,** *Argopecten irradians* Lamarck (Lat. *irradiare,* to irradiate) (pl. XXXIX, 20), is about 50 to 75 mm. (2 to 3 in.) in size. This common edible scallop of the Northeast generally has a drab shell, colored pale brown or gray, but some have a pleasing light reddish tinge; rarely there are darker rays, and one of the valves is white. The valves are not very inflated, the ears are about equal, and there are seventeen to nineteen roundish ribs. This is a northern species, formerly ranging to Nova Scotia in the Pleistocene, and now living in bays from Cape Cod to Long Island and New Jersey.

The subspecies *Argopecten irradians concentricus* Say (pl. XLIV, 8), is found more to the south, from Virginia to Florida and Louisiana. It differs from typical *irradians* in that the lower, lighter-colored valve is noticeably deeper than the upper one, and the nineteen to twenty ribs are squarish rather than round in cross section. This and the previous species were formerly placed in *Aequipecten* Fischer, but they do not closely resemble the type species of that genus.

The **Mossy Scallop,** *Aequipecten muscosus* Wood (Lat. *aequus, pecten,* equal comb, *muscus,* moss) (pl. XLIV, 9), is 37 mm. (1 1/2 in.) in size. Both valves are fairly swollen and the colors are rich, either bright yellow, orange, red or brown, occasionally mottled. The eighteen to twenty ribs are armed with strong concave scales. This species is commonly covered with sponges—probably the "moss" of the name—and in such specimens the scales are very strongly developed. This species ranges from North Carolina to Texas and the West Indies.

The **Sea Scallop,** *Placopecten magellanicus* Gmelin (Gr. *plaks,* Lat. *pecten,* plate comb; Ferdinand Magellan) (pl. XVI, 10), is quite large, reaching as much as 200 mm. (8 in.) in size. It is almost circular, and the only slightly inflated valves are quite smooth, though sculptured with numerous shallow radial striations. This is an inhabitant from deeper water, but single valves or recognizable fragments are not uncommon on beaches. It forms the basis for a deep-sea scallop industry, and it ranges from Labrador to North Carolina.

The **Lion's Paw,** *Nodipecten nodosus* Linnaeus (Lat. *nodus pecten,* knot comb; *nodosus* knotty) (pl. XVI, 7), reaches 145 mm. (5 4/5 in.) (rarely 7 in.) in size. This striking species is bright red, deep orange, or even purplish red in color. The surface is sculptured with numerous riblets, and in addition, seven to nine large ribs irregularly armed with large, hollow nodules or blisterlike swellings. This species cannot be mistaken for any other. It ranges from North Carolina to Texas and the West Indies. Specimens are rather abundant in offshore waters, and are sometimes found on beaches, especially after a hard blow. This species was formerly placed in the genus *Lyropecten* Conrad, but this is now considered to be a genus restricted to extinct species.

---

FAMILY:

# PLICATULIDAE
(*kitten's paws*)

These small, fanlike shells with strong, radiating surface ridges look sufficiently like cat's paws to merit their English appellation. They live cemented to bits of coral and pebbles in warmer waters.

Genus *Plicatula* Lamarck

*Plicatula gibbosa* Lamarck
    Kitten's Paws
      Pl. XXXVIII, 11

ETYMOLOGY: Lat. *plicatus*, folded, plaited; *gibbus*, hunched.

SIZE: 25 mm. (1 in.) in length and height.

DISTRIBUTION: North Carolina to the Gulf States and the West Indies.

CHARACTERISTICS: Shell small, strong, generally fan shaped, with several large, strong, radiating ridges. Color whitish, with reddish brown markings on the ridges. Each valve has two strong hinge teeth fitting into corresponding notches on the opposing valve.

This species is not easily confused with any other shell, even though only single valves are generally found on the beaches, and the shells, like all species that live fixed to hard substrates, are often distorted in shape. Their strong texture keeps the shell from deteriorating even in a pounding surf, and thus this is one of the commonest beach shells everywhere in its range.

FAMILY:

# SPONDYLIDAE

(*spiny oysters*)

These shells are large and colorful, with many, long graceful spines. They live cemented to hard objects in the warmer offshore waters. Damaged valves are often found washed onto beaches. Like the scallops, they have sensitive light detectors arranged in the form of eyes along the edge of the mantle.

Genus *Spondylus* Linnaeus

*Spondylus americanus* Hermann
Atlantic Spiny Oyster

Pl. XVI, 4

ETYMOLOGY: Gr. *spondylus*, vertebra.

SIZE: 80 to 95 mm. (3 1/5 to 3 4/5 in.) in length, 90 to 112 mm. (3 3/5 to 4 1/2 in.) in height.

DISTRIBUTION: Florida, Texas, and the West Indies to Brazil.

CHARACTERISTICS: Shell large, heavy, usually with large, strong spines frondlike at the tips. Color white, with yellow, orange, or shades of rose or red near the umbones. Each valve has two strong, rectangular hinge teeth fitting into corresponding notches on opposing valve.

Little need be said about the handsome spiny oysters; they are among the most spectacular and highly desirable of all bivalve shells. Living specimens may be found attached to rocks and corals in depths of ten or more feet of water. Single valves when found on shore are generally badly worn, often without spines, with only low, radiating ridges remaining on the surface. Even in this beach-worn condition, however, the peculiar hinge teeth, which are said to have been the inspiration for the first mechanical door hinge, betray the true identity.

SUPERFAMILY:

# ANOMIACEA

FAMILY:

# ANOMIIDAE
(*jingle shells*)

In these shells the upper valve is thin, glassy, or scaly; the lower valve, chalky and with a large hole, through which a limy byssus attaches the animal to a hard substrate. This is a small family living in warm and temperate seas.

## KEY TO GENERA
## ANOMIA AND PODODESMUS

| | | |
|---|---|---|
| * | Surface of upper valve smooth, shiny, golden yellow to brown; range Nova Scotia southward to Brazil | *Anomia simplex* |
| * | Surface of upper valve roughened | |
| ** | Shell small, 20 mm. (4/5 in.), drab, tan white; range Maine to North Carolina | *A. squamula* |
| ** | Shell larger, 45 mm. (1 4/5 in.), whitish brown; range Florida to the West Indies | *Pododesmus rudis* |

Genus *Anomia* Linnaeus

*Anomia simplex* Orbigny
  Common Jingle Shell

  Pl. XXXVIII, 12

ETYMOLOGY: Gr. *anomoios*, unlike, dissimilar; Lat. *simplex*, simple, plain.

SIZE: 40 mm. (1 3/5 in.) in length and height.

DISTRIBUTION: Nova Scotia to the Gulf states, the West Indies, and Brazil.

CHARACTERISTICS: Shell small, glossy, thin. Color lemon-yellow, golden, brownish, or pale buff. Upper valve highly variable and irregular but generally inflated; lower valve flat, much stronger, white, with a large hole near the hinge.

This is one of the commonest shells in protected bay areas and huge numbers of the upper, more colorful, valve may litter these beaches. The animal lives fixed to rocks or to oyster or other shells by a strong calcified byssuslike extension that passes through the hole in the lower valve. Even after the shell has been removed this byssus still remains fixed to the substrate. Sometimes brilliant jet black shells are found, but these are merely dead shells that have been trapped in black mud or oil deposits and are artificially discolored. Jingle shells that become fixed to scallop or ark shells take on the characteristic radiating ridging of those shells and look quite different from the usual *Anomia*. The English name probably comes from the pleasant jingling sound the shells make when large numbers of loose ones are being rolled over on shore by waves. The Latin generic name refers to the extreme variability of the shells.

The **Prickly Jingle Shell,** *Anomia squamula* Linnaeus (Lat. *squamula*, scaly) (pl. XXXVIII, 13), is only half the size of *A. simplex*. It is yellowish white and much flatter and by no means so attractive an object as the latter. Its surface is not smooth and shiny but much roughened by radiating lines of prickly scales. It is a northern species ranging from Labrador to North Carolina. Formerly known as *A. aculeata* Gmelin (Lat. *aculeus,* thorn or prickle), a later name.

The **Rough Jingle Shell,** *Pododesmus rudis* Broderip (Gr. *pous demos,* foot ligament; Lat. *rudis,* rough) (pl. XXXVIII, 14), reaches 45 mm. (almost 2 in.). Its shape is very variable, but the white lower valve with a hole near the beak is always flatter than the whitish brown upper one. The interior is pearly, and the surface is very roughened, with scaly, indistinct growth lines. Abbott reports that it is moderately common in crevices of coral boulders just below the low-water mark. It ranges from Florida to Texas and the West Indies.

SUPERFAMILY:

# LIMACEA

---

FAMILY:

# LIMIDAE
(*file shells*)

These shells are obliquely oval, generally rather thin, and either smooth or rather weakly sculptured. They resemble the Pectinidae, but are not as strongly ridged. Like the scallops, they are good swimmers, darting about trailing their numerous filamentlike, colorful tentacles. They are found in warmer seas, often in shallow water, living in crevices and under rocks, where they construct nests of shells and pebbles held together with byssuslike threads.

---

## KEY TO GENUS LIMA

| | |
|---|---|
| * Shell opaque, light to dark brown | |
| ** Shell sculpture rough, ribs imbricated | *Lima scabra* |
| ** Shell sculpture smooth, satiny | *L. s. tenera* |
| * Shell often translucent, always white | |
| ** Ribs strong, spinose | *L. lima* |
| ** Ribs weak, smooth | *L. pellucida* |

---

Genus *Lima* Bruguière

*Lima lima* Linnaeus
Spiny File Shell

Pl. XXXIX, 21

ETYMOLOGY: Lat. *lima*, file.

SIZE: 45 mm. (1 4/5 in.) in length, 55 mm. (2 1/5 in.) in height.

DISTRIBUTION: Southeastern Florida to Texas and the West Indies.

CHARACTERISTICS: Shell 37–50 mm. (1 1/2–2 in.) in height, rather fragile, irregularly oval. Hinge ears unequal in size. Color pure white. Surface sculptured with numerous radiating spinose ribs.

*Lima,* like *Pecten* (see page 367), are able to flit through the water by manipulating their valves and mantle margins. But many species construct nests of byssal threads in which are caught bits of broken shell and rock. In these nests, they spend their entire lives if they are not disturbed. If the nest is broken open, however, they flit away rapidly and set about constructing a new one. The mantle edge is armed with long waving tentacles, which, at least in some species, have been shown to secrete an ill-tasting fluid that predators quickly learn to avoid. *Lima lima* is moderately common under coral boulders in shallow water.

The **Rough File Shell,** *Lima scabra* Born (Lat. *scaber* rough) (pl. XXXIX, 22), is about the same size as *Lima lima.* It differs in having a more evenly oval shape and many more, narrower ribs. These ribs do not have sharp spines, but are coarse, covered with low scales arranged like the tiles on a roof. The color is light to dark brown, and the shell is opaque. When *L. scabra* flits about, it shows a fiery red to bright orange red fleshy interior with vivid red tentacles, a very beautiful sight. Sometimes individuals spend their lives in nests constructed inside holes bored by *Lithophaga;* shells of such animals are strongly constricted laterally, and the shape is rectangular rather than oval. This species ranges from North Carolina to Texas and the West Indies. The form *L. scabra tenera* Sowerby (pl. XXXVIII, 15) differs only in having a much smoother, almost satiny shell, with narrower, lower, smoother ribs. It is found together with *L. scabra.*

The **Pellucid File Shell,** *Lima pellucida* C. B. Adams (Lat. *pellucere,* to shine through) (pl. XXXVIII, 16), is smaller, 16 mm. (2/3 in.) in length, 25 mm. (1 in.) in height. It is white and translucent. The surface is covered with fine, smooth, wavy radiating ribs. The hinge ears are almost equal in size. This species ranges from North Carolina to the West Indies, and single valves are sometimes found on the beach.

SUPERFAMILY:
# OSTREACEA

---

FAMILY:
# OSTREIDAE
(*oysters*)

The rough irregular shells of the edible oysters are well known to all epicureans of sea food. The gray shells may be overgrown with other shells and algae, but in the warmer seas, many are more colorful, some having reddish or yellowish green shells. These oysters are worldwide in distribution, commonly found on hard substrates to which the lower valve is securely cemented. The pearls formed by these oysters are not nacreous, and are seldom of commercial value. This is a very ancient group, dating from the upper Triassic about 180 million years ago. Some extinct oysters attained gigantic dimensions and weight, reaching the size of a pizza pan and weighing several pounds.

---

## KEY TO GENERA OSTREA AND CRASSOSTREA

* Shell purplish red, margins strongly scalloped — *Ostrea frons*
* Shell light colored, gray or yellowish, margins smooth or lightly crenulated
** Muscle scars purple, shell elongate, margin smooth — *Crassostrea virginica*
** Muscle scars white, almost central, shell oval
*** Umbones prominent, turned sharply to one side, interior white, margins smooth — *Ostrea permollis*
*** Umbones not prominent, not turned to one side, interior greenish gray, margins crenulate — *O. equestris*

Genus *Ostrea* Linnaeus

*Ostrea equestris* Say
  Horse Oyster

  Pl. XXXIX, 23

ETYMOLOGY: Gr. *ostreon*, oyster; Lat. *eques*, horsemen.

SIZE: 39 mm. (1 3/5 in.) in length, 36 mm. (1 1/2 in.) in height.

DISTRIBUTION: Virginia to Texas and the West Indies.

CHARACTERISTICS: Shell generally oval but often distorted, color dull to
  brownish, interior grayish green. Lower valve with a high, crenulated
  margin. Muscle scars almost central.

This species resembles the common edible Eastern Oyster (see below),
and also plays an important economic role. The two species' shells,
however, are not easily confused. The Horse Oyster, which is also
known as the Crested Oyster because of the crenulated margin of
the lower valve, is more southerly in its distribution, and it lives
in more saline waters than its northern relative.

The **Leafy Oyster,** *Ostrea frons* Linnaeus (Lat. *frons,* a leaf) (pl.
XXXIX, 24), reaches 30 mm. (1 1/5 in.) in length and 54 mm. (about
2 1/5 in.) in height, but it is frequently smaller. It is readily recognized by its color, which is reddish purple on the outside and whitish
inside. In addition, the shell has strong folds, which terminate in a
strong, zigzag margin. Frequently the shells develop grasping projections, termed claspers, along a central ridge of the lower valve;
by this means the bivalve becomes attached to mangrove roots and
other objects. The species, which ranges from Florida and Louisiana
to the West Indies, is a favorite food of raccoons, and is therefore
also called the Coon Oyster. Some writers place it in the genus *Lopha*
Röding.

The **Sponge Oyster,** *Ostrea permollis* Sowerby (Lat. *per mollis,*
very soft) (pl. XL, 1), is 25 mm. (1 in.) in length and 30 mm. (1 1/5
in.) in height. The shape is variable, but the species is most readily
recognized by its thin, translucent, and rather smooth shell and its
light yellowish color. The prominent umbones are flattened to the
surface and abruptly turned to one side. This species lives in the
"bread sponge," where only the margins show beyond the surface of
the sponge. It is a fairly common species, ranging from North
Carolina to the West Indies.

The **Eastern Oyster,** *Crassostrea virginica* Gmelin (Lat. *crassus,*
Gr. *ostreon*, thick oyster) (pl. XLI, 1), can grow up to 150 mm.

(6 in.) in length, and very old specimens develop a shell that can be as thick as 1 inch. The shape is elongate but exceedingly variable, depending upon the substrate on which it grew. Nevertheless, the shells that house this tasty morsel are readily recognizable. They are rough on the outside, dirty white, and frequently overgrown with seaweed and covered by other mollusks. The interior is white, with purple muscle scars and a purple stain along the edges. This species, ranging from the Gulf of Saint Lawrence to the Gulf of Mexico and the West Indies, is one of the most important invertebrates in commercial fisheries. The Eastern Oyster was formerly placed in the genus *Ostrea*, but was removed to *Crassostrea* Sacco because of important morphological and reproductive differences.

SUBCLASS:

# HETERODONTA

(*differentiated teeth*)

ORDER:

# VENEROIDA

SUPERFAMILY:

## LUCINACEA

FAMILY:

## LUCINIDAE

(*lucina shells*)

These shells are generally circular, compressed or inflated, white or light colored, and smooth or weakly sculptured. The hinge teeth are weak. This is mainly a warm-water group, but some representatives are found in temperate seas.

## KEY TO FAMILY LUCINIDAE

* Shell without hinge teeth                                        *Anodontia*
* Shell with hinge teeth
** Shell inflated, shiny, surface with chevronlike sculpture    *Divaricella*

  ∗ ∗ Shell with radial and/or concentric sculpture
∗ ∗ ∗ Shell compressed, sculpture strong, rarely beaded      *Codakia*
∗ ∗ ∗ Shell inflated, sculpture various                      *Lucina*

---

# KEY TO GENUS LUCINA

  ∗ Shell large, 35 to 55 mm. (1 2/5 to 2 1/5 in.)
  ∗ ∗ Shell with deep axial furrow                            *Lucina pensylvanica*
  ∗ ∗ Shell without furrow
∗ ∗ ∗ Shell white                                             *L. floridana*
∗ ∗ ∗ Shell yellow to orange                                  *L. pectinata*
  ∗ Shell small, 6 to 10 mm. (1/4 to 2/5 in.)
  ∗ ∗ Shell with about 8 strong, widening axial
      furrows, concentric threads fine                        *L. amianta*
  ∗ ∗ Radial and concentric markings about equal
∗ ∗ ∗ Scales present where radial and concentric
      furrows cross, ventral margin strongly beaded           *L. nassula*
∗ ∗ ∗ Scales absent, inner ventral margin finely
      denticulate                                             *L. multilineata*

---

Genus *Lucina* Bruguière

*Lucina pensylvanica* Linnaeus
  Pennsylvania Lucina

  Pl. XL, 2

ETYMOLOGY: Juno Lucina was the Roman goddess of childbirth; Linnaeus's
  spelling of *pensylvanica* must be preserved for this shell.

SIZE: 54 mm. (about 2 1/5 in.) in length, 53 mm. (about 2 1/5 in.) in height.

DISTRIBUTION: North Carolina to southern Florida.

CHARACTERISTICS: Shell medium, almost circular, moderately strong,
  inflated. Color pure white under a thin yellowish periostracum.
  Concentric ridges pronounced but thin and delicate, posterior radial
  furrow very strong. Hinge teeth small, weak.

With the species of the subclass Heterodonta (Gr. *heteros odous*,
different teeth) we come to the largest group of present-day
bivalves. They all have more or less equal-sized adductor muscles,

and are hence considered to be isomyarin (Gr. *isos mya,* equal sea mussel) in contrast to the Anisomyaria, which we have dealt with so far. In addition, the heterodonts usually have two different types of hinge teeth—the *heteros* part of the subclass name—cardinal teeth, smaller, vertical teeth under the umbones and lateral teeth, usually longer, more or less horizontal teeth lying to one or both sides of the umbo. In the case of Lucinidae, these teeth, with some exceptions, are usually small. This and the following species were recently placed in the genus *Linga* de Gregorio by specialists.

The Pennsylvania Lucina is fairly common in shallow water. It is readily recognized by the deep, slightly curved furrow that runs from the umbo to the posterior ventral margin. The distinct but delicate concentric ridges are usually lost in beach shells, which then become smooth and glossy. It is in this condition that the shells are commonly found in beach drift in Florida.

The **Miniature Lucina,** *Lucina amianta* Dall (Gr. *amiantos,* unsoiled) (pl. XL, 3), is only 6 to 10 mm. (1/4 to 2/5 in.) in size. The pure white shell is inflated, quite strong, and marked with eight to nine widening radial ribs crossed by numerous delicate concentric lines. In well-preserved specimens there is a radial row of eight to twelve small scales along the posterior margin. This species ranges from North Carolina to Texas, where it lives buried in mud or fine sand in bays and inlets.

The **Many-lined Lucina,** *Lucina multilineata* Tuomey & Holmes (Lat. *multus lineatus,* many lined) (pl. XL, 4), resembles *L. amianta* in size, shape, and color. It differs in being more swollen and in having only a very finely reticulated surface, the concentric ridges being somewhat stronger than the radiating lines, thus presenting a much smoother appearance. It has the same range and habitat as *L. amianta.* Recently put in the genus *Parvilucina* Dall.

The **Florida Lucina,** *Lucina floridana* Conrad (pl. XL, 5), is about 34 mm. (1 2/5 in.) in length and 36 mm. (1 1/2 in.) in height. The shell is white and thin, with a brownish, flaking periostracum. The surface is smoothish, marked only by irregular growth lines; radiating lines are lacking. This species is a Gulf form, ranging from the west coast of Florida to Texas. It is commonly found dead on beaches. Assigned to the genus *Pseudomiltha* Conrad by specialists.

The **Comb Lucina,** *Lucina pectinata* Gmelin (Lat. *pecten,* comb) (pl. XL, 6), is 55 mm. (2 1/5 in.) long, 50 mm. (2 in.) high. The shell is pale yellow to orange, the surface marked with fine, unequal, concentric ridges. The hinge plate is rather wide, with strong, lateral teeth in the left valve fitting into corresponding sockets in the opposing right valve. This is a mud-dwelling species ranging from North Carolina to Texas and the West Indies.

The **Basket Lucina,** *Lucina nassula* Conrad (diminutive of Lat. *nassa,* straw fishing basket) (pl. XL, 7), is 10 mm. (2/5 in.) in size. It is white, with elegant, reticulated sculpture of twenty radiating and about twenty concentric ridges, which are produced in tiny, raised scales at the points where the ridges cross. The lower margin is denticulated by the ends of the radiating ridges. The species ranges from North Carolina to Texas and the Bahamas. This and the previous species were formerly placed in the genus *Phacoides.*

# KEY TO GENUS ANODONTIA

* Shell with smooth, yellow orange interior    *Anodontia alba*
* Shell with pustulose white interior    *A. philippiana*

The **Buttercup Lucina,** *Anodontia alba* Link (Gr. *an odous,* without tooth; Lat. *albus,* dead white) (pl. XL, 8), is 50 mm. (2 in.) in diameter. It is almost circular, moderately well inflated, rather smooth, and without hinge teeth. It is white externally, but the interior is brilliant yellow orange. It was formerly known as *Loripinus chrysostoma* Philippi (Gr. *chrysos, stoma,* gold mouth). The Buttercup Lucina is a common species ranging from North Carolina to the West Indies, and is much used in shellcraft.

**Philippi's Lucina,** *Anodontia philippiana* Reeve (R. A. Philippi was a German malacologist of the nineteenth century) (pl. XLI, 2), is about 75 mm. (3 in.) in diameter, and differs from *A. alba* in being all white inside and out. The interior, moreover, is not smooth but strongly pimpled. This is an inhabitant of deeper water, but the inflated, rather light shell enables it to float into shore when dead. It ranges from North Carolina to Texas and the West Indies. It was formerly called *Loripinus schrammi* Crosse.

# KEY TO GENUS CODAKIA

* Shell large, 80 mm. (3 1/5 in.), compressed, ribs
  beaded, interior marked with yellow and red          *Codakia orbicularis*
* Shell small, 13 mm. (1/2 in.), all white, ribs smooth   *C. orbiculata*

The **Tiger Lucina,** *Codakia orbicularis* Linnaeus (Senegalese *codok*, shell; Lat. *orbiculus*, small circle or disk) (pl. XLI, 3), is about 80 mm. (3 1/5 in.) in diameter. It is a common species, readily recognized by its large size and circular and strongly compressed white valves, which are frequently flushed internally with a yellow stain below the umbo and sometimes stained with pink along the hinge margin. The surface is thickly sculptured with narrow radial ribs crossed by fine, concentric threads, making them look weakly beaded. In this species, the lunule, a small, usually heart-shaped depression in front of the umbones, is deep, and nearly all of it rests on the right valve. The Tiger Lucina ranges from Florida to the West Indies. The English name, despite its puzzling applicability, has become quite common among collectors and shellcrafters.

The **Dwarf Tiger Lucina,** *Codakia orbiculata* Montagu (Lat. *orbiculatus,* circular) (pl. XL, 9), is about 13 mm. (1/2 in.) in diameter. It looks like a miniature edition of *C. orbicularis,* but it is more swollen, though still quite compressed; the surface sculpture is stronger; and the shell color is white. The lunule is large, elongate heart shaped, and rests equally on both valves. This is a common species ranging from North Carolina to the West Indies.

# KEY TO GENUS DIVARICELLA

* Shell 20 mm. (4/5 in.), margins smooth    *Divaricella quadrisulcata*
* Shell 30 mm. (1 1/5 in.), margins
  denticulate; southern range only          *D. dentata*

The **Cross-hatched Lucina,** *Divaricella quadrisulcata* Orbigny (Lat. *divaricare,* to spread, stretch apart; and *quadrisulcatus,* four-furrowed) (pl. XL, 10), is about 20 mm. (4/5 in.) in size. It is quite swollen, almost globular, white, and shiny, and the surface has prominent grooves that bend obliquely downward at both ends, giving the sculpture a chevronlike appearance. This is a species from deeper water, but single valves are common on the beaches. The species ranges from Massachusetts to the West Indies.

The **Dentate Lucina**, *Divaricella dentata* Wood (pl. XL, 11), is larger, reaching 30 mm. (1 1/5 in.), and differs chiefly by having fine teeth instead of smooth edges. It is a southern species, ranging from North Carolina to the West Indies.

SUPERFAMILY:

# CHAMACEA

FAMILY:

# CHAMIDAE
(*jewel boxes*)

A family of thick, irregular, roughly sculptured shells, commonly with brilliant colors. They live fixed to hard substrates below the tide lines in warm waters. In many ways they resemble some of the smaller *Spondylus* (see pages 371–2), differing, however, in the nature of the hinge.

## KEY TO GENERA CHAMA, PSEUDOCHAMA, AND ARCINELLA

* Umbones turned to the left, right valve is attached                                      *Pseudochama radians*
* Umbones turned to the right, left valve is attached
** Valves about equal, lower valve little if at all attached                               *Arcinella cornuta*
** Lower valve distinctly larger than the upper, and strongly cemented to the substrate
*** Shell richly colored, surface with more or less developed foliations                    *Chama macerophylla*

∗ ∗ ∗ Shell color subdued, surface with low, wavy
ridges
        *C. congregata*

---

Genus *Chama* Linnaeus

*Chama macerophylla* Gmelin
Leafy Jewel Box

Pl. XLI, 4

ETYMOLOGY: Lat. *chama*, gaper; Gr. *makros phyllon*, long leaf.

SIZE: 75 mm. (3 in.) in length, 60 mm. (2 2/5 in.) in height.

DISTRIBUTION: North Carolina to Florida, Gulf of Mexico, and the West
Indies.

CHARACTERISTICS: Shell large, umbones turning to right. Color bright,
variable: lemon yellow, reddish brown, deep to pale purple, orange,
pink or white, or in combinations. Lower (left) valve larger, deeper,
strongly attached to hard substrate; upper (right) valve flatter, circular;
valves thickly covered with long, scaly or leaflike lamellations.

These shells display the freshest, brightest colors of any mollusks; in
quiet waters the lamellations can grow as long as the spines of the
Spiny Oyster, *Spondylus* (see page 371). Jewel boxes live below the
tidal line, strongly cemented by the lower valve to coral, rocks, or any
hard, anchored object. A large number of very handsome ones were
once found on the hulk of a submerged steamer. The free upper
valve is frequently thrown on shore, where it becomes a rather unsightly bit of calcium, distinguished from *Spondylus* by its smaller
size and characteristic heterodont hinge teeth.

    The **Corrugated Jewel Box,** *Chama congregata* Conrad (Lat. *con-
gregatio,* a society, a gathering) (pl. XL, 12), is only 25 mm. (1 in.)
in size. It differs from the Leafy Jewel Box in having a smoother
surface, without the leaflike foliations. The surface instead is sculptured by wavy, moderately elevated radiating ridges crossed by
roughened concentric growth lines. The color is dull red or brown.
Like *C. macerophylla,* the umbones turn to the left. This is a rather
common species found attached to pen shells (*Atrina*), ark shells
(*Arca*), and other mollusk species, or to bits of broken coral rock
that offer a sufficiently wide surface. It ranges from North Carolina
to the Gulf of Mexico and the West Indies.

    The **False Jewel Box,** *Pseudochama radians* Lamarck (Gr. *pseudes,*

Lat. *chama*, false gaper; Lat. *radiare*, to emit rays) (pl. XL, 13),
is about 40 mm. (1 3/5 in.) in size. It has a heavy, dull white, cream-
colored, or dull purplish red shell, the interior usually stained with
brown. The surface is pitted and further roughened by low radiating
ribs and low, crude foliations. This species, like all members of the
genus *Pseudochama* Odhner, is fixed by the right valve, and the
umbones curve to the left. Thus, in outline it is a mirror image of
*C. macerophylla*. The False Jewel Box ranges from southern Florida
to Texas and the West Indies.

The **Spiny Jewel Box,** *Arcinella cornuta* Conrad (diminutive of
Lat. *arcus*, a bow; and *cornutus*, horned) (pl. XL, 14), is 35 mm.
(1 2/5 in). in length and 40 mm. (1 3/5 in.) in height. The shell is
thick, rather globular, and white, with brownish stains near the
umbo. The surface is ornamented with seven to nine radiating rows
of strong, longish spines. The shell is usually free, but sometimes it
is cemented to small bits of shell or stones. It ranges from North
Carolina to Florida, Texas, and the West Indies. *Arcinella arcinella*
Linnaeus, limited to the West Indies, has many more rows (seventeen
to twenty-five) of narrower and lower spines. Both these species were
formerly placed in the genus *Echinochama* (spiny gaper), a later
name (pl. XLI, 5).

SUPERFAMILY:

# GALCOMMATACEA
# =ERYCINACEA AND LEPTONACEA

FAMILY:

# LEPTONIDAE
(*leptons*)

The shells of the Leptonidae (Gr. *lepton*, a small coin, from *leptos*,
fine, delicate) are small to minute, white or reddish; hinge teeth
weak. They are found intertidally and in moderate depths from the
tropics to the colder waters. Many of these tiny bivalves live commensally or even parasitically on other marine invertebrates. Some
species attach themselves by byssal threads to the undersides of
crustaceans, and others inhabit the burrows these creatures build.

Because of their small size, leptons are often overlooked, and when found, identification of many species is not easy. Collectors frequently take them for the juvenile forms of larger bivalves. New species are still being discovered, and only the handful of experts who have studied them can be relied upon to give valid determinations.

Genus *Mysella* Angas

*Mysella planulata* Stimpson
Flat Lepton.

Pl. XL, 15

ETYMOLOGY: Diminutive of Gr. *mya*, sea mussel; and Lat. *planus*, flat, level.

SIZE: 5 mm. (1/5 in.) in length, 2.5 mm. (about 1/10 in.) in height.

DISTRIBUTION: Greenland to Texas and the West Indies.

CHARACTERISTICS: Shell very small, thin, compressed, depressed oval, or wedge shaped. Color white to reddish brown. Umbones small, not central, near posterior end.

This tiny shell need not be confused with the equally small *Gemma gemma*, whose range it shares. *Mysella* is more compressed, thinner, and more fragile, and the umbo is not central. It lives attached to buoys, eel grass, and jetties, but dead shells are fairly common in drift at the high-water line. This species has also been called *Rochefortia planulata*, after Rochefort, a French naturalist.

The genus *Aligena* H. C. Lea (Lat. *aliger*, winged) (pl. XLIV, 10), of the family Kelliidae, is another group of very small bivalves. They differ from the *Mysella* in that the shell is more strongly inflated, the umbones are centrally placed, and chiefly, in the two tiny cardinal teeth, one in each valve, that diverge from the umbo and project outward like a comma or a tiny finger. These bivalves are more swollen than *Gemma*, and have thinner shells, which are not denticulated marginally. The species *Aligena elevata* Stimpson is the commonest *Aligena* in our area. It measures about 6 mm. (1/4 in.) in length and about 5 mm. (1/5 in.) in height. It lives in shallow water from Massachusetts to North Carolina.

# CARDITACEA

# CARDITIDAE

(*cardita or little heart clams*)

These shells are small, heavy, and strongly sculptured axially. They are found in all seas, often at great depths.

Genus *Carditamera* Conrad

*Carditamera floridana* Conrad
  Florida Cardita

  Pl. XLI, 6

ETYMOLOGY: Diminutive of Gr. *kardia*, heart.

SIZE: 25 mm. (1 in.) in height, 40 mm. (1 3/5 in.) in length.

DISTRIBUTION: Southern Florida to Texas and Mexico.

CHARACTERISTICS: Shell small, elongate-oval, swollen, solid, and strong.
  Color whitish to gray, with small brownish broken color bars. Surface
  has about fifteen to twenty strong, rounded radiating ribs beaded by
  the concentric growth lines.

This is an abundant species in shallow water, and forms a prominent part of the beach shell drift, especially on the west coast of Florida. The shape and sculpture prevent confusion with any other species. It is also widely used in shellcraft. Long known as *Cardita floridana.*

The **Northern Cardita,** *Cyclocardia borealis* Conrad (Gr. *kyklos, kardia*, circle heart; Lat. *boreas*, north wind) (pl. XL, 16), is about 25 mm. (1 in.) in length and height. Like the Florida Cardita, it is thick and strong and sculptured with about 20 strong, rounded, roughened radiating ribs. However, it is obliquely heart shaped, and the color is whitish under a thick, velvety, dull brownish periostracum. It is sometimes called the Cod Clam, because its shells are frequently found in the stomachs of codfish. These strong shells withstand a great deal of heavy surf, and single valves are found on many ocean beaches. They range from Labrador to Cape Hatteras. Formerly placed in the genus *Venericardia* Lamarck (Lat. *Venus*, Gr. *kardia*, little Venus heart), a group of extinct heart shells.

SUPERFAMILY:
# CRASSATELLACEA

FAMILY:
# ASTARTIDAE
(*astarte clams*)

These shells are usually small, quite thick and heavy, and white under a strong, dark-colored periostracum; hinge teeth are large, well developed. This is a small family living mainly in cold seas, with some representatives in shallow, temperate waters.

## KEY TO GENUS ASTARTE

* Shell larger, reaching 40 mm. (1 3/5 in.) in length; range northern, to Massachusetts only     *Astarte borealis*
* Shell smaller, reaching only 25 mm. (1 in.) in length; range more southern, to Cape Hatteras
** Shell surface smooth     *A. castanea*
** Shell surface with wide concentric ridges     *A. undata*

Genus *Astarte* Sowerby

*Astarte castanea* Say
    Chestnut or Smooth Astarte

    Pl. XL, 17

ETYMOLOGY: Astarte was the Greek form of the name of Ashtaroth, the Phoenician goddess of fertility; Lat. *castanea*, chestnut.

SIZE: 25 mm. (1 in.) in length and height.

DISTRIBUTION: Nova Scotia to Cape Hatteras, North Carolina.

CHARACTERISTICS: Shell small, heavy, very thick, smooth, trigonal in shape. Color whitish under a strong black or chestnut brown periostracum. Umbones high, slightly hooked; margins finely crenulated.

This species is easily recognized by its small, heavy, smooth shell, and, if not worn off, by its strong brown periostracum. Dead shells are fairly common on the beaches, and fine live specimens can be collected in sand on Cape Cod, Long Island, and elsewhere. The soft parts of the clam have a brilliant scarlet color, which contrasts pleasingly with the glossy chestnut. Shells with an almost black periostracum were named *A. castanea picea* Gould; and those with a dull yellowish brown color, *A. castanea procera* Totten. These forms are merely color variations of this species.

Astarte is the Phoenician counterpart of the Roman Venus. Several other names of the pagan love goddess have been given to these beautiful bivalves, possibly because Venus rose from the sea in a Venus-like shell.

The **Wavy Astarte**, *Astarte undata* Gould (Lat. *undatus*, wavy) (pl. XLI, 7), is slightly smaller, 20 mm. (4/5 in.) in size, and more broadly triangular, with lower umbones than *A. castanea*. It differs mostly, however, by having the surface marked with about fifteen strong, rounded concentric ridges. This species ranges from Labrador to deep waters off Chesapeake Bay, but it is found in shallow water as far south as New Jersey. It is said to be the commonest *Astarte* in New England.

The **Boreal Astarte**, *Astarte borealis* Schumacher (Lat. *boreas*, north wind) (pl. XLI, 8), is usually about 40 mm. (1 3/5 in.) in length and 25 mm. (1 in.) in height. It is quite variable in shape and surface sculpture. Some specimens have high curved umbones and show concentric ridges only near them; others have lower umbones and oval outlines and concentric lines covering nearly the entire shell. But these ridges are narrower and smaller and more numerous than the ridges in *A. undata*. The species, which ranges from the Arctic seas to Massachusetts Bay is sometimes found washed up on shore in Maine and Massachusetts.

FAMILY:

# CRASSATELLIDAE

(*crassinella clams*)

Most members of this family tend to be heavy, bulky shells with massive hinge plates, quite unlike the single crassetellid that we discuss, which is small and has a narrow hinge plate. This is an ancient bivalve family reaching back to the Devonian Period, some 350 million years ago.

Genus *Crassinella* Guppy

*Crassinella lunatula* Conrad
    The Crescent Crassinella

    Pl. XLII, 1

ETYMOLOGY: Diminutive of Lat. *crassus*, thick, heavy; and *lunatus*, moon-shaped.

SIZE: 8 mm. (1/3 in.) in diameter.

DISTRIBUTION: Massachusetts Bay to Florida, Texas, and the West Indies.

CHARACTERISTICS: Shell small, triangular, with two straight sides and a rounded lower edge. Umbones high, pointed; the color white, yellowish, or, in the southern part of the range, pinkish. Sculpture variously ridged, from barely defined to quite strong.

This species somewhat resembles *Parastarte* because of its triangular shape, but it is much larger and the surface sculpture, when present, is stronger. This is a shallow water inhabitant that is common in gravelly or shelly bottoms. *C. mactracea* Linsley has recently been shown to be the same species.

SUPERFAMILY:

# CARDIACEA

---

FAMILY:

# CARDIIDAE
(*cockle or heart shells*)

The shells in this family are generally swollen and heart-shaped, especially when viewed from the side, smooth and glossy, or strongly sculptured radially; hinge teeth are small. This is one of the larger bivalve families, with representatives in all seas. They are often used for food, especially in Europe. Most species have a strong, sickle-shaped foot that enables the animal to leap about in a lively manner. Though present also in temperate and even colder water, the most richly colored and sculptured heart shells are found in the tropics.

---

## KEY TO FAMILY CARDIIDAE

* Shell surface smooth *Laevicardium*
* Shell surface sculptured, usually with strong radiating ribs
** Ribs roughened by scales and/or spines *Trachycardium*
** Ribs generally smooth or lightly marked with concentric growth lines
*** Shell quite small, 15 mm. (3/5 in.), thin, ribs wide, flat *Cerastoderma*
*** Shell larger, 25 to 80 mm. (1 to 3 1/5 in.), color tawny with brownish blotches, ribs strong
**** Shell up to 80 mm. (3 1/5 in.), evenly ovate, gently domed at both sides, or in one subspecies, with a more strongly descending posterior ridge *Dinocardium*
**** Shell about 25 mm. (1 in.), with strongly descending, almost perpendicular posterior edge *Americardia*

Genus *Dinocardium* Dall

*Dinocardium robustum* Lightfoot
  Giant Atlantic Cockle

Pl. XLI, 9

ETYMOLOGY: Gr. *deinos kardia*, mighty heart; Lat. *robustus*, strong, hard.

SIZE: 75 to 106 mm. (3 to 4 in.) in length, 85 to 104 mm. (3 2/5 to 4 in.) in height.

DISTRIBUTION: Virginia to northern Florida, Texas, and the Gulf of Mexico.

CHARACTERISTICS: Shell large, inflated, obliquely circular, moderately heavy. Exterior color pale buff, occasionally with reddish brown color patches, posterior slope mahogany red shading to purplish; interior rose to brownish rose. Surface has numerous strong, wide, smooth radiating ribs. Hinge teeth small but well developed.

This large cockle is readily recognized by its brownish color and the strong ribs, which are only slightly marked with growth lines. Less commonly seen in collections than Van Hyning's Cockle, described below, it is replaced in central and southern Florida by that subspecies.

**Van Hyning's Cockle,** *Dinocardium robustum vanhyningi* Clench & L. C. Smith (T. Van Hyning, who died in 1948, was the director of the Florida State Museum in Gainesville) (pl. XLI, 10), differs mainly in being more obliquely elongate and somewhat triangular in shape. In addition, it is usually larger, and shows more vivid color. This is the common Florida cockle which figures so greatly in shellcraft. It has a peculiarly restricted range, on the west coast of Florida from Clearwater to Cape Sable.

The **Prickly Cockle,** *Trachycardium egmontianum* Shuttleworth (Gr. *trachys kardia*, rough heart; named for Egmont Key, Florida) (pl. XLI, 11), is about 40 to 60 mm. (1 3/5 to 2 2/5 in.) in size. It is somewhat elongate and circular, and the twenty-seven to thirty-one radiating ribs are strongly marked with imbricated scales, that is, scales arranged like tiles on a roof; the scales are more strongly developed on the posterior side of the valves. Externally the shells are whitish or tawny gray, with yellow brown or purplish patches; internally they are marked with salmon or light purple areas. This species ranges from North Carolina to Florida and the West Indies.

The **Yellow Cockle,** *Trachycardium muricatum* Linnaeus (Lat.

*muricatus,* from *murex,* purple snail or a pointed stone) (pl. XLI, 12), is about 60 mm. (2 2/5 in.) in size. It differs from *T. egmontianum* by being almost circular in outline and in that the thirty to forty radiating ribs are armed with only small, toothlike scales, which are absent from the upper area of the valves. The external color is commonly light cream, with irregular patches of brownish red, but many specimens show shades of yellow or orange. Florida specimens usually have a yellow wash over most of the interior, the reason for its Floridian English name. This species has a large range from North Carolina to Argentina, including the West Indies and the Gulf of Mexico.

**Morton's Cockle,** *Laevicardium mortoni* Conrad (Lat. *laevis,* Gr. *kardia,* smooth heart; Samuel G. Morton, 1799–1851, was an American naturalist) (pl. XVI, 2), is a small shell, 15 to 25 mm. (3/5 to 1 in.) in size. It is rather thin but strong, and the surface is quite smooth, marked only by weak growth lines. Smooth, very weak radiating ribs can be seen, rather than felt, in the interior. Externally the shell is dirty white, with occasional individuals showing pretty brown zigzag markings; the interior is shining yellow, with a deep purple patch on the posterior side. This species ranges from Nova Scotia to Florida and the Gulf of Mexico. In Long Island, New York, where it is abundant in muddy bottoms in shallow water, it is called the Duck Clam, because it is eagerly eaten by several species of migrating ducks.

The **Egg Cockle,** *Laevicardium laevigatum* Linnaeus (Lat. *laevis,* smooth) (pl. XVI, 3), is also smooth and shining, but the shell is more elongate and much larger, reaching 70 mm. (almost 3 in.) in length and 60 mm. (2 2/5 in.) in height. The external color is varied, pure white, with patches of rose or brown, or yellow to orange brown with similar patches. Internally there are pale or intense yellow, orange, or pinkish purple shades. The surface often shows about sixty radiating ridges, which are so fine that they cannot be felt. This is a species found more to the south, ranging from North Carolina to Texas, the Caribbean area, and Brazil. It was formerly erroneously called *Laevicardium serratum* Linnaeus, an Indo-Pacific species. **Ravenel's Egg Cockle,** *L. pictum* Ravenel, is smaller, more oblique and more brightly colored. It lives in deep water from South Carolina to the Gulf of Mexico, but specimens are occasionally found in fish stomachs. (Pl. XLI, 13.)

The **American Cockle,** *Americardia media* Linnaeus (America, and Gr. *kardia,* American heart; Lat. *medius,* middle) (pl. XVI, 8), is about 40 mm. (1 3/5 in.) in size. It has strong, inflated valves and a sharply descending, almost vertical posterior ridge, which gives the shell, when seen from above, a broad triangular outline. There are thirty-three to thirty-six strong radiating ribs; the ribs on the vertical side are armed with rough plates, while the others are quite smooth. The color is white, well mottled with reddish brown. This species lives in shallow water and ranges from North Carolina to Florida and the West Indies. It was formerly called *Trigoniocardia media*.

The **Dwarf Northern Cockle,** *Cerastoderma pinnulatum* Conrad (Gr. *kerastes derma*, horny skin; Lat. *pinnula*, little feather or pen) (pl. XLI, 14), is quite small, reaching only 15 mm. (3/5 in.) in size. It is thin, obliquely circular in outline, and sculptured with twenty-two to twenty-eight flattened and gently rounded ribs; the ribs have thin, slightly arched scales. The color is cream or white, often with a brownish infusion. This is a northern species, ranging from Labrador to deep water off North Carolina, and it is found in shallower water north of Cape Cod. It is a common shell in the stomachs of fish taken off New England.

SUPERFAMILY:

# MACTRACEA

FAMILIES:

# MACTRIDAE AND MESODESMATIDAE
(*surf clams*)

These shells are mostly large, fragile to moderately strong, and either smooth, marked only by prominent growth lines, or concentrically ridged. Under the umbo is a central spoonlike pit to accommodate a dark, tough resilium. Generally shallow-water shells, found in all seas.

# KEY TO FAMILIES
# MACTRIDAE AND MESODESMATIDAE

\* Shell small, less than 20 mm. (4/5 in.)

\*\* Shell swollen, posterior ridge well
developed       *Mulinia lateralis*

\*\* Shell compressed, posterior ridge absent       *Spisula solidissima*
(juvenile)

\* Shell large, 40 mm. (1 3/5 in.) and larger

\*\* Chondrophore, with subcentral shell
ridge separating it from the ligament

\*\*\* Shell oval, moderately thin, yellowish,
smooth       *Mactra fragilis*

\*\*\* Shell oblique, fragile, white, surface with
strong concentric ridges       *Raeta plicatella*

\*\* Chondrophore without shelly ridge

\*\*\* Shell wedge shaped, with umbones near
posterior end       *Mesodesma arctatum*

\*\*\* Shell with umbones more or less central

\*\*\*\* Shell obliquely triangular, very heavy,
periostracum persistent       *Rangia cuneata*

\*\*\*\* Shell more or less oval, posterior and
anterior margins equally rounded,
periostracum deciduous

\*\*\*\*\* V-shaped cardinal tooth strong, laterals
with smooth sides; distribution northern,
reaching Rhode Island only       *Spisula polynyma*

\*\*\*\*\* V-shaped cardinal tooth weak, laterals
strongly ridged on the sides

\*\*\*\*\*\* Shell very large, 150 to 200 mm. (6 to 8
in.); northern distribution to Virginia
only       *S. solidissima*

\*\*\*\*\*\* Shell smaller, 75 to 100 mm. (3 to 4 in.);
distribution from Virginia southward       *S. s. raveneli*

---

Genus *Mactra* Linnaeus

*Mactra fragilis* Gmelin
Fragile Surf Clam

Pl. XLIV, 11

ETYMOLOGY: Gr. *maktra*, kneading trough; Lat. *fragilis*, brittle.

SIZE: 60 mm. (2 2/5 in.) in length, 38 mm. (1 1/2 in.) in height.

DISTRIBUTION: North Carolina to Florida, Texas, and the West Indies.

CHARACTERISTICS: Shell rather large, thin but strong, oval. Color white, under a thin yellowish periostracum. Surface smooth, marked only with fine, irregular growth lines. The posterior slope has two small radiating ridges; chondrophore with a low, almost central axial ridge separating it from the internal ligament.

This is a common surf clam found living in sand in shallow water in Florida. Dead valves are also frequently found on the beaches. It is readily recognized by the large, thin, white shell—which can reach 100 mm. (4 in.) in length in exceptional specimens—and the two radiating posterior ridges. The Mactridae, in addition to an external or internal ligament to hold the two valves together, also have a dark brown chitinous resilium, which rests in a small triangular cavity located just under the umbo, called the "chondrophore" (Gr. *chondros phora,* grain carrier). The chondrophore acts as a spring opposing the two adductor muscles, which pull the valves together. In the genus *Mactra* the chondrophore is provided with a low, shelly ridge, in the genus *Spisula* Gray the chondrophore is without such a structure.

The **Atlantic Surf Clam,** *Spisula solidissima* Dillwyn (Lat. *spissus,* thick, compact; augmentative of *solidus,* whole, entire) (pl. XLI, 15), is the largest bivalve on the eastern coast of North America, growing up to 225 mm. (9 in.) long, though the usual size is nearer 150 mm. (6 in.) in length and 113 mm. (4 1/2 in.) in height. The mature shell is heavy, thick, and broadly triangular with evenly rounded edges, and is yellowish white in color under a thin, brownish periostracum that is usually removed in beach populations by the action of sand and waves. There is also a very fragile, V-shaped cardinal tooth, which is commonly broken when the two shells are forced apart. In addition, the long lateral teeth have the sides strongly scored with sharp, oblique ridges. Small, immature specimens are sometimes confused with *Mulinia lateralis,* but they are less swollen and lack the posterior ridge. The Atlantic Surf Clam ranges from Nova Scotia to Virginia.

**Ravenel's Surf Clam,** *Spisula solidissima raveneli* Conrad (Edmund Ravenel, 1797–1871, was an American malacologist) (pl. XLI, 16), is smaller, only 70 mm. (2 4/5 in.) in length and proportionately lower, more elongate, and smoother. This is the southern race of *S. solidissima;* it ranges from Virginia to Florida and Texas. It was formerly mistaken for *S. solidissima similis* Say, which is apparently merely a juvenile *solidissima*.

**Stimpson's Surf Clam,** *Spisula polynyma* Stimpson (Gr. *polys nêma,* many filament) (pl. XLIV, 12), is a northern species, ranging only from the Arctic seas to Rhode Island; it also occurs on the West Coast to Puget Sound, as well as in Japan. It reaches 125 mm. (5 in.) in length, and differs from *S. solidissima* in being higher and shorter, with the anterior end somewhat shorter than the posterior. The V-shaped cardinal tooth is stronger and more likely to survive the separation of the valves, and the sides of the longish lateral teeth are smooth, without ridges. It is said to occur plentifully at low water in Eastport and other coastal areas of Maine.

The **Dwarf Surf Clam,** *Mulinia lateralis* Say (*mulinia* is an artificial word without meaning; Lat. *lateralis,* from *latus,* side) (pl. XLII, 2), is a much smaller species, reaching only 14 mm. (about 3/5 in.) in length and 12 mm. (1/2 in.) in height. It is swollen and triangular in shape, with a distinct but rounded posterior ridge. The chondrophore is much smaller proportionately than in juvenile *S. solidissima,* which also lack the posterior ridge and are much less inflated. The color is a nondescript grayish white under a light buff periostracum. This is an abundant species in quiet waters ranging from the Gulf of Saint Lawrence to northern Florida and Texas.

The **Channeled Surf Clam,** *Raeta plicatella* Lamarck (*raeta* is an artificial word without meaning; diminutive of Lat. *plica,* fold) (pl. XLI, 17), is 50 to 75 mm. (2 to 3 in.) in size. The shell is pure white, thin, and fragile. In shape it is obliquely oval; the surface is pleasingly ornamented with handsome, raised concentric ridges. The hinge teeth are much reduced. This is a fairly common species found from North Carolina to Texas and the Caribbean. It was formerly called *Anatina canaliculata* Say, a later name, and it was placed in the genus *Labiosa,* which is a synonym of *Anatina.*

The **Wedge Rangia,** *Rangia cuneata* Sowerby (Sander Rang, 1784–1859, was a French malacologist; Lat. *cuneus,* wedge) (pl. XLI, 18), is about 50 mm. (2 in.) in size. The shell is thick, heavy, and obliquely triangular or wedge shaped. The chondrophore is deep and the umbones elevated. In color the shell is whitish, under a strong olive green or brownish periostracum. This is a very abundant species, ranging from Virginia to northern Florida and the Gulf of Mexico. *Rangia* is so abundant locally that the city of Mobile, Alabama, is said to be built on the bones of the dead bivalve.

The **Arctic Wedge Clam,** *Mesodesma arctatum* Conrad (Gr. *mesos desma,* middle band; Arctic) (pl. XLIV, 13), is 40 mm. (1 3/5 in.)

in length, and 25 mm. (1 in.) in height. It is readily recognized by its wedge-shaped shell, with the umbones shifted to the posterior side. In addition, the shell is strong, compressed, grayish white in color, with a thin yellowish periostracum. The chondrophore is large and spoon shaped. The shells resemble a large, unhandsome *Donax* (see page 415). They live in shallow water in sand, tending to congregate around the inlets to bays. The range is from Canada to northern New Jersey, and they are common on the beaches of Cape Cod and eastern Long Island, New York. The genus *Mesodesma* Deshayes has recently been removed from the family Mactridae and placed in its own family, Mesodesmatidae.

SUPERFAMILY:

# SOLENACEA

FAMILY:

# SOLENIDAE
(*razor clams*)

The true razor clams are characterized by elongated, narrow, generally fragile shells with small hinge teeth. The equal valves gape at both ends. They burrow actively in sandy bottoms, and are found in shallow depths in most seas. These clams are considered by many gourmets to be the tastiest of all mollusks.

## KEY TO GENERA SOLEN, ENSIS, AND SILIQUA

* Shell length at least four times that of height, ends truncated
** Shell straight, periostracum pale greenish     *Solen viridis*
** Shell curved, periostracum yellowish green with brown or purplish triangular areas
*** Shell large, 150 mm. (6 in.); distribution Canada to South Carolina     *Ensis directus*

* * * Shell small, 75 mm. (3 in.); distribution southern
    Florida to Texas                                      *E. minor*
  * Shell length less than four times that of height, ends
    rounded
  * * Shell fragile, periostracum purplish, internal ridge
    slanted anteriorly                                    *Siliqua costata*
  * * Shell strong, periostracum pale yellow, internal ridge
    slanted posteriorly                                   *S. squama*

---

Genus *Solen* Linnaeus

*Solen viridis* Say
  Green Razor Clam

  Pl. XLII, 3

ETYMOLOGY: Gr. *solen*, pipe, tube; Lat. *viridis*, green.

SIZE: 50 mm. (2 in.) in length, 10 mm. (2/5 in.) in height.

DISTRIBUTION: Rhode Island to northern Florida and the Gulf states.

CHARACTERISTICS: Shell medium, rather fragile, elongate, compressed
    cylindrical, straight, smooth. Color white, under a varnishlike green
    periostracum; hinge teeth terminal, small, one on each valve. Ends
    truncated, gaping.

The razor or jackknife clams are readily recognized by their long,
sometimes curved shape, which makes them look like handles of
old-fashioned barber's straight razors. The Green Razor Clam is a
moderately common shell in shallow water in inlets and bay areas,
on sand or mud flats. It is less common in the northern part of its
distribution. The clam lives in the sand, and can dig in with amazing speed by alternately compressing its foot to a knifelike thinness
and forcing it through the subsurface, then swelling it like an anchor
and pulling down the rest of the shell by contracting its muscles.
Once the foot is anchored in the sand, it is useless to try to pull out
the clam; the shell will break and the animal will tear in half, but
the foot will not pull free.

  The superfamily Solenacea, together with the next succeeding
ones (Myacea, Gastrochaenacea, Hiatellacea, and Pholadacea), in
some systematic arrangements of the bivalves, are combined in a
suborder called the *Adapedonta* (Gr. *a dapedon*, without a floor or

base) because the hinge teeth do not rest on a well-formed hinge plate.

The **Common Razor Clam,** *Ensis directus* Conrad (Lat. *ensis,* sword; *directus,* straight) (pl. XLIV, 14), is a much larger bivalve, reaching 150 mm. (6 in.) in length, 30 mm. (1 1/4 in.) in height. The shell is moderately strong, curved, and covered by a brilliant, yellowish green periostracum that has a large, elongated, triangular brownish or purplish region. Both ends gape, and are sharply truncated. The members of the genus *Ensis* Schumacher all have a single narrow cardinal tooth in the left valve and two teeth in the right valve, between which the left valve tooth rotates. In addition, each valve has a long posterior tooth behind the cardinals. This is a northern species, ranging from Canada to South Carolina. It is often harvested for human food.

The **Lesser Razor Clam,** *Ensis minor* Dall (pl. XLI, 19), reaches only 75 mm. (3 in.) in length. It closely resembles *E. directus,* but it is more fragile and more pointed at the hingeless end. It is found from Florida to Texas.

The **Fragile Razor Clam,** *Siliqua costata* Say (Lat. *siliqua,* the pod of a leguminous plant; *costatus,* ribbed) (pl. XLIV, 15), reaches 45 mm. (1 4/5 in.) in length, 18 mm. (3/4 in.) in height. The shell is thin, fragile, smooth, oblong oval, the ends rounded. Within the valves there is a white, rather strong, riblike ridge extending from the umbo vertically to the opposite edge, slanting to the front, and widening out as it proceeds. There is a polished violaceous periostracum, greenish olive near the edges. The internal rib alone is sufficient to identify the species, even when the rest of the fragile shell is broken away. This is a moderately common species living in clean shallow water, where it digs into the mud or sand. It ranges from Canada to New Jersey.

The **Scaly Razor Clam,** *Siliqua squama* Blainville (Lat. *squama,* fish scale) (pl. XLI, 20), is 60 mm. (2 2/5 in.) in length, 18 mm. (3/4 in.) in height. The shell, which is heavier, is white, with a strong, glossy yellowish periostracum, the posterior of which is wrinkled—possibly the "scales" of the Latin name. The internal rib is strong and pointed toward the back. This is a rather rare northern beach shell ranging from Newfoundland to Cape Cod, but it is often found in fish stomachs, and isolated valves are occasionally thrown up on the shore.

# TELLINACEA

---

# TELLINIDAE
(*tellin shells*)

These shells are very small to rather large, oval or elongate oblong, fragile to quite sturdy, glossy and smooth to dull, and variously but weakly sculptured. Hinge teeth are small, but well developed. There is usually a slight but pronounced twist at the posterior end. These animals burrow in sand and possess long and active siphons. They are found in all seas, but they are more abundant and more colorful in warmer seas. Though the species and genera differ widely in shape, sculpture, and color, they can be recognized by the weak twist to the right at the posterior end and the presence of two usually small cardinal teeth, one of which is split in two (bifid). They are generally active bivalves living buried in sand or mud and communicating with the water by means of long and extremely lively spihons.

---

## KEY TO GENERA AND SUBGENERA OF FAMILY TELLINIDAE

| | |
|---|---|
| * Shell with crested dorsal margin | *Tellidora* |
| * Shell with smooth dorsal margin | |
| ** Shell sculpture of oblique scissulations crossing concentric lines | |
| *** Scissulations variously flexed on posterior slope | *Strigilla* |
| *** Scissulations not flexed on posterior slope | *Scissula* |
| ** Shell sculpture of concentric lines only, occasionally with microscopic axial scratches | |
| *** Lateral teeth absent in both valves | *Macoma* |
| *** One or more lateral teeth present | |
| **** Lateral tooth present in right valve only, shells generally small, fragile | *Angulus* |

**\* \* \* \*** Lateral tooth or teeth present in both valves, shells
generally large, strong                                    *Tellina*

---

# KEY TO GENUS TELLINA

**\*** Shell high oval, length only little greater than height

**\* \*** Shell smaller, 38 mm. (1 1/2 in.) in length          *T. lineata*

**\* \*** Shell larger, 94 mm. (about 3 4/5 in.) in length

**\* \* \*** Shell heavy, not glossy, color dull white          *T. fausta*

**\* \* \*** Shell lighter, glossy, frequently with yellow, pink,
orange or red stains                                       *T. laevigata*

**\*** Shell elongate, length almost twice as great as height

**\* \*** Shell with pronounced concentric sculpture

**\* \* \*** Shell dull, concentric lines evenly spaced, surface with
zigzag lines or speckles                                   *T. listeri*

**\* \* \*** Shell glossy, concentric lines interrupted by narrower
or wider spaces on the posterior section; streaks and
speckles absent

**\* \* \* \*** Shell generally white or with suffusions of pale pink
or yellow generally near umbo; distribution North
Carolina to Florida but absent on Keys                     *T. alternata*

**\* \* \* \*** Shell pinkish rose or purplish, interior darker;
distribution Florida Keys                                  *T. angulosa*

**\* \*** Shell smooth, concentric sculpture very fine, almost
microscopic

**\* \* \*** Shell strong, varnished, length more than twice the
height                                                     *T. radiata*

**\* \* \*** Shell thin, moderately glossy, length less than twice
the height                                                 *T. magna*

---

Genus *Tellina* Linnaeus

*Tellina radiata* Linnaeus
Sunrise Tellin

Pl. XVI, 6a & b

ETYMOLOGY: Gr. *tellinê*, a kind of shellfish; Lat. *radiatus*, emitting rays.

SIZE: Up to 114 mm. (4 1/2 in.) in length, 53 mm. (2 1/8 in.) in height.

DISTRIBUTION: South Carolina to British Guiana.

CHARACTERISTICS: Shell large, strong, elongate, moderately inflated, smooth. Color glistening creamy white or rayed with pink or yellow, or with pink or yellow area near umbones; interior with yellow flush. Umbones usually bright red.

This is probably the most spectacular of all tellins, and one of the most beautiful bivalves in our area. Its glossy surface and bright colors never fail to win the admiration of all viewers. For this reason it is extensively used in shellcraft. Not all specimens are rayed; some are all white or have a yellow or pink blotch near the umbones. Shells with this color have been called *T. radiata unimaculata* Lamarck (Lat. *unus macula,* one spot) but this is an unacceptable varietal name. The Sunrise Tellin is less common in Florida than in the West Indies.

The **Great Tellin,** *Tellina magna* Spengler (Lat. *magnus,* great) (pl. XLIV, 16), reaches 122 mm. (4 4/5 in.) in length and 65 mm. (2 3/5 in.) in height. It is elliptical in shape, the front end widely and evenly rounded. The shells are rather thin and sculptured by regular, closely spaced concentric growth lines and some microscopic radial scratches, mainly on the anterior slope. The color is white or pink, sometimes with weak rays; the right valve is more strongly colored. This largest of the tellins is rather rare; it lives in sand just below the low-tide line and ranges from southern Florida to the West Indies.

**Lister's Tellin,** *Tellina listeri* Röding (Martin Lister, 1638–1712, was an English naturalist and author of an important shell iconography), is smaller, about 79 mm. (2 3/4 in.) in length, 41 mm. (1 3/5 in.) in height. The shell is elongate, dull, and sculptured with many strong, evenly spaced concentric lines. The posterior section has two strong ridges, and is twisted to the right. The shell is white to purplish brown; the interior is often suffused with yellow. This species ranges from North Carolina to the West Indies and southward. It was formerly called *Tellina interrupta* Wood, a later name. (Pl. XLIV, 17.)

The **Alternate Tellin,** *Tellina alternata* Say (pl. XLI, 21), extends to 72 mm. (2 3/4 in.) in length and 40 mm. (1 3/5 in.) in height. It is elongate-triangular in shape, with a widely rounded anterior end and a moderately pointed and twisted posterior. The sculpture consists of series of numerous evenly spaced, fine, concentric grooves, the individual series separated by broad, smooth bands. The sculpture of the left valve has broader bands and fewer striations. The glossy shell is nearly always white, but many individuals have pink or yellowish suffusions. This large shell is one of the commonest larger tellins in our area; it ranges from Cape Hatteras to Florida and Texas.

The **Angulate Tellin,** *Tellina angulosa* Gmelin (Lat. *angulosus,* full of angles) (pl. XLII, 4), is similar to *T. alternata,* and replaces it in southern Florida and the Caribbean. It is much more elongate, and has a tendency to show a posterior orange red ray. It is also thinner and somewhat translucent.

The **Smooth Tellin,** *Tellina laevigata* Linnaeus (Lat. *laevigatus,* smooth) (pl. XLIV, 18), reaches 94 mm. (about 3 3/4 in.) in length and 78 mm. (about 3 in.) in height. The shell is unevenly oval in shape, the surface smooth except for microscopic growth lines. The color is variable: generally the shell is white with yellow, pink, orange or red near the umbo, but in some individuals these colors permeate the entire shell or are arranged in a radial pattern. It differs from *T. radiata* chiefly in the almost oval shape of the shell. The range is from southern Florida, where it is not very common, to the West Indies.

The **Rose Petal Tellin,** *Tellina lineata* Turton (Lat. *linea,* line) (pl. XLIII, 1), is small, reaching 38 mm. (1 1/2 in.) in length, 25 mm. (1 in.) in height. The smooth, glossy shell is irregularly high oval in shape, with a narrower, pointed, and twisted posterior end. The sculpture consists of fine concentric grooves. The color is pure white, usually strongly flushed with bright pink or red. This is a fairly common species ranging from Florida to the Gulf of Mexico, the West Indies, and southward. Its English name comes from its frequent use in shellcraft for that purpose.

The **Faust** or **Lucky Tellin,** *Tellina fausta* Pulteney (Lat. *faustus,* favorable, lucky) (pl. XLIII, 2), is a massive tellin reaching 98 mm. (4 in.) in length and 90 mm. (3 1/2 in.) in height. The shell is almost orbicular in shape, and heavy and solid in consistency. The irregular, rather weak, concentric sculpture is crossed by extremely fine radial scratches. The color is usually dull white externally, somewhat polished and yellow tinged internally. The lateral teeth in both valves are well developed, especially strong in the right valve. *T. fausta* resembles *T. laevigata* in shape, but it is heavier, less glossy, less colorful, and the lateral teeth are more strongly developed. This is a fairly common shell ranging from the Florida Keys and Bahamas to the West Indies. Some authors call the shell *Arcopagia fausta* (Lat. *arcus,* arc, Gr. *pagios,* firm, solid) but others consider *Arcopagia* to be merely a subgenus.

The **White-crested Tellin,** *Tellidora cristata* Recluz (*telli,* first two syllables of *Tellina,* and Gr. *dora,* gift; Lat. *cristatus,* crested), reaches 35 mm. (1 2/5 in.) in length. It need be confused with no other tellin. The four rows of strong crests on the anterior and posterior dorsal margins of both valves, and the few wide rounded surface ridges are unique among our tellins. The color is white and a periostracum is lacking. This bizarre species is fairly common in shallow water on the west coast of Florida. It ranges from North Carolina to Florida and Texas. (Pl. XLII, 5.)

---

## KEY TO SUBGENUS ANGULUS

* Shell comparatively large, reaching 25 mm. (1 in.) in length
** Posterior dorsal margin slope gradual, pallial sinus low, basal line coinciding only briefly with pallial line         *Tellina (Angulus) mera*

** Posterior dorsal margin slope short, steep, pallial sinus high, basal line coinciding with pallial line for most of its length         *T. (A.) tampaensis*
* Shell small, less than 20 mm. (4/5 in.)
** Shell only about 10 mm. (2/5 in.) in length
*** Shell colorful, yellow, pink, or peach, posterior twist present         *T. (A.) sybaritica*
*** Shell white, sometimes tinged faintly with yellow, posterior twist absent         *T. (A.) tenella*
** Shell 16 to 18 mm. (2/3 to 3/4 in.) in length
*** Shell with rather strong, well-spaced, regular concentric lines         *T. (A.) versicolor*
*** Shell with faint, irregular concentric growth lines only
**** Shell very fragile, translucent, frequently pink; northern distribution         *T. (A.) agilis*
**** Shell stronger, opaque, white with yellow infusion, never pink; southern distribution         *T. (A.) texana*

---

Subgenus *Angulus* Megerle von Muhlfeld

*Tellina (Angulus) agilis* Stimpson
   Agile Tellin

    Pl. XLIII, 3

ETYMOLOGY: Gr. *tellinê*, a kind of shellfish; Lat. *angulus*, bent, crooked; Lat. *agilis*, agile, nimble.

SIZE: 16 mm. (2/3 in.) in length, 11 mm. (2/5 in.) in height.

DISTRIBUTION: Gulf of Saint Lawrence to Georgia.

CHARACTERISTICS: Shell small, depressed oval, moderately inflated, quite thin, translucent and fragile, glossy. Color white, frequently with more or less large blotches of bright pink. Sculpture of weak concentric growth lines only. Pallial sinus strongly impressed, its anterior margin rather far from anterior muscle scar.

The tellin members of the subgenus *Angulus* can be readily recognized. They are small shells, the largest reaching no more than 25 mm. (1 in.) in length, but most species are less than 20 mm. (4/5 in.). The surface sculpture consists of weakly incised concentric growth lines. There is a lateral tooth in the right valve only, the left valve being without one. Though it is relatively easy to recognize tellins belonging to the subgenus *Angulus,* it is a more difficult matter to identify the species themselves, especially the smaller ones. One of the important differentiating or diagnostic features is the shape and the size of the pallial sinus and its relation to the pallial line and the muscle scars. The pallial line is a line near, and running concentrically with, the ventral margin of the shells. It marks the point of attachment of the marginal muscles of the mantle. The pallial sinus is an indentation of the pallial line, varying in size, that occurs in the posterior part of the shell. The reader is referred to the text figure below for clarification. The use of the pallial sinus for identification purposes is made harder by the fact that the lines delimiting it and the muscle scars are not always clearly visible. Before reference is made to the figures, therefore, the reader is advised to darken the lines with a soft pencil after carefully determining where they occur on his specimen.

The **Texan Tellin,** *Tellina texana* Dall (not illus.), replaces *T. agilis* in the south. The two species are about the same size, but the valves of *T. texana* are thicker, more compressed, and white, rarely with a yellowish suffusion, never pink. In addition, the pallial sinus is less strongly impressed, and the anterior margin is closer to the anterior muscle scar. This species ranges from North Carolina to Florida, the Gulf of Mexico, and Cuba. More northern records rest upon erroneous identifications of *T. agilis.*

The **Delicate Tellin,** *Tellina tenella* Verrill (Lat. *tenellus,* somewhat tender or delicate) (pl. XLIII, 4), is a smaller species, only

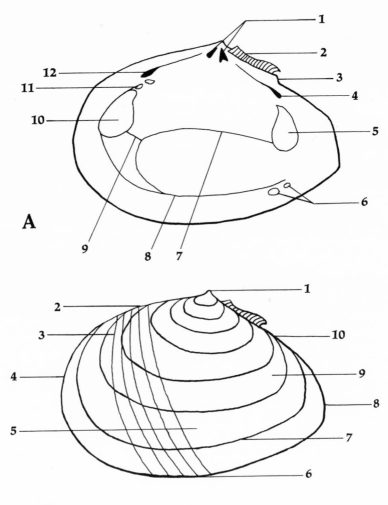

Diagrammatic representation of the shell morphology of a generalized *Tellina*. *Fig. A: Internal view of a right valve. 1. Cardinal complex with the single anterior laminate cardinal tooth and the bifid cardinal tooth. 2. Ligament. 3. Nymphal callosity. 4. Posterior lateral tooth. 5. Posterior adductor muscle scar. 6. Cruciform muscle scars. 7. Pallial sinus. 8. Pallial line. 9. Interlinear scar. 10. Anterior adductor scar. 11. Pedal retractor scars. 12. Anterior lateral tooth. Fig. B: External view of a left valve. 1. Umbo. 2. Anterior dorsal margin. 3. Oblique sulcus or scissulation. 4. Anterior margin. 5. Disc. 6. Ventral margin. 7. Concentric sculpture. 8. Posterior margin. 9. Posterior slope. 10. Posterior dorsal margin. (After Boss, 1966, p. 220.)*

10 mm. (2/5 in.) in length, 6 mm. (1/4 in.) in height, but similar to *T. agilis*. It is a rarer species that has not been well understood. According to Dr. Boss (1968), it may be distinguished from *T. agilis* "by its arcuate ventral margin, its elongate concave anterior dorsal margin, and its shorter and more blunt posterior truncation." There is no posterior twist. In addition, the pallial sinus approaches the anterior muscle scar more closely, and the surface sculpture is stronger and more widely spaced. *T. tenella* ranges from Massachusetts to the west coast of Florida and Mississippi.

**DeKay's Tellin,** *Tellina versicolor* DeKay (Lat. *versicolor,* of various colors) (pl. XLIII, 5), reaches 17.5 mm. (3/4 in.) in length, 9 mm. (about 2/5 in.) in height. It resembles *T. agilis* in texture, color, and somewhat in shape. It differs in its sculpture, which consists of widely spaced, moderately incised concentric lines. The pallial sinus is very close to the anterior muscle scar, sometimes touching it. This is a fairly common shell in the more southern part of its range, which extends from Cape Cod, Massachusetts, to Florida, Texas, and the West Indies.

The **Sybarite Tellin,** *Tellina sybaritica* Dall (Sybaris was a Greek city in Italy known for its love of luxury and pleasure) (pl. XLIII, 6), reaches only 11 mm. (about 1/2 in.) in length and 6 mm. (1/4 in.) in height. The colorful "sybaritic" shell is elongate, rather solid, bluntly pointed behind, and with the characteristic tellin posterior twist. Its color is white, richly suffused with red, pink, yellow, or peach, sometimes arranged as rays. It is closest to *T. tenella,* but differs in being more swollen, more colorful, and having a rounded instead of a truncated posterior margin with a distinct twist to the right. This species ranges from North Carolina through Florida and the West Indies southward. It is fairly common in shallow water.

The **Pure Tellin,** *Tellina mera* Say (Lat. *meris,* pure, unmixed) (pl. XLII, 6), is one of the larger members of the subgenus *Angulus,* reaching 25 mm. (1 in.) in length and 22 mm. (7/8 in.) in height. It has a high ovate shape, and the shell is thin but rather strong, weakly sculptured with irregular concentric growth lines. This is a common species ranging from Florida to the Bahamas and the West Indies.

The **Tampa Tellin,** *Tellina tampaensis* Conrad (pl. XLIII, 7), reaches 24 mm. (1 in.) in length and 18 mm. (3/4 in.) in height. It differs from *T. mera* in having the posterior dorsal (upper) margin sharply sloping; in *T. mera* this slope is more gradual. In addition, in *T. tampaensis* the pallial sinus is higher, raised in a sharp angle above, and its basal margin coincides for most of its length with the pallial line; in *T. mera* the pallial sinus is barely raised above and the basal margin coincides only briefly with the pallial line. The color of *T. tampaensis* is white, rarely suffused with pale peach; the sculpture is rather strong. The Tampa Tellin ranges from Florida to Texas and the West Indies.

---

# KEY TO SUBGENUS SCISSULA

* Shell with long, gradually sloping posterior
  margin, umbones almost central      *Tellina (Scissula) similis*
* Shell with short, steeply sloping posterior
  margin, umbones shifted posteriorly
** Shell strong, white      *T. (S.) candeana*
** Shell thin, fragile, pink or red      *T. (S.) iris*

---

Subgenus *Scissula* Dall

*Tellina (Scissula) similis* Sowerby
   Candy Stick Tellin

   Pl. XLII, 7

ETYMOLOGY: Gr. *tellinê*, a kind of shellfish; Lat. *scissus*, split, divided; *similis*, like, resembling.

SIZE: 27 mm. (about 1 in.) in length, 18 mm. (3/4 in.) in height.

DISTRIBUTION: Southeast coast of Florida to the West Indies and southward.

CHARACTERISTICS: Shell small, dull, oval, thin but fairly strong, posterior margin obliquely truncated, bent to the right. Color white, sometimes suffused with yellow, red, or apricot, often arranged in narrow broken rays. Surface sculpture of irregular concentric growth lines crossed by very fine, evenly spaced threads, which run diagonally across the shell; these oblique threads are absent on the posterior slope.

This species, like all members of the subgenus *Scissula*, shows the diagonally incised lines called "scissulations." These are very fine, and must be seen under some magnification. Dr. Boss believes that these peculiar markings help the animal to maintain its horizontal position in the sand when it withdraws its long siphons. *Tellina similis* is a fairly common shell on the southeast coast of Florida, where it can be found living in sand banks. Its lively colors suggested its English name.

The **Wedge Tellin,** *Tellina candeana* Orbigny (Lat. *candere,* to be glittering white) (pl. XLIII, 8), is 16 mm. (2/3 in.) in length and 10 mm. (2/5 in.) in height. It has the oblique scissulations of all members of the subgenus *Scissula,* but it is a heavier shell than *T. similis,* and has an elongate-triangular shape with a short, steep posterior slope, giving it a wedge shape, something like a coquina clam, *Donax* (see page 415). The concentric markings are stronger on the narrow posterior slope. The left valve is more inflated than the right. The color is usually white, but some faintly pink individuals can also be found. This species ranges from southern Florida to the West Indies. It is especially abundant on the west coast of Florida.

The **Rainbow Tellin,** *Tellina iris* Say (Lat. *iris,* rainbow) (pl. XLIII, 9), is 15 mm. (3/5 in.) in length and 9 mm. (2/5 in.) in height. The shell is trigonal in shape, with a short, sharply descending posterior slope. It is quite thin, fragile, and translucent, and the widely spaced scissulations are less oblique. The color is white or glassy, with some suffusion of red or pink. There are often white rays on the posterior portion. This is a fairly common shell on intertidal flats ranging from North Carolina to Florida and Texas.

---

# KEY TO GENUS STRIGILLA

* Shell generally white
** Shell moderately inflated, scissulations few, strong,
   widely spaced                                      *Strigilla mirabilis*
** Shell very inflated, almost globular, scissulations
   numerous, closely set, mainly West Indian          *S. pisiformis*
* Shell pink or rose colored                     *S. carnaria*

---

Genus *Strigilla* Turton

*Strigilla mirabilis* Philippi
   Remarkable Scraper

   Pl. XLIII, 10

ETYMOLOGY: Lat. *strigilis,* ancient Roman tool for scraping the body after a bath; *mirabilis,* wonderful.

SIZE: 14 mm. (3/5 in.) in length, 13 mm. (1/2 in.) in height.

DISTRIBUTION: North Carolina to Yucatán, Mexico.

CHARACTERISTICS: Shell small, solid, inflated, high oval. Color shining white, sometimes with a yellow tinge. Sculpture of concentric lines crossed by steep, diagonal scissulations, which are bent or flexed in a repeated zigzag pattern on the posterior slope.

The shells of the genus *Strigilla,* like the subgenus *Scissula,* also have scissulations, but in this case the scissulations are steeper, more strongly incised, easily visible, and variously flexed or bent on the posterior slope. The sculpture of *S. mirabilis* superficially resembles that of the Cross-hatched Lucina, *Divaricella quadrisulcata* (see page 383), but in the latter the markings are bent in the middle, making them look like chevrons. Moreover, the lucina is larger, more inflated, and has fine denticulations along the margin of the shell; these are missing in the *Strigilla.*

The **Pink Scraper,** *Strigilla carnaria* Linnaeus (Lat. *caro, carnis,* flesh) (pl. XLII, 8), is a larger species, reaching 28 mm. (1 1/8 in.) in length, 26 mm. (about 1 in.) in height. The exterior white color is richly suffused with pink, sometimes disposed in bands. The scissulations on the posterior slope are flexed in a large, acute angle. This species ranges from Florida to the West Indies and southward.

The **Pea Scraper,** *Strigilla pisiformis* Linnaeus (Lat. *pisum,* pea) (pl. XLIII, 11), is an abundant West Indian species imported in large numbers into Florida for shellcraft. It is 13 mm. (about 1/2 in.) in length and quite swollen, almost globular. The pink color, if present, is concentrated in the umbonal region. The scissulations are narrower and more closely set than in *S. mirabilis.*

# KEY TO GENUS MACOMA

* Shell dull, chalky; northern distribution
* * Shell thin, small, 25 mm. (1 in.), occasionally pink     *Macoma balthica*
* * Shell strong, larger, 50 mm. (2 in.), dirty white only     *M. calcarea*
* Shell quite glossy, occasionally delicately iridescent
* * Shell elongate, small, white, fragile     *M. tenta*
* * Shell high oval, stronger; southern distribution only

* * * Shell 40 mm. (1 3/5 in.), with peach, yellow, or
    orange flush, rather thin            *M. brevifrons*
* * * Shell white only, 60 mm. (2 2/5 in.), heavier    *M. constricta*

---

Genus *Macoma* Leach

*Macoma balthica* Linnaeus
    Baltic Macoma

    Pl. XLIII, 12

ETYMOLOGY: Possibly from Gr. *makos*, length, or simply coined for its euphonious sound; the spelling by Linnaeus of Baltic must be preserved for this species name.

SIZE: 25 mm. (1 in.) in length, 18 mm. (3/4 in.) in height.

DISTRIBUTION: Arctic seas to Georgia; also northern Europe.

CHARACTERISTICS: Shell medium, thin, compressed, widely oval, almost circular. Color usually dirty white, sometimes pinkish, chalky, dull; periostracum thin, grayish or yellowish, usually worn off the umbonal region. Posterior bluntly pointed, twisted to the right. Lateral teeth wanting.

This is a very common species in bays and inlets, living in mud or sandy mud in shallow water. The members of the genus *Macoma* can be recognized by the absence of lateral teeth in both valves and by the fact that the pallial sinus is smaller in one valve than in the other. The shells are usually white or unattractively gray, with a nondescript, flaking periostracum.

The **Chalky Macoma,** *Macoma calcarea* Gmelin (Lat. *calcarius*, pertaining to lime) (pl. XLIII, 13), is a larger species, reaching 50 mm. (2 in.) in length. The shell is moderately strong, less circular, and a dull, chalky white, covered by a grayish periostracum. The pallial sinus is relatively longer than in *M. balthica*, and it approaches the anterior muscle scar much more closely. *M. calcarea* is a cold-water species ranging from Greenland to New York.

The **Elongate Macoma,** *Macoma tenta* Say (Lat. *tentus*, stretched out) (not illus.), is 18 mm. (3/4 in.) in length, 10 mm. (2/5 in.) in height. The shell is small and fragile and quite narrowly elongate, with the posterior dorsal margin steeper and lower than the anterior. The color is white or yellowish and faintly iridescent. This is a very common species, in shallow water on sand, ranging from Massachusetts to Florida, Texas, and the West Indies.

The **Constricted Macoma,** *Macoma constricta* Bruguière (pl. XLII, 9), is the largest of the local Macomas, reaching 65 mm. (almost 2 1/2 in.) in length and 40 mm. (1 3/5 in.) in height. The rather high oval shell is dull white but delicately iridescent, marked with weak irregular growth lines only. The posterior margin is roundly truncated and twisted to the right. This is a common shallow-water species ranging from Florida to Texas and the West Indies.

The **Short Macoma,** *Macoma brevifrons* Say (Lat. *brevis frons*, short leaf) (pl. XLII, 10), reaches 25 mm. (1 in.) in length, 18 mm. (3/4 in.) in height. The shell is oblong, rather polished, and white, with a peach or orange flush near the umbones. The periostracum is light brown. This species ranges from deep water off New Jersey to shallow water in Florida and Texas. Its narrower oval shape, smaller size, thinner texture, and faint touches of color will distinguish it from *M. constricta*.

FAMILY:

# DONACIDAE

(*wedge shells*)

The shells of this family are small, strong, often colorful, and usually wedge shaped, with the umbones placed near the posterior end. This is an agile group of bivalves, living near the shore in warmer seas and burrowing actively in the sand. Some tropical species attain 75 mm. (3 in.) or more in length.

These active little clams live in the wash area of sandy beaches, accompanying the tide as it advances and recedes. As the water of a wave washes over the area where *Donax* lies buried in the sand, the clams leap out and are carried along by the advancing water. When the wash recedes, they anchor themselves with their long siphons and pointed foot, then quickly upend and dig in. They frequently occur in vast numbers, and the bright and varied colors make them, despite their small size, the most colorful objects on the beach. They cook into a famous chowder, and the coquina stone, used for building in such places as Florida and Bermuda, consists largely of their compacted shells.

# KEY TO GENERA DONAX AND IPHIGENIA

* Shell triangular, umbo almost central      *Iphigenia brasiliana*
* Shell wedge shaped, umbo near posterior edge
** Shell with well-marked radiating sculpture and pronounced posterior ridge
*** Shell large, 20 mm. (4/5 in.) in length, colorful; range Virginia to Florida      *Donax variabilis*
*** Shell smaller, 15 mm. (3/5 in.) in length, less colorful; range New York to Virginia      *D. fossor*
** Shell without radiating sculpture, posterior ridge weak, rounded      *D. parvulus*

---

Genus *Donax* Linnaeus

*Donax variabilis* Say
     Coquina Clam

     Pl. XLIII, 14

ETYMOLOGY: Gr. and Lat. *donax*, dart; also a kind of shellfish in Pliny; Lat. *varie*, with diverse colors.

SIZE: 20 mm. (4/5 in.) in length, 11 mm. (about 1/2 in.) in height.

DISTRIBUTION: Long Island, New York, to Florida.

CHARACTERISTICS: Shell small, glossy, strong, wedge-shaped, with a short, steeply sloping posterior margin. Color bright, variable: white, yellow, pink, purple, bluish, mauve, commonly with rays of darker shade. Umbones not central, near posterior end; margins crenulate. Sculpture of concentric growth lines and fine, noticeable radial striations, stronger over the posterior area.

North of Virginia these clams, since they live in less favorable conditions, tend to be smaller and less colorful. The forms comprising these populations have been called *Donax fossor* Say (Lat. *fossor*, digger), but a recent study tends to show that they are merely a depauperate form of *D. variabilis*. However, this point has not finally been settled; it has met with vigorous opposition by some malacologists, who contend that *D. fossor* is a valid species. (Pl. XLIII, 15.)

The **Lesser Donax,** *Donax parvulus* Philippi (Lat. *parvulus*, petty, slight) (not illus.), reaches only 15 mm. (3/5 in.) in length. It resembles *D. variabilis*, and has long been taken for its juvenile form. However, according to Dr. Morrison of the U.S. National Museum, it differs in having a thicker shell without any radiating structures, and thus has a smooth posterior area. In addition, the posterior ridge, which is rather high in *D. variabilis*, is flatter and rounder in *D. parvulus*. Hence he considers it to be a valid species. It ranges from Ocracoke Island, North Carolina, to Saint Lucie County, Florida, living together with colonies of *D. variabilis*.

The **Giant False Donax**, *Iphigenia brasiliana* Lamarck (Iphigenia was the daughter of Agamemnon; originally described from Brazil) (pl. XLIII, 16), is rather large, 60 mm. (2 2/5 in.) in length, 40 mm. (1 3/5 in.) in height. Although in the family Donacidae, the shells of the genus *Iphigenia* Schumacher do not resemble the true *Donax*. The rather thin shell is almost triangular in outline, and the umbones are almost centrally placed. The surface is smooth and the color cream, with the umbo area purple or orange. The periostracum is thin, glossy, and brownish. This moderately common species ranges from southern Florida to the West Indies, and south to Uruguay.

FAMILIES:

# PSAMMOBIIDAE AND SOLECURTIDAE

*(sand clams)*

The shells in these families resemble those of the family Tellinidae, but they are without the posterior twist. The hinge teeth are weak, the external ligament large, and the siphons long. Most forms gape slightly, especially at the posterior end. The shape is variable and not easily defined conchologically. In the Psammobiidae (Gr. *psammos*, sand) the shells are generally more or less oval, the length being less than twice the height. The Solecurtidae (Gr. *solen*, a pipe, tube; and Lat. *curtus*, short) differ in having oblong or rectangular shaped shells, the length being more than twice the height. These animals burrow in mud and sand, usually in warmer seas, but some of the Solecurtidae range to Massachusetts.

# KEY TO FAMILIES SOLECURTIDAE AND PSAMMOBIIDAE

| | |
|---|---|
| \* Shell oblong, length almost 2 1/2 times greater than width (family Solecurtidae) | |
| \*\* Shell smaller, 38 mm. (1 1/2 in.) in length, purplish, with internal radial rib | *Tagelus divisus* |
| \*\* Shell large, 60 mm. (2 2/5 in.), white, without internal rib | *T. plebeius* |
| \* Shell oval, length only slightly greater than height (family Psammobiidae) | |
| \*\* Shell quite small, 17 mm. (about 3/4 in.), varicolored | *Heterodonax bimaculatus* |
| \*\* Shell larger, 60 to 70 mm. (2 2/5 to 2 4/5 in.) in length | |
| \*\*\* Shell surface strongly roughened by radial ridges and concentric striae, varicolored | *Asaphis deflorata* |
| \*\*\* Shell surface smooth, color pink and white | *Sanguinolaria sanguinolenta* |

---

Genus *Sanguinolaria* Lamarck

*Sanguinolaria sanguinolenta* Gmelin
Blood-stained Sand Clam

Pl. XLIII, 17

ETYMOLOGY: Lat. *sanguis*, blood; *lintus*, flexible.

SIZE: 62 mm. (2 1/2 in.) in length, 42 mm. (1 3/4 in.) in height.

DISTRIBUTION: Southern Florida to the Gulf states and the West Indies.

CHARACTERISTICS: Shell rather large, thin, smooth, moderately depressed, oval in shape with narrowed posterior end; left valve flatter than the right. Color white, with a pink flush around the umbones; interior pink. Periostracum thin, flaking, brown.

The gory name given to this species is hardly deserved for our pale pinkish American form. In Europe, however, some *Sanguinolaria* really do look blood-stained. *Sanguinolaria sanguinolenta* is rather rare in Florida. It has been confused with *Sanguinolaria cruenta*

Lightfoot, a different species. The family Psammobiidae has also been called Gariidae or Sanguinolariidae, both of which are later names.

The **Gaudy Sand Clam,** *Asaphis deflorata* Linnaeus (Gr. *asaphes,* indistinct, dim; Lat. *deflorescere,* to shed blossoms) (pl. XVI, 5), is 70 mm. (2 3/4 in.) in length, 45 mm. (1 2/3 in.) in height. It is most easily recognized by its moderately raised oval shape and especially by the rough surface sculpture consisting of numerous strong, narrow, slightly wavy radiating ridges roughened by less strongly incised concentric furrows. The color is variable (like fading blossoms?); the shells can be whitish or yellowish, stained with red, yellow, blue, or purplish. In the interior the colors are brighter. This is a moderately common intertidal species found in southeastern Florida and the West Indies. This and the following three species belong to the family Solecurtidae.

The **Vulgar Sand Clam,** *Tagelus plebeius* Lightfoot (from *le tagal,* an arbitrary word made up by Adanson in 1757; Lat. *plebeius,* of the common people) (pl. XLIV, 19), is 56 mm. (2 1/5 in.) in length, 21 mm. (1 3/4 in.) in height. This species is best recognized by its elongate shape with the upper and lower margins almost straight and parallel, the anterior and posterior ends gently rounded. The surface is smooth, buff white under a thick brownish periostracum. This species, formerly called *Tagelus gibbus* Spengler (Lat. *gibbus,* hunch), ranges from Massachusetts to Florida, Texas, and the West Indies. It lives in rather deep burrows in sand in shallow water. Dead beach specimens are sometimes locally abundant.

The **Divided Sand Clam,** *Tagelus divisus* Spengler (Lat. *divisus,* divided, separated) is a smaller species, reaching only 38 mm. (1 1/2 in.) in length and 13 mm. (about 1/2 in.) in height. It is similar in shape to *T. plebeius,* but the ventral margin is slightly arched, the periostracum is rather glossy, and the color whitish purple. The Latin name comes from a weak internal radial rib running diagonally across the center of the valves, dividing them in two. This structure is absent from *T. plebeius. Tagelus divisus* is found from Massachusetts to Florida, the Gulf states, and the West Indies. (Pl. XLIII, 18.)

The **False Donax,** *Heterodonax bimaculatus* Linnaeus (Gr. *heteros donax,* differing donax; Lat. *bi maculatus,* twice spotted) (pl. XLII, 11), is only 17 mm. (about 3/4 in.) in length, 15 mm. (3/5 in.) in height. It is unevenly oval, with a rounded anterior and a bluntly pointed posterior end. This smooth surface is sculptured with concentric growth lines crossed by fine radial scratches. The color may be white, blue, purple, red, orange, or any combination arranged either in rays or as flecking. The Latin name comes from some specimens that have two oblong reddish spots within. This species is found in southern Florida and the West Indies, living with *Donax* on sandy beaches.

FAMILY:

# SEMELIDAE
(*semeles*)

These shells superficially resemble the tellins. They are oval, with a centrally placed umbo, and have weak sculpture. The ligament at the umbo has a small chitinous resilium. This is a generally warm-water group, burrowing in sand and mud in shallow water. Some deep-water and temperate-water forms are also known. Like other families with long siphons, they have a deep pallial sinus.

## KEY TO GENERA SEMELE, CUMINGIA, AND ABRA

* Shell very small, 6 mm. (1/4 in.), white, smooth — *Abra aequalis*
* Shell larger, 18 to 40 mm. (3/4 to 1 3/5 in.), surface ridged and/or colored
** Shell white only, posterior edge pointed; range north to Nova Scotia — *Cumingia tellinoides*
** Shell with yellow, pink, purple or reddish stains internally, posterior end rounded; range to North Carolina only
*** Shell almost circular, height and width almost equal, surface sculpture of rather strong concentric ridges — *Semele proficua*
*** Shell oval, length greater than width
**** Surface relatively smooth, shell thin — *S. purpurascens*
**** Surface strongly cancellated, shell strong — *S. bellastriata*

Genus *Semele* Schumacher

*Semele proficua* Pulteney
 White Semele

   Pl. XLII, 12

ETYMOLOGY: Semele (pronounced SEM-e-lee) in Greek mythology was the
  mother of Dionysus; Lat. *proficio*, useful.

SIZE: 25 to 40 mm. (1 to 1 3/5 in.) in length, 23 to 35 mm. (1 to 1 2/5 in.)
  in height.

DISTRIBUTION: North Carolina, Texas, and the West Indies to Argentina.

CHARACTERISTICS: Shell small, almost circular, moderately strong, umbo
  nearly central. Color dirty white externally, interior glossy with
  suffusion of yellow and occasionally blotches of brownish red, or with
  pink or reddish radial rays. Surface sculpture of rather strong
  concentric lines and microscopic radial striations. Teeth relatively
  small, weak.

This rather common, roundish bivalve is easily recognized by its
weak dentition, concentric sculpture, and glossy, colorful interior.
The specimens in which the internal color takes the shape of rays
has been called subspecies *radiata* Say, but the name is not needed.
The animal lies on its left side, buried in sand in shallow water. One
collector found some specimens, several feet above the sea bottom,
living in dead oyster shells attached to a sunken wreck.

   The **Purple Semele,** *Semele purpurascens* Gmelin (Lat. *purpura,*
purple) (pl. XLII, 13), reaches 36 mm. (1 1/2 in.) in length and 31
mm. (1 1/4 in.) in height. It differs from *S. proficua* in having a
more oval shape, a thinner but more colorful shell, and a relatively
smooth surface with minute oblique lines. The color, variably orange
or purplish, sometimes in the form of specks, appears on the outer
surface of the shells as well as internally. This species ranges from
North Carolina to Florida, Texas, the West Indies, and south to
Brazil.

   The **Cancellate Semele,** *Semele bellastriata* Conrad (Lat. *bella
striata,* beautifully striated) (pl. XLIV, 19), is smaller, reaching 23
mm. (about 1 in.) in length and 17 mm. (about 3/4 in.) in height.
It is oval in shape, and readily recognized by its cancellate surface,
which in some individuals is cancellate only at both ends, and concentrically ridged in the middle. In some specimens the cancellations
give rise to a beaded sculpture. In color it is yellowish white, with

reddish or purple specks. It ranges from North Carolina to Florida, Texas, the West Indies, and south to Brazil.

The **Tellin-shaped Cumingia,** *Cumingia tellinoides* Conrad (Hugh Cuming, 1791–1865, was a famous English collector; Gr. *tellin oidea,* resembling a tellin) (pl. XLII, 14), is only 12 to 18 mm. in length. It is oval in shape, with a prominent, contracted posterior end. The color is uniformly chalky white, and the surface has narrow, sharp concentric lines. The resilium rests in a pit much like that of the Mactridae. This is a mud burrower, and ranges from Nova Scotia to Florida and Texas. The *Cumingia* in the Lower Keys and the West Indies has stronger and more widely separated concentric ridges. This form has been called *Cumingia antillarum* Orbigny.

The **Common Abra,** *Abra aequalis* Say (Gr. *abros,* graceful, pretty; Lat. *aequalis,* equal or smooth) (pl. XLV, 1), is a tiny shell only 6 mm. (1/4 in.) in diameter. It is lopsided circular, swollen, white, and quite smooth. It ranges from North Carolina to Florida and Texas, and at times is found on the beach in huge quantities.

# CORBICULACEA

# CORBICULIDAE

The shells in this family are small to moderately large, with a well-developed periostracum and strong anterior and posterior lateral teeth. This is a widely distributed family mostly in warmer areas, where it is found in brackish as well as in fresh water, generally burrowing in soft substrates.

## KEY TO FAMILIES CORBICULIDAE AND DREISSENIDAE

* Shell fan shaped, umbo terminal, *Mytilus*-like, septum under umbo *Mytilopsis leucophaeata*
* Shell oval or triangular, umbo more or less central
** Shell triangular-oval, found only in fresh water *Corbicula manilensis*
** Shell found in salt or brackish water
*** Shell rounded triangular, periostracum fuzzy, brown or greenish *Polymesoda caroliniana*
*** Shell depressed triangular, posterior extended beaklike, ventrally twisted, periostracum thin, shiny *Pseudocyrena floridana*

Genus *Corbicula* Megerle von Mühlfeld

*Corbicula manilensis* Philippi
  Asiatic Clam

  Pl. I, 3a & b

ETYMOLOGY: Lat. *corbicula*, little basket; Manila, chief city of the
  Philippine Republic.

SIZE: 22 to 64 mm. (1 to 2 1/2 in.) in length, 20 to 50 mm. (4/5 to 2 in.) in
  height.

DISTRIBUTION: Throughout the United States; in the Atlantic slope, at the
  time of writing, in the Altamaha, Delaware, and Santee River systems.

CHARACTERISTICS: Shell small to medium, ovate to trigonal. Periostracum
  glossy, yellow green, rayed in juvenile forms, usually eroded at
  umbones. Surface sculpture of regular concentric ridges. Lateral teeth
  strong, serrated. Interior blue or purple, polished.

This clam from southeast Asia was first detected in the Columbia
River in the state of Washington in 1938. It spread rapidly along the
West Coast, and by 1959 it had reached the Tennessee River system.
It finally appeared on the Atlantic coast in the Altamaha River in
1971, and the next year it was found in numerous localities in the
Delaware River between Trenton and Philadelphia. It can be ex-
pected to expand its range rapidly into other coastal river systems.

The Asiatic Clam has proved to be a serious pest, its chief
danger lying in its amazingly rapid population buildups. As a result,
it clogs water systems, drives out native freshwater mollusks, and
renders the river sand and gravel in which it pullulates unfit for
building purposes. Its rapid increase in numbers and its swift extension of range show no signs of abating. The application of
chlorine has been found to be an effective control method, at least
in drinking water systems.

The proliferation of this foreign clam in our inland waters is one of
the most striking recent examples of what can result when a species is
introduced into a favorable area lacking natural enemies. Without
biological controls, *C. manilensis* has become a widespread nuisance.
Unhappily, this is only one of numerous such instances of human
intrusion, intentional or not, in the delicately balanced web of inter-
relationships among our flora and fauna.

The shell superficially resembles the freshwater mussels (family Unionidae) (see pages 318–28), but it actually belongs with the freshwater Fingernail Clams, genera *Sphaerium* and *Pisidium* (see pages 329–31). It differs from native Corbiculidae in having serrated lateral teeth. It reproduces without an intermediate parasitic glochidial stage, a factor that aids its rapid population growth.

The **Carolina Marsh Clam,** *Polymesoda caroliniana* Bosc (Gr. *poly mesos,* many center), is 25 to 40 mm. (1 to 1 3/5 in.) in height and length. The rather strong shell is rounded triangular in shape and swollen, with a rather strong, shiny but minutely roughened, brownish or greenish periostracum. The interior is white, rarely with a purple stain; the umbones are usually eroded. This common species lives in mud in estuaries and in brackish, occasionally even fresh water, but never above the influence of the tidal flow. Dead shells are common in salt marshes, from Virginia to northern Florida, and Texas. (Pl. XLII, 15.)

The **Florida Marsh Clam,** *Pseudocyrena floridana* Conrad (Gr. *pseudes* false, and *Cyrena,* the name of a nymph and a different but related bivalve genus), is 25 mm. (1 in.) in length. It is more variable in shape than *Polymesoda caroliniana,* and in general more elongate, and the posterior ventral margin is slightly sinuous and somewhat pointed. The periostracum is thin, shiny. The surface is marked with irregular growth lines only, and the color is dirty white flushed with pink or light purple. There is also a purple area in the white interior. This species is found from northern Florida to Key West and Texas. Orbigny's *P. maritima* may be an earlier name for this marsh clam. (Pl. XLII, 16.)

SUPERFAMILY:

# DREISSENACEA

---

FAMILY:

# DREISSENIDAE
(*false mussels*)

The shells of this family have the narrow triangular shape of the true mussels (family Mytilidae), but differ in having a short septum or shelf at the umbo. They are found in fresh and brackish water, and in many northern European countries are considered to be pests in canals, ditches, and rivers.

Genus *Mytilopsis*

*Mytilopsis leucophaeata* Conrad
　　Conrad's False Mussel

　　Pl. XLV, 2

ETYMOLOGY: Lat. *mytilos*, Gr. *opsis*, mussel like; Gr. *leukos phaetein*, white, shining.

SIZE: 15 to 20 mm. (3/5 to 4/5 in.) long, 8 mm. (1/3 in.) wide.

DISTRIBUTION: Hudson River above New York to Florida, Texas, and Mexico.

CHARACTERISTICS: Shell small, fragile, not nacreous within; elongate triangular in shape with a small, shelflike extension under the terminal umbo; color bluish brown to pale buff, occasionally with darker zigzag markings.

Despite its shape, this small shell need not be confused with small mytilids. The calcareous, rather than pearly or nacreous, interior and the small shelf under the umbo serve readily to distinguish it. Like *Mytilus*, it commonly forms large clumps held together by short byssal threads. It can live in fresh as well as brackish water, but never very far from the sea. Formerly placed in the genus *Congeria* Partsch (Lat. *congeries*, heap or pile). The family is named for a Dr. Dreissens, a European pharmacist.

SUPERFAMILY:

# ARCTICACEA

---

FAMILY:

# ARCTICIDAE
(*black quahogs*)

The shells are large and thick, nearly circular. The wrinkled periostracum is heavy and dark colored. This small family is confined largely to colder seas. See key, page 427.

Genus *Arctica* Schumacher

*Arctica islandica* Linnaeus
    Black Quahog

    Pl. XLII, 17

ETYMOLOGY: Named for the Arctic and for Iceland.
SIZE: 75 to 100 mm. (3 to 4 in.) in length and height.

DISTRIBUTION: Newfoundland to off Cape Hatteras, in deeper water.

CHARACTERISTICS: Shell large, almost circular, heavy, chalky. Color white
    under a coarse, blackish brown periostracum. Pallial sinus and lunule
    absent.

This large clam is rare south of Massachusetts, where shells are
often washed up after a storm. The juveniles, with a thinner, lighter-
colored shell, can be confused with the true quahog, *Mercenaria mercenaria*, but the shape is rounder, the lunule and pallial sinus are
lacking, and there is a posterior lateral tooth, characters that serve
to differentiate this species. The Black Quahog is widely fished for
human consumption, and is sold as canned or frozen clam meat.

SUPERFAMILY:
# VENERACEA

FAMILY:
# VENERIDAE
(*venus clams*)

The shells in the family are tiny to large, oval or heart shaped, with
a prominent umbo, generally directed toward the front, and are
commonly strikingly sculptured and colored. This is a very large
family with representatives in all seas, living at various depths.
Though an ancient group, first appearing in the Cretaceous, it is
today undergoing its most flourishing stage, with more species and
genera living at the present time than in past geological periods.
Many students regard the Veneridae as the best evolved of the
Heterodonta.

    The Veneridae can all be distinguished easily from the Cardiidae, which they may resemble in shape, by the fact that they all have a lunule and frequently also an escutcheon, two structures lacking in the Cardiidae. The lunule is a small, heart-shaped depression lying in front of the umbones; the escutcheon is a generally smaller, lozenge-shaped area lying opposite, behind the umbones. In the Cardiidae the areas around the umbones are not so marked. Venerologists, even after much study and work, are not yet agreed upon many basic points of taxonomy.

## KEY TO FAMILIES
## ARCTICIDAE AND VENERIDAE

* Shell tiny, about 3 mm. (1/8 in.)
* * Height more or less equal to length, usually with purple or lavender stain     *Gemma*
* * Height distinctly greater than length, color buff to brown     *Parastarte*
* Shell larger, 10 to 150 mm. (2/5 to 6 in.)
* * Shell small to medium, 15 to 35 mm. (3/5 to 1 2/5 in.)
* * * Shell strongly rostrate posteriorly, umbones not central     *Anomalocardia*
* * * Shell weakly or not at all rostrate, umbones nearly central
* * * * Shell with reticulate or cancellate surface
* * * * * Shell trigonal, umbones small and directed upward, reticulations weak     *Gouldia*
* * * * * Shell heart shaped, umbones large and directed backward, reticulations strong     *Chione*
* * * * Shell not reticulated, marked only by concentric sculpture
* * * * * Shell small, 15 mm. (3/5 in.), inner margins with oblique striae     *Transennella*
* * * * * Shell larger, 25 to 30 mm. (1 to 1 1/5 in.), heart shaped, inner margin smooth     *Pitar*
* * Shell very large, 50 to 150 mm. (2 to 6 in.) and larger
* * * Shell subcircular in outline
* * * * Shell moderately inflated, periostracum strong, dark brown or black; northern distribution     *Arctica*
* * * * Shell very compressed, periostracum thin, yellow, southern distribution     *Dosinia*

\* \* \* Shell trigonal, heart shaped or elongate

\* \* \* \* Shell smooth, periostracum glossy, color
brownish                                        *Macrocallista*

\* \* \* \* Shell not smooth, periostracum lacking, color
gray or whitish

\* \* \* \* \* Shell surface cancellated; southern distribution
only                                             *Periglypta*

\* \* \* \* \* Surface sculpture weak, predominantly
concentric, often with purplish stains           *Mercenaria*

# KEY TO GENUS MERCENARIA

\* Shell often with purple color stains, moderately
large and heavy, central area of shell smooth    *Mercenaria mercenaria*

\* No purple color, shell very large and heavy,
rough concentric sculpture over entire shell     *M. campechiensis*

Genus *Mercenaria* Schumacher

*Mercenaria mercenaria* Linnaeus
Hard-shelled Clam or Quahog

Pl. XLV, 3

ETYMOLOGY: Lat. *merces*, hire, pay, reward.

SIZE: 75 to 100 mm. (3 to 4 in.) in length, 50 to 75 mm. (2 to 3 in.) in height.

DISTRIBUTION: Canada to Florida.

CHARACTERISTICS: Shell medium, heavy, thick, obliquely ovate or heart
shaped, swollen. Grayish white or ash colored, usually with rich purple
blotch or area inside. Surface marked with numerous narrow, low
concentric folds and growth lines, central area smooth and moderately
shining; margin crenulate. Juvenile forms have distinct raised
concentric lamellae near the umbones.

The quahog (prounced CO-hawg, based on an Indian word for the
bivalve) is the best-known representative of the Veneridae family

on the eastern coast of the United States. It lives in large numbers in bays, where it burrows in mud or sandy mud. Next to the oyster, *Crassostrea virginica*, it is probably the most commercially important American bivalve. The Indians utilized the shell to make the money they called "wampum," and it is this use that possibly suggested its name to Linnaeus. The shells vary somewhat in shape, some individuals being comparatively lower and longer than others, but there is never confusion as to their identity. The young shells of about 15 mm. (3/5 in.) look quite different because of the prominently raised lamellae near the umbones, which, however, are worn away as the shell matures. Among many populations there are individuals that vary slightly in color, and some of these forms have been given names: mature shells that lack the purple color stains have been called *M. alba* Dall, and those prettily marked with brownish zigzag markings *M. notata* Say. These forms are not recognized as valid species. Populations in the western Gulf of Mexico are a subspecies, *Mercenaria mercenaria texana* Dall.

The **Southern Quahog,** *Mercenaria campechiensis* Gmelin (named for the Gulf of Campeche, Mexico) (pl. XLV, 4), is similar, but it is much larger, 125 to 150 mm. (5 to 6 in.), and heavier. The shell is chalky white, and the interior never contains a purplish stain. The entire surface is covered with low, narrow concentric ridges with no smoothish central area as in *M. mercenaria*. The species ranges from Chesapeake Bay to Florida, Texas, and the West Indies.

**Lister's Venus,** *Periglypta listeri* Gray (Gr. *peri, glyptos,* nearly carved; Martin Lister, 1638–1712, was an English physician and naturalist) (pl. XLII, 18), is 82 mm. (about 3 1/5 in.) in length and 64 mm. (about 2 3/5 in.) in height. It is more rounded than *Mercenaria*, and most easily recognized by the cancellate surface sculpture. The numerous narrow, radiating lines are crossed by raised, somewhat heavier and slightly beaded concentric lamellae or ridges. The color is grayish, and the posterior muscle scar usually has a light brown stain. This species ranges from southeastern Florida to the West Indies, and is occasionally found on beaches. Formerly placed in the genus *Antigona* (Antigone was a daughter of Oedipus), which is actually an East Indian group of Venus clams.

# KEY TO GENUS CHIONE

* Shell larger, 35 mm. (1 2/5 in.) in length
** Concentric ribs few but high, lamellar       *Chione cancellata*
** Concentric ribs numerous but low       *C. intapurpurea*
* Shell smaller, 10 to 15 mm. (2/5 to 3/5 in.) in length
** Shell 15 mm. (3/5 in.), surface cancellate, radiating
and concentric structures about equal in strength       *C. pygmaea*
** Shell 10 mm. (2/5 in.), surface with wide radiating
ridges, concentric markings weak, threadlike       *C. grus*

---

The **Cross-barred Venus,** *Chione cancellata* Linnaeus (Gr. *chion,* snow—Chione was the daughter of Boreas, the north wind; Lat. *cancelli,* a grating-like lattice) (pl. XLVI, 1), is about 38 mm. (1 1/2 in.) in length, 33 mm. (1 1/3 in.) in height. It has the oblique heart shape of a Venus clam, but the sculpture is marked by a small number of strong, raised concentric ribs with a series of lower radiating ridges underlying them. The exterior is usually grayish white, sometimes with brown markings, and the interior strongly suffused with purple. This is an abundant venerid living in shallow water from South Carolina to Florida, Texas, and the West Indies.

The **Purple Venus,** *Chione intapurpurea* Conrad (Lat. *intus purpura,* inside purple) (pl. XLVI, 2), is about the same size, 35 mm. (1 2/5 in.) in length, 30 mm. (1 1/5 in.) in height. It is readily distinguished from *C. cancellata* by having numerous lower and more closely set concentric ridges. The radiating sculpture is quite weak. The color is deep cream with heavy brown markings, and the interior is smooth and purple. This is a rarer shell than *C. cancellata,* inhabiting deeper waters. It is found from North Carolina to Florida, Texas, and the Gulf of Mexico.

The **Gray Pygmy Venus,** *Chione grus* Holmes (Gr. *grus,* gritty, or Lat. *grus,* crane) (pl. XLVI, 3), is small, 10 mm. (2/5 in.) in length, 7 mm. (about 1/4 in.) in height. The shell is transversely oblong, marked with some rather wide radiating ridges crossed by fine, threadlike concentric lines. The color is grayish white, sometimes faintly pinkish or orange, and the interior has a purplish band. This Venus shell is common in shallow water and in beach drift. It ranges from North Carolina to Key West, Texas, and Mexico.

The **White Pygmy Venus,** *Chione pygmaea* Lamarck (pl. XLV, 5), is larger, 15 mm. (3/5 in.) in length, 11 mm. (about 1/2 in.)

in height. The shell is also transversely oblong, but it differs from *C. grus* in having a stronger cancellated surface, the radiating lines and concentric ridges being of about equal strength. The color is white, flecked with brown, the interior all white. This species is fairly common in shallow water, ranging from southeastern Florida to the West Indies.

---

## KEY TO GENUS TRANSENNELLA

* Shell rostrate posteriorly, elongate     *Transennella conradina*
* Shell ovate or rounded-trigonal
** Shell pure white, rarely with brown flecks;
   range Key West to West Indies     *T. cubaniana*
** Shell glossy, exterior white or bluish white
   with brown bands or spots or chevron
   markings, interior commonly purple or
   orange; range North Carolina to West Indies     *T. stimpsoni*

---

The Lattice Venus Clams, genus *Transennella* Dall (Lat. *transenna*, lattice), are small, 10 to 17 mm. (2/5 to 3/4 in.) in length and about 9 mm. (about 2/5 in.) in height. All the members of this genus are characterized by the inner margins of the valves being grooved with fine, oblique striae, the lowest ones running parallel to the ventral growth lines on the outside of the shell. These markings are readily visible under slight magnification. The three commonest species can be distinguished as follows:

**Conrad's Lattice Venus,** *Transennella conradina* Dall (Timothy A. Conrad, 1804–1877, was an American paleontologist and conchologist) (pl. XLV, 6), is the largest of the three, reaching 17 mm. (about 3/4 in.) in length. It differs from the others in being rostrate or pointed behind. It is glossy white or cream, and marked with pale brown zigzag markings. Southern Florida to the West Indies.

The **Cuban Lattice Venus,** *Transennella cubaniana* Orbigny (not illus.), is more ovate and less elongate. It is the smallest, reaching only 10 mm. (2/5 in.). The color is pure white, rarely flecked with irregular brown dots. Florida Keys to the West Indies.

**Stimpson's Lattice Venus,** *Transennella stimpsoni* Dall (William Stimpson, 1832–1872, was an American naturalist particularly interested in Florida) (not illus.), reaches about 15 mm. (3/5 in.)

in length. It is not pointed and is the most colorful of the three. The shell is white or cream, variegated with brown bands or spots, purple or orange inside especially toward the middle. North Carolina to the West Indies.

The **Pointed Venus,** *Anomalocardia auberiana* Orbigny (Gr. *anamolos kardia,* irregular heart; Auber was a collector in the West Indies) (pl. XLVI, 4), is 18 mm. (3/4 in.) in length, 12 mm. (about 1/2 in.) in height. It is most easily recognized by its long pointed shape, the posterior end being well extended in a beaklike process. The umbones are not central but are shifted to the front end. The varicolored surface—white through brown and green, often with brown or purplish streaking—is well marked by prominent, rounded concentric ridges. These ridges serve to separate this species from the Florida Marsh Clam, *Pseudocyrena floridana* (see page 424), which also has a rostrate shape but is smooth. The Pointed Venus ranges from southern Florida to Texas, Mexico, and Central America, and is a common beach shell. It has occasionally been misidentified as *A. brasiliana* Gmelin, a larger West Indian species. Formerly known as *A. cuneimeris* Conrad (Lat. *cuneus,* wedge; Gr. *meris,* part of morsel), which is a later name.

The **Gem Venus Clam,** *Gemma gemma* Totten (Lat. *gemma,* a precious stone) (pl. XLVI, 5), is a minute clam only about 3 mm. (1/8 in.) in diameter. It is prettily engraved with numerous fine, concentric furrows. The color is gleaming white with more or less extensive purple or lavender areas, and the margins are finely crenulated. This excessively abundant tiny clam was at one time taken to be young *Mercenaria mercenaria.* It ranges from Nova Scotia to Florida and Texas. A form with a more restricted purplish area was named *G. purpurea* Lea (synonym: *fretensis* Rehder); and a completely white bay form, *G. manhattensis* Prime. The validity of these latter names has not been established.

The **Brown Gem Clam,** *Parastarte triquetra* Conrad (Gr. *para Astarte,* near Astarte, the goddess of love and the name of a genus of clams; Lat. *triquetrus,* three-cornered) (pl. XLVI, 6), is about the same size. It differs in being much higher proportionately, with a more elevated umbo and a wider hinge area. The color is buff or brown, but dead beach shells have a pinkish purple tinge. This species is restricted to the two coasts of peninsular Florida.

# KEY TO GENUS PITAR

* Shell grayish, with brownish areas; northern
  distribution            *Pitar morrhuanus*
* Shell whitish, with brownish markings arranged in
  radiating bands; southern distribution      *P. fulminatus*

---

The **Codfish Venus,** *Pitar morrhuanus* Linsley (*pitar* is a Senegalese word introduced by Adanson; Lat. *morrhua,* codfish) (pl. XLVI, 7), is 25 to 35 mm. (1 to 1 2/5 in.) in size. It has the obliquely ovate or heart-shaped form of *Mercenaria,* but differs in being more swollen, less heavy, and in having smooth, noncrenulated margins. The sculpture consists only of rather heavy, irregular concentric growth lines. The color is gray, with several rust-colored or darker gray areas. This species, which is commonly eaten by codfish, is found in shallow water. It ranges from the Gulf of Saint Lawrence to North Carolina.

The **Lightning Venus,** *Pitar fulminatus* Menke (Lat. *fulmen,* lightning flash) (pl. XLVI, 8), is the same size as *P. morrhuanus,* and is similar in shape, shell texture, and smooth margin. It differs in being chalky white in color, ornamented with brown zigzag markings generally arranged in a radiating pattern of narrower or wider rays. This is a southern species ranging from North Carolina to Florida and the West Indies.

**Gould's Wax Venus,** *Gouldia cerina* C. B. Adams (Augustus A. Gould, 1805–1866, was an American naturalist especially interested in the shells of New England; Lat. *cerinus,* wax-colored) (pl. XLVI, 9), is 13 mm. (1/2 in.) in length, 10 mm. (2/5 in.) in height. The small shell is compressed and trigonal in shape, with small umbones; the surface is reticulate, the concentric lines somewhat more prominent than the crossing radiating striae. The color is yellowish white, occasionally with light brown zigzag markings or flecks, the white interior purple tinged near the umbones. This is a fairly common species ranging from North Carolina to Florida and the West Indies. This species was formerly placed in the genus *Gafrarium* Röding (possibly from Gr. *graphis,* a pointed writing style).

# KEY TO GENUS MACROCALLISTA

* Shell elongate-oval    *Macrocallista nimbosa*
* Shell rounded-trigonal   *M. maculata*

---

The **Sunray Venus,** *Macrocallista nimbosa* Lightfoot (Gr. *makros,* large, *callista,* very beautiful, or Callista, name of a nymph; Lat. *nimbosus,* rainy, stormy) (pl. XVI, 9), is a large species, reaching 115 mm. (4 1/2 in.) in length and 60 mm. (2 1/2 in.) in height. The shell is very elongate-oval, rather compressed, strong, and smooth, with a glossy periostracum; the basic color is fawn, with radiating brown bands made up of irregular block-shaped spots. The interior is white, with a pinkish flush in the center. This pretty shell is common in shallow sandy areas, and storms sweep large numbers on shore. It ranges from North Carolina to Florida and Texas. Recently it has begun to be fished in large quantities for human consumption.

The **Spotted Venus,** *Macrocallista maculata* Linnaeus (Lat. *macula,* stain or blemish) (pl. XLV, 7), is 50 mm. (2 in.) in size. It has the smooth shell, lacquered periostracum, and fawn base color with brown markings of *M. nimbosa,* but it differs in being rounded-trigonal in shape and in having the brown surface markings thickly and irregularly distributed over the surface, sometimes in a vaguely checkerboard design. This is a common shell ranging from North Carolina to Florida and the West Indies.

---

# KEY TO GENUS DOSINIA

* Concentric ridges strong   *Dosinia elegans*
* Concentric ridges weak    *D. discus*

---

The **Elegant Venus,** *Dosinia elegans* Conrad (*dosin* is a Senegalese term introduced in 1757 by Adanson) (pl. XLVI, 10), reaches 75 mm. (3 in.) in length and 65 mm. (2 3/5 in.) in height. The shell is disk-like, almost circular, heavy, and quite flatly compressed. The color is white, and the surface is heavily marked by numerous strong concentric ridges. There is also a thin, yellowish periostracum. This is an abundant species living in shallow water on sandy bottoms. It is frequently cast up on shore, both valves stoutly joined together by a strong ligament. It ranges from western Florida to Texas and Mexico.

The **Disk Venus,** *Dosinia discus* Reeve (pl. XLV, 8), is readily distinguished by having the concentric ridges more numerous, much smaller, finer, and less prominent. In other respects, it is similar to its elegant congener, but it is somewhat less abundant. It ranges from Virginia to Florida, the Gulf states, and the Bahamas.

FAMILY:

# PETRICOLIDAE
(*false piddock*)

These shells are white, thin but sturdy, elongate, with the umbo near the anterior end and the surface strongly sculptured. This is a group of wide distribution, burrowing in clay, peat, coral, and rock.

## KEY TO GENERA PETRICOLA AND RUPELLARIA

* Shell elongate, length about twice the height     *Petricola pholadiformis*
* Shell elongate or triangular, length not much greater or equal to the height
** Surface sculpture in superficial calcareous coating     *P. lapicida*
** Surface sculpture part of shell     *Rupellaria typica*

Genus *Petricola* Lamarck

*Petricola pholadiformis* Lamarck
   False Angel Wing

   Pl. XLVI, 11

ETYMOLOGY: Lat. *petra cola*, rock dwelling; *pholas formis*, Pholas-like.

SIZE: 40 mm. (1 3/5 in.) in length, 18 mm. (3/4 in.) in height.

DISTRIBUTION: Gulf of Saint Lawrence to Gulf of Mexico and southward.

CHARACTERISTICS: Shell medium, elongate, thin but strong, umbones near the rounded anterior end. Color chalky white. Sculpture of low ridges radiating from the umbo, those on the anterior portion shorter, more elevated, and armed with strong, toothlike scales. Interior glossy, marked with indentations corresponding to the external sculpture.

This is a common species that bores into peat and clay, occasionally into water-logged wood. The shells must not be confused with the true piddocks of the family Pholadidae (see pages 442–6), which they resemble in habits and general appearance. But whereas *Petricola*, being a heterodont bivalve, has distinct, pointed cardinal teeth, the Pholadidae lack all signs of any hinge dentition. A form of *P. pholadiformis* that is shorter and broader in outline, with more numerous radiating ribs and with shorter, grooved hinge teeth, has been called *P. pholadiformis lata* Dall. This latter form ranges from Maine to South Carolina.

The **Southern False Angel Wing,** *Petricola lapicida* Gmelin (Lat. *lapicida*, stone cutter) (pl. XLVI, 12), is about 25 mm. (1 in.) in length and height. The shell is rounded, inflated, white; the sculpture, which is not part of the shell surface but consists of a deposited calcareous coating, presents a crisscross pattern formed of zigzag radiating ribs crossed by concentric growth lines. This is a fairly common species inhabiting burrows in coral rock. It ranges from southern Florida to the West Indies.

**Jonas's Rock Borer,** *Rupellaria typica* Jonas (diminutive of Lat. *rupes*, cliff or steep rock; and the word for typical) (pl. XLVI, 13), is 30 mm. (1 1/5 in.) long, 20 mm. (4/5 in.) high. The shell is variable in shape, but generally well rounded and inflated in front and more or less compressed and rostrate behind. The surface is sculptured with numerous wavy, well-marked radiating lines. The color is grayish white stained internally with buff or orange. This common species, found burrowing in coral rock, ranges from North Carolina to Texas, Mexico, and the West Indies. It was recently incorrectly placed in the genus *Pseudoirus,* a Japanese genus of nonburrowing bivalves.

ORDER:

# MYOIDA

(*degenerate teeth*)

SUPERFAMILY:

## MYACEA

FAMILY:

## MYIDAE

(*soft-shelled clams*)

These shells are chalky, grayish, and oval, though commonly distorted in shape; the left valve has a spoonlike chondrophore; the periostracum is thin, flaky. The adults live in deep burrows in mud, especially in bays, and feed through strong, extendible siphons. When exposed at low tide, they react to the tread of approaching footsteps and quickly retract the siphon, expelling a jet of water into the air. This defensive behavior betrays their presence.

# KEY TO GENUS MYA

* Shell generally oval, posterior rounded, pallial sinus long and narrow; distribution southward to North Carolina        *Mya arenaria*
* Shell widely truncate behind, pallial sinus wide and shallow; distribution southward to Nahant, Massachusetts        *M. truncata*

---

Genus *Mya* Linnaeus

*Mya arenaria* Linnaeus
   Soft-shelled Clam, Steamer

   Pl. XLV, 9

ETYMOLOGY: Gr. and Lat. *mya*, sea mussel; Lat. *arena*, sand.

SIZE: Ordinarily 85 mm. (3 1/2 in.) in length, 45 mm. (1 3/4 in.) in height.

DISTRIBUTION: Labrador to South Carolina; introduced on the West Coast.

CHARACTERISTICS: Shell medium to large, thin, wrinkled, widely elliptical, gaping at both ends, chalky. Periostracum thin, grayish, flaky. A long, spoon-shaped structure, the chondrophore, present in the left valve to receive the resilium, the right valve with a corresponding groove. No true hinge teeth.

This prolific bivalve goes under several popular names: it is simply "clam" in New England—where the Hard Clam (*Mercenaria*) (see page 428) is a "quahog"—"long clam" in eastern Long Island, and "soft clam" or "steamer" in New York City. It is also called "nanny nose" (from the Indian *maninose*) by fishermen in Delaware and Maryland. It is among the most important food mollusks in our area. Diners who have eaten steamers that were not sufficiently cleaned before cooking can appreciate the appropriateness of the use of *arenaria* (sandy) as part of the Latin name. The small immature forms, before they begin burrowing, can always be recognized by the spoon-shaped chondrophore.

   The **Gaper Soft-shelled Clam,** *Mya truncata* Linnaeus (Lat. *truncatus*, cut off, mutilated) (pl. XLIV, 20), differs from *M. arenaria* in having an abruptly truncate and widely gaping posterior end. The pallial sinus is wide and shallow, the depth being equal to or less than its width. It is this feature that will distinguish true *M. truncata* from the distorted valves of *M. arenaria*, which may look like the former because they have a falsely truncate end. In *M. arenaria* the pallial sinus is long and narrow, the length about twice the size of the width. *M. truncata* ranges circumpolarly, reaching only to Nahant, Massachusetts, on the East Coast of North America. It is a favorite food of many birds and fish, as well as of walruses and humans.

FAMILY:

# CORBULIDAE
(*box clams*)

These shells are small, usually whitish, and oblong, with strong concentric ridges on the surface. The left valve is smaller, and fits into the right along the lower margin. This family is widely distributed in temperate seas.

## KEY TO GENUS CORBULA

* Shell white or grayish
** Shell grayish, with sculpture of narrow, closely set
    concentric lines                                    *Corbula contracta*
** Shell white, with concentric lines wider and more
    widely spaced                                       *C. caribaea*
* Shell pinkish or red                                  *C. dietziana*

Genus *Corbula* Bruguière

*Corbula contracta* Say
  Contracted Box Clam

  Pl. XLV, 10

ETYMOLOGY: Lat. *corbula*, little basket.

SIZE: 10 mm. (2/5 in.) in length, 6 mm. (1/4 in.) in height.

DISTRIBUTION: Cape Cod, Massachusetts, to Florida, Texas, and the West Indies.

CHARACTERISTICS: Shell small, triangular, inflated, moderately strong; rounded in front, somewhat pointed and truncate behind. Color white. Left valve fits snugly into right valve. Surface sculpture of closely and regularly spaced, well-incised concentric lines.

This is a common shallow-water species living in bays and inlets in sand or mud. The genus can best be recognized by the snug fit of the left valve into the right valve, like the closely fitting cover on a box.

**Dietz's Box Shell,** *Corbula dietziana* C. B. Adams (named for a Mr. Dietz) (pl. XLV, 11), differs mainly in being pink or red instead of white or gray. The shape tends to be distorted, with the posterior end usually more pointed. The surface sculpture is weak and irregular. This is a southern species, not commonly found, ranging from North Carolina to Florida, Texas, and the West Indies.

The **Caribbean Box Shell,** *Corbula caribaea* Orbigny (the author's spelling of "Caribbean" must be preserved, under the rules of the International Commission of Zoological Nomenclature) (pl. XLV, 12), is 9 mm. (about 2/5 in.) long. It differs from *C. contracta* in being white rather than gray, in being somewhat thinner, less swollen, and with more widely spaced concentric lines. It ranges from Massachusetts to Florida, Texas, and the West Indies. *C. swiftiana* C. B. Adams is thought to be the same species, but the *Corbula* are still not clearly understood. This is a common species in the south, rarer in the north.

SUPERFAMILY:

# GASTROCHAENACEA

FAMILY:

# GASTROCHAENIDAE
(*burrowing gaper clams*)

The shells are small, chalky, and petal shaped, and do not enclose all of the soft parts; hinge teeth are absent. They live in burrows in coral rock or in bottle-shaped cells, which they construct in the empty valves of other bivalves. Found only in warmer seas.

# KEY TO GENERA GASTROCHAENA AND SPENGLERIA

* Shell with concentric sculpture only      *Gastrochaena hians*
* Shell with posterior triangular area heavily sculptured with transverse lamellae      *Spengleria rostrata*

---

Genus *Gastrochaena* Spengler

*Gastrochaena hians* Gmelin
     Burrowing Gaper Clam

ETYMOLOGY: Gr. *gaster chainein*, stomach gaping; Lat. *hiare*, to gape.

SIZE: 18 mm. (3/4 in.) in length, 10 mm. (2/5 in.) in height.

DISTRIBUTION: North Carolina to Texas and the West Indies.

CHARACTERISTICS: Shell small, petal shaped, chalky, fragile; anterior gaping widely below. Color white. Sculpture of weak concentric lines. Hinge teeth absent.

This species usually lives in bottle-shaped burrows dug in coral rock or thick mollusk shells. Here it can be found side by side with other burrowing species. It can also live in a thin shelly cell constructed by the clam inside the valves of dead *Arca*. The fragile shell does not permit itself to be extracted unbroken from its burrow or cell. This species at one time was confused with G. *cuneiformis* Spengler, a Pacific species. *Rocellaria* is a synonym of the genus *Gastrochaena*.

**Spengler's Burrowing Gaper Clam,** *Spengleria rostrata* Spengler (L. Spengler was a German conchologist; Lat. *rostratus*, beaked) (pl. XLV, 13), is 25 mm. (1 in.) in length. The shell differs from *Gastrochaena hians* in that the posterior end is truncate instead of rounded, and most important, that the posterior slope has a raised triangular area that is heavily sculptured with low, transverse plates or lamellae. This species, ranging from southeastern Florida to the West Indies, is less common than *Gastrochaena*. It also lives in burrows, but as far as is known, it does not construct cells.

# PHOLADACEA

# PHOLADIDAE
*(piddock clams or angel wings)*

These shells are small to rather large, white, greatly gaping and incapable of containing all of the soft parts; periostracum grayish, thin, flaky. The surface is strongly sculptured, especially at the anterior rounded end, which serves as the boring tool; hinge teeth and ligament are absent. The interior has long chondrophores; accessory valves are commonly present. Found in all seas, burrowing in wood, clay, coral, peat, and rocks.

Since the Pholadidae live in burrows in various kinds of hard substrates, they do not need any special devices like ligaments or hinge teeth to keep the valves together and in place. Their cramped quarters, together with the adductor muscles and in some cases the mantle, provide sufficiently for that purpose. Because of the absence of the ligament, the pholads and the shipworms (family Teredinidae) (see pages 446–7) are in some systems of bivalve arrangement put into a superfamily called Adesmacea (Gr. *a desmos*, without a band or ligament).

## KEY TO FAMILY PHOLADIDAE

    * Shell with a transverse furrow
    ** Mature shell without a callum, only mesoplax
      present                             *Zirfaea crispata*
    ** Mature shell with a callum, metaplax and
      mesoplax present
  * * * Shell larger, up to 40 mm. (1 3/5 in.), umbo
      covered by a long, sickle-shaped flange;
      usually burrowing in wood            *Martesia striata*
  * * * Shell smaller, 15 mm. (3/5 in.), umbo masked
      by thin, platelike covering, the umbonal
      reflection; usually burrowing in shell or
      shelly rock                     *Diplothyra smithii*

* Shell without transverse furrow
* * Umbonal flange supported by 10 to 14 strong
  vertical septa                                      *Pholas campechiensis*
* * Umbonal flange unsupported or with only
  1 septum
* * * Shell large, up to almost 200 mm. (8 in.) in
  length, posterior end rounded, sculpture
  strong, apophyses wide, spoon shaped              *Cyrtopleura costata*
* * * Shell smaller, up to 70 mm. (2 4/5 in.) in
  length, posterior end mostly truncated,
  apophyses long, narrow                            *Barnea truncata*

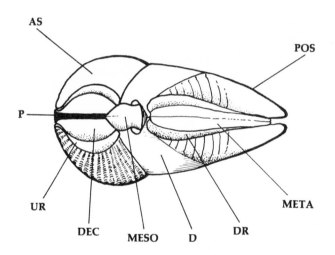

*Some morphological structures of a pholadid bivalve. AS—anterior slope; POS—posterior slope; META—metaplax; DR—dorsal reflection of valve; D—disc; MESO—mesoplax; DEC—dorsal extension of callum; UR—umbonal reflection; P—periostracum between valves. (After Kennedy, 1974, p. 12.)*

Genus *Cyrtopleura* Tryon

*Cyrtopleura costata* Linnaeus
    True Angel Wing

Pl. XLIV, 21

ETYMOLOGY: Gr. *kyrtos pleura*, arched side; Lat. *costatus*, ribbed.

SIZE: Reaching 183 mm. (7 1/4 in.) in length, 75 mm. (3 in.) in height.

DISTRIBUTION: Fall River, Massachusetts, to the West Indies and southward.

CHARACTERISTICS: Shell large, inflated, thin but strong, elliptical, rounded at
    both ends. Color white under a thin, straw-colored, flaking
    periostracum, some southern populations with an irregular pink
    band. Sculpture of strong radiating ribs armed with large, regularly
    spaced scales, crossed by weak concentric lines, sculpture stronger on
    both slopes; radial sculpture is reflected in the glossy interior of the
    valves. Hinge teeth and ligament absent. Umbones near anterior end,
    covered by a shelly reflection. A long spoonlike process, called the
    "apophysis" (pl. apophyses), is present in each of the valves under
    the umbones.

This beautiful species is too well known to require much description.
Spread out, the two valves do indeed resemble the English name by
which they are widely known. The animals live in sandy mud or
clay at or just below the low-water mark in bays and inlets. They
inhabit burrows, which can be as deep as two feet or more. In
most Pholadidae there are one to three accessory plates fixed to the
dorsal surface. These are the protoplax (front plate), the mesoplax
(middle plate), and metaplax (hind plate). In *Cyrtopleura* the protoplax, except in fully adult individuals, is chitinous; the mesoplax is
triangular and rather heavy, and the metaplax is lacking.

The **False Angel Wing,** *Barnea truncata* Say (*barnea* is an artificial word without meaning; Lat. *truncatus*, cut off) (pl. XLV, 14),
reaches 70 mm. (2 3/4 in.) in length, and 25 mm. (1 in.) in height.
This species differs from *Cyrtopleura costata* by having weaker and
less scaly surface sculpture, which disappears at the truncated, posterior end. The apophyses are long, slender, and curved. The animals
live in burrows, in clay or mud or peat, in shallow protected waters.
The species ranges from Canada to Texas, the West Indies, and
southward. In western Florida and Texas the shells have a rounded
rather than a truncated posterior end.

The **Campeche Angel Wing,** *Pholas campechiensis* Gmelin (Gr.
*pholas*, lurking in a hole) (pl. XLV, 15), reaches 110 mm. (4 3/8 in.)

in length, 35 mm. (1 3/8 in.) in height. The shell is elongate, elliptical, almost flattened-cylindrical in shape, and the sculpture is weaker. Its most distinguishing characteristic, however, is the presence of ten to fourteen vertical septa located between the umbonal reflection and the umbones. (In *Cyrtopleura* there is only a single septum, and in *Barnea* none.) All three accessory plates are present. This species, according to Dr. Turner, is not often taken alive, because it probably lives in burrows in deeper water. However, beach specimens are not rare, and even if the valves are largely destroyed, the species can be recognized by the fact that the umbonal area is strengthened by the septa, which survives to the last. *Pholas campechiensis* ranges from North Carolina to the Gulf states, and the West Indies and southward.

The **Common Piddock**, *Zirfaea crispata* Linnaeus (possibly from Lat. *sirpea*, a basketwork of rushes, but most likely an artificial word without meaning; Lat. *crispare*, to curl or crisp) (pl. XLIV, 22), reaches 93 mm. (3 3/4 in.) in length, 49 mm. (2 in.) in height, but is often smaller. The shell is broadly rounded, truncate posteriorly and widely gaping at both ends. There is a deep furrow that runs obliquely from the umbo to the middle of the opposite margin, and divides the valves into two almost equal sections. The anterior area is covered by coarse radiating ribs, which bear rather strong scales, especially near the margins; the area behind the furrow is relatively smooth. The furrow is more prominent in younger individuals. Only a mesoplax is present. This species, in addition to clay and peat, is also found in waterlogged bits of wood thrown up on the beach. The piddocks can be collected here by breaking open and examining the softened wood. The shape of the valves can be distorted by the hardness of the matrix in which the animal burrows. This piddock ranges from Labrador to New Jersey.

The **Striate Piddock**, *Martesia striata* Linnaeus (Lat. *martes*, marten, a carnivorous mammal; *striare*, to furrow) (not illustrated), can reach 44 mm. (1 3/4 in.) in length and 19 mm. (3/4 in.) in height, but its size depends on the size of the wood in which it lives. The shell is variable in shape, but generally it is pear shaped with a shorter or longer anterior end. The juvenile shell has a wide posterior gape, but in adult forms this gape is covered by a rounded shield of calcium termed a "callum." This species resembles *Zirfaea* in the presence of the furrow, but differs in having a sickle-shaped flange extending over the umbones and forming a funnel-shaped pit below. Moreover, the sculpture on the anterior portion is weaker, and the scales are either absent or very small. A meso- and a metaplax are present, protoplax lacking. The variability of this species is so great that Dr. Turner found more than thirty synonyms given to various shapes or juvenile stages of this species. Its range is normally from North Carolina to Florida, the Gulf coast, the West Indies, and southward, but specimens in driftwood have been found as far north as Massachusetts.

**Smith's Piddock,** *Diplothyra smithii* Tryon (Gr. *diploos thyra* double door; Sanderson Smith, 1832–1915, was a prominent malacologist from Long Island, New York) (pl. XLVI, 14), is a small shell, 15 mm. (3/5 in.) in length, 9 mm. (about 2/5 in.) in height. The shell is pear shaped and white or light brown, under a thin, yellow, flaking periostracum; it is solid, with a callum, in the adult state. There is a weak transverse furrow, as in *Martesia* and *Zirfaea;* the umbonal reflection is thin and pressed close to the umbo. This small species burrows in live oyster shells, and has been found in other shells and shell rock as well. It probably avoids wood. Its small size, shelly habitat, and appressed umbonal reflection will identify it. It ranges from Provincetown, Massachusetts, to Florida and Texas.

---

FAMILY:

# TEREDINIDAE

(*shipworms*)

The bivalved shells of this family are small, concave, saddle-shaped, with filelike surface sculpture. Shipworms live in long, calcium-lined burrows in wood and their destructive burrowing habit requires the shipping industry to spend vast amounts of money yearly to combat this maritime menace.

Genus *Teredo* Linnaeus

*Teredo navalis* Linnaeus
Common Shipworm

Pl. XLV, 16

ETYMOLOGY: Lat. *teredo,* a worm; and *navalis,* pertaining to ships.

SIZE: Shells 6 to 8 mm. (1/5 to 1/3 in.) long, length of rest of body depends on thickness of the wooden shelter.

DISTRIBUTION: Both coasts of North America, also Europe, and Africa.

CHARACTERISTICS: Shell small, concave, saddle-shaped, surface sculpture of filelike, denticulated ridges placed at right angles to each other. Body encased in long shelly tube lining the wooden burrow. Terminal pallets very small, paddle-shaped.

This most unlikely-looking mollusk nevertheless is one closely related to the piddocks (family Pholadidae). The small shells are set at the head of a long smooth burrow which they excavate with their filelike surface sculpture. The elongated soft anatomy is further protected by a long, fragile, shelly tube lining the burrow. If the clam is taken alive, two tiny featherlike pallets can be seen at the opposite end near the outer surface of the burrowed wood. They serve to close off the narrow end of the tube from contaminated or otherwise dangerous water. In the genus *Teredo* the pallets are shaped like tiny, short-handled paddles. This species is one of the notorious shipworms that cause so much damage to untreated wood pilings, wharfs, or wooden barges in our saltwater harbors. But the Teredinidae are also useful, in that they destroy floating logs and trees that could seriously damage ships.

The shells of shipworms are commonly collected by breaking open bits of waterlogged wood on beaches. The presence of *Teredo* is betrayed by minute surface holes, the point of entry of the larval shipworm.

**Gould's Shipworm,** *Bankia gouldi* Bartsch (possibly from the proper name Bank; Augustus A. Gould, 1805–1866, was an American malacologist) (pl. XLIV, 23), has a shell that is practically identical with *Teredo navalis*. The only difference between the genera lies in the pallets which in *Bankia* are elongate and composed of a series of conelike, calcareous sections connected by a central core. Most of the taxonomical distinctions in the family Teredinidae rest upon the structure of the pallets. Clench and Turner (1946) call this species "the most widespread and abundant species on the Atlantic coast." It ranges from New Jersey to the West Indies and southward.

SUBCLASS:

# ANOMALODESMATA
(*irregular hinges*)

ORDER:

# PHOLADOMYOIDA

SUPERFAMILY:

## PANDORACEA

FAMILY:

## PANDORIDAE
(*pandoras*)

The shells are much compressed, right valve very flat, left valve somewhat swollen, hinge teeth small. *Pandora*, the only genus in the family, is widely distributed, with most species occurring in the cooler waters of the northern hemisphere.

## KEY TO GENUS PANDORA

* Shell oblong, posterior end almost vertical, length
  only slightly greater than height; range Canada to
  Cape Hatteras                                         *Pandora gouldiana*

* Shell elongate, boat shaped, posterior strongly
  sloping, length almost twice height; range Cape
  Hatteras to Texas                                    *P. trilineata*

---

Genus *Pandora* Bruguière

*Pandora gouldiana* Dall
    Gould's Pandora

   Pl. XLVI, 15

ETYMOLOGY: Gr. *pas, pan doron*, all gifted—Pandora was the Eve of Greek
    mythology; Augustus A. Gould, 1805–1866, was an American
    malacologist.

SIZE: 35 mm. (1 2/5 in.) in length, 27 mm. (1 in.) in height.

DISTRIBUTION: Gulf of Saint Lawrence to New Jersey.

CHARACTERISTICS: Shell small, rounded-oblong, extremely compressed,
    pearly under a thin, chalky surface layer. Umbones tiny, at anterior
    end. Dorsal margin with a strong, concave squarish ridge tapering to
    an upward directed extension, or rostrum, posteriorly. Right valve flat,
    left valve somewhat convex, prominently divided into two sections by a
    shallow groove running diagonally from umbo to opposite margin.

This species is most easily recognized by the extremely compressed
valves, the inner pearly layer, and the strong, concave dorsal ridge,
which alone permits recognition even when the rest of the shell is
broken or destroyed. This is a fairly common species in shallow
water in muddy bays or inlet waters. Dead valves, or recognizable
fragments, are frequently found in beach drift.

The **Three-lined Pandora,** *Pandora trilineata* Say (Lat. *tri linea,*
three line) (pl. XLV, 17), is 30 mm. (1 1/5 in.) in length, 14 mm.
(about 3/5 in.) in width. It differs from *P. gouldiana* chiefly in shape.
Whereas the latter is oblong in shape, with the length only a little
greater than the height, *P. trilineata* is elongate, the ventral margin
strongly sloping upward, and the length almost twice the height.
Moreover, the pointed extension of the dorsal ridge is longer in
*P. trilineata.* This is a southern form, ranging from Cape Hatteras
to Florida and Texas.

FAMILY:

# LYONSIIDAE

(*glass clams*)

These shells are small, glassy, hinge teeth lacking, periostracum thin, with minute projections. There are only a few species of this family living generally in shallow waters, although some occur at great depths.

Genus *Lyonsia* Turton

*Lyonsia hyalina* Conrad
  Northern Glass Clam

  Pl. XLV, 18

ETYMOLOGY: W. Lyons (1766–1849) was an English naturalist; Lat. *hyalus*, glass.

SIZE: 17 mm. (about 3/4 in.) in length, 8 mm. (1/3 in.) in height.

DISTRIBUTION: Nova Scotia to South Carolina.

CHARACTERISTICS: Shell small, rounded-oblong, height about one-half length, swollen; pearly, glassy, extremely thin. Umbones prominent, near the anterior end. Posterior end obliquely truncate, periostracum drawn up into a number of fine radiating wrinkles that look like surface sculpture.

This is a common shallow-water species living partly buried in clay and mud bottoms. The curious periostracum is covered with minute, hairy fringes, which serve to trap bits of sand grains to cover the shell. The thin, glassy shell texture is so characteristic that even fragments can be identified as belonging to this species.

The **Floridian Glass Clam,** *Lyonsia hyalina floridana* Conrad, differs only in being more elongate, with the height only one-third the length. It is found from the west coast of Florida to Texas.

FAMILY:

# PERIPLOMATIDAE

(*spoon clams*)

The shells of this family are small, fragile, whitish, opaque, with two spoonlike internal chondrophores, one in each valve. The relatively few species are widely distributed, generally in shallow water.

## KEY TO GENUS PERIPLOMA

* Umbones almost central, chondrophores directed
  downward; range from Nova Scotia to North
  Carolina                                          *Periploma leanum*
* Umbones anterior, chondrophores directed
  posteriorly; range South Carolina to Texas        *P. margaritaceum*

Genus *Periploma* Schumacher

*Periploma leanum* Conrad
    Lea's Spoon Clam

    Pl. XLVI, 16

ETYMOLOGY: Gr. *periplem*, I sail about; Isaac Lea, 1792–1886, was an American conchologist.

SIZE: 18 mm. (3/4 in.) in length, 7 mm. (about 1/4 in.) in height.

DISTRIBUTION: Nova Scotia to North Carolina.

CHARACTERISTICS: Shell small, oval, opaque, rather weak, brittle, smooth. Color white under a thin yellowish periostracum. Umbones almost central, with a downward-pointing, spoon-shaped condrophore under the umbo in each valve.

This frail shell is often found thrown up on shore by strong ocean waves on the outer beaches. It is surprising how well these fragile creatures survive the force of the waves. This is a fairly common species, living just below the low-tide line in sandy locations. The smooth shell and the spoon-shaped chondrophore are enough to enable one to recognize the species.

The **Unequal Spoon Clam,** *Periploma margaritaceum* Lamarck (pl. XLVI, 17), is about the same size as *P. leanum.* It differs in being roundly quadrate in shape, with barely rounded sides. The beaks are not centrally located but are placed at the anterior end. The two spoon-shaped chondrophores under the umbones are directed backward toward the posterior end. This fairly common species ranges from South Carolina to Florida and Texas. It is especially abundant off Texas. Better known as *P. inequale* C. B. Adams (Lat. *inaequalis,* not equal), a synonym.

# CHAPTER V

# OTHER MARINE MOLLUSKS

In this final chapter are the species of scaphopods (tusk and tooth shells), cephalopods (Ram's Horn Shell and Paper Nautilus), and polyplacophorans (chitons) the collector might expect to find in this region. All the representatives of these three classes, Scaphopoda, Cephalopoda, and Polyplacophora, are marine inhabitants. Although only a few species belonging to these groups are found living intertidally in our area, some, such as the scaphopods, which live offshore, are occasionally found in beach drift. The chitons occur more commonly in the West Indian region on rocks and stony corals, but they are common intertidal constituents along the rocky shores of our West Coast.

# CLASS:
# SCAPHOPODA
*(tusk and tooth shells)*

The scaphopods (meaning boat footed or digger footed) have tube-like shells, open at both ends. They superficially resemble diminutive elephant tusks (family Dentaliidae), or tiny canine teeth of a carnivore (family Siphonodentaliidae). Thus, the common names, tusk and tooth shells, are applied respectively to the representatives of these families. The shell is slightly to moderately curved, and the posterior end is attenuated. The shell may be sculptured with longitudinal or annular ribs, or less commonly it is smooth. The body can be completely withdrawn inside the tubular shell, to which it is attached on the dorsal side by muscles. A head is lacking, but the mouth is situated in a projection of the pharynx. A well-developed radula is present. Extending from the snout are many filamentous tentacles, called "captacula," which terminate in tiny food-gathering capsules. Adapted for burrowing in soft substrates, the foot lacks an operculum.

These marine mollusks are largely subtidal inhabitants of sandy and muddy substrates. The shell is held in an oblique position by the foot, which extends out of the larger opening of the tube, half-buried in the sea bottom. The exposed contractile tentacles catch tiny organisms from the bottom sediment and pass them by means of minute hairs, termed "cilia," to the mouth. Most species live on the continental shelf, although many occur at greater depths, some in the deepest oceanic trenches. Less than 400 living species of scaphopods are known. Shallow-water species are occasionally washed ashore, and may be found in beach drift.

## KEY TO GENERA DENTALIUM AND CADULUS

  \* Shell very small, usually less than 10 mm.
     (2/5 in.) in length, tube-shaped with swollen
     central section
\*\* Shell with 4 shallow apical notches            *Cadulus carolinensis*

| | |
|---|---|
| ** Shell with 4 deep notches | *C. quadridentatus* |
| * Shell large, 25 to 50 mm. (1 to 2 in.) in length, shaped like an elephant tusk | |
| ** Shell hexagonal in cross section | *Dentalium texasianum* |
| ** Shell circular in cross section | |
| *** Shell wider, dull white, apex with narrow pear-shaped slit; range northern | *D. entale stimpsoni* |
| *** Shell narrow, glossy, often pinkish, apex with 4 long narrow slits; range southern | *D. eboreum* |

FAMILY:

# DENTALIIDAE

(*tusk shells*)

The tusklike shells of this family are small to medium sized, usually 25 to 50 mm. (1 to 2 in.), although some attain 120 mm. (5 in.) in length. Most are white; a few tropical species are greenish or reddish. The cylindrical tube is long and tapering to a point at the posterior (apical) end. The surface may be smooth, but more commonly it is ribbed longitudinally, or rarely has annular ribs. Primitive man used tusk shells for money and adornment. Like the tooth shells, they are widely distributed everywhere but the Arctic seas.

Genus *Dentalium* Linnaeus

*Dentalium entale stimpsoni* Henderson
   Stimpson's Tusk Shell

   Pl. XLVII, 1

ETYMOLOGY: Lat. *dens dentis*, tooth; *entalis*, inner; William Stimpson, 1832–1872, was a malacologist from New England.

SIZE: 25 to 50 mm. (1 to 2 in.) in length, 2 to 4 mm. (1/12 to 1/6 in.) in width.

DISTRIBUTION: Nova Scotia to Cape Cod, Massachusetts.

CHARACTERISTICS: Shell long, tusk shaped. Color ivory white. Apex chalky, eroded, with a tiny, elongate, pear-shaped slit.

The Scaphopoda constitute a small group of mollusks commonly living in deep water. Some species from the tropics are handsomely sculptured and colored, but the few species easily available to the local collector are not very showy, their only attraction being their peculiar shape, like a tiny elephant's tusk. *D. entale stimpsoni* lives commonly offshore in sandy bottoms, but occasionally specimens can be found on shore after severe storms. The local populations are considered to represent a subspecies of those occurring in European waters.

The **Ivory Tusk Shell,** *Dentalium eboreum* Conrad (Lat. *ebur,* ivory) (pl. XLVII, 2), is narrower, glossier, more delicate, and the color is often pinkish. The apical end has four long, narrow slits and about twenty surface scratches. This is a common shallow-water species ranging from North Carolina to the West Indies and Brazil.

The **Texas Tusk Shell,** *Dentalium texasianum* Philippi (pl. XLVII, 3), reaches 35 mm. (1 2/5 in.) in length. The rather thick, dull, grayish white shell is sculptured with vertical ribs, the interspaces being flat. As a result, the shell in cross section is not round, as in the other species of *Dentalium* discussed, but hexagonal. This is a fairly common species ranging from North Carolina to the Gulf states. It lives in open bays and inlets, half sunken in mud and clay bottoms. *Dentalium americanum* Chenu may prove to be an earlier name.

---

FAMILY:

# SIPHONODENTALIIDAE
(*tooth shells*)

The shells in this family are small, usually less than 10 mm. (2/5 in.) in length. They are white, tubelike, generally with a swollen central portion. They somewhat resemble a tiny canine tooth.

Genus *Cadulus* Philippi

*Cadulus carolinensis* Bush
  Carolina Tooth Shell

  Pl. XLVII, 4

ETYMOLOGY: Lat. *cadulus,* a small jar or pail.

SIZE: 10 mm. (2/5 in.) in length.

DISTRIBUTION: North Carolina to Florida.

CHARACTERISTICS: Shell small, white, tubelike, swollen centrally, with 4 shallow notches on the narrower (apical) end.

The Carolina Tooth Shell lives in 3 to 100 fathoms, but dead specimens are not uncommon in sand and beach drift. The 4 shallow notches at the narrower end serve to distinguish this species from the following one.

The **Four-cusped Tooth Shell,** *Cadulus quadridentatus* Dall (Lat. *quadri dentatus,* four toothed) (pl. XLVII, 5), is very similar to the Carolina Tooth Shell, but it has 4 deep notches at the narrower end. It lives very much like the former species, but its range extends southward to the West Indies.

# CEPHALOPODA

*(octopuses and squids)*

The octopuses and squids, which, together with the chambered nautilus, make up this class, are the most active and advanced of the mollusks, and in size, vigor, and intelligence outclass all other marine invertebrates. However, in our area, the shells of only three species are worthy of the collector's attention; the other animals are either shell-less or have an internal glassy "pen" or limy "cuttle bone."

The **Spirula** or **Ram's Horn Shell,** *Spirula spirula* Linnaeus (diminutive of Lat. *spira,* a spiral) (pl. XLVII, 6), is a handsome little object about 25 mm. (1 in.) in diameter. It is pearly white, and wound into three loose coils that are not in contact. The coils are sculptured externally with a series of constrictions, each one of which corresponds to the presence of one of the internal partitions, so that the entire shell is divided internally into a series of concave chambers. A small tube, called the "siphuncle," connects the chambers and terminates as a tiny opening in the last partition. The shells are common objects especially on tropical and subtropical beaches such as Florida. In our area they have been found as far north as Nantucket Island, having been carried there by an arm of the Gulf Stream. In life, the shell is found inside this small, ten-armed pelagic cephalopod. This little creature, though rarely found alive, must occur on the high seas in prodigious numbers.

The **Paper Nautilus,** *Argonauta argo* Linnaeus (named for the Argonauts who sailed on the ship *Argo* to find the Golden Fleece), and the **Brown Paper Nautilus,** *Argonauta hians* Lightfoot (Lat. *hiare,* to gape) (pl. XLVII, 7 & 8), produce very handsome, fragile, shell-like structures. We call them "shell-like" because they are not true shells; they are secreted by a pair of weblike appendages, not by the mantle. They are actually the receptacles in which the female carries her eggs until they hatch. The "shell" is a boatlike structure composed of a large, gaping body whorl and a single, rapidly widening whorl behind. The shell of *A. argo* is pearly white, ornamented with numerous narrow radial ridges that end in small, dark marginal nodules. *A. hians* has a tan or brown shell, with fewer, heavier, and more irregular ridges terminating in strong dark nodules at the upper margin. These shell receptacles attain 250 mm. (10 in.) in length, and unbroken specimens are highly prized. Shells of both species are occasionally cast up on shore, chiefly in Florida, but specimens have been taken as far north as New Jersey. The lucky finder of even a small specimen can count that day among his unforgettable ones. In spite of their intelligence, no cephalopod has ever learned to raise its webbed tentacles, and using them like sails, to sail before the wind. The idea is poetical but unproven. The interested reader should consult Lane's (1957) book, *The Kingdom of the Octopus*, for an authoritative account of the life history of the cephalopods.

# CLASS:
# POLYPLACOPHORA

(*chitons*)

---

The polyplacophorans (many-plate bearers) are primitive mollusks with an elongate, limpetlike body bearing a shell composed of eight overlapping plates, or valves. The limy plates are joined to each other marginally by a thick, skinlike girdle, which may be ornamented by scales, spines, or bristles. Better known as chitons, a name derived from the Greek name for the outer garment worn by men in classical times, these mollusks have a small anterior head lacking eyes or tentacles. Some species have light-sensitive spots in the integument covering the plates. The mouth is provided with a radula to rasp off algae growing on the rocks or other hard substrates to which these animals adhere. Others prey on small animals, such as tiny crustaceans.

Chitons occur in the intertidal zone to the oceanic depths. There are approximately 600 living species that are widely distributed, mostly in temperate and warmer seas. They move by crawling on their muscular foot, and clamp down tightly when disturbed by wave action or by predators. When dislodged from their footing, they curl up into a ball, much as a pill bug does when it is disturbed. Living specimens can be removed from their domicile by inserting the blade of a knife or other sharp instrument under the foot. To prevent them from curling up, specimens should be tied by string or strips of cloth to a flat surface, such as strips of plastic or wooden tongue depressors. They can either be preserved intact in 70 percent alcohol, or the foot and other soft parts can be removed, leaving the girdle to hold the plates together.

The chitons were formerly placed in the class Amphineura with the wormlike solenogasters, a small group of mollusks that lack a shell. The latter are separated from the polyplacophorans and comprise the class Aplacophora, meaning, appropriately, nonplate bearers.

# KEY TO THE POLYPLACOPHORANS

\* Girdle covered with rounded scales, no
hairs

\*\* Shell long, narrow, length three times the
width                                              *Stenoplax floridana*

\*\* Shell oval, length little greater than width

\*\*\* Shell small, 8 mm. (1/3 in.) in length,
color olive or brown, surface sculpture of
fine pustules; range from Tampa, Florida,
to the West Indies                                 *S. papillosus*

\*\*\* Shell large, 25 mm. (1 in.) in length, color
reddish, surface sculpture of concentric
growth lines; range from Arctic seas to
Connecticut                                        *Ischnochiton ruber*

\* Girdle with hairs, or fuzzy

\*\* Hairs sparse, scattered, color generally
gray, buff or reddish brown; range from
Cape Cod to Florida                                *Chaetopleura apiculata*

\*\* Hairs thick, girdle fuzzy, surface usually
much eroded; range from southern Florida
to the West Indies                                 *Acanthopleura granulata*

# ORDER:
# NEOLORICATA

# CHAETOPLEURIDAE,
# ISCHNOCHITONIDAE
# AND CHITONIDAE

The families of chitons are characterized largely by the nature of the girdle, the kind of toothlike projections on the valves that are inserted into the girdle, and the composition of the plates. In the family Chaetopleuridae, the spicules on the girdle are interspersed with either fibrous hairs or calcareous spines, and the central areas of the valves are beaded or have rows of pustules arranged longitudinally. The family Ischnochitonidae generally has finely scaled girdles, and the insertion teeth of the valves are smooth or weakly grooved. In the family Chitonidae, the girdles have large, overlapping scales or bristly spines. The insertion teeth have the outer bottom surfaces fluted or deeply incised.

Genus *Chaetopleura* Shuttleworth

*Chaetopleura apiculata* Say
    Gray or Hairy Chiton

    Pl. XLVII, 9

ETYMOLOGY: Gr. *chaites pleura*, hairy side; diminutive of Lat. *apex*, tip or summit.

SIZE: 17 to 25 mm. (about 3/4 to 1 in.) in length; 10 to 16 mm. (2/5 to 2/3 in.) in width.

DISTRIBUTION: Cape Cod, Massachusetts, to Florida.

CHARACTERISTICS: Shell moderate, flat, oblong to oval, the eight valves
    slightly keeled centrally. Color buff to gray or reddish brown, interior
    blue, girdle mottled with cream and brown. Surface sculpture of fine
    tubercles on the sides of the valves, with wavy, beaded vertical lines
    on the center. Girdle narrow, granulose, with short scattered hairs.

*Chaetopleura apiculata* can be collected in shallow water by haul-
ing up and carefully examining submerged rocks and the undersides of dead clam shells. Abbott reports that on the west coast of
Florida, where this species attaches itself to the shells of *Atrina,* the
color is shades of mauve, yellow, or white, with a darker stripe along
the center. Sometimes the valves of dead chitons are freed when the
girdle deteriorates. When found in this condition they are called,
because of their shape, "butterfly shells" or "mermaid teeth." Determining to what species such disarticulated valves belong, especially
with the girdle missing, is a task best left to the experts.

The **Red Northern Chiton,** *Ischnochiton ruber* Linnaeus (Gr.
*ischnos chiton,* slender tunic; Lat. *ruber,* ruddy) (pl. XLVII, 10), is
15 to 25 mm. (3/5 to 1 in.) in length. The valves are rounded centrally and rather smooth, and they vary in color from tan suffused
with orange red patches to entirely red. The interior is bright pink.
The surface sculpture consists of well-marked concentric growth
lines. The reddish brown girdle is covered with minute smooth
scales. This species ranges from the Arctic seas to Connecticut and
lives, like *Chaetopleura,* on hard objects in shallow water. It is also
found in Europe and on the West Coast. This and the following two
species belong to the family Ischnochitonidae.

The **Florida Slender Chiton,** *Stenoplax floridana* Pilsbry (Gr.
*sten plax,* narrow plate) (pl. XLVII, 11), reaches 25 to 40 mm. (1 to
1 3/5 in.) in length and 8 to 12 mm. (1/3 to 1/2 in.) in width. The
elongate, narrow shell is enough to identify it. The color is whitish
or buff, mottled with blackish olive or gray; the interior is a mix-
ture of pink and white, sometimes entirely white or rosy. There are
wavy, often beaded lines on the valves. The blue or gray girdle is
covered with smooth, tiny scales. This is a moderately common species ranging from Miami to Key West and the Dry Tortugas.

The **Pitted Chiton,** *Stenoplax papillosus* C. B. Adams (Lat. *papilla,*
pimple) (pl. XLVII, 12), is the smallest of the local chitons, reaching
only 8 mm. (1/3 in.) in length and 6 mm. (about 1/4 in.) in width.
The oval, mottled olive or brown valves are moderately keeled
centrally and thickly sculptured with minute papillae; the interior is
white. The narrow white and brown or olive brown girdle is covered

with tiny, overlapping scales. This is a reasonably common species frequently found on *Atrina* shells. It is found from Tampa to the lower Keys and the West Indies. This and the previous species were formerly placed in the genus *Ischnochiton*.

The **Fuzzy** or **Granulated Chiton,** *Acanthopleura granulata* Gmelin (Gr. *acanthos pleura*, spine side; Lat. *granulum*, small grain) (pl. XLVII, 13), is large, 50 to 75 mm. (2 to 3 in.) in length. It is readily reccgnized by its thick, fuzzy whitish girdle with occasional black areas. The granulated surface is brownish, and the commonly eroded sculpture is faint. The interior of the valves is brown centrally, with a light green edge. This is the common chiton found on the rocks of breakwaters along the shore walks of Miami and other Floridian cities, where it lives just at or below the high-tide line. It ranges from southern Florida to the West Indies. This species belongs to the family Chitonidae.

# BIBLIOGRAPHY

**Abbott, R. T.**

1944.  The genus *Modulus* in the western Atlantic. *Johnsonia* (Harvard Univ.), 1, no. 14; 1–6, pls. 1, 2.

1950.  Snail invaders. *Natural History Magazine,* 59, no. 2; 80–85, illus.

1950.  The genera *Xancus* and *Vasum* in the western Atlantic. *Johnsonia,* 2, no. 28; 201–219, pls. 89–95.

1954.  *American seashells.* Princeton, N.J.: D. Van Nostrand Co., Inc., 541 pp., 40 pls. (24 in color), text figs.

1954.  Review of the Atlantic periwinkles, *Nodilittorina, Echininus,* and *Tectarius. Proceedings U.S. National Museum,* 103; 449–464, figs. 55–57.

1964.  *Littorina ziczac* (Gmelin) and *L. lineolata* Orbigny. *Nautilus,* 78; 65–66.

1968.  *Seashells of North America.* New York: Golden Press, 280 pp., illus. in color.

1968.  The helmet shells of the world (Cassidae). Pt. 1, *Indo-Pacific Mollusca,* 2, no. 9; 202 pp., 187 pls. (8 in color).

1974.  *American seashells* (second edition). New York: Van Nostrand Reinhold, vi + 663 pp., 24 pls. in color, 3,000 text figs.

**Andrews, J.**

1972.  *Sea shells of the Texas coast.* Austin: Univ. Texas Press, 17 + 298 pp., profusely illustrated.

**Baker, F. C.**

1911.  *The Lymnaeidae of North and Middle America.* Chicago Academy Sciences Special Publication 3, 16 + 539 pp., 58 pls., 51 figs.

1928.   The fresh water Mollusca of Wisconsin, 2 parts. *Wisconsin Geological and Natural History Survey*, Bulletin 70, Univ. Wisconsin, Madison, Pt. 1, Gastropoda, 20 + 507 pp., 1–28 pls., 202 figs. Pt. 2, Pelecypoda, 6 + 495 pp., pls. 29–105, figs. 203–299.

**Bales, B. R.**

1940.   The rock dwellers of the Florida Keys. *Nautilus*, 54, pp. 39–42.

**Bartsch, P.**

1908.   Notes on the fresh-water mollusk *Planorbis magnificus* and descriptions of two new forms of the same genus from the southern states. *Proceedings U.S. National Museum*, 33; 697–700, pl. 57.

**Basch, P. F.**

1959.   The anatomy of *Laevapex fuscus*, a freshwater limpet. Museum Zoology, Univ. Michigan, *Miscellaneous Publications* no. 108; 56 pp., 15 figs.

1963.   A review of the Recent freshwater limpet snails of North America. *Bulletin Museum Comparative Zoology* (Cambridge, Mass.), 129, no. 8; 401–461, 19 figs.

**Bequaert, J. C.**

1942.   *Cerithidea* and *Batillaria* in the western Atlantic. *Johnsonia*, 1, no. 5; 1–11, pls. 1–5.

1943.   The genus *Littorina* in the western Atlantic. *Johnsonia*, 1, no. 7; 1–27, pls. 1–7.

**Berry, E. G.**

1943.   The Amnicolidae of Michigan. Museum Zoology, Univ. Michigan, *Miscellaneous Publications* no. 57; 68 pp., 9 pls., 10 figs., 10 maps.

**Borkowski, T. V., and M. R. Borkowski**

1969.   The *Littorina ziczac* species complex. *Veliger*, 11, no. 4; 408–414, pl. 66, 4 figs.

**Boss, K. J.**

1966. The subfamily Tellininae in the western Atlantic. The Genus *Tellina* (Pt. 1), *Johnsonia*, 4, no. 45; 217–272, pls. 127–142.

1968. The subfamily Tellininae in the western Atlantic. The Genus *Tellina* (Pt. 2) and *Tellidora. Johnsonia*, 4, no. 46; 273–344, pls. 143–160.

1969. The subfamily Tellininae in the western Atlantic. The Genus *Strigilla. Johnsonia*, 4, no. 47; 345–367, pls. 164–171.

1972. The genus *Semele* in the western Atlantic. *Johnsonia*, 5, no. 49; 1–32, pls. 1–12.

**Boss, K. J., and A. S. Merrill**

1965. The family Pandoridae in the western Atlantic. *Johnsonia*, 4, no. 44; 181–215, pls. 115–126.

**Burch, J. B.**

1962. *How to know the Eastern land snails.* Dubuque, Iowa: Wm. C. Brown Co., 215 pp., 519 figs., 7 pls.

1972. Freshwater Spaeriacean clams of North America. *Biota of Freshwater Ecosystems Identification Manual* no. 3 (Washington, D.C.); 31 pp., 34 figs.

**Call, R. E.**

1886. On the genus *Campeloma* Rafinesque, with a revision of the species, Recent and fossil. *Bulletin Washburn College Laboratory Natural History* (Topeka, Kan.), 1, no. 5; 149–165, pls. 3–6.

**Clarke, A. H., Jr., and C. O. Berg**

1959. The freshwater mussels of central New York. *New York State College of Agriculture, Memoir* 367 (Cornell Univ.); 79 pp., 7 pls., 1 map.

**Clench, W. J.**

1942. The genus *Conus* in the western Atlantic. *Johnsonia*, 1, no. 6; 1–40, pls. 1–15.

1942. The genus *Ficus* in the western Atlantic. *Johnsonia*, 1, no. 2; 1, 2, 1 pl.

1944. The genera *Casmaria, Galeodea, Phalium* and *Cassis* in the western Atlantic. *Johnsonia*, 1, no. 16; 1–16, pls. 1–8.

1946. The genera *Bathyaurinia, Rehderia* and *Scaphella* in the western Atlantic. *Johnsonia*, 2, no. 22; 41–60, pls. 24–31.

1947. The genera *Purpura* and *Thais* in the western Atlantic. *Johnsonia*, 2, no. 23; 61–91, pls. 32–40.

1962. A catalogue of the Viviparidae of North America with notes on the distribution of *Viviparus georgianus* Lea. *Museum Comparative Zoology, Occasional Papers on Mollusks*, 2, no. 27; 261–287, pls. 44–45.

1964. The genera *Pedipes* and *Laemodonta* in the western Atlantic. *Johnsonia*, 4, no. 42; 117–127, pls. 76–79.

**Clench, W. J., and R. T. Abbott**

1941, 1945. The genus *Strombus* in the western Atlantic. *Johnsonia*, 1, no. 1, 1–14, pls. 1–10; no. 18, p. 1 (1945).

1942. The genera *Tectarius* and *Echininus* in the western Atlantic. *Johnsonia*, 1, no. 4; 1–4, pls. 1–3.

1943. The genera *Cypraecassis, Morum, Sconsia* and *Dalium* in the western Atlantic. *Johnsonia*, 1, no. 9; 1–8, pls. 1–4.

**Clench, W. J., and C. G. Aguayo**

1943. The genera *Xenophora* and *Tugurium* in the western Atlantic. *Johnsonia*, 1, no. 8; 1–8, 1 pl.

**Clench, W. J., and I. Pérez Farfante**

1945. The genus *Murex* in the western Atlantic. *Johnsonia*, 1, no. 17; 1–58, pls. 1–29.

**Clench, W. J., and S. L. H. Fuller**

1965. The genus *Viviparus* in North America. *Museum Comparative Zoology, Occasional Papers on Mollusks*, 2, no. 32; 385–412, pl. 64–68.

**Clench, W. J., and L. C. Smith**

1944. The family Cardiidae in the western Atlantic. *Johnsonia,* 1, no. 13; 1–32; pls. 1–13.

**Clench, W. J., and R. D. Turner**

1946. The genus *Banksia* in the western Atlantic. *Johnsonia,* 2, no. 19; 1–28, pls. 1–16.

1948. The genus *Truncatella* in the western Atlantic. *Johnsonia,* 2, no. 25; 149–164, pls. 65–73.

1951. The genus *Epitonium* in the western Atlantic, pt. 1. *Johnsonia,* 2, no. 30; 249–288, pls. 108–130.

1952. The genera *Epitonium, Depressiscala, Cylindriscala, Nystiella* and *Solutiscala* in the western Atlantic. *Johnsonia,* 2, no. 31; 289–356, pls. 131–177.

1955. The North American genus *Lioplax* in the family Viviparidae. *Museum Comparative Zoology, Occasional Papers on Mollusks,* 2, no. 19; 1–20, pls. 1–4.

1956. The family Melongenidae in the western Atlantic. *Johnsonia,* 3, no. 35; 161–188, pls. 94–109.

1956. Freshwater mollusks of Alabama, Georgia, and Florida from the Escambia to the Suwannee River. *Bulletin Florida State Museum,* 1, no. 3; 97–239, 9 pls.

1957. The family Cymatiidae in the western Atlantic. *Johnsonia,* 3, no. 36; 189–244, pls. 110–135.

1960. The genus *Calliostoma* in the western Atlantic. *Johnsonia,* 4, no. 40; 1–80, pls. 1–56.

**Cox, I. (editor)**

1957. *The Scallop. Studies of a shell and its influence on humankind.* London: *Shell Transport and Trading Co., Ltd.,* 135 pp., profusely illustrated in color.

**Dazo, B. C.**

1965. The morphology and natural history of *Pleurocera acuta* and *Goniobasis livescens. Malacologia,* 3, no. 1; 1–80, 7 pls.

**Dodge, H.**

1957.  A historical review of the mollusks of Linnaeus; part 5, the genus *Murex* of the class Gastropoda. *Bulletin American Museum Natural History*, 113, no. 2; 77–223.

**Emerson, W. K., and A. D'Attilio**

1963.  A new species of *Latiaxis* from the western Atlantic. *American Museum Natural History, Novitates*, no. 2149; 1–9, 6 figs.

**Emerson, W. K., and E. L. Puffer**

1953.  A catalogue of the molluscan genus *Distorsio*. *Proceedings Biological Society Washington*, 66; 93–108.

**Ewald, J. J.**

1963.  Living examples of *Auriculastra pellucens* and its larval history. *Nautilus*, 77, no. 1; 11–14.

**Feininger, A., and W. K. Emerson**

1972.  *Shells*. New York: Viking Press, 295 pp., profusely illustrated.

**Foster, R. W.**

1946.  The genus *Mya* in the western Atlantic. *Johnsonia*, 2, no. 20; 29–35, pls. 17–21.

**Fretter, V., and A. Graham**

1962.  *British prosobranch mollusks*. London: The Ray Society. xvi + 755 pp., text figs., tables.

**Goodrich, C.**

1929.  The nomenclature of ecological varieties. *Nautilus*, 42; 114–118.

**Gould, S. J.**

1968.  Phenotypic reversion to ancestral form and habit in a marine snail. *Nature*, 220, no. 5169; 804.

**Harman, W. N.**

1968.   Replacement of pleurocerids by *Bithynia* in polluted waters of central New York. *Nautilus,* 81, no. 3; 77–83.

**Harman, W. N., and C. O. Berg**

1971.   The freshwater snails of central New York. *Search* (Ithaca, N.Y.), 1, no. 4; 1–68, 194 figs.

**Harman, W. N., and J. L. Forney**

1970.   Fifty years of change in the molluscan fauna of Oneida Lake, New York. *Limnology and Oceanography,* 15, no. 3; 454–460.

**Harry, H. W.**

1966.   Studies on bivalve molluscs of the genus *Crassinella* in the northwestern Gulf of Mexico: Anatomy, ecology and systematics. *Publications Institution Marine Science* (Texas), 11; 65–89, 17 figs., 1 map.

1969.   A review of the living Leptonacean bivalves of the genus *Aligena. Veliger,* 11, no. 3; 164–181, 40 text figs.

1969.   Anatomical notes on the mactrid bivalve, *Raeta plicatella* Lamarck, 1818, with a review of the genus *Raeta* and related genera. *Veliger,* 12, no. 1; 1–23, 20 text figs.

**Heard, W. H., and R. H. Guckert**

1970.   A re-evaluation of the Recent Unionacea of North America. *Malacologia,* 10, no. 2; 333–355, 3 figs.

**Henderson, J. B.**

1920.   A monograph of the East American scaphopod mollusks. *U.S. National Museum Bulletin,* 111; 6 + 177 pp., 20 pls.

**Herrington, H. B.**

1962.   A Revision of the Sphaeriidae of North America. Museum Zoology, Univ. Michigan, *Miscellaneous Publications,* no. 118; 74 pp., 7 pls., 1 fig.

**Holle, P. A., and C. F. Dineen**

1959.   Studies on the genus *Melampus. Nautilus,* 73; 28–35, pls. 5, 6, and vol. 73, pp. 46–51.

**Hollister, S. C.**

1958.   A review of the genus *Busycon* and its allies, Pt. 1, *Palaeontographica Americana,* 4, no. 28; 1–126, pls. 8–18, 3 text figs.

**Hubendick, B.**

1946.   Systematic monograph of the Patelliformia. *Kungl. Svenska Vetenskapsakademiens Handlingar* (Stockholm), 23, no. 5; 1–93, 6 pls., 20 text figs.

1951.   Recent Lymnaeidae, *Kungl. Svenska Vetenskapsakademiens Handlingar* (Fjarde Serien), 3, no. 1; 1–223, 369 figs., 5 pls.

**Jacobson, M. K., and W. K. Emerson**

1971.   *Wonders of the world of shells: Sea, land, and freshwater.* New York: Dodd, Mead and Co. 80 pp., illustrations. (An introduction to mollusks.)

1971.   *Shells from Cape Cod to Cape May, with special reference to the New York City area.* New York: Dover Publications, xix + 152 pp., paperbound. Revised and enlarged edition of *Shells of the New York City area.* Larchmont, N.Y.: Argonaut Books Inc., 1961.

**Johnson, C. W.**

1934.   List of marine Mollusca of the Atlantic coast from Labrador to Texas. *Proceedings Boston Society Natural History,* 40, no. 1; 204 pp.

**Johnson, R. I.**

1970.   The systematics and zoogeography of the Unionidae of the southern Atlantic Slope region. *Bulletin Museum Comparative Zoology,* 140, no. 6; 263–449, 22 pls., 5 text figs.

1972. The Unionidae of peninsular Florida. *Bulletin Florida State Museum Studies,* 16, no. 4; 181–249, 12 figs.

**Keen, A. M.**

1971. *Sea shells of tropical West America. Marine mollusks from Baja California to Peru.* Stanford, Calif.: Stanford Univ. Press. 2nd ed., xiv + 1064 pp., 22 color plates, black and white figs., maps.

**Kennedy, G. L.**

1974. West American Cenozoic Pholadidae (Mollusca: Bivalvia). Memoir San Diego Society Natural History, no. 8; 217 pp., 103 pls.

**Lane, F. W.**

1957. *The kingdom of the octopus: the life history of the Cephalopoda.* New York: Sheridan House; 287 pp., 53 pls. (5 in color).

**La Rocque, A.**

1956. Variation of carinae in *Valvata tricarinata. Nautilus,* 70; 13–14.

**Laursen, D.**

1953. The genus *Ianthina. Dana-Report* (Carlsberg Foundation, Copenhagen), 38; 40 pp., 1 pl., 41 figs.

**McGraw, B. M.**

1959. The ecology of the snail *Lymnaea humilis* Say. *Transactions American Microscopical Society,* 78, no. 1; 101–121, 4 figs.

**McLean, J. H., and W. K. Emerson**

1970. *Calotrophon,* A New World Muricid genus. *Veliger* 13, no. 1; 57–62, figs. 8–17.

**McLean, R. A.**

1951. The Pelecypoda or bivalve mollusks of Porto Rico and the Virgin Islands. New York Academy Sci., *Scientific Survey Porto Rico and the Virgin Islands,* 17, pt. 1; 183 pp., 26 pls.

## Mazÿck, W. G.

1913. Catalog of Mollusca of South Carolina. *Contributions Charleston Museum*, 2; 16 + 39 pp.

## Merrill, A. S., and R. E. Petit

1965, 1969. Mollusks new to South Carolina. Pt. 1, *Nautilus* 79, no. 2; 58–66 [1965]; Pt. 2, *Nautilus* 82, no. 4; 117–122 [1969].

## Moore, D. R.

1969. Systematics, distribution, and abundance of the West Indian micromollusk *Rissoina catesbyana* Orbigny. *Transactions Gulf Coast Association Geological Societies*, 19; 425–426.

## Moore, R. C. (editor)

1969. *Treatise on invertebrate paleontology*, Part N, vol. 1 (of 3), Mollusca 6, Bivalvia, xxxviii + 489 pp., illus.; Part N, vol. 2 (of 3), Mollusca 6, Bivalvia, 460 pp., illus. Lawrence: Geological Society America and Univ. Kansas.

## Morrison, J. P. E.

1964. Notes on American Melampidae. *Nautilus*, 77; pp. 119–121.

1968. Four American *Hastula* species. *Texas Conchologist*, 4, no. 9; 67–70.

1971. Western Atlantic *Donax*. *Proceedings Biological Society Washington*, 83, no. 48; 545–568, 2 pls.

## Morton, J. E.

1967. *Molluscs* (4th revised edition). London: Hutchinson Univ. Library. 244 pp., 41 figs.

## Newell, N. D.

1965. Classification of the Bivalvia. *American Museum Natural History, Novitates*, no. 2206; 1–25, 3 figs.

**Olsson, A. A.**

1956. Studies on the genus *Olivella*. *Proceedings Academy Natural Sciences Philadelphia*, 108; 155–225, pls. 8–16, 1 text fig.

**Pérez Farfante, I.**

1943. The genera *Fissurella, Lucapina* and *Lucapinella* in the western Atlantic. *Johnsonia*, 1, no. 10; 1–20, 5 pls.

1943, 1945. The genus *Diodora* in the western Atlantic. *Johnsonia*, 1, no. 11; 1–20, 6 pls.; no. 18; 4–6 (1945).

**Pilsbry, H. A.**

1890. Preliminary notices of new Amnicolidae. *Nautilus* 4; 52–53.

1905. Land shells of the Florida Keys. *Nautilus*, 19; 37–41.

1920. Review of the *Thysanophora plagioptycha* group. *Nautilus*, 33; 93–96, figs. 1–4.

1934. Review of the *Planorbidae* of Florida, with notes on other members of the family. *Proceedings Academy Natural Sciences Philadelphia*, 86; 29–66, pls. 7–11, figs. 1–7.

1939–1948. *Land mollusca of North America (north of Mexico)*. Monograph 3, Academy of Natural Sciences of Philadelphia, Pennsylvania, vol. 1, part 1, 1938, part 2, 1940, 1,003 pp., 580 figs.; vol. 2, part 1, 1946, part 2, 1948, 1,113 pp., 585 figs.

**Pilsbry, H. A., and R. A. McLean**

1939. A new *Arca* from the Western Indian region. *Notulae Naturae* (Academy of Natural Sciences, Philadelphia), no. 39; 1–2, 1 fig.

**Poirier, H.**

1954. An up-to-date systematic list of 3200 seashells from Greenland to Texas: Translation, explanation and gender of their names. Privately issued, mimeographed, 215 pp.

**Porter, H. J., and J. Tyler**

1971. Sea shells common to North Carolina. North Carolina Dept. Natural and Economic Resources, Information Series, 36 pp., illus.

**Porter, H. J., and D. A. Wolfe**

1971. Mollusca from North Carolina commercial fishing grounds for the Calico Scallop, *Argopecten gibbus* (Linné). *Journal Conchyliologie* (Paris), 109, no. 3; 91–109.

**Puffer, E. L., and W. K. Emerson**

1954. Catalogue and notes on the gastropod genus *Busycon*. *Proceedings Biological Society Washington*, 67; 115–150.

**Pulley, T. E.**

1959. *Busycon perversum* (Linné) and some related species. Rice *Institute Pamphlet* (Houston), 46, no. 1; 70–89, figs. 1–9.

**Radwin, G. E., and A. D'Attilio**

1972. The systematics of some New World Muricid species (Mollusca, Gastropoda), with descriptions of two new genera and two new species. *Proceedings Biological Society Washington*, 85, no. 28; 323–352, 26 figs.

**Robertson, R.**

1958. The family Phasianellidae in the western Atlantic. *Johnsonia*, 3, no. 37; 245–283, pls. 136–148.

1971. Sexually dimorphic Archaeogastropods and radulae. *American Malacological Union Annual Report for 1970*, pp. 75–78, 1 pl.

**Rogers, J. E.**

1960. *The shell book.* Boston: Charles T. Branford Co., 485 pp., 87 plates (8 in color). Reprint of 1908 edition, with the names brought up to date in an appendix by Harald A. Rehder.

**Russell, H. D.**

1941.    The Recent mollusks of the family Neritidae of the western Atlantic. *Bulletin Museum Comparative Zoology,* 88, no. 4; 347–404, pls. 1–7, 4 figs.

**Solem, G. A.**

1974.    *The shell makers: Introducing mollusks.* New York: John Wiley & Sons, xii + 289 pp. (illus., some in color).

**Soot-Ryen, T.**

1955.    A report on the family Mytilidae. *Allan Hancock Pacific Expeditions* (Univ. Southern California, Los Angeles), 20, no. 1; 1–154, 10 pls., 78 figs.

**Stingley, D. V.**

1952.    *Crepidula maculosa* Conrad. *Nautilus,* 65; 83–85, pl. 7, figs. 7–10.

**Thompson, F. G.**

1969.    Some hydrobiid snails from Georgia and Florida. *Quarterly Journal Florida Academy Sciences,* 32, no. 4; 241–265, 11 figs.

**Turner, R. D.**

1948.    The family Tonnidae in the western Atlantic. *Johnsonia,* 2, no. 26; 165–191, pls. 74–85.

1954.    The family Pholadidae in the western Atlantic and the eastern Pacific, Part I—Pholadinae. *Johnsonia,* 3, no. 33; 1–64, pls. 1–34.

1955.    The family Pholadidae in the western Atlantic and the eastern Pacific, Part II—Martesiinae, Jouannetiinae and Xylophaginae. *Johnsonia,* 3, no. 34; 65–160, pls. 35–93.

1966.    *A survey and illustrated catalogue of the Teredinidae.* Cambridge, Mass.; Museum Comparative Zoology. 265 pp., 64 pls.

**Turner, R. D., and K. J. Boss**

    1962.    The genus *Lithophaga* in the western Atlantic. *Johnsonia,*
             4, no. 41; 81–116, pls. 57–75.

**Turner, R. D., and J. Rosewater**

    1958.    The family Pinnidae in the western Atlantic. *Johnsonia,*
             3, no. 38; 285–326, pls. 149–171.

**Vagvolgyi, J.**

    1968.    Systematics and evolution of the genus *Triodopsis. Bulletin
             Museum Comparative Zoology,* 136, no. 7; 145–254, 7
             pls., 25 figs.

**Vokes, E. H.**

    1971.    Catalogue of the genus *Murex* Linné (Mollusca: Gastro-
             poda); Muricinae, Ocenebrinae. *Bulletin American Paleon-
             tology,* 61, no. 268; 1–141.

**Waller, T. R.**

    1969.    The evolution of the *Argopecten gibbus* stock (Mollusca:
             Bivalvia), Memoir 3, *Journal Paleontology,* 43, no. 5;
             suppl. 1–125, pls. 1–8, 13 figs.

**Walter, H. J.**

    1969.    Illustrated biomorphology of the "Angulata" lake form
             of the basommatophoran snail *Lymnaea catascopium* Say.
             *Malacological Review,* no. 2; 102 pp., 91 figs.

**Weaver, C. S., and J. E. du Pont**

    1970.    *Living volutes; A monograph of the recent Volutidae of
             the world.* Greenville: Delaware Museum Natural History;
             xv + 375 pp., illus., maps, 79 color plates, text figs.

**Wells, H. W., and M. J. Wells**

    1962.    The distinction between *Acteocina candei* and *Retusa
             canaliculata. Nautilus,* 75, no. 3; 87–93.

**Wilcox, J.**

1896. Notes on mollusks in Florida. *Nautilus,* 10, no. 3; 27–29.

**Wurtz, C. B.**

1949. *Physa heterostropha* (Say). *Nautilus,* 63; 20–33, pl. 2, 1 fig.


## CANADIAN REFERENCES

**Athearn, A. D., and A. H. Clarke**

1962. The freshwater mussels of Nova Scotia. *National Museum of Canada Bulletin,* no. 183; 11–41, pls. 1–4, 6 maps.

**Bousfield, E. L.**

1960. *Canadian Atlantic Sea Shells.* Ottawa: National Museum of Canada, 72 pp., 13 pls.

**Clarke, A. H.**

1961. Freshwater mollusks of James Bay watershed. *Annual Report American Malacological Union for 1961,* pp. 11–12.

1973. The freshwater molluscs of the Canadian Interior Basin. *Malacologia,* 13, nos. 1–2; 4 + 509 pp., 28 pls., 9 text figures, 87 maps.

**Clarke, A. H., et al.**

1968. The land snail fauna of Fundy National Park, New Brunswick. *National Museum of Canada Bulletin* no. 223, 22 pp., 1 map.

**Johnson, C. W.**

1926. A list of the mollusks collected by O. Bryant along the coasts of Labrador, New Foundland and Nova Scotia. *Nautilus,* 39, 128–135; 40, 21–25.

**LaRocque, A.**

1953. *Catalogue of the Recent mollusks of Canada.* National Museum of Canada Bulletin, no. 129, 406 pp.

**MacMillan, G. K.**

1954. A preliminary survey of the land and freshwater gastropoda of Cape Breton, Nova Scotia, Canada. *Proceedings Nova Scotia Institute of Science,* 23; pp. 389–408.

# INDEX

Roman numerals in boldface refer to photographic plates.

## A Note About the Authors

William K. Emerson has been a curator at the American Museum of Natural History since 1955. From 1960 to 1974 he was chairman of the Department of Living Invertebrates at the Museum. He is past president of the American Malacological Union and the Western Society of Malacologists.

Morris K. Jacobson taught foreign languages for many years in the New York City high school system. He is an associate in malacology at the Museum.

Together Dr. Emerson and Mr. Jacobson have written three books: *Shells of the New York City Area* (1961), *Shells from Cape Cod to Cape May* (1971), and *Wonders of the World of Shells* (1971). Dr. Emerson is also the co-author, with Andreas Feininger, of *Shells* (1972) and, with Arnold Ross, of *Wonders of Barnacles* (1974).

## A Note About the Type

The text of this book was set in a film version of Palatino, a type face designed by the noted German typographer Hermann Zapf. Named after Giovanbattista Palatino, a writing master of Renaissance Italy, Palatino was the first of Zapf's type faces to be introduced to America. The first designs for the face were made in 1948, and the fonts for the complete face were issued between 1950 and 1952. Like all Zapf-designed type faces, Palatino is beautifully balanced and exceedingly readable.

*Composed, printed, and bound by American Book–Stratford Press, Saddle Brook, New Jersey.*

*Color plates engraved and printed by Universal Printing, St. Louis, Missouri.*

*Typography and binding design by Virginia Tan.*